Ellen Smith-Dennis
A Grammar of Papapana

Pacific Linguistics

Managing editor
Alexander Adelaar

Editorial board members
Wayan Arka
Danielle Barth
Don Daniels
Nicholas Evans
Gwendolyn Hyslop
David Nash
Bruno Olsson
Bill Palmer
Andrew Pawley
Malcolm Ross
Dineke Schokkin
Jane Simpson

Volume 659

Ellen Smith-Dennis

A Grammar of Papapana

An Oceanic Language of Bougainville, Papua New Guinea

DE GRUYTER
MOUTON

ISBN 978-1-5015-2073-0
e-ISBN (PDF) 978-1-5015-0997-1
e-ISBN (EPUB) 978-1-5015-0989-6
ISSN 1448-8310

Library of Congress Control Number: 2020951681

Bibliographic information published by the Deutsche Nationalbibliothek
The Deutsche Nationalbibliothek lists this publication in the Deutsche Nationalbibliografie;
detailed bibliographic data are available on the Internet at http://dnb.dnb.de.

© 2022 Walter de Gruyter Inc., Boston/Berlin
This volume is text- and page-identical with the hardback published in 2020.
Photo credit: Ellen Smith-Dennis
Typesetting: Integra Software Services Pvt. Ltd.
Printing and binding: CPI books GmbH, Leck

www.degruyter.com

To Laurence – may you travel through life with curiosity and determination xxx

Acknowledgements

Work on this book spans nearly a decade of my life, starting with my doctoral research in Australia and continuing into the early years of my academic career in England. Researching Papapana and its speakers has been a fascinating, exciting and sometimes daunting experience, and I have learnt so many different things along the way. I feel very privileged to have had such a rewarding opportunity and I would like to thank the people who have made it possible.

Firstly, I should acknowledge that my doctoral research was part of a project funded by a Major Documentation Project grant (MDP0206) from the Endangered Language Documentation Programme (ELDP) at the School of Oriental and African Studies, University of London. I would like to thank ELDP for funding this project and my principal PhD supervisor Bill Palmer for securing this funding. I would also like to thank the Faculty of Social Sciences Research Development Fund and the Centre for Applied Linguistics at the University of Warwick for funding and supporting my fieldwork in 2018.

This book would not have been possible without the cooperation and hard work of the Papapana speech community. I am indebted to them for welcoming me into their community, for collaborating with me and for their friendships. I am especially grateful to Casilda Vavetaovi-Atuvia and Helen Kiara for their generous hospitality. Thank you to everyone who told me stories, especially Helen, Francis Abea, John-Wayne Abea, Kathy Apo, Leo Geare, Kevin Moko, Margaret Oavi, Cicilia Pako, Soa Scolastica and Rose Vave. Thank you to those people who good-naturedly answered my questions in elicitation sessions and patiently assisted me with transcription and translation, especially Casilda, Francis, Gerard Epa, Maureen Magua, Georgina Rereo and Max Wabe.

I would like to thank my wonderful PhD supervisors Bill Palmer and Catriona Malau, who taught me so much and who have continued to be supportive in my career. Thank you especially to Bill who has always encouraged me to publish this grammar and who has provided invaluable advice and interesting discussion over the past few years, from the beginnings of the book proposal to the final revisions. I would also like to thank an anonymous reviewer for their very detailed and helpful feedback. All remaining errors and weaknesses are of course my own.

Thank you to my family and friends, especially my parents, for always being there for me no matter where I am in the world, and for your love and encouragement. Thank you to the Dennis family for being my home away from home in Australia, and to the Smiths for helping me settle back into life and work in England – I am so grateful to you all for your continued support, even when it means I/we move away from you or when my fieldwork has caused worry!

Finally, I would like to thank my husband Jeff, whom I met at the start of my PhD and who has always supported me in my work, whether it's meant a long-distance relationship, travelling in the Pacific, or moving to another hemisphere. I am so grateful that you're such an adventurer, that you completely embraced life in Bougainville and that you're so good at striking up conversations with strangers! Thank you for your encouragement and enthusiasm in the field, for putting up with me when I've been stressed, and for making me laugh and switch off. This book has been almost as much a part of your life as mine and it would've been a lot harder to write it without you. Here's to the next chapter!

Mata:na

Contents

Acknowledgements —— VII

List of figures —— XIX

List of tables —— XXI

Abbreviations —— XXIII

Glossing convention —— XXV

Chapter 1
Introduction —— 1
1.1	Background and focus —— 1	
1.2	Previous research and documentation —— 2	
1.3	Fieldwork and methodology —— 4	
1.3.1	Introductions and approvals —— 4	
1.3.2	Field sites —— 5	
1.3.3	Project management —— 7	
1.3.4	Participant recruitment, payment and consent —— 9	
1.3.5	Data collection —— 10	
1.3.5.1	Lexical and grammatical elicitation recordings —— 11	
1.3.5.2	Text recordings —— 12	
1.3.5.3	Other linguistic data: participant observation, elicitation, community materials —— 13	
1.3.5.4	Photographs —— 14	
1.3.5.5	Sociolinguistic and genealogical data: informal interviews, genealogical profiles and participant observation —— 15	
1.3.6	Data processing —— 16	
1.3.6.1	Elicitation and text recordings —— 16	
1.3.6.1.1	Secure storage —— 16	
1.3.6.1.2	Transcription and translation —— 17	
1.3.6.1.3	Metadata —— 17	
1.3.6.2	Photographs —— 19	
1.3.6.3	Sociolinguistic, genealogical and other linguistic data —— 19	
1.3.7	Data analysis and presentation —— 19	
1.3.8	Archiving and access to data, annotations, metadata and other project outcomes —— 20	

1.3.9	Follow-up and scoping visit	—— 21
1.4	Book organisation and typological overview	—— 23
1.4.1	Background and sociolinguistic context	—— 23
1.4.2	Phonology —— 23	
1.4.3	Word classes —— 24	
1.4.4	Nouns, noun phrases, noun class, number and possession —— 26	
1.4.5	Verbs and the verb complex —— 28	
1.4.6	Clause types and structures —— 29	
1.4.7	Complex sentences —— 31	

Chapter 2
Language background and sociolinguistic context —— 32

2.1	The name and location of the Papapana language	—— 32
2.2	Genetic affiliation —— 35	
2.3	Papapana speakers —— 38	
2.4	The history of Papapana language contact —— 41	
2.4.1	Linguistic diversity in Papua New Guinea and Bougainville —— 41	
2.4.2	Migration in pre-colonial times —— 42	
2.4.3	European colonisation, plantations and missions —— 47	
2.4.3.1	Plantations —— 47	
2.4.3.2	Missionaries: churches and education —— 50	
2.4.4	Mid–20th century educational policies and independence —— 51	
2.4.5	The Bougainville Crisis —— 52	
2.4.6	The 21st century —— 53	
2.5	Papapana language use 2011–2018 —— 54	
2.5.1	Home —— 54	
2.5.1.1	Intermarriage and intergenerational transmission —— 54	
2.5.1.2	Multilingualism and other L1s —— 57	
2.5.1.3	Intergenerational transmission patterns —— 58	
2.5.2	Work and administration —— 60	
2.5.3	Education —— 61	
2.5.4	Religion, social events and media —— 64	
2.6	Papapana's ethnolinguistic vitality —— 65	

Chapter 3
Phonology —— 68
3.1 Segmental phonology —— 68
3.1.1 Vowels —— 68
3.1.1.1 Monophthongs: phonemes and allophones —— 68
3.1.1.2 Vowel length —— 70
3.1.1.3 Diphthongs and vowel sequences —— 72
3.1.2 Consonants —— 76
3.1.2.1 Consonant phonemes —— 77
3.1.2.2 Allophonic variation —— 77
3.1.2.3 Glide insertion —— 79
3.1.2.4 Glottal epenthesis —— 80
3.1.3 Phonological variation and change —— 81
3.2 Orthography —— 82
3.2.1 Orthographic representation of vowels —— 82
3.2.2 Orthographic representation of consonants —— 83
3.3 Phonotactics —— 85
3.3.1 Syllable structure —— 85
3.3.2 Phonological word structure —— 85
3.4 Reduplication —— 87
3.4.1 Monosyllabic copying —— 88
3.4.2 Disyllabic copying —— 90
3.4.3 Multiple reduplication —— 91
3.5 Stress —— 92
3.5.1 Regular stress assignment —— 92
3.5.2 Reduplication and stress —— 94
3.5.3 Proclitics and stress —— 95
3.5.4 Suffixes, enclitics and stress —— 97

Chapter 4
Nouns and noun phrase structure —— 99
4.1 Nominals and noun phrase structure —— 99
4.2 Pronouns —— 104
4.2.1 Independent pronouns —— 104
4.3 Nominal derivation —— 106
4.3.1 Zero derivation —— 107
4.3.2 Reduplication —— 109
4.3.2.1 Nominalised verbs —— 109
4.3.3 Reduplication and derivational *-na* —— 112
4.3.3.1 Derived location nouns —— 112

4.3.3.2	Derived dyadic nouns —— 114	
4.4	Compound nouns and complex kinship terms —— 115	
4.4.1	Compounds and the construct suffix *-i* or *-ni* —— 116	
4.4.2	Compounds with partitive and collective nouns —— 119	
4.4.3	Compounds with lexicalised *toi ~ tei* 'person' and *tai* 'people' —— 121	
4.4.4	Compounds with *mata* 'trait' —— 123	
4.4.5	Complex kinship terms —— 125	
4.5	Demonstratives —— 127	
4.5.1	Demonstrative modifiers —— 128	
4.5.1.1	Person-based demonstratives —— 128	
4.5.1.2	Distance-based demonstratives —— 131	
4.5.1.3	Co-occurrence of person-based and distance-based demonstratives —— 132	
4.5.2	Demonstrative pronouns —— 133	
4.6	Adjectives and adjective phrases —— 135	
4.6.1	Adjective phrase modifiers —— 137	
4.6.2	Bare adjectives —— 141	
4.6.3	Adjective *etawa* 'big' and augmentative *-eta ~ -ota* —— 142	
4.6.4	Adjective phrases and elided nouns —— 143	
4.7	Miscellaneous postnominal modifiers —— 144	
4.7.1	Exhaustive *panapana* —— 145	
4.7.2	Limiting *ora ~ ara* —— 145	
4.7.3	Intensifiers *poto* and *mamangi* —— 146	
4.7.4	Intensifier *papanusu* —— 148	
4.7.5	Emphatic *tobi* —— 148	
4.7.6	Associative *vowa ~ vewa* —— 149	
4.7.7	Additive *tomana* —— 150	
4.7.8	*=re* '(an)other' —— 151	
4.8	Attributive PP with *merei* —— 151

Chapter 5
Noun class, number and possession —— 154

5.1	Noun class —— 154
5.1.1	Personal nouns —— 155
5.1.2	Class I nouns —— 158
5.1.3	Class II nouns —— 161
5.1.4	Location nouns —— 164
5.1.5	Noun class assignment: flexibility and irregularity —— 169
5.2	Number —— 171

5.2.1	Lexical plurals —— **171**	
5.2.2	Associative plural *nia* —— **173**	
5.2.3	Reduplication —— **175**	
5.3	Articles —— **176**	
5.3.1	Specific articles: *e-, na=, nau ~ nu=* —— **178**	
5.3.2	Inverse number marking and the plural article *bau* —— **182**	
5.3.3	Non-specific articles: *ta=, tau* —— **185**	
5.3.4	Diminutive singular articles: *si=, sau ~ su=* —— **186**	
5.3.5	Diminutive plural article *ani* —— **189**	
5.3.6	Partitive article *pei* —— **190**	
5.3.7	Dual and plural collective articles *mena* and *mamena* —— **191**	
5.4	Numerals and numeral phrases —— **192**	
5.4.1	Counting system —— **192**	
5.4.2	Cardinal and ordinal numeral modifiers —— **195**	
5.4.3	Numerals and elided nouns —— **202**	
5.5	Possession —— **203**	
5.5.1	Direct possessive construction —— **204**	
5.5.2	Indirect possessive construction —— **208**	
5.5.3	Indirect possessor proclitics and elided nouns —— **213**	
5.5.4	Possessor stacking —— **215**	
5.5.5	Prepositional possessive construction —— **216**	
5.6	Quantifiers and quantifier phrases —— **218**	
5.6.1	*na:* 'some, other' with possessed NP complement or PP complement —— **219**	
5.6.2	*na:* 'some, other' and *ta:* 'some' with plural NP complement —— **220**	
5.6.3	*na:* 'some, other' with partial NP complements —— **221**	
5.6.4	*a'aisi* 'many' —— **224**	

Chapter 6
Verbs and the verb complex —— 228

6.1	Verbs and verb complex structure —— **228**	
6.2	Verbal derivation and compounding —— **231**	
6.2.1	Zero derivation —— **231**	
6.2.2	Reduplication —— **233**	
6.2.3	Verbal compounding —— **233**	
6.2.4	Valency —— **234**	
6.3	Argument marking —— **234**	
6.3.1	Alignment and grammatical relations —— **234**	
6.3.2	Subject-indexing and object-indexing clitics —— **237**	

6.3.2.1	Subject-indexing proclitics —— 238	
6.3.2.2	Object-indexing enclitics —— 240	
6.3.3	Emphatic *to* —— 241	
6.4	Verb types —— 245	
6.4.1	Intransitive verbs —— 248	
6.4.2	Monotransitive verbs —— 250	
6.4.2.1	A-verbs —— 251	
6.4.2.2	U-process verbs —— 252	
6.4.3	Ditransitive verbs —— 253	
6.4.4	Ambitransitive verbs —— 254	
6.4.4.1	U-process verbs —— 254	
6.4.4.2	A-verbs —— 255	
6.5	Valency-changing operations —— 257	
6.5.1	Transitive =*i* and applicative *i* —— 258	
6.5.1.1	Transitive =*i* —— 259	
6.5.1.2	Applicative *i* —— 264	
6.5.2	Causative *va-* —— 267	
6.5.3	Detransitivising *ta-* —— 269	
6.5.4	Applicative comitative *me* —— 269	
6.5.5	Object incorporation and transivity discord —— 274	
6.5.5.1	Object incorporation —— 275	
6.5.5.2	Transitivity discord —— 276	
6.5.6	Reciprocal/Reflexive *vei* —— 277	
6.5.6.1	Reciprocal —— 278	
6.5.6.2	Reflexive —— 281	
6.6	Verb serialisation —— 282	
6.6.1	Verb types and component wordhood —— 283	
6.6.2	SVC semantic types and composition —— 287	
6.6.2.1	Same-subject monotransitive directional —— 288	
6.6.2.2	Intransitive directional —— 288	
6.6.2.3	Switch-subject monotransitive directional —— 290	
6.6.2.4	Causative —— 291	
6.6.2.5	Cause-effect —— 292	
6.6.2.6	Similarity and manner —— 292	
6.7	Directionals —— 293	
6.7.1	Geocentric directionals *tae*, *dini* and *batabata* —— 294	
6.7.2	Deictic directionals *mai* and *nao* —— 298	
6.7.3	Sequential directionals *mei* and *no* —— 299	
6.7.4	Allative directional *vowa ~ vewa* —— 302	
6.8	Adverbs in the VC —— 303	

6.8.1	Preverbal —— 304	
6.8.2	Postverbal —— 307	
6.8.2.1	Syntactic position —— 308	
6.8.2.2	Reduplication and alternate forms —— 310	
6.8.2.3	Interaction with TAM —— 312	

Chapter 7
Tense, aspect, mode and negation —— 314

7.1	Tense, aspect and mode —— 314
7.1.1	Distinctions, markers and postverbal subject-indexing —— 314
7.1.2	Unmarked —— 318
7.1.3	Past tense *ara* —— 320
7.1.4	Irrealis mode *=i* —— 321
7.1.4.1	Future tense and present habitual: *=i* —— 321
7.1.4.2	Past habitual: *pei* and *=i* —— 323
7.1.4.3	Apprehensive mode: *te* and *=i* —— 325
7.1.4.4	Hypothetical conditional: *awa* and *=i* —— 326
7.1.5	Optative mode *eri* —— 329
7.1.5.1	Optative mode: *eri*, PSI and *=i* —— 329
7.1.5.2	Proximative aspect: *eri* and PSI —— 332
7.1.5.3	Counterfactual conditional: *awa* and *eri* —— 333
7.1.6	Imperfective aspect: PSI and reduplication —— 335
7.1.6.1	Continuous and habitual aspect, present —— 336
7.1.6.2	Continuous aspect, future —— 340
7.1.6.3	Continuous aspect, past —— 340
7.1.7	Repetitive aspect *vare ~ vae* —— 342
7.1.8	Completive aspect *osi* —— 344
7.2	Imperative and hortative —— 346
7.3	Negation —— 348
7.3.1	Verbal assertive negation: *ae* —— 349
7.3.2	Prohibitives: *ae/te* and verbal reduplication —— 352

Chapter 8
Obliques, adjuncts and clause-level adverbs —— 356

8.1	Adjunct noun phrases —— 357
8.1.1	Class I temporal nouns —— 357
8.1.1.1	Temporal duration —— 357
8.1.1.2	Temporal location —— 358
8.1.2	Location nouns —— 360
8.1.2.1	Absolute Location nouns —— 360

8.1.2.2	Familiar Location nouns —— 363	
8.1.2.3	Relational Location nouns —— 365	
8.1.2.4	Lexicalised Relational Location nouns —— 367	
8.1.3	Bound noun *peite-* 'own' —— 370	
8.2	Deictic locationals —— 371	
8.3	Adposition phrases —— 373	
8.3.1	Preposition *te* —— 374	
8.3.1.1	*te* with possessor proclitics —— 374	
8.3.1.2	*te* with Personal nouns —— 375	
8.3.1.3	*te* with Class I/II nouns —— 376	
8.3.1.4	*te* with other articles and numerals —— 379	
8.3.2	Preposition *eangoiena* 'until' —— 381	
8.3.3	Preposition *avosia* 'like' —— 382	
8.3.4	Nascent postposition *tomana* 'with' —— 383	
8.4	Clause-level adverbs —— 386	
8.4.1	Spatial, manner and modal adverbs —— 386	
8.4.2	Modal adverbs *eangoiena* and *avirua* —— 388	
8.4.2.1	Ability: *eangoiena* —— 389	
8.4.2.2	*avirua* 'not yet' —— 389	

Chapter 9
Clause types and structures —— 391

9.1	Declarative clauses and core arguments —— 391	
9.1.1	Intransitive —— 392	
9.1.2	Monotransitive —— 395	
9.1.3	Ditransitive —— 397	
9.2	Imperative and hortative clauses —— 399	
9.3	Interrogative clauses —— 401	
9.3.1	Polar questions —— 401	
9.3.2	Content questions and interrogative terms —— 402	
9.3.2.1	Core arguments —— 403	
9.3.2.2	Adnominal —— 406	
9.3.2.3	Clausal adjunct —— 411	
9.3.2.3.1	Temporal —— 411	
9.3.2.3.2	Reason —— 412	
9.3.2.3.3	Location —— 413	
9.3.2.3.4	Manner —— 414	
9.3.2.4	Interrogative terms in declarative clauses —— 415	
9.4	Existential clauses —— 417	
9.4.1	Existential verb *po* 'stay/exist' —— 417	

9.4.2	Existential verb *tonu* 'stand' —— **419**
9.4.3	Existential verb *a'aisi* 'be many' —— **420**
9.5	Negative clauses —— **420**
9.5.1	Negative existential verb *aruai* 'be not' —— **421**
9.5.2	Verbal assertive negation: *aruai* 'no' —— **422**
9.6	Verbless clauses —— **423**
9.6.1	Nominal predicates —— **423**
9.6.1.1	Identity —— **424**
9.6.1.2	Possession —— **426**
9.6.1.3	Location —— **427**
9.6.1.4	Negative nominal predicates —— **428**
9.6.2	Interrogative predicates —— **430**
9.6.3	Locative PP predicates —— **431**
9.6.4	Attributive PP predicates —— **431**
9.6.5	Numeral predicates —— **432**
9.6.6	Adjectival predicates —— **433**
9.6.7	Existential clauses —— **436**
9.6.8	Possessive clauses with *pea* —— **437**

Chapter 10
Complex sentences —— 441

10.1	Coordination and coordinators —— **441**
10.1.1	Conjunction and adversative coordination —— **442**
10.1.1.1	Clause coordination —— **442**
10.1.1.2	Phrase coordination —— **444**
10.1.1.3	Phrase coordination with dual independent pronouns —— **449**
10.1.2	Disjunction —— **450**
10.1.2.1	Clause coordination —— **450**
10.1.2.2	Phrase coordination —— **451**
10.1.3	Sequential coordination —— **452**
10.1.4	Asyndesis —— **453**
10.2	Relative clauses —— **457**
10.2.1	Position and relativiser —— **458**
10.2.2	Relativised function —— **459**
10.2.2.1	Relativised NP as subject —— **460**
10.2.2.2	Relativised NP as object —— **462**
10.2.2.3	Relativised NP as adjunct —— **465**
10.2.2.4	Relativised NP as genitive —— **466**
10.3	Adverbial clauses and subordinators —— **467**
10.3.1	Condition —— **468**

10.3.2	Apprehensive —— 470	
10.3.3	Purpose —— 472	
10.3.3.1	*tena* 'in order to' —— 472	
10.3.3.2	*tenava* 'so that' —— 475	
10.3.3.3	*merei* 'in order to' —— 476	
10.3.4	Temporal location —— 477	
10.3.4.1	Elapsed time: *inao tani* 'ago' —— 478	
10.3.4.2	Duration: *eangoiena* 'until' —— 478	
10.3.5	Spatial location: *avoa* 'where' —— 480	
10.3.6	Reason: *avisi* 'because' —— 480	
10.3.7	Result: *arogani* 'therefore' —— 483	
10.3.8	Concession —— 484	
10.3.8.1	*marana* 'even though' —— 484	
10.3.8.2	*po'ovira* 'even though' —— 486	
10.3.9	Similarity and manner: *avosia* 'like' —— 487	
10.4	Complement clauses —— 488	
10.4.1	Finite complements —— 488	
10.4.1.1	Asyndesis —— 489	
10.4.1.2	Subordinator *avosia* —— 491	
10.4.1.3	Subordinator *avosia* and object-indexing —— 495	
10.4.1.4	Interrogative complementizers —— 496	
10.4.2	Non-finite complements —— 497	
10.4.3	Reported speech —— 502	
10.4.3.1	Finite complements —— 502	
10.4.3.1.1	Direct —— 502	
10.4.3.1.2	Indirect —— 504	
10.4.3.2	Non-finite complements —— 507	

References —— 509

Appendix 1 Pronominal paradigms —— 521

Appendix 2 25 demonstrative scenes (Wilkins 1999) —— 523

Index —— 527

List of figures

Figure 1.1 Helen Kiara inside cooking house, Barora, 2011 —— 5
Figure 1.2 Helen Kiara's house in Barora, 2011 —— 6
Figure 1.3 Casilda Vavetaovi-Atuvia, Teperoi church, 2013 —— 7
Figure 1.4 Teperoi Primary School site, 2011 —— 7
Figure 1.5 Margaret Oavi with plants, Teperoi, 2011 —— 13
Figure 2.1 Papapana in Papua New Guinea —— 33
Figure 2.2 Bougainville: Papapana villages Koikoi and Iraka, and other important locations —— 34
Figure 2.3 Papapana villages —— 35
Figure 2.4 Genealogical tree for Papapana (based on Ross 2004c) —— 36
Figure 2.5 Locations of Northwest Solomonic languages (from Ross 1988: 216) —— 37
Figure 2.6 A Northwest Solomonic genetic tree (from Ross 1988: 217) —— 38
Figure 2.7 Proportion within each village of L1/fluent speakers, L2/semi-speakers and people with passive or no Papapana knowledge —— 40
Figure 2.8 Numbers of L1/fluent speakers, L2/semi-speakers and passive bilinguals in each location —— 41
Figure 2.9 Oceanic and Papuan languages of Bougainville and Northwestern Solomon Islands (from Evans 2009) —— 44
Figure 2.10 Teperoi, circa 1931 —— 47
Figure 2.11 Teperoi beach, circa 1931 —— 49
Figure 2.12 Teperoi catechists, circa 1931 —— 50
Figure 2.13 Francis Abea, Teperoi Elementary School, 2012 —— 63
Figure 2.14 A classroom in Teperoi Elementary School, 2018 —— 63
Figure 6.1 Objects: direct and indirect, primary and secondary —— 236
Figure 6.2 Proto-Oceanic verb classes (after Evans 2003: 87, 306) —— 246
Figure 6.3 Geocentric coordinates —— 294
Figure 10.1 Adverbial Desententialisation Hierarchy —— 474

List of tables

Table 1.1   Recording file name key —— 18
Table 1.2   Metadata fields —— 18
Table 2.1   Speakers by location —— 39
Table 2.2   Bougainville languages speaker numbers —— 43
Table 2.3   Intermarriage patterns —— 56
Table 2.4   Multilingualism in Papapana villages —— 58
Table 2.5   Speakers by age —— 59
Table 2.6   Proportion of speakers in age group —— 59
Table 3.1   Monophthong phonemes —— 69
Table 3.2   Contrastive sets: Monophthongs —— 69
Table 3.3   Monophthong formant measurements —— 69
Table 3.4   Contrastive sets: Long vowels —— 71
Table 3.5   Vowel phonemes: Diphthong formant measurements —— 73
Table 3.6   Diphthongs —— 73
Table 3.7   Contrastive sets: Diphthongs —— 74
Table 3.8   Vowel sequences —— 76
Table 3.9   Consonant phonemes —— 77
Table 3.10 Contrastive sets: Consonant voicing distinctions —— 77
Table 3.11 Contrastive sets: Consonant manner distinctions —— 78
Table 3.12 Contrastive sets: Consonant place distinctions —— 79
Table 3.13 Orthography: Vowels —— 83
Table 3.14 Orthography: Diphthongs —— 83
Table 3.15 Orthography: Consonants —— 84
Table 3.16 Root structures —— 86
Table 4.1   Noun phrase structure: pre-head —— 100
Table 4.2   Noun phrase structure: post-head —— 100
Table 4.3   Independent pronouns —— 104
Table 4.4   Derived nouns: Zero derivation —— 107
Table 4.5   Derived nouns: Reduplication —— 110
Table 4.6   Colour terms —— 137
Table 4.7   Adjective subclass —— 137
Table 5.1   Noun classes —— 155
Table 5.2   Personal nouns —— 156
Table 5.3   Examples of Class I nouns —— 159
Table 5.4   Examples of Class II nouns —— 163
Table 5.5   Location nouns —— 165
Table 5.6   Articles —— 177
Table 5.7   Syntactic positions of articles —— 177
Table 5.8   Counting system —— 193
Table 5.9   Cardinal and ordinal numeral modifiers —— 195
Table 5.10 Direct possessor suffixes —— 205
Table 5.11 Directly possessed nouns —— 207
Table 5.12 Indirect possessor proclitics —— 208
Table 5.13 Indirectly possessed nouns —— 212

Table 6.1	Verb complex structure: preverbal	229
Table 6.2	Verb complex structure: postverbal	229
Table 6.3	Subject-indexing proclitics	238
Table 6.4	Object-indexing enclitics	240
Table 6.5	Valency and verb types in Papapana	247
Table 6.6	Intransitive 1 verbs	249
Table 6.7	Monotransitive A-verbs	252
Table 6.8	Monotransitive U-process verbs	253
Table 6.9	Ambitransitive U-process verbs	254
Table 6.10	Ambitransitive A-verbs: Group 1	256
Table 6.11	Ambitransitive A-verbs: Group 2	257
Table 6.12	Transitive structures with singular objects	260
Table 6.13	Proto-Oceanic transitive structures (adapted from Evans 2008: 291)	262
Table 6.14	Ditransitive structures with singular objects	265
Table 6.15	SVC verb types	284
Table 6.16	SVC semantic types and composition	287
Table 6.17	Postverbal adverbs: meanings and functions	308
Table 7.1	TAM constructions	316
Table 7.2	Postverbal subject-indexing (PSI) enclitics	317
Table 7.3	Imperfective aspect: PSI and reduplication patterns	336
Table 7.4	Imperfective aspect: Examples of Group 1 verbs	339
Table 7.5	Imperfective aspect: Examples of Group 2 verbs	339
Table 7.6	Imperfective aspect: Examples of Group 3 verbs	340
Table 9.1	Functions of interrogative terms in verbal clauses	403
Table 10.1	Adverbial clauses	468
Table 10.2	Verb categories and finite clausal complement types	489
Table 10.3	Verb categories with non-finite complements	497

Abbreviations

A	actor
ADJ	adjective
AP	adjective phrase
BRA	Bougainville Revolutionary Army
ELAR	Endangered Language Archive
GEOG	geographic direction verb
L1	first language
L2	second language
LOCO	locomotion verb
NP	noun phrase
NUM	numeral
NumP	numeral phrase
O	object
O1	primary object
O2	secondary object
PMV	Public Motor Vehicle
PNG	Papua New Guinea
PNGDF	Papua New Guinea Defence Force
PNWS	Proto-Northwest Solomonic
POc	Proto-Oceanic
PP	preposition phrase
PSI	postverbal subject indexing
PWO	Proto-Western Oceanic
QP	quantifier phrase
S	subject
SIL	Summer Institute of Linguistics
SVC	serial verb construction
TAM	tense, aspect, mode
U	undergoer
V	verb
V1	first verb in a series
V2	second verb in a series
VC	verb complex
VP	verb phrase
VTPS	Viles Tok Ples Skul 'village language school'

Glossing conventions

1	first person	OPT	optative
2	second person	PART	partitive
3	third person	PERS	Personal
AN	animate	PL	plural
APPL	applicative	PRO	pronoun
APPR	apprehensive	PROX	proximal
ART	article	PSSR	possessor
ASSOC	associative	PST	past
ATTRIB	attributive	PURP	purposive
AUG	augmentative	RD	reduplicant
CAP	capability	REAL	realis
CAUS	causative	REL	relativiser
CF	counterfactual	REP	repetitive
CLI	Class I	R/R	reciprocal/reflexive
CLII	Class II	SBJ	subject
COLL	collective	SEQ	sequential
COM	comitative	SG	singular
COMPL	completive	SPEC	specific
COND	conditional	SUBR	subordinator
CONST	construct morpheme	TR	transitive
DEM1	demonstrative 1		
DEM2	demonstrative 2		
DER	derivational morpheme		
DET	determiner		
DETR	detransitiviser		
DIM	diminutive		
DU	dual		
DIST	distal		
EMPH	emphatic		
EXCL	exclusive		
HORT	hortative		
HUM	human		
INAN	inanimate		
INCL	inclusive		
INTS	intensifier		
IPFV	imperfective		
IRR	irrealis		
LOC	locative		
NEG	negative		
MED	medial		
NHUM	non-human		
NSPEC	non-specific		
OBJ	object		
OBL	oblique		
ORD	ordinal		

Chapter 1
Introduction

1.1 Background and focus

This book provides a comprehensive grammatical description of Papapana, a previously undocumented and under-described, highly endangered Northwest Solomonic (Oceanic, Austronesian) language. Papapana is spoken by 99 fluent speakers on the northeast coast of Bougainville island, in the Autonomous Region of Bougainville, Papua New Guinea (PNG), an area of the Pacific known as Melanesia. Northwest Solomonic languages are found from Nissan island in Bougainville in the north-west to the south-eastern tip of Santa Ysabel island in the Solomon Islands. Like the rest of PNG, the Autonomous Region of Bougainville is an area of considerable linguistic diversity where language contact between speakers of Oceanic and non-Austronesian languages is pervasive.

This grammar initially arises from my doctoral project, which involved a year's fieldwork documenting Papapana to core documentation level, comprising a corpus of time-aligned translated transcriptions of digital audio and video recordings, that are accompanied by full metadata and relevant photographic materials. This grammar is further informed by other project outputs, which include materials for community use to assist in linguistic and cultural maintenance and promote vernacular literacy: a short dictionary, pedagogical readers and illustrated vocabulary books for particular cultural domains (see §1.3.5.3). In addition, I compiled genealogical and sociolinguistic profiles of the Papapana community members and documented the socio-cultural context of Papapana. My doctoral thesis (Smith 2015a) constituted a comprehensive reference grammar of Papapana and a partial investigation of language contact phenomena in the Papapana speech community: I examined contact-induced grammatical change (under the influence of neighbouring non-Austronesian languages) and language shift and endangerment (due to the influence of the creole Tok Pisin). The research on contact-induced change and on ethnolinguistic vitality were developed in Smith (2016a) and Smith (2016b) respectively and will therefore not be included in this book. However, my research on the history of language contact and on language use is included in more depth in chapter 2, and throughout the book at the relevant points, reference will be made to grammatical features which exhibit evidence of contact-induced change. This book is thus not a publication of my thesis, but a substantial development of the grammatical description, which was the main focus of my thesis.

The grammar has been developed rather significantly. There are many new additions to the description based on data which I have now had the opportunity to fully analyse and the space to include. Based on my research on reduplication (Smith 2016c), grammaticalisation (Smith-Dennis 2018) and mode (Smith-Dennis 2019; Smith-Dennis, in press), I have enhanced the analysis and description of certain verbs and verbal morphology. I have also refined my analyses of previously nameless morphemes and I have significantly revised my analysis of noun phrase structure and the syntactic relationship between articles, numerals, quantifiers and nouns. This monograph has also benefited from an additional three-week visit to Bougainville in April 2018, during which I had the opportunity to collect further audio and video recordings. I was able to check and further investigate some areas of the lexicon and grammar, and I gathered updated sociolinguistic information, which is included in chapter 2.

Accordingly, this book describes Papapana on various levels, including phonology, morphology and syntax in noun phrases and the verb complex, and syntax at the clause- and sentence-level. This book also describes the sociolinguistic and historical context within which Papapana is spoken. Throughout the grammar, I relate the described phenomena to the current research on typological and Oceanic linguistics. Typologically unusual features of Papapana include its patterns of verbal reduplication and multiple reduplication (Smith 2016c), inverse-number marking in the noun phrase, and postverbal subject-indexing, which interacts with reduplication or mode markers to express a range of meanings. Papapana also displays a partial shift from left-headedness to right-headedness, especially evident in its clause orders, obliques and possessive constructions; these features are likely the result of Papuan (non-Austronesian) contact and also raise questions about Papapana's exact genetic affiliation within the Northwest Solomonic subgroup (Smith 2016a), which could be further informed by the cross-linguistic comparisons to other Northwest Solomonic languages made throughout this grammar.

1.2 Previous research and documentation

This is the first comprehensive grammar of Papapana, and moreover, the first full reference grammar of any Oceanic language of Northern Bougainville, despite this being a region displaying considerable linguistic innovation and language contact phenomena, with numerous typologically significant features. Indeed, less than 10% of Oceanic languages in Melanesia are well described and Lynch, Ross and Crowley (2002: 21) argue that this area must be the focus for research over the coming decades.

Previous research and documentation on Papapana includes a preliminary draft dictionary (Palmer 2007b) which was compiled from a 200 item Summer Institute of Linguistics (SIL) survey questionnaire collected by Allen and Hurd in 1963, and six hours of primary data collected by Palmer from two speakers in elicitation sessions in the field in 2006. These audio recordings are accompanied by annotations and the data is archived and disseminated online (Palmer 2007c). No grammar studies exist. Due to the limited prior research, it was particularly necessary to consult research on related languages when analysing and describing Papapana.

Comparative research on Bougainville languages includes Lincoln's (1976a) *Austronesian Languages: Bougainville Province*, in which Lincoln endeavours to define the subgroups of the Oceanic languages of Bougainville by examining lexicostatistics, lexical and grammatical innovations, consonant correspondences and sound correspondences. In *Proto-Oceanic and the Austronesian languages of Western Melanesia*, Ross (1988) describes Northwest Solomonic group typology and provides evidence to show that these languages are descended from a single proto-language, Proto-Northwest Solomonic (PNWS) (see Figure 2.6 in §2.2).

Five of the grammar sketches in *The Oceanic Languages* (Lynch, Ross, and Crowley 2002) describe Northwest Solomonic languages: Taiof, spoken in northern Bougainville (Ross 2002b), Banoni, spoken in southwest Bougainville (Lynch and Ross 2002), Sisiqa (or Sengga), spoken in central Choiseul in the Solomon Islands (Ross 2002a), Kokota, spoken on Santa Isabel in the Solomon Islands (Palmer 2002) and Roviana, spoken on New Georgia in the Solomon Islands (Corston-Oliver 2002). Other grammar sketches and theses of Northwest-Solomonic languages include those of Kubokota (or Ghanongga), spoken in the New Georgia archipelago, Solomon Islands (Chambers 2009); Mono-Alu, spoken in the Bougainville Straits (Fagan 1986); Banoni, spoken in south Bougainville (Lincoln 1976b); Nehan (Todd 1978) and Teop (Mosel and Thiesen 2007) both spoken in northern Bougainville (the latter being based on Mosel's extensive documentary work of Teop).

There are only three published reference grammars of Northwest Solomonic languages, all of which are spoken in the Solomon Islands: Kokota, spoken on Santa Isabel (Palmer 2009), and Hoava (Davis 2003) and Ughele (Frostad 2012), both spoken in the New Georgia archipelago.

Other research on Northwest Solomonic languages includes two studies of ergativity in Roviana (Corston 1996) and Nehan (Glennon 2014) and Mosel and various collaborators' research into Teop gender (Mosel and Spriggs 1999a), negation (Mosel and Spriggs 1999b) and valency (Mosel 2007, 2010).

This literature survey shows that the reference grammars of Northwest Solomonic languages that do exist focus on languages of the Solomon Islands, and the only grammatical description of Northwest Solomonic languages in

Northern Bougainville are sketch grammars or articles on specific grammatical topics. This grammar therefore fills an important gap in terms of grammatical descriptions of North Bougainville languages, makes a significant contribution to the field of Oceanic linguistics and to future comparative linguistic and typological research, and may help clarify the exact subgrouping of Papapana within the Northwest Solomonic subgroup.

1.3 Fieldwork and methodology

The grammar is mostly based on data that I collected during two fieldwork trips to PNG as part of my doctoral project: my first fieldwork trip took place from June 2011 to March 2012, and the second from March to May 2013. This section describes introductions and approvals (§1.3.1), the field sites (§1.3.2), project management (§1.3.3), participant recruitment, payment and consent (§1.3.4), data collection methods (§1.3.5), data processing (§1.3.6), data analysis and presentation (§1.3.7) and archiving and access to data, annotations, metadata and other project outcomes (§1.3.8). This grammar has also benefited from an additional three-week visit to PNG in April 2018 (§1.3.9). For any references to places or languages, please see Figures 2.1 to 2.3 in §2.1, Figure 2.6 in §2.2 and Table 2.2 in §2.4.2. Sociolinguistic information such as speaker numbers, language use and ethnolinguistic vitality are described in chapter 2.

1.3.1 Introductions and approvals

While conducting fieldwork in Bougainville in 2006, my doctoral supervisor Bill Palmer (The University of Newcastle, Australia) had recorded two Papapana speakers in the Torau-speaking village of Rorovana (see §1.2). These speakers expressed an interest in documenting Papapana and Bill subsequently secured a Major Documentation Project grant for this purpose from the Endangered Language Documentation Programme (ELDP), based at the School of Oriental and African Studies (SOAS) at the University of London. I was recruited as a PhD researcher on this project. With no way of contacting speakers in advance, I planned to arrive in Bougainville and establish connections with the Papapana community either through people in the provincial capital Buka or by visiting the main Papapana village of Teperoi.

As it transpired, establishing connections with the community was far quicker and easier than I anticipated. Prior to leaving Australia, an Australian friend introduced me to her Papua New Guinean friend, who happened to be travelling to Port Moresby at the same time as myself. In Port Moresby, this friend introduced me to a Bougainvillean lady, whose uncle in Bougainville knew Papapana community member John Konnou. By the time I arrived in Buka two days later, word of my arrival had already reached John and shortly after I landed, he found me at my guesthouse. I spent two days in Buka and John kindly took me to the relevant government offices to seek local approval, before introducing me to the Papapana community and establishing me in my first field site.

1.3.2 Field sites

My first field site was the Papapana village of Barora. John Konnou accompanied me to Barora where he had arranged for me to stay with his first cousin-in-law, Helen Kiara (see Figure 1.1). John believed this would be the best location for me as Helen lived in a "permanent" house (i.e. one with concrete foundations), had a generator, a rainwater tank and a small store in the house (see Figure 1.2). I lived in Barora from June to September 2011.

Figure 1.1: Helen Kiara inside cooking house, Barora, 2011.

Figure 1.2: Helen Kiara's house in Barora, 2011.

In order to work on transcriptions and translations of the audio recordings that I had collected, I had to travel around six kilometres to Teperoi as there were only a few people who were able and willing to assist me with this work, and they lived and/or worked in Teperoi. I initially worked only with the Teperoi Primary School head teacher Casilda Vavetaovi-Atuvia, and the elementary teacher Francis Abea. Travelling to Teperoi could be extremely time-consuming and difficult, and the timing of my arrival could be unpredictable, which was not ideal when Casilda and Francis were only available during the school break-times (after school was not an option as then it was too late for transport back to Barora). I therefore decided that it made more sense practically to live in Teperoi where I would have contact with not only more Papapana speakers but with Casilda, Francis and other literate speakers who could assist with transcription and translation.

The Teperoi Primary School site had five timber houses on stilts, which teachers rented. By September 2011 Casilda (see Figure 1.3) had moved into one of these houses (the furthest on the right in Figure 1.4) from the nearby Papapana village of Koikoi and she invited me to live with her family: her Teop-speaking husband Jerry Atuvia, her teenage daughter and, from December 2011, her baby son. I lived in Teperoi with Casilda's family from September 2011 to March 2012, and again from March to May 2013.

1.3 Fieldwork and methodology — 7

Figure 1.3: Casilda Vavetaovi-Atuvia, Teperoi church, 2013.

Figure 1.4: Teperoi Primary School site, 2011.

1.3.3 Project management

Woodbury (2003: 47) asserts that a corpus should be large and its production should be ongoing, distributed and opportunistic and for this to happen, documentation projects "must be designed to put easily available, easy-to-use, well-diffused technologies in the hands of as many people as possible, and to train them to make high quality recordings" (Woodbury 2003: 47). Community members should therefore not only be active as the producers of the language data but also as co-researchers in the collection and analysis of data. Indeed, in the 21st century, documentary linguistics saw a change in ideologies from the early 20th century approach of fieldwork *on* a language, the 1960s approach of fieldwork *for* a language community and the 1980s approach of fieldwork *with* a language community, to fieldwork *by* the language community (Grinevald 2003: 58–60). The ideologies of fieldwork *with* or *by* a language community adhere to one of Dwyer's (2006: 38–40) five principles for carrying out ethical language documentation: the principle of reciprocity and equity. This principle asserts that the research relationship must be consultative, continuously negotiated and respectful and research should be planned collaboratively. These ideologies are evident in language documentation projects today and this is the approach I adopted in my own fieldwork as described below and in §1.3.6.1.2 where I discuss how community members acted as co-researchers in the transcription, translation and analysis of Papapana. It might also be advantageous for a speaker to collect recorded data as it may mitigate against possible effects of "foreigner talk", that is, speakers might behave differently when being recorded by another fluent speaker. However, it was not possible for me to recruit speakers to collect recorded data because speakers were apprehensive about using the equipment, especially without me present.

During my fieldwork, I held regular meetings to facilitate and focus the activities of participants and foster a spirit of project ownership and community involvement. The first of these meetings took place the day after I arrived in Barora, at the Sunday church service in Teperoi. John Konnou introduced me to the wider community and I established the project. I sought approval and guidance on culturally appropriate ways of proceeding, we discussed project objectives in relation to community needs, we determined recordings to be made, including genres and topics and we identified speakers whom it would be appropriate to record (see §1.3.5.1 and §1.3.5.2), as well as those interested in assisting with transcription and translation (see §1.3.6.1.2). After church services, there were often announcements and I regularly took this as an opportunity to update the wider community about the progress of the project, seek input and encourage further participation. In October 2011 I even had the opportunity to give a Powerpoint presentation in one of the school buildings. I presented the background context to the project, the progress and direction of the project and the outcomes to date, such as audio recordings. Prior to my departure in March 2012, I ran a meeting to consult with the community about the progress and direction of the project, options for storing materials, the creation of community-oriented outputs and any restrictions the community would like to place on data access. When I returned in 2013, I ran similar meetings to recommence and to conclude the project.

1.3.4 Participant recruitment, payment and consent

Community members were supportive of the project and the project seemed to generate some enthusiasm for the language; for example, one evening in Barora, community members crowded around my laptop to listen to excerpts of audio recordings and look at the draft dictionary I had begun to compile. This then prompted some Papapana speakers to teach Papapana words to the non-Papapana-speaking community members.

In total, I recorded forty-three Papapana speakers, that is, around 40% of the population of fluent speakers. Of these, seventeen speakers were video-recorded either as well as or instead of being audio-recorded. I did what I could to encourage more speakers to participate in audio or video recordings, but of course I had to respect an individual's choice to not participate. One Papapana speaker did not want their voice to be recorded and played elsewhere, some speakers were reluctant to be recorded out of shyness, and some were reluctant because of their insecurity about their competency, while other speakers simply had other priorities or commitments.

60% of the recorded participants were women and around 70% of the text recordings were with women: this could be because I am female and women felt more comfortable working with me than the men did. The arrival of my partner, Jeff, in January 2012 certainly facilitated my work in this respect. Jeff involved himself in all aspects of village life and was allowed to participate in men's activities that I was not, such as fishing or collecting bamboo to make smoking pipes. As a result, I had more interaction with men in the community and opportunities arose to record accounts of these activities, where previously I had struggled to record such accounts.

8% of recorded participants were under the age of thirty, 26% were in their thirties, 30% in their forties, 19% in their fifties and 16% were over sixty years old. A range of age groups is therefore represented, given the fact that fluent and confident speakers were generally older than thirty years old (see §2.3).

Most of the participants were housewives or subsistence farmers, but 16% worked in the education sector and 5% worked as skilled tradespersons. A few of the older speakers had previously worked in nursing, administration or skilled trades.

The recruitment of research assistants to transcribe and translate the recordings was restricted by the fact that only five individuals were identified as fluent speakers and also as literate (in any language), and of those, three were teachers. My principal research assistants were Casilda Vavetaovi-Atuvia, Francis Abea, and the Secretary of the Chiefs Committee Maureen Magua. I was also assisted by Francis' sister Georgina Rereo, and later their brother Max Wabe, while another speaker, Gerard Epa, assisted me for a short period while he was visiting from Port Moresby. Some of these speakers also contributed to text recordings, while others preferred to participate in elicitation recordings.

The Papapana speakers who participated in the project gave generously of their time and were interested in the project, and many did not expect payment. Nevertheless, for ethical reasons, I ensured that every participant was paid as compensation for their time and as a token of gratitude. I sought guidance about payment and appropriate rates from community leaders at the project outset. The hourly rate of pay for transcription and translation work was based on the average hourly teacher wage, while a set payment was given for a recording session.

An important feature of documentary linguistics outlined by Woodbury (2003: 47) is that a corpus should be ethical, that is, it "should respect intellectual property rights, moral rights, as well as both individual and cultural sensitivities about access and use" (Austin and Grenoble 2007: 16). Another two of Dwyer's (2006: 38–40) principles involve doing no harm and obtaining informed consent, which should relate not just to the recording of data, but also to the archiving and dissemination of data. Accordingly, I obtained informed consent in writing for all participants who were recorded or photographed. Unfortunately the information sheets and consent forms were not translated into Tok Pisin in time so if a participant could not read English, then I or another community member would translate the information into either Tok Pisin or Papapana. It should be noted that while obtaining informed consent is a necessary part of conducting human research within my culture, this concept was completely unknown to community members and they were often bewildered by the process. The wishes of each participant and the community have been adhered to in relation to data access and dissemination of documentation outputs. All participants agreed to be referenced by their name rather than a pseudonym.

1.3.5 Data collection

To fulfil the aims of my doctoral project and thesis, from which this book arises, I employed a number of data collection methods and collected a broad range of data types: audio and video recordings of lexical and grammatical elicitation (§1.3.5.1), audio and video recordings of texts (§1.3.5.2), notes on linguistic data obtained through participant observation, unrecorded elicitation, and the creation of community materials (§1.3.5.3), photographs (§1.3.5.4), and sociolinguistic and genealogical data obtained through informal interviews, compiling genealogical profiles and participant observation (§1.3.5.5). See §1.3.8 for details on accessing the audio, video and photographic data.

All audio documentation was gathered using a solid state digital audio recorder and recordings were made as WAV files at 48KHz 24bit. Video documentation was recorded in MiniDV format and audio input to video recordings was taken from audio recorder output channels to ensure maximal quality. Photographs were mainly captured on my own digital SLR camera or occasionally on another digital camera, and always as JPEG files. Lanyard microphones were generally used to increase range of capture and reduce risk of interference but sometimes I used the stereo microphones built in to the audio recorder, or a microphone mounted on the video recorder.

1.3.5.1 Lexical and grammatical elicitation recordings

Lüpke (2009: 62) identifies three types of communicative events which result from different data collection methods. One of these is elicitation, such as word lists, paradigm lists and acceptability judgements. Elicitations are heavily influenced linguistically by the researcher and only created for the sake of the researcher.

In total I audio-recorded 48.5 hours of lexical and grammatical elicitation sessions: around four hours were recorded in Barora and three hours in Teperoi during my first field trip, while the remaining forty-one hours were recorded in Teperoi during my second field trip.

In Barora, I elicited a basic wordlist of around 350 words using pictures, props and translation from Tok Pisin, or occasionally English. I also elicited basic clause structures, possessed noun phrases, and a few complex sentences. However, my competency in Tok Pisin limited further elicitation at that point, so I moved on to recording texts.

In Teperoi, in December 2011 and January 2012 I conducted more elicitation sessions focusing on numerals, tense, aspect and mode (TAM), pronouns and possession. The main elicitation methods I employed were translation and back translation, but also included data manipulation and grammaticality judgements. These sessions were conducted in Tok Pisin (or English, as one particular participant during those months was fluent in English).

The large majority of elicitation took place during my second field trip in Teperoi in 2013. Back in Australia, between the two field trips, I had analysed the data collected during the first field trip and drafted my thesis chapters. The process of drafting my thesis chapters allowed me to identify gaps and uncertainties in my description of Papapana. I returned to Bougainville in 2013 with sixteen elicitation session plans designed to obtain the missing information or to test hypotheses. By this point I was much more competent and fluent in Tok Pisin which greatly benefited this data collection. During this field trip I analysed the data I had collected and on the basis of my findings, I planned and conducted a further thirteen sessions. These sessions were conducted in Tok Pisin and/or English, and the elicitation methods I employed included translation, back translation, asking questions about data already recorded, data manipulation, grammaticality judgements, stimulus tools such as pictures, and scenario-based questionnaires (which are discussed in §4.5 and §7.1).

Elicitation sessions were generally conducted with two to four speakers in order to collect a range of data and opinions, and to allow data to be checked and confirmed at the same time as collection. When there was disagreement or uncertainty among speakers, the data was checked with and/or elicited from other speakers in a subsequent elicitation session. The elicitation sessions were invaluable as a more structured approach to language learning and analysis, and provided information about Papapana that it was not possible to deduce from the text recordings or observed communication.

1.3.5.2 Text recordings

The other two types of communicative events identified by Lüpke (2009: 62) are observed communicative events and staged communicative events. With observed communicative events, such as narratives, the only influence of the researcher is their presence. Staged communicative events, such as when speakers are asked to describe objects, represent a kind of middle ground between observed communicative events and elicitations because they are staged for linguistic purposes but use non-linguistic prompts and are thus less likely to be directly influenced by the researcher.

In total I recorded 10.5 hours of text sessions, which were generally observed communicative events but also included staged communicative events: fifty-one minutes were recorded in Barora and 9.5 hours in Teperoi during my first field trip, while eight minutes were recorded in Teperoi during my second field trip. Almost five hours of these recordings were simultaneously captured on video and proportionately represent the topics and genres targeted for audio capture. The text recordings are generally monologues and include the following genres: custom description, contemporary lifestyle description, procedural description, geographical description, identification of flora and fauna and description of their uses, personal narrative, traditional narrative, account of local or personal history, personal opinion. Some text recordings were of songs, either in isolation or as part of a custom description or traditional narrative.

Often participants had a clear idea of what they wanted to talk about but when they did not, I suggested topics to prompt them. Sometimes the ideas for text recording sessions would arise during general discussion with community members; for example, while walking around the village, I asked for the name of a tree in Papapana and that prompted the paramount chief's wife, Margaret Oavi, to bring me plant samples and teach me their uses and Papapana names (see Figure 1.5). On other occasions, I identified particular genres or topics that were under-represented in the corpus and invited speakers to participate if they were able to assist in collecting this data. The audience was often just myself but sometimes the speaker would tell the story to an organised or impromptu audience (which may of course have lead speakers to speak differently).

Figure 1.5: Margaret Oavi with plants, Teperoi, 2011.

1.3.5.3 Other linguistic data: participant observation, elicitation, community materials

Some linguistic data was not audio- or video-recorded but handwritten in my notebooks. This includes lexicon, expressions, sentences and grammatical features I was taught or acquired as the result of living in the community and participating in village activities. The data collected in informal settings was always checked and confirmed later with other speakers in more formal settings. Everett (2001) argues for the advantages of learning the language under study monolingually, through participation in community life, observing language in use and constant interaction with speakers on a daily basis. Although the first two methods were possible, constant interaction in Papapana was not possible because Tok Pisin is the primary means of communication in the community (see §2.5). It was also not practically possible to live with a family in which both parents spoke Papapana. Nevertheless, my hosts Helen and Casilda were Papapana speakers and I learnt a lot from living with them as I could practice and ask questions about Papapana on a daily basis. Helen was interested in the project and contributed considerably to elicitation and text recordings, especially while I was living in Barora. Casilda had a keen interest in the project and contributed significantly to elicitation sessions, and transcription and translation. She is a natural linguist and has a great grasp of the grammar and semantics of Papapana. She is skilled at translating and explaining the meanings of lexemes and grammatical features, which was facilitated by her good command of English and her knowledge of grammatical terminology.

Other linguistic data recorded in my notebooks includes data collected as part of lexical, orthographic and grammatical elicitation sessions that it was not possible to record, and of sessions during the second field trip in which I worked with speakers to create community materials. The community materials comprise of a short dictionary, four pedagogical readers (based on the SIL Shell books) and ten illustrated vocabulary books for the alphabet, numbers, colours and particular cultural domains (fish, marine animals, birds, plants, things/animals in the village, geographic/meteorological phenomena, body parts). Checking the draft dictionary provided information on the lexicon, phonology and orthography, and creating illustrated trilingual vocabulary books for particular cultural domains was a great source of lexical data and grammatical information such as noun class and nominal modifiers. The community materials themselves served as visual elicitation materials for lexical data that it would otherwise have been difficult to collect; for example, showing pictures of fish for which I already had the English or scientific names was a much more effective method of eliciting Papapana fish names than if speakers had listed fish names or shown me fish that I was unable to identify. The pedagogical readers were also a good source of some lexical data and grammatical information.

1.3.5.4 Photographs

There are currently around 200 digital photographs in the documentation collection that capture local flora and fauna (mainly shells and plants), cultural artefacts, socio-cultural activities, speakers and the local environment. These photographs are often associated with items or activities mentioned in a particular text recording, while others capture an item that individuals brought to show me and teach me the name and use of. It was not possible to identify and translate the name of a number of items, thus the photographs provide a record of the word's referent. For other items, the photographs have proven useful in identification and translation of items and names that it was not possible to identify and translate in the field.

1.3.5.5 Sociolinguistic and genealogical data: informal interviews, genealogical profiles and participant observation

I collected sociolinguistic and genealogical data through informal interviews, compiling genealogical profiles, and participant observation.

I conducted around fifteen informal interviews with speakers and/or community members in Barora in 2011 and six in Teperoi in 2013. Questions focused on linguistic repertoires, perceptions of language ability, present and past language use, language attitudes, and the history of Papapana people and their contact with other speech communities.

At the beginning of my first field trip I tried to establish how many people were fluent in Papapana. However, it was difficult to establish how many people lived in each house, let alone how many of them spoke Papapana, because people often left the village during the day to attend to duties such as gardening or fishing, and when they were in the village, people were not necessarily inside or outside their own house. It was therefore more accurate to record the genealogical relationships of the community members and then to establish which language(s) each person spoke. By the end of my first field trip I had collected genealogical data for inhabitants of the Papapana villages Barora, Peuni, Koikoi and Teperoi and rough data for those in Maras and Iraka. During my second field trip I checked, updated and expanded this data, and subsequently accounted for around 800 individuals who lived in the Papapana villages or were closely related to its inhabitants. The data I collected for an individual included: name(s); gender; age; location; linguistic repertoire; competency in Papapana (first language/fluent speakers with full productive ability, second language/semi-speakers with partial productive ability, or people with only passive understanding). I was not able to meet every single individual so some of the information was obtained from their relatives, and despite my best efforts, some of the data is unknown or approximate. For the speakers who participated in audio or video recordings, their competency in Papapana was self-evident but for others I relied on speakers' judgements.

Participant observation is a primary source of the sociolinguistic data presented in this book. Throughout my fieldwork, I carried a notebook with me to record information and observations about language use, language contact, language attitudes, government and educational policies, the historical, geographic and environmental context, and the socio-cultural context. In order to make accurate observations and obtain this information, it was necessary to gain the community's trust and I achieved this through the way in which I managed the project, as outlined in §1.3.3 and §1.3.4, and by participating in community life (e.g. preparing local food, attending church etc.). I also obliged community members in sharing my personal photographs and stories about my own culture to foster trust and friendships. The arrival of my partner Jeff facilitated my interaction and involvement in the community, not only from a work perspective as mentioned in §1.3.4, but also because kin relationships are important in the Papapana community and so having my "man" present normalised me as a person and provided another topic of conversation. Jeff's presence also gave me more flexibility in terms of visiting other villages because I had a companion, whereas previously I had to rely on community members to accompany me to other villages as they were reluctant to let me travel on my own.

1.3.6 Data processing

This section describes how the data described in §1.3.5 was stored securely and processed (including time-aligned transcription and translation in ELAN and analysis in Toolbox), and the metadata conventions that were employed.

1.3.6.1 Elicitation and text recordings

1.3.6.1.1 Secure storage

In the field I uploaded audio data to my laptop and to an external hard-drive, which was stored in a separate location to minimise risk. I also backed up this data on CDs. Video tapes were carried back to Australia and securely stored until they could be digitised, after which they were also backed up on an external hard-drive.

Audio recordings were reduced to 48kHz 16bit for import into ELAN and export from ELAN to Toolbox. After video recordings were digitised, they were imported into the existing ELAN file. There is one Toolbox database comprising all exported ELAN files to ease the process of searching for data and comparing results from different sessions. The ELAN and Toolbox files were similarly backed up on external hard-drive and CD in the field.

Most elicitation annotation and analysis were recorded in a notebook. I took photographs of these notes in the field and backed them up on external hard-drive. The annotation and analysis from the 2013 elicitation sessions has subsequently been typed into Word documents to ease the process of searching for and analysing data.

1.3.6.1.2 Transcription and translation

All text recordings from both field trips, and some elicitation recordings from the first field trip, have time-aligned transcription and translation in ELAN and have been exported to Toolbox. Elicitation recordings from the second field trip do not have time-aligned transcription and translation, but do have annotations and analytical notes in Word. All time-aligned transcriptions, translations and annotations were completed in the field. The recording metadata spreadsheet (see §1.3.8 for details on accessing it) shows which recordings have time-aligned transcription and translation in ELAN and details of who assisted in these annotations.

The process of time-aligned transcription and translation of text recordings was hugely time-consuming, and often tedious. All research assistants showed great patience in this process. At the beginning of my fieldwork, I asked the research assistant to identify the boundaries of a sentence and I then segmented the audio file in ELAN (however, the boundaries did not always match sentence boundaries so I had to adjust them later). Then we would listen to a segment and the research assistant would write the transcription into a notebook. I then typed this into the ELAN file. Once all transcription was complete, we would then check the transcription and the research assistant would provide a translation into Tok Pisin or English, and I would type the translation in English into ELAN. Later on, I began to segment the audio file myself prior to working with the research assistant. By the end of my fieldwork, to allow more than one research assistant to be working simultaneously and to speed up the process, I had begun to give research assistants an mp3 player to listen to the recording and transcribe it independently in a notebook. This was possible as they were now more competent and confident in their transcription skills. Then I would type this transcription into ELAN on my own, and often write a rough translation, then later check the transcription and translation with the same or a different research assistant. The transcription and translation process was invaluable in my acquisition of Papapana not only because it was an opportunity to ask speakers about semantic, grammatical or cultural issues that arose, but also because it gave me concentrated and constant exposure to Papapana.

1.3.6.1.3 Metadata

The audio and video files have been labelled in accordance with the requirements of the Endangered Language Archive (ELAR).[1] An example file name is *ES1-PPNE006-001A.wav*. Table 1.1 shows the meaning of the sequence of letters and numbers in a file name.

---

[1] ELAR is part of the library at the School of Oriental and African Studies (SOAS) at the University of London, England.

Table 1.1: Recording file name key.

File name letter/ number	Meaning
ES	The initials of the fieldworker and file creator, Ellen Smith
1 or 2	First fieldwork trip, or second fieldwork trip
PPN	Papapana ISO code
E or T	Elicitation session, or Text session
001	Session number
-001	Session part number (some sessions were recorded in parts with breaks in between)
A or B	Track code (some sessions or session parts were recorded across more than one audio track when a recording was unexpectedly interrupted). Alternatively, the *A* track contains the introductory metadata information that was usually recorded at the start of a track.
a or b	Two files were mistakenly labelled with the same session number and these small case letters distinguish between the two separate files.
.wav, .mp4, .eaf or .txt	The file type: audio, video, ELAN annotation file, or text file for use in Toolbox

Audio, video, transcription and text files that represent the same recording are thus labelled identically except for the file type. This identical label is the *bundle identifier*. A bundle minimally contains an audio file but may also contain a video file of the same recording. Table 1.2 shows the metadata that is recorded for audio files, video files and both (see §1.3.8 for details on accessing the recording

Table 1.2: Metadata fields.

File type	Metadata
Audio	Device, microphone, sampling rate and size, original sampling rate and size
Video	Device, format, original format
Audio and video	Recording duration, date, location, creator, participants, comments (such as audience), languages used, genre, content and access rights
Annotation	Main annotator, co-annotator
Annotation Text	Main annotator, co-annotator

metadata spreadsheet). A bundle may contain an annotation file and annotation text file, in which case the metadata recorded for the annotation file includes the annotator's names. A bundle may also contain associated images. A particular image may be associated with more than one bundle and therefore the metadata for the image is recorded in a separate metadata file (see §1.3.6.2). Similarly, information about the participant is recorded in a separate metadata file.

1.3.6.2 Photographs

In the field I uploaded photographic data to my laptop and to an external hard-drive. Sometimes it was necessary to edit the photograph by changing orientation, cropping or improving the quality. The photographs and other illustrative material (including several videos of activities without speech) have been labelled in accordance with the requirements of ELAR. The metadata recorded for images includes: device, format, date, location, creator, content, comments and access rights.

1.3.6.3 Sociolinguistic, genealogical and other linguistic data

As a means of backing up the data in the field, handwritten sociolinguistic and genealogical data and handwritten linguistic data were photographed, or typed into a Word document or entered into the Toolbox dictionary. In between the two field trips I used a commercial software program, Family Tree Maker, to enter the genealogical information and produce various family trees in PDF format. During my second field trip I used paper copies of these documents to check information and then regularly updated the Family Tree Maker database. Once complete I was able to convert this to GEDCOM[2] files and export to an Excel spreadsheet. Unfortunately it was not possible to retain the genealogical relationships in Excel but the format did allow me to more easily generate demographic figures. All these files were backed up on external hard-drive and CD.

1.3.7 Data analysis and presentation

The grammatical analysis of Papapana is based on all the data that I collected (see §1.3.5). In the grammatical description of Papapana, I have endeavoured to exemplify my analysis with spontaneously produced utterances from text

---

2 GEDCOM stands for GEnealogical Data COMmunication and is a proprietary and open specification for exchanging genealogical data between different genealogy software.

recordings but where that was not possible, I have used elicited data. I have also sometimes used elicited data when it more clearly exemplifies the analysis than text data.

The source of the data is indicated in the reference numbers given after each example. The reference numbers reflect the file names as described in §1.3.6.1.3. An audio file name such as *ES1-PPNE006-001A.wav* is reduced to *1-E006* thus indicating the fieldwork trip, the session type (elicitation 'E' or text 'T') and the session number. If the session was recorded in parts and/or as different tracks, the session part number and/or track code are also given, e.g. *1-E006-1A*. When data comes from a time-aligned text recording, the time of the segment (in hours, minutes, seconds and milliseconds) is given after the rest of the reference, e.g. *1-T063-00:00:17.130*. Since elicitation recordings are not time-aligned, no time is given. Where data comes from unrecorded elicitation sessions, the example is referenced as *Fieldnotes* and accompanied by the date those notes were taken. When analysis is built on the corpus as a whole (such as when analysing a common word like *naorawi* 'the/a man', which occurs in many different texts) no reference is given.

Particular elicitation methods and tools are referenced and/or discussed at the relevant points. When relevant, linguistic data is also presented with explanations providing the context for an utterance, since "the annotation of cultural/contextual information is vital to reconstructing, within the linguist's grammar, the sinew and fiber of the speaker's grammar" (Everett 2001: 186).

My analysis is written in terms of "basic linguistic theory" (Dixon 2010) which "has supplemented traditional grammar with a variety of ideas from structuralism, generative grammar [. . .] and typology" (Dryer 2006: 211). As such the terminology that is used should be understood by the majority of linguists, and is relevant for Papapana.

1.3.8 Archiving and access to data, annotations, metadata and other project outcomes

Archiving is a significant concern in documentary linguistics as it ensures materials are available to potential users in the future. Raw data should be archived not only "to keep the data safe [. . . but also] to let others know what has been recorded" (Bowern 2008: 60). Archiving materials involves preparation of the recorded data, annotations and metadata so that "the information it contains is maximally informative and explicitly expressed, encoded for long-term accessibility and safely stored with a reputable organisation that can guarantee long-term curation" (Austin 2006: 100).

Documentation outcomes from my doctoral project have been archived with ELAR (Smith 2015b).[3] ELAR is a digital repository and the Papapana collection can be accessed by any registered ELAR user (registration is free).[4] The collection includes all text and elicitation audio, video and photographic data, all ELAN and Toolbox Text files, all metadata, my doctoral thesis and all community materials (a short dictionary, four pedagogical readers and ten illustrated vocabulary books for particular cultural domains).[5] The elicitation annotations and analytical notes in Word are yet to be organised into a more useable format and archived.

In consultation with the community, it was agreed that documentation outcomes should be made accessible to the Papapana community through local institutions such as the National Research Institute of Papua New Guinea in Port Moresby, the University of Papua New Guinea in Port Moresby and Buka, the SIL library in Buka, and the Teperoi Primary School. In 2015 I posted these institutions copies of my thesis and all community materials. In 2018, I posted further copies to the Papapana community and Teperoi school, the Unity Library in Buka, and the Department of Education in Buka.

1.3.9 Follow-up and scoping visit

In April 2018, I visited Bougainville for three weeks in order to scope out the feasibility of future linguistic research on the island. I aimed to establish and re-establish connections with local gatekeepers and potential participants in the communities, and to test data collection methods. Since my last field trip in 2013, I had maintained contact with some community members (mostly Casilda and Francis), but contact was sporadic and unreliable due to poor mobile phone networks and lack of mains electricity and postal addresses in the villages.

Over the three weeks of the 2018 visit, I visited homes in Teperoi, Maras, Koikoi, Peuni and Barora, and attended two church services in Teperoi, after which I was able to give short announcements. Much of this time was spent re-establishing and strengthening my friendships and connections. I brought

---

3 The collection can be found at http://elar.soas.ac.uk/deposit/0313
4 For more information on access protocols, see https://www.soas.ac.uk/elar/using-elar/access-protocol/
5 The ELAN (and Text) files in this deposit require further work to make the orthography and word boundaries in the transcriptions more consistent, and to make some of the translations more accurate. Examples in this book that have been taken from these ELAN files have been corrected in these areas.

photographs as gifts, informed the community of the completion of my thesis and my work on this book, and I showed them the draft dictionary, pedagogical readers and vocabulary books that I had made. It was rewarding to see their positive reactions to these materials and to show them concrete outputs from my doctoral project. I explained that I had returned to visit them, and to explore the possibilities of working with them again. I was delighted to be welcomed back warmly and enthusiastically, and to be given permission to return again for future research. With this in mind, I asked some community members to help me test some data collection methods, and to help me with the completion of this book by answering some questions about Papapana. I also sought opinions on the types of community materials they would like to result from future research. In addition, I made new connections with teachers in Teperoi and Asitavi, and during my time in Buka, I met John Konnou, and I was able to gain support for future research from official institutions and organisations, and to scope out possibilities for dissemination of future research.

During my doctoral project, I did not collect any conversational data and I was keen to test out methods for collecting this type of data. I tried recording observed communicative events whereby one speaker would tell a story about their local or personal history to the other speakers and they would then ask questions or discuss as a group; however this was only really successful in one of the five recordings and in the others, more of a monologue was produced. I also successfully recorded one staged communicative event where I asked Francis and a male elder to discuss a collection of photographs. In total, I video-recorded six dialogue sessions in Teperoi, amounting to 1 hour 5 minutes. Overall, six speakers took part in these recordings; three women and three men, all of whom I had worked with in 2011–2013. With Casilda's help, I used ELAN to transcribe and translate (into English or Tok Pisin) the utterances that were of interest or that I could not understand on my own, but these annotations are minimal due to the time constraints of the visit.

I also conducted and audio-recorded three elicitation sessions, amounting to 2 hours 15 minutes in total. Two of these sessions were with Casilda in Asitavi and one in Teperoi with a group of four women (of which three I had worked with in 2011–2013). These recordings are associated with annotations and analysis in Word.

During this visit, I kept a field diary in which I recorded sociolinguistic insights from conversations and my observations, and in which I noted lexical or grammatical features of the language that I observed, asked about, or that speakers taught me when they were correcting my spoken Papapana!

As before, I recorded the elicitation sessions using a solid state digital audio recorder and audio was recorded as WAV files at 48KHz 24bit. I used the built-in stereo microphone, or lanyard omnidirectional microphones. I recorded the dialogue sessions using a digital video camcorder, recording in AVCHD format. I used a directional stereo microphone mounted on the camcorder for all recordings, except one where the audio input to the video recording was taken from audio recorder output channels. I followed the same metadata conventions and the same procedures for secure data storage as described in §1.3.6. I have also continued the same practice for labelling and referring to recordings, with the addition of *D* to indicate dialogue sessions, and my new initials *ESD*. As with previous research, I obtained informed consent for these recordings and have adhered to the participants' wishes in relation to access and dissemination. All participants agreed to be referenced by their name rather than a pseudonym.

1.4 Book organisation and typological overview

This section outlines the book's organisation and provides an overview of the typological features of Papapana, pointing out particular areas of interest.

1.4.1 Background and sociolinguistic context

This introductory chapter has detailed the background to and focus of this book, previous research on and documentation of Papapana and related languages, and explained the methodology employed in data collection, processing, analysis and archiving. Chapter 2 *Language background and sociolinguistic context* discusses the language name and location, Papapana's genetic affiliation, speaker numbers and trends, and language contact, use and endangerment.

1.4.2 Phonology

Chapter 3 *Phonology* describes segmental phonology (including the phoneme inventory, allophones, phonological and morpho-phonological processes, and phonological variation and change), the orthography, phonotactics, reduplication patterns, and stress.

Papapana has five monophthongs /i; e; a; ɔ; u/. The three front unrounded vowels exhibit contrastive vowel length. Seventeen vowel combinations are attested in Papapana, of which seven are realized as, but are not phonemically, diphthongs: /ei; ai; ae; au; aɔ; ɔi; ɔe/. Papapana's consonant system consists of fourteen phonemes: /p; b; t; d; k; g; ʔ; m; n; ŋ; r; β; s; w/. The phonemes /r/ and /β/ exhibit allophonic variation: [ɾ] and [r] occur in free variation, as do [β],

[w] and [v]. Certain intervocalic environments trigger glottal epenthesis or glide creation, either of the labial-velar approximant [w] or the voiced palatal approximant [j]. The syllable structure is (C)V(V), except for non-lexicalized loanwords which allow codas and consonant clusters. Reduplication involves monosyllabic and disyllabic copying for both derivational and inflectional functions, but some verbs also display the cross-linguistically rare phenomenon of multiple reduplication to express a subtype of imperfective aspect (Smith 2016c). Multiple reduplication in Papapana may involve two monosyllabic reduplicants or a monosyllabic reduplicant followed by a disyllabic reduplicant. Feet are left-aligned syllabic trochees and word stress is predictable with primary stress falling on the first syllable of the first foot, which is unusual for Oceanic languages since stress usually falls on the penultimate syllable of a word. Furthermore, stem-medially, long vowel or diphthong formation is dependent on whether or not this results in extrametricality.

1.4.3 Word classes

Oceanic languages have figured prominently in typological and theoretical debates on distinguishing word classes, with some languages claimed to have no distinction between content words such as nouns and verbs, and others claimed to have distinct language-specific classes, which in some cases are multifunctional (van Lier 2016). Papapana does have distinct word classes including nouns, verbs, adjectives and adverbs. Word classes are defined in individual chapters. Chapter 4 defines nouns, pronouns, adjectives and demonstratives. Chapter 5 describes class, number and possession, for which nouns can be specified, and defines articles, numerals and quantifiers. Chapter 6 defines verbs, adverbs and directionals, while Chapter 7 describes tense, aspect, mode and negation for which verbs can be specified. Chapter 8 defines deictic locational words and adpositions, as well as clause-level adverbs. Chapter 9 defines interrogative terms and chapter 10 defines coordinators and subordinators.

I distinguish word classes based on formal criteria including inflectional morphology, derivational morphology, and syntactic distribution, that is, the constituents with which a word is compatible and the relative order of those constituents. These constituents often relate to the morphosyntactic categories for which a word is specifiable, such as noun class, possession, transitivity or aspect. I also describe the functions of a word class, but I do not use functions as defining criteria because there is not a one-to-one correspondence between form and function.

Derivational morphology in Papapana includes reduplication, a derivational suffix and to some extent, compounding. Words can also be derived from other word classes through zero-derivation.⁶ In this case, there is no change in form and the word class is identifiable only through inflectional morphology and/or syntactic distribution. For example, in (1), the first instance of *'a'ade'e* is a verb because it is the head of a verb complex (see below) which is marked by subject- and object-indexing clitics, and mode and aspect markers, while the second instance of *'a'ade'e* is a noun because it is marked by a specific article which agrees with the noun class of the noun.

(1)   *Anau*   ***u=ri***   ***'a'ade'e=i=a=u***
      1SG   1SG.SBJ=OPT   narrative=TR=3SG.OBJ=1SG.IPFV
      ***nu='a'ade'e* . . .**
      SPEC.CLII=narrative
      'I want to tell a story . . . '
      (1-T063-00:00:17.130)

Taking nouns and verbs as an example, the reason that I argue for zero-derivation is because firstly, not all nouns can be zero-derived as verbs, and not all verbs can be zero-derived as nouns. For example, *orete* 'to walk' and *vurau* 'to run' are both intransitive verbs which express the manner of movement, but while *orete* can be zero-derived as a noun denoting 'walking', *vurau* is reduplicated to *vuvurau* to denote 'car'. Secondly, nouns are not derived from a particular class of verb vis-a-vis transitivity or semantic class nor are verbs derived from a particular noun class. Thirdly, unlike lexical flexibility, zero-derivation "results in output forms with non-productively derivable semantics" (van Lier 2016: 203). Thus, when a noun is zero-derived from a verb, not only is noun class assignment varied and unpredictable, but the resulting noun might denote an action, resultative state or entity, instrument, abstract noun and so on (see §4.3.1). For example, while *orete* 'to walk' denotes 'walking' as a noun, *ari* 'to dig' denotes 'grave/hole' as a noun, not 'digging'. It is often difficult to determine which direction the zero-derivation has occurred in but I have generally made the decision based on the prototypical meaning of nouns and verbs as denoting objects or persons, and actions and events respectively, and/or based on the predictability of the meaning. I have also considered the relative frequency with which the word occurs as a noun or verb or otherwise in the corpus, and in some cases, cognates in related languages; for example, *'a'ade'e* is cognate with *kakadeke* 'narrative' in Torau (Palmer fieldnotes).

---

6 An alternate term for *zero derivation* is *conversion*. By using the term *zero derivation* I am not claiming there is a zero derivational morpheme.

1.4.4 Nouns, noun phrases, noun class, number and possession

Chapter 4 *Nouns and noun phrase structure* describes nominals (pronouns and nouns) and noun phrase structure, derived and compound nouns, and word classes and phrases which can modify nouns, including demonstratives, adjectives and adjective phrases, miscellaneous modifiers and an attributive preposition phrase. Chapter 5 *Noun class, number and possession* describes noun class and nominal number (including articles and numerals), possession, and quantifier phrases, which take noun phrase or preposition phrase complements.

A noun phrase (NP) may function as the core argument of a verbal or nonverbal predicate, a clausal adjunct, the complement of an adposition or quantifier, a possessor NP modifier and as a predicate in a verbless clause. Some nouns can also have an adnominal function in compounds and complex kinship terms. Nouns may be derived through zero derivation, reduplication, or reduplication and a derivational suffix. Papapana has three types of compound nouns, two of which may involve the *construct suffix -i* or *-ni* and reflect the Proto-Oceanic (POc) non-specific possessor constructions, while the third type involves the noun *mata* 'trait', a reduplicated verbal root and verbal morphology.

Papapana has the four separate pronominal paradigms that are widespread in Oceanic languages: independent pronouns, possessor suffixes, subject-indexing proclitics and object-indexing enclitics. In addition, Papapana has possessor proclitics which are not synchronically segmentable into a possessive constituent and possessor suffix, as in other Oceanic language, and postverbal subject-indexing (PSI) enclitics. All pronominal paradigms classify referents according to first, second or third person, with an inclusive/exclusive distinction in the first person, and distinguish between singular and plural number. Independent pronouns also distinguish dual and trial number. The other type of pronouns are the demonstrative pronouns. Papapana does not have possessive, interrogative, reflexive, reciprocal or relative pronouns.

The classification of nouns has a semantic basis and there are four noun classes in Papapana: a) Personal (including proper names, and four kinship terms referring to ancestors or taboo relationships), b) Class I (including nouns denoting units of time and periods of the day, celestial bodies, meteorological phenomena, marine vertebrates, fruit and nuts, and kinship terms that refer to kin who are in the same generation as the referent or have been acquired through marriage), c) Class II (including nouns denoting liquids, light and fire, body parts, birds, land-dwelling vertebrates, insects, marine invertebrates, plants and kinship terms that refer to kin who are in the generation below the referent) and d) Location (including institutionalised place names, nouns denoting familiar places, and locative part nouns such as 'inside'). Papapana also exhibits a very interesting pattern observed elsewhere in Northwest Solomonic languages where two words that have the same phonological form, but a different, though related, meaning can belong to different noun classes.

Nominal number can be expressed through lexical plurals and in some cases by reduplication, but this is not productive. Personal nouns can be marked by an associative plural marker *nia*. Otherwise, nouns are not inflected for number and instead nominal number is indicated by articles, numerals or quantifiers. The nominal number of core arguments is reflected in the verb complex by subject- and/or object-indexing clitics.

Articles are either independent or clitics, and precede the noun. They can code specificity and non-specificity, noun class, number, and semantic features such as diminutive and partitive categories. The noun class system interacts with number in a remarkable way involving inverse number marking, which is found in other Northwest Solomonic languages but is a typologically rare phenomenon.

The counting system is a combination of quinary and decimal. The numeral modifiers 'one' and 'two' are marked by *au* when they modify Class II nouns, while unusually, 'three' makes a human/non-human distinction. Ordinals are generally derived by means of the causative prefix and the cardinal numeral modifiers.

There are two quantifiers denoting 'other, some' and one indicating abundance. Quantifiers head a quantifier phrase (QP), which has a possessed or plural NP complement, a preposition phrase (PP) complement, or a partial NP complement in which the head has been elided.

In possessive constructions there is a formal distinction based on the semantic difference between inalienable and alienable nouns, which is expressed by direct and indirect constructions respectively. The direct construction is head-marking. Papapana also expresses possession via a preposition. Unlike many Oceanic languages, Papapana does not have possessive classifiers denoting different kinds of possessive relationship.

There is a person-based demonstrative paradigm and a further paradigm based on distance relative to the speaker: these can operate separately or together. Adjectives occur in an adjective phrase (AP) with an article that agrees in noun class and/or number with the head noun that the AP is modifying, though a small group of adjectives can also modify a noun without being marked by an article.

While articles are always prenominal, and there is a set of miscellaneous nominal modifiers that are always postnominal, Papapana shows considerable variation in the position of numeral phrases, possessor NPs, demonstratives, and adjectives and APs in the NP: this reflects the mixture of left-headedness and right-headedness in Papapana more generally and may be attributed to contact with Papuan languages of the region (see Smith 2016a). Similarly, QPs may be left- or right-headed.

1.4.5 Verbs and the verb complex

Chapter 6 *Verbs and the verb complex* describes verbs and the structure of the verb complex, verbal derivation and compounding, argument marking and alignment, verb types and valency-changing operations, and verb serialisation. Verbs can be modified by directionals and adverbs. Chapter 7 *Tense, aspect and mode* describes tense, aspect and mode (TAM) marking, imperative and hortative clauses, and negation within the verb complex.

Verbs function primarily as predicates and may be derived through zero-derivation or reduplication. Compound verbs are not common. The *verb complex* (VC) refers to the verbal head (or sequence of verbs in a serial construction) with its accompanying modifiers: subject-indexing and object-indexing clitics, the emphatic marker *to*, TAM markers, negative markers, directionals and adverbs. The verbal head and its modifiers occur in a fixed structural relationship and the term *verb complex* is used as a descriptive device to capture this relationship. The VC does not include arguments and the object-indexing enclitics are considered to be agreement rather than pronominal objects because they can co-occur with coreferential lexical object NPs (and sometimes with free conominal pronouns); therefore, without the inclusion of the object NP, the VC does not equate to a verb phrase (VP) (see §6.3.2). Whether or not Papapana even has a VP is open to further research.

Papapana is nominative-accusative in its formal marking of core arguments, and makes a distinction between primary and secondary objects. Core arguments are indexed in the VC by subject proclitics and object enclitics, and sometimes postverbal subject-indexing (PSI) enclitics, which belong to three of Papapana's six pronominal paradigms. Subject proclitics are not portmanteau forms combining with TAM markers, as attested in several Northwest Solomonic languages.

Verbs may be intransitive, monotransitive, ditransitive or ambitransitive. Valency-changing operations include a postverbal applicative marker, a causative prefix, a detransitivising prefix, a preverbal applicative comitative marker, object incorporation, transitivity discord and a reflexive/reciprocal marker (which co-occurs with reduplication in reciprocal constructions).

Up to two verbs can occur in a serial verb construction (SVC). Papapana SVCs are nuclear and asymmetrical. Semantically, there are three directional SVCs, one causative SVC, one cause-effect SVC and one SVC which involves the verb *vowa ~ vewa* 'be like' and expresses similarity or manner.

Directionals belong to a small closed class of words which can optionally modify a verb. There are four types: geocentric directionals which occur immediately after the verb, deictic directionals which occur at the end of the VC, sequential directionals which are in preverbal position, and a postverbal allative directional which requires a locative phrase and which is polysemous with the verb *vowa ~ vewa* 'be like' and the adnominal associative marker.

Adverbs in Papapana express temporal and aspectual notions, manner, spatial location and degree. Three are preverbal but the rest are postverbal. Some of these adverbs are also attested at the clausal level, while others may function in the NP as general modifiers.

Papapana has a complex system of TAM marking in which verbal reduplication and various combinations of preverbal and postverbal markers are used to make TAM distinctions. Present tense is unmarked but past and future tense are marked. Five aspectual distinctions are encoded: habitual, continuous, proximative, repetitive and completive. Four mode distinctions are encoded: hypothetical conditional, counterfactual conditional, optative and apprehensive. Imperative and hortative clauses may carry either no TAM marking, or the irrealis mode enclitic. Most Northwest Solomonic languages display PSI, which reflects former possessor indexing. In Papapana, PSI enclitics function with the optative mode marker to indicate optative mode or proximative aspect, and with various patterns of verbal reduplication to indicate habitual or continuous aspect.

Within the VC, negation of verbal assertive predicates is expressed by a preverbal negative marker, while imperatives are negated by verbal reduplication and either the preverbal negative marker or the apprehensive mode marker. The apprehensive mode marker is also used in conjunction with the irrealis mode enclitic in an apprehension-causing adverbial clause.

1.4.6 Clause types and structures

Chapter 8 *Obliques, adjuncts and clause-level adverbs* discusses the internal characteristics of obliques and other clause-level adjuncts, and the position of obliques and adjuncts in the clause. Clause-level adjuncts in Papapana can be noun phrases, deictic locational words, adposition phrases and clause-level adverbs. Chapter 9 *Clause types and structures* describes declarative verbal clauses with core arguments, imperative and hortative clauses, interrogative clauses, verbal existential clauses, verbal negative clauses and verbless clauses. For each clause type, I discuss clause structure.

Obliques may be licenced by the prepositions *eangoiena* 'until', *avosia* 'like' and *te*, or the nascent postposition *tomana* 'with', *Te* expresses temporal location, static location of an entity, or the goal or source to or from which movement or action is directed. *Te* may also mark possession and sometimes the semantic roles of instrument, addressee, recipient and beneficiary. Some Class I nouns referring to time, Location nouns (some of which are marked by the locative case prefix *i-*), deictic locational words and the bound noun *peite-* 'own' can function as adjuncts. Obliques are typically expressed as preposition phrases in Northwest Solomonic languages, whereas the nascent postposition *tomana* is atypical and may have grammaticalised as a comitative marker from the Papapana additive marker denoting 'too' under the influence of the neighbouring Papuan language Rotokas. The position of obliques and adjuncts in the clause is variable. Most often, obliques and adjuncts are clause-final, but they may also occur clause-initially, and sometimes they can occur between an argument NP and the VC.

Adverbs operating at the clausal level may be spatial, manner or modal adverbs, and can occur clause-initially, clause-finally or between an argument NP and the VC.

Constituent order in declarative verbal clauses shows considerable variation. In intransitive clauses, verb-final clause order is the basic clause order and the pragmatically marked clause order when the subject is Topic, while verb-initial clause order is highly restricted. In pragmatically unmarked monotransitive clauses, both SVO and SOV order are possible and frequent and found across a variety of text genres, produced by a range of speakers. The pragmatically marked monotransitive clause order involves a clause initial Topic position. In ditransitive clauses the order is either verb medial or verb final. The variation in constituent order is also argued to be the result of Papuan contact (Smith 2016a).

In interrogative clauses, intonation patterns and tags mark polar questions, while content questions are formed by employing one of seven interrogative terms. Monotransitive interrogative clauses which inquire about core arguments are always verb-final, with the known argument NP occurring clause-initially and the interrogative constituent occurring clause-medially. In contrast, ditransitive interrogative clauses which inquire about one of the object arguments are subject-initial, with the interrogative constituent occurring between the subject and the VC, and the known object argument occurring after the VC. A NP containing an adnominal interrogative term occurs clause-initially. When an interrogative term functions as an adjunct, it is either clause-initial or between the subject and VC.

Imperative and hortative clauses do not differ in clause order from other clauses, but are less likely to contain a subject NP. Verbal existential clauses in Papapana employ one of three existential verbs. The form *aruai* may function as the negative answer to questions, the tag *o aruai* 'or not', a negative existential verb, and as a clausal negative marker with verbal assertive predicates, which may or may not also be marked by the preverbal negative marker.

Papapana does not have copula verbs. In verbless clauses in Papapana the predicate may be a NP which expresses identity (proper inclusion or equation), possession or location, or may be negated. The subject NP and the predicate NP are juxtaposed and there is no overt marking to indicate the function of the NP. The predicate of a verbless clause may also be an interrogative term, a locative PP, an attributive PP, a numeral phrase, or an adjective phrase. A verbless existential clause can consist of just the predicate NP with no subject NP, but the predicate noun must be modified by a numeral or negative marker. There are also verbless possessive clauses involving *pea* 'possession' which is followed by a possessum noun marked by a possessor suffix; in such a construction the coreferent possessor NP is the subject.

1.4.7 Complex sentences

Finally, Chapter 10 *Complex sentences* describes coordination, relative clauses, adverbial clauses and complement clauses.

Papapana coordinating constructions may be asyndetic, or syndetic and employ one of three coordinators expressing conjunction or adversative coordination, disjunction and sequential coordination. Some coordinators may conjoin NPs and PPs as well as clauses. Dual independent pronouns can coordinate NPs, as well as having an inclusory function.

Relative clauses are externally headed and postnominal, and there is no formal difference between restrictive and non-restrictive relative clauses. A relativiser signals the beginning of the relative clause and connects the relative clause to the matrix noun. All grammatical relations can be relativised except the object of a comparative, though a relativised NP as possessor is somewhat limited. The relativised function is indicated by the gap strategy, and if the relativised function is subject or object, then the subject or object enclitic may be an overt expression of the relativised noun, as is common in Oceanic languages.

Papapana has conditional and apprehensive adverbial clauses, and adverbial clauses expressing purpose, temporal location, spatial location, reason, result, concession and similarity/manner. The adverbial clause may be linked asyndetically to the main clause that it modifies or linked by a subordinator.

Complement clauses only function as object arguments, and may be either finite or non-finite. Both finite and non-finite complement clauses may occur in reported speech sentences. Finite complements may be formally unmarked, as is typical of Oceanic languages or linked to the matrix clause by a subordinator. A complement introduced by a subordinator may or may not be indexed by object enclitics in the VC of the matrix clause. Non-finite complement clauses are introduced by a subordinator. There is no one-to-one correspondence between the verb category and the structural type of the complement, and even a single verb may take different types of complement.

Chapter 2
Language background and sociolinguistic context

This chapter presents sociolinguistic and historical information about Papapana to contextualise the language. The name of the language and its geographical location are discussed in §2.1 and its genetic affiliation in §2.2. The number, proportion and distribution of Papapana speakers are described in §2.3 and the historical and current language contact situation is discussed in §2.4. Finally, language use and endangerment are discussed in §2.5 and §2.6. This chapter intends to provide socio-historical and cultural background to text recording excerpts and grammatical features of the language, and to show the type and intensity of language contact that has induced some of Papapana's linguistic variation and change. Similarly, some variation, or speakers' uncertainty about linguistic features, can be explained by Papapana's declining ethnolinguistic vitality. Throughout the grammar, I make cross-linguistic comparisons with related Oceanic languages and consider diachronic explanations for synchronic Papapana; therefore, the current chapter is also important in establishing the genetic relationships and historical contact between these languages and their communities. While some of the research presented in this chapter also appears in Smith (2016a) and Smith (2016b), this chapter is much more detailed and is updated with sociolinguistic data collected in 2018.

2.1 The name and location of the Papapana language

Papapana is a language of Papua New Guinea (PNG), spoken on the northeast coast of Bougainville island, in the Autonomous Region of Bougainville (see Figure 2.1).

The Papapana speech community originates in the village of Teperoi but in 2011–2018 the community was also located in five other villages north and south of Teperoi: Peuni, Koikoi, Maras, Barora and Iraka (see Figure 2.2 for the location of Koikoi and Iraka in Bougainville, along with other important locations, and see Figure 2.3 for the relative locations of all six Papapana villages). Peuni, Barora and Iraka villages were each situated in one clearing. In 2011–2013, Maras consisted of seven sites situated north and south of the Maras bridge, and both east and west of the highway, while Koikoi consisted of six sites; one was north of a river on the west side of the highway, three more were situated south of the

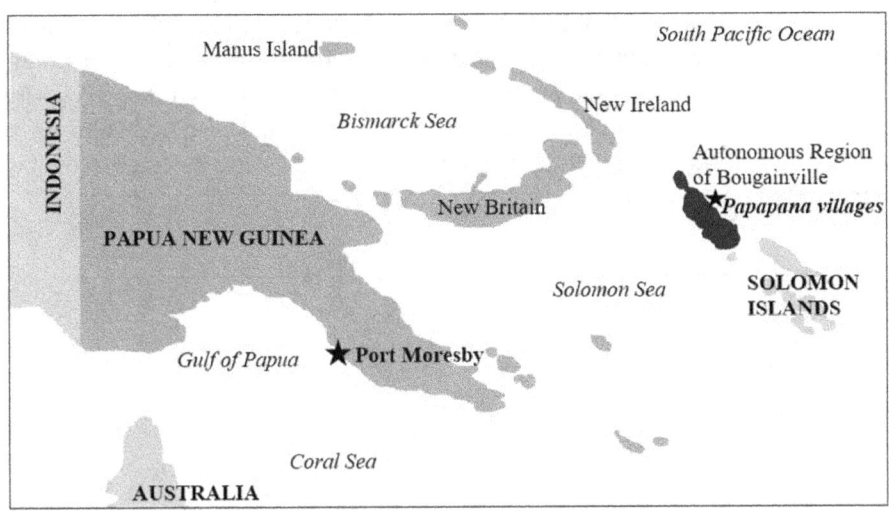

Figure 2.1: Papapana in Papua New Guinea.

river along the west side of the highway, while two were south of the river but to the east of the highway, next to the beach. Teperoi itself was spread out along a narrow track of roughly 1.5 kilometres running adjacent to the shoreline. The first few settlements along this track were considered by community members to be Makomako village. Access to Teperoi proper was only possible through Makomako and there was no clear divide between the two. The track ended in a large clearing which was the centre of Teperoi. Beyond this there was a smaller track leading to the Teperoi Primary School site.

The name *Papapana* is an endonym and can describe the Papapana people, land, culture and language. There are no dialects. Speakers were unsure of the origin of *Papapana* but two reported meanings are 'the place where men live' and 'people from the beach'. Another possible origin is reduplication of *papana* 'side' or *pana* 'part'. It seems quite likely though that *Papapana* comes from the closely related Uruava language where *pa-papa-na* denotes 'uncles (mother's brothers)' (Palmer 2007d). This is supported by accounts that Papapana ancestors were part of a migration from the south in the mid–19th century which settled first in the area around Kieta and Arawa (the once Uruava-speaking area), before moving north up the Bougainville eastern coast (see §2.4.2).

One of Papapana's exonyms *Auta* is used by Rotokas speakers and reportedly translates as 'down below' in Rotokas (Rotokas speakers live in the mountains surrounding the Papapana villages). *Auta* was even used on the Teperoi church sign.

Torau and Teop speakers call Papapana people *Numanuma*, due to their proximity to the Numanuma plantation (see Figure 2.2). Indeed Togolo (2005), a Torau speaker, notes that his grandfather was fluent in the Numanuma language. The endonym *Papapana* is generally also used in the literature (Allen and Hurd 1963; Lewis, Simons and Fennig 2014), though the language has also been referred to as *Papapa* (Wurm and Hattori 1981–83) and *Teperoi* (Lanyon-Orgill and King 1942).

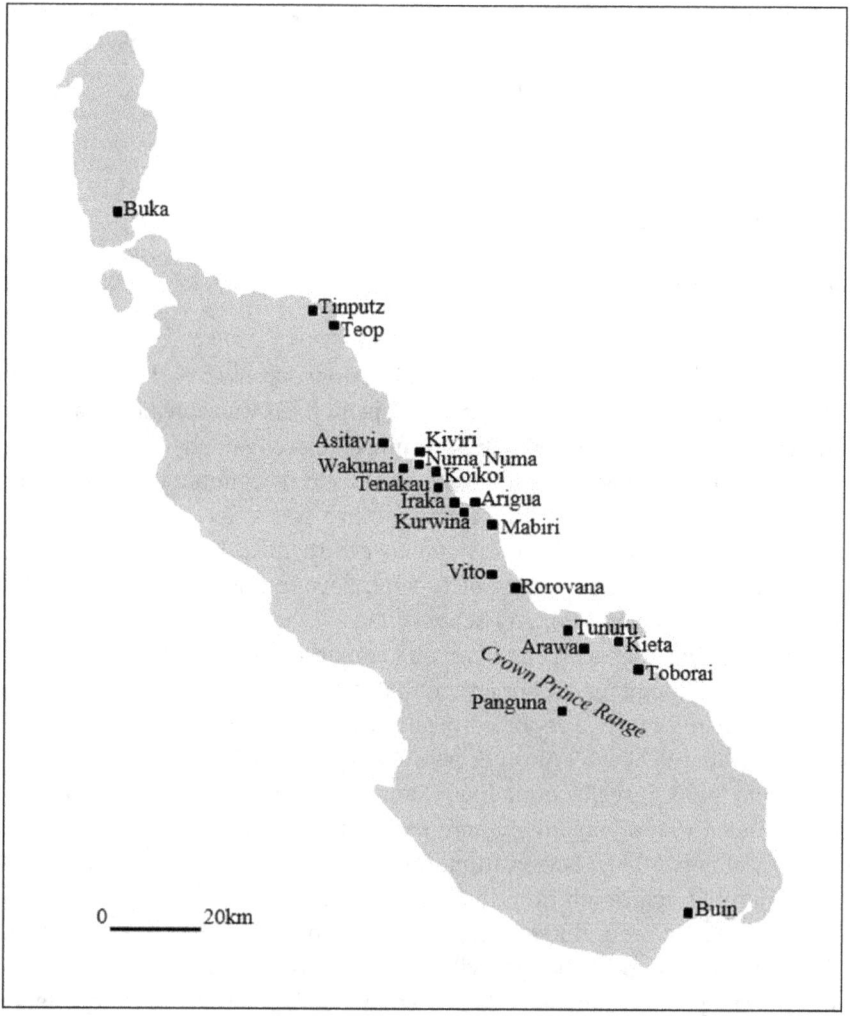

Figure 2.2: Bougainville: Papapana villages Koikoi and Iraka, and other important locations.

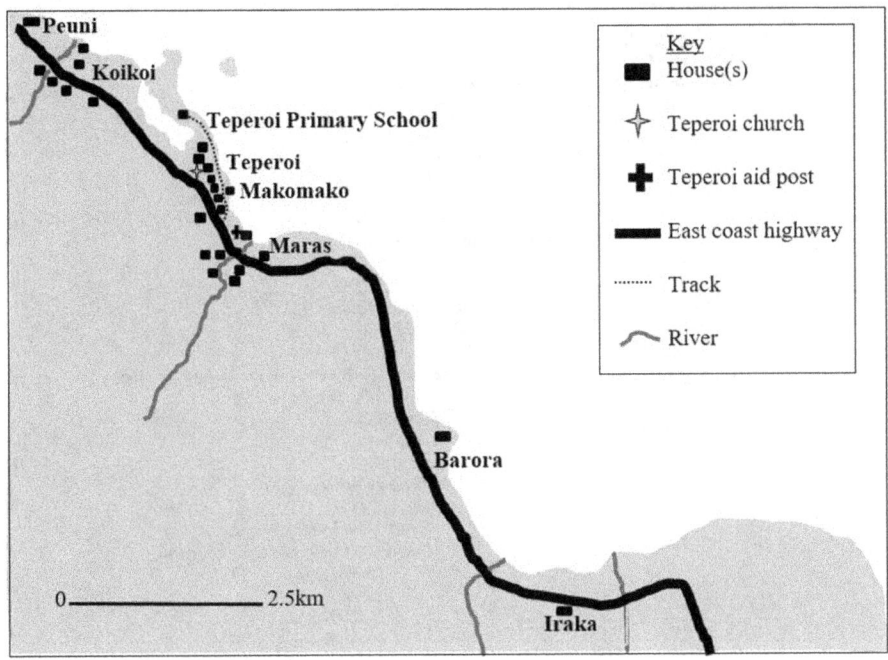

Figure 2.3: Papapana villages.

2.2 Genetic affiliation

Figure 2.4 shows the genealogical tree for Papapana.[7] This tree is developed from Ross (2004c) with the addition of the more recently identified first order subgroup of Oceanic, Temotu (Ross and Næss 2007), and the addition of two languages listed by *Ethnologue* (Lewis, Simons and Fennig 2014), Tomoip and Minigir, though the source identifying the genetic affiliation of these languages is unclear. The numbers of languages per group are taken from Ethnologue (Lewis, Simons and Fennig 2014). In the genealogical tree, the term *linkage* refers to "a group of communalects which have arisen by dialect differentiation" (Ross 1988: 8). There are two types of linkages: (i) a *chain*, "where communalects are typically spread along a coastline, each related most closely to its neighbour on either side" and (ii) a *network*, "where communalects are scattered over a land area or an archipelago, typically having neighbours on more

---

[7] Higher order subgroups which are not relevant to Papapana are not shown.

```
Austronesian (1257)
    Malayo-Polynesian (1237)
        Central/Eastern Malayo-Polynesian linkage (720)
            Eastern Malayo-Polynesian family (554)
                Oceanic family (513)
                    Temotu (10)
                    Admiralties family (31)
                    St.Matthias group (2)
                    Yapese (1)
                    Central/Eastern Oceanic (228)
                    Western Oceanic linkage (241)
                        North New Guinea linkage (106)
                        Papuan Tip linkage (64)
                        Meso-Melanesian linkage (71)
                            Bali-Vitu (2)
                            Willaumez linkage (4)
                            New Ireland/Northwest Solomonic linkage (65)
                                Tungak/Nalik family (6)
                                Tabar linkage (2)
                                Madak linkage (3)
                                Tomoip (1)
                                St. George linkage (53)
                                    Minigir (1)
                                    South New Ireland languages (12)
                                    Northwest Solomonic linkage (40)
                                        Choiseul (4)
                                        Santa Isabel (7)
                                        New Georgia (13)
                                        Piva-Banoni (2)
                                        Mono-Uruava (4)
                                        Nehan-North Bougainville (10)
                                            Papapana
                                            Solos
                                            Nehan
                                            Petats
                                            Halia
                                            Taoif
                                            Saposa
                                            Hahon
                                            Tinputz
                                            Teop
```

Figure 2.4: Genealogical tree for Papapana (based on Ross 2004c).

than two sides, and often sharing different innovations with several of these" (Ross 1988: 8).

Papapana belongs to the Oceanic branch of the large Austronesian language family. Within the area occupied by Oceanic language speakers, three subregions can be delineated based on geographical, socio-cultural, physical and linguistic factors: Micronesia to the north, Polynesia to the east and Melanesia to the west. Melanesia encompasses Vanuatu, New Caledonia, and Fiji in the southeast, to the Solomon Islands, the Bismarck Archipelago (New Britain, New Ireland and the Admiralties) and New Guinea in the northwest (Pawley 2006). In the Melanesian region, there are both Oceanic and non-Oceanic Austronesian languages as well as over 800 *Papuan* languages (see §2.4.1). The Oceanic group has six first order subgroups consisting of over 500 languages. One of these, Western Oceanic, contains 241 languages including in PNG most Oceanic languages of New Britain, New Ireland and the Western Solomon Islands in the Meso-Melanesian linkage, while other Oceanic languages of PNG belong to the Papuan Tip linkage, North New Guinea linkage, or are part of the Admiralties subgroup of Oceanic, rather than the Western Oceanic subgroup.

Within the Meso-Melanesian linkage there is the New Ireland/Northwest Solomonic linkage which contains the St. George linkage. Papapana is a member of the Northwest Solomonic linkage within the St. George linkage. Northwest Solomonic languages stretch from Nissan island (PNG) in the northwest to the boundary between the Maringe and Bugotu languages on the southeastern tip of Santa Ysabel island (Solomon Islands) (Ross 1988). The location of these languages can be seen in Figure 2.5 while their genetic affiliation is shown in Figure 2.6.

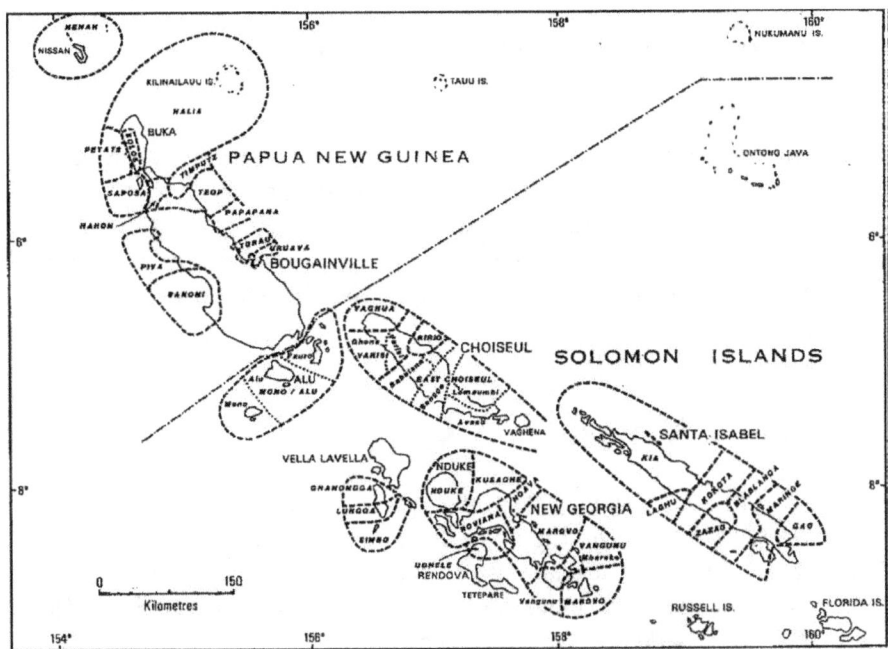

Figure 2.5: Locations of Northwest Solomonic languages (from Ross 1988: 216).

On the basis of the limited data available at the time, Ross (1988) placed Papapana in the Nehan-North Bougainville subgroup of Northwest Solomonic,

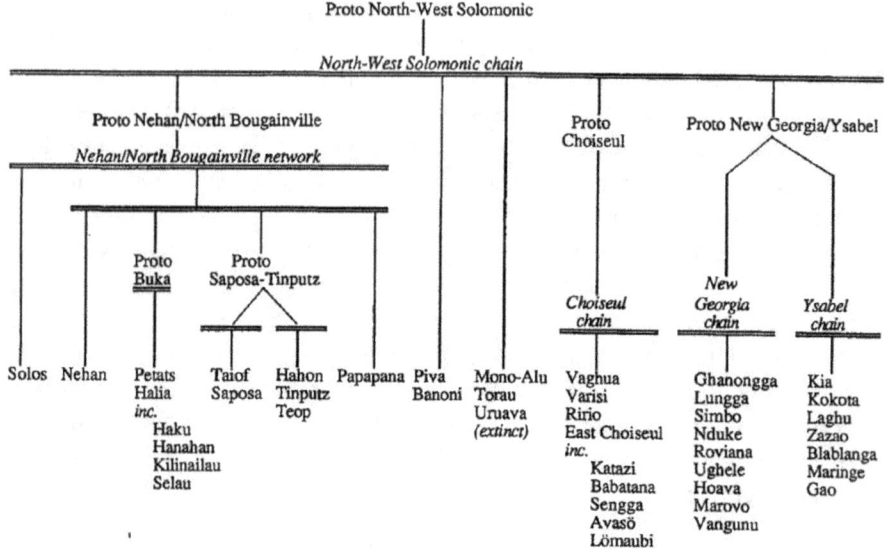

Figure 2.6: A Northwest Solomonic genetic tree (from Ross 1988: 217).

containing the languages of northern Bougainville and Buka; however, there are similarities in lexicon and syntax which raise the possibility that Papapana is related more closely to Uruava, or perhaps even Mono and Torau (Bill Palmer, pers.comm.). This is further supported by evidence of contact-induced grammatical change in Papapana (Smith 2016a) and by the migration patterns described in §2.4.2.

2.3 Papapana speakers

Papapana is listed as having 100 speakers in 1963 (Oliver 1973: 188), 150 speakers in 1977 (Wurm 2012) and more recently 120 speakers (Lewis, Simons and Fennig 2014). The genealogical data I collected in the field (see §1.3.5.5 and §1.3.6.3) allowed me to calculate the number of Papapana speakers, their location, and the population of each Papapana village.

In May 2013, the total number of fluent, first language (L1) Papapana speakers with full productive ability was 106, there were fifty-five second language (L2) or semi-speakers with partial productive ability, and there were around 136 people who could understand Papapana but not speak it and could thus be considered passive bilinguals.[8] Table 2.1 shows the number of these different types of speaker by location. The "elsewhere" category in Table 2.1 includes other locations in Bougainville or PNG, and locations outside PNG. There were seventeen L1/fluent speakers elsewhere in Bougainville, one in Port Moresby and one in Australia; nine L2/semi-speakers elsewhere in Bougainville, three elsewhere in PNG and one in Australia; and nineteen passive bilinguals elsewhere in Bougainville and ten elsewhere in PNG. Note that a few of the L1/fluent speakers and L2/semi-speakers were not related to the Papapana people but had grown up in the Papapana villages, while a few passive bilinguals were also not related to the Papapana people in any way but were immigrants in the community.

Taking into consideration only the speakers who were residing in the six Papapana villages, L1/fluent Papapana speakers accounted for 17%, L2/semi-speakers accounted for 8%, and passive bilinguals accounted for 21% of the population. Taking into account the speakers who were living elsewhere (since they may visit the Papapana villages), fluent Papapana speakers constituted 21%, semi-speakers 11% and people with passive knowledge 27% of the total population.

Table 2.1: Speakers by location.

Location	Population of location	L1/fluent speakers		L2/semi-speakers		Passive bilinguals	
Peuni	21	3	14%	4	19%	7	33%
Koikoi	47	7	15%	3	6%	10	21%
Teperoi	224	47	21%	17	8%	45	20%
Maras	91	13	14%	7	8%	14	15%
Barora	68	10	15%	9	13%	24	35%
Iraka	59	7	12%	2	3%	7	12%
Elsewhere		19		13		29	
TOTAL	510	106	17–21%	55	8–11%	136	21–27%

Figure 2.7 shows the proportion of L1/fluent speakers, L2/semi-speakers, passive bilinguals and people with no knowledge of Papapana out of the total population

---

[8] Since May 2013, the number of fluent speakers has decreased by at least seven due to the death of speakers.

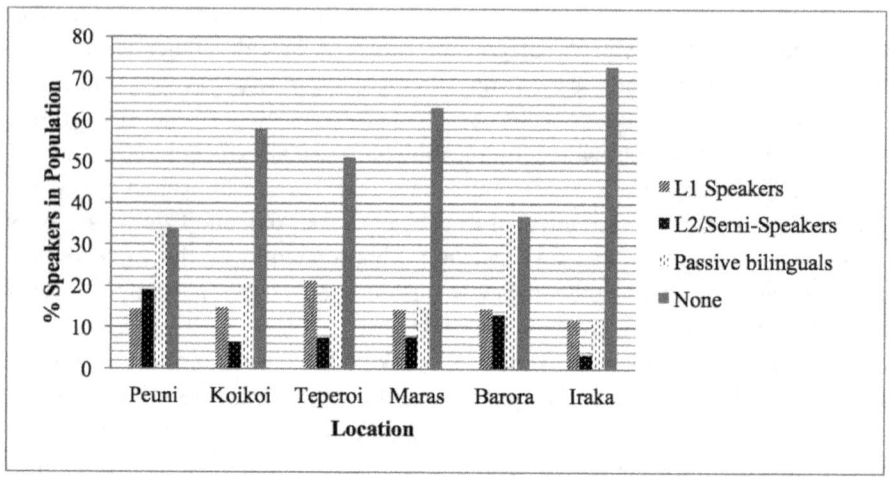

Figure 2.7: Proportion within each village of L1/fluent speakers, L2/semi-speakers and people with passive or no Papapana knowledge.

of each village. Teperoi had the highest proportion of L1/fluent speakers, which is perhaps because Teperoi is the original and main Papapana village. Peuni had the highest proportion of L2/semi-speakers and Barora had the highest proportion of people who could understand Papapana but not speak it. Peuni had the smallest population of all six villages and therefore it would not take many speakers to constitute a high proportion, while Barora is a small village in terms of land area with the houses very close together; this might increase exposure to the language and thus foster more L2/semi-speakers and passive bilinguals. Iraka had the lowest proportion of all three types, which might be attributed to its distance from the other villages thus decreasing the chance of contact with other Papapana speakers. In every village, there were more people without any knowledge of Papapana than with it.

Using the data above, it is also possible to take the numbers of L1/fluent speakers, L2/semi-speakers and passive bilinguals and show how these people are geographically distributed (Figure 2.8). The majority of the total number of fluent Papapana speakers lived in Teperoi, followed by locations other than the six Papapana villages. A smaller number of fluent speakers lived in Maras and Barora, while Peuni, Koikoi and Iraka contained the smallest number of fluent Papapana speakers out of the total number of fluent speakers. The same pattern is found with the numbers of L2/semi-speakers and passive bilinguals, though more of these speakers live in Maras than in Barora.

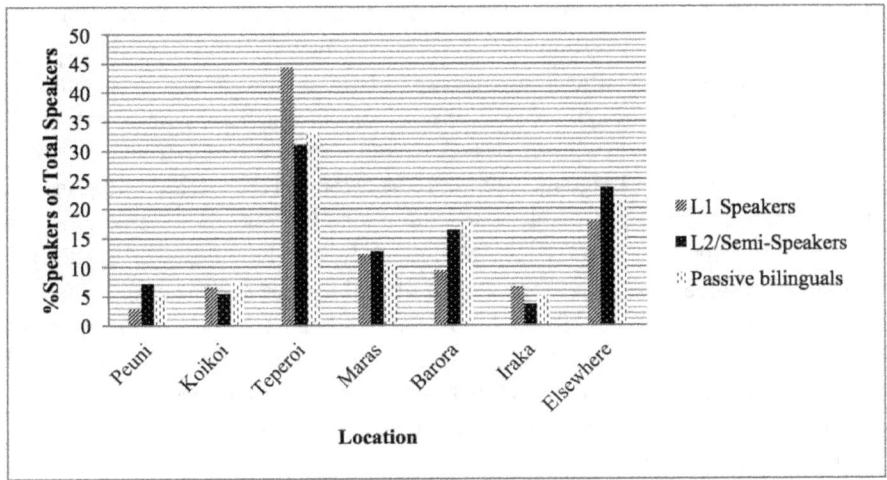

Figure 2.8: Numbers of L1/fluent speakers, L2/semi-speakers and passive bilinguals in each location.

Using the data above, it is possible to summarise that the total number of Papapana speakers, be it L1/fluent or L2/semi-speakers, was 161 in 2013, which was 32% of the population of the six villages, while the total number of people with knowledge of Papapana, to whatever extent, was 297, which was 58% of the population.

2.4 The history of Papapana language contact

This section describes the languages of PNG and Bougainville (§2.4.1), and the history of language contact and use in the Papapana community over the last century or so, from migration in pre-colonial times (§2.4.2), European colonisation (§2.4.3), national independence (§2.4.4) and the Bougainville civil war (§2.4.5), to the present day (§2.4.6). For any references to places in Bougainville, please see Figure 2.2 and Figure 2.3 in §2.1, where relevant population centres discussed here, such as villages, plantations and mission centres, are marked.

2.4.1 Linguistic diversity in Papua New Guinea and Bougainville

PNG is one of the most linguistically diverse countries in the world: 836 different languages are spoken by between six and seven million people. Papua New

Guinean languages account for roughly 13.2% of the world's languages but only 0.1% of the world's population and 0.4% of the world's land area (Nettle and Romaine 2000: 80). The official languages of PNG are English, Tok Pisin and Hiri Motu. Aside from these, Papua New Guinean languages generally have very small speaker bases: more than half have less than 1000 speakers (see Wurm 2003: 25).

Of PNG's 836 living languages, around 230 belong to the Oceanic subgroup of the Austronesian language family while the remaining 600 or so languages are non-Austronesian (Wurm 2003: 25). Non-Austronesian languages in the Pacific area are often given the cover term *Papuan* but this does not mean that the languages belong to one family. Instead most Papuan languages belong to five major groups of genetically interrelated languages, but with the possible exception of two groups, these groups are not related to each other. A sixth eastern geographical group probably comprises several small unrelated groups of languages, totalling thirty-four languages (Wurm 2003). PNG is clearly a classic case of a residual zone, that is, a zone which has high diversity and is "inhabited by small groups, from many different stocks, with many different language types, among whom bilingualism or multilingualism is the norm" (Nettle and Romaine 2000: 38).

The Autonomous Region of Bougainville has a population of around 234,280 people, according to the 2011 census. The province is home to twenty-three local languages: eight are Papuan, thirteen belong to the Northwest Solomonic subgroup of Western Oceanic and three belong to the Ellicean subgroup of Central-Eastern Oceanic. Table 2.2 shows the number of speakers per language (Lewis, Simons and Fennig 2014). Figure 2.9 shows the location of the languages spoken on Buka and Bougainville islands. The Ellicean languages and Nehan are spoken on atolls north of Buka island.

2.4.2 Migration in pre-colonial times

Buka and Bougainville islands, both part of the Autonomous Region of Bougainville, were first populated by Papuan language speakers around 30,000 years ago (Tryon 2005: 33), probably from the north through the Bismarck Archipelago (Regan and Griffin 2005: 475). Around 3,000 years ago, Austronesian language speakers arrived from the north (Regan and Griffin 2005: 475). For more information on these migrations, see Oliver (1973) and Spriggs (2005). The Austronesians continued south into the Solomon Islands and beyond, but much later, the descendants of some of those who had settled on the islands immediately south of Bougainville, resettled along Bougainville's eastern coast (Oliver 1991: 3).

According to Oliver (1991: 3), in the most recent of these movements, the ancestors of Torau speakers, founded the present day community of Rorovana

Table 2.2: Bougainville languages speaker numbers.

Language group		Name	Speakers
Papuan (69,000 speakers)	South Bougainville	Buin (Telei, Kugara)	26,500
		Nasioi (Kieta)	20,000
		Motuna (Siwai)[9]	6,600
		Nagovisi (Sibbe)	6,000
	North Bougainville	Rotokas	4,320
		Konua (Rapoisi)	3,500
		Eivo (Askopan)	1,200
		Keriaka (Ramopa)	1,000
Austronesian (53,556 speakers)	Northwest Solomonic (Western Oceanic)	Halia	25,000
		Nehan (Nissan)	6,500
		Teop	5,000
		Tinputz (Vasui)	3,900
		Solos	3,200
		Petats (Majugan)	2,000
		Saposa	1,400
		Hahon	1,300
		Banoni (Tsunari)	1,000
		Torau (Rorovana)	600
		Piva (Lawunuia)	550
		Papapana	106
		Uruava	0
	Ellicean (Central-Eastern Oceanic)	Takuu (Mortlock)	1,750
		Nukumanu (Tasman)	700
		Nukuria (Nahoa)	550

---

9 To be consistent with the literature I use the name *Motuna*, but it should be noted that the Papapana speech community refer to *Motuna* as *Siwai*.

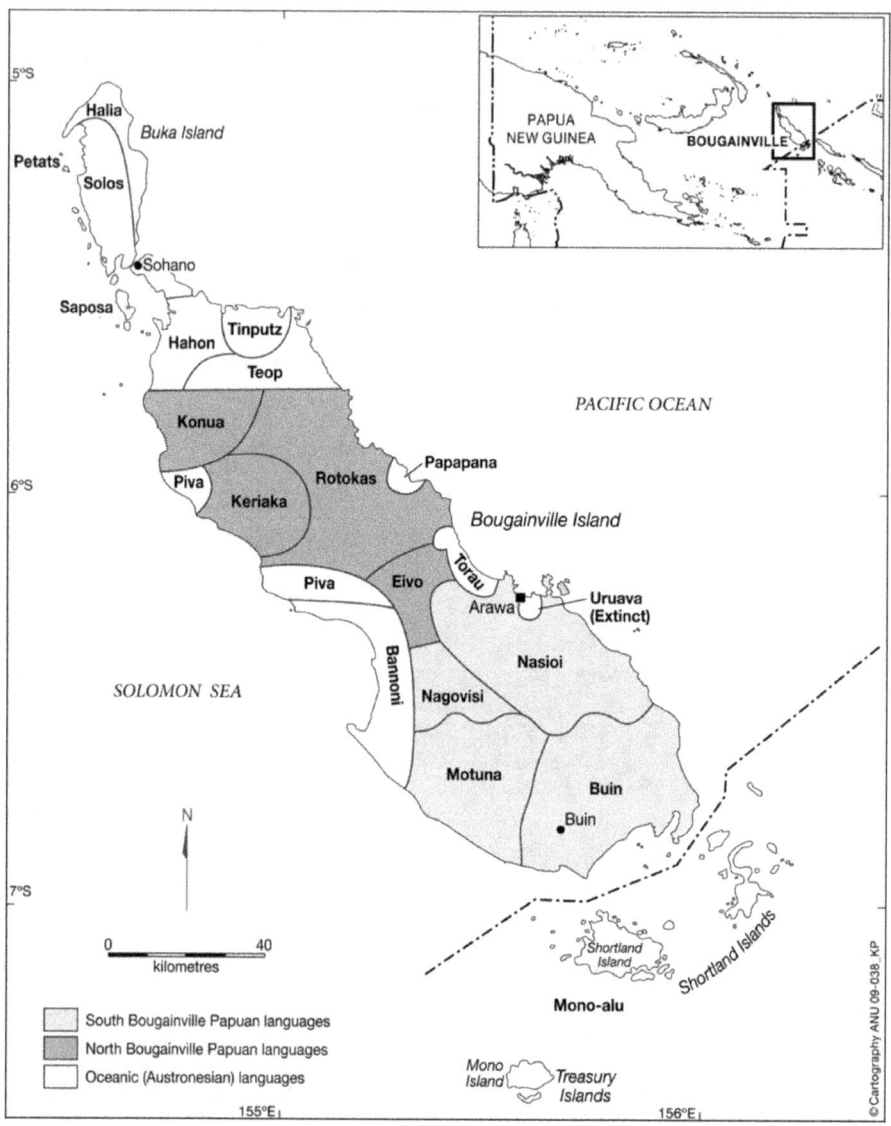

Figure 2.9: Oceanic and Papuan languages of Bougainville and Northwestern Solomon Islands (from Evans 2009).

around 1890. The ancestors of Papapana speakers are aligned with those of Torau speakers in migrating from the Shortland Islands "only a few generations ago", while the ancestors of Uruava speakers also arrived from the Shortland Islands but earlier than the Torau (Oliver 1991: 5). According to Laracy (1969: 235), who references the Catholic missionary McHardy's notes, migrators from the Shortland Islands first landed at a village called Lavelai on the southeast coast in 1860 after a dispute over a woman.[10] Next, they went to Toborai, south of Kieta (the area where Uruava used to be spoken), where they settled temporarily, before fleeing from locals and heading north to Numanuma (north of the contemporary Papapana-speaking area, but recall that Numanuma is an exonym for Papapana). At Numanuma they were forced out by the mountain people so they went south again to Rorovana (the contemporary Torau-speaking area). An account reported to Terrell and Irwin (1972: 333) at Asitavi by three people from Rorovana also aligns with this story, and current Torau elders in Rorovana reported to a friend of mine that they arrived in Rorovana about 150–160 years ago, i.e. mid–19th century. Thurnwald's notes, referred to by Terrell and Irwin (1972: 328), contradict this somewhat by claiming that the starting place for the migration was the south-eastern coast of Bougainville, that the motivation for the migration was harassment from Gorai, the leader of the Shortland Islands, and that after Numanuma the migrators settled south and inland at Vito (a contemporary Torau-speaking village), and did not return to the coast until Gorai's death in 1894. Terrell and Irwin (1972) also relate an account from Ratovai, a Teperoi leader, in which he reported that a leader at Lavelai came to Numanuma after a conflict with the Torau and settled there with a leader of Wakunai village.

What all these accounts have in common is that they suggest that Papapana ancestors were part of a migration from the south in the mid–19th century which settled first in the area around Kieta and Arawa (the once Uruava-speaking area), moved north up the Bougainville eastern coast to the contemporary Papapana-speaking area before moving south again, with a possible halt in Vito, before settling on the coast in the late–19th century. It is unknown whether Papapana ancestors stayed behind in the Numanuma area, or whether they returned there later after the final settlement. Papapana community members reported to me on separate occasions that the Papapana ancestors arrived from the Solomon Islands before the Torau and Uruava, and that the second migration was to the Torau area, and the final migration to the Uruava area. If these members meant that the second and final migrations were from the Papapana area, then these accounts also align with those outlined already.

It does however appear that the history of the Papapana community is further complicated by intermarriage and further migrations. Papapana community members reported that the first clans to arrive were Naroa (with

---

10 Unfortunately it is unclear where exactly Lavelai was located and so it does not appear in Figure 2.2.

the dove as their totemic symbol), Naororo (sea eagle) and Tagoni (eagle), while Ma'eara (*girigau* 'bird species') and Tuvio (hornbill) settled later, after European colonisation. This is supported by the fact that *aroa* and *tagori* are the names of Uruavan clans (with *aroa* also denoting 'pigeon') (Palmer 2007d) and are cognate with the Papapana clan names *naroa* and *tagoni*, while *ma'eara* might be related to *keara* 'older same sex sibling' in Teop (Palmer 2014) given it is likely POc *k has undergone a sound change to /ʔ/ in Papapana (see §3.1.2.4). The sixth Papapana clan is Barisi (flying fox totem). In text recording ES2-T001, a Papapana elder recounted the genealogical history of his clan Barisi and reported that their origins lie in intermarriage between a Papapana speaker and a mountain-dweller seven generations ago. The Papapana speaker may well have migrated from the south as well, as *barrio* 'flying fox' was the name of an Uruavan clan too (Palmer 2007d). It is thus possible that Naroa, Naororo, Tagoni and Barisi clans came from the south in the mid–19th century, while Ma'eara and Tuvio clans came later from the north.

Further evidence to support the claim that immigrants from the north settled in the Papapana-speaking area comes from the caption to the Catholic missionary McHardy's photograph (Figure 2.10) which reads "Looking up the main street of Teperoi – the village, even in its houses, shows traces of two different tribes: the round one in the left foreground is after the style of Buka and the north, whereas those in the background are like Kieta houses".[11] Furthermore, the German trader Parkinson's travelogue, translated in Oliver (1991: 36), reports that the village of Bagovegove (near the Numanuma plantation and where a Papapana elder's ancestors lived, as recounted in ESD3-D006 and ESD3-D007) was destroyed several times but after its last reconstruction in 1898 (post-colonisation), "it has survived unscathed, mainly because of its reinforcement by immigrants from north Bougainville and east Buka".

During the time prior to European settlement, Papapana community members report that contact was only with Rotokas speakers for the purposes of trade and intermarriage. Rotokas was the intergroup language since Rotokas speakers greatly outnumbered Papapana speakers. The isolation of the Papapana community is supported by the caption to another of McHardy's photographs from circa 1931: "[. . .] a peculiar people these; the village seems to be isolated; in language, custom, even in physical appearance, they seem to differ from other villages [. . .]".

---

[11] MAW Acc 205/20 – photo album of Fr Emmet McHardy sm, Marist Archives, Wellington, New Zealand. Figures 2.10–2.12 and photograph captions referred to here are all from this source, whom I gratefully acknowledge.

Figure 2.10: Teperoi, circa 1931.

2.4.3 European colonisation, plantations and missions

Bougainville was colonised in 1886, when Buka and Bougainville were included in German New Guinea. In 1899 the German Imperial government officially assumed administration over German New Guinea. During World War I (1914–1918), Australian military forces occupied the island until it became a League of Nations mandatory power in 1918. In 1942, during World War II, the Japanese invaded and Bougainville became the site of World War II battles between the Japanese and The United States of America and Australia. In 1945 the Japanese surrendered and Australia controlled Bougainville as a United Nations mandatory power until PNG's independence in 1975. For more information on European colonisation, see Griffin (2005), Oliver (1991, 1973), Regan and Griffin (2005) and Sack (2005).

2.4.3.1 Plantations

With European colonisation came the introduction of a plantation economy. The first commercial plantation in Bougainville was at Kieta (Sack 2005: 88), the Numanuma plantation had been established north of Teperoi by 1912 (Laracy

2005a: 140) and by 1968 there were plantations to the north and south of the Papapana-speaking area: Numanuma, Koikoi, Tenekau, Kurwina and Arigua. The manual labour in these plantations was supplied mainly by indigenes who were also employed to work on plantations elsewhere in the Pacific, including Samoa and the British Solomon Islands (Oliver 1991: 31). Papapana community members, including Motuna speakers, reported that speakers of the South Bougainville Papuan languages Buin and Motuna were employed to work in the plantations surrounding Teperoi. Papapana speakers suggested that the plantation owners employed labourers from further afield as it reduced the chances of them escaping and returning home. Papapana speakers not only had contact with the migrant labourers due to their proximity to the plantations, but they would have also been labourers themselves. As a result of plantation labour, contact subsequently increased and extended beyond Rotokas speakers to other speech communities, leading to more trade and intermarriage, and perpetuating multilingualism.

In addition to having contact with speakers of other local languages, Papapana speakers would have had increasing exposure to Tok Pisin, which owes its origins largely to plantation activities in Samoa in the early 1880s and its introduction from there into German New Guinea. For more information on the origins of Tok Pisin and the various versions of its history, see Baker (1993, 1995, 1996), Goulden (1990), Keesing (1988) and Mühlhäusler (1976, 1979, 1982, 1987).

The establishment of the plantations also decreased the land size occupied by the Papapana speech community. While Papapana has always been a minority immigrant language, community members reported to me that the Papapana community did once occupy a much larger area of land along the coast, stretching from Kiviri point in the north to the area around the Arigua plantation in the south (see Figure 2.2 in §2.1). This is supported by the caption to McHardy's photograph (Figure 2.11) which reads "A snap on the beach near Teperoi – a fair sized village about forty miles up the coast from Tunuru" and the caption to another of McHardy's photographs: "Obviously, from the remains of old gardens, etc. the village was very big at no distant date – but now they seem to be dwindling fast. The two Catechists there have more last minute baptisms to make than any others I know".[12]

The decreased land and community size may also be attributed to conflict. As mentioned in §2.4.2, the village of Bagovegove was destroyed three times by hostile mountain-dwellers in the 1880s and 1890s (Parkinson's travelogue, translated in Oliver 1991: 36). Furthermore, Shortland Islands leader Gorai "on one

---

12 The mention of last minute baptisms is a reference to high death rates, as the baptisms would be performed quickly before the person died.

Figure 2.11: Teperoi beach, circa 1931.

occasion [. . .] sent a fleet of his war canoes to the village of Numanuma [. . .] and killed a score of its people to avenge the killing of a white trader with whom he was friendly" (Oliver 1991: 18). The white trader in question was a Mr. Ferguson:

> The inhabitants of this strip of coast, known as the Numanuma area, have on occasion been hostile to whites as well as to their inland neighbours. In the 1870s, for example, the small trading steamer *Ripple* was attacked here by the local people; its captain, a Mr Ferguson, was murdered, along with several of his crew [. . .] Revenge was not long in coming. It happened that Captain Ferguson enjoyed the friendship of the Shortland chief, Gorai, and the latter sent a fleet of warriors who wiped out Numanuma and its inhabitants during a month long campaign.
> (Parkinson's travelogue, translated in Oliver 1991: 36–37)

The knock-on effect of decreased land was that by the mid–20th century, the Papapana villages were overpopulated. Overpopulation, family disputes and the desire to be closer to particular crops, led certain families to reclaim their ancestors' land and settle the villages of Maras, Barora and Iraka in the mid–20th century. In the 1990s the village of Peuni was settled for similar reasons, and then from there, the settlements at Koikoi were established, the last one as recently as 2010.

2.4.3.2 Missionaries: churches and education

European settlers also introduced their religious beliefs, and established churches and schools at mission stations. The Catholic Society of Mary (Marists) established the first mission station near Kieta in 1901 (Laracy 2005b: 126), the Methodists set up missionaries in Siwai (the Motuna-speaking area) in 1922 (Laracy 2005b: 126), and the Seventh Day Adventists arrived in 1924 (Regan and Griffin 2005: 476). The closest Marist missions to Teperoi were Asitavi to the north (established 1935) and Mabiri to the south (established in 1958) (Laracy 1976) but the Papapana people had their own Catechists in the village by the time the missionary McHardy visited in circa 1931 (McHardy 1935): the caption to McHardy's photograph (Figure 2.12) reads "The two Catechists at Teperoi on their house [. . .]". Although these Catechists had been trained and thus there had been some missionary contact before McHardy arrived, it is unknown whether any missionary had actually visited Teperoi before McHardy.

Figure 2.12: Teperoi catechists, circa 1931.

At least until 1914, Catholic missionaries in PNG usually used their parishioners' languages, whereas Protestant missionaries tended to resort to a lingua franca (Ross 1996: 595). Nevertheless, the arrival of Protestant competition in Bougainville, prompted the Marists to make greater use of Tok Pisin, teach English in some mission schools and recruit English-speaking staff (Laracy 2005b: 126). By 1968 the Bible Society of Papua New Guinea had translated the New Testament into Tok Pisin, and the whole Bible by 1989.

Aside from the language contact brought about through new religious practices and education, a Papapana community member also reported to me that along with the establishment of a police force, the new religious beliefs meant there was less conflict and less fear of outsiders and so people were more willing to travel outside of the Papapana villages, again increasing exposure to other languages.

2.4.4 Mid–20th century educational policies and independence

Prior to the 1950s, most education was conducted (by non-government agencies) in the vernaculars for local primary schools, and in either Tok Pisin or a regional vernacular for higher level schools (Jenkins 2005: 7–8). Under the 1954 Education Ordinance, the teaching of English and the use of English as a medium of instruction were the official educational policy from 1956 (Ross 1996: 597). After independence in 1975, this policy ceased to be successful and instead Tok Pisin, Hiri Motu and local languages were used. Indeed, much teaching was conducted in Tok Pisin as more and more teachers were PNG citizens rather than expatriates: these teachers tended to have never used English beyond their own school studies, and they were often assigned to schools outside their language area (Jenkins 2005: 8).

In Bougainville, in 1979, the provincial government decided to introduce the community-based Viles Tok Ples Skul (VTPS) ('village language school') scheme. During the 1980s, Papua New Guinean educational policies focused on strengthening local traditional cultures and values and raising literacy levels in local languages, Tok Pisin, Hiri Motu and English. By the end of the 1980s, VTPS had become a widespread phenomenon and a national language policy had been approved by the Department of Education, which "encouraged the use of vernacular languages for initial education, and the maintenance of vernacular literacy in the formal education system" (Litteral 2001: 1). A 1997 declaration made every one of the country's local languages official languages that could be used in basic elementary education along with Tok Pisin, Hiri Motu and English.

2.4.5 The Bougainville Crisis

In 1969, vast copper ore deposits were discovered in the Crown Prince Range, near Panguna in southern Bougainville, and this led to the establishment of a huge copper mine by Bougainville Copper Limited. When the Panguna mine began production in 1972, it was the world's largest open cut copper mine and generated nearly half of PNG's export revenue. In terms of language contact, the mine seems to have increased the use of Tok Pisin in the region:

> The company's operations affected, from east to west, Torau, Nasioi, Nagovisi and Banoni speakers. Had there been a dominant local language, it might have been possible to encourage its use; in the absence of such a language, it was Pidgin which became the common means of communication with the majority of employees and with most villagers.
> (Vernon 2005: 263)

Panguna mine became politically contentious with disputes over land tenure and allegations of environmental damage and inequitable distribution of mining revenues. Negotiations between landowners and mine owners broke down and in May 1989 Francis Ona and the Bougainville Revolutionary Army (BRA) sabotaged mining operations and Panguna mine shut down after its power cables were blown up. On 26th June 1989, the PNG government declared a state of emergency and in September 1989 the Papua New Guinea Defence Force (PNGDF) were sent to quell the resistance. This response enraged Bougainvilleans and prompted a civil war, the Bougainville Crisis, which lasted from 1989 until 1997. The BRA fought against the PNGDF and The Resistance, a paramilitary group that aligned itself with the PNG government. In total, 10,000–15,000 people died either through fighting or indirectly, such as due to lack of medical attention. The Crisis ended in 1997, largely as the result of New Zealand brokered negotiations, and a Peace Agreement was finalised in 2000, with the establishment of the Autonomous Bougainville Government. In 2005, the first president was elected, Joseph Kabui, and Francis Ona died, leaving the BRA leadership in question. The mine was still a "No Go Zone" during my last fieldtrip in 2018.

The Crisis has significantly impacted on Bougainville, causing huge social and economic change, massive population displacement, a breakdown in law and order, and a decline in the educational system, which at one point was one of the best in PNG (Litteral 2001). For the Papapana people, the Crisis caused significant population displacement as many people were forced to hide in the bush or relocate to Care Centres, while some community members joined the BRA. My corpus includes stories of escape, capture, or life in the Care Centres during this time. The displacement increased contact with other local languages and increased the need for Tok Pisin as a lingua franca, especially in the PNG government Care Centres where Tok Pisin was the dominant language.

2.4.6 The 21st century

Since the Bougainville Crisis, there has been increased mobility of Papapana speakers to population centres. In PNG, population centres might be towns, government stations, regional schools, plantations, mines, factories, or even large mission compounds (Landweer 2012: 164). The increased mobility can be attributed to the desire to gain access to employment, to sell and purchase produce in markets, to access educational and medical services, to seek entertainment such as sporting events, or to participate in important religious celebrations in larger parishes. It has become increasingly easier to travel to towns such as Buka and Arawa, government stations such as Wakunai and mission compounds and local high schools such as those at Asitavi, due to Public Motor Vehicles (PMVs) travelling daily between Arawa and Buka, as well as local PMVs travelling around the Wakunai district, and the completion in 2012 of a bridge network along the east coast highway. In April 2018, the main road on Buka island had been tarmacked and work had begun on tarmacking the roads on the east coast highway.

Some Papapana community members have moved between villages because they wish to be closer to assets such as running water or particular crops. People have moved into or out of the Papapana community for marriage, work or entertainment. In the year between my first two field trips alone (2011–2013), there had been movement of at least twenty-three individuals with knowledge of Papapana (8% of the total number of people with knowledge of Papapana).

There is also increased contact due to media and technology. In PNG, television is almost exclusively in English, national radio is in English, Tok Pisin and Hiri Motu and provincial radio is in Tok Pisin or the larger local languages, while national newspapers are in English or Tok Pisin and provincial newspapers are in Tok Pisin or sometimes a local language (Lynch 1998: 268). For more information, see Mühlhäusler, Philpott and Trew (1996). A few of the Papapana community members had mobile phones and when I returned to Teperoi in 2013, several of the teachers had DVD televisions and one had a laptop which they would use to watch films or music videos, however, usage depended on whether they had money to fuel their generators and charge the devices. In April 2018, a few more community members had mobile phones and some had speaker systems for playing music, but again usage varied depending on power sources. There were however small solar panel chargers in use among a range of community members, either for phones/speakers or for torches.

2.5 Papapana language use 2011–2018

In the Papapana villages between 2011 and 2013, language domains included the home (§2.5.1), work and administration (§2.5.2), education (§2.5.3), and religion, social events and media (§2.5.4). These domains are discussed in more detail in the following sections, and language use in each domain is described. For more information on the cultural and social context of Melanesia and Bougainville see Ogan (2005), Oliver (1973, 1991), Regan (2005) and Sillitoe (1998).

2.5.1 Home

In the six Papapana villages between 2011 and 2013, homes consisted of separate buildings for sleeping and cooking. The buildings for sleeping were usually on stilts and either constructed from timber or sago palm leaves, sometimes with corrugated iron roofs or doors. Inside there might be one room or several. A household might have more than one sleeping house. The buildings for cooking were usually constructed from sago palm leaves and contained a fire and food preparation area. Often the building was divided into two, with the second area used as an eating area. Otherwise, food was eaten outside around the building. Mealtimes could therefore be quite communal; even if there was an eating area, it usually had open windows and people came and went during mealtimes. General relaxation took place outside. Neighbours were generally family members and often more immediate family members had houses which were closer to each other. Thus, the idea of being "at home" means being around the buildings in which people sleep and cook, and "home" denotes the village setting rather than an actual house. The people with whom an individual might have contact are grandparents, parents, children, siblings, cousins, in-laws and so on. The genealogical and sociolinguistic data I collected in the field (see §1.3.5.5 and §1.3.6.3) allowed me to ascertain the following information on intergenerational language transmission and multilingualism.

2.5.1.1 Intermarriage and intergenerational transmission

The language spoken in the home domain relates to intergenerational language transmission: "whether parents and older members of the community are speaking the language with and around children and young people" (Florey 2005: 45). Intergenerational language transmission is linked with mixed or inter-ethnic marriages, since in these marriages the parents have different native languages and have to make a choice about which language to transmit to their children. Of course, intergenerational language transmission is also an issue in intra-ethnic marriages where parents share the same native language but one or both parents might be bilingual and have to decide which language to use with their children. Community members reported to me that before the Bougainville Crisis there was much less intermarriage, it tended to be limited to Rotokas speakers, and Papapana speakers were proud of the fact they did not marry outside of their community. However, as a result of the increase in contact historically, there has been a huge increase in intermarriage in the Papapana community in the last decade or so.

In May 2013, thirty-one of the fluent Papapana speakers were married to each other in intra-ethnic marriages: fourteen couples and one polygamous marriage between a man and two sisters. Of these fifteen intra-ethnic marriages, one couple had fully passed Papapana on to both of their children (who were under the age of ten) and another to their eldest offspring only; two couples' eldest offspring were fluent speakers and younger offspring were semi-speakers; another two couples' eldest offspring were fluent speakers and middle offspring semi-speakers; and three couples had some or all offspring who were semi-speakers. In the remaining six marriages, no Papapana transmission had taken place, or at best their offspring only had passive knowledge.

There were also five Papapana-speaking widows who had been married to Papapana-speaking men. One of these, the eldest Papapana speaker, had fully passed Papapana on to all her offspring. Another widow had four offspring of whom one was a fluent speaker and one a semi-speaker. Some or all of the other three widows' offspring were semi-speakers.

The larger majority of fluent Papapana speakers, totalling fifty-nine speakers, were married to spouses in inter-ethnic marriages.

Table 2.3 shows the number of spouses of different L1 backgrounds, whether the spouse was male or female, and whether the spouse lived with the Papapana speaker in one of the six Papapana villages, or outside of the Papapana villages. The majority of Papapana speakers who had married inter-ethnically had remained in one of the six Papapana villages, with more men marrying into the community than women. More Papapana-speaking men had also married and lived outside of the community with their wives, than Papapana-speaking women.

Of these partnerships, only two women had managed to bring up some or all of their offspring with Papapana as L1. One of these women married a Rotokas-speaking man and their two eldest, both daughters, spoke Rotokas. However, only one daughter spoke Papapana fluently while the other, who had moved away, spoke Papapana with less confidence and proficiency. The other woman, a widow who had passed on Papapana, had married a Torau-speaking man and their offspring were all apparently bilingual in Papapana and Torau. Two of these

Table 2.3: Intermarriage patterns.

L1 Background	Husbands, in	Husbands, outside	Wives, in	Wives, outside
Tok Pisin (Papapana ancestors)	2		3	
Rotokas	3	1	2	5
Buin	7 (1 dead)		1	
Motuna		1	2	
Nasioi			1	
Tinputz	1		2	
Torau	2 (1 dead)	3		3
Halia	3		4	
Nehan	1		1	
Teop	1			
Eivo	1			
Other (incl. English)	5	1	1	2
TOTAL	26	6	17	10

offspring lived with their own families in Teperoi while the other five lived elsewhere, four in a Torau-speaking village. The children in these four families all spoke Torau, as did the children of another Papapana woman who had married into the Torau community.[13]

A further eight of the inter-marriage partnerships had brought up some or all of their offspring to be semi-speakers. Some of the other semi-speakers descended from three deceased Papapana-speaking mothers who had married Papuan language-speaking men. Another two semi-speakers were L2 speakers who had grown up in Teperoi but whose parents were Motuna speakers and had moved to the area. In another family, a Torau-speaking man had married a Rotokas-speaking woman and they had lived in Teperoi. Now deceased, this

---

13 In contrast, one Papapana-speaking woman's offspring spoke their father's language Buin but not Papapana because they had been brought up in the Buin area, though the mother and two of her offspring were living in a Papapana village in May 2013.

couple spoke Papapana as a L2, as did three of their offspring who spoke it fluently and another three who were semi-speakers.

2.5.1.2 Multilingualism and other L1s

A discussion of what language is spoken in the home domain normally involves ascertaining what language(s) parents speak to each other and to their children. Section 2.5.1.1 showed that in the families of the fluent Papapana speakers, Papapana had rarely been transmitted or was rarely being transmitted to the children: only 40% of the intra-ethnic marriages had succeeded in fully transmitting Papapana to some or all of their children and only 3.4% of the inter-ethnic marriages had succeeded. However, as described in §2.5.1, in the Papapana villages the boundaries of the home extend beyond the parents and their children, and furthermore, children can acquire language from a range of people of different ages, including their peers. It is therefore useful to know what other languages were being spoken around the villages between 2011 and 2013.

While Tok Pisin was the intergroup language, many Papapana-speaking adults were multilingual, not only in Tok Pisin and occasionally English, but also in other local languages: 14% spoke Rotokas, 13% spoke Torau, 2% spoke Teop, 2% spoke Buin, 1% Tinputz and 1% spoke Motuna. Some of these individuals spoke another local language because it was the language of their spouse or a parent, but most fluent Papapana speakers who had multilingual repertoires did so because of social contact with other speech communities over their lifetime, suggesting multilingualism used to be pervasive in the community. This in turn was supported by reports from Papapana speakers of their parents' linguistic repertoires, for example, the previous paramount chief spoke Papapana, Rotokas, Nasioi and Nagovisi.

In addition to the languages spoken by spouses and by multilingual Papapana speakers, there were other individuals present in the community who had different L1s and who must be included if one wishes to gain a full picture of language contact in the Papapana villages. Table 2.4 shows the number of speakers of different L1s per village. Where speakers were multilingual, they are included in the main count for their primary language and in square brackets for the language they identified with least. The numbers in square brackets are not considered in the calculation of the proportion of speakers out of the total population of 510 as otherwise there would be more than 510 tokens. Overall most people's L1 was Tok Pisin (including some people who were not of Papapana descent), followed by Papapana. There were over twenty people with Rotokas as their L1 (six of whom also had another L1). After that, the language groups which were represented by over ten speakers were Halia, Motuna, Buin and Torau.

Table 2.4: Multilingualism in Papapana villages.

	Peuni	Koikoi	Teperoi	Maras	Barora	Iraka	TOTAL	
Tok Pisin	9	32	145	68	47	37	338	66%
Papapana	3	7	47	13	10	7	86	17%
Rotokas	1	3	4[3]	3[3]	5	4	20[6]	4%
Halia	1	1	9		1	1	13	3%
Motuna		2	4	5		1	12	2%
Buin	1	[1]	3[1]	1[1]	1	2	8[3]	1.5%
Torau	4		2[3]	[2]			6[5]	1.1%
Nasioi		1	[1]			4	5[1]	1%
Nehan	2	1	2				5	1%
Other (PNG)		1	1	1		2	5	1%
Tinputz			3[2]				3[2]	0.6%
Nagovisi					3		3	0.6%
Other (Solomons)			1		1		2	0.4%
Teop			1[1]				1[1]	0.2%
Eivo						1	1	0.2%
Banoni		[1]					[1]	0.2%

2.5.1.3 Intergenerational transmission patterns

Having considered marriage patterns and success of Papapana transmission within particular families and the number of languages spoken as L1 in the Papapana villages, one might wonder which generations had succeeded or were succeeding in transmitting Papapana. Table 2.5 presents the distribution of fluent speakers, semi-speakers and passive bilinguals by each age group. It can be calculated that 95% of fluent speakers were above the age of thirty, while except for one or two individuals, all semi-speakers and passive bilinguals were under the age of forty. This shows that in 2013 there were speakers in the parental generation who had had Papapana transmitted to them but, with the exception of one couple (who had two Papapana-speaking sons under the age of ten), were not transmitting the language to their own children.

Table 2.5: Speakers by age.

Age group		L1/fluent speakers	L2/semi-speakers	Passive bilinguals	TOTAL
Children	0–9	2	1	7	10
	10–19	0	7	48	55
Parents	20–29	3	13	45	61
	30–39	23	33	33	89
Grandparents	40–49	40	1	2	43
	50–59	24	0	0	24
Great-Grandparents	60–69	11	0	1	12
	70–79	1	0	0	1
	80–89	2	0	0	2
TOTAL		106	55	136	297

Table 2.6 presents the proportion of fluent speakers within each age group, using the population of an age group across all six villages. Table 2.6 shows that only 1.8% of children under ten in Papapana villages spoke Papapana while 0% of children between ten and twenty spoke Papapana, only 4% of adults in their 20s and 21% of adults in their 30s spoke Papapana, while after the age of 40 years old, over 65% of each age group spoke Papapana. This shows that the grandparental generation were not especially successful in transmitting Papapana to their children, who in turn were even less successful.

Table 2.6: Proportion of speakers in age group.

Age group		Total population of age group in Papapana villages	L1/fluent speakers		L2/semi-speakers		Passive bilinguals	
Children	0–9	114	2	1.8%	0	–	7	6%
	10–19	142	0	–	8	6%	46	32%
Parents	20–29	76	3	4%	9	12%	33	43%
	30–39	81	17	21%	24	30%	18	22%

Table 2.6 (continued)

Age group		Total population of age group in Papapana villages	L1/fluent speakers		L2/semi-speakers		Passive bilinguals	
Grandparents	40–49	49	33	67%	1	2%	2	4%
	50–59	31	20	65%	0	–	0	–
Great-Grandparents	60–69	12	9	75%	0	–	1	8%
	70–79	1	1	100%	0	–	0	–
	80–89	2	2	100%	0	–	0	–
TOTAL		508	87		42		107	

The percentage of parents in their 20s and 30s who spoke Papapana to some extent is higher than those who spoke it fluently: 12% and 30% compared to the aforementioned 4% and 21%. This shows that the grandparental generation did partially succeed in transmitting some Papapana to their children, but more of them did not fully succeed. Only 2% of the over 40s spoke Papapana partially, suggesting that it is more a case of all or nothing for older speakers.

Three people of the grandparent generation were passive bilinguals (and at least one of these speakers was an immigrant), but otherwise all passive bilinguals were under 40: 6% and 32% of children, 43% and 22% of parents.
Overall, grandparent and great-grandparent generations were generally the fluent speakers, parents in their 30s were often semi-speakers, while younger parents and children had passive knowledge of Papapana at best.

2.5.2 Work and administration

Within the villages between 2011 and 2013, work included housework, building shelters, cooking, fishing, hunting, gathering and gardening, and copra/cocoa production. Gardens were most often located outside of the village. Fishing, hunting, gathering and copra/cocoa production also took place outside of the village, while some community members went to markets at Wakunai, or further to Arawa and Buka, to sell and buy produce. In 2013, a small market was established on the main highway, just south of Maras bridge, and thus easily accessible to those living in Maras and Teperoi. Another occupation within the

Papapana villages was teacher, while some community members worked in other towns as tradesmen, teachers, nurses or in local government. Work inside the village could be considered part of the home domain (see §2.5.1), or educational domain (see §2.5.3) while work outside of the village was more distinct. Papapana might be used among fluent speakers in the external work domain but it was most certainly not the language of that domain and it was less likely to be used given the increased chance of non-Papapana speakers being present.

Between 2011 and 2013, the Papapana speech community had a chief system that consisted of a Paramount Chief, Chairman of Chiefs, Vice Chairman of Chiefs, a Secretary and Treasurer and then one or two Clan Chiefs for each of the six clans. In May 2013, all the main chiefs lived in Teperoi or Maras, while each village had one or two clan chiefs. The Secretary and many of the clan chiefs were female. All chiefs were fluent Papapana speakers and met once a month. Without being privy to these meetings, I cannot say what language was used. Speakers said they used Papapana, but Tok Pisin may well have been used too. The entire community met about once a month but there were also regular announcements after church on Sundays and minor meetings were scheduled among particular groups (such as the women's prayer group), clans or villages as and when it was necessary. Clan chiefs were responsible for disseminating information and decisions that had been made at chief meetings. At meetings in which the entire community was present, Tok Pisin was used since a large majority of community members did not speak or understand Papapana. Regional government and administration outside of the six Papapana villages was most certainly conducted in Tok Pisin, or another local language. The fact that Papapana had no status at the regional level is evident in the fact that the sign on the Teperoi church said *Auta Parish*, *Auta* meaning 'Papapana' in the neighbouring Rotokas language.

2.5.3 Education

The Papua New Guinean educational system begins with Elementary School, continues with Primary School and Secondary School, and concludes with High School. Teperoi has both an Elementary and Primary School. In 2013, Teperoi school had been following the 2003 Elementary Language Syllabus, which states that "The students' first language is to be used as a medium of instruction for the first three years of education" (NDOE 2003: iv).[14] The students'

---

14 It was announced in January 2013 (Taita 2013) that the government had made it policy that English should be the official language of instruction at elementary level and that this policy

L1 is referred to elsewhere in the syllabus as the students' "vernacular" and this is defined as "'tokples', which is also called 'mother tongue' in many countries. The vernacular in PNG could be one of the PNG's 850 local languages including Tok Pisin, Hiri Motu and English" (NDOE 2003: 1). Teachers and students are expected to "speak well the language of instruction" in order to meet the syllabus outcomes, and teachers "need to read and write fluently the vernacular of the students" (NDOE 2003: 1). English is introduced at Elementary 1 level and as medium of instruction at Primary level.

In Teperoi, Papapana is the "tokples" even though it is not everyone's L1. However, it is difficult to achieve the objective of using Papapana as the medium of instruction because the teachers themselves had different language backgrounds: in 2011–2013, only the first year of Elementary was taught by a fluent Papapana speaker. Nevertheless, in April 2018, all three Elementary teachers were Papapana speakers. The second problem with achieving the objective of using Papapana as the medium of instruction was that the students had different language backgrounds. The syllabus does recognise Tok Pisin as a "vernacular", but in Teperoi "tokples" means Papapana, and Tok Pisin would not be considered "tokples" by any means. It was difficult therefore to achieve the syllabus objectives when the children did not speak their "tokples" and when some children spoke an entirely different "tokples". The third obstacle in achieving the goal was lack of permanent teaching materials and the resources to create and store them. In reality, there was a makeshift blackboard, the teacher Francis Abea used songs and games, and he had created some paper flashcards of words or sentences (see Figure 2.13). Other materials, such as story books Francis had created, had been destroyed or lost. Otherwise, there were no written Papapana materials in the community, even though Papapana does have an established orthography (see §3.2). In April 2018, the situation had certainly improved. As well as all three Elementary teachers being Papapana-speakers, there were two new, secure, weather-tight classrooms for the Elementary school, which were certainly more "print rich" (albeit not in Papapana) (see Figure 2.14). In 2015, I had also sent the school my thesis, draft dictionary, four pedagogical readers (based on the SIL Shell books) and ten illustrated vocabulary books (see §1.3.5.3). I was not able to ascertain how and how much the readers and

---

should be implemented in February 2013. However, this was not being implemented when I left in May 2013 and still does not seem to be in place: the 2015 Elementary Language syllabus follows the same policy outlined here, that is, "the children's first language is to be used as a medium of instruction for the first three years of elementary education" (NDOE 2015: iv) which "in some communities [. . .] will be Tok Ples while in others is in Tok Pisin" (NDOE 2015: 2).

Figure 2.13: Francis Abea, Teperoi Elementary School, 2012.

Figure 2.14: A classroom in Teperoi Elementary School, 2018.

vocabulary books were used though, nor to find out what other Papapana teaching materials the three teachers made.

In 2013, given the aforementioned obstacles, it was not surprising that even in Francis' Elementary Prep classes Papapana was not used consistently as the medium of instruction. Instead Papapana was taught effectively as an L2 in Language classes, with the medium of instruction being Papapana and Tok Pisin. English was also taught as an L2 alongside Papapana, in preparation for Elementary 1 where English is introduced as a subject. In Maths classes and Community and Culture classes, Papapana was sometimes used for numbers and naming objects respectively, but Tok Pisin was used as the medium of instruction. In 2018, it was reported to still be the case that Papapana is sometimes, but not always, used as the medium of instruction, and is sometimes used in Maths and Language classes. Even though there are Papapana-speaking teachers for all Elementary classes, there is "bridging" between the "tok ples" and Tok Pisin and English in Elementary 1 and 2. Thus it is highly unlikely that students will become literate in Papapana. This chance is further diminished by the fact that not all 'Papapana' children attended school in Teperoi; for some children it was too far to walk and they went to school elsewhere or not at all.

2.5.4 Religion, social events and media

Between 2011 and 2013, Teperoi village had a Catholic church while Barora also had a small building which was used as a church. Church sermons, readings and prayers were conducted in Tok Pisin. Songs were also conducted in Tok Pisin, though occasionally English songs or Papapana songs were sung. According to one community member, funerals and marriages within the church were conducted in Tok Pisin, but traditional ceremonies outside the church were conducted in Papapana. When there were more Papapana speakers present, such as at one of the women's prayer meetings, more Papapana songs were sung and preaching might be conducted in a mixture of Papapana and Tok Pisin.

Between 2011 and 2013, quite often on Sunday afternoons, community members gathered at the school grounds and played football and volleyball, sometimes just for entertainment and sometimes in preparation for tournaments in Bougainville or at national level. Community members also met for fundraising events, such as a school fundraiser which took place for a whole week on the school grounds and included sports tournaments, live music and food stalls. In 2018, community members had set up a volleyball net in the centre of Teperoi and seemed to play regularly. Social events such as these which took place within

Teperoi or another Papapana village were conducted in a mixture of Papapana and Tok Pisin depending on the participants of a particular conversation. Social gatherings such as these which took place outside of the six villages, for example, in the district capital Wakunai, were conducted in Tok Pisin, though Papapana speakers might speak Papapana among themselves.

Within the village setting, a few community members had generators and televisions with DVD players, so occasionally villagers were exposed to television shows, films and music videos in English, Tok Pisin, Solomons Pijin and other local languages such as Rotokas.

2.6 Papapana's ethnolinguistic vitality

To assess the extent of endangerment of a language, we need to assess how much the language is used. The number and quality of domains, and the proportion of speakers within a community are thus crucial indicators of linguistic vitality: the more domains and the higher the proportion of speakers, the greater the chance of the language being used. Intergenerational transmission is also an indicator as it reflects the extent to which the language is used in the home and school domains and at the same time, the interruption of intergenerational transmission leads to demographic changes which further perpetuate endangerment. For more on the distinction between indicators and causes of language endangerment, and on assessing ethnolinguistic vitality, see Himmelmann (2010) and Smith (2016b).

As this chapter has shown, Papapana is now spoken by less than 20% of the total population of the community, intergenerational transmission has almost ceased, and Tok Pisin is the dominant language of all domains (though Papapana may be used among Papapana speakers in these domains and is used to a limited degree in elementary school). Papapana is thus undoubtedly one of the world's languages that is likely to disappear within this century.

Papapana is endangered because there has been considerable language shift to Tok Pisin. This shift to Tok Pisin is not unique to the Papapana community: in other parts of PNG "language shift to Tok Pisin is now proceeding in many communities at an alarming pace" (Dobrin 2005: 42) with an increasing number of younger Melanesians growing up speaking Tok Pisin exclusively, or with greater confidence than their parents' vernaculars (Lynch, Ross and Crowley 2002: 28). Certainly, where Tok Pisin was known by around half of the population twenty years ago, it is now spoken by more than three-quarters of the population (Wurm 2012: 444). Language shift is caused "by shifts in personal and group values and goals" (Kulick 1992: 9). Such attitudes concern the usefulness and worth of the language: "speakers abandon their native tongue in adaptation to an environment where use of that language is no longer advantageous" (Grenoble and Whaley 1998: 22). However, the complicated issue is identifying the environmental changes that bring about the decreased efficacy of a language in a community (Grenoble and Whaley 1998: 22).

Like the rest of PNG, colonisation and recent globalisation in Bougainville have introduced new economic bases (see §2.5.2) in which Tok Pisin is dominant so knowledge of Tok Pisin offers considerable economic advantages to Papapana speakers. Furthermore, contact between Papapana speakers and speakers of other languages, both inside and outside of the community, has increased considerably over the past century (as described in §2.4 and §2.5.1), thus there has been more need for and exposure to a lingua franca like Tok Pisin. However, Tok Pisin could be added to a Papapana speaker's linguistic repertoire, without abandoning their vernacular, as happens in other speech communities in Bougainville. In the Papapana community this has not happened because of a number of interrelated factors (see Smith 2016b). Firstly, the community's coastal location has made them more vulnerable to contact with outsiders and to more sustained contact (since plantations and mission stations were established along the coast). Secondly, the Papapana speech community has always been a minority immigrant group (see §2.4.2 and §2.4.3) and thus the apparent increase in death rates in the early 1900s, and recent migration, immigration, displacement and increased mobility have all caused a more noticeable and rapid decrease in number and proportion of speakers. This in turn reduces the efficacy of Papapana and could also have affected the community's sense of identity. It is also possible that subconsciously there has been a shift from ethnic identity to regional/national identity which has promoted the use of Tok Pisin even further (a change seen elsewhere in PNG; see Kulick 1992 and Wurm 2012: 444). Furthermore, Papapana is not viewed by its speakers as a powerful language because of its small speaker numbers. Thirdly, coupled with a decreasing speaker base, the weak representation in institutions such as school, church and the media adds to the occasions when Papapana is not used and affects its perceived importance and speakers' motivations to use the language. Low speaker numbers also mean it is difficult to support the use of Papapana (e.g. by creating resources) in these institutions. Finally, a change in attitudes may also be attributed to the perception of Papapana as an endangered language: community members may feel that it is not beneficial to speak or transmit Papapana as it has no future. As Papapana becomes more endangered, there are fewer fluent speakers and there is a certain level of shame among semi-speakers that they do not have a high level of proficiency in Papapana; this results in a reluctance to speak Papapana, which of course further exacerbates the situation. The interaction of all these factors has led to changes in Papapana speakers' attitudes towards their language: Tok Pisin has gained prestige and usefulness and so it has been added to their multilingual repertoire, but Papapana has lost prestige and usefulness and is therefore being abandoned.

Chapter 3
Phonology

This chapter describes the Papapana phoneme system and phonological variation (§3.1), the orthography (§3.2), phonotactics (§3.3), reduplication (§3.4) and the stress regime (§3.5).

3.1 Segmental phonology

This section outlines the phonemes, allophones and phonological and morphophonological processes in the vowel system (§3.1.1) and the consonant system (§3.1.2). Like most Oceanic languages, Papapana is a non-tonal language. Length plays a role in the vowel system. This section concludes with some brief observations on phonological variation and change (§3.1.3).

3.1.1 Vowels

The Papapana vowel system consists of five monophthongs (§3.1.1.1). The three front unrounded vowels exhibit contrastive vowel length (§3.1.1.2). Seventeen vowel combinations are attested in Papapana, of which seven are diphthongs, though the phonemic status of these diphthongs is unclear (§3.1.1.3). Morphophonological processes involving vowels include loss of a word-final echo vowel in three syllable verb roots when the transitive enclitic =i attaches directly to the verb (see §6.5.1.1).

3.1.1.1 Monophthongs: phonemes and allophones

The Papapana vowel system has five monophthongs (see Table 3.1), which is typical of Oceanic languages. The three front vowels are unrounded, while the back vowels are both rounded, which is a common correlation cross-linguistically. The sets of minimal pairs in Table 3.2 show that the monophthongs are in contrastive distribution.

In order to accurately identify the monophthongs used in Papapana, I conducted an acoustic analysis in the Praat program. I used a wordlist of at least ten words per vowel, spoken by two to four different speakers ranging in age and gender. Table 3.3 shows the range of the frequencies in Hertz of the first and second formants of each vowel. The acoustic analysis confirmed my identification of /e/

Table 3.1: Monophthong phonemes.

Vowel	Description
/i/	close, front, unrounded (cardinal 1)
/e/	close-mid, front, unrounded (cardinal 2)
/a/	open, front, unrounded (cardinal 4)
/ɔ/	open-mid, back, rounded (cardinal 6)
/u/	close, back, rounded (cardinal 8)

Table 3.2: Contrastive sets: Monophthongs.

Contrast	Minimal pairs			
/i/ /e/	/peri/	'to find'	/pere/	'unripe/uncooked'
/i/ /a/	/ini/	'here'	/ani/	2SG
/i/ /ɔ/	/mimi/	'urine'	/mɔmɔ/	'seaweed species'
/i/ /u/	/ami/	1EXCL.PSSR=	/amu/	2SG.PSSR=
/e/ /a/	/mate/	'die'	/mata/	'eye'
/e/ /ɔ/	/te/	OBL	/tɔ/	EMPH
/e/ /u/	/ate/	'liver'	/atu/	'to make'
/a/ /ɔ/	/βatu/	'stone'	/βɔtu/	'to leave'
/a/ /u/	/tama/	'father'	/tamu/	'to eat'
/ɔ/ /u/	/naʊnɔ/	'tree'	/naʊnu/	'leaf'

Table 3.3: Monophthong formant measurements.

Vowel	Formant 1	Formant 2
/i/	281–461 Hz	1906–2383 Hz
/e/	362–479 Hz	1685–2108 Hz
/a/	522–991 Hz	1391–1897 Hz
/ɔ/	375–595 Hz	940–1387 Hz
/u/	316–422 Hz	912–1681 Hz

but the frequencies of the first formant for /i/ and /u/ indicated that these vowels were sometimes articulated with a lower tongue position than one might expect, while the second formant frequency for /u/ suggested a slightly more fronted tongue position on occasions. It should be noted that the recording conditions were unfortunately not always ideal, which may account for the unexpected frequencies. My acoustic analysis confirmed my perception that /a/ and /ɔ/ were sometimes articulated with a slightly higher tongue position, approximating [æ] and [ɐ], and [o] respectively; however, there was no consistency among the speakers nor were there distinct environments in which these allophones occurred. Instead, these allophones are in free variation.

In some speakers' casual speech, I perceived /a/ to be realised as a schwa [ə] in word-final syllables. Also in casual speech, the phoneme /i/ shows allophonic variation in that the voiced palatal approximant [j] occurs as an allophone of /i/ when /i/ is word-initial before the short vowel /a/ in a monomorphemic word, as in (1). Alternatively, [j] is inserted between /i/ and the following vowel (see §3.1.2.3). In Hoava too, the combinations /ia/ and /iu/ are pronounced with a glide as [ja] and [ju] (Davis 2003: 25) and in Kokota, high vowels have glide allophones in casual speech when they are the first vowel in a VV sequence that is not eligible for diphthong formation (Palmer 2009: 13, 17).

(1)   /i/ → [j] / #_ [a]
      /iaʔa/   'Mum'   →   [jaʔa]
      /bau iana/   'PL fish'   →   [bau jana]
      / bau iaβa/   'PL slaked lime'   →   [bau jaβa]

3.1.1.2 Vowel length

Vowel length is contrastive in Papapana for the three front unrounded vowels /i/, /e/ and /a/, but has a low functional load. I perceived a difference in length for /i/, /e/ and /a/ but not for /ɔ/ and /u/, and my acoustic analysis in Praat confirmed these length contrasts. The sets of minimal or near-minimal pairs in Table 3.4 show that in Papapana /iː/, /eː/ and /aː/ are phonemes. Table 3.4 shows the duration of the vowels in these pairs in seconds for three different speakers.

Contrastive vowel length is also demonstrated by the fact that vowels of different length are not in complementary distribution, there is no correspondence between vowel length and a word's syllabic structure, and stress does not play a role.

Table 3.4: Contrastive sets: Long vowels.

Contrast	Minimal pairs				
		Length (sec)		Length (sec)	Length difference (sec)
/i/ /iː/	[ˈsi.βa] 'hot'	0.073958	[ˈsiː.pa] 'pot stand'	0.184390	0.110432
		0.100723		0.180175	0.079452
		0.117812		0.168538	0.050726
/e/ /eː/	[ˈte.na] OBL	0.083362	[ˈteː.na] 'who'	0.144481	0.061119
		0.083869		0.214730	0.130861
/a/ /aː/	[ˈna.ni] 'there'	0.084099	[ˈnaː.ni] 'day'	0.217455	0.133356
		0.091288		0.216793	0.125505
		0.112595		0.246172	0.133577

Although long vowels are not attested in word-final syllables, they can occur in either word-medial (2b) or word-initial (3b) syllables. There is no correlation between vowel length and phonological environment as a short vowel (a) and a long vowel (b) may be preceded and followed by the same phonemes, as in (2) and (3):

(2) a. /βiβirɔʔɔ/ 'around' b. /βiβiːru/ 'milkwood'

(3) a. /patu/ 'head' b. /paːtɔ/ 'duck'

There is no correspondence between vowel length and the number of syllables in a word as both short vowels (a) and long vowels (b) can appear in words with the same number of syllables:

(4) a. [a.si.ɾe] 'turmeric' b. [βi.βiː.ɾu] 'milkwood'

(5) a. [ka.tɔ.pɔ] 'toe/finger nail' b. [maː.mi.dɔ] 'slowly'

Stress also does not affect vowel length as both stressed (6)–(7) and unstressed (8) syllables may contain both short (a) and long vowels (b):

(6) a. [ˈme.ɾeɪ] OBL b. [ˈpeː.pe] 'shell species'

(7) a. [ˈta.mu.te] 'mango' b. [ˈaː.ma.ni] 1EXCL

(8) a. [ˈtaʊ.βa.si] 'four' b. [ˈtɔ.ɾaː.ɾa] 'axe'

As the pairs of examples in (9) to (10) demonstrate, long vowels frequently occur when morphological concatenation results in the adjacent co-occurrence of two identical vowels (a). It is only by testing the roots in other morphosyntactic environments (b) that it is possible to show that the long vowel is not phonemic when the vowel length crosses morpheme boundaries and results from concatenation.

(9) a. [iːnu]
      i-inu
      LOC-house
      'in the house'

    b. [baʊ inu]
      bau inu
      PL   house
      'houses'

(10) a. [naːgana]
      na=agana
      SPEC[CLI]=root
      'root'

    b. [baʊ agana]
      bau agana
      PL   root
      'roots'

Although distinctive vowel length is not common in Western Oceanic languages (Lynch, Ross and Crowley 2002: 35), it is attested in other Northwest Solomonic languages such as Banoni (Lynch and Ross 2002: 441). However, asymmetrical vowel length contrasts are not attested in Northwest Solomonic languages and within the Oceanic group, they are only found in a few Vanuatu languages. In Southeast Ambrym, there are six vowels and vowel length is contrastive (albeit with a very low functional load) but the data do not provide evidence for the existence of contrastive /oː/ while /æː/ is attested in only one word and is in free variation with /æa/ (Crowley 2002: 660). In Dorig (François 2005: 461) and Lelepa (Lacrampe 2014: 14) vowel length is contrastive only for /a/. In fact, cross-linguistically, low vowels such as /a/ are more likely than other vowels to be long (Gordon 2017: 76), therefore, Papapana is unusual since it is the front vowels which demonstrate contrastive vowel length.

3.1.1.3 Diphthongs and vowel sequences

In Papapana, the non-identical vowel sequences [ei], [ai], [ae], [au], [ao], [ɔi] and [ɔe] undergo a process of diphthong formation. All diphthongs are closing diphthongs. For four of these, the tongue moves towards but does not completely reach [i] or [u] and thus the tongue arrives at the lax counterparts of these cardinal vowels, [ɪ] and [ʊ]. The difference between [aɪ], [aʊ] and [ɔɪ] and [ae], [ao] and [ɔe] is shown by an acoustic analysis which confirms that tongue height does not increase as much for the latter three diphthongs: Table 3.5 shows the range of the frequencies in Hertz of the first and second formants for the starting and ending position of each diphthong, as measured in the acoustic analysis.

Table 3.5: Vowel phonemes: Diphthong formant measurements.

Diphthongs	Start position		End position	
	Formant 1	Formant 2	Formant 1	Formant 2
[aɪ]	695–922 Hz	1631–1696 Hz	428–561 Hz	1283–2606 Hz
[ae]	788–949 Hz	1436–1510 Hz	561–641 Hz	1410–2406 Hz
[aʊ]	677–733 Hz	1079–1603 Hz	468–553 Hz	725–1097 Hz
[aɔ]	631–766 Hz	1174–1502 Hz	545–615 Hz	800–1047 Hz
[ɔɪ]	516–626 Hz	872–1084 Hz	411–508 Hz	1762–2494 Hz
[ɔe]	451–670 Hz	696–1133 Hz	505–635 Hz	1760–2298 Hz

An examination of the stress regime in Papapana demonstrates that these vowel sequences are indeed diphthongs as they combine to form the nucleus of a single, heavy syllable in both root and stem forms, as shown in Table 3.6; however, their underlying phonemic status is unclear. Evidence that the diphthongs

Table 3.6: Diphthongs.

Diphthong	Monomorphemic root		Stem
[eɪ]	[a.βu.teɪ]	'brother-in-law'	No data
[aɪ]	[naɪ]	'forehead'	[naɪ.na] nai-na forehead-3SG.PSSR 'his forehead'
[ae]	[bae]	'shoulder'	[bae.na] bae-na shoulder-3SG.PSSR 'his shoulder'
[aʊ]	[maʊ.nu]	'woman'	No data
[aɔ]	[naɔ]	'to go'	[e.naɔ.wi] e=nao=i 3SG.SBJ=go=IRR 'he/she will go'
[ɔɪ]	[ɔɪ.na]	3PL	No data
[ɔe]	[nɔe]	'to put'	No data

are likely not to be phonemes comes from reduplication in which only the first vowel of a diphthong is reduplicated (see §3.4), and from CVVCV verb roots such as *gaunu* 'write' where the final vowel very likely reflects a Proto-Northwest Solomonic echo vowel added after word-final Proto-Oceanic consonants; the final /u/ would not be an echo vowel if the diphthong /au/ were phonemic (see §6.5.1.1 for more detail).

Although the phonemic status of diphthongs is unclear, the pairs in Table 3.7 show a contrast between monophthongs and diphthongs.

Table 3.7: Contrastive sets: Diphthongs.

Contrast	Minimal pairs			
[e] [eɪ]	[bebe]	'spleen'	[beɪbeɪ]	'butterfly'
[a] [aɪ]	[ate]	'liver'	[aɪte]	'Dad'
[a] [ae]	[ta]	NSPEC[CLI]=	[tae]	'up'
[a] [aʊ]	[kakaʊ]	'dog'	[kaʊkaʊ]	'sweet potato'
[a] [aɔ]	[ara]	PST	[araɔ]	'brother'
[ɔ] [ɔɪ]	[tɔ]	EMPH	[tɔɪ]	'person'
[ɔ] [ɔe]	[nɔ]	go.SEQ	[nɔe]	'to put'

Diphthongs also frequently occur when morphological concatenation results in the adjacent co-occurrence of two non-identical vowels as in (11)–(17), but these diphthongs are clearly not phonemic:

(11) [eɪrɔmɔ]
   e=iromo
   3SG.SBJ=drink
   'he drank'

(12) [naɪŋani]
   na=ingani
   SPEC[CLI]=Canarium.Indicum
   'Canarium Indicum'

(13) [naepu]
    na=epu
    SPEC[CLI]=cloud
    'clouds'

(14) [nauβi]
    na=uvi
    SPEC[CLI]=yam
    'yam'

(15) [naɔrawi]
    na=orawi
    SPEC[CLI]=man
    'the man'

(16) [nasinɔɪna]
    na=sino-ina
    SPEC[CLI]=bone-3PL.PSSR
    'their bones'

(17) [misiɔdɔemani]
    mi=siodo=emani
    1EXCL.SBJ=work=1EXCL.IPFV
    'we are working'

Aside from the vowel sequences involved in the diphthongs, there are ten other attested vowel sequences in monomorphemic roots, as shown in Table 3.8. The vowel sequences [iu], [ɔu] and [uɔ] are not attested in monomorphemic roots. The ten vowel sequences do not form diphthongs as they belong to separate syllables, as Table 3.8 shows, and a glide is usually created between the two vowels (see §3.1.2.3).

These vowel sequences may also occur as the result of morphological concatenation, as can the vowel sequences [iu], [ɔu] and [uɔ], as in (18)–(20).

(18) [nuwapiju]
    nu=api-u
    SPEC.CLII=thigh-1SG.PSSR
    'my thigh'

Table 3.8: Vowel sequences.

Vowel combination	Monomorphemic root	
[ie]	[i.je]	'leg'
[ia]	[bi.si.ja]	'back'
[iɔ]	[βi.si.jɔ]	'body'
[ea]	[me.ja]	'tongue'
[eɔ]	[ba.re.jɔ]	'breadfruit'
[eu]	[u.be.ju]	'cave'
[ɔa]	[ma.nɔ.wa]	'neck'
[ui]	[ba.ba.ku.wi]	'shark'
[ue]	[tu.we]	'language'
[ua]	[tu.wa]	'to paddle'

(19) [nukatɔpɔwu]
 nu=katopo-u
 SPEC.CLII=nail-1SG.PSSR
 'my fingernail/toenail'

(20) [ɔwaputuwɔmu]
 o=aputu=omu
 2SG.SBJ=sleep=2SG.IPFV
 'you are sleeping'

3.1.2 Consonants

The Papapana consonant system consists of fourteen phonemes (§3.1.2.1). Some Papapana consonant phonemes exhibit allophonic variation (§3.1.2.2) while certain intervocalic environments trigger glide insertion (§3.1.2.3) or glottal epenthesis (§3.1.2.4). A morpho-phonological process involving consonants entails a word-final syllable beginning with /t/ undergoing a sound change to [s] when (as mentioned in §3.1.1) word-final echo vowels in three syllable verb roots are lost when the transitive enclitic =i attaches to the verb (see §6.5.1.1 for more detail). This consonant sound change reflects the sound change of POc and PNWS *t to s/_i in Papapana (Ross 1988: 219).

3.1.2.1 Consonant phonemes

Table 3.9 presents the fourteen consonants used in the Papapana phoneme system. The consonant phonemes cross four places of articulation and can be articulated in five different manners. One of the Papapana consonant phonemes /w/ is labial-velar and therefore inherently has two simultaneous places of articulation. Although Ross (1988: 218) reports that POc *w was lost in the Northwest Solomonic group, Papapana is like Taiof (Ross 2002b: 426) in having /w/ as a phoneme. Only oral stops make a voicing distinction. Voiced consonants are in bold typeface in Table 3.9. Unlike in many Melanesian Oceanic languages, voiced oral stops are not prenasalised.

Table 3.9: Consonant phonemes.

	Bilabial		Alveolar		Velar		Glottal	Labial-velar
Oral stop	p	**b**	t	**d**	k	**g**	ʔ	
Nasal stop	m		n		ŋ			
Tap			ɾ					
Fricative	β		s					
Approximant								w

The minimal pairs or near-minimal pairs in Tables 3.10, 3.11 and 3.12 demonstrate consonant phoneme contrasts by voicing status, manner of articulation and place of articulation.

Table 3.10: Contrastive sets: Consonant voicing distinctions.

Con	Bilabial		Alveolar		Velar	
Voiceless	/pɔtɔ/	INTS	/tua/	'to paddle'	/kaʊmɔ/	'sea-crab'
Voiced	/bɔtɔ/	'to be born'	/dua/	'bad'	/gaʊnu/	'to write'

3.1.2.2 Allophonic variation

Some Papapana consonant phonemes exhibit allophonic variation. The alveolar tap /ɾ/ is sometimes lightly trilled by some speakers but this is not contrastive; the allophones [ɾ] and [r] are in free variation in all environments. In other Northwest Solomonic languages such as Taiof the alveolar trill is a phoneme

Table 3.11: Contrastive sets: Consonant manner distinctions.

	Bilabial		Alveolar		Velar	
Oral stop /Nasal	/bɔni/	'night'	/dua/	'bad'	/agana/	'root'
	/mɔni/	'money'	/nua/	'two'	/ŋanaŋana/	'moon'
Oral stop /Tap	N/A		/tɔa/	'chicken'	N/A	
			/rɔa/	'to plant'		
Oral stop /Fricative	/bɔtu/	'boat'	/ta=aʊ/	NSPEC=CLII	N/A	
	/βɔtu/	'to leave'	/sa=aʊ/	DIM=CLII		
Oral stop /Approximant	/batu/	'to clean (wall)'	N/A		/garu/	'Casuarina tree'
	/watu/	'smoke'			/watu/	'smoke'
Nasal /Tap	N/A		/anaʊ/	1SG	N/A	
			/arɔ/	'brother'		
Nasal /Fricative	/mɔri/	'citrus fruit'	/nɔ/	'mosquito'	N/A	
	/βɔri/	'to talk'	/sɔ/	1INCL.SBJ=		
Nasal /Approximant	/maʔa/	'to give'	N/A		/reβaŋa/	'centipede'
	/wa/	'to say'			/etawa/	'big'
Tap /Fricative	N/A		/ʔurita/	'octopus'	N/A	
			/ʔusia/	'child'		
Tap /Approximant	N/A		N/A		N/A	
Fricative / Approximant	/βatu/	'stone'	N/A		N/A	
	/watu/	'smoke'				

(Ross 2002b: 426) while in Roviana the degree of trilling depends on stress (Corston-Oliver 2002: 467).

The voiced bilabial fricative [β] is in free variation with the voiced labio-dental fricative [v] as allophones of /β/ in all environments, though there is a tendency for the voiced bilabial fricative to precede rounded vowels. The voiced bilabial fricative also occurs in free variation with the voiced labial-velar approximant allophone [w] as allophones of /β/, in the environment shown in (21):

(21) /β/ → [w] / [aʊ] _ [a]
/taʊβasi/ 'four' → [taʊβasi] and [taʊwasi]

Table 3.12: Contrastive sets: Consonant place distinctions.

	Voiceless Plosives		Voiced Plosives		Nasals	
Bilabial	/pusi/	'cat'	/bua/	'full'	/maʊnu/	'woman'
/Alveolar	/atutusi/	'to chase'	/dua/	'bad'	/naʊnu/	'leaf'
Bilabial	/papasi/	'quickly'	/baʊ/	PL	/mɔnɔ/	'turtle'
/Velar	/kakaʔi/	'small'	/gaʊ/	'green jobfish'	/nɔŋɔnɔ/	'to hear'
Bilabial	/pusi/	'cat'	N/A		N/A	
/Glottal	/ʔusi/	'shell species'				
Alveolar	/tura/	'fire'	/dɔβi/	'to spit'	/nana/	'branch'
/Velar	/kura/	'betel catkin'	/gɔgɔβi/	'ripe banana'	/ŋanaŋana/	'moon'
Alveolar	/i-ata/	'LOC-above'	N/A		N/A	
/Glottal	/iaʔa/	'Mum'				
Velar	/kaʊkaʊ/	'sweet potato'	N/A		N/A	
/Glottal	/ʔaɔʔaɔ/	'Bougainville crow'				

In Papapana, the phoneme is assumed to be underlyingly bilabial because the allophone [β] occurs more often than the allophones [v] and [w], and speakers judged [β] to be the "correct" pronunciation.

3.1.2.3 Glide insertion
In accordance with the Maximum Onset Principle (Kahn 1976) the melody of the back rounded vowels /u/ and /ɔ/ (and their associated diphthongs /aʊ/ and /aɔ/), and another vowel may create an onset consisting of the voiced labial-velar approximant [w], as in (22)–(25):

(22) /natui/ 'tomorrow' → [natuwi]
    /tue/ 'language' → [tuwe]
    /aruaɪ/ 'no' → [aruwaɪ]

(23) /aʊ=araɔ/ '1SG.PSSR[CLI]=brother' → [aʊwaraɔ]

(24) /tɔa/ 'chicken' → [tɔwa]

(25) /naɔi/ 'rain' → [naɔwi]

Similarly, the melody of the front vowels /i/ or /e/ (or their associated diphthongs /eɪ/, /aɪ/, /ɔɪ/, /ae/ and /ɔe/) and another vowel may create an onset consisting of the voiced palatal approximant [j], as in (26)–(29):

(26) /nu=ie-na/ 'SPEC.CLII=leg-3SG.PSSR' → [nuwijena]
     /ʔusia/ 'child' → [ʔusija]
     /kiɔkiɔ/ 'chick' → [kijɔkijɔ]

(27) /βeβeɪɔŋɔ/ 'clothing' → [βeβeɪjɔŋɔ]
     /aɪa/ 3SG → [aɪja]
     /mɔɪa/ 'vegetable' → [mɔɪja]

(28) /bea/ 'maybe' → [beja]
     /bareɔ/ 'breadfruit' → [barejɔ]
     /ubeu/ 'cave' → [ubeju]

(29) /ae=a/ 'buy=3SG.OBJ' → [aeja]
     /vɔea/ 'crocodile' → [vɔeja]

3.1.2.4 Glottal epenthesis

The glottal stop is phonemic in Papapana; however, it may also occur as epenthetic glottal insertion in reduplicated forms to break the hiatus between two identical vowels as in (30):

(30) /a~aβeru/ 'RD~steal (thief)' → [aʔaβeru] 'RD~steal (thief)'

Forms with epenthetic glottal insertion have to be distinguished from those where the glottal stop is intervocalic at a morpheme boundary but phonemic, as in (31)–(32), since the surface forms can look superficially similar.

(31) [naʔareɪ]
    na='arei
    SPEC[CLI]=ant
    'ant'

(32) [naʔɔru]
    na='oru
    SPEC[CLI]=snake
    'snake'

It is likely that POc *k has undergone a sound change to /ʔ/ in Papapana as /ʔurita/ 'octopus' can be considered a reflex of POc *kurita 'octopus', while the lexeme /ʔaʔadeʔe/ 'narrative' can be considered cognate with *kakadeke* 'narrative' in Torau (Palmer fieldnotes). This sound change may still be in progress as I noticed that one speaker would pronounce /kɔkɔbunu/ 'short' as [ʔɔʔɔbunu].

3.1.3 Phonological variation and change

I observed and confirmed several variations in pronunciation which seem to reflect sound changes in progress:
1. In certain words, such as those in (33) and (34), there is variation between the back vowel /ɔ/ and the front vowels /e/ or /a/, but the forms with front vowels are considered by speakers to be recent innovations used mainly by younger speakers.

(33) [mɔɪsibuaβa] and [meɪsibuaβa] 'old woman'
 [sɔɪdaʔɔ] and [seɪdaʔɔ] 'old man'
 [pɔʔuɾi] and [peʔuɾi] 'basket'
 [aβɔa] and [aβea] 'where'
 [βɔwa] and [βewa] 'be like'

(34) [ɔra] and [ara] 'only'

2. In certain words, such as those in (35)–(37), there is variation between the front vowel /e/ and the back vowel /ɔ/, and between the front vowel /i/ and the back vowels /ɔ/ or /u/. The forms with back vowels are considered to be a recent innovation used mainly by younger speakers.

(35) [egɔ] and [ɔgɔ] 'well'
 [eta] and [ɔta] -AUG

(36) [riβu] and [ruβu] 'to put'

(37) [si] and [sɔ] 1INCL.SBJ=

3. The attributive preposition/purposive subordinator /meɾeɪ/ is pronounced by younger speakers with the voiceless bilabial oral stop /p/ instead of the voiced bilabial nasal stop /m/. This is an unusual sound change since it involves a difference in both voicing and manner of articulation.

There was no difference in the morphosyntactic and phonological distribution of these variant forms, nor did speakers report semantic or pragmatic differences (though of course the absence of such reports does not mean such differences do not exist). The variation instead seems to be free and to reflect phonological change subject to the age of the speaker, though younger speakers were not tested for individual variation.

As with the preposition/subordinator *merei*, other variations in pronunciation apply to particular morphemes so are allomorphic, but unlike *merei* they were not attributed to the speech of younger speakers. For example, the coordinator /taʊ/ 'and' is variably pronounced as [taʊ] or [ta], while the numeral /taʊβasi/ 'four' is variably pronounced as [taʊβasi] or [aːβasi]. Both pairs of allomorphs involve a reduction from the diphthong [aʊ], and are in free variation, possibly motivated by speech formality. Similarly, the polymorphemic Class II specific and diminutive articles *na=au* and *sa=au* are sometimes reduced from [naʊ] and [saʊ] to [nu] and [su] but the choice between the allomorphs here is lexically conditioned.

3.2 Orthography

Papapana is traditionally not a written language, it has not been standardised and few speakers are literate in Papapana. Nevertheless, an orthography was developed by Casilda Vavetaovi-Atuvia at a fortnight-long Vernacular Literacy Writers Workshop held in 2004 in Tsiroge, Northwest Bougainville and run by the Summer Institute of Linguistics (SIL). The orthography is generally phonemic. Among those speakers that are literate, there is considerable variation in orthographic choices made from speaker to speaker, and even a great deal of variation in the choices made by one individual. Loanwords from English and Tok Pisin are written in their original orthography.

3.2.1 Orthographic representation of vowels

The orthographic representations of the vowel phonemes can be seen in Table 3.13. Occasionally the phoneme /i/ was represented by <ie> but since this was not common, I use only <i> here. Long vowels were very occasionally represented by an apostrophe or hyphen but I use a colon here to avoid confusion with the glottal stop and the notation in interlinear glossing used to separate segmentable morphemes. However, if morphological concatenation results in the adjacent co-occurrence of two identical vowels and this creates a long variant of the vowel in question, I represent both vowels to make the morphology transparent

Table 3.13: Orthography: Vowels.

Vowel	Orthographic Symbol
/i/	i
/iː/	iː
/e/	e
/eː/	eː
/a/	a
/aː/	aː
/ɔ/	o
/u/	u

and differentiate between surface and phonemic long vowels (see §3.1.1.2). It should be noted that wherever possible I have represented phonemic long vowels but due to the lack of representation in native orthography it may be the case that some phonemic long vowels are unknowingly not represented in this grammatical description.

As the phonemic status of diphthongs is unclear, there is no need to differentiate diphthongs used in monomorphemic roots and those created by morphological concatenation (see §3.1.1.3). The orthographic representations of the diphthongs are shown in Table 3.14.

Table 3.14: Orthography: Diphthongs.

Diphthong	Orthographic Symbol
/eɪ/	ei
/aɪ/	ai
/ae/	ae
/aʊ/	au
/aɔ/	ao
/ɔɪ/	oi
/ɔe/	oe

3.2.2 Orthographic representation of consonants

The orthographic representations of the consonant phonemes are shown in Table 3.15. It is worth noting that speakers prefer the use of the hyphen to

Table 3.15: Orthography: Consonants.

Consonant	Orthographic Symbol
/p/	p
/b/	b
/t/	t
/d/	d
/k/	k
/g/	g
/ʔ/	'
/m/	m
/n/	n
/ŋ/	ng
/r/	r
/β/	v
/s/	s
/w/	w

represent the glottal stop, although the use of the apostrophe is also attested. For the purposes of this grammatical description I have opted to use the apostrophe to disambiguate between the glottal stop and the notation in interlinear glossing used to separate affixal morphemes. One or two speakers also used <gn> to represent the velar nasal stop /ŋ/ but the majority used <ng> and it is this digraph which I have chosen to use here since it is the most common in written Papapana. Literate speakers represented the allophones of /β/, that is [β], [v] and [w], as either <v> or <w>. Since these allophones represent the single phoneme [β], I have chosen for this grammatical description to use only <v> as the orthographic symbol for /β/ as it is the symbol most commonly used by speakers and it avoids confusion with the symbol <w> for the phoneme /w/. Speakers sometimes orthographically represented the creation of the voiced labial-velar approximant [w] with the symbol <w>, and the voiced palatal approximant [j] in intervocalic environments as a hyphen or apostrophe. Since in this situation, [w] and [j] are phonetic and not phonemic, I do not represent them in the orthography. However, in the case of epenthetic glottal insertion, I do represent the glottal stop because without this orthographic symbol, the two identical vowels the glottal stop separates would appear incorrectly to form a long vowel.

3.3 Phonotactics

This section outlines Papapana syllable structure (§3.3.1), and phonological word structure (§3.3.2).

3.3.1 Syllable structure

Papapana employs a simple syllable structure consisting of an optional onset and a vowel nucleus; for example, the first syllable in [i.nu] 'house' does not have an onset, while the second syllable does. Codas are prohibited, except in English or Tok Pisin loanwords such as Tok Pisin [siks.ti] 'sixty' or [bi.kos] 'because'. Papapana syllables are therefore always open and are typical of Oceanic languages in which syllable structures tend to be a simple CV type (Lynch, Ross, and Crowley 2002: 34).

When present, onsets consist of one consonant and allow any of the consonant phonemes to appear. Consonant clusters in the onset are only attested in loanwords, such as Tok Pisin [sku.na] 'ship', [sku.ru] 'school' and [stɔ.a] 'store'. These consonant clusters all contain the voiceless alveolar fricative /s/ followed by a voiceless alveolar or velar oral stop, /t/ or /k/. Sometimes the vowel [i] is inserted between these consonant clusters to align with Papapana phonology; for example, some speakers would pronounce the loanword /sku.ru/ 'school' as [si.ku.ru].

Papapana nuclei can be simple or complex, containing either a monophthong (thus being *monomoraic*, or *light*) or a long vowel or diphthong (thus being classified as *bimoraic*, or *heavy*). The maximum number of moras per syllable is therefore two. The syllable structure can be described as (C)V(V) and possible Papapana syllable structures are consequently V, VV, CV, CVV. In a limited set of loanwords, CCV, CVC and CVCC are possible.

3.3.2 Phonological word structure

The minimal Papapana word is at least one trochaic foot, which can either be disyllabic, or a bimoraic syllable with a diphthong or long vowel nucleus; for example, *tau* /tau/ 'and'. Syllables which are monomoraic do not constitute words (except for the Tok Pisin loan *o* 'or', and arguably the preposition *te*, which is discussed in §8.3.1). Monomoraic syllables may constitute roots, but these do not usually occur in isolation as such roots are verbs or nouns to which affixes or clitics attach, thus satisfying word minimality and allowing stress assignment to occur, as in (38). If a monomoraic root does occur in isolation, there is compensatory lengthening to allow it to constitute a word.

(38) wa   → e=wa
     [wa]   ['e=wa]
     say   3SG.SBJ=say
     'to say' 'he said'

Table 3.16 shows examples of how the five possible syllable structures can combine in various ways to form roots of up to six syllables. VV represents a long vowel or diphthong. The minimal root in Papapana consists of a single syllable, be it monomoraic or bimoraic, though bimoraic is more common. Roots of one, two, three or four syllables are common. Since several affixes and clitics may be attached to roots, stems of five or more syllables are much more common than roots of this length.

Table 3.16: Root structures.

Number of syllables	Syllable structure	Lexeme	
1	VV	/ɔɪ/	'to take'
	CV	/wa/	'to say'
	CVV	/taʊ/	'and'
2	V.CV	/i.nu/	'house'
	V.CVV	/a.naʊ/	1SG
	VV.V	/aɪ.a/	3SG
	VV.CV	/aɪ.na/	3PL
	CV.CV	/bɔ.rɔ/	'pig'
	CV.CVV	/bu.kaʊ/	'dolphin'
	CVV.CV	/βaʊ.nu/	'new'
	CVV.CVV	/kaʊ.kaʊ/	'sweet potato'
3	V.CV.VV	/a.ru.aɪ/	'no'
	V.CV.CV	/a.si.ta/	'plant species'
	VV.CV.CV	/aː.ma.ni/	1EXCL
	CV.V.CV	/pɔ.a.na/	'village'
	CV.CV.V	/ma.nɔ.a/	'neck/ten'
	CV.CV.CV	/da.ra.mu/	'water/river'
	CV.CV.CVV	/ma.ka.reɪ/	'spear'
	CVV.CV.CV	/geː.re.re/	'white'

Table 3.16 (continued)

Number of syllables	Syllable structure	Lexeme	
4	V.CV.CV.CV	/a.ta.ma.ta/	'friend'
	CV.CV.V.CV	/vi.tu.a.si/	'young'
	CV.CV.CV.CV	/ka.ra.βɔ.na/	'lobster'
5	V.CV.V.CV.CV	/a.de.a.ra.mu/	'taro species'
	CV.CV.V.CV.CV	/ka.pɔ.a.si.si/	'plant species'
	CV.CV.CV.CV.CV	/kɔ.pu.kɔ.pu.ri/	'seaweed species'
	CV.CV.CV.CVV.V	/bi.bi.ra.kaɪ.ɔ/	'bird species'
	CV.CV.CVV.V.CV	/ma.ta.βaɔ.a.na/	'emperor fish'
6	V.CV.CV.CV.CV.CV	/a.ga.βa.ta.pa.ra/	'plant species'
	CV.CV.CV.CV.CV.CVV	/ka.mu.ka.ka.te.ʔiː/	'crab species'

3.4 Reduplication

Reduplication can have either derivational or inflectional functions in Papapana. For both, reduplication involves leftward copying and is continuous, as the reduplicant is to the left of and adjacent to the material that is copied. Reduplicants may be monosyllabic (§3.4.1) or disyllabic (§3.4.2). Cross-linguistically, leftward copying is the most common directionality (Rubino, 2005: 14) and reduplicative constructions are most likely to be continuous (Rubino, 2005: 18), and in Northwest Solomonic languages too, leftward continuous reduplication is typical. Papapana is typologically unusual, however, as some verbs also display the cross-linguistically rare phenomenon of multiple reduplication to express a subtype of imperfective aspect (Smith 2016c). Multiple reduplication in Papapana may involve two monosyllabic reduplicants or a monosyllabic reduplicant followed by a disyllabic reduplicant (§3.4.3).

Derivational reduplication is phonologically unpredictable as the reduplicant may copy the initial syllable or the first two syllables of the base to derive nouns from verbs (§4.3.2.1), adjectives from nouns (§4.6) and verbs from other categories (§6.2.2). Disyllabic copying may additionally derive adjectives from other adjectives (§4.6) and there is one attested instance in my data of disyllabic reduplication deriving a noun from another noun (§4.3.2). There are also some postverbal adverbs which may have undergone disyllabic reduplication (§6.8.2.2).

Monosyllabic reduplication and the derivational suffix *-na* may derive location nouns from verbs (§4.3.3.1) while disyllabic reduplication and the derivational suffix *-na* may derive augmented dyadic nouns from nouns expressing kinship (§4.3.3.2). In addition, monosyllabic reduplication and the derivational suffix -*na* derive an Absolute Location noun from a Relational Location noun, and disyllabic reduplication and the derivational suffix -*na* derive a numeral from another numeral (§4.3.3).

Inflectional reduplication occurs in the verb complex (VC) in prohibitive constructions, reciprocal constructions, or to mark continuous or habitual aspect. In prohibitive constructions, either the preverbal negative marker *ae* or the preverbal apprehensive mode marker *te* function in conjunction with either monosyllabic or disyllabic verbal reduplication (§7.3.2). In reciprocal constructions, the reciprocal marker *vei* is used and the reduplicant copies either the initial syllable or the first two syllables of the verb (§6.5.6.1). All four types of verbal reduplication operate with postverbal subject-indexing (PSI) enclitics in the VC to mark continuous or habitual aspect (§7.1.6). Reduplication also seems to mark nominal pluralisation in some cases, though this is not a productive process (§5.2.3).

All monosyllabic and disyllabic reduplicants behave phonologically in the same way, regardless of their function or their occurrence with other morphemes, and the remainder of this section discusses the formal properties of monosyllabic and disyllabic reduplication.

3.4.1 Monosyllabic copying

The reduplicant may copy the initial syllable of the base as in (39)–(42). Reduplication has a derivational function in (39) and (40), where it derives a noun from a verb and an adjective from a noun respectively (see §4.3.2.1 and §4.6). Verbal reduplication has an inflectional function in (41) and (42), where it co-occurs with the preverbal apprehensive mode marker *te* in a prohibitive (41) and with PSI enclitics in the VC to express continuous aspect (42) (see §7.3.2 and §7.1.6).

(39) /dɔβi/ 'to spit' → /dɔdɔβi/ 'lung'

(40) /reβasi/ 'blood' → /rereβasi/ 'red'

(41) /ɔte tɔtɔnu/
 o=te to~tonu
 2SG.SBJ=APPR RD~stand
 'don't stand'

(42) /ewawaena/
　　　e=wa~wa=ena
　　　3SG.SBJ=RD~talk=3SG.IPFV
　　　'he is talking'

As (43) and (44) show, if the initial syllable of the base consists of a diphthong, only the first vowel of the diphthong is copied, and it is accompanied by any preceding onset consonant: this is support for the hypothesis that diphthongs are not phonemic. Papapana is thus similar to Hoava, where vowels can be combined into pairs with the weight of two syllables and words beginning with CVV only reduplicate the first syllable, despite the fact that disyllabic copying occurs in the language (Davis, 2003: 25, 32). In Torau too, inflectional reduplication copies only the melody of the first vowel of a diphthong, accompanied by any preceding onset consonant; however, in Torau, the copied single mora then lengthens to generate a complete bimoraic foot with the melody of the copied vowel (except when the copied mora of the base is not preceded by an onset consonant) (Palmer, 2007a: 510).

(43) /βeɪɔŋɔ/　'to get into'　→　/βeβeɪɔŋɔ/ 'clothes'

(44) /ɔema/　'taro garden'　→　[ɔʔɔemana]
　　　　　　　　　　　　　　　　o~'oema-na
　　　　　　　　　　　　　　　　RD~taro.garden-DER
　　　　　　　　　　　　　　　　'bush (lit. taro garden place)'

In the three vowel-initial verbs in (45)–(47), and the verb *ubete* 'to lie down', the verb loses the initial vowel prior to reduplication, however, the motivation for this is unclear.

(45) /irɔmɔ/　'to drink'　→　[erɔrɔmɔena]
　　　　　　　　　　　　　　e=ro~romo=ena
　　　　　　　　　　　　　　3SG.SBJ=RD~drink=3SG.IPFV
　　　　　　　　　　　　　　'he is drinking'

(46) /umunu/　'to sit'　→　[ɔae mumunu]
　　　　　　　　　　　　　　o=ae　　　　　mu~munu
　　　　　　　　　　　　　　2SG.SBJ=NEG　RD~sit
　　　　　　　　　　　　　　'don't sit'

(47) /ɔrete/   'to walk'   → [irereteina]
                                      i=re~rete=ina
                                      3PL.SBJ=RD~walk=3PL.IPFV
                                      'they are walking'

If the initial syllable of the base is onset-less, only the nucleus is reduplicated and epenthetic glottal insertion occurs between the reduplicant vowel and the base vowel to break the hiatus between the two identical vowels, as in (48) (if the glottal stop were part of the onset there would be a glottal stop between the subject proclitic and the reduplicant).

(48) [eja?aputuwena]
     e=a~'aputu=ena
     3SG.SBJ=RD~sleep=3SG.IPFV
     'he sleeps'

If the root is monoyllabic then of course the whole base is reduplicated, giving the appearance of full reduplication:

(49) /de/   'to carry'   → /dede/ 'bag'

3.4.2 Disyllabic copying

The second type of reduplication involves disyllabic copying of an entire initial foot as in (50)–(53). Reduplication has a derivational function in (50) and (51), deriving a different adjective from the noun *revasi* 'blood' (50) (c.f. example 40), and, with the derivational suffix, an augmented dyadic noun from a kinship term noun (51) (see §4.6 and §4.3.3.2). Reduplication has an inflectional function in (52) and (53), negating an imperative and expressing imperfective aspect respectively (see §7.3.2 and §7.1.6).

(50) /reβasi/   'blood'   → /reβareβasi/ 'bloody'

(51) /sina/   'mother'   → /sinasinana/
                                   sina~sina-na
                                   RD~mother-DER
                                   'mother and two daughters'

(52) /ɔte βɔʔɔβɔʔɔ/
    o=te   vo'o~vo'o
    2SG.SBJ=APPR RD~call.out
    'don't shout'

(53) /etamutamuena/
    e=tamu~tamu=ena
    3SG.SBJ=RD~eat=3SG.IPFV
    'he is eating'

When the base includes a diphthong after the first syllable, only the first vowel of the diphthong is copied:

(54) /raβaɪ/   'dirt'   → /raβaraβaɪ/ 'black/dirty'

If the root is disyllabic with no diphthongs then of course the whole base is reduplicated giving the appearance of full reduplication, as in (55) and (56), where reduplication derives a noun from a verb and a noun from another noun respectively.

(55) /tɔʔɔ/   'to cut' → /tɔʔɔtɔʔɔ/ 'knife'

(56) /pute/   'wind'   → /putepute/ 'fan'

3.4.3 Multiple reduplication

Multiple reduplication of the verb involves either two monosyllabic reduplicants occurring next to each other at the left margin of the base (57) or the monosyllabic reduplicant occurring at the leftmost margin, followed by the disyllabic reduplicant and then the base (58). Multiple verbal reduplication always and only co-occurs with PSI enclitics in the VC to express habitual aspect (see §7.1.6).

(57) /esisisiriena/
    e=si~si~siri=ena
    3SG.SBJ=RD~RD~read=3SG.IPFV
    'she reads'

(58) /etatamutamuena/
 e=ta~tamu~tamu=ena
 3SG.SBJ=RD~RD~eat=3SG.IPFV
 'he eats'

3.5 Stress

Word stress in Papapana is *bounded*, that is, main stress is located at a fixed distance from the word boundary. Secondary stress is not prominent and requires further research to determine, and there is no lexical stress in Papapana. This section describes regular stress assignment in Papapana (§3.5.1) and then discusses stress patterns when reduplicants (§3.5.2), proclitics (§3.5.3), and suffixes and enclitics attach to the root (§3.5.4). An interesting aspect of morphophonology is that stem-medially, long vowel or diphthong formation is dependent on whether or not it results in extrametricality (§3.5.4). The analysis of stress is based on speakers' and my perception and on observing the intensity of the waveform in Praat. Further phonetic research is required to determine the phonetic components that bring about the perception of stress.

3.5.1 Regular stress assignment

In Papapana, feet are left-aligned syllabic trochees and word stress is predictable with primary stress falling on the first syllable of the first foot of the root. This differs from canonical Oceanic languages in which stress falls on the penultimate syllable of a word (Lynch, Ross, and Crowley 2002: 35). Reduplicants, affixes and clitics to either side of the root do not generally alter stress assignment (see §3.5.2 to §3.5.4).

Feet consisting of a light syllable followed by a heavy syllable (such as CVCVV or VCVV) demonstrate that stress in Papapana is *syllabic* or *quantity insensitive*, meaning syllable weight does not influence foot construction. Examples (59) and (60) demonstrate that Papapana employs a syllabic trochee foot type rather than a moraic trochee foot type:

(59) /bukaʊ/   'dolphin'   → [ˈbu.kaʊ]   *[bu.ˈkaʊ]

(60) /enaɪ/   DEM2   → [ˈe.naɪ]   *[e.ˈnaɪ]

Disyllablic monomorphemic roots, such as those in (61)–(65), show that feet in Papapana are trochaic, regardless of whether the syllable nucleus is light or heavy, i.e. whether the syllable contains a monophthong (61)–(62), a long vowel (63)–(64) or a diphthong (65):

(61) /bɔrɔ/ 'pig' → [ˈbɔ.rɔ]

(62) /ɔba/ 'hibiscus' → [ˈɔ.ba]

(63) /βaːgi/ 'now' → [ˈβaː.gi]

(64) /aːmu/ 2PL → [ˈaː.mu]

(65) /βaʊnu/ 'new' → [ˈβaʊ.nu]

Trisyllabic monomorphemic roots, such as those in (66)–(70), demonstrate that feet are parsed from the left margin, that is, stress is left-aligned, regardless of whether the syllable nucleus is light (66)–(67) or heavy (68)–(70).

(66) /manɔa/ 'neck' → [ˈma.nɔ.wa]

(67) /aβɔa/ 'where' → [ˈa.βɔ.wa]

(68) /βaːsina/ 'before' → [ˈβaː.si.na]

(69) /aːmani/ 1EXCL → [ˈaː.ma.ni]

(70) /taʊtɔnɔ/ 'three' → [ˈtaʊ.tɔ.nɔ]

Lexemes consisting of two feet, such as (71)–(73), demonstrate that the leftmost foot carries primary stress and is thus the head foot (though the rightmost foot is the head foot when there is disyllabic reduplication, see §3.5.2).

(71) /kaβururu/ 'rice' → [ˈka.βu.ˌru.ru]

(72) /βɪtuasi/ 'young' → [ˈβɪ.tu.ˌa.si]

(73) /atamata/ 'friend' → [ˈa.ta.ˌma.ta]

3.5.2 Reduplication and stress

In reduplicated forms when the reduplicant copies the initial syllable of the base, such as in (74)–(76), the reduplicant does not participate in stress assignment:

(74) /buburisi/   'womb'   → [bu.ˈbu.ɾi.si]

(75) /βuβuɾaʊ/   'car'   → [βu.ˈβu.ɾaʊ]

(76) /ɔɔemana/   'bush'   → [ɔ.ˈʔɔe.ma.na]¹⁵

In reduplicated forms, when the reduplicant copies an entire initial foot, such as in (77)–(79), the reduplicant does participate in stress assignment but primary stress still rests on the base; therefore, rather than the leftmost foot carrying primary stress, the rightmost foot is the head foot.

(77) /tamutamu/   'food'   → [ˌta.mu~ˈta.mu]

(78) /aɾiaɾi/   'hole'   → [ˌa.ɾi~ˈa.ɾi]

(79) /ɾaβaɾaβaɪ/   'black'   → [ˌɾa.βa~ˈɾa.βaɪ]

In Papapana, the reduplicant is thus not part of the same prosodic domain as the base. Monosyllabic reduplicants do not form a foot so are not stressed at all, whereas disyllabic reduplicants form a foot and can therefore be assigned stress (although they do not cause primary stress to shift).

Some forms, such as (80), which are not synchronically reduplicated, show irregular stress assignment but this could be because they are diachronically reduplicated:

(80) /kɔkɔbunu/   'short'   → [kɔ.ˈkɔ.bu.nu]

Other forms, such as (81), which may be diachronically reduplicated are regularly stressed. This could indicate that the forms which demonstrate regular stress assignment were derived at an earlier date than those which exhibit

---

15 As §3.1.2.4 and §3.4.1 explain, there is epenthetic glottal insertion in reduplicated forms to break the hiatus between two identical vowels.

irregular stress assignment, and perhaps in time forms such as *kokobunu* in (80) may also adopt the regular stress regime.

(81) /kukuɾaka/   'finger'   → [ˈku.ku.ˌɾa.ka]

3.5.3 Proclitics and stress

Articles and subject-indexing proclitics form phonological but not prosodic words with roots. The proclitic specific articles /na/ and /nu/ do not participate in stress assignment as (82)–(88) show for roots with two, three and four syllables.

(82) /na=bɔrɔ/   'SPEC[CLI]=pig'   → [na.ˈbɔ.rɔ]

(83) /nu=kaɾa/   'SPEC.CLII=pandanus'   → [nu.ˈka.ɾa]

(84) /nu=βanaɪ/   'SPEC.CLII=plant.sp'   → [nu.ˈβa.naɪ]

(85) /na=maʊnu/   'SPEC[CLI]=woman'   → [na.ˈmaʊ.nu]

(86) /nu=pɔtutu/   'SPEC.CLII=Barringtonia.asiatica' → [nu.ˈpɔ.tu.tu]

(87) /nu=gɔraβiβi/ 'SPEC.CLII=vine.sp'   → [nu.ˈgɔ.ɾa.ˌβi.βi]

(88) /nu=mamiɔke/   'SPEC.CLII=papaya'   → [nu.ˈma.mi.ˌɔ.ke]

The subject proclitics also do not participate in stress assignment as (89) to (93) show for roots of two, three or four syllables.

(89) /mu=tamu/   '2PL.SBJ=eat'   → [mu.ˈta.mu]

(90) /e=dɔβi/   '3SG.SBJ=spit'   → [e.ˈdɔ.βi]

(91) /mi=siɔdɔ/   '1EXCL.SBJ=work'   → [mi.ˈsi.ɔ.dɔ]

(92) /u=ɔrete/   '1SG.SBJ=walk'   → [u.ˈɔ.ɾe.te]

(93) /u=gaganini/   '1SG.SBJ=play'   → [u.ˈga.ga.ˌni.ni]

However, if the specific article /na/ cliticises to a vowel-initial noun root, it forms a long vowel as in (94), or a diphthong as in (95)–(98); due to this fusion, the article becomes part of the base and is thus relevant for stress assignment. Similarly, if the 2SG subject-indexing proclitic /ɔ/ cliticises to a verb root beginning with /i/ or /e/, or if the 3SG subject-indexing proclitic /e/ cliticises to a verb root beginning with /i/, they form a diphthong, as in (99) and (100). The stress, which is normally assigned to the first syllable of the root, is adjusted and falls on the article or subject-indexing proclitic, because it is no longer prosodically possible to assign stress to the first syllable of the root as that first syllable now forms part of a long vowel or diphthong. Stress assignment therefore follows diphthongization.

(94) /na=aβu/   'SPEC[CLI]=ash'   → ['naa.βu]

(95) /na=inu/   'SPEC[CLI]=house'   ['naɪ.nu]

(96) /na=epu/   'SPEC[CLI]=cloud'   ['nae.pu]

(97) /na=ɔba/   'SPEC[CLI]=hibiscus'   ['naɔ.ba]

(98) /na=uβi/   'SPEC[CLI]=yam'   ['naʊ.βi]

(99) /ɔ=irɔmɔ/   '2SG.SBJ=drink'   ['ɔɪ.ɾɔ.mɔ]

(100) /e=irɔmɔ/   '3SG.SBJ=drink'   ['eɪ.ɾɔ.mɔ]

There are three attested monosyllabic noun roots but I only have an audio recording of one of these nouns, /nɔ/ 'mosquito'. There are several monosyllabic verb roots. The article or the subject-indexing proclitic forms a foot with the root to allow stress assignment, and it is the article or subject proclitic which carries the stress, following regular stress assignment patterns, as in (101)–(104):

(101) /na=nɔ/   'SPEC[CLI]=mosquito'   → ['na.nɔ]

(102) /ɔ=naɔ/   '2SG.SBJ=go'   → ['ɔ.naɔ]

(103) /e=wa/   '3SG.SBJ=say'   → ['e.wa]

(104) /mi=pɔ/   '1EXCL.SBJ=stay'   → ['mi.pɔ]

3.5.4 Suffixes, enclitics and stress

Affixation and cliticisation to the right of the root, such as direct possessor suffixes and PSI enclitics, do not alter stress alignment and stress remains left-aligned with the suffix or enclitic participating in the stress regime, as in (105) to (108):

(105) /patu-mani/ 'head-1EXCL.PSSR' → ['pa.tu.ˌma.ni]

(106) /katɔpɔ-na/ 'nail-3SG.PSSR' → ['ka.tɔ.ˌpɔ.na]

(107) /uɾupesi-mani/ 'anus-1EXCL.PSSR' → ['u.ɾu.ˌpe.si.ma.ni]

(108) /e=ɾi dɔβi=ena/ '3SG.SBJ=OPT spit=3SG.IPFV' → ['e.ɾi 'do.βi.ˌe.na]

If the resulting stem has an odd number of syllables the suffix or enclitic is extrametrical as in (109)–(112):

(109) /sinɔ-na/ 'bone-3SG.PSSR' → ['si.nɔ.na]

(110) /βetaka-mani/ 'brain-1EXCL.PSSR' → ['βe.ta.ˌka.ma.ni]

(111) /uɾupesi-u/ 'anus-1SG.PSSR' → ['u.ɾu.ˌpe.si.ju]

(112) /u=ɾi dɔβi=ɔu/ '1SG.SBJ=OPT spit=1SG.IPFV' → ['e.ɾi 'do.βi.jɔu]

When two vowels are adjacent due to morphological concatenation, a long vowel or diphthong may be formed as in (113) to (116), even if this results in extrametricality as in (115):

(113) /patu-u/ 'head-1SG.PSSR' → ['pa.tuː]

(114) /sinɔ-u/ 'bone-1SG.PSSR' → ['si.nɔu]

(115) /katɔpɔ-u/ 'nail-1SG.PSSR' → ['ka.tɔ.pɔu]

(116) /u=ɾi tua=u/ '1SG.SBJ=OPT paddle=1SG.IPFV' → ['u.ɾi 'tu.wau]

However, stem-medially, long vowel or diphthong formation depends on whether extrametricality will result. In (117)–(119), the two vowels form a diphthong because this allows two feet to be created and extrametricality to be avoided, whereas in (120) and (121), the diphthong or long vowel is not created as that would result in extrametricality.

(117) /βetaka-iɾa/ 'brain-1INCL.PSSR' → [ˈβe.taˌkaɪ.ɾa]
 *[ˈβe.taˌka.i.ɾa]

(118) /katɔpɔ-iɾa/ 'nail-1INCL.PSSR' → [ˈka.tɔˌpɔɪ.ɾa]
 *[ˈka.tɔˌpɔ.i.ɾa]

(119) /mi=siɔdɔ-emani/ '1EXCL.SBJ=work=1EXCL.IPFV' → [ˈmi.siˌɔ.dɔe.ma.ni]
 *[ˈmi.siˌɔ.dɔ.e.ma.ni]

(120) /e=ɾi dɔβi=ina/ '3SG.SBJ=OPT spit=3SG.sIPFV' → [ˈe.ɾi ˈdo.βiˌi.na]
 *[ˈe.ɾi ˈdo.βiː.na]

(121) /e=siɔdɔ=ena/ '3SG.SBJ=work=3SG.IPFV' → [ˈe.siˌɔ.dɔ.we.na]
 *[ˈe.siˌɔ.dɔwe.na]

Chapter 4
Nouns and noun phrase structure

This chapter describes nominals and noun phrase structure (§4.1), pronouns (§4.2), derived nouns (§4.3), compound nouns and complex kinship terms (§4.4) and word classes and phrases which can modify nouns, including demonstratives (§4.5), adjectives and adjective phrases (§4.6), miscellaneous postnominal modifiers (§4.7) and an attributive preposition phrase (§4.8). Chapter 5 describes noun class and nominal number (including articles and numerals), possession, and quantifier phrases, which take noun phrase or preposition phrase complements.

4.1 Nominals and noun phrase structure

In Papapana, there are two formally distinct subcategories of nominals: pronouns and nouns. Pronouns belong to a closed word class and subtypes include independent (§4.2.1) and demonstrative (§4.5.2). The semantic and morpho-syntactic characteristics which identify these words as pronouns are described in those sections. A noun phrase (NP) whose head is a pronoun can function as the core argument of a verbal or non-verbal predicate. Independent pronouns can also function as possessor NPs or be the complement of prepositions.

Nouns, including derived nouns (§4.3) and compound nouns (§4.4), belong to an open class and belong to one of four noun classes: Personal, Class I, Class II and Location. The semantic and morpho-syntactic characteristics which identify these different nouns are discussed in depth in §5.1. Nouns can also be categorised according to whether they are inalienably or alienably possessed (§5.5), but this classification does not correlate with and is separate from noun class. Except for Personal proper name nouns, some Location nouns and a limited number of exceptions from other classes, all nouns are always marked by either an article (§5.3), a numeral modifier (§5.4), or a possessor proclitic or suffix (§5.5). The possessor proclitics, the specific, non-specific and singular diminutive articles, and the numeral modifiers *'aria* 'one' and *nua* 'two' attach to the Class II marker *au* when the head noun belongs to Class II (§5.3–5.5). They do not attach to the Class I marker *ata* when the head noun belongs to Class I; *ata* is only present in indirectly possessed NP predicates when the head noun has been elided (see §5.5.3), or in some quantifier phrases (QP) headed by the quantifier *na:* 'some, other' when the head of the NP complement has been elided (see §5.6.3).

Nouns may also be modified by demonstratives (§4.4.5), adjectives and adjective phrases (§4.6), a modifier from a miscellaneous group (§4.7) or a preposition phrase (PP) expressing either possession (see §5.5.5 and §8.3) or attribution (§4.8 and §8.3). Nouns may also be modified by interrogative terms (see §9.3.2) and externally headed relative clauses (see §10.2). The types and combinations of modifiers permitted depend on the noun type and are discussed in the relevant sections. Conjoined NPs are discussed in §10.1.

A NP whose head is a noun can function as the core argument of a verbal or non-verbal predicate, a clausal adjunct, the complement of an adposition, the complement of a quantifier, the predicate in a verbless clause, or a possessor NP. NPs headed by Location nouns typically only function as predicates in verbless clauses or as adjuncts. Some nouns can also have an adnominal function in compounds and complex kinship terms (see (§4.4)).

Table 4.1 and Table 4.2 show the NP structure when the head is a Class I or II noun, since these nouns have the least restrictions in terms of modifiers. Not

Table 4.1: Noun phrase structure: pre-head.

PRE-HEAD PERIPHERY				CORE					HEAD
DEM	ASSOC.PL	PSSR NP	AP/ADJ	PSSR= or SPEC or NSPEC	NumP	DIM	CLI/II or PL or DIM.PL or PART or DU.COLL or PL.COLL	COLL	NOUN

Table 4.2: Noun phrase structure: post-head.

HEAD	POST-HEAD PERIPHERY						
NOUN -DER or -CONST	-AUG or -PSSR and Root	MISC MOD.	NumP	DEM	AP /ADJ	PSSR NP	PP	REL.CL

all constituents occur in one NP but possible combinations are discussed and exemplified below. The most minimal NP consists only of the head noun, though usually Personal, Class I and Class II nouns are marked by an article, numeral or possessor, thus a NP usually consists of the head and at least one constituent from the core.

The head position may contain only the head noun, or a morphologically complex head noun: the derivational suffix (see §4.3.3) is mutually exclusive with the construct suffix and modifying root that together form compounds (§4.4), while the augmentative suffix (§4.6.3) or the possessor suffixes (§5.5.1) can co-occur with compound nouns as in (1) and (2) (though they are not attested with nouns derived by -na). The relative position of the augmentative suffix and possessor suffixes is not known. Possessor proclitics (§5.5.2) and possessor suffixes are mutually exclusive. Unlike possessor proclitics, possessor suffixes can co-occur with prenominal specific articles (3) (see §5.3.1).

(1) *bau vuni-i*   ***naono-eta***
    PL   trunk-CONST tree-AUG
    'the big tree trunks'
    (1-T034-00:06:59.360)

(2) *nu=mata-i*   ***puru-mu***
    SPEC.CLII=eye-CONST flower-2SG.PSSR
    'your eyelash (lit. your eye flower)'
    (2-E011)

(3) ***na=vavine-u***
    SPEC[CLI]=sibling-1SG.PSSR
    'my cousin'
    (1-T042-00:09:33.250)

The core of the NP is configurationally ordered and includes the head. In prehead position, possessor proclitics and the specific/non-specific articles (§5.3) are mutually exclusive. Following this are numeral modifiers (§5.4.2), then singular diminutive articles (§5.3), and then either the Class II marker *au* or a non-singular article (§5.3). Example (5) shows all four of these prenominal positions filled. Closest to the head is the collective marker *vei* which occurs with derived nouns (§4.3), compound nouns headed by *mata* 'trait' (§4.4.4) and in adjective phrases (AP) when they have a collective reference (§4.6.1). *Vei* can be preceded by *nu=* which is analysed as a phonologically reduced form of the specific article *na* and the Class II marker *au*; thus *vei* follows the Class II marker. None of these constituents can appear in any other position except for numeral modifiers which may alternatively occur in the post-head periphery.

(4)   E=mate   asi=ina   **ena=nua**   **sa=au**   'usia. . .
        3SG.SBJ=die leave=3PL.OBJ 3SG.PSSR=two DIM=CLII child
        'He died leaving his two poor children. . .'
        (1-T030-00:03:53.913)

In the outer layer of the NP, in pre-head position, the relative position of demonstratives (§4.5.1), the associative plural *nia* (§5.2.2), possessor NPs including *te:na ~ te:a* 'whose' (see §5.5 and §9.3.2.2) and adjectives and APs (§4.6) is unknown as these are not attested together in a NP (see the relevant sections for examples of these constituents). The adnominal interrogative terms, *te:na ~ te:a* 'whose', *mata* 'what kind', *avete* 'which' and *tauvita* 'how many' are also prenominal (see §9.3.2). *Te:na ~ te:a* 'whose', like possessor NPs, precedes specific articles or possessor proclitics. *Tauvita* may or may not precede a specific article but *avete* and *mata* do not. Nevertheless, *avete* and *mata* do precede the Class II marker. The exact position of these interrogative terms is unknown.

In the outer layer of the NP, in postnominal position, a miscellaneous modifier (§4.7) such as exhaustive *panapana* is attested as preceding demonstratives as in (5). The miscellaneous modifier *=re* '(an)other' (see §4.7.8) cliticises to the noun or to a directly possessed noun marked by a possessor suffix (6). The exact relative ordering of postnominal numeral phrases (§5.4.2), demonstratives (§4.5.1), adjectives and APs (§4.6) and possessor NPs (§5.5) is unclear, again because these are not all attested together in a NP (see the relevant sections for examples of these constituents). In fact when these types of modifiers co-occur, it is usually the case that one is prenominal and the other is postnominal. However, occasionally two or three of these constituents may co-occur postnominally, as in (7) which shows a demonstrative preceding an AP, and (8) which shows a numeral, demonstrative and AP in succession, though it is also possible for a demonstrative to precede a numeral (9). The reason for this variation is unclear (see §4.5.1.1 and §5.4.2).

(5)   . . .i=oi~oi=ina   **na='usia**   *panapana* *mama*. . .
        3PL.SBJ=RD~call=3PL.OBJ SPEC[CLI]=child all   DEM1
        '. . .they called all the children. . .'
        (1-T043a-00:02:01.844)

(6) **Na=vavine-u=re** ini vowa e=pei
SPEC[CLI]=sibling-1SG.PSSR=REP here like 3SG.SBJ=PST.IPFV
po~po=na=i...
RD~stay=3SG.IPFV=IRR
'[I came and stayed with]...my other cousin here where she was living.'
(1-T042-00:09:47.190)

(7) I=mei tamu te=**na=au obutu mama**
3PL.SBJ=come.SEQ eat OBL=SPEC=CLII canoe DEM1
nu=vaunu.
SPEC.CLII=new
'They came and ate off the new canoe.'
(1-T043-00:02:11.904)

(8) **Na=inu** tautono mama na=etawa
SPEC[CLI]=house three DEM1 SPEC[CLI]=big
i=to po=ina i-nongana.
3PL.SBJ=EMPH stay=3PL.IPFV LOC-beach
'Those three big houses are on the beach.'
(3-E002)

(9) **Na=iana** mama tautono e=ma'a=ina.
SPEC[CLI]=fish DEM1 three 3SG.SBJ=give=3PL.OBJ
'He gave them these three fish.'
(1-T029-00:08:46.817)

The same numerals and adjectives can appear in both pre-head and post-head positions (see §5.4.2 and §4.6.1) and for each category the prenominal and postnominal positions are mutually exclusive, that is, there cannot simultaneously be two adjectives or two numerals in one NP (and of course the latter would be hard to interpret anyhow). Likewise, prenominal and postnominal possessor NPs are mutually exclusive (see §5.5). The same demonstrative can appear in both prenominal and postnominal positions; however, there can be more than one demonstrative in a NP (see §4.5.1). There can be one or two demonstratives in prehead position, one or two in posthead position, or a particular demonstrative occurs prenominally while another simultaneously occurs postnominally (see examples in §4.5.1). PPs expressing possession (§5.5.5) or attribution (§4.8), and relative clauses (§10.2) are always postnominal and are furthest away from the head noun.

4.2 Pronouns

Papapana has the four separate pronominal paradigms that are widespread in Oceanic languages: independent pronouns (§4.2.1), possessor suffixes (§5.5.1), subject-indexing proclitics (see §6.3.2.1) and object-indexing enclitics (see §6.3.2.2). In addition, Papapana has possessor proclitics (§5.5.2) (which, unlike many other Oceanic languages, are not synchronically segmentable into a possessive constitutent and possessor suffix) and postverbal subject-indexing (PSI) enclitics (§7.1.1). All six pronominal paradigms (see aforementioned sections or Appendix 1) classify referents according to first, second or third person and distinguish between singular and plural. There is an inclusive (speaker and addressee) and exclusive (speaker and non-speech act participant) distinction in the first person plural. Independent pronouns additionally distinguish dual and trial number. Other subtypes of pronouns include demonstrative pronouns (§4.5.2). Papapana does not have possessive, interrogative, reflexive, reciprocal or relative pronouns. Pronouns do not have articles in Papapana and they can function as arguments or NP predicates. Independent pronouns can also function as possessor NPs or be the complement of prepositions.

4.2.1 Independent pronouns

Table 4.3 shows the closed class of independent pronouns in Papapana; they make four number distinctions, three person distinctions, and an exclusive vs. inclusive distinction in the first person. Trial number forms specify exactly three individuals as their referent, as (10) demonstrates. There is no gender or case distinction.

Table 4.3: Independent pronouns.

	1EXCL	1INCL	2	3
SG	anau ~ aniau		ani ~ anio	aia
DU	auami	auara	auamu	auana
	ami=nua anua	era=nua anua	amiu=nua anua	nua anua
TR	ami=atono	era=atono	amiu=atono	oina=atono
PL	a:mani	arira	a:mu	aina

(10) *Charlie enai na=chairman.   Anau na=treasurer.*
Charlie DEM SPEC[CLI]=chairman 1SG SPEC[CLI]=treasurer
Ta secretary John Aimo.
and secretary John Aimo
Ami=atono *te=na=board*
1EXCL.PSSR=three.HUM OBL=SPEC[CLI]=board
mi=tonu=emani.
1EXCL.SBJ=stand=1EXCL.IPFV
'Charlie is the chairman. I'm the treasurer. And the secretary is John Aimo. We three constitute the board (lit. We three are standing on the board).'
(1-T081-00:00:17.560)

The 1SG pronoun *anau* and the 2SG pronoun *ani* have very likely undergone phonological reduction historically from *aniau* and *anioi* respectively. The 1963 Summer Institute of Linguistics (SIL) survey documented *aniau* and *anioi* for these pronouns, as did Palmer during his 2006 fieldwork. I noticed the occasional use of *aniau* for 1SG and *anio* (not *anioi*) for 2SG during my fieldwork and *aniau* is attested in three text recordings. For two of these recordings, the speaker was in her 70s, while for the other recording, the speaker was in her late 40s and was one of the speakers whom Palmer recorded. It may be a coincidence but both these women had Torau spouses and had previously lived in a Torau-speaking village; this (along with age) has perhaps contributed to their more conservative language. There is therefore synchronic free variation between 1SG *anau* and *aniau* and 2SG *ani* and *anio*, though given the rare uses of *aniau* and *anio*, this is a change which is perhaps nearly complete.

Papapana has two sets of dual independent pronouns. The first set in Table 4.3 begin with *aua* while the remainder of the form is similar to the possessor suffixes (see §5.5.1). It is unclear what the origin of these forms is and if they are diachronically morphologically complex. The other set of dual independent pronouns are formed periphrastically and are comprised of the cardinal numeral modifier for Class I nouns *nua* 'two' (see §5.4.2) and the noun *anua* 'person', and are marked for possession by the plural possessor proclitics, except for 3DU. It is common for dual pronouns in Oceanic languages to contain an element that is historically related to the numeral 'two' (Lynch, Ross, and Crowley 2002: 35). I did not observe a grammatical, semantic or pragmatic distinction between the two sets of dual independent forms, though the periphrastic forms were used less often.

In Papapana, independent pronouns may function alone as a NP, but they may also be postmodified by the exhaustive, emphatic or limiting modifiers (see §4.7) as in (11)–(13). They cannot co-occur with any other nominal modifiers.

(11) **Aina panapana** . . .i=vaene tae=a na=namu.
3PL all 3PL.SBJ=climb up=3SG.OBJ SPEC[CLI]=Malay.apple
'They all . . .climbed up the Malay apple tree.'
(1-T022-00:01:07.630)

(12) **A:mani tobi** mi=roroto=ina
1EXCL 1EMPH 1EXCL.SBJ=see=3PL.OBJ
na=vanua i=to paga=ina.
SPEC[CLI]=people 3PL.SBJ=EMPH shoot =3SG.OBJ
'We ourselves saw the people they shot/We ourselves saw the people shot them.'
(1-T103-00:15:21.775)

(13) Ta enai **aia** ora si=atutusi=a=i.
and after 3SG only 1INCL.SBJ=chase=3SG.OBJ=IRR
'And then we follow him only.'
(1-T097-00:11:43.671)

Independent pronouns function as subject (11)–(12) or object (13) arguments; possessors modifying a directly or indirectly possessed noun (see §5.5.1 and §5.5.2); or complements of the preposition *te* or *avosia* (see §5.5.5 and §8.3.3). They may co-occur with subject-indexing proclitics (and sometimes object-indexing enclitics) (see §6.3.2), possessor suffixes (§5.5.1), and possessor proclitics (§5.5.2): their function and status as optional or obligatory constituents is discussed in these sections. The first set of dual independent pronouns listed in Table 4.3 may also coordinate NPs or function as inclusory pronouns (see §10.1.1.3).

4.3 Nominal derivation

Papapana derives nouns by zero derivation (§4.3.1), reduplication (§4.3.2), and a derivational suffix, which may function alone or in combination with reduplication (§4.3.3). The prenominal collective marker *vei* co-occurs with derived nouns and a particular type of compound noun (see §4.4.4), resulting in a NP with a collective meaning, as well as occurring in adjective phrases when they have a collective reference (§4.6.1). *Vei* is polysemous as *vei* is also a reciprocal/reflexive marker in the verb complex (VC) and it is believed to be a reflex of POc **paRi-* which Pawley (1973: 150–151) reconstructed as a collective/associative, reciprocal, and iterative marker (see §6.5.6).

4.3.1 Zero derivation

Nouns can be derived through zero derivation from many, but by no means all, verbs. Nouns are not derived from a particular class of verb, nor do the resulting derived nouns belong to a particular class of noun. The verbs, from which the nouns are derived, do not belong to a particular transitivity category nor to a semantic class of verb (see §6.4); for example, *orete* 'walk' is intransitive while *ari* 'dig' is ambitransitive and *po* 'stay' is a state verb while *siodo* 'work' is an action verb. As Table 4.4 shows, the meaning of the resulting noun and noun class assignment are varied and largely unpredictable: nouns denoting actions belong to Class I, and resultative states and entities belong to Class II but other nouns such as instruments are less easily accounted for.

Table 4.4: Derived nouns: Zero derivation.

Verb		Noun	Noun class
po	stay/exist	living	Class I
ma	chew	chewing	Class I
orete	walk	walking	Class I
usi	scrape	scraper	Class I
siodo	work	job	Class I
vo'o	call out	voice	Class II
ari	dig	grave/hole	Class II
matautu	fear	fear	Class II
nai	marry	marriage	Class II
aporo	cut	scissors	Class II
tete	enter	ladder	Class II

Examples (14a) to (16a) show a derived noun as the head of an intransitive subject NP, a monotransitive subject NP and as an object NP respectively. Examples (14b)–(16b) show the verb root functioning as the head of the VC.

(14) a. ***Na=orete***   *e=ae*   *mata=na.*
SPEC[CLI]=walk 3SG.SBJ=NEG good=3SG.IPFV
'Walking is not good.'
(2-E002)

b. ***Mi=pei***   ***orete*** *ora nao=i*   *i-maria,*   *Vakonaia.*
1EXCL.SBJ=PST.IPFV walk only thither=IRR LOC-thing Wakunai
'We used to just walk to where's-it-called, Wakunai.'
(1-T011-00:00:42.820)

(15) a. ***Nu=matautu***   *e=adu~adu=a=ena*
SPEC.CLII=fear 3SG.SBJ=RD~destroy=3SG.OBJ=3SG.IPFV
oina=au   *atu~atu.*
3PL.PSSR=CLII RD~make
'Fear destroys their custom.'
(2-E002)

b. "*O=ae*   ***matautu?***"
2SG.SBJ=NEG fear
"'Weren't you afraid?'"
(1-T074-00:03:34.330)

(16) a. …*u=to*   *asi=a*   ***na=siodo***   *mama*…
1SG.SBJ=EMPH leave=3SG.OBJ SPEC[CLI]=work 1DEM
'…I left this job…'
(1-T097-00:13:43.376)

b. …***e=pei***   *me-na*   *siodo=ena=i*   *na=siapani.*
3SG.SBJ=PST.IPFV COM-PL.OBJ work=3SG.IPFV=IRR SPEC[CLI]=Japan
'…he was working with the Japanese.'
(1-T034-00:13:27.980)

NPs headed by a zero-derived noun and marked by an article and the collective marker *vei* have a collective meaning (17)–(18).

(17) *Na:=bau* ***na=vei***   ***burisi***   *na=ava*   *de=ina.*
some=PL SPEC[CLI]=COLL give.birth SPEC[CLI]=sea take=3PL.OBJ
'The sea took some of the layers (chickens).'
(1-T105-00:18:23.840)

(18) **nu=vei** **toko**
 SPEC.CLII=COLL worship
 'congregation'
 (2-E005)

4.3.2 Reduplication

In Papapana, derivational reduplication involves either monosyllabic or disyllabic copying (see §3.4) and may derive nouns from verbs (§4.3.2.1) or adjectives from nouns or other adjectives (see §4.6). There are also some postverbal adverbs which may have undergone reduplication (see §6.8.2.2). There is one attested instance in the data of disyllabic reduplication deriving the noun *putepute* 'fan' (Class II) from another noun *pute* 'wind' (Class I).

4.3.2.1 Nominalised verbs

A noun can be derived from a verbal root through reduplication, a common process of nominalising verbs in Oceanic languages (Lynch, Ross, and Crowley 2002: 38). This can be seen in (19a) where the root *tamu* is an intransitive verb while in (19b) *tamutamu* is a noun derived via reduplication.

(19) a. *Nani te=na=garasi* **mi=tamu.**
 there OBL=SPEC[CLI]=grass 1EXCL.SBJ=eat
 'We ate there on the grass.'
 (1-T071-00:05:52.450)
 b. *. . .i=atu=a* **tamu~tamu** *nani.*
 3PL.SBJ=make=3SG.OBJ RD~eat there
 '. . .they made food there.'
 (1-T049-00:05:21.540)

The resulting nouns are marked by an article (either Class I or II singular articles, or the plural article *bau*), although *tamutamu* 'food' and *to'oto'o* 'knife' do not when singular. There is no grammatical, semantic or phonological motivation for which type of reduplication is employed, though monosyllabic reduplication is far more common. As Table 4.5 shows, noun class assignment (see §5.1) is fairly predictable, with food and objects belonging in Class I and body parts in Class II, along with an instrument and resultative entity, but noun class assignment of humans is less predictable. In other Northwest Solomonic languages, nouns derived from verbs by reduplication may also refer to the object undergoing the action of the verb or the object created as a result of the action, as in Hoava (Davis, 2003: 45).

Table 4.5: Derived nouns: Reduplication.

	Verb		Noun		Noun class
Mono-syllabic	vurau	run	vu~vurau	car	Class I
	de	take	de~de	bag	Class I
	umunu	sit	mu~munu	chair	Class I
	averu	steal	a~'averu	thief	Class I
	pita	step	pi~pita	foot	Class II
	veiongo	get into	ve-veiongo	clothing	Class II
	burisi	give birth	bu~burisi	womb	Class II
	dovi	spit	do~dovi	lung	Class II
	moroko	lie	mo~moroko	liar	Class II
Di-syllabic	tamu	eat	tamu~tamu	food	Class I
	to'o	cut	to'o~to'o	knife	Class II
	atu	make	atu~atu	custom	Class II
	vaene	climb	vae~vaene	climber	Class II

Examples (20)–(21) show a deverbal noun as the head of an intransitive subject NP, and object NP.

(20) **Na=vu~vurau**   e=to   naomai.
     SPEC[CLI]=RD~run 3SG.SBJ=EMPH come
     'The car came.'
     (1-T071-00:03:05.350)

(21) . . .tau si=panisi=ina=i   **bau atu~atu te   arira.**
     and   1INCL.SBJ=change=3PL.OBJ=IRR PL RD~make OBL 1INCL
     '. . .and we change our customs.'
     (1-T089-00:10:21.736)

The roots *mate* 'to die' and *ari* 'to dig' behave interestingly. A NP headed by *mate* has different references depending on its noun class: 'dead body' when

Class I but 'sickness' or 'death' when Class II. When reduplicated, *mate* has a further reference of 'sick person' and belongs to Class II. The root *ari* is marked by a Class II article to denote 'grave/hole' but when reduplicated it denotes 'cemetery' and belongs to Class II, which is unusual since locations usually belong to Class I. The other alternative is that the reduplication is a method of pluralisation, indicating 'many graves'. Indeed, reduplication is connected with nominal number in confined constructions (see §4.3.3.2) and nominal pluralization can be marked by reduplication, though this is not a productive process (see §5.2.3).

For some NPs headed by abstract nouns, the collective marker *vei* may also appear between the article and the root, giving the NP a collective meaning:

(22) **Na=vei**   ta~tavone   avosia   e=to   ae
     SPEC[CLI]=COLL   RD~help   like   3SG.SBJ=EMPH   NEG
     po=na=i.
     stay=3SG.IPFV=IRR
     'People don't help. (lit. Helping, like, it doesn't exist.)'
     (1-T093-00:03:50.175)

(23) **Nu=vei**   no~nongono   va:gi   e=ae   agai
     SPEC.CLII=COLL   RD~hear   now   3SG.SBJ=NEG   really
     po=na   avosia   va:sina.
     stay=3SG.IPFV   like   before
     'Today they don't listen like before. (lit. Listening today doesn't really exist like before.)'
     (1-T079-00:00:54.630)

Sometimes the verb is a derived intransitive verb, whereby a monotransitive or ambitransitive verb has syntactically incorporated its generic object. This verb is then nominalized via reduplication as in (24)–(25).

(24) ...*i=pei*   *po=ina=i*   *na=vanua=ma*
     3PL.SBJ=PST.IPFV   stay=3PL.IPFV=IRR   SPEC.CLII=people=ma
     nu=vei   ani~ani   vanua.
     SPEC.CLII=COLL   RD~eat   people
     '...people were living as cannibals.'
     (1-T034-00:02:53.026)

(25) **nu=vei   ago~agoto si'ini**
     SPEC.CLII=COLL RD~hold   spear
     'army'
     (2-E005)

4.3.3 Reduplication and derivational -na

In Papapana, the derivational suffix -*na*, usually in conjunction with monosyllabic reduplication, derives location nouns from verbs (§4.3.3.1), while the derivational suffix -*na* derives minimal dyadic nouns from nouns expressing kinship, and the derivational suffix and disyllabic reduplication derive augmented dyadic nouns from nouns expressing kinship (§4.3.3.2). Disyllabic reduplication and the derivational suffix -*na* also derive the numeral *manomanoana* 'one thousand' from the numeral *manoa* 'ten' while monosyllabic reduplication and the derivational suffix -*na* derive the Absolute Location noun *mumurina* 'future' from the Relational Location noun *muri* 'behind'. The suffix -*na* is identical in form to the 3SG direct possessor suffix -*na* but I analyse it as a derivational suffix because it has a broad derivational function, the meanings of the derived nouns are not related to possession and I believe it most likely reflects the POc nominalising suffix *-ŋa (Ross 1988: 70).

4.3.3.1 Derived location nouns

The derivational suffix -*na* can derive a noun denoting a location in which the activity referred to by the verb takes place. In (26)–(27), there is no reduplication of the verb root.

(26) *na=vamaunisi-**na***
     SPEC[CLI]=rest-DER
     'resting house (lit. resting place)'
     (2-E005)

(27) *vamamatau-**na***
     teach-DER
     'school (lit. teaching place)'
     (Fieldnotes 2013)

Examples (28) and (29) show the derivational suffix -*na* deriving a location noun from a verb but in conjunction with monosyllabic reduplication of the verbal root.

It is unclear how productive this morphology is as examples such as (26)–(29) only arose through elicitation and there are only a few instances in my data. Nevertheless, this morphology is typical of Northwest Solomonic languages: in Banoni (Lynch and Ross 2002: 442) and Roviana (Corston-Oliver 2002: 472), the nominalising suffix -*ana* and reduplication also derive locative nouns from verbs, while in Kubokota (Chambers, 2009: 73) nominalised verbs with reduplicated roots and the nominalising suffix -*na* often describe the location where the action occurs.

(28) *na=**si**~siodo-**na***
SPEC[CLI]=RD~work-DER
'workplace'
(2-E006)

(29) *na=**ta**~tamu-**na***
SPEC[CLI]=RD~eat-DER
'eating place/food garden'
(2-E006)

A derived intransitive verb, whereby a monotransitive or ambitransitive verb has incorporated its object, can be nominalized via reduplication of the verbal root and the derivational suffix on the noun (30), while in (31) the verb and the reciprocal/reflexive marker *vei* are nominalized via reduplication of *vei* and the derivational suffixed to the verb. Elsewhere in the Northwest Solomonic group, Kubokota also allows verbal morphology to be included in nominalisations (Chambers, 2009: 73). It is possible that in (30 and (31) a noun has first been derived by reduplication from a verb and then this noun has been further derived into a location noun by -*na*.

(30) ***de**~de   matau-**na***
RD~take knowledge-DER
'school (lit. knowledge-taking place)'
(Fieldnotes 2013)

(31) ***ve**~vei   tago-**na***
RD~R/R exchange-DER
'market (lit. mutual/reciprocal exchanging place)'
(Fieldnotes 2013)

Example (27) represents an alternative to example (30) and this could reflect the fact that 'school' is a culturally imported concept and it is usually referred to by the Tok Pisin loan *skuru*, so examples (27) and (30) could be spontaneous attempts to create a Papapana word for 'school'. Example (30) suggests the verb *vamamatau* 'to teach' could actually derive from the noun *matau* 'knowledge'. Other speakers in text recordings use *vamamatau* as a noun denoting 'school' when usually as a zero-derived noun *vamamatau* denotes 'teacher'. Similarly, the verb *tago* 'to exchange' may be zero-derived as a noun denoting either 'exchange', or 'market' (when in an oblique with the preposition *te*, see example (46) in §10.1.4).

4.3.3.2 Derived dyadic nouns

The derivational suffix *-na* derives a minimal dyadic noun from a noun expressing kinship. The minimal dyadic noun refers to two people who are on either side of the relationship in question (32)–(34). A minimal dyadic noun is always modified by the dual collective article *mena* (see §5.3.7). Example (34) shows that minimal dyadic nouns may also be modified by adjectives.

(32) . . .*i=pei   po=ina=i   mena   tama-na.*
     3PL.SBJ=PST.IPFV stay=3PL.IPFV=IRR DU.COLL father-DER
     '. . .the father and child remained.'
     (1-T031-00:48.960)

(33) *Ta   anau   au=bau   'usia u=asi=ina,*
     and 1SG   1SG.PSSR=PL   child 1SG.SBJ=leave=3PL.OBJ
     mena   vavine-na   ta   sa=au   sina-ina   tomana.
     DU.COLL sibling-DER and   DIM=CLII mother=3PL.PSSR too
     'And I left my children, two sisters, and their poor/young aunty too.'
     (1-T065-00:04:00.640)

(34) *Enai   **mena   panu-na   vaunu** nani i=po=ina.*
     after DU.COLL spouse-DER new   there 3PL.SBJ=stay=3PL.IPFV
     'Then the new couple live there.'
     (1-T076-00:00:41.040)

The derivational suffix *-na* and disyllabic reduplication of a kinship noun together derive an augmented dyadic noun that refers to three or more people who are on either side of the relationship in question (35)–(37). Augmented dyadic nouns are always modified by the plural collective article *mamena* (see §5.3.7). Example (37) shows that augmented dyadic nouns may also be marked by possessor proclitics.

(35) **Mamena sina~sina-na** *i=naomai.*
      PL.COLL RD~mother-DER 3PL.SBJ=come
      'The (step)mother and her children came.'
      (1-T050-00:03:50.990)

(36) **Mamena tubu~tubu-na** *i=nao* *i-daramu.*
      PL.COLL RD~grandparent-DER 3PL.SBJ=go LOC-river
      'A grandmother and her (two) grandchildren went to the river.'
      (1-T073-00:00:27.860)

(37) *au=mamena* *tama~tama-na*
      1SG.PSSR=PL.COLL RD~father-DER
      'my family'
      (2-E005)

It is possible that it is actually the NP with this particular constructional frame (*mena* and *-na*, or *mamena*, disyllabic reduplication and *-na*) that is dyadic, rather than the noun. Indeed kinship nouns with derivational *-na* are not attested without the collective articles *mena* and *mamena*. However, these articles do mark other types of nouns which do not have derivational morphology (see §5.3.7), hence I do not consider *mena* and *mamena* to be part of the derivational morphology in (35)–(37).

4.4 Compound nouns and complex kinship terms

Papapana has three types of compound nouns. In the first, noun or verb roots modify head nouns which may or may not be marked by the *construct suffix -i* or *-ni* (see §4.4.1 and §4.4.2, the latter of which have a partitive or collective noun as the head). The second type is similar, with a lexicalized head noun *toi ~ tei* 'person' or *tai* 'people' being modified by a noun or verb root (§4.4.3). In the third type, the head noun *mata* 'trait' is modified by a reduplicated verbal root to which PSI enclitics attach (§4.4.4). There is one more compound-like construction in which a possible noun *pea* 'possession' is followed by a possessum noun marked by a possessor suffix: this only functions as a predicate expressing possession and is discussed in §9.6.8. Section §4.4.5 describes complex kinship terms which contain a head noun marked by a 1SG or 3SG direct possessor suffix and followed by a modifiying root (usually nominal): these constructions are likely undergoing a process of lexicalization.

4.4.1 Compounds and the construct suffix -*i* or -*ni*

Nouns and verbs may modify head nouns in compound noun constructions in which the head noun may or may not be marked by a *construct suffix* -*i* (38)–(40) or -*ni* (41)–(42) (see below for discussion of this term) or sometimes neither (43) (see below for further discussion of the absence of the construct suffix). Example (39) is the only example here where the modifying element is a verb. Example (42) shows a compound whose head noun is derived through reduplication from a verb, while (43) shows a compound whose modifying noun is derived from a verb via the derivational suffix and monosyllabic reduplication of a verb root (like the derived location nouns in §4.3.3.1). Except for (41), all the compound nouns here are marked either by possessor proclitics (42), specific articles (for example in (38)), or the plural article *bau* (40). Modifying nouns are not marked by articles or possessor proclitics, which is evidence that these are compounds, not a series of NPs.

(38) **na=mata-i** *api*
 SPEC[CLI]=door-CONST bamboo
 'bamboo door'
 (2-E023)

(39) **na=noa-i** *irupu*
 SPEC[CLI]=k.o.grouper-CONST go.inside
 'scorpionfish'
 (2-E023)

(40) **bau nauno-i** atovo
 PL tree-CONST sago
 'sago trees'
 (2-E003)

(41) **Tue-ni** *Papapana* u=a~'atu=au.
 language-CONST Papapana 1SG=RD~make=1SG.IPFV
 'I speak Papapana.'
 (2-E002)

(42) *Anau u=ri   'a'ade'e=i=a=u*
     1SG   1SG.SBJ=OPT narrative=TR=3SG.OBJ=1SG.IPFV
     ami=atu~atu-ni   **va:sina,** bau
     1EXCL.PSSR[CL1]=RD~make-CONST before   PL
     tubu-mani.
     grandparent-1EXCL.PSSR
     'I want to tell a story about our customs in the past, our ancestors.'
     (1-T076-00:00:19.590)

(43) **na=inu   be~beata-na**
     SPEC[CLI]=house RD~excrete-DER
     'toilet (lit. excretement/excreting house)'
     (2-E005)

The status of these constructions as compound nouns is supported by further morpho-syntactic evidence: possessor suffixes and the augmentative suffix normally directly attach to the head noun they modify, but in a compound noun, they attach to the newly created compound base, rather than to the first root, as in (44) and (45).

(44) **nu=mata-i   puru-mu**
     SPEC.CLII=eye-CONST flower-2SG.PSSR
     'your eyelash (lit. your eye flower)'
     (2-E011)

(45) . . .*i=to   vurau nao=i   tena* **bau vuni-i**
     3PL.SBJ=EMPH run   thither=IRR OBL PL trunk-CONST
     naono-eta. . .
     tree-AUG
     '. . .they run to the big tree trunks. . .'
     (1-T034-00:06:59.360)

These compound nouns seem to reflect POc inalienable and alienable non-specific possessor constructions which were expressed with the prepositions *qi and *ni respectively; these intervened between the possessum and possessor as in (46):

(46) Inalienable *a natu qi boRok
                 ART child qi pig
                 'a piglet' (lit. 'child of pig')

Alienable *a polo ni niuR
ART liquid ni coconut
'coconut water' (lit. 'liquid of coconut')
(Ross 1998a: 249, after Hooper 1985 and Lichtenberk 1985)

Ross (1998a: 250) states that the "majority of reflexes of *qi, and some of *ni, are phonologically bound to the preceding noun as suffixes or enclitics. Oceanic linguists label a suffix that reflects *qi or *ni a 'construct suffix'". It seems reasonable to hypothesise that in Papapana, -ni is a reflex of *ni and -i is a reflex of *qi, and that the head of the compound noun represents the possessum while the modifying noun represents the possessor. Nevertheless, the Proto-Oceanic inalienable/alienable distinction has been lost or at least mixed up, as the nouns that occur with -i are both alienable and inalienable. It could even be that -i is a phonologically reduced form of -ni as a speaker confirmed that (47a) and (47b) were both possible. Ross (1998a: 248) highlights that "non-specific 'possessors' are often not really possessors at all but generic nouns used attributively" and argues that "POc nonspecific possession was (and in modern Oceanic languages still is) simply a subfunction of the broader function of attribution". This certainly appears to be the case for Papapana.

(47) a. *nana-**ni**   tamute*
       branch-CONST mango
       'mango branch'
       (Fieldnotes 2013)
    b. *nana-**i**   tamute*
       branch-CONST mango
       'mango branch'
       (Fieldnotes 2013)

In Western Oceanic languages, non-specific possessor constructions tend to be lost altogether and their functions are either replaced by the specific constructions or by simple juxtaposition (Ross 2004c: 514). The latter situation is likely occuring in Papapana, with a modifying nominal root directly following the head noun: examples (48a)–(49a) show compound nouns where -i was absent in text data, but elicitation sessions revealed that the presence of -i was also acceptable (48b)–(49b) and in fact deemed by speakers to be "original Papapana". The absence of -ni or -i renders Papapana compound nouns more similar to Teop compound nouns which consist of a head noun modified by an immediately following nominal (Mosel and Thiesen 2007).

(48) a. *nu='usia   maunu*
        SPEC.CLII=child woman
        'girl'
        (1-T029-00:23:32.433)
     b. *nu='usia-i   maunu*
        SPEC.CLII=child-CONST woman
        'girl'
        (2-E023)

(49) a. *bau inu   atovo*
        PL   house sago
        'sago houses'
        (1-T001-00:04:12.590)
     b. *bau inu-i   atovo*
        PL   house-CONST sago
        'sago houses'
        (2-E023)

4.4.2 Compounds with partitive and collective nouns

The partitive noun *pei* refers to part of an entity. Although phonologically identical to the partitive article (§5.3.6), as a partitive noun *pei* may itself be marked by articles (50)–(52) or by possessor proclitics (53). The partitive noun is the head of the NP while the noun which *pei* denotes a part of functions as a modifier in postnominal position. Note that in (51)–(52), the modifying nouns are derived from verbs via reduplication, or reduplication and the derivational suffix. The modifying noun is not marked by an article, which is evidence that these constructions are not a series of NPs. Although the head noun is not marked by the construct suffix, it is possible for compounds to lack the construct suffix (see §4.4.1) and the status of these constructions as compound nouns is supported by (50) where the augmentative suffix attaches to the newly created compound base, rather than to the first root.

(50) ...*bau pei   naono-ota mi=to   de=ina=i*...
        PL   part tree-AUG   1EXCL=EMPH   take=3PL.OBJ=IRR
        '...we get big pieces of wood...'
        (1-T085-00:03:24.830)

(51) **ta=pei**   **tamu~tamu**
NSPEC[CLI]=part RD~eat
'a piece of food'
(2-E023)

(52) **Ta=pei**   **bu~burisi-na,**   *ta=pei*   mata,
NSPEC[CLI]=part RD~give.birth-DER NSPEC[CLI]=part good
e=pei   *aruai=ena=i. . .*
3SG.SBJ=PST.IPFV be.not=3SG.IPFV=IRR
'There was no maternity ward, no good place. . .'
(1-T034-00:16:53.740)

(53) *"Enai* **au=pei**   *tanga*   *enai."*
DEM2 1SG.PSSR=part shell.money DEM2
'"That's my (shell) necklace."'
(1-T029-00:13:25.570)

Collective nouns refer to a collection of items of the same kind. As in Teop (Mosel and Spriggs 1999a: 332), the collective noun in Papapana is the head of the NP and determines its noun class, while the noun denoting the collected item functions as a modifier, directly following the head noun. There are three collective nouns which belong to Class I and refer to groups of human referents (54), other animate referents (55) and inanimate referents (56). The head noun in (54)–(56) is not marked by the construct suffix but is marked by an article, while the modifying noun is not marked by an article, which is evidence that these are not a series of NPs. Further research could show that these are actually nouns modifying nouns, but I analyse them as compounds for the time being because they have the same structure as the compounds which lack the construct suffix in §4.4.1.

(54) *na=gumu*   *'usia*
SPEC[CLI]=group.HUM child
'group of children'
(2-E005)

(55) *na=navo*   *boro*
SPEC[CLI]=group.AN pig
'herd of pigs'
(2-E005)

(56) na=gona   kaukau
     SPEC[CLI]=group.INAN sweet.potato
     'bundle of potatoes'
     (2-E005)

4.4.3 Compounds with lexicalised *toi ~ tei* 'person' and *tai* 'people'

The nouns *toi ~ tei* 'person' and *tai* 'people' never occur independently but are always modified by a following noun indicating the place where the person is from (57)–(58), or by a verb indicating what the person does (59), or occasionally by an adjective (60). The alternate forms *toi* and *tei* are a reflection of the first phonological variation described in §3.1.3. I hypothesise that *toi ~ tei* 'person' and *tai* 'people' are lexicalisations of the head nouns *to* 'person' and *ta* 'people' and the construct suffix *-i*, and thus, with the modifying noun or verb, form a compound which reflects the compounds described in §4.4.1. Although **to* 'person' and **ta* 'people' do not exist in Papapana, they perhaps once did because in the closely related Teop *too* denotes 'person' and *ta* denotes 'people' (Mosel and Spriggs 1999a: 329).

(57) . . .*e-tama-u*   *e=oi=a*   mai   toi   sikuna*. . .
     PERS-father-1SG.PSSR 3SG.SBJ=take=3SG.OBJ hither person ship
     '. . .my father brought a white man (lit. ship person). . .'
     (1-T034-00:16:25.250)

(58) *E=roroto=ina*   tai   Teperoi. . .
     3SG.SBJ=see=3PL.OBJ people Teperoi
     'She saw Teperoi people. . .'
     (2-T001-00:00:35.188)

(59) a. **toi   bui**
        Person dance
        'dancer'
        (2-E003)
     b. **toi   ena**
        Person sing
        'singer'
        (2-E003)

Usually such a compound is not modified in any way, but it is possible for these compounds to be marked by articles such as *sau* or *bau* (60)–(61) and possessors (62):

(60) *Ta   sa=au   vena   e=to   ara   mate **sa=au***
     and   DIM=CLII individual   3SG.SBJ=EMPH   PST   die   DIM=CLII
     toi   vituasi.
     person   young
     'And the poor one who died was just a young guy.'
     (1-T103-00:12:27.700)

(61) . . .*na:=**bau** tai   Buka*. . . *i=de=ina   mai*. . .
     some=PL   people Buka   3PL.SBJ=take=3PL.OBJ   hither
     '. . .some Buka people. . . they brought them. . .'
     (1-T034-00:15:15.810)

(62) . . .*i=tavone=ami   **au=bau**   toi   poana*. . .
     3PL.SBJ=help=1EXCL.OBJ   1SG.PSSR=PL   person   village
     '. . .my relatives (lit. my villagers) helped us. . .'
     (1-T023-00:01:08.525)

When it is a verb that modifies *toi ~ tei* and *tai*, certain verbal properties may be incorporated, such as aspect (63), object enclitics (64) and object NPs (65).

(63) ***toi   si~siodo***
     person   RD~work
     'workaholic (lit. person who always works)'
     (2-E006)

(64) ***Toi   peri=a   e=ma'=i=a,*   Ebauka.*
     person   find=3SG.OBJ   3SG.SBJ=give=TR=3SG.OBJ   Ebauka
     'He gave her to the person who found her, Ebauka.'
     (2-T001-00:00:77.635)

(65) *Treasurer, e-maria,   **mama toi   si~sia=a***
     treasurer   PERS-thing   DEM1   person RD~look.after=3SG.OBJ
     moni   na=vatu   *enai   Maureen.*
     money   SPEC[CLI]=money   DEM2   Maureen

'The treasurer, what's-their-name, this person who looks after money, that's Maureen.'
(1-T081-00:00:46.150)

4.4.4 Compounds with *mata* 'trait'

The noun *mata* 'trait' occurs in a compound noun construction in which *mata* is followed by a reduplicated verbal root to which PSI enclitics attach (66). The compound usually functions as a nominal predicate (see §9.6.1.1) and it denotes a trait of habitually carrying out the action denoted by the reduplicated verb. I analyse the bound morphemes as PSI enclitics rather than as direct possessor suffixes (the two paradigms are identical in form as PSI enclitics diachronically reflect former possessor indexing; see §7.1.1) because the meaning of the construction is not related to possession but to habitual action and in the VC, PSI enclitics interact with reduplication to express habitual aspect (see §7.1.6). Although the compound only occurs once in the text data, it is a productive construction and is attested in several elicitation recordings with different speakers, as well as being a construction I heard and used during my fieldwork.

(66) Anau **nu=mata**   **ro~romo=u.**
     1SG SPEC.CLII=trait RD~drink=1SG.IPFV
     'I'm an alcoholic (lit. I drink (a lot) / I'm a drinker).'
     (1-T088-00:27:26.500)

When the subject is singular, *mata* is marked by the Class II specific article *nu=* as in (67)–(68), whereas when the subject is plural, *mata* is marked by the Class II specific article *nu=* and the collective marker *vei* as in (69)–(70). *Vei* also occurs with derived nouns that have a collective reference (see §4.3.1 and §4.3.2) and in adjective phrases which modify plural nouns (see §4.6.1). The PSI enclitic is coreferential in number and person with the subject NP, and reduplication is monosyllabic when the subject is singular (67)–(68) but disyllabic when the subject is plural (69)–(70). Although nouns can be derived from a verbal root through reduplication, it is not possible for the same verbal root to undergo either monosyllabic or disyllabic reduplication (see §4.3.2), therefore these compounds do not appear to be composed of a deverbal noun (derived by reduplication). Instead, the reduplicant and PSI enclitics attach to the verbal root, operating together, before this stem forms a compound with *mata* (and does so obligatorily since a reduplicated verbal root with PSI enclitic cannot stand alone).

(67) Ben **nu=mata** **vo~vori=na.**
 Ben SPEC.CLII=trait RD~talk=3SG.IPFV
 'Ben talks (a lot). / Ben is a talker.'
 (2-E007-2B)

(68) Na=orawi **nu=mata** **te~tepe=na.**
 SPEC[CLI]=man SPEC.CLII=trait RD~cut=3SG.IPFV
 'The man carves. / The man is a carver.'
 (2-E015)

(69) Na='usia mama **nu=vei** mata vori~vori=ina.
 SPEC[CLI]=child DEM1 SPEC.CLII=COLL trait RD ~talk=3PL.IPFV
 'These children talk (a lot). / These children are talkers.'
 (2-E023)

(70) Oina=bau sinoni **nu=vei** mata tepe~tepe=ina.
 3PL.PSSR=PL husband SPEC.CLII=COLL trait RD~cut=3PL.IPFV
 'Our husbands carve. / Our husbands are carvers.'
 (2-E023)

The construction can include other verbal morphology such as adverbs, as in (71).

(71) Bau kakau mama **nu=vei** mata ore~orete papasi=ina.
 PL dog DEM1 SPEC.CLII=COLL trait RD~walk quickly=3PL.IPFV
 'These dogs walk about quickly. / Those dogs are quick walkers.'
 (2-E023)

It is also possible for the reduplicated verb in this compound to belong to the subclass class of intransitive verbs which are zero-derived from adjectives (see §6.4.1): such a compound denotes an ongoing state and may function as a nominal predicate as in (72).

(72) Na=maunu **nu=mata** sa~sare=na.
 SPEC[CLI]=woman SPEC.CLII=trait RD~happy=3SG.IPFV
 'The woman is always happy.'
 (2-E028-1)

4.4.5 Complex kinship terms

There are three kinship terms which are marked by direct possessor suffixes (see §5.5.1) and followed by a modifier: *tua- pea* 'uncle' (73), *asi- maunu* 'same sex female sibling/cousin' (75) and *tu- maunu* 'daughter' (74). Unlike the former two terms, *tu- maunu* 'daughter' does not fill a gap in the Papapana lexicon, as 'daughter' can also be expressed by modifying *'usia* 'child' with *maunu* (see (48) in §4.4.1). It is possible that *tu-* could be a reflex of POc **natu* 'child' (Ross 1988: 153) while *asi* in *asi- maunu* 'same sex female sibling/cousin' (75) is likely cognate with Banoni *kasi* 'same sex sibling' (Palmer 2014). The etymology of *tua- pea* 'uncle' (73) is unclear. Elsewhere in the Northwest Solomonic group, *tua* denotes 'grandparent' in Mono-Alu, *pean* denotes 'child' in Petats, *pea* denotes 'big' in Solos (Palmer 2014) and *-pe* denotes 'younger (of kin)' in Uruava (Palmer 2007d), while *tuani* denotes 'old' in Papapana but to derive a denotation of 'uncle' from any of these forms seems incongruous.

There are no attested instances of articles marking *tua- pea* 'uncle' (73) nor *tu- maunu* 'daughter' (74). *Asi- maunu* 'same sex female sibling/cousin' is usually not marked by articles either (75a) but (75b) and (75c) show that it can be marked by articles and numeral modifiers respectively (though these give conflicting evidence regarding noun class).

(73) a. **Tua-u**   *pea* *e=wa. . .*
       uncle-1SG.PSSR pea 3SG.SBJ=say
       'My uncle said. . .'
       (1-T042-00:00:37.510)
   b. **Tua-na**   *pea* *e=naomai. . .*
       uncle-3SG.PSSR pea 3SG.SBJ=come
       'Her uncle came. . .'
       (1-T088-00:29:12.978)

(74) **tu-na**   *maunu*
     child-3SG.PSSR woman
     'her daughter'
     (2-E006)

(75) a. **Asi-na**   *maunu* *e=vare*   *oa=re.*
       sister-3SG.PSSR woman   3SG.SBJ=REP cry=REP
       'Her sister cried again.'
       (1-T007-00:02:51.640)

b. *"Iai   sa=au   asi-u   maunu=ma*
   PROX DIM=CLII sister-1SG.PSSR woman=ma
   u=oi=a=i...
   1SG.SBJ=call=3SG.OBJ=IRR
   "'I will call her my dear/little sister...'"
   (1-T068-00:01:06.440)
c. *"Anau   nua   asi-u   maunu*
   1SG   two[CLI]   sister-1SG.PSSR   woman
   i=me-a   tua=au   mai...
   3PL.SBJ=COM-SG.OBJ   paddle=1SG.OBJ   hither
   "'My two sisters paddled here with me...'"
   (1-T101-00:03:57.268)

It cannot be argued that these three kinship terms are compound nouns as the modifiers follow the possessor suffixes, whereas for compound nouns, possessor suffixes attach to the modifying noun and the compound noun is treated as a single stem (see §4.4.1). Instead it can be argued that these directly possessed kinship nouns are simply being modified by a noun, akin to a directly possessed noun being modified by a bare adjective (see (120) in §4.6.2).

That these constructions are synchronically polymorphemic is supported by the change in possessor suffix (though only 1SG or 3SG are attested) and also by data such as (76) and (77) which show *asi- maunu* being marked by the dual and plural collective articles *mena* and *mamena*, which most commonly mark derived dyadic nouns (§4.3.3.2). These examples can clearly be analysed as derived minimal and augmented dyadic nouns as they refer to two (76) or three (77) people who are on either side of the relationship in question. There is no sense of possession either and thus, as with other minimal and augmented dyadic nouns, *-na* in these examples can be analysed as the derivational suffix. Furthermore, as per other augmented dyadic nouns, there is disyllabic reduplication of the kinship noun *asi* in (77). The position of the modifier *maunu* is also compatible with this analysis as (34) in §4.3.3.2 shows an adjective following the derivational suffix.

(76) *E=atunu=ina   mena   asi-na   maunu.*
     3SG.SBJ=attack=3PL.OBJ DU.COLL   sister-DER   woman
     'She hit the two sisters.'
     (1-T007-00:01:13.450)

(77) . . .*oina=atono,* **mama mamena asi~asi-na maunu**
     3PL.PSSR=three.HUM DEM1 PL.COLL RD~sister-DER woman
     i=pei sado=i.
     3PL.SBJ=PST.IPFV walk=IRR
     '. . .they three, these three sisters used to walk around.'
     (1-T101-00:00:43.617)

The above suggests that the kinship constructions are polymorphemic; however, there is also evidence which suggests that they are undergoing a process of lexicalisation and are treated as monomorphemic: a few instances such as (78) and (79) show the kinship terms being marked by both the direct possessor suffixes and the possessor proclitics, with (78) suggesting *tu- maunu* belongs to Class II because of the Class II marker *au*. Since these kinship terms seem to be lexicalized and there are only three of them, I have not included a noun modifier in the postnominal outer layer of the NP in §4.1.

(78) **Ena=au tu-na maunu** *e=pei varona=i.*
     3SG.PSSR=CLII child-3SG.PSSR woman 3SG.SBJ=PST.IPFV know=IRR
     'Her daughter knew.'
     (1-T044-00:04:07.480)

(79) *I=pei vowa=i=ma nani,*
     3PL.SBJ=PST.IPFV be.like=IRR=ma there
     na: **ena=nua asi-na maunu.**
     other 3SG.PSSR=two[CLI] sister-3SG.PSSR woman
     'They (went around) like this there, her other two sisters'
     (1-T101-00:01:22.297)

4.5 Demonstratives

Papapana has a closed class of five demonstratives, that code the deixis of a noun in relation to a spatial reference point. From text data and basic elicitation data alone it was very difficult to establish the basis of the Papapana demonstrative system. I therefore used Wilkins' (1999) demonstrative questionnaire and recreated twenty-five scenes (see Appendix 2) in real life, asking speakers to say something about a single object within the particular context created. I carried this out on two separate occasions with different groups of speakers. Himmelmann (1996) outlines four uses of demonstratives: situational use, discourse deictic use, tracking use and recognitional use. In the elicitations sessions in which I created particular scenes, and in some of the text data, the demonstratives were used situationally, that is "the entity picked out by the demonstrative is present in the situation of the utterance" (Cleary-Kemp 2007: 326). In the text data, demonstratives may also be used for tracking, that is to "refer to participants in the discourse, allowing the hearer to keep track of what is happening to whom" (Cleary-Kemp 2007: 326). Unfortunately, it was not possible to fully investigate the other uses of demonstratives.

Papapana has two demonstratives that are person-based, *mama* 'near speaker' and *enai* 'near addressee', with a further paradigm based on distance relative to the speaker, *iai* 'proximal', *ioi* 'medial', *io'o* 'distal'. I hypothesise that *iai, ioi* and *io'o* are polymorphemic, beginning with the Papapana locative case prefix *i-*. Indeed the POc oblique proform *i-ai* 'there' consisted of the preposition *i* and a locative anaphor (Lynch, Ross, and Crowley 2002: 104). The Papapana deictic locational paradigm correlates with the distance-based demonstrative paradigm (see §8.2). In Oceanic languages, demonstrative systems tend to be based on person or distance, but it is possible to have a combination of the two, as in Papapana and also for example in Saliba (Ross 2004a: 177). The demonstrative system in Papapana does not make distinctions based on visibility, nor does it distinguish the number or noun class of the referent. Established boundaries in lived space do not make a difference to the application of demonstratives. The demonstratives are never modified by any other constituent, and can be either nominal modifiers (§4.5.1) or pronouns (§4.5.2).

4.5.1 Demonstrative modifiers

A noun can be modified by the person-based demonstratives *mama* 'near speaker' and/or *enai* 'near addressee' (§4.5.1.1), the distance-based demonstratives *iai* 'proximal', *ioi* 'medial', or *io'o* 'distal' (§4.5.1.2), or *mama* and one of the distance-based demonstratives (§4.5.1.3).

4.5.1.1 Person-based demonstratives

The person-based demonstrative *mama* 'near speaker' can postmodify a head noun when the speaker is referring to something that is in contact with their own body (e.g. scene 3 in (Wilkins 1999)) as in (80), or as in (81) where the speaker is holding the plant that they are telling me about, or when the speaker is talking about an object immediately in front of him/herself and out of the addressee's reach (e.g. scenes 7 in (Wilkins 1999)) as in (82). When a speaker is referring to something that they are pointing to or touching on the body of the addressee (e.g. scene 4 in (Wilkins 1999)), *mama* was also used to modify the noun (83). In such cases, the entity could be seen as near the speaker because the speaker is physically in contact with it (or very nearly).

(80) **Na='arei**   **mama** *e=abe~abe=au=ena.*
SPEC[CLI]=ant DEM1 3SG.SBJ=RD~walk=1SG.OBJ=3SG.IPFV
'This ant is walking about on me.'
(Fieldnotes 16/04/13)

(81) **Tavea**   **mama** *mi=roa~roa=ina=mani. . .*
plant.sp DEM1 1EXCL.SBJ=RD~plant=3PL.OBJ=1EXCL.IPFV
'We plant this *tavea*. . .'
(1-T058-00:00:54.420)

(82) *Anau u=mate-i=a=au*   **nu=buku**   **mama.**
1SG 1SG.SBJ=like=TR=3SG.OBJ=1SG.IPFV SPEC.CLII=book DEM1
'I like this book.'
(Fieldnotes 03/04/13)

(83) **Na='arei**   **mama** *e=abe~abe=ena*   *te*   *ani.*
SPEC[CLI]=ant DEM1 3SG.SBJ=RD~walk=3SG.IPFV OBL 2SG
'This ant is walking about on you.'
(Fieldnotes 16/04/13)

The person-based demonstrative *enai* 'near addressee' can postmodify a head noun when the speaker is referring to something on the addressee's body that the speaker is not (nearly) physically in contact with, or something that is on the addressee's side that is furthest away from the speaker when they are sitting next to each other (e.g. scenes 5 and 10 in (Wilkins 1999)) as in (84) and (85). In (86) the speaker is recounting an attack during the Bougainville Crisis and is referring to tree trunks that have been mentioned previously in the discourse so *enai* has more of a tracking function here and could be interpreted more as 'not near speaker' rather than 'near addressee' (in this case, me).

(84) **Na='arei**   **enai** *e=abe~abe=ena*   *te*   *ani.*
SPEC[CLI]=ant DEM2 3SG.SBJ=RD~walk=3SG.IPFV OBL 2SG
'That ant is walking about on you.'
(Fieldnotes 16/04/13)

(85) *Anau u=mate=i=a=au* **na=bara** *enai.*
1SG 1SG.SBJ=like=TR=3SG.OBJ=1SG.IPFV SPEC[CLI]=ball DEM2
'I like that ball.'
(Fieldnotes 16/04/13)

(86) *Avosia i=to no ta'opo=i tena* **bau vuni naono**
like 3PL.SBJ=EMPH go.SEQ hide=IRR OBL PL trunk tree
enai.
DEM2
'Like they went and hid in those tree trunks.'
(1-T034-00:07:17.390)

The person-based demonstratives can co-occur to modify a head noun when the speaker is referring to something that is close to both or in between the speaker and the addressee (e.g. scenes 17 in (Wilkins 1999)), as in (87) where *mama* follows the head noun but precedes *enai*. *Mama* and *enai* were also used together to refer to a book which was below me and the speaker when we were stood together on a balcony. In (88) *mama* and *enai* also co-occur and have a tracking function: the speaker is referring back to a language just mentioned in the discourse, which is known to both the speaker and the addressee (me).

(87) *Anau u=mate=i=a=au* **na=bara** **mama enai,**
1SG 1SG.SBJ=like=TR=3SG.OBJ=1SG.IPFV SPEC[CLI]=ball DEM1 DEM2
i-butona e=po=na.
LOC-middle 3SG.SBJ=stay=3SG.IPFV
'I like that ball, it's in the middle.'
(Fieldnotes 16/04/13)

(88) **Na=au** *tue* **mama enai**
SPEC=CLII language DEM1 DEM2
na=vanua panapana i=varon=i=a=ina.
SPEC[CLI]=people all 3PL.SBJ=know=TR=3SG.OBJ=3PL.IPFV
'Everybody knows this language.'
(1-T083-00:01:38.540)

Demonstratives are commonly postnominal in Northwest Solomonic languages such as Kubokota (Chambers 2009: 60), Kokota (Palmer 2002: 503) and Teop (Mosel and Thiesen 2007) but there are some Oceanic languages where demonstratives are prenominal (Lynch, Ross, and Crowley 2002: 40), such as Banoni (Lynch and Ross 2002: 445). Demonstrative modifiers are usually in postnominal position in Papapana, as presented above. However, the text data also shows some variation, with both person-based demonstratives occurring on their own before the head noun, as in (89) and (90) which have a situational and tracking function respectively. When the person-based demonstratives co-occur, it is possible for *enai* to precede the head noun, and *mama* to follow it, as in (91), where the demonstratives have a situational function. This is another instance of the mixture of left-headedness and right-headedness found in Papapana.

(89) **Mama nua ta'apena.**
DEM1 two[CLI] part
'(I'm weaving) these two parts.'
(1-T062-00:08:56.780)

(90) *E=pei tavone=i=a=i sa=au moisibuava*
3SG.SBJ=PST.IPFV help=TR=3SG.OBJ=IRR DIM=CLII old.woman
*tau **enai** sa=au 'usia, mena tubu-na.*
and DEM2 DIM=CLII child DU.COLL grandparent-DER
'He used to help the poor old woman and that poor boy, the grandmother and grandchild.'
(1-T029-00:04:08.954)

(91) "*A:mani mi=mate poto=i=a=mani*
1EXCL 1EXCL.SBJ=like INTS=TR=3SG.OBJ=1EXCL.IPFV
enai *pei tanga **mama**.*"
DEM2 PART shell.money DEM1
"'We really want that necklace (that you're wearing).'"
(1-T029-00:16:03.170)

In terms of their position relative to other postnominal elements, demonstratives can precede adjective phrases (see (7) and (8) in §4.1), follow the modifier *panapana* 'all' (see (5) in §4.1), but their position relative to postnominal numerals is variable (compare (8) and (9) in §4.1).

4.5.1.2 Distance-based demonstratives

The distance-based demonstratives postmodify a head noun and indicate the distance relative to the speaker: *iai* 'proximal', *ioi* 'medial', or *io'o* 'distal'. In (92) the object was in the middle of and equidistant from the speaker and addressee, but was within five paces of the speaker. Example (93) is from a traditional narrative and is the speech uttered by a man who has just drunk some water, while example (94) is also from a traditional narrative and the man is telling his mother about a woman who is, at that point in the story, is at the beach, while the man and his mother are at their house. Thus, the distance-based demonstratives are used situationally in these stories.

(92) ***Nu=buku iai amu=au?***
SPEC.CLII=book PROX 2PL.PSSR=CLII
'Is this book yours?'
(Fieldnotes 03/04/13)

(93) *"**Nu=daramu** **iai** siopa-u e=putu*
SPEC.CLII=water PROX stomach-1SG.PSSR 3SG.SBJ=break.off
osiosi=a."
osiosi=3SG.OBJ
"'This water is breaking my stomach.'"
(1-T044-00:01:38.840)

(94) *"**Na=maunu** io'o u=to oi=i=a mai."*
SPEC[CLI]=woman DIST 1SG.SBJ=EMPH take=TR=3SG.OBJ hither
"'I brought back that woman.'"
(1-T003-00:02:01.210)

4.5.1.3 Co-occurrence of person-based and distance-based demonstratives

The distance-based demonstratives, which indicate the distance relative to the speaker, can be used in conjunction with the person-based demonstrative *mama* 'near speaker', but are incompatible with *enai* 'near addressee'. In such constructions, both demonstratives are postnominal, with *mama* preceding the distance-based demonstrative as in (95), where the speaker is referring to a fish in the canoe next to him. The object might be in the middle of the speaker and addressee, and it may or may not be equidistant from the speaker and addressee, or the speaker and addressee could be stood together and the object is a little way away from them (e.g. scenes 8, 19, 20 and 22 in (Wilkins 1999)): whatever the scenario, *iai* refers to the distance from the speaker, as in (96).

(95) *"**Na=iana** **mama iai** au=ata."*
SPEC[CLI]=ball DEM1 PROX 1SG.PSSR=CLI
"'This fish is mine.'"
(1-T029-00:01:30.120)

(96) *Anau u=mate=i=a=au*   ***nu=buku***   ***mama***
      1SG   1SG.SBJ=like=TR=3SG.OBJ=1SG.IPFV   SPEC.CLII=book   DEM1
      iai.
      DEM
      'I like this book.'
      (Fieldnotes 03/04/13)

If the speaker and addressee are together and the object is further away, such as between five and twenty paces (e.g. scenes 12, 13, 14 and 21 in (Wilkins 1999)), *mama* may be followed by *ioi*, regardless of whether the object is or is not close to a third party:

(97) **Na=bara**   ***mama ioi***   *na=mata.*
      SPEC[CLI]=ball   DEM1   MED   SPEC[CLI]=good
      'This ball is good.'
      (Fieldnotes 16/04/13)

If the object is further away, such as more than twenty paces (e.g. scenes 13 and 15 in (Wilkins 1999)), *mama* may be followed by *io'o*, regardless of whether the object is or is not close to a third party, and regardless of its visibility:

(98) **Na=bara**   ***mama io'o***   *na=mata.*
      SPEC[CLI]=ball   DEM1   DIST   SPEC[CLI]=good
      'That ball is good.'
      (Fieldnotes 16/04/13)

4.5.2 Demonstrative pronouns

The forms in both demonstrative paradigms can be pronouns and retain the distinctions described in §4.5.1. They are never modified by any other constituent. While demonstratives could be analysed as as heads of a phrase which may or may not have a complement NP, and while they could possibly be assigned to a determiner category, I have opted to analyse them as modifiers or pronouns because further reseach is needed to account for their variable order in relation to other words (c.f. examples (8) and (9) in §4.1) and in relation to each other (c.f. examples (88) and (91) in §4.5.1.1).

In (99)–(100) the person-based demonstrative pronouns *mama* 'near speaker' and *enai* 'near addressee' function as objects, while in (101) *enai* functions as the subject of a nominal predicate and is referring to a ball that is closer to the addressee when the speaker and addressee are sitting at different ends of a large cleared space (e.g. scene 17 in (Wilkins 1999)).

(99) *I=ani~ani=a=ina* **mama.**
 3PL.SBJ=RD~eat=3SG.OBJ=3PL.IPFV DEM1
 'They eat this (shell, that I'm holding).'
 (1-T107-00:08:10.100)

(100) "**Enai** *avoa o=de=a?*"
 DEM2 where 2SG.SBJ=take=3SG.OBJ
 '"Where did you get that (necklace, that you're wearing)?"'
 (1-T029-00:15:57.040)

(101) **Enai** *amu=bara awa?*
 DEM2 2SG.PSSR[CLI]=ball correct
 'That's your ball right?'
 (Fieldnotes 16/04/13)

In (102) the distance-based demonstrative pronoun *iai* 'proximal' is the subject of a nominal predicate and is referring to a book that is inside a room under a window when the speaker is outside the window peering in and the addressee is at the other end of the room (e.g. scene 17 in (Wilkins 1999)). In (103) *iai* 'proximal' is also the subject of a nominal predicate and is referring to the story the speaker is about to tell me.

(102) **Iai** *amu=au buku awa?*
 PROX 2SG.PSSR=CLII book correct
 'This is your book right?'
 (Fieldnotes 03/04/13)

(103) **Iai** *atu~atu-ni va:sina te a:mani.*
 PROX RD~make-CONST before OBL 1EXCL.PSSR
 'This (story/custom) is one of our traditional customs.'
 (1-T047-00:00:24.460)

The distance-based demonstratives, which indicate the distance relative to the speaker, can be used in conjunction with the person-based demonstrative *mama* 'near speaker', as in (104) where *mama iai* functions as the subject of a predicate

NP and refers to a shell that the speaker is holding and telling me about. The head noun of the predicate NP is also modified by *iai*.

(104) **Mama iai**   *nu=oirau*   *iai.*
      DEM1 PROX   SPEC.CLII=k.o.shell PROX
      'This (shell) is the great green turban shell.'
      (1-T017-00:02:14.800)

4.6 Adjectives and adjective phrases

Adjectives belong to a medium-sized open word class in Papapana and denote qualities or attributes. Adjective roots are generally underived but can be derived through reduplication from nouns or other adjectives (see below). All Papapana adjectives can occur in an adjective phrase (AP) with an article that agrees in noun class and/or number with the head noun that the AP is modifying (§4.6.1). If the head noun is plural, the collective marker *vei* follows the article in the AP. Adjectives in APs can be negated with *ae* and postmodified by intensifiers. APs may be prenominal or postnominal. A small subclass of adjectives may also behave in this way or they may directly precede or follow the head noun they modify, but without being marked by an article (§4.6.2). One of these adjectives appears to have developed into an augmentative suffix (§4.6.3). APs can function alone in a NP when the head noun is elided (§4.6.4). APs can also function as predicates in verbless clauses (see §9.6.6). A subclass of intransitive verbs is derived through zero-derivation from adjectives (see §6.4.1).

Papapana is unusual in having a class of adjectives because in Oceanic languages, stative meanings are generally expressed by intransitive verbs (Lynch, Ross and Crowley 2002: 40). However, this is not the only method. Ross (1998b), outlines seven Proto-Oceanic adjectival categories including "adjectival nouns" which "serve as modifiers of a noun" and have "the predicate syntax of a noun" (Ross 1998b: 97), and "adjectival verbs" which "serve as modifier of a noun (i.e., need no relative-clause marking)" and have "the predicate syntax of a stative verb" (Ross 1998b: 91). The Nehan-North Bougainville languages Nehan and Halia are described as having adjectival nouns: in Nehan, when an adjective is the head of a NP, it can only be used predicatively, but in Halia, the predicative construction is also an attributive construction (Ross 1998b: 95–96).

I define the words denoting qualities or attributes in Papapana as *adjectives* and not as nouns or verbs because, despite having some things in common with each, they are different from nouns and verbs in several ways. Firstly, although adjectives in APs are marked with an article, this article agrees in noun class and/or number with the head noun that the AP is modifying and thus adjectives are distinct from nouns because they are not independently assigned a noun class, whereas nouns, including those derived from verbs, are (see §4.3). It is common in languages where nouns and adjectives have similar morphology, for an adjective to be able to take any noun class marking but for a noun to be restricted to one class (Aikhenvald 2000: 20). Secondly, the plural article *bau* never marks adjectives, whereas it does mark nouns, including those derived from verbs. Instead the collective marker *vei* is used to mark plurality on adjectives, and this can also be used with derived nouns (see §4.3) and compound nouns with *mata* 'trait' (see §4.4.4), resulting in a NP with a collective meaning. Thirdly, adjectives in APs can be premodified by the negative marker *ae*, whether they are AP modifiers in a NP, or AP predicates in a verbless clause. This makes adjectives similar to verbs as negative *ae* is a preverbal marker in the VC, but different to nouns as NP predicates are postmodified by the negator *aruai* (see §9.6.1.4). However, adjectives are different to verbs because, as just mentioned, when a verb is zero-derived as a noun and marked by an article, it can be marked by the plural article *bau* and it is independently assigned noun class. Furthermore, when a verbal root (or nominal root) modifies a noun, such as in a compound, it is not possible to mark it with an article (see §4.4). Additionally, in the VC intransitive verbs derived through zero derivation from adjectives constitute a subclass of intransitive verbs because, unlike other intransitive U-stative verbs, their valency can be increased by applicative *i*, as well as causative *va-* (see §6.4.1). On a related note, nouns are not zero-derived from adjectives; for example, *sare* 'happy' is not attested as a noun meaning 'happiness', nor is *dua* 'bad' attested as a noun denoting 'the bad'.

In Papapana, adjective roots are generally underived, such as those describing dimension, age and value in Table 4.7 in §4.6.2 and others such as *sare* 'happy' and *tubu* 'fat'. However, there are a few adjectives which are derived through disyllabic reduplication from nouns, such as *pi'i~pi'ita* 'dirty' from *pi'ita* 'rubbish'. Colour terms are mostly derived through monosyllabic or disyllabic reduplication from nouns or other adjectives (see Table 4.6). Such adjectives express the meaning 'similar to X', a meaning which Moravcsik (1978: 323) identifies as close to the meaning of *attenuation*, one of the universal semantic properties of reduplication. Indeed, in Oceanic languages, it is common for colour terms to be derived through reduplication (Blust 2001). Various Oceanic languages, for example, derive 'yellow' from 'turmeric', as does Papapana, reflecting the reconstruction of Proto Malayo-Polynesian **ma-kunij* 'yellow' from **kunij* 'turmeric' (Blust 2001: 27). Some adjectives in Papapana may be diachronically reduplicated but are not synchronically reduplicated; for example, synchronically there is not a word *bukoi* from which *bubukoi* 'multicoloured' can be claimed to derive.

Table 4.6: Colour terms.

Root		Adjective	
revasi	blood	re~revasi	red
asire	turmeric	asi~asire	yellow
namana	ocean	nama~namana	blue
mero'o	mud	mero~mero'o	brown
ravai	dirt	rava~ravai	black
pere	unripe	pere~pere	green
-	-	bubukoi	multicoloured
-	-	ge:rere	white
–	–	ovaovani	orange

Table 4.7: Adjective subclass.

etawa	big
kaka'i	small
sirorai	long/tall
kokobunu	short
vaunu	new
dua	bad

4.6.1 Adjective phrase modifiers

All adjectives can occur in an AP with an article that agrees in noun class and/or number with the head noun that the AP is modifying, as in (105)–(109), where the NP containing the AP functions as the subject of a verbless clause (105), an intransitive clause (106), a monotransitive clause (107), and the object of a monotransitive clause (108). For a few adjectives in Papapana (*sare* 'happy, *nami* 'sad' and *dua* 'bad'), both allomorphs of the Class II specific article, *nau* and *nu=*, are attested with the adjective in an AP, even though only *nu=* is found as a clitic on the head noun (109). In Taiof and Teop too, postmodifying adjectives are preceded by an article agreeing in noun class with the head noun (Ross 2002b: 430; Mosel and Thiesen 2007).

(105) **Na=poana**   **na=kaka'i**   tagena Teperoi.
SPEC[CLI]=village SPEC[CLI]=small near Teperoi
'The small village is near Teperoi.'
(2-E004)

(106) **Na=inu**   **na=vaunu**   e=po=na   Teperoi.
SPEC[CLI]=house SPEC[CLI]=new 3SG.SBJ=stay=3SG.IPFV Teperoi
'The new house is in Teperoi.'
(2-E004)

(107) **Na=orawi**   **na=mata**
SPEC[CLI]=man SPEC[CLI]=good
e=ae   atun=i=a   ena=maunu.
3SG.SBJ=NEG attack=TR=3SG.OBJ 1SG.PSSR[CL1]=woman
'The good man did not attack his wife.'
(2-E004)

(108) Anau u=vaene=i=a   **nu=naono**   **nu=pere~pere.**
1SG 1SG.SBJ=climb=TR=3SG.OBJ SPEC.CLII=tree SPEC.CLII=RD~unripe
'I climbed the green tree.'
(2-E004)

(109) a. **Nu='usia**   **na=au sare**   e=nao   Buka.
SPEC.CLII=child SPEC=CLII happy 3SG.SBJ=go Buka
'The happy child went to Buka.'
(2-E011)
b. **Nu='usia**   **nu=sare**   e=nao   Buka.
SPEC.CLII=child SPEC.CLII=happy 3SG.SBJ=go Buka
'The happy child went to Buka.'
(2-E011)

The AP may precede (110a) or follow (110b) the head noun. This is another instance of the mixture of left-headedness and right-headedness found in Papapana.

(110) a. Anau u=irom=i=a   **nu=sisiva**   **nu=daramu.**
1SG 1SG.SBJ=drink=TR=3SG.OBJ SPEC.CLII=hot SPEC.CLII=water
'I drank the hot water.'
(2-E004)

b. *Anau u=irom=i=a* **nu=daramu nu=sisiva.**
   1SG 1SG.SBJ=drink=TR=3SG.OBJ SPEC.CLII=water SPEC.CLII=hot
   'I drank the hot water.'
   (2-E004)

In postnominal position the AP follows demonstrative modifiers:

(111) **Na=inu** *mama na=vaunu* Peter *ena=ata.*
   SPEC[CLI]=house DEM1 SPEC[CLI]=new Peter 3SG.PSSR=CLI
   'This new house is Peter's.'
   (2-E004)

When the head noun is plural, the adjective does not take the same article as the head. Instead, if the head noun is marked by the plural article *bau* the adjective is marked by *na=vei* (112)–(113), while if the head noun is marked by the diminutive plural article *ani*, the adjective is marked by *ani vei* (114). The collective marker *vei* also co-occurs with derived nouns and a particular type of compound noun, resulting in a NP with a collective meaning (see §4.3.1 and §4.3.2, and §4.4.4). As (113) shows, the adjective itself may be postmodified by a modifier such as the intensifier *poto* (see §4.7.3 and §6.8.2).

(112) . . .*i=to* *ru~ruvu=ina=ina,* **bau taramina**
   3PL.SBJ=EMPH RD~put=3PL.OBJ=3PL.IPFV PL thing
   na=vei *takarau*. . .
   SPEC[CLI]=COLL rusty
   '. . .they used to put them, the rusty things. . .'
   (1-T071-00:03:54.110)

(113) *I-ata* **bau vanao na=vei** *etawa poto*
   LOC-above PL tree sp. SPEC[CLI]=COLL big INTS
   i=pei *po=ina=i.*
   3PL.SBJ=PST.IPFV stay=3PL.IPFV=IRR
   'There were really big *vanao* trees above.'
   (1-T034-00:07:48.090)

(114) **Ani** *naono ani* **vei** *kaka'i i=noe*
   DIM.PL tree DIM.PL COLL small 3PL.SBJ=put
   tae=ina *te=na=ari.*
   up=3PL.OBJ OBL=SPEC.CLI=dig
   'They put a few small sticks on top of the hole.'
   (1-T035-00:09:17.880)

An adjective can be negated with *ae*, the negative marker found in the VC. The negative marker occurs between the article and the adjective root. Note that the AP is prenominal in (115)–(116) but postnominal in (117).

(115) *E=po~po=na*   **na=ae**   *pi'i~pi'ita*
      3SG.SBJ=RD~stay=3SG.IPFV SPEC[CLI]=NEG RD~rubbish
      na=inu.
      SPEC[CLI]=house
      'She lives in a clean (lit. not dirty) house.'
      (2-E004)

(116) *Aia de~de=a=na*   **na=ae**   *bua*
      3SG RD~take=3SG.OBJ=3SG.IPFV SPEC[CLI]=NEG full
      na=govi.
      SPEC[CLI]=bottle
      'He carried the empty (lit. not full) bottle.'
      (2-E004)

(117) **Na=orawi**   **na=ae**   *tubu e=nao*   *Buka.*
      SPEC[CLI]=man SPEC[CLI]=NEG fat 3SG.SBJ=go Buka
      'The thin (lit. not fat) man went to Buka.'
      (2-E004)

So far the examples show Class I and II nouns being modified, and not Personal nouns. Personal nouns are often modified by bare adjectives as in §4.6.2, but when an article is present, it is not the Personal article. Instead, there is a choice: *nau* ~ *nu=* indicates the referent is nearby or visible (118a) whereas *na=* indicates that the referent is far away or not visible (118b). This is similar to the use of the diminutive article *si=* for Class I nouns when they are proximal but *sau* when they are distal, and the use of *sau* for Class II nouns when they are proximal (see §5.3.4).

(118) a. **E-tubu-na**   *nu=tubu*   *e=nao*   *Buka.*
         PERS-grandparent-3SG.PSSR SPEC.CLII=fat 3SG.SBJ=go Buka
         'His fat grandmother (whom I saw) went to Buka'
         (2-E028-1)
      b. **E-tubu-na**   *na=tubu*   *e=nao*   *Buka.*
         PERS-grandparent-3SG.PSSR SPEC[CLI]=fat 3SG.SBJ=go Buka
         'His fat grandmother (whom I didn't see) went to Buka'
         (2-E028-1)

4.6.2 Bare adjectives

A small subclass of adjectives may behave in the way described in §4.6.1 and form APs, or they may directly precede or follow the head noun they modify, but without being marked by an article that agrees in noun class and/or number with the head noun and without being able to be marked by negative *ae* nor intensifiers. Compare (105) in §4.6.1 in which *kaka'i* 'small' is marked by an article, and (119) below where it is not. Such adjectives therefore do not form APs and they function only attributively, and not as predicates in verbless clauses (see §9.6.6), nor can they function alone in a NP when the head noun is elided (see §4.6.4).

The adjectives in this subclass describe dimension, age, value and colour (see Tables 4.5 and 4.6); these are the four core semantic types typically associated with adjective word classes (Dixon 2004: 3). In examples (119) and (120) the adjectives describe dimension, while (121) and (122) have lexicalised meanings.

(119) **Na=poana** kaka'i tagena Teperoi.
SPEC[CLI]=village small near Teperoi
'The small village is near Teperoi.'
(2-E004)

(120) **E-tama-na** sirorai e=nao Buka.
PERS-father-3SG.PSSR tall 3SG.SBJ=go Buka
'His tall father went to Buka.'
(2-E028-1)

(121) **Na=visio** mamanana na=maunu
SPEC[CLI]=body brown SPEC[CLI]=woman
i=atun=i=a=i. . .
3PL.SBJ=attack=3SG.OBJ=IRR
'The redskins attacked the woman. . .'[16]
(1-T034-00:22:41.626)

---

[16] Even though the adjective here is 'brown', the translation is 'redskin' because that is the Tok Pisin term referring to mainland Papua New Guineans.

(122) . . .*bau visio ge:rere* o=roroto=ina=i iai.
   PL body white 2SG.SBJ=see=3PL.OBJ=IRR PROX
   '. . .you'll see the white people.'
   (1-T107-00:02:36.300)

Like APs, bare adjectives can follow the head noun as in (119)–(122), or precede it (123)–(124).

(123) *Na=orawi   na=sirorai   ta **kokobunu sa=au***
   SPEC[CLI]=man SPEC[CLI]=tall and short DIM=CLII
   ***maunu** i=nao.*
   woman 3PL.SBJ=go
   'The tall man and the short woman went.'
   (2-E004)

(124) ***Sirorai** e-sina-na   e=nao   Buka.*
   tall PERS-mother-3SG.PSSR 3SG.SBJ=go Buka
   'Her tall mother went to Buka.'
   (2-E028-1)

4.6.3 Adjective *etawa* 'big' and augmentative *-eta ~ -ota*

The adjective *etawa* 'big' may be shortened to *eta* as (125) shows:

(125) a. *E-sina-u   kaka'i ta **e-tama-u**   etawa*
      PERS-mother-1SG.PSSR small and PERS-father-1SG.PSSR big
      i=nao.
      3PL.SBJ=go
      'My small mother and big father went.'
      (2-E004)
   b. *E-sina-u   kaka'i ta **e-tama-u**   eta*
      PERS-mother-1SG.PSSR small and PERS-father-1SG.PSSR big
      i=nao.
      3PL.SBJ=go
      'My small mother and big father went.'
      (2-E004)

The shortened form has developed into an augmentative suffix *-eta ~ -ota*. The alternate forms are a reflection of the phonological variation described in

§3.1.3. This suffix occurs frequently in the data and can modify all nouns, including Class I nouns (126), Class II nouns (127) and possessed nouns (128):

(126) *Na=naoi   e=pei   si'i~si'i=ena=i,*
      SPEC[CLI]=rain 3SG.SBJ=PST.IPFV RD~rain=3SG.IPFV=IRR
      na=naoi-eta.
      SPEC[CLI]=rain-AUG
      'The rain was falling, the heavy rain.'
      (1-T034-00:23:10.431)

(127) **Nu=api-ota**   *e=ara   no   tepe=a.*
      SPEC.CLII=bamboo-AUG 3SG.SBJ=PST go.SEQ cut=3SG.OBJ
      'He went and cut a big bamboo (plant/leaf).'
      (1-T026-00:01:53.50)

(128) **Ena=arao-eta**   *e=wa...*
      3SG.PSSR[CLI]=brother-AUG 3SG.SBJ=say
      'His elder brother said...'
      (1-T035-00:06:15.954)

Evidence for its status as a suffix comes from (129) in which the head noun is also modified by a demonstrative. The augmentative suffix precedes the demonstrative, whereas APs follow demonstrative modifiers (see (111) in §4.6.1).

(129) *E=to   nao te=na=novo,   **na=novo-ota**   enai...*
      3SG.SBJ=EMPH go   OBL=SPEC.CLI=reef SPEC[CLI]=reef-AUG DEM2
      'He went to the big, that big reef...'
      (1-T029-00:04:35.295)

4.6.4 Adjective phrases and elided nouns

As shown in (130)–(131), APs can function alone in a NP when the head noun is elided but anaphorically recoverable. Such APs do not have generic reference. The adjective is marked by an article agreeing in noun class and/or number with the elided, antecedent noun.

(130) **Na=mata**   i=va-tonu=a.
SPEC[CLI]=good   3PL.SBJ=CAUS-stand=3SG.OBJ
'They built a good one (hospital).'
(1-T034-00:38:08.180)

(131) E=to   taosi. **Sa=au**   kokobunu ora.
3SG.SBJ=EMPH   finish   DIM=CLII   short   only
'It's finished. It's just a short one (story).'
(1-T074-00:03:46.620)

If the antecedent noun is plural, the adjective is marked with *na=vei* or *ani vei*:

(132) **Na=vei**   sirorai o=atu=i   nasipuna.
SPEC[CLI]=COLL   long   2SG.SBJ=make=IRR   sometimes
'You make long ones (banana rolls) sometimes.'
(1-T036-8-00:02:37.900)

(133) **Enai ani   vei   kaka'i ora**   mi=roroto=ina...
DEM2   DIM.PL COLL small   only   1EXCL.SBJ=see=3PL.OBJ
'We saw those small ones (waves) only...'
(1-T105-00:20:08.020)

4.7 Miscellaneous postnominal modifiers

There is a small group of modifiers that do not belong to a coherent class but share the properties of functioning as nominal modifiers and occurring as the first postnominal element in the outer layer of the NP (see Table 4.1 and Table 4.2). Exhaustive *panapana* 'all' (§4.7.1), limiting *ora ~ ara* 'just/only' (§4.7.2) and intensifying *poto* and *mamangi* (§4.7.3) may also modify other nominal modifiers and quantifiers (as described below) and occur underived as adverbs in the VC (see §6.8.2). The Location noun intensifier *papanusu* (§4.7.4) and emphatic *tobi* (§4.7.5) function only as nominal modifiers. *Vowa ~ vewa* 'like' (§4.7.6) is polysemous and is also a directional morpheme in the VC and a serial verb (see §6.7.4 and §6.6) while *tomana* 'too' (§4.7.7) has grammaticalised as a nascent comitative postposition (see §8.3.4). The clitic *=re* denotes '(an)other' (§4.7.8) and also occurs as a discontinuous repetitive aspect marker with preverbal *vare ~ vae* (§7.1.7). None of these postnominal modifier forms can be nouns or adjectives and none (except *vowa ~ vewa*) can be verbs.

4.7.1 Exhaustive *panapana*

The exhaustive modifier *panapana* denotes 'all'. It is attested modifying independent pronouns (134), Class I nouns (135) and (136), and Location nouns (137). In a comparative construction (see §6.4.1), *panapana* can also modify the head noun in the object NP (the comparand) which gives a superlative interpretation (138). Example (5) in §4.1 shows that *panapana* precedes postnominal demonstratives.

(134) **Aina panapana** i=vaene   tae=a   na=namu.
       3PL   all   3PL.SBJ=climb up=3SG.OBJ   SPEC[CLI]=Malay.apple
       'They all climbed up the Malay apple tree.'
       (1-T022-00:01:07.630)

(135) . . .*na=vanua*   *panapana* i=naomai.
           SPEC[CLI]=people all   3PL.SBJ=come
           '. . .everybody came.'
           (1-T029-00:14:05.060)

(136) **Tauvasi ta'apena panapana** ini   o=sogo   vewa=ina=i.
       four   part   all   here   3SG.SBJ=push   be.like=3PL.OBJ=IRR
       'All four parts you push in here like (this).'
       (1-T027-2-00:02:55.860)

(137) *I=tua*   *i-ata*   *panapana.*
       3PL.SBJ=paddle   LOC-above   all
       'They went and paddled all the way out.'
       (1-T064-00:01:48.760)

(138) *Nu=kakau*   mama   e=kaka'i   mamangi=ina=na
       SPEC.CLII=dog DEM1   3SG.SBJ=small   INTS=3PL.OBJ=3SG.IPFV
       na=kakau   *panapana.*
       SPEC[CLI]=dog   all
       'This dog is much smaller than all dogs (i.e. this dog is the smallest of all).'
       (2-E005)

4.7.2 Limiting *ora ~ ara*

The limiting modifier *ora ~ ara* denotes 'just' or 'only'. The alternate forms are a reflection of the phonological variation described in §3.1.3. *Ora ~ ara* modifies an independent pronoun in (139) and a Class II noun in (140). In (141) it follows a numeral in a NP in which the head noun has been elided, while in (142) it modifies an elided noun in a partial NP that is the complement of a quantifier (see §5.6.3).

(139) *Enai* **aina ora** *i=pei* *agoto=ina=i* *bau atu*...
after 3PL only 3PL.SBJ=PST.IPFV hold=3PL.OBJ=IRR PL make
'Then only they would hold the ways...'
(1-T034-00:05:53.715)

(140) ***Nu='usia*** *ora e=toto.*
SPEC.CLII=child only 3SG.SBJ=live
'Only the child lived.'
(1-T029-00:02:37.640)

(141) ***Nu='aria*** *ora e=pei po~po=ena=i*
SPEC.CLII=one only 3SG.SBJ=PST.IPFV RD~stay=3SG.IPFV=IRR
o~'oema-na ***papanusu.***
RD~taro.garden-DER INTS
'There was only one (breadfruit tree) in the deep forest'
(1-T035-00:00:25.140)

(142) ***Na:=bau ora*** *i=pei nao=i, na:=bau aruai.*
some=PL only 3PL.SBJ=PST.IPFV go=IRR some=PL NEG
'Only some (people) would go, others wouldn't.'
(1-T105- 00:02:53.432)

4.7.3 Intensifiers *poto* and *mamangi*

There are only a few examples in my data of the intensifiers *poto* and *mamangi*. In the following examples, *poto* modifies Location nouns (143)–(144), a quantifier (145) and an adjective (146) while *mamangi* modifies a Class I noun denoting a period of the day (147), and a quantifier (148). Although *poto* therefore seems to have a wider distribution than *mamangi*, a speaker in elicitation session ESD3-E001 indicated that it was possible to use the two interchangeably in all the examples below. As other speakers later confirmed, the difference between *poto* and *mamangi* is that *mamangi* is stronger than *poto*, for example, *navanua a'aisi poto* denotes 'lots of people' whereas *navanua a'aisi mamangi* denotes 'lots and lots of people'. Similarly, *namata poto* means 'very good' whereas *namata mamangi* means 'extremely good'.

(143) *"Na=nganangana io'o **i-ata** **poto***
SPEC[CLI]=moon DIST LOC-above INTS
e=po~po=na ioi."
3SG.SBJ=RD~stay=3SG.IPFV DIST
'"The moon is over there at the very top."'
(1-T091-00:02:48.431)

(144) ***Va:sina poto,*** *sa=au maunu e=pei*
before INTS DIM=CLII woman 3SG.SBJ= PST.IPFV
ara po~po=na=i. . .
PST RD~stay=3SG.IPFV=IRR
'Long long ago, a young woman lived. . .'
(1-T003-00:00:31.890)

(145) *. . .na=vanua **a'aisi poto** i=pei*
SPEC[CLI]=people many INTS 3PL.SBJ=PST.IPFV
ara po=ina=i.
PST stay=3PL.IPFV=IRR
'Very many people stayed. . . [here in our village in the past].'
(1-T029-00:00:19.890)

(146) *Taramina mama **na=mata** **poto** iai.*
thing DEM1 SPEC[CLI]=good INTS PROX
'This thing was very good.'
(1-T022-00:00:55.750)

(147) *"Maisia **tuimatamata mamangi,** o=matono=i. . ."*
okay morning INTS 2SG.SBJ=wake=IRR
'"Okay early in the morning, wake up. . ."'
(1-T042-00:07:43.200)

(148) *. . .**na=kauto** **a'aisi mamangi***
SPEC[CLI]=Terminalia.Catappa many INTS
i=mangano i-ata.
3SG.SBJ=hang LOC-above
'. . .very many Terminalia Catappa nuts were hanging above.'
(1-T033-00:01:12.240)

4.7.4 Intensifier *papanusu*

The intensifier *papanusu* only modifies Location nouns and denotes 'deep' as in (149)–(151), or 'high' as in (152) (as explained in §6.7.1, movement away from the shoreline out to sea is conceived as 'up'):

(149) *Na:=bau i=pei no be~bete=ina=i*
some=PL 3PL.SBJ=PST.IPFV go.SEQ RD~sleep=3PL.IPFV=IRR
o~'oema-na papanusu.
RD~taro.garden-DER INTS
'Some were sleeping in the deep forest.'
(1-T103-00:04:59.900)

(150) . . .***i-namana papanusu*** *e=no de na=iana a'aisi.*
LOC-ocean INTS 3SG.SBJ=go.SEQ take SPEC[CLI]=fish many
'. . .he goes and catches lots of fish in the deep ocean.'
(1-T099-00:01:28.840)

(151) *E=to pu **i-bana** **papanusu** te=na=tatopu.*
3SG.SBJ=EMPH fall LOC-inside INTS OBL=SPEC.CLI=hole
'He fell deep inside in the hole.'
(2-E004)

(152) *Aia e=nao **i-ata** **papanusu** i-namana.*
3SG 3SG.SBJ=go LOC-above INTS LOC-ocean
'He went really far out on the ocean (lit. high above on the ocean).'
(2-E004)

4.7.5 Emphatic *tobi*

The emphatic modifier *tobi* most often modifiers independent pronouns (153) but may also modify Location nouns (154). The preverbal emphatic marker *to* may derive from *tobi* (see §6.3.3).

(153) ***Anau tobi*** *u=de=a=ma na=po mama.*
1SG EMPH 1SG.SBJ=take=3SG.OBJ=ma SPEC[CLI]=stay DEM1
'I myself took this position (of chief).'
(1-T079-00:00:42.730)

(154) *Va:sina aruai, bau sipunu merei* **i-poana** **tobi.**
 before NEG PL spoon ATTRIB LOC-village EMPH
 'In the past no, all the spoons were from the village itself.'
 (1-T102-00:01:54.531)

4.7.6 Associative *vowa ~ vewa*

The postnominal modifier *vowa ~ vewa* 'like' associates the head noun with something mentioned elsewhere in the discourse. The alternate forms *vowa* and *vewa* are a reflection of the phonological variation described in §3.1.3. *Vowa ~ vewa* 'like' most often modifies the Class I noun *taramina* 'thing' (155) but is also attested modifying other Class I and Class II nouns (156)–(157). The form *vowa ~ vewa* 'like' is also a postverbal allative directional in the VC (§6.7.4) and a serial verb denoting 'in the way of, be like' (see §6.6) which can occur with a PP headed by *avosia* (§8.3.3), with the interrogative term *avoa* 'how' (§9.3.2.3.4) or with a finite complement clause introduced by *avosia* (§10.4.1). Smith-Dennis (2018a) argues that these forms are heterosemous and have developed due to polygrammaticalisation of a Proto-Oceanic directional verb.

(155) **Taramina vewa** *e=pei* *ae ta~tavotu=ena=i.*
 thing like 3SG.SBJ=PST.IPFV NEG RD~arrive=3SG.IPFV=IRR
 'Something like this didn't use to happen.'
 (1-T040-00:00:34.500)

(156) **Enai bau kain orawi vewa** *u=pei*
 DEM2 PL kind man like 1SG.SBJ=PST.IPFV
 ta~tavone=ina=u.
 RD~help=3PL.OBJ=1SG.IPFV
 'I used to help the kinds of men like this.'
 (1-T088-00:15:12.600)

(157) *Aina i=varona* **na=au** **eva** **vowa** *e=naomai.*
 3PL 3PL.SBJ=know SPEC=CLII celebration like 3SG.SBJ=come
 'They know a celebration like (this) happens.'
 (1-T076-00:02:03.560)

4.7.7 Additive *tomana*

The additive marker *tomana* is postnominal in a NP and denotes 'too'. In the following examples *tomana* modifies an independent pronoun (158), a Class II noun (159)–(160), and an Absolute Location noun (161). Example (162) shows that *tomana* can co-occur with the emphatic modifier *tobi* in the NP while examples (115)–(116) in §8.3.4 demonstrate that *tomana* precedes preposition phrases and relative clauses. It is likely that the additive marker has grammaticalised as the comitative marker in Papapana, perhaps under the influence of the the Papuan language Rotokas (see §8.3.4).

(158) *"**Anau tomana** u=nao."*
 1SG too 1SG.SBJ=go
 '"I too am going."'
 (1-T074-00:02:02.480)

(159) ***Pei tovu tomana*** *e=ma'=i=a.*
 PART sugarcane too 3SG.SBJ=give=TR=3SG.OBJ
 'A piece of sugarcane too he gave her.'
 (1-T029-00:09:17.690)

(160) *"**Au=au 'usia tomana** e=eri me-na*
 1SG.PSSR=CLII child too 3SG.SBJ=OPT COM-PL.OBJ
 nao=amu=ena."
 go=2PL.OBJ=3SG.IPFV
 '"My son too wants to go with you."'
 (1-T042-00:02:30.240)

(161) *Ta **va:gi tomana**...*
 and now too
 'And today too...'
 (1-T098-00:04:12.962)

(162) *Avosia **anau tobi tomana**...*
 like 1SG EMPH too
 'Like I myself too...'
 (1-T097-00:13:33.639)

4.7.8 =re '(an)other'

In the VC, the preverbal repetitive aspect marker *vare ~ vae* (§7.1.7) may occur as a discontinuous morpheme with *vare ~ vae* occurring preverbally and the enclitic *=re* as the final postverbal element as in the VC in (165). The form *=re* can also cliticise to the head of a NP to denote '(an)other' as in (163)–(165), forming a phonological word with its host. In (163) *=re* attaches to the head noun, while in (164) it cliticises to a directly possessed noun marked by a possessor suffix. Without evidence showing its co-occurrence with other postnominal modifiers, it is assumed for now to occupy the same position in the NP as other miscellaneous modifiers, immediately after the head position.

(163) *Ta* **au=arao=re** *aruai.*
  and 1SG.PSSR[CLI]=brother=REP NEG
  'And I have no other brother.'
  (1-T034-00:32:31.856)

(164) **Na=vavine-u=re** *ini vowa e=pei*
  SPEC[CLI]=sibling-1SG.PSSR=REP here like 3SG.SBJ=PST.IPFV
  po~po=na=i...
  RD~stay=3SG.IPFV=IRR
  '[I came and stayed with]...my other cousin here where she was living.'
  (1-T042-00:09:47.190)

(165) **Na:=ata na=boni=re,**
  some=CLI SPEC[CLI]=day=REP
  mi=vae no gono mai=re na=kauto.
  1EXCL.SBJ=REP go.SEQ collect hither=REP SPEC[CLI]=Indian.almond
  'Another day, we went and picked Indian almonds again.'
  (1-T010-00:00:37.460)

4.8 Attributive PP with *merei*

The preposition *merei* is the head of a preposition phrase (PP) which follows the head noun it modifies and expresses the origin or purpose of the referent of the head noun. A PP with *merei* may be the predicate in a verbless clause (see §9.6.4). There is an allomorph *perei* which occurs infrequently in the data and was considered by speakers to be a feature of the speech of younger speakers (see §3.1.3). *Merei* can also have a quantifier phrase complement, though this only occurs once in my data (see §5.6.1). *Merei* may also function as a purposive subordinator (see §8.3 and §10.3).

When *merei* has a complement NP which consists of an underived nominal root, *merei* usually expresses the origin of the referent of the head noun. In (166) the underived nominal root is an Absolute Location noun while in (167) it is a case-marked Familiar Location noun and in (168) a deictic locational word. In (169) *merei* expresses the purpose of the referent of the head noun.

(166) *Nasipuna* **bau wokman merei Koikoi**
sometimes PL workman ATTRIB Koikoi
i=pei va-oto=ami nao=i.
3PL.SBJ=PST.IPFV CAUS-board=1EXCL.OBJ thither=IRR
'Sometimes the workmen from Koikoi gave us a lift.'
(1-T011-00:00:59.870)

(167) . . .***na=vu~vurau merei** i-tanana e=mei tu'u.*
SPEC[CLI]=RD~run ATTRIB LOC-road 3SG.SBJ=come.SEQ meet
'. . .a car from the road came and met (us).'
(1-T042-00:02:08.030)

(168) . . .***na='usia merei ini.** . . i-poana*
SPEC[CLI]=child ATTRIB here LOC-village
na=matau i=t=eri de=a=ina=i. . . .
SPEC[CLI]=knowledge 3PL.SBJ=EMPH=OPT take=3SG.OBJ=3PL.IPFV=IRR
'. . .the youth from here, in the village, want to gain knowledge. . .'
(1-T098-00:09:02.629)

(169) ***na=beke merei kavura***
SPEC[CLI]=bag ATTRIB copra
'the copra bag'
(2-E005)

When *merei* has a complement NP which consists of a noun zero-derived from a verb as its complement, it usually expresses purpose (170)–(172). In (172) a verb and its object noun have been nominalised.

(170) **Bau inu   merei   aputu,** bau haus   toirete,   i=atu
  PL   house ATTRIB sleep   PL   house toilet   3PL.SBJ=make
  tani=ina.
  already=3PL.OBJ
  'They had already made the sleeping houses (lit. the house for sleeping) and toilets.'
  (1-T002-214.010)

(171) *Iara* **ena=nganangana=ma   merei   burisi   e=to**
  then 3SG.PSSR[CLI]=month=ma ATTRIB give.birth 3SG.SBJ=EMPH
  naomai.
  come
  'Then her due date (lit. her month for giving birth) came.'
  (1-T029-00:02:24.061)

(172) **nu=kara   merei   atu   vonata**
  SPEC[CLI]=pandanus ATTRIB make bed
  'the pandanus for making beds'
  (2-E005)

Chapter 5
Noun class, number and possession

This chapter describes noun class (§5.1) and nominal number (§5.2). Except for Personal proper name nouns, Location nouns and a limited number of exceptions from other classes, all nouns occur in a noun phrase (NP) with either an article (§5.3), a numeral modifier (§5.4), or a possessor proclitic or suffix (§5.5). Nominal number can also be expressed by quantifiers (§5.6).

5.1 Noun class

Noun class in Papapana is not related to animacy, biological gender, physical shape or size, or sociocultural function, nor is there an individual/mass distinction between the classes or a formal basis for categorisation; however, noun class does have a semantic basis and it is possible to identify semantically associated groups of nouns that belong to each class. Loanwords such as *skuru* 'school' (from Tok Pisin) are subject to these semantic criteria and are assigned to noun classes accordingly. For some nouns of certain semantic classes, noun class is predictable, while for others it is not, as the following discussion exemplifies. Note that I use the term *noun class* since the term *gender* is often used for languages where there is a distinction between masculine and feminine entities (Aikhenvald 2000: 19) and Papapana does not make such a distinction. Furthermore, to maintain consistency and avoid confusion I use the term *noun class* even when discussing languages where the term *gender* is used in the literature.

There are four noun classes in Papapana: Personal (§5.1.1), Class I (§5.1.2), Class II (§5.1.3) and Location (§5.1.4). These reflect the *personal, common* and *local* noun classes found in Proto-Oceanic and many Oceanic subgroups. In Papapana, the Personal class has two subtypes; kinship terms and proper names. The Location class consists of terms referring to spatial and temporal location and has four subtypes; absolute, familiar, relational and lexicalised relational. Class I and Class II consist of common and abstract nouns from a range of semantic categories.

Table 5.1 presents a summary of the syntactic justification for these noun classes, which is discussed in further detail in §5.1.1–§5.1.4. Personal nouns can all be pluralised by the associative plural marker *nia* (see §5.2.2) but only kinship terms are marked by the article *e-*. Class I nouns are marked by the articles *na=*, *ta=* and *si=*, while Class II nouns are marked by the articles *nau ~ nu=*,

5.1 Noun class

Table 5.1: Noun classes.

	Article	Other	PP *te*
Personal Kinship	*e-*	nia	Yes
Personal Proper	Ø	nia	Yes
Class I	*na=, ta=, si=*	Possessor proclitic does not attach to Class II *au*	Yes
Class II	*nau ~ nu=, tau, sau*	Possessor proclitic can cliticse to Class II *au*	Yes
Location Absolute	Ø	No locative case prefix, not possessed	No
Location Familiar	Ø	Locative case prefix, not possessed	No
Location Relational	Ø	Locative case prefix, can be directly possessed	No
Location Lexicalised Relational	Ø	No locative case prefix, diachronically possessed	No

tau, and *sau* (portmanteau forms including the Class II marker *au*). When possessor proclitics modify a noun and there is no other prenominal modifier, the possessor proclitic cliticises to *au* for Class II nouns but directly to the noun if it belongs to Class I. Personal, Class I and Class II nouns can all be the complement of the preposition *te*. Location nouns do not have articles and they cannot occur in a preposition phrase (PP) headed by *te*. The subtypes are differentiated based on whether they can be marked by the locative case prefix *i-* and whether they can be directly possessed. Section 5.1.5 discusses a hybrid noun, nouns which are polysemous but belong to different noun classes, and nouns which do not belong to the expected noun class.

5.1.1 Personal nouns

All Personal nouns can be marked by the associative plural marker *nia* (1) which unifies the class as it does not occur with any other type of noun (see §5.2.2). All Personal nouns can be complements of the preposition *te* as in (2) (see §8.3.1.2).

(1) . . .*nia*   *e-sina-u*   *i=nao*
     ASSOC.PL PERS-mother-1SG.PSSR 3PL.SBJ=go
     te=na=bisiu.
     OBL=SPEC[CLI]=banana.garden
     '. . .my mother and companions went to the banana garden.'
     (1-T042-00:01:16.770)

(2) "*Anau te   ia'a u=nao~nao=u.*"
     1SG   OBL Mum 1SG.SBJ=RD~go=1SG.IPFV
     "'I'm going to Mum.'"
     (1-T031-00:09:30.360)

The Personal noun class can be divided into two subtypes (see Table 5.2). The first contains four kinship terms that refer to kin who are in the generation above the referent, and/or whom must be respected. The reciprocal term for a man's mother-in-law and a woman's son-in-law is included in this category since it is a cultural taboo for a woman's husband and mother to speak to or look at each other, or be in close proximity. These nouns can be marked with the specific article *e-* when singular as in (3) (see §5.3.1) and they are bound because they are always directly possessed. The second subtype consists of proper names, including two kinship terms of endearment: these nouns are never possessed and are never marked by the article *e-*, as in (2) and (4).

Table 5.2: Personal nouns.

Kinship terms: generation above, high status	
tubu	grandparent, parent-in-law (of a woman)
sina	mother, aunt
tama	father
noa	mother-in-law (of a man), son-in-law (of a woman)
Proper names	
Ebauka	Ebauka (male name)
Aunu	Aunu (female name)
aite	Dad
ia'a	Mum

(3) Enai=ma **e-sina-ina**   e=atunu=ina.
    after=ma PERS-mother-3SG.PSSR 3SG.SBJ=attack=3SG.OBJ
    'Then their mother attacked them.'
    (1-T007-00:01:10.140)

(4) Iara **Ebauka** e=vo'u=i=a   **Nabebe.**
    then Ebauka 3SG.SBJ=call=TR=3SG.OBJ Nabebe
    'Then Ebauka called Nabebe.'
    (2-T001-2-00:01:42.141)

Personal nouns in Papapana are not marked by a unique diminutive article but by the Class II diminutive article *sau ~ su=* (see §5.3.4) and when a Personal noun referent is nearby or visible, a modifying adjective may be marked by the Class II specific article *nau ~ nu=*, whereas when the referent is far away or not visible, the modifying article is marked by *na=* (see §4.6.1). This is similar to the use of the Class II diminutive article *sau* for Class II nouns when they are proximal (see §5.3.4). When pluralized, Personal nouns are marked by the plural article *bau* rather than inverse number marking (see §5.3.2) and are enumerated with *nua* 'two': similarly Class I nouns are enumerated with *nua* 'two' and are more often marked for plurality by *bau* than inverse number marking (see §5.3.2). Thus Personal nouns behave somewhat like Class II nouns and somewhat like Class I nouns: further research is required to determine whether Personal nouns are in fact variably assigned Class I and Class II membership, or whether the forms *nau ~ nu=* and *sau ~ su=* are syncretic between Class II and the Personal class when the noun is singular.

The Personal noun class in Papapana resembles the typical Oceanic *personal* noun class which includes personal proper names and sometimes kinship terms denoting particular individuals (Lynch, Ross, and Crowley 2002: 37) and thus in keeping with the literature on Oceanic languages, I name this noun class in Papapana *Personal*. Papapana demonstrates a minor reduction in the semantic scope of the personal class from Proto-Oceanic since only four kinship terms are included. Indeed, the kinship term *vavine* 'cross sex sibling/cousin' belongs in Class I in Papapana, whereas its cognate *fafine* 'cross sex sibling' in Taiof belongs in the personal class (Ross 2002b: 428). Across the Northwest Solomonic group there have been diverse changes in the semantic scope of the personal class from POc; for example, Kubokota's personal class contains only personal names and the interrogative pronoun (Chambers 2009) while Teop's I-E noun class consists of proper names of persons, some kinship terms, people who have a particular social status, and pets (Mosel and Spriggs 1999a, Mosel and Thiesen 2007).

5.1.2 Class I nouns

Class I nouns can be marked by the specific article *na=* (5), the non-specific article *ta=* (6), or the diminutive article *si=* (7) (see §5.3.1, §5.3.3 and §5.3.4). In the absence of an article, the possessor proclitics (8) and numeral modifiers 'one' (9) and 'two' (10) are not marked when they modify a Class I noun (see §5.5.2 and §5.4.2). All Class I nouns can head NPs which are complements of the preposition *te* (11) (see §8.3.1.3).

(5) **Na=orawi**   e=ara   naomai. . .
SPEC[CLI]=man   3SG.SBJ=PST   come
'A man came. . .'
(1-T065-00:00:23.470)

(6) "**Ta=maunu**   o=to   muni=a=mu?"
NSPEC[CLI]=woman   2SG.SBJ   hide=3SG.OBJ=2SG.IPFV
"'Are you hiding a woman?'"
(1-T029-00:21:14.460)

(7) **Si=daramu**   e=to   no   amun=i=a.
DIM.CLI=river   3SG.SBJ=EMPH   go.SEQ   look=TR=3SG.OBJ
'He saw a stream.'
(1-T012-00:02:07.513)

(8) **Ami=vamamatau**   na=orawi   e=wa=ami. . .
1EXCL.PSSR[CL1]=teach   SPEC[CLI]=man   3SG.SBJ=say=1EXCL.OBJ
'Our teacher, a man, said to us. . .'
(1-T042-00:04:50.200)

(9) Mi=to   no   po   **na='aria**   wik
1EXCL.SBJ=EMPH   go.SEQ   stay   SPEC[CLI]=one   week
te=na='uru.
OBL=SPEC[CLI]=island
'We went and stayed on the island for one week.'
(1-T103-00:10:29.671)

(10) "**Nua**   matuana   i=to   oa~oa=ina."
two[CLI]   spirit   3PL.SBJ=EMPH   RD~cry=3PL.IPFV
"'Two spirits are crying.'"
(1-T026-00:03:22.280)

(11) *Te=**na**=perete*   *te=na=au*   *daramu*   *e=to*
OBL=SPEC[CLI]=plate   OBL=SPEC=CLII   water   3SG.SBJ=EMPH
ruvu=i=a.
put=TR=3SG.OBJ
'He put it on the plate in the water.'
(1-T073-00:00:57.900)

The Class I noun class in Papapana comprises collective and partitive nominals; nouns denoting celestial bodies, units of time and periods of the day; meterological phenomena and natural forces; locations and landmarks; spiritual beings and certain humans; kinship terms that refer to kin who are in the same generation as the referent or have been acquired through marriage; fish and other marine vertebrates; fruit and nuts; and prepared food. The hypernyms *iana* 'fish' and *vua* 'fruit' also belong in Class I. Some nouns denoting plant parts, geological entities and objects (made from plants or other materials), and some abstract nouns belong to Class I, while others belong to Class II but noun class assignment is arbitrary and has no apparent phonological or semantic basis. Table 5.3 shows examples of nouns in Class I.

Table 5.3: Examples of Class I nouns.

Collective and partitive nominals	
gumu	group (human)
pei	part/piece
Celestial bodies, unit of time and periods of the day[17]	
nganangana	moon/month
kirok	o'clock
na:ni	day
Meterological phenomena and natural forces	
naoi	rain
magaru	earthquake

---

[17] Some of the nouns referring to time are loans from Tok Pisin, as are the names of weekdays and months. Similarly, clock time can be expressed using the Tok Pisin loan *kirok* 'o'clock' but telling the time is not very important in Papapana culture, especially as many speakers do not have clocks/watches!

Table 5.3 (continued)

Locations and landmarks	
sigasiga	hill
'uru	island
nongana	beach
vuna	coast
ava	sea
daramu	river
poana	village

Spritual beings, generic human terms, people with particular social status	
toituna	God, chief
atamata	friend

Kinship terms: same generation, acquired through marriage	
arao	same sex male sibling/cousin
vanisi	father-in-law (of a man), son-in-law (of a man)

Marine vertebrates	
pano	trevally species
bukau	dolphin

Fruit and nuts and prepared food	
mamioke	papaya fruit
ingani	Canarium Indicum nut
menaga	bananas boiled, mashed, rolled, baked in coconut cream

Some plant parts	
nana	big branch
'epita	stick
agana	root

Some geological entities	
kavururu	earth, soil, ground
watu	stone

Some objects: made from plants or other materials	
tange	boat, ship
bero	bell
mata	door
kabekabe	bag (of any kind)
'ave	woven bag
avutu	leaf bundle

Table 5.3 (continued)

vutunu	bow (bamboo)
anini	arrow (sago)
tora:ra	axe
petata	tray/basket (woven leaves)
Some abstract	
matau	knowledge
'ire	anger

Papapana's Class I resembles Teop's I-A class which also includes landmarks, fruit and nuts, and things not made from plant materials (Mosel and Spriggs 1999a, Mosel and Thiesen 2007), and therefore I label this noun class *Class I* in Papapana.

5.1.3 Class II nouns

Class II nouns can be marked by the specific article *nau ~ nu* (12), the non-specific article *tau* (13) or the diminutive article *sau* (14) (see §5.3.1, §5.3.3 and §5.3.4). As discussed in §5.3 these articles can be analysed as portmanteau forms consisting of *na=*, *ta=* or *sa=* and the Class II marker *au*. In the absence of an article, the possessor proclitics (15) and numeral modifiers 'one' (16) and 'two' (17) are also marked by *au* when they modify a Class II noun (see §5.5.2 and §5.4.2). All Class II nouns can head NPs which are complements of the preposition *te* (18) (see §8.3.1.3).

(12) *O=dari=a=i*   *eangoiena* **na=au**   **dada**
       2SG.SBJ=rub=3SG.OBJ=IRR until   SPEC=CLII coconut.milk
       e=to   *taosi.*
       3SG.SBJ=EMPH   finish
       'You rub it until the coconut milk is done.'
       (1-T036-9-00:01:24.920)

(13) *"Maisia si=atu=a=i* **ta=au** *obutu-eta."*
okay 1INCL.SBJ=make=3SG.OBJ=IRR NSPEC=CLII canoe-AUG
'"Okay let's make a big canoe."'
(1-T101-00:09:05.489)

(14) *U=eri roros=i=a=u* **sa=au**
1SG.SBJ=OPT see=TR=3SG.OBJ=1SG.IPFV DIM=CLII
tubu-u.
grandparent-1SG.PSSR
'I wanted to see my dear grandmother.'
(1-T088-00:44:14.750)

(15) **"*Ami=au*** *'usia e=eri nai=a=na*
1EXCL.PSSR=CLII child 3SG.SBJ=OPT marry=3SG.OBJ=3SG.IPFV
na=maunu mama."
SPEC[CLI]=woman DEM1
'"Our child wants to marry this woman."'
(1-T024-00:00:46.499)

(16) ***nu='aria=au*** *marei*
SPEC.CLII=two=CLII bird
'two birds'
(2-E023)

(17) *. . .u=vare agoto=ina* **nua=au** **nima-na**.
1SG.SBJ=REP hold=3PL.OBJ two=CLII arm-3SG.PSSR
'. . .I again held its two arms.'
(1-T106-00:01:22.180)

(18) *Te=na=perete te=na=au daramu e=to*
OBL=SPEC[CLI]=plate OBL=SPEC=CLII water 3SG.SBJ=EMPH
ruvu=i=a.
put=TR=3SG.OBJ
'He put it on the plate in the water.'
(1-T073-00:00:57.900)

Class II noun class in Papapana consists of nouns denoting liquids, light and fire; kinship terms that refer to kin who are in the generation below the referent; body parts and bodily products; birds; land-dwelling vertebrates; insects; marine invertebrates including shells; and plants including seaweeds. The hypernyms

5.1 Noun class

marei 'bird' and *nauno* 'tree' also belong in Class II. Some nouns denoting plant parts, geological entities, objects made from plant materials, and some abstract nouns belong to Class II while others belong to Class I. Table 5.4 shows examples of the nouns in Class II.

Table 5.4: Examples of Class II nouns.

Liquids, light and fire	
iruvu	soup
tura	fire
watu	smoke
Kinship terms: generation below	
'usia	child, fraternal niece/nephew (of a woman)
adope	grandchild, daughter-in-law
Body parts and bodily products	
patu	head
vunu	hair
mimi	urine
Birds (vertebrate)	
vevevata	eagle
toa	chicken
Land vertebrates	
kakau	dog
'oru	snake
Insects (invertebrate)	
kikiriri	cicada
beibei	butterfly
Marine invertebrates and shells	
karavona	lobster
'urita	octopus
nare	coral
bokoboko	serpent's head cowrie shell
Plants and seaweed	
mamioke	papaya tree
ingani	Canarium Indicum tree
momo	kind of seaweed

Table 5.4 (continued)

Some plant parts	
naunu	leaf
vuni	trunk
peoga	small branch
Some geological entities	
vuno	volcanic sand
mero'o	mud
Some objects: made from plants	
obutu	canoe
putepute	fan (leaf, woven)
makarei	spear (fishing, wooden)
si'ini	spear (any kind)
totopi	bow (sago)
pako	war club
vonata	mat
'a'u	tall wooden pestle and mortar
Some abstract	
matautu	fear
nai	marriage
mate	death
tue	language
atuatu	custom
'a'ade'e	narrative

Papapana's Class II resembles Teop's II class which also includes light and fire, plants, plant parts other than fruit, things made from plant materials and some kinship terms (Mosel and Thiesen 2007) and Taiof's Class II which contains nouns denoting plants, objects made from wood and non-count nouns (Ross 2002b): accordingly, I have labelled this noun class *Class II* in Papapana.

5.1.4 Location nouns

The Location noun class in Papapana reflects the typical Oceanic *local* noun class consisting of nouns referring to "a specific location, a time, or an intrinsically located part of something" (Ross 2007a: 232) including institutionalised place names, nouns denoting familiar places in the environment such as 'home' and 'village', and directly suffixed locative part nouns such as 'inside' (Lynch, Ross, and Crowley 2002: 37). As examples (19)–(23) below show, Location nouns are not marked by articles in Papapana and indeed in Oceanic languages "NPs with ... locative/temporal reference generally do not appear with any article" (Lynch, Ross, and Crowley 2002: 38). NPs with Location nouns as the head cannot occur in a PP with *te* but function instead as adjuncts as in (19)–(22) below (see also §8.1.2).

There are four subtypes of location nouns, shown in Table 5.5: (i) Absolute Location, (ii) Familiar Location, (iii) Relational Location and (iv) lexicalised Relational Location. As will be discussed further below, only Familiar Location and Relational Location nouns are marked by the locative case prefix *i-*, which is a reflex of the POc preposition *i* used with local NPs that did not have articles (Ross 2007b: 284). No other prenominal modifier may intervene between *i-* and the noun in Papapana and *i-* forms a phonological word with the noun it marks, thus I analyse it as a prefix.

Table 5.5: Location nouns.

Absolute	
Marasi	Maras
o'oemana	bush
nasinaina	day before yesterday
naonava	yesterday
va:gi	now, today
natui	tomorrow
va:sina	before, past
mumurina	future
nani'ira	sunrise
nasipuna	sometimes
Familiar	
inu	house
tanana	road
poana	village
nongana	beach
ava	sea
namana	ocean
daramu	river
nganisi	sky

Table 5.5 (continued)

abata	bachelor house
navi	afternoon
naviboni	evening
boni	night
Relational	
ata	above
vuna	below/coast
bana	inside
ota	outside
butona	middle
muri	behind
mata	in front
Body parts, e.g. *patu*	head
Lexicalised Relational	
obetena	under
gegetena	next to
tagena / tage-	near

Absolute Location nouns do not occur with the locative case prefix *i-* and they are never possessed (19)–(20). Some are attested with modifiers such as *ora ~ ara* 'only' and the intensifier *poto* (20), which can modify other nouns (see §4.7.2–4.7.3). Absolute Location nouns include all proper place names and the noun *o'oemana* 'bush'. It is quite common in Oceanic languages for words denoting important locations such as 'bush' to behave differently to other local nouns. As Table 5.5 shows, the Absolute Location class also include six nouns that refer to time relative to the point of speaking, one that refers to a period of the day and one that refers to frequency. *Mumurina* 'future' appears to be derived through monosyllabic reduplication and the derivational suffix *-na* from the Familiar Location noun *muri* 'behind'.

(19) *Iai=ma   si=nao   dini   nao   **Manetai**=ma.*
     PROX=ma 1INCL.SBJ=go down thither Manetai=ma
     'Then we went down to Manetai.'
     (1-T002-00:02:58.630)

(20) ***Va:sina poto,*** sa=au maunu e=pei ara
before INTS DIM=CLII woman 3SG.SBJ=PST.IPFV PST
po~po=na=i...
RD~stay=3SG.IPFV=IRR
'Long long ago, a young woman lived...'
(1-T003-00:00:31.890)

The subtype of Familiar Location nouns comprises the exhaustive list of nouns in Table 5.5 that express familiar geographic locations and periods of the day; these are marked by the locative case prefix *i-* but they are never directly possessed:

(21) Tau ***i-ava*** mi=de~de=a=mani mama.
and OBL=sea 1EXCL.SBJ=RD~take=3SG.OBJ=1EXCL.IPFV DEM1
'And we got it from the sea.'
(1-T107-00:01:04.200)

Relational Location nouns refer to "a part of the reference object or to a location in relation to the reference object" (Ross 2007a: 230) and the group comprises the seven nouns listed in Table 5.5, as well as body parts. Relational Location nouns are marked by the locative case prefix *i-* (22)–(23) and they can be directly possessed (23).

(22) I=to naovo=ina=i ***i-ata...***
3PL.SBJ=EMPH fly=3PL.OBJ=IRR LOC-above
'They flew them above...'
(1-T034-00:29:00.380)

(23) O=no sapo=a ***i-ata-na*** na=inu.
2SG.SBJ=go.SEQ clean=3SG.OBJ LOC-above-3SG.PSSR SPEC[CLI]=house
'Go and clean the top of the house.'
(2-E029-1)

The group of lexicalised Relational Location nouns comprises three invariant terms which obligatorily take a PP complement headed by *te* as in (24)–(25) or NP complement headed by another Location noun as in (26). The three lexicalised Relational Location nouns are not marked by the locative case prefix *i-*. The form *tage-* can be directly possessed with different person and number possessor suffixes as in (27) and (28). Example (27) shows *tage-* with a 1SG possessor suffix, and this contrasts with (24) in which *tagena* has a PP complement consisting of the preposition *te* and the 1SG independent pronoun *anau*. The behaviour of *tage-* suggests that the forms *obetena*, *gegetena*, and *tagena* may be diachronically divisible into a root and the 3SG possessor suffix *-na*. Indeed, in Longgu (Southeast Solomonic), *gege-* denotes 'next to' (Hill and Goddard 1997: 265) and it is likely cognate with Papapana *gegetena*. Synchronically, *obetena*, *gegetena*, and *tagena* are monomorphemic but the process of lexicalisation from directly possessed Relational Location nouns to complement-taking lexicalised Relational Location nouns is not entirely complete with *tage-* as it occurs both lexicalised with *-na* and a complement and in its unlexicalised form with direct possessor suffixes. Note that *tage* is also a monotransitive verb denoting 'approach' (see §6.6.2) but it is unclear whether the noun derives from the verb or vice-versa.

(24) *Aia e=tonu=ena* ***tagena** te anau.*
 3SG 3SG.SBJ=stand=3SG.IPFV near OBL 1SG
 'He is standing next to me.'
 (2-E026)

(25) *U=aputu* ***obetena** te=na=vuni kauto.*
 1SG.SBJ=sleep under OBL=SPEC[CLI]=trunk terminalia.catappa
 'I slept under the Terminalia catappa tree.'
 (1-T033-00:00:51.630)

(26) *. . .e=pei bio~bio=na nao=i **obetena**
 i-inu.*
 3SG.SBJ=PST.IPFV RD~sweep=3SG.IPFV thither=IRR under
 LOC-house
 '. . .she was sweeping under the house.'
 (1-T067-00:00:51.800)

(27) *E=to noe=ina na=koko'i **tage-u.***
 3SG.SBJ=EMPH put=3PL.OBJ SPEC[CLI]=taro near-1SG.PSSR
 'He put the taros near me.'
 (2-E019)

(28) *U=mate=i=a=au enai na=bara
 mama **tage-mu.***
 1SG.SBJ=like=TR=3SG.OBJ=1SG.IPFV DEM2 SPEC[CLI]=ball
 DEM1 near-2SG.PSSR
 'I like that ball next to you.'
 (Fieldnotes 16/04/13)

5.1.5 Noun class assignment: flexibility and irregularity

In Papapana every noun is assigned to a particular noun class. The only case of a *hybrid* noun, that is, a noun that can take agreement in more than one class and whose agreement form depends on the type of target involved (Corbett 1991: 183), is the semantically empty noun *maria*: when *maria* is marked by the Personal specific article it denotes 'what's-their-name', with the Class I and II specific articles it denotes 'what's-it-called' and with the locative case prefix *i-*, it denotes 'where's-it-called'. The speaker often recalls the noun they had forgotten and this follows *maria*, as in (29)–(32).

(29) *A:mani=ma **e-maria**, Glen Tovirika, e=to sare=ami.*
 1EXCL=ma PERS-thing Glen Tovirika 3SG.SBJ send=1EXCL.OBJ
 'What's-their-name, Glen Tovirika, sent us.'
 (1-T034-00:30:21.680)

(30) *E=garu **na=maria**, na=bareo.*
 3SG.SBJ=harvest SPEC[CLI]=thing SPEC[CLI]=breadfruit
 'He harvested what's-it-called, breadfruit.'
 (1-T035-00:07:12.388)

(31) ***Nu=maria**, nu=tura e=amun-i=a.*
 SPEC.CLII=thing SPEC.CLII=fire 3SG.SBJ=look=TR=3SG.OBJ
 'He saw the what's-it-called, the fire.'
 (1-T012-00:00:39.300)

(32) *Mi=pei orete ora nao=i **i-maria**, Vakonaia.*
 1EXCL.SBJ=PST.IPFV walk only thither=IRR LOC-thing Wakunai
 'We used to just walk to where's-it-called, Wakunai.'
 (1-T011-00:00:42.820)

Papapana also exhibits a very interesting pattern observed elsewhere in Northwest Solomonic languages such as Teop (Mosel and Sprigss 1999a, Mosel and Thiesen 2007) where two words that have the same phonological form, but a different, though related, meaning can belong to different noun classes. As Tables 5.3 and 5.4 show, nouns denoting the names of plants belong to Class II, whereas the names of their fruit or nuts belong to Class I: for example *mamioke* as a Class II noun denotes 'papaya tree' but as Class I it denotes 'papaya fruit'. Similarly, the lexeme *daramu* denotes 'river' in Class I but 'water' in Class II, and *mata* denotes 'door' in Class I but 'eye' in Class II ('door' might be understood as related to 'eye' if one thinks of a door as the eye of a house and indeed it is common in Northwest Solomonic languages for the lexeme denoting 'eye' to also denote 'doorway').

As Tables 5.3 and 5.5 show, some nouns referring to spatial location, and the noun *boni,* which refers to temporal location, can be either a Familiar Location noun or a Class I noun. When the noun *boni* is a Familiar Location noun it denotes 'night' whereas when it is a Class I noun it denotes 'twenty-four hours' or it can be modified by the augmentative suffix to denote 'midnight'. When nouns that denote spatial locations are Familiar Location nouns, the referent is a home or familiar location in the local environment which is identifiable to the speaker and addressee (33), whereas when such nouns are Class I nouns, the referent is a general location (34). This is a common distinction in Oceanic languages (Ross 2007a: 234; Ross 2007b: 283). Familiar Location nouns typically function as adjunct NPs (33) whereas Class I nouns can be the complement of prepositions in oblique adjuncts (34) or function as core arguments (35) and can be further modified, such as by a relative clause (35). Similarly, body parts are usually Class II nouns, but can be Relational Location nouns when they function as adjuncts expressing spatial orientation (see §8.1.2.3).

(33) *Na:=bau i=pei ubete=ina=i **i-tanana**. . .*
some=PL 3PL.SBJ=PST.IPFV lay=3PL.IPFV=IRR LOC-road
'Some were lying on the road. . .'
(1-T002-00:04:51.530)

(34) *Avosia a:mani mi=pei ta'opo=ina=i **tena**
bau tanana.*
SUBR 1EXCL 1EXCL.SBJ=PST.IPFV hide=3PL.OBJ=IRR OBL
PL road
'So we used to hide from them on the roads.'
(1-T034-00:28:14.155)

(35) *Mi=atutusi=a **na=tanana** mama
e=pei vori~vori=i=a=ena=i.*
1EXCL.SBJ=chase=3SG.OBJ SPEC[CLI]=road REL
3SG.SBJ=PST.IPFV RD~talk=TR=3SG.OBJ=3SG.IPFV=IRR
'We followed the road she used to talk about.'
(1-T042-00:04:34.500)

As with many noun class systems, there are some nouns in Papapana which do not belong to the expected noun class. There are a few nouns in Class I that belong to a semantic category overwhelmingly represented by Class II: these include four of the forty-five body part terms elicited during my fieldwork, *u'u* 'finger', *ingani* 'kidney', *iminio* 'vein' and *vuri* 'egg', and two of the twenty-three shell names elicited, *tuvini* 'Triton trumpet' and *'oro* 'Triton trumpet species'. Of the forty-two fish names elicited, two belong in Class II, *tanoana* 'salted fish' and *oini'a* 'convict surgeon fish', while the marine vertebrate *mono* 'turtle' also belongs in Class II. It is possible to offer explanations for only some of these exceptions. It is feasible that since eggs are a food source, this motivates their unexpected class membership since food belongs in Class I, while the Triton trumpet shell is a culturally important item used as a horn, thus the assignment to Class I might mark that property (see Dixon 1968: 120). Speakers were unsure of the motivations for the other body parts, fish and marine animals not belonging to the expected noun class.

For abstract nouns and nouns belonging to the semantic classes of plant parts, objects made from plant parts and geological entities, noun class is unpredictable. Furthermore, the distribution is equal across noun classes so that it is not even possible to say that a particular class contains nouns belonging to a particular semantic category with a few exceptions. The reason for this irregularity could lie in the origin of the nouns, which may have entered Papapana from varying source languages, or it could be attributable to the language death process.

5.2 Number

Number is not marked inflectionally on nouns in Papapana, which is typical of Oceanic languages (Lynch, Ross, and Crowley 2002: 37). Instead, nominal number is expressed through articles (§5.3), numerals (§5.4) and quantifiers (§5.6), and is reflected in subject and object agreement in the verb complex (VC). Before describing these strategies, this section describes other ways in which nominal number can be expressed in Papapana: lexical plurals (§5.2.1), the associative plural marker *nia* which only marks Personal nouns (§5.2.2), and reduplication, which seems to mark nominal pluralisation in some cases, but is not a productive process (§5.2.3).

5.2.1 Lexical plurals

In most Meso-Melanesian languages, particular referents may have distinct singular and plural forms (Palmer 2012: 448). In Papapana there are only two attested lexical plurals and both reference important human terms. In (36) *orawi* 'man' (36a) is not pluralised by the plural article *bau*, but by a suppletive plural form *vanua* (36b), which also denotes 'people' (36c): while *orawi* triggers singular subject-indexing in the VC, *vanua* triggers plural subject-indexing. In (37) the singular and plural forms *maunu* 'woman' and *burimaunu* 'women' are clearly related, but the singular form is marked by the Class I article *na=*. Instead of using the plural article *bau*, *buri* is used. Again the grammatical number of the head nouns triggers singular and plural subject-indexing in the VC in (37a) and (37b) respectively. Since *buri* denotes 'many' and *maru* 'women' in Uruava (Palmer 2007d), it is likely that *burimaunu* is diachronically divisible in Papapana; however, synchronically it is monomorphemic and *buri* is not a productive morpheme. In fact, there are even some occurrences in the text data of *burimaunu* where it is marked by the plural article *bau* and even one occurrence where it is marked by the Class I article *na=*, showing that it truly is synchronically monomorphemic.

(36) a. **Na=orawi**   e=ara   naomai. . .
        SPEC[CLI]=man 3SG.SBJ=PST come
        'A man came. . .'
        (1-T065-00:00:23.470)
    b. Enai **na=vanua**   i=to   tua   tae.
        then SPEC[CLI]=people 3PL.SBJ=EMPH paddle up
        'Then the men paddled out.'
        (1-T101-00:12:29.475)
    c. **Na=vanua**   i=nao=i   i-ava.
        SPEC[CLI]=people 3PL.SBJ=go=IRR LOC-sea
        'People would go to sea.'
        (1-T077-00:01:57.360)

(37) a. **Na=maunu**   e=mate   nani.
        SPEC[CLI]=woman 3SG.SBJ=die there
        'The woman died there.'
        (1-T029-00:02:35.436)
    b. Iara **burimaunu** i=tua   tae.
        then women   3PL.SBJ=paddle up
        'Then the women paddle out.'
        (1-T020-00:02:46.430)

5.2.2 Associative plural *nia*

Nia is a morpheme which only marks Personal nouns and has an associative meaning, denoting a group of individuals who are associated with the named referent: in (38) the named referent is referred to with a Personal proper name while in (39) the named referent is referred to with a directly possessed Personal kinship term, and plural number is reflected in the 3PL subject-indexing in the VC.[18]

(38) *Nasinaina   nu=kakau   u=to de=a   te*
day.before.yesterday SPEC.CLII=dog 1SG   take=3SG.OBJ OBL
nia   Anita.
ASSOC.PL Anita
'The day before yesterday I got the dog from Anita and companions.'
(1-T106- 00:00:18.500)

(39) *. . .**nia**   e-sina-u   i=nao*
ASSOC.PL PERS-mother-1SG.PSSR 3PL.SBJ=go
te=na=bisiu.
OBL=SPEC[CLI]=banana.garden
'. . .my mother and companions went to the banana garden.'
(1-T042-00:01:16.770)

In (40) *nia* marks two directly possessed Personal kinship nouns, while in (41) and (42) Personal nouns are conjoined by a coordinator and 3DU independent pronoun respectively (see §10.1.1.2 and §10.1.1.3 for phrase coordination). The associative meaning is less explicit in these translations but nonetheless *nia* still marks these coordinated NPs as plural and still refers to a group of individuals, as evidenced by the plural subject or object-indexing clitics in the VC.

(40) "*Anau **nia**   e-sina-u   e-tama-u*
1SG   ASSOC.PL PERS-mother-1SG.PSSR PERS-father-1SG.PSSR
i=ara   asi=au. . ."
3PL=PST leave=1SG.OBJ
"'My mother and father left me. . ."'
(1-T003-00:01:03.550)

---

18 Although not strictly a number value or category of number (see Corbett 2000: 101–111 for a discussion of differences between associatives and number), I describe *nia* here as it is used exclusively with Personal nouns and thus unifies the class, and it is necessary to contrast it with articles and quantifiers, also discussed in this chapter.

(41) ...iara e=va-tavotu=**ina** nia **Aunu, Siopaimasi**
 then 3SG.SBJ=CAUS-arrive=3PL.OBJ ASSOC.PL Aunu Siopaimasi
 tau Abea.
 and Abea
 '...then she gave birth to Aunu, Siopamasi and Abea.'
 (2-T001-2-00:02:40.793)

(42) ...*nia aite auana ia'a* mi=to ari=**ina.**
 ASSOC.PL Dad 3DU Mum 1EXCL.SBJ dig=3PL.OBJ
 '...we had buried Dad and Mum.'
 (1-T030-00:03:12.127)

The distribution of *nia* is unlike other prenominal modifiers. Although specific articles, non-specific articles, singular diminutive articles and non-singular articles have different syntactic positions (see Table 5.7), they do not co-occur, so if *nia* were an article, it would not co-occur with the Personal article *e-*. Instead, I considered whether *e-* is actually a class marker, and that *nia* could be a dedicated Personal class plural article; however, then one might expect that if *nia* and *e-* co-occur, the plural article *bau* and *e-* should also be able to co-occur, but that is not the case. Instead *bau* and *e-* are mutually exclusive. Like quantifiers, *nia* precedes articles; however, *nia* differs from quantifiers as it cannot function independently, and it does not fit with the semantic definition of quantifiers as a class that gives a relative or indefinite indication of quantity (see §5.6). It seems most likely that *nia* derives from a 3PL pronoun and that the following NPs are complements of this pronoun. Some Meso-Melanesian languages without overt plural markers pluralise NPs periphrastically in this way, giving the pronoun the appearance of a plural article, especially in languages where this plural pronoun does not occur with an article (Palmer 2012: 449). Example (43) from Kubokota (which does mark the complement NP with an article) demonstrates the use of a pronominal head to mark plurality.

(43) **Kubokota**[19]
 ria na tinoni paleka=di
 3PL DET people wound=3PL.POS
 'the wounded people'
 (Chambers 2009: 62)

---

[19] Chambers' abbreviations in interlinear glosses follow the Leipzig glossing rules except POS 'possessive pronoun'.

The pronominal /ria/ is a reflex of the Proto-Western Oceanic (PWO) 3PL pronoun *idri[a]* (Ross 1988: 385) and given that Kubokota /r/ and Papapana /n/ are sound correspondences that are reflexes of POc *r* (Ross 1988: 220), it is likely that *nia* is related to *ria*.

5.2.3 Reduplication

As in many Meso-Melanesian languages (Palmer 2012: 453), the one morphological strategy Papapana does seem to employ to mark nominal pluralisation involves disyllabic reduplication, and this is reflected in the 3PL subject-indexing in the VC if the nominal is subject or primary object. However, this is not a productive process and (except examples (46a) and (47a)) the NP contains other modifiers which mark plurality: the plural collective article *mamena* (44), the postnominal modifier *panapana* 'all' (45) or the plural article *bau* as in (46b) and (47b). Note that *mamena* also marks augmented dyadic nouns, which have been derived by disyllabic reduplication of a kinship noun and the derivational suffix *-na* (see §4.3.3.2). Interestingly, in (46a) the singular noun is derived by monosyllabic reduplication from a verb, while in (46b) disyllabic reduplication derives the plural noun from the verb. In (47a) the augmentative suffix attaches to the reduplicated noun to give a lexicalised meaning 'chief/elder' and this noun occurs twice as frequently without any further marker of plurality as in (47a), than it does with one. In (47b) the noun is marked by the plural article *bau* and the NP is the complement of the quantifier *na:bau* 'some'.

(44) a. ***I**=vei   vare atu   ma'ata=i   **mamena natu~natu.***
        3PL.SBJ=R/R REP make be.heated=IRR PL.COLL   RD~clan
        'All the clans would cook together again.'
        (1-T072-00:02:42.730)
    b. ***Mamena boni~boni,** i-ava   e=nao=i.*
        PL.COLL RD~day   LOC-sea   3SG.SBJ=go=IRR
        'Every day, he would go to sea.'
        (1-T026-00:00:47.740)

(45) ***Natu~natu panapana** i=vei   ta~tavone=i.*
     RD~clan   all   3PL.SBJ=R/R RD~help=IRR
     'All clans helped each other.'
     (1-T093-00:02:57.580)

(46) a. **do~dovi-u**
RD~spit-1SG.PSSR
'my lungs'
(2-E001)

b. **bau dovi~dovi-ina**
PL RD~spit-3SG.PSSR
'their lungs'
(Fieldnotes 2013)

(47) a. **Vanu~vanua-eta i**=to umunu=i nasipuna...
RD~people-AUG 3PL.SBJ sit=IRR sometimes
'Sometimes when the chiefs meet...'
(1-T093-00:03:15.850)

b. *Tau* **bau vanu~vanua-ota na:**=bau i=mate tani.
and PL RD~people-AUG some=PL 3PL.SBJ=die already
'And some elders had already died.'
(1-T105-00:11:31.256)

5.3 Articles

In Papapana, articles belong to a closed class and can code specificity and nonspecificity, noun class, number, and semantic features such as diminutive (see Table 5.6). Papapana also has a partitive article *pei* which does not distinguish noun class, and collective articles *mena* and *mamena* which also do not distinguish noun class but make a dual and plural number distinction respectively. Articles are not obligatory in Papapana, but nouns are usually marked by them, or a numeral modifier (§5.4), or possessor proclitic or suffix (§5.5).

Articles occur in a pre-head position in Papapana, which is typical of articles in Oceanic and Northwest Solomonic languages (Lynch, Ross, and Crowley 2002: 38). The specific/non-specific articles, singular diminutive articles and non-singular articles (plural *bau*, diminutive plural *ani*, partitive *pei* and collective *mena* and *mamena*) have different syntactic positions (see Table 5.7, and Table 4.1 and Table 4.2 in Chapter 4) but cannot co-occur. Specific/non-specific articles precede numerals (48), diminutive articles follow numerals (49), while the non-singular articles occupy the same syntactic position as the Class II marker *au*, following numerals (51) and possessor proclitics (52) but immediately preceding the head noun as in (50)–(52) (or collective marker *vei*). The evidence for these syntactic positions is discussed in the relevant subsections below. The Class II specific article *nau ~ nu=*, non-specific article

5.3 Articles

Table 5.6: Articles.

Type	Noun class	Number	
		SG	PL
Specific	Personal	e-	bau
	Class I	na=	bau nau ~ nu=
	Class II	nau ~ nu=	bau na=
Non-specific	Personal	N/A	N/A
	Class I	ta=	bau
	Class II	tau	bau
Diminutive	Personal	sau ~ su=	?
	Class I	si=	ani
	Class II	sau ~ su=	ani

Table 5.7: Syntactic positions of articles.

Indirect alienable possessor proclitic OR Specific/Non-specific articles	Numeral modifier	**Singular diminutive articles**	**Non-singular articles** OR Class II marker	Collective marker	Head noun

tau and diminutive article *sau* ~ *su*= can be analysed as portmanteau forms consisting of *na*=, *ta*= or *sa*= and the Class II marker *au* (see §5.3.1, §5.3.3 and §5.3.4). This is because the numeral modifiers *'aria* 'one' (48) and *nua* 'two', the diminutive article (49) and the possessor proclitics are also marked by *au* when they modify a Class II noun (see §5.4.2, §5.3.4 and §5.5.2).

(48) ***nu='aria=au   marei***
 SPEC.CLII=one=CLII bird
 'one bird'
 (2-E023)

(49) E=mate   asi=ina   **ena=nua**   sa=au   'usia...
3SG.SBJ=die leave=3PL.OBJ 3SG.PSSR=two DIM=CLII child
'He died leaving his two poor children...'
(1-T030-00:03:53.913)

(50) **Ami=bau**   'usia i=to   ara nao te=na=skuru
1EXCL.PSSR=PL   child 3PL.SBJ PST go OBL=SPEC[CLI]=school
reareana...
far
'Our children went to school far away...'
(1-T090- 00:00:23.980)

(51) Enai **nua mena   panu-na**   na=bomb   atunu=ina.
after two DU.COLL spouse-DER SPEC.CLII=bomb attack=3PL.OBJ
'Then a bomb killed a couple.'
(1-T096-00:01:04.515)

(52) **Au=mamena   tama~tama-na**
1SG.PSSR=PL.COLL   RD~father-DER
'my family'
(2-E005)

5.3.1 Specific articles: *e-, na=, nau ~ nu=*

The most prevalent articles in Papapana are the specific articles: Personal noun class *e-*, Class I *na=* and Class II *nau ~ nu=*. These articles appear to be reflexes of the POc personal determiner **e* and the POc common non-human determiner **na*, reported in Lynch (2002: 224).

The article *nau* can be analysed as consisting of the specific article *na=* and the Class II marker *au*; the absence of this marker indicates Class I. Evidence for this analysis comes from NPs in which there is a numeral modifier or possessor proclitic (see §5.4.2 and §5.5.2). The phonologically reduced allomorph *nu=* is actually more pervasive than *nau*; however, in oblique expressions, it is *nau* which occurs with the preposition *te* to give *tenau* (c.f. **tenu*), regardless of the article used when the NP is a core argument (see §8.3.1). Class II nouns are either marked by *nau* or *nu=* and cannot occur with both, as (53) and (54) show. There is no discernible phonological or semantic motivation for the selection of *nau* or *nu=*, thus assignment is rather unpredictable. Three of the twenty-three bird names elicited during my fieldwork occurred with *nau* (*pupu* 'hornbill', *sisi* 'lorikeet', and *'o* 'heron'), one of the twenty-one shell names occurred with *nau* (*usi* 'shell species'), while five of the forty-five plant names (whose English translations are unknown) occurred with *nau* (*mago, pipi, tomo, vo'u, tabu*). Other Class II nouns which are marked by *nau* are *nare* 'coral', *vani* 'stingray', *gori* 'jellyfish', *watu* 'smoke' and *nai* 'marriage'.

(53) a. . . . *e-tama-na*   *e=vae*   *de=a=i*
PERS-father-3SG.PSSR   3SG.SBJ=REP   take=3SG.OBJ=IRR
nu=obutu.
SPEC.CLII=canoe
'. . .his father got the canoe again.'
(1-T031-00:03:21.950)

b. **. . .e-tama-na*   *e=vae*   *de=a=i*
PERS-father-3SG.PSSR   3SG.SBJ=REP   take=3SG.OBJ=IRR
na=au   ***obutu.***
SPEC=CLII   canoe
'. . .his father got the canoe again.'

(54) a. ***Na=au***   *tue*   *mama*   *enai*
SPEC=CLII   language   DEM1   DEM2
na=vanua   *panapana*   *i=varon=i=a=ina.*
SPEC[CLI]=people   all   3PL.SBJ=know=TR=3SG.OBJ=3PL.IPFV
'Everybody knows this language.'
(1-T083-00:01:38.540)

b. ****Nu=tue***   *mama*   *enai*
SPEC.CLII=language   DEM1   DEM2
na=vanua   *panapana*   *i=varon=i=a=ina.*
SPEC[CLI]=people   all   3PL.SBJ=know=TR=3SG.OBJ=3PL.IPFV
'Everybody knows this language.'

In terms of the status of the articles *na=* and *nu=* as proclitics, evidence comes from the formation of long vowels or diphthongs when morphological concatenation results in the adjacent co-occurrence of two identical or non-identical vowels respectively, as in (55). The personal non-specific article *e-* is analysed as a prefix because it only ever attaches to the head noun and it participates in stress assignment, whereas the other articles do not (see §3.5.3).

(55) a. [namu]
    na=inu
    SPEC[CLI]=house
    'a/the house'
  b. [naɔrawi]
    na=orawi
    SPEC[CLI]=man
    'a/the man'
  c. [nuurisi]
    nu=urisi
    SPEC.CLII=rope
    'a/the rope

As shown in §5.4, the specific articles *na* and *nu* can precede *'aria* 'one' and *nanamoa* 'first'. They do not co-occur with possessor proclitics (but do co-occur with possessor suffixes) and therefore I argue that they are in the same syntactic position as possessor proclitics, that is, the leftmost margin of the NP core. Indeed, in PPs with *te*, *te* either immediately precedes the specific articles *na*, *nau* and *e-*, or immediately precedes a possessor proclitic, whereas it does not immediately precede other core prenominal modifiers (see §8.3.1).

Singular Personal kinship term nouns in Papapana occur with the prefixed article *e-* and are always directly possessed, as in (56) to (58). Consequently, they always refer to a particular referent and are thus specific. The possessor suffixes have a deictic value, corresponding to an identifiable person. Since nouns that are grammatically possessed by identifiable nouns are also identifiable, Personal kinship term nouns are thus always definite. It is not possible for these nouns to be generic or indefinite in Papapana. The Personal article is cognate with the personal article in other Northwest Solomonic languages such as Taiof (Ross 2002b: 429), Teop (Mosel and Spriggs 1999a, Mosel and Thiesen 2007) and Kubokota (Chambers 2009: 89–90), though in Teop and Kubokota the personal article can mark personal names, whereas in Papapana the Personal article does not mark Personal proper name nouns.

(56) . . .***e-tama-na** **nu='usia*** *e=wa=i=a*
    PERS-father-3SG.PSSR SPEC.CLII=child 3SG.SBJ=say=TR=3SG.OBJ
    ***e-sina-na**. . .*
    PERS-mother-3SG.PSSR
    '. . .the child's father said to his mother. . .'
    (1-T031-00:02:06.520)

(57) "**Anau e-tama-u**   e=mate. . ."
      1SG   PERS-father-1SG.PSSR   3SG.SBJ=die
      "'My father died. . .'"
      (1-T029-00:07:28.659)

(58) Ta   **e-tubu-ina**   e=to   nao. . .
      and   PERS-grandparent-3PL.PSSR   3SG.SBJ=EMPH   go
      'And their grandmother went. . .'
      (1-T073-00:01:16.240)

Singular nouns belonging to Class I in Papapana can be marked by the specific article proclitic *na=*. The following examples show that this article expresses specificity rather than definiteness: in (59a) the referent *iana* 'fish' is introduced to the discourse for the first time and is indefinite, while in (59b) *iana* 'fish' is definite because it is accessible to the hearer having been previously mentioned in the discourse in (59). In both these examples the referent *iana* 'fish' is specific because it is a particular referent.

(59) a. *Peter   e=roros=i=a*   **na=iana-eta**. . .
         Peter   3SG.SBJ=see=TR=3SG.OBJ   SPEC[CLI]=fish-AUG
         'Peter saw a big fish. . .'
         (1-T016-00:00:35.135)
      b. *e=to   atutusi=a   nao*   **na=iana**.
         3SG.SBJ   chase=3SG.OBJ   thither   SPEC[CLI]=fish
         '. . .he chased the fish.'
         (1-T016-00:00:52.010)

Singular nouns belonging to Class II in Papapana can be marked by the specific article *nau* or the phonologically reduced allomorph *nu=*. The following examples show that this article expresses specificity rather than definiteness: in (60a) the referent *tura* 'fire' is introduced to the discourse for the first time and is indefinite, whereas in (60b) *tura* 'fire' is definite because it is accessible to the hearer having been previously mentioned in the discourse in (60). In both these examples the referent *tura* 'fire' is specific because it is a particular referent.

(60) a. Iara mi=atu=a=i=ma   ***nu=tura.*** . .
      then 1EXCL.SBJ=make=3SG.OBJ=IRR=ma[20] SPEC.CLII=fire
  b. *mi=va-udu-i=a=i=ma*   ***nu=tura.***
     1EXCL.SBJ=CAUS-be.alight=TR=3SG.OBJ=IRR=ma SPEC.CLII=fire
     'Then we make a fire. . . we light the fire.'
     (1-T038-00:02:07.985)

5.3.2 Inverse number marking and the plural article *bau*

In Papapana the noun class system interacts with number in a remarkable way involving inverse number marking whereby "the marking of singular number in one noun could be by the same formal means as are used for marking plural in another" (Corbett 2000: 159). This typologically rare phenomenon is found in other Northwest Solomonic languages such as Nehan (Baerman 2007; Corbett 2000: 163–65; Ross 1988: 252, 299, 301) and Teop (Corbett 2000: 163–65; Mosel and Spriggs 1999a; Mosel and Thiesen 2007). In Papapana the specific article *na=* marks singular nouns when it occurs with Class I nouns (61a), but plural when it occurs with Class II nouns (63), while the specific article *nau* ~ *nu=* marks singular Class II nouns (62) but plural Class I nouns (61b).

(61) a. ***na=epu***
      SPEC[CLI]=cloud
      'a cloud'
      (2-E003)
  b. ***na=au***   *epu*
      SPEC=CLII cloud
      'clouds'
      (2-E003)

(62) ***Nu='usia***   *ora* *e=toto.*
     SPEC.CLII=child only 3SG.SBJ=live
     'Only the child lived.'
     (1-T029-00:02:37.640)

---

[20] *=ma* attaches to all word classes and may be a discourse marker but this requires further research to confirm.

(63) . . .*i=oi~oi=ina*   ***na='usia***   ***panapana mama***. . .
      3PL.SBJ=RD~call=3PL.OBJ   SPEC[CLI]=child   all   DEM1
      '. . .they called all the children. . .'
      (1-T043a-00:02:01.844)

It is also common to mark plurality for nouns belonging to all noun classes with the plural article *bau*, an independent morpheme that precedes the head noun. Indeed, it is common for plural marking lexemes to be independent in Meso-Melanesian languages (Palmer 2012: 451). It is feasible that *bau* derives from a quantifier as in the closely related Northwest Solomonic language Torau there is a quantifier that is similar in phonological form, *beau* 'many' (Palmer fieldnotes). However, *bau* does not behave syntactically like other Papapana quantifiers, and it can co-occur with quantifiers. Instead, I analyse *bau* as an article because it is mutually exclusive, thus cannot co-occur, with other articles. Nevertheless, the articles occupy different syntactic positions and *bau* appears to occupy the same position in the NP as the Class II marker *au* (see also §5.5.3 and §5.6 for further similarities). This is shown by the fact that (if there are no other intervening modifiers such as numerals or diminutive articles) the possessor proclitics attach directly to the noun if it is Class I singular, to the Class II marker *au* if the noun is Class II singular, or to *bau* if the Class I or II noun is plural (see §5.5.2 for more).

In Papapana *bau* seems to be replacing the inverse number marking system. Inverse number marking does not exist at all for Personal nouns which always employ *bau* (64); this is contrary to Teop (Mosel and Spriggs 1999a, Mosel and Thiesen 2007) where some I-E class nouns behave like I-A class nouns, adopting the class II singular article *o* to mark plurality while other I-E class nouns use a distinct personal plural article.

(64) a. ***E-sina-ina***   *e=mate*   *asi=ina*.
        PERS-mother-3PL.PSSR   3SG.SBJ=die   leave=3PL.OBJ
        'Their mother died leaving them.'
        (1-T026-00:00:24.680)
     b. ***Bau sina-ina***   *i=vori~vori=ina=ina=i*. . .
        PL   mother-3PL.PSSR   3PL.SBJ=RD~talk=3PL.OBJ=3PL.IPFV=IRR
        'Their mothers talk to them. . .'
        (1-T025-00:01:47.050)

In Papapana, inverse number marking is almost obsolete for Class I nouns which are marked by *bau* the large majority of the time (65b). Some speakers accepted inverse number marking for some nouns, but not for others such as *inu* 'house' (65c), while other speakers never accepted inverse number marking.

(65) a. mi=atu=a　　　　　　　　**na=inu**
　　　 1EXCL.SBJ=make=3SG.OBJ SPEC[CLI]=house
　　　 'we made a house'
　　　 (2-E003)
　　b. mi=atu=ina　　　　　　　**bau inu**
　　　 1EXCL.SBJ=make=3PL.OBJ PL　 house
　　　 'we made houses'
　　　 (2-E003)
　　c. *mi=atu=ina　　　　　　　**nu=inu**
　　　 1EXCL.SBJ=make=3PL.OBJ SPEC.CLII=house
　　　 'we made houses'
　　　 (2-E003)

For Class II nouns, inverse number marking and the plural article *bau* are both common, with no difference in the meaning between the two, as in (66).

(66) a. nu=patu-na
　　　 SPEC.CLII=head-3SG.PSSR
　　　 'his/her head'
　　　 (2-E003)
　　b. na=patu-ina
　　　 SPEC[CLI]=head-3PL.PSSR
　　　 'their heads'
　　　 (2-E003)
　　c. bau patu-ina
　　　 PL　 head-3PL.PSSR
　　　 'their heads'
　　　 (2-E003)

Nouns denoting fruit or nuts belong to Class I (and thus are marked by *na=* when singular (67a)) whereas nouns denoting the names of the plants belong to Class II (and thus are marked by *nau ~ nu=* when singular (68a)) (see §5.1.5). It is therefore not an option to use inverse number marking to pluralise fruit/nuts and fruit/nut-bearing plants. Instead, for nouns denoting fruit/nuts, the plural article *bau* is used as in (67b). For nouns denoting the plant, inverse number marking can only arise when the plant has no fruit/nuts: when it does have fruit/nuts, the name of the plant functions as a nominal modifier in a compound noun (see §4.4.1) as in (68b).

(67) a. *na=bareo*
SPEC[CLI]=breadfruit
'a/the breadfruit'
(2-E003)
b. *bau bareo*
PL breadfruit
'the breadfruits'
(2-E003)

(68) a. *nu=bareo*
SPEC.CLII=breadfruit
'the breadfruit tree'
(2-E003)
b. *bau naono-i bareo*
PL tree-CONST breadfruit
'the breadfruit trees'
(2-E003)

5.3.3 Non-specific articles: *ta=, tau*

The non-specific articles, *ta=* for Class I nouns (69) and *tau* for Class II nouns (70), arise very infrequently. These articles are cognate with the non-specific articles *ta* and *to* in Teop (Mosel and Spriggs 1999a: 324–325) and *ta* and *tu* in Taiof (Ross 2002b: 429) and are likely reflexes of the POc indefinite determiner **ta*, which marked common non-human nouns (Lynch 2001: 224; Lynch, Ross, and Crowley 2002: 71). As §5.3.1 showed though, Papapana articles do not make a distinction in definiteness, but in specificity and in (69)–(70), *ta=* and *tau* do not mark nouns which refer to specific people/objects. The article *tau* can be analysed as consisting of the non-specific article *ta=* and the Class II marker *au*; the absence of this marker indicates Class I. Since Personal nouns are always possessed, they are always specific and therefore they are not marked by the non-specific articles.

(69) "*Ta=maunu   o=to   muni=a=mu?*"
NSPEC[CLI]=woman 2SG.SBJ hide=3SG.OBJ=2SG.IPFV
"'Are you hiding a woman?'"
(1-T029-00:21:14.460)

(70) *"Maisia   si=atu=a=i   ta=au   obutu-eta."*
     okay   1INCL.SBJ=make=3SG.OBJ=IRR   NSPEC=CLII   canoe-AUG
     "'Okay let's make a big canoe.'"
     (1-T101-00:09:05.268)

Evidence for the status of *ta=* as a proclitic comes from (71) in which a diphthong is formed when morphological concatenation results in the adjacent co-occurrence of two non-identical vowels, and from the fact that *ta=* attaches directly to the noun if it belongs to Class I, but to *au* when the noun belongs to Class II (compare (69) and (70) above). In terms of syntactic position, the non-specific articles clearly precede Class II marker *au* but otherwise it is my assumption that they occur in the same position as the specific articles rather than the singular diminutive articles; the infrequency of occurrence and semantic incomptability with other prenominal modifiers make it impossible to know for sure.

(71) [tamueta]
     ta=inu-eta
     NSPEC[CLI]=house-AUG
     'a big house'
     (2-E008)

5.3.4 Diminutive singular articles: *si=, sau ~ su=*

In Papapana there is a set of diminutive articles expressing 'small', or 'dear' or 'poor' in the sense of endearment or sympathy: it is common cross-linguistically for the diminutive category to have semantic extensions into the semantic realm of affection and endearment (Dahl 2006). Sometimes other constituents in the clause provide the meaning 'small', but usually such constituents are absent and therefore the meaning 'small' or 'poor' must come from the article itself.

Singular Class I nouns can be marked by *si=* (72), while singular Class II nouns (73) and Personal nouns (74) are marked by *sau ~ su=*. The Class II diminutive articles resemble the Class II specific articles so *sau* can be analysed as consisting of the diminutive article *sa=* and the Class II marker *au;* however, the Class I diminutive article is not *sa=* but *si=*. For the Class I diminutive article, there may have been a sound change from /a/ to /i/, perhaps under the influence of Teop which has a diminutive particle *si* which can occur with articles (Mosel and Thiesen 2007), or perhaps *si=* is a borrowing from Teop which replaced *sa=*.

(72) **Si=daramu** e=to no amun=i=a.
DIM.CLI=river 3SG.SBJ=EMPH go.SEQ see=TR=3SG.OBJ
'He went and saw a stream.'
(1-T012-00:02:07.513)

(73) ***sa=au*** *marei*
DIM=CLII bird
'small bird'
(2-E023)

(74) U=eri roros=i=a=u ***sa=au***
1SG.SBJ=OPT see=TR=3SG.OBJ=1SG.IPFV DIM=CLII
tubu-u.
grandparent-1SG.PSSR
'I wanted to see my dear grandmother.'
(1-T088-00:44:14.750)

The singular diminutive articles precede Class II marker *au* but follow numerals as in (75). This example is problematic because the noun referent is plural, not singular. It could therefore be argued that *si=* and *sau ~ su=* only mark singularity in the absence of other number marking to the contrary. They are certainly not plural though as there is a dedicated diminutive plural article, *ani* (see §5.3.5).

(75) E=mate asi=ina ena=nua ***sa=au*** *'usia*
3SG.SBJ=die leave=3PL.OBJ 3SG.PSSR=two DIM=CLII child
'He died leaving his two poor children. . .'
(1-T030-00:03:53.913)

Nouns that have the same phonological form, but a different, though related, meaning (see §5.1.5) can belong to different noun classes and the diminutive articles are applied accordingly: compare (72) and (76) where 'river' is Class I but 'water' is Class II.

(76) *sa=au daramu*
DIM=CLII water
'little bit of water'
(2-E011)

The Class II noun *'usia* 'child' can be marked by the Class II diminutive article *sau*, or by the phonologically reduced allomorph *su=*, as shown in (77) and (78). *Su=* is only attested with *'usia*. The fact that *'usia* can be marked by either of the allomorphs contrasts with the use of the Class II specific article allomorphs, where a noun is marked by either *nau* or *nu=* (see §5.3.1). Some speakers reported no semantic or pragmatic difference between *sau* and *su=* with *'usia* and indeed in translations of texts there often is not, as shown in (77) and (78). Other speakers indicated that *sau 'usia* denoted 'poor child' while *su'usia* denoted 'poor boy' as in (79).

(77) Ta   **sa=au**   *'usia mama*   sa=au   maru.
      and DIM=CLII   child DEM1   DIM=CLII orphan
      'And this poor child was a poor orphan.'
      (1-T035-00:01:23.910)

(78) E=de   tae=ina   mai   **su='usia**. . .
      3SG.SBJ=take up=3PL.OBJ   hither DIM.CLII=child
      'The poor child took them up. . .'
      (1-T031- 00:04:47.820)

(79) **Su='usia**   e=roroto=ina=na=i.
      DIM.CLII=child   3SG.SBJ=watch=3PL.OBJ=3SG.IPFV=IRR
      'The poor boy watched them.'
      (1-T029- 00:04:48.710)

Class I nouns, such as *babakui* 'shark', can be marked by either Class I *si=* or Class II *sau* (though, rather arbitrarily, Class I noun *maunu* 'woman' can only be marked by *sau*). Speakers were sometimes unsure of the difference with some Class I nouns, but for other Class I nouns speakers claimed that a switch from *si=* to *sau* marked a switch from proximal to distal as in (80). For Class II nouns, such as *tura* 'fire', *sau* marks proximal (81) but elicitation during my April 2018 fieldwork showed that a switch to *si=* for Class II nouns was not permitted (81).

(80) a. *si=babakui*
         DIM.CLI=shark
         'the small shark (nearby)'
         (2-E028-1)

b. *sa=au   babakui*
   DIM=CLII shark
   'the small shark (far away)'
   (2-E028-1)

(81) a. *sa=au   tura*
   DIM=CLII fire
   'the small fire (nearby)'
   (2-E028-1)
   b. **si=tura*
   DIM.CLI=fire
   'the small fire (far away)'

It therefore remains unclear whether some nouns can definitely be marked by both diminutive articles, and if so, what the difference in meaning really is, if any. Nevertheless, the alleged switch from proximal to distal meaning is interesting as it mirrors the inverse-number marking system. However, instead of the articles marking number, they mark distance (as well as having a diminutive function). Consequently, the marking of proximal in one noun is by the same formal means as the marking of distal in another. This phenomenon is even more interesting when one considers that POc had three demonstrative/spatial deictics, **e/*ne* 'near speaker', **a/*na* 'near addressee' and **o/*no* 'distant from both speaker and addressee' (Ross 1988: 100), and Mosel and Spriggs (1999a: 342) argue that Teop articles developed from these demonstratives (finding support for this hypothesis in the semantic rules of noun class assignment). While I do not think the semantic rules of noun class assignment in Papapana reflect the deictic categories of proximity and distance, I do think the examples above and (118) in §4.6.1 support the suggestion that Papapana specific articles could have developed from these demonstratives. These deictic features could then have been extended from the specific articles to the diminutive articles.

5.3.5 Diminutive plural article *ani*

While *si=* and *sau ~ su=* mark a singular noun, *ani* is the diminutive plural article. *Ani* does not distinguish noun class and does not co-occur with the Class II marker *au*: in (82) it marks a Class I noun and in (83) a Class II noun; therefore it seems to occupy the same position in the NP as other non-singular articles. There is no data showing *ani* marking a Personal noun.

(82) **ani   arao**
     DIM.PL brother
     'little brothers'
     (2-E011)

(83) . . .**ani   'usia** i=pei   ara   vavana=ina   nao=i.
     DIM.PL child 3PL.SBJ=PST.IPFV PST spearfish=3PL.OBJ thither=IRR
     '. . .some small children went spearfishing.'
     (1-T058-00:00:15.680)

5.3.6 Partitive article *pei*

The partitive article *pei* in Papapana refers to part of an entity and denotes 'piece of'. In my data, the nouns marked by *pei* are all Class II nouns, as in (84)–(85), and further research is required to determine whether *pei* is restricted to Class II nouns or not.

The partitive article *pei* is independent and precedes the head noun. Although phonologically identical to the partitive noun (§4.4.2), the partitive article does not co-occur with other articles like the partitive noun does, and it behaves like other articles because adjectives may be marked by *pei* to agree with the head noun they modify, as in (86). *Pei* does not co-occur with other prenominal modifiers nor with the Class II marker *au* (despite all the attested examples being Class II nouns) so it could be that its syntactic position is the same as *au*, and the other non-singular articles.

(84) **pei   daramu**
     PART water
     'a bit of water'
     (2-E006)

(85) **Pei   tovu   tomana** e=ma'=i=a.
     PART sugarcane too   3SG.SBJ=give=TR=3SG.OBJ
     'A piece of sugarcane too he gave her.'
     (1-T029-00:09:17.690)

(86) **pei   arava pei   maro**
     PART dry   PART fabric
     'old sarong (lit. old bit of fabric)'
     (2-E004)

5.3.7 Dual and plural collective articles *mena* and *mamena*

The dual and plural collective articles are independent and most commonly mark dyadic nouns which have been derived from kinship nouns (see §4.3.3.2); *mena* marks a minimal dyadic noun which refers to two people who are on either side of the relationship in question as in (87) and (89) while *mamena* marks augmented dyadic nouns which refer to at least three people (88). The collective articles can, however, modify other nouns; *mena* marks dual number as in (90) while *mamena* marks plural number for a range of Class I nouns such as *gono* 'banana' in (91). I label these articles *collective* because they refer to pairs or groups. *Mamena* can also mark nouns which have undergone disyllabic reduplication and which are grammatically plural; however reduplication to mark nominal pluralisation is not a productive process and does generally co-occur with other markers of plurality such as *mamena* (see §5.2.3).

These articles cannot co-occur with other articles but can co-occur with possessor proclitics (88) and numerals (89), the latter example showing that the collective articles follow numeral modifiers in the NP. The collective articles obviously do not mark singular number and, like the other non-singular articles, they do not combine with the Class II marker; therefore, I tentatively suggest that the collective articles occur in the same syntactic position as the other non-singular articles and the Class II marker.

(87) . . .*i=pei*   *po=ina=i*   **mena**   *tama-na.*
3PL.SBJ=PST.IPFV stay=3PL.IPFV=IRR DU.COLL father-DER
'. . .the father and child remained.'
(1-T031-00:48.960)

(88) ***au=mamena***   *tama~tama-na*
1SG.PSSR=PL.COLL RD~father-DER
'my family'
(2-E005)

(89) *Enai* **nua mena**   **panu-na**   *na=bomb*   *atunu=ina.*
after two DU.COLL spouse-DER SPEC.CLII=bomb attack=3PL.OBJ
'Then a bomb killed a couple.'
(1-T096-00:01:04.515)

(90) *Maisia anau u=ri*   *vare 'a'ade'e=i=a=u*
okay 1SG 1SG.SBJ=OPT REP narrative=TR=3SG.OBJ=1SG.IPFV

nu='a'ade'e   mena   atamata.
SPEC.CLII=narrative   DU.COLL   friend
'Okay I want to tell a story again about two friends.'
(1-T064- 00:00:19.860)

(91) ...*mamena* *gono,*   *kaukau,*   *i=no*   *ari~ari=i.*
     PL.COLL   banana   sweet.potato   3PL.SBJ=go.SEQ   RD~dig=IRR
     '...they dig all the bananas and sweet potato.'
     (1-T066- 00:00:47.680)

5.4 Numerals and numeral phrases

Although Tok Pisin cardinal and ordinal numerals are frequently borrowed, Papapana does have its own counting system (§5.4.1). Some of the numerals used in counting have a slightly different form when they are cardinal or ordinal numeral modifiers in a NP, and in postnominal position, there is some evidence that the numeral itself can be modified (§5.4.2). Cardinal and ordinal numerals can also occur alone in a NP when the head noun is elided but anaphorically recoverable (§5.4.3). Numeral phrases can also function as predicates (§9.6.5).

5.4.1 Counting system

Table 5.8 shows the numerals used in counting. As the syntactic distribution of the numeral modifiers can only be determined by considering the formal properties of the counting numerals, this section first describes the formal and semantic properties of numerals before describing the slightly different forms of cardinal and ordinal numeral modifiers and their syntactic distribution in §5.4.2.

As Table 5.8 shows, Papapana has unique lexical items for 'zero' to 'five', and compounds that are formed additively for 'six' to 'nine'. Any numerals involving these units use the same forms. The word *toatoa* 'on top of' in the compounds is optional and only two speakers out of nine used it in elicitation and it is attested only once in the text recordings when the numeral is a modifier. There is a unique lexical item for 'ten' and subsequent decades are formed multiplicatively. 'One thousand' is derived from 'ten' by disyllabic reduplication and the derivational suffix *-na*, and thousands are formed multiplicatively. Interestingly, 'one hundred' is formed by multiplying fifties, therefore counting between 'one hundred' and 'one thousand' involves counting in fifties, with the

Table 5.8: Counting system.

	Papapana	Literal translation
0	*aruai*	
1	*na'aria*	
2	*nuata*	
3	*tautono*[21]	
4	*tauvasi*	
5	*pepeitaunima*	
6	*pepeitaunima na'aria [toatoa]*	five one [on top of]
7	*pepeitaunima nuata [toatoa]*	five two [on top of]
8	*pepeitaunima tautono [toatoa]*	five three [on top of]
9	*pepeitaunima tauvasi [toatoa]*	five four [on top of]
10	*numanoa*	
11	*numanoa na'aria [toatoa]*	ten one [on top of]
12	*numanoa nuata [toatoa]*	ten two [on top of]
13	*numanoa tautono [toatoa]*	ten three [on top of]
14	*numanoa tauvasi [toatoa]*	ten four [on top of]
15	*numanoa pepeitaunima [toatoa]*	ten five [on top of]
16	*numanoa pepeitaunima na'aria [toatoa]*	ten five one [on top of]
17	*numanoa pepeitaunima nuata [toatoa]*	ten five two [on top of]
32	*numanoa pepeitaunima tautono [toatoa]*	ten five three [on top of]
32	*numanoa pepeitaunima tauvasi [toatoa]*	ten five four [on top of]
20	*nuau manoa*	two tens
21	*nuau manoa na'aria [toatoa]*	two tens one [on top of]
30	*tautoi manoa*	three tens
40	*tauvasi manoa*	four tens
50	*pepeitaunima manoa*	five tens
60	*pepeitaunima nu'aria manoa*	five one tens
70	*pepeitaunima nuau manoa*	five two tens
80	*pepeitaunima tautoi manoa*	five three tens
90	*pepeitaunima tauvasi manoa*	five four tens
100	*nuau pepeitaunima manoa*	two five-tens
110	*nuau pepeitaunima manoa ta numanoa*	two five-tens and ten
150	*tautoi pepeitaunima manoa*	three five-tens
1000	*manomanoana*	
2000	*nuau manomanoana*	two thousands

decades in between fifties being formed additively with the coordinator *tau ~ ta* 'and' (such as for '110' in Table 5.8). When numerals are formed multiplicatively, the multiplying numeral occurs in its numeral modifier form; for example, instead

---

[21] This is variably pronounced as /tautɔnu/ and /tautɔnɔ/.

of *nuata manoa 'two tens', it is *nuau manoa* 'two tens'. According to Lynch, Ross, and Crowley (2002: 39), such a counting system is a combination of quinary and decimal, with 6–9 being compounds involving the form for 5, along with a separate lexical item for 10, but not separate stems for 100 and 1000. Proto-Oceanic had a decimal number system (Ross 1988: 183), with numerals from one to ten, and many Northwest Solomonic languages such as Sisiqa (Ross 2002a: 459) and Taiof (Ross 2002b: 429) use decimal systems, so Papapana is slightly unusual in its counting system, with the formation of hundreds being a particularly interesting feature. Since the neighbouring Papuan language Rotokas uses a quinary system (Robinson 2011: 125) the combination of decimal and quinary systems in Papapana may be the result of language contact.

In terms of the forms themselves, *nuata* 'two' could be analysed as consisting of the cardinal numeral modifier *nua* 'two' and the Class I marker *ata*, similar to the pattern found with possessed NPs functioning as non-verbal predicates (see §5.5.3) and in quantifier phrases (§ 5.6.3). Support for *nuata* 'two' being polymorphemic, diachronically and possible synchronically, comes from the fact that Papapana *nua* is likely a reflex of POc *rua* 'two' as Papapana underwent a sound change from POc *r > n (Ross 1988: 220). It is also likely that diachronically, *tautono*, *tauvasi* and *pepeitaunima* were polymorphemic: *tau* could be a reflex of the POc counting prefix *ka- (Lynch, Ross, and Crowley 2002: 89) with *tono*, *vasi*, and *nima* being reflexes of PNWS *vati 'four' (Ross 1988: 225) and POc *tolu 'three' and *lima 'five' (Ross 1988: 344). The *pepei* in *pepeitaunima* 'five' may relate to *pepei* 'side' while *nima*, as is very common cross-linguistically, is probably etymologically related to *nima* 'hand'.

Interestingly, the lexeme *manoa* also denotes 'neck', which is a Class II noun and the numeral *numanoa* 'ten' begins with what looks like the Class II specific article *nu=*. Similarly, *na'aria* 'one' begins with what appears to be the Class I specific article *na=*. Ross (1988: 313) proposes a Proto-New Ireland NP structure in which the numeral was the head of the phrase and the enumerated noun was the grammatical possessor, which implies that numerals could be treated as nouns of quantity, and indeed in Northwest Solomonic languages such as Taiof, numerals are nouns and they are preceded by the Class I article *a* (Ross 2002b: 429). Considering this, one could suggest that Papapana numerals are nouns, with *na'aria* 'one' belonging to Class I but *numanoa* 'ten' and other plural numbers belonging to Class II, since numerals formed multipicatively (i.e. two tens, six tens, seven tens, two fifties, two thousands) employ the cardinal numeral modifiers marked for Class II (*nu'aria* or *nu'ariau* 'one' and *nuau* 'two'). The question of whether numerals are nouns will be returned to in §5.4.2.

5.4.2 Cardinal and ordinal numeral modifiers

This section first describes the formal and semantic properties of cardinal and ordinal numerals (see Table 5.9 for an overview) as this provides evidence for their syntactic distribution. In the NP, numeral modifiers occur in one of two fixed positions in the NP, either prenominally or sometimes postnominally (see below and Table 4.1 and Table 4.2 in Chapter 4). In Meso-Melanesian languages, numerals typically follow the head noun (Ross 1988: 358), but there are Northwest Solomonic languages, such as Sisiqa (Ross 2002a) and Roviana (Corston-Oliver 2002) in which numerals are prenominal. The variation in syntactic distribution is another instance of the mixture of left-headedness and right-headedness found in Papapana.

Table 5.9: Cardinal and ordinal numeral modifiers.

	Cardinal		Ordinal	
1	'aria 'aria or 'aria=au	one (Class I) one (Class II)	nanamoa	first
2	nua nua=au	two (Class I) two (Class II)	va-nua va-nua=au	second (Class I) second (Class II)
3	atono tautoi	three (Human) three (Non-human)	va-atono or va-tautono va-tautoi	third (Human) third (Non-human)
4	tauvasi ~ aavasi	four	va-tauvasi	fourth
5	pepeitaunima	five	va-pepeitaunima	fifth
10	numanoa	ten	?	

For the numbers 'one' (92)–(93) and 'two' (94)–(95), and for any compound numerals involving these numbers such as 'six' (96) the cardinal numeral modifier forms differ slightly from those used in counting: *na'aria* 'one' (92) and *nua* 'two' (94) for Class I nouns, and *nu'aria* or *nu'ariau* 'one' (93) and *nuau* 'two' (95) for Class II nouns. In the text data, there are no examples of enumerated Personal nouns but elicitation data revealed that a Personal noun could be modified by *nua* 'two' (97).

(92) *Mi=to   no   po   **na='aria   wik***
     1EXCL.SBJ=EMPH go.SEQ stay SPEC[CLI]=one week
     te=na='uru.
     OBL=SPEC[CLI]=island
     'We went and stayed on the island for one week.'
     (1-T103-00:10:29.671)

(93) ***nu='aria=au***   *marei*
     SPEC.CLII=one=CLII bird
     'one bird'
     (2-E023)

(94) *"**Nua**   **matuana** i=to   oa~oa=ina."*
     two[CLI] spirit   3PL.SBJ=EMPH RD~cry=3PL.IPFV
     '"Two spirits are crying."'
     (1-T026-00:03:22.280)

(95) …*avosia **nua=au**   **orona=ma**   i=pu mai.*
     SUBR   two=CLII   possum=ma   3PL.SBJ=fall hither
     '…like two possums had fallen down.'
     (1-T077-00:01:19.170)

(96) ***Pepeitaunima na='aria   nganangana** nani   u=pei*
     five   SPEC[CLI]=one   month   there 1SG.SBJ=PST.IPFV
     no   po=u.
     go.SEQ   stay=1SG.IPFV
     'I went and stayed there for six months.'
     (1-T088-00:09:29.235)

(97) *Va:gi **nua**   **tubu-u**   i=po=ina.*
     now   two[CLI]   grandparent-1SG.PSSR   3PL.SBJ=stay=3PL.IPFV
     'Two of my grandparents are alive now.'
     (2-E003)

For the number 'three' (98)–(99) and for any compound numerals involving this number such as 'eight' (100), there are two cardinal numeral forms used as nominal modifiers but remarkably these make a human/non-human distinction rather than being marked for noun class: *atono* 'three' for humans (98) and *tautoi* 'three' for non-humans (99)–(100). If there were a noun class distinction, *'usia* 'child' and *marei* 'bird' would both be marked with the same numeral, since they are both Class II nouns.

(98) *Pauline tau Kingsford* **atono** *'usia aruai.*
Pauline and Kingsford three.HUM child NEG
'Pauline and Kingsford don't have three children.'
(2-E026)

(99) *I-bana e=po=ena* **tautoi** **na:ni.**
LOC-inside 3SG.SBJ=stay=3SG.IPFV three.NHUM day
'She stays inside for three days.'
(1-T066-00:01:31.210)

(100) ***pepeitaunima tautoi marei***
five three.NHUM bird
'eight birds'
(Fieldnotes 2013)

For the numbers 'four' (101), 'five' (102) and 'ten' (103), and any compound numerals involving these numbers such as 'nine' (104), the cardinal numerals listed in Table 5.8 are used and there is no noun class or human/non-human distinction. Occasionally *aavasi* 'four' was used instead of *tauvasi* when enumerating humans as in (105), suggesting a human/non-human distinction, but *aavasi* is also attested with *kakau* 'dog' and it is therefore more likely that *aavasi* is an allomorph in free variation with *tauvasi*.

(101) ***tauvasi naono***
four tree
'four trees'
(2-E003)

(102) ***Pepeitaunima vuri*** *te=na=epita.*
five egg OBL=SPEC[CLI]=nest
'Five eggs are in the nest.'
(2-E026)

(103) ...***numanoa*** *yia*   *i=nao*   *tani.*
       ten   year 3PL.SBJ=go already
       '...ten years ago.'
       (2-E021-1)

(104) *E=pei*   *ara siodo=ena=i*   *Teperoi* ***pepeitaunima***
       3SG.SBJ=PST.IPFV PST work=3SG.IPFV=IRR Teperoi five
       tauvasi nganangana.
       four   month
       'He was working in Teperoi for nine months'
       (2-E019)

(105) *Va:sina* ***aavasi tubu-u***   *i=pei*
       before   four   grandparent-1SG.PSSR 3PL.SBJ=PST.IPFV
       po=ina=i.
       stay=3PL.IPFV=IRR
       'Before, four of my grandparents were alive.'
       (2-E003)

Papapana has a distinct ordinal numeral modifier, *nanamoa,* denoting 'first'. In prenominal position only (106), *nanamoa* follows the specific articles, while it postnominal position it does not (107)–(108). There is no noun class distinction; *kakau* 'dog' (106) and *obutu* 'canoe' (107) are Class II nouns while *inu* 'house' (108) is a Class I noun.

(106) *nu=nanamoa   kakau*
       SPEC.CLII=first dog
       'the first dog'
       (2-E023)

(107) *nu=obutu   nanamoa*
       SPEC.CLII=canoe first
       'the first canoe'
       (2-E003)

(108) *na=inu   nanamoa*
       SPEC[CLI]=house first
       'the first house'
       (2-E003)

Ordinal numerals are "most commonly derived from cardinal numerals" (Dryer 2007b: 164) and except for 'first', this is indeed the case in Papapana: ordinals are derived by the prefix *va-*, which is homophonous with the causative prefix. Other Northwest Solomonic languages such as Banoni (Lynch and Ross 2002: 443) and Kokota (Palmer 2002: 504) also derive ordinals from cardinals by a morpheme that is formally identical to the causative marker. Since ordinal numerals are derived from cardinal numerals in Papapana, the ordinal numerals make the same noun class distinction for 'second' and the same human/non-human distinction for 'third' as the cardinal numerals (see Table 5.9) as shown in (109)–(110). Perhaps due to the infrequency with which ordinal numeral modifiers are used, speakers showed variation in terms of whether they derived 'third (human)' from the cardinal numeral modifier *atono*, as in (110), or from the numeral used in counting, *tautono* (111). In the text data, there are no examples of Personal nouns modified by ordinal numerals and it proved impossible to elicit such a noun phrase in elicitation sessions; whether this is because it is conceptually incongruous or whether it is ungrammatical is a matter for further research.

(109) a. ***va-nua***   *inu*   **Class I**
     ORD-two[CLI] house
     'the second house'
     (2-E003)
    b. ***va-nua=au***   *marei*   **Class II**
     ORD-two=CLII bird
     'the second bird'
     (2-E003)

(110) a. *amu=au*   *'usia*   ***va-atono***   **Human**
     2SG.PSSR=CLII child ORD-three.HUM
     'your third child'
     (2-E003)
    b. ***va-tautoi***   *marei*   **Non-human**
     ORD-three.NHUM bird
     'the third bird'
     (2-E003)

(111) ***va-tautono*** *'usia*   *te*   *anau*
     ORD-three   child OBL 1SG
     'my third child'
     (2-E003)

In Papapana, cardinal and ordinal numeral modifiers may either precede or follow the head noun, as the following pairs of examples demonstrate, but most often they precede it.

(112) a. **va-nua** nganangana
 ORD-two[CLI] month
 'the second month'
 (2-E003)
 b. nganangana **va-nua**
 month ORD-two[CLI]
 'the second month'
 (2-E003)

(113) a. amu=sinoni **va-tauvasi**
 2SG.PSSR[CLI]=husband ORD-four
 'your fourth husband'
 (2-E003)
 b. **va-tauvasi** nganangana
 ORD-four month
 'the fourth month'
 (2-E003)

As Table 4.1 and Table 4.2 in §4.1 and (114) below show, in pre-head position, numeral modifiers occur in the NP core, after the position containing possessor proclitics or specific/non-specific articles, but before the position containing diminutive articles (which in turn precede the position which contains either non-singular articles or the Class II marker *au*). Numerals are not attested with non-singular articles, presumably because the non-singular articles are redundant when the noun is enumerated. The forms *'ariau* and *nuau* can be analysed as consisting of the numeral modifiers *nua* and *'aria* and the Class II marker *au*; the absence of this marker indicates Class I. Indeed, as (114) shows, *nua* can be detached from *au* by an intervening diminutive article. Furthermore, *na* in *na'aria* and *nu* in *nu'aria* seem to be the Class I and II specific articles respectively and hence in prenominal position, the numerals arguably follow the specific articles (which I have shown occur in the same position as possessor proclitics; see §5.3.1). It is also the case that *nanamoa* 'first' follows the specific articles in prenominal position. Other numerals do not co-occur with specific articles. Although it is possible that diachronically *numanoa* 'ten' was morphologically divisible, synchronically it is not because if it were, then (103) would be **na=manoa yia* since *yia* 'year' is a Class I noun.

(114) E=mate   asi=ina   **ena=nua**   sa=au   **'usia**. . .
      3SG.SBJ=die leave=3PL.OBJ 3SG.PSSR=two DIM=CLII child
      'He died leaving his two poor children. . .'
      (1-T030-00:03:53.913)

In post-head position, numeral modifiers occur in the outer layer of the NP, after miscellaneous modifiers, but the exact relative ordering of postnominal numerals, demonstratives, adjective phrases, and possessor NPs is unclear: for example, there is variation in the relative position of the numeral and demonstrative in (115) and (116).

(115) **Na=inu   tautono mama na=etawa**
      SPEC[CLI]=house three   DEM1   SPEC[CLI]=big
      i=to   po=ina   i-nongana.
      3PL.SBJ=EMPH stay=3PL.IPFV LOC-beach
      'Those three big houses are on the beach.'
      (3-E002)

(116) **Na=iana   mama tautono** e=ma'a=ina.
      SPEC[CLI]=fish   DEM1   three   3SG.SBJ=give=3PL.OBJ
      'He gave them these three fish.'
      (1-T029-00:08:46.817)

In §5.4.1 I mentioned Ross' (1988: 313) proposal that the Proto-New Ireland numeral was the head noun in the NP and the enumerated noun was the grammatical possessor. There is some, albeit limited, evidence to support the numeral being a noun in synchronic Papapana. Firstly, speakers occasionally added *-i* to the numeral as in (117) (and to the interrogative term *tauvita* 'how many'; see §9.3.2.2). This could be a variation in pronunciation but it may instead be the construct suffix found synchronically in Papapana compounds, which reflect Proto-Oceanic inalienable and alienable non-specific possessor constructions (see §4.4.1). In this case, *pepeitaunima* 'five' would be the head noun and the following noun *vuri* 'egg' would be the modifier.

(117) *pepeitaunima-i vuri*
      five-CONST   egg
      'five eggs'
      (2-E023)

Secondly, in two text recordings, both the noun as well as the cardinal numeral *'aria* 'one' (118)–(119) were marked by an article, and the numeral is followed by the limiter *ora ~ ara* in (119). This could suggest that the numeral is a noun. Alternatively, instead of the numeral phrase containing only the head numeral in (118)–(119), it contains modifiers and is marked by an article agreeing with the head noun. This does not entail that numerals are nouns; after all, adjective phrases (whether adnominal or predicates) are marked by an article agreeing with the head noun or head of the subject NP.

(118) . . .*nu='aria   nu='usia   e=tavotu.*
      SPEC.CLII=one SPEC.CLII=child 3SG.SBJ=arrive
      '. . .one child was born.'
      (1-T043b-00:04:40.800)

(119) *Bau   poana mama na=au   tue   nu='aria   ora*
      PL   village DEM1 SPEC=CLII language SPEC.CLII=one only
      i=pei   vori~vori, iai   Papapana.[22]
      3PL.SBJ=PST.IPFV RD~talk   PROX   Papapana
      'These villages spoke only one language, Papapana.'
      (1-T034-00:02:32.445)

Given the limited data presented in (117)–(119), and the fact that it is only *'aria* 'one' and prenominal (but not postnominal) *nanamoa* 'first' which are marked by specific articles, I do not analyse numerals as nouns nor as NP heads. Instead in prenominal position, I analyse *'aria* 'one' and *nanamoa* 'first' as adnominal constituents that are separate from and follow the specific articles, while (118)–(119) represent adnominal numeral phrases marked by an article agreeing with the head noun.

5.4.3 Numerals and elided nouns

In Papapana, cardinal and ordinal numerals can occur alone in a NP when the head noun is elided but anaphorically recoverable, i.e. their interpretation depends on the interpretation of an antecedent NP. There is only one recorded example of this with a cardinal numeral modifier, forming a phrase in which it

---

[22] This utterance expresses habitual aspect but it is unclear why the verbal reduplication is not accompanied by PSI enclitics.

is modified by the limiter *ora*, and the numeral is marked by an article agreeing in noun class with the elided, antecedent noun.

(120) ***Nu='aria*** *ora e=pei po~po=ena=i...*
SPEC.CLII=one only 3SG.SBJ=PST.IPFV RD~stay=3SG.IPFV=IRR
'There was only one (breadfruit tree)...'
(1-T035-00:00:25.140)

When the ordinal numerals occur without nouns (121)–(123), the form for 'second' is not *va-nua* or *va-nua=au* but *vataunua*. As *vataunua* was also used as an ordinal numeral modifier in three instances, it may be that *taunua* reflects an earlier version of the numeral 'two', with *tau* being a reflex of the POc counting prefix **ka-*. There are very few examples in the text data of ordinal numerals functioning on their own and in elicitation sessions, it did not come easily to speakers. The numeral in (123) agrees with the elided, antecedent noun in terms of animacy (human vs. non-human).

(121) ...***nanamoa*** *e=to ara tavotu...*
first 3SG.SBJ PST arrive
'...the first (of my children) was born...'
(1-T083-00:02:24.300)

(122) ***Vataunua*** *Teperoi e=naovo.*
second Teperoi 3SG.SBJ=fly
'The second (bird) flew to Teperoi.'
(2-E028-2)

(123) ***Va-tautono*** *te=na='uru e=naovo.*
ORD-three OBL=SPEC[CLI]=island 3SG.SBJ=fly
'The third (bird) flew to the island.'
(2-E028-2)

5.5 Possession

Papapana has three types of possessive constructions. I will refer to the modifying NP in possessive constructions as the *possessor* and the noun that is modified by the possessor NP as the *possessum*. See §9.6.1 and §9.6.8 for possessive clauses, where possession is predicated at the clausal level.

In possessive constructions Papapana makes a formal distinction based on the semantic difference between inalienable and alienable nouns: this is a lexical category distinct from noun class and nouns are either one or the other in Papapana. The direct construction expresses inalienable possession (§5.5.1), while the indirect construction expresses alienable possession (§5.5.2). The indirect possessor proclitics can attach to a class or plural marker when the head noun has been elided in a possessed NP functioning as a non-verbal predicate (§5.5.3). Possessive constructions are recursive and consequently Papapana may exhibit possessor stacking (§5.5.4). A prepositional possessive construction also expresses alienable possession (§5.5.5), but may be used in conjunction with both the direct inalienable and indirect alienable construction for pragmatic purposes. Remnants of the Proto-Oceanic non-specific possessor constructions are evident in compound nouns (see §4.4.1).

In direct and indirect possessive constructions, possessor NPs may precede or follow the possessum in the outer layers of the NP (see Table 4.1, Table 4.2 and discussion in §4.1); therefore, as with other modifiers such as numerals, Papapana exhibits both right- and left-headed alignment. With the exception of Mono, Torau and Uruava (Evans and Palmer 2011), possessor NPs are postposed in Northwest Solomonic languages such as Taiof (Ross 2002b: 430) and Sisiqa (Ross 2002a: 460). Like Mono, Torau and Uruava, the right-headed alignment in Papapana is argued to be the result of contact with Papuan languages (Smith 2016a). Possessor NPs containing independent pronouns, Personal, Class I and Class II nouns are expressed by the same constructions: this is typologically less common in the world's languages (Dryer 2007b: 182).

5.5.1 Direct possessive construction

The direct possessive construction involves a pronominal possessor suffix attaching to the possessum as in (124)–(132); this reflects the Proto-Oceanic direct construction in which "the possessor may be a possessive affix or a separate word" (Lichtenberk 1985: 95). The direct possessive construction is head-marking, which is typical of Meso-Melanesian and Oceanic languages (Palmer 2012: 455). Table 5.10 shows the possessor suffixes in Papapana; they make two number distinctions, three person distinctions, and an exclusive vs. inclusive distinction in the first person plural.

Table 5.10: Direct possessor suffixes.

	1EXCL	1INCL	2	3
SG	-u		-mu	-na
PL	-mani	-ira	-miu	-ina

The possessor suffixes can co-occur with the specific articles as in (124) (unlike the possessor proclitics which never co-occur with specific articles; see §5.5.2), plural article *bau* (125) or numeral modifiers (126) or if the possessum is a Relational Location noun, it is marked by the locative case prefix *i-* (127).

(124) . . .*bikos* **nu=visio-na**   *e=ravaravai=ena.*
      because SPEC.CLII=body-3SG.PSSR 3SG.SBJ=black=3SG.IPFV
      '. . . because his skin was black.'
      (1-T029-00:19:19.350)

(125) *I=mei*   *tue=ami*
      3PL.SBJ=come.SEQ scold=1EXCL.OBJ
      bau sina-mani   ta   **bau tama-mani.**
      PL mother-1EXCL.PSSR and PL   father-1EXCL.PSSR
      'Our mothers and fathers scolded us.'
      (1-T011-00:01:47.979)

(126) . . .*u=vare*   *agoto=ina*   **nua=au**   **nima-na.**
      1SG.SBJ=REP hold=3PL.OBJ two=CLII arm-3SG.PSSR
      '. . .I again held its two arms.'
      (1-T106-00:01:22.180)

(127) *Nu=pen*   **i-butona-ira**   *e=po=na.*
      SPEC.CLII=pen LOC-middle-1INCL.PSSR 3SG.SBJ=stay=3SG.IPFV
      'The pen is in the middle of us.'
      (2-E026)

The possessor suffix may be the only reference to the possessor as in (124)–(127) or it may agree with a possessor NP, in which case the possessor suffix is still obligatory. When a possessor NP expressing the possessor occurs, it may either follow or precede the possessum as in (128) and (129) respectively. In the following examples, the possessor NP is headed by a Class II noun (128), Class I noun (129), Personal proper name (130) and even an independent pronoun (131)–(132), the latter of which is interesting and further research could reveal the circumstances under which pronominal possessors are doubled in this way.

(128) . . .*e-tama-***na**   ***nu=*'usia**   *e=wa=i=a*
PERS-father-3SG.PSSR SPEC.CLII=child 3SG.SBJ=say=TR=3SG.OBJ
e-sina-na. . .
PERS-mother-3SG.PSSR
'. . .the child's father said to his mother. . .'
(1-T031-00:02:06.520)

(129) **na=inu**   *na=mata-**na***
SPEC[CLI]=house SPEC[CLI]=door-3SG.PSSR
'the house's door'
(2-E006)

(130) **Rosu** *nu=mata-**na***   *e=tapipi.* . .
Satan SPEC.CLII=eye-3SG.PSSR 3SG.SBJ=close
'Satan's eye closed. . .'
(1-T035-00:05:43.298)

(131) **a:mani** *bau tama-**mani***
1EXCL PL father-1EXCL.PSSR
'our fathers'
(Fieldnotes 2013)

(132) *Nu=pen*   *e=po=na*   *i-butona-**ira***
SPEC.CLII=pen 3SG.SBJ=stay=3SG.IPFV LOC-middle-1INCL.PSSR
auara.
INCL.DU
'The pen is in the middle of us.'
(2-E026)

The direct possessive construction encodes all body parts, some bodily products, Relational Location nouns (which express locative parts) and some kinship terms (including all Personal kinship terms); such nouns are typically inalienably possessed in Oceanic languages (Lynch, Ross, and Crowley 2002: 41; Ross 2004c: 511). The direct construction in Papapana also encodes parts of a persona and parts of inanimate entities. Personal kinship terms and body parts are obligatorily possessed in Papapana and are therefore bound nouns. Relational Location nouns (which express locative parts) are optionally possessed by the direct construction, which is not unusual in Oceanic languages. Indeed in Proto-Oceanic (POc) "when a noun was viewed as semantically inalienable, like the inside of an object, it was monovalent (i.e. directly possessed, with a possessor suffix), but the same noun could also have zero valency if used in a context where inalienability was irrelevant" (Ross 2007b: 234).

Table 5.11 shows examples of directly possessed nouns in Papapana. Papapana is similar to Taiof (Ross 2002b: 430), Banoni (Lynch and Ross 2002: 460) and Sisiqa (Ross 2002a: 445) in which some kinship terms, some anatomical parts and some parts of wholes are inalienably possessed. The prototypical inalienable noun in Papapana thus expresses a part-whole relation, while kinship terms are not prototypical representatives. Indeed, the kinship terms which are inalienably possessed are the four Personal kinship terms and the

Table 5.11: Directly possessed nouns.

Body parts	
patu	head
vunu	hair
nima	hand
Some bodily products	
tae	excrement
mimi	urine
revasi	blood
sogana	smell
tongana	sweat
Relational Location nouns	
ata	above
vuna	below
bana	inside
Parts of persona	
vatono	name
abeabe	image/reflection
Parts of inanimate entities	
mata	door
batubatu	wall

Table 5.11 (continued)

tamana	outrigger
naunu	leaf
Some kinship terms	
tubu	grandparent, parent-in-law (of a woman)
sina	mother, aunt
tama	father
noa	mother-in-law (of a man), son-in-law (of a woman)
vavine	cross sex cross sex sibling/cousin

Class I kinship term *vavine* 'cross sex sibling/cousin'. Since the cognate *fafine* 'cross sex sibling' in Taiof belongs to the personal class (Ross 2002b: 428), it could be that the distribution of kinship terms across inalienably and alienably possessed constructions is a reflection of noun class diachronically.

5.5.2 Indirect possessive construction

The indirect construction involves pronominal possessor proclitics as in (133)–(145). These make two number distinctions, three person distinctions, and an exclusive vs. inclusive distinction in the first person plural, as Table 5.12 shows. As will be discussed in further detail below, the possessor proclitics attach to the head noun if it is a singular Class I noun, but otherwise they attach to the Class II marker *au*, or another prenominal article or modifier.

Table 5.12: Indirect possessor proclitics.

	1EXCL	1INCL	2	3
SG	au=		amu=	ena=
PL	ami=	era=	amiu=	oina=

The possessor proclitics are in the same syntactic position as the specific/non-specific articles, that is, the leftmost margin of the NP core. Consequently, the possessor proclitics do not co-occur with the specific/non-specific articles, however they can co-occur with numerals and other articles (see Table 4.1 and Table 4.2 in §4.1).

In (133) the possessum belongs to Class I noun class, whereas in (134) the possessum is a Class II noun. The possessor proclitics attach to the numeral modifier (see §5.4.2), which attaches to the Class II marker *au* in (134).

(133) "***Au=nua**   arao   i=wa...*"
    1SG.PSSR=two[CLI] brother   3PL.SBJ=say
    '"My two cousins said..."'
    (1-T042-00:01:51.940)

(134) ***Au=nua=au***   *'usia   i=to   ara tavotu=ma.*
    1SG.PSSR=two=CLII   child   3PL.SBJ=EMPH   PST   arrive=ma
    'My two children were born.'
    (1-T083-00:02:24.300)

In (135) the possessum belongs to Class I, whereas in (136) the possessum is a Class II noun. The possessor proclitics attach to the singular diminutive articles (see §5.3.4), which attaches to the Class II marker *au* in (136). It is even possible to have NPs which contain a possessor prolitic, numeral, diminutive article and *au* (137).

(135) ***Ena=si=arao***   *e=wa...*
    3SG.PSSR=DIM.CLI=brother   3SG.SBJ=say
    'His little brother said...'
    (1-T035-00:02:34.446)

(136) ***Ena=sa=au***   *'usia iai   e=po=ena=i=ma.*
    3SG.PSSR=DIM=CLII   child PROX 3SG.SBJ=stay=3SG.IPFV=IRR=ma
    'His poor child stayed behind.'
    (1-T031-00:03:34.270)

(137) *E=mate   asi=ina   **ena=nua   sa=au***   *'usia...*
    3SG.SBJ=die leave=3PL.OBJ 3SG.PSSR=two DIM=CLII child
    'He died leaving his two poor children...'
    (1-T030-00:03:53.913)

When the possessum is plural, the possessor proclitics attach to the plural article *bau*. *Bau* does not distinguish noun class as shown by (138) and (139) in which the possessums belong to Class I and II respectively. The possessor proclitics may also attach to the plural collective article (140).

(138) . . .*i=de=ina=i* **au=bau paga**. . .
3PL.SBJ=take=3PL.OBJ=IRR 1SG.PSSR=PL shoot
'. . .they got my guns. . .'
(1-T103-00:16:01.325)

(139) *"**Anau au=bau** 'usia i=ae eangoi=ina*
1SG 1SG.PSSR=PL child 3PL.SBJ=NEG be.able=3PL.IPFV
i=manene=i. . ."
3PL.SBJ=return=IRR
'"My children can't go back. . ."'
(2-T001-2-00:04:16.718)

(140) ***au=mamena** tama~tama-na*
1SG.PSSR=PL.COLL RD~father-DER
'my family'
(2-E005)

When there is no other prenominal modifier between the possessor proclitics and the possessum, the possessor proclitics attach to the head noun if it is a singular Class I noun (141), but otherwise they attach to the Class II marker *au* when the possessum is a Class II singular noun (142).

(141) ***Ami=vamamatau** na=orawi e=wa=ami.* . .
1EXCL.PSSR[CL1]=teach SPEC[CLI]=man 3SG.SBJ=say=1EXCL.OBJ
'Our teacher, a man, said to us. . .'
(1-T042-00:04:50.200)

(142) *"**Ami=au** 'usia e=eri nai=a=na*
1EXCL.PSSR=CLII child 3SG.SBJ=OPT marry=3SG.OBJ=3SG.IPFV
na=maunu mama."
SPEC[CLI]=woman DEM1
'"Our child wants to marry this woman."'
(1-T024-00:00:46.499)

The possessor proclitic may be the only reference to the possessor in Papapana as in all the examples so far, except (139) above and (143) below where it co-occurs with a possessor NP. In this case, the possessor proclitic is still obligatory, and may either precede or follow the possessum as in (139) and (143) respectively. While in (143) the possessor NP is headed by a Personal proper name, in

(139) it is an independent pronoun, which is again interesting and further research could reveal why pronominal possessors are doubled in this way.

(143) . . .*i=no*   *atunu=ina*   ***ena=bau***   *adope*   Isio.
3PL.SBJ=go.SEQ   attack=3PL.OBJ   3SG.PSSR=PL   grandchild   Devil
'. . .they went and killed the Devil's grandchildren.'
(1-T022-00:03:04.750)

In Oceanic indirect constructions the possessum is preceded or followed by an independent possessive constituent which is marked by a possessor suffix (Lynch, Ross, and Crowley 2002: 40). Excluding 1EXCL and 1INCL, the possessor proclitics in Papapana are identical to the possessor suffixes except for the addition of an initial vowel /a/, /e/ or /ɔ/. The 1INCL possessor proclitic form has a different initial vowel to the possessor suffix, /e/ instead of /i/, while the 1EXCL form is *ami=* compared with *-mani*. Synchronically, the Papapana possessor proclitics are not segmentable into a possessive constituent and a possessor suffix; however, given the similarity between the possessor suffixes and proclitics, it is likely that diachronically they were segmentable and that the initial vowels are reflexes of the PNWS possessive constituents **na-* and **sa-*, which expressed general possession, and **ye* which expressed consumable possession (Ross 1988: 185–186). Indeed, most Melanesian and Micronesian Oceanic languages distinguish different kinds of alienable possession by means of different constituents termed *classifiers*: in Western Melanesia a distinction is often made between consumable and non-consumable (Lynch, Ross, and Crowley 2002: 41). Papapana does not have possessive classifiers denoting different kinds of possessive relationship, as shown by (144) and (145) where the possessor proclitic for a consumable noun is the same as that for an unconsumable noun.

(144) ***Ami=bau***   *'usia*   *i=to*   *ara*   *nao*   *te=na=skuru*
1EXCL.PSSR=PL   child   3PL.SBJ   PST   go   OBL=SPEC[CLI]=school
reareana. . .
far
'Our children went to school far away. . .'
(1-T090- 00:00:23.980)

(145) . . .***ami=bau   kaukau tobi   mi=pei***
1EXCL.PSSR=PL potato   EMPH 1EXCL.SBJ=PST.IPFV
ani~ani=ina=ami=i
RD~eat=3PL.OBJ=1EXCL.IPFV=IRR
'. . .we would just eat our potatoes.'
(1-T096-00:02:08.139)

The indirect possessive construction is used for all other nouns including those kinship terms and bodily products that are not directly possessed. It is unclear why some bodily products are considered inalienable and others alienable; however, more kinship terms are alienably possessed than inalienably possessed, and as described in §5.5.1 those that are inalienably possessed are all Personal nouns, with one exception. Table 5.13 shows examples of indirectly possessed nouns in Papapana.

Table 5.13: Indirectly possessed nouns.

Some kinship terms	
arao	same sex male sibling/cousin
'usia	child, fraternal niece/nephew (of a woman)
adope	grandchild, daughter-in-law
vanisi	father-in-law
sinoni	husband
maunu	wife
Some bodily products	
'ou	cough
ngoroa	snot
pisi	wind
apuapu	sore
Other	
vevesi	thought/choice
magura	coconut
watu	stone/money
inu	house
poana	village
tue	language
koko'i	taro
daramu	water
skiotu	skirt
vonata	bed
boro	pig

5.5.3 Indirect possessor proclitics and elided nouns

In some possessed NPs functioning as non-verbal predicates expressing equation, it is possible for the indirect possessor proclitics to be present but the head noun to be elided. As discussed below, the possessor proclitic attaches to the Class I marker *ata*, Class II marker *au* or plural article *bau*, which raises questions about Papapana NP structure.

As described in §9.6.1.1, possessed NPs can function as predicates expressing equation, as in (146)–(147) where the noun is inalienable and so directly possessed, and in (148) where the noun is alienable and so indirectly possessed. In (147) there is also a prenominal coreferential possessor NP.

(146) *Iai* **nu=ie-u.**
PROX SPEC.CLII=leg-1SG.PSSR
'This is my leg.'
(2-E028-2)

(147) *Mama* **nu=boro** **nu=ie=na.**
DEM1 SPEC.CLII=pig SPEC.CLII=leg-3SG.PSSR
'This is the pig's leg.'
(2-E028-2)

(148) "*Iai* **ena=iana...**"
PROX 3SG.PSSR[CLI]=fish
'"This is his fish..."'
(1-T031-00:05:11.960)

In (146)–(148) the subject NP is headed by a demonstrative pronoun referring to the possessum. When the subject NP is headed by a noun referring to the possessum as in (149)–(152), there is no need for the predicate NP to also contain the possessum, thus it is elided, leaving the possessor proclitic and possibly a coreferential possessor NP as in (150). However, the possessor proclitic attaches to the Class I marker *ata*, Class II marker *au* or plural article *bau*, which agree with the elided noun in class and/or number, and thus also agree with the subject NP. This is similar to adjective phrase and some numeral phrase predicates, which also agree with the class (or animacy) of the subject NP (see §4.6.1 and §9.6.6). The corpus only shows this type of possessed NP predicate when the possessum is alienable; this is likely to be because inalienable nouns are usually obligatorily possessed bound nouns so it would not be possible for the subject NP to be unpossessed.

(149) *"Na=iana   mama iai   **au=ata**."*
    SPEC[CLI]=fish DEM1 PROX 1SG.PSSR=CLI
    '"This fish is mine."'
    (1-T029-00:01:30.120)

(150) *Na=inu   mama na=vaunu   **Peter ena=ata**.*
    SPEC[CLI]=house DEM1 SPEC[CLI]=new Peter 3SG.PSSR=CLI
    'This new house is Peter's.'
    (2-E004)

(151) *Nu=naono   nu=vaunu   **ami=au**.*
    SPEC.CLII=tree SPEC.CLII=new 1EXCL.PSSR=CLII
    'The new tree is ours.'
    (2-E002)

(152) *Bau inu   vaunu **ami=bau**.*
    PL   house new   1EXCL.PSSR=PL
    'The new houses are ours.'
    (2-E002)

The presence of *ata* in (149) is interesting because when the head noun is present, *ata* is absent as in (148): **iai ena=ata iana* 'this is his fish' is not grammatical. This contrasts with *au* and *bau* which are present regardless of whether the noun is elided or not (compare (151) and (152) with (142) and (144) in §5.5.2). Thus in full NPs, the lack of a class marker indicates singularity and Class I, whereas the presence of *au* indicates singularity and Class II, and the presence of *bau* indicates plurality. Diachronically, *ata* may have been present in the same prenominal position in the NP as Class II *au*, but synchronically we only see *ata* in these possessed NP predicates and in quantifier phrases (QP) headed by the quantifier *na:* 'some, other' (see §5.6.3). In these QPs, the NP complement of the quantifier is also not a full NP as it only consists of *ata, au* or *bau* and the head noun has been elided but its class and/or number is reflected by *ata, au,* or *bau,* and its referent is recoverable from the discourse context or from an apposed NP. It could also be the case that in the counting system *nuata* 'two' is analysable as *nua=ata*, switching to *nua=Ø* when modifying Class I nouns, and *nua=au* when modifying Class II nouns (see §5.4), but note that *nuata* is only ever a number used to count, it is not a NP predicate or a partial NP complement. Even if we analysed the possessor proclitics as outside the NP, like quantifiers, with both perhaps belonging to the category of determiner (along with specific/non-specific articles), then we still have to account for a NP consisting only of *ata, au* and *bau*, which raises questions for further research about Papapana NP structure and whether *ata, au* and *bau* should be considered phrasal heads.

5.5.4 Possessor stacking

Possessive constructions are recursive, thus a modifying possessor NP may itself be possessed as in (153) and (154).

(153) *Te* **e-sina-na** **e-tama-na**
OBL PERS-mother-3SG.PSSR PERS-father-3SG.PSSR
oina=vevese.
3PL.PSSR[CL1]=choice
'It (marriage) was of his/her parents' choice.'
(1-T024-00:00:20.320)

(154) . . .*mi=ara* *tua* *mai* *a:mani* **au=sinoni**
1EXCL.SBJ=PST paddle hither 1EXCL 1SG.PSSR[CL1]=husband
ena=bau *toi* **poana,** *toi* *Rorovana.*
3SG.PSSR=PL person village person Rorovana
'. . .we paddled here (with) my husband's relatives, the Rorovana people.'
(1-T023-00:00:31.300)

In (153) and (154), the modifying possessor NP precedes the possessum, but the position is variable as shown in the following pairs of examples: in (155) both the possessor NP and the possessum are directly possessed, in (156) the possessor NP is directly possessed and the possessum indirectly possessed, while in (157) both the possessor NP and the possessum are indirectly possessed.

(155) a. **e-tubu-u** *nu=patu-na*
PERS-grandparent-1SG.PSSR SPEC.CLII=head-3SG.PSSR
'my grandmother's head'
(2-E005)
b. *nu=patu-na* **e-tubu-u**
SPEC.CLII=head-3SG.PSSR PERS-grandparent-1SG.PSSR
'my grandmother's head'
(2-E005)

(156) a. **e-sina-u**   ena=inu
       PERS-mother-1SG.PSSR   3SG.PSSR[CLI]=house
       'my mother's house'
       (2-E005)
   b. ena=inu   **e-sina-u**
       3SG.PSSR[CLI]=house   PERS-mother-1SG.PSSR
       'my mother's house'
       (2-E005)

(157) a. **au=maunu**   ena=au   obutu
       1SG.PSSR[CLI]=wife   3SG.PSSR=CLII   canoe
       'my wife's canoe'
       (2-E005)
   b. ena=au   obutu   **au=maunu**
       3SG.PSSR=CLII   canoe   1SG.PSSR[CLI]=wife
       'my wife's canoe'
       (2-E005)

5.5.5 Prepositional possessive construction

Papapana also expresses possession via a preposition linking the possessed NP and the possessor NP; it is typical of Oceanic languages to have this third kind of possessive construction (Lichtenberk 1985; Lynch, Ross, and Crowley 2002: 42) and it is employed in some Northwest Solomonic languages, such as Banoni (Lynch and Ross 2002: 466), Roviana (Corston-Oliver 2002: 479–480), Sisiqa (Ross 2002a: 460–461) and Teop (Mosel and Thiesen 2007).

In Papapana, the preposition *te* forms a PP constituent with a possessor NP and the construction is thus dependent marked (see also §8.3). The PP follows the possessum. The head of the possessor NP may be a Personal noun (158b)–(159), Class I noun (160) or independent pronoun (158a). No examples with a Class II noun are attested, although there is no evidence that Class II nouns are not allowed in such a construction. Prepositional possessive constructions may only express alienable possession with alienably possessed nouns as in (158)–(160), so an inalienable noun such as *mata* 'eye' cannot be possessed in the prepositional construction (161). Although Location nouns do not occur in PPs with *te*, and thus cannot be possessors in a possessive PP, a Location noun can be the possessum, as in (159)–(160).

(158) a. ...**na='usia**   **te**   **a:mani**   mi=va-tavotu=ina
       SPEC[CLI]=child OBL 1EXCL 1EXCL.SBJ=CAUS-arrive=3PL.OBJ
       nani,
       there
   b. **na=adope**   **te**   **Kaie.**
       SPEC[CLI]=grandchild OBL Kaie
       '...we gave birth to our children there, Kaie's grandchildren.'
       (1-T030-0:01:35.957)

(159) I=tua   dini   mai   **i-poana**   **te**   **e-sina-na.**..
       3PL.SBJ=paddle down hither LOC-village OBL PERS-mother-3SG.PSSR
       'They paddled back to his mother's place...'
       (1-T003-00:01:44.840)

(160) ...iara na=maunu   i=oi   asi=a
       then SPEC.CLI=woman 3PL.SBJ=take leave=3SG.OBJ
       nao=i   **i-inu**   **te=na=orawi.**
       thither=IRR LOC-house OBL=SPEC[CLI]=man
       '...then they take the woman to the man's home.'
       (1-T024-00:01:41.520)

(161) *****nu=mata**   **te**   **aia**
       SPEC.CLII=eye OBL 3SG
       'his eye'

There is no perceived semantic or pragmatic difference between the prepositional possessive construction, and direct and indirect possessive constructions: when presented with (162) from a text recording, speakers found it acceptable to substitute *nutura te ani* with *amuau tura* (163), deeming the meanings to be identical. Further research is required to confirm this analysis.

(162) **Nu=tura**   **te**   **ani** maria e=sisiva=ena=i...
       SPEC.CLII=fire OBL 2SG thing 3SG.SBJ=hot=3SG.IPFV=IRR
       'Your fire must be hot...'
       (1-T036-9-00:01:41.460)

(163) **amu=au** tura
2SG.PSSR=CLII fire
'your fire'
(2-E005)

The prepositional possessive construction may occur on its own, or in conjunction with either the direct (164) or indirect (165) possessive construction. The combination emphasises or contrasts the possession.

(164) *Na=orawi nu=buku e=noe=a*
SPEC.CLI=man SPEC.CLI=book 3SG.SBJ= put=3SG.OBJ
i-patu-na te=na=au 'usia.
LOC-head-3SG.PSSR OBL=SPEC=CLII child
'The man put the book on the child's head.'
(2-E015)

(165) *Ta e=pei siodo=ena=i,* **ena=siodo** *te*
and 3SG.SBJ=PST.IPFV work=3SG.IPFV=IRR 3SG.PSSR[CLI]=job OBL
aia avosia na=carpenter tomana, e-tama-u.
3SG like SPEC.CLI=carpenter too PERS-father-1SG.PSSR
'And he was working, his job was also a carpenter, my father.'
(1-T034-00:18:15.430)

5.6 Quantifiers and quantifier phrases

Papapana has a closed lexical class of three *quantifiers* which indicate relative or indefinite quantity. The quantifier *na:* denotes 'some, other', *ta:* denotes 'some' and *a'aisi* indicates abundance. The notion of 'few' may be expressed by the partitive noun (§4.4.2) or partitive article (§5.3.6). *Na:* can head a quantifier phrase (QP) which has a possessed NP complement, or PP complement (§5.6.1), while *na:* and *ta:* can head a QP which has a NP complement marked by the plural article *bau* (§5.6.2). *Na:* can also head a QP that has a partial NP complement consisting only of the class markers *ata* and *au*, or the plural article *bau*: here the head of the complement NP has been elided but its referent is recoverable either from the discourse context or from an apposed NP (§5.6.3). Finally, *a'aisi* 'many' heads a QP that may or may not have a complement NP (§5.6.4). QPs can function as arguments or adjuncts of a verb, or in one case (173), as the complement of a PP headed by *merei*.

5.6.1 *na:* 'some, other' with possessed NP complement or PP complement

QPs headed by the quantifier *na:* 'some, other' always have a complement; either a possessed NP or a PP headed by *te*. The fact that *na:* precedes PPs is evidence that it is the head of a QP, rather than being an adnominal constituent in a NP: if *na:* 'some, other' were an adnominal constituent in a NP then it would follow the preposition *te*, rather than be separated from the NP by the preposition as it is in (169)–(172).

The attested NP complements all begin with a possessor proclitic (166)–(168). The head of the NP may belong to Class I (166) or Class II (167) noun class, and hence may or may not be marked by the Class II marker *au*. The head of the NP may also be plural and marked by *bau* (168).

(166) **Na: au=arao** *e=wa=au...*
 other 1SG.PSSR[CLI]=brother 3SG.SBJ=say=1SG.OBJ
 'My other cousin said to me...'
 (1-T042-00:01:04.490)

(167) **na: au=au obutu**
 other 1SG.PSSR=CLII canoe
 'my other canoe'
 (3-E001)

(168) ...**na: ami=bau** *burimaunu tena visit=ina...*
 other 1EXCL.PSSR=PL women SUBR visit=3PL.OBJ
 '...to visit some of our women...'
 (1-T053-00:04:24.560)

The attested PP complements are all headed by the preposition *te* (169)–(172). This type of construction occurs quite frequently in the text data and speakers confirmed that it was acceptable on several occasions.

(169) *E=to tua nao* **na: te=na='uru.**
 3SG.SBJ=EMPH paddle thither other OBL=SPEC[CLI]=island
 'He paddled to another/the other island.'
 (1-T091-00:02:10.476)

(170) *Mi=to   nao,   mi=no   ubete* **na:**
      1EXCL.SBJ=EMPH go   1EXCL.SBJ=go.SEQ   lay   other
      te=na=poana.
      OBL=SPEC[CLI]=village
      'We went, we went and slept in another/the other village.'
      (1-T103-00:01:54.573)

(171) *Na=orawi   e=pei   umunu=ena=i   **na:***
      SPEC[CLI]=man 3SG.SBJ=PST.IPFV sit= 3SG.IPFV=IRR   other
      te=na=au   naono.
      OBL=SPEC=CLII   tree
      'The man was sitting on another/the other tree.'
      (3-E001)

(172) **Na:**   ***te=na=au   obutu*** *e=tua.*
      other   OBL=SPEC=CLII canoe 3SG.SBJ=paddle
      'He paddled in another/the other canoe.'
      (3-E001)

Example (173) shows that a QP with a PP complement can itself even be the complement of the attributive preposition *merei*. Such PPs are postnominal modifiers expressing the origin or purpose of the head noun (see §4.8).

(173) *...marana   burimaunu o   na=vanua   merei   **na:***
      even.though women   or SPEC.CLI=people ATTRIB other
      te=na=poana,   *i=vamamatau=ina=ina   oina=bau*
      OBL=SPEC[CLI]=village 3PL.SBJ=teach=3PL.OBJ=3PL.IPFV 3PL.PSSR=PL
      'usia   te   oina=au   tue.
      child OBL 3PL.PSSR=CLII language
      '[In other villages] ...even though the women or men are from other villages, they teach their children in their language.'
      (1-T083-00:04:57.130)

5.6.2 *na:* 'some, other' and *ta:* 'some' with plural NP complement

QPs headed by the quantifier *na:* 'some, other' (174)–(175) or *ta:* 'some' (176)–(177) can have a plural NP complement which has been marked by the plural article *bau*. The quantifier forms a phonological word with *bau* resulting in *na:bau* and *ta:bau*. However, the quantifiers do not form phonological words with the possessed nouns or preposition *te* in (166)–(173) so I do not analyse *na:* or *ta:* as clitics there. The quantifier *ta:* 'some' occurs so infrequently in the corpus that its existence did not become apparent until the end of my second fieldwork trip.

In (174) the head of the NP complement has also been marked for plurality by reduplication, in addition to *bau* (see §5.2.3), while in (175) the head of the NP complement is a compound noun (see §4.4.1). In (177) the NP complement contains a modifying adjective phrase *navei dua* 'bad' (see §4.6.1), and the head noun has been derived from a verb via reduplication.

(174) *U=nongono   avosia **na:=bau poa~poana iai,***
       1SG.SBJ=hear SUBR   other=PL RD~village PROX
       na=tonu   vewa iai   e=tete.
       SPEC[CLI]=wave   like PROX 3SG.SBJ=enter
       'I heard that in some places, a wave like this came inside.'
       (1-T105-00:15:36.720)

(175) *Enai eangoiena va:gi **na:=bau vanua-i***   *sikuna i=ara*
       after until   now   some=PL people-CONST ship   3PL.SBJ=PST
       naomai.
       come
       'So until today some foreigners (lit. ship people) came.'
       (1-T034-00:39:15.380)

(176) *. . .tena vae atu=ina   **ta:=bau taramina.***
       SUBR   REP make=3PL.OBJ some=PL thing
       '. . .to do some things again.'
       (1-T103-00:13:14.375)

(177) ***Ta:=bau atu~atu   na=vei   dua***
       some=PL RD~make SPEC[CLI]=COLL bad
       i=pei   ae   atu=ami=i.
       3PL.SBJ=PST.IPFV NEG   make=1EXCL.OBJ=IRR
       'They would not do any bad things to us.'
       (1-T025-00:01:24.200)

5.6.3 *na:* 'some, other' with partial NP complements

QPs headed by the quantifier *na:* 'some, other' often have a complement that is not a full NP, but consists only of the Class I marker *ata* (178), the Class II marker *au*, or the plural article *bau* (179)–(181). The quantifier forms a phonological word with these morphemes, resulting in *na:ata, na:au* and *na:bau*. The head of the complement NP has been elided but its class and/or number is reflected by *ata, au*, or *bau*, and its referent is anaphorically recoverable from the discourse context. That the head noun has been elided is further supported by the fact that other (usually) postnominal modifying constituents are present: an attributive PP in (180) (see §4.8) and a limiting modifier in (181) (see §4.7.2).

(178) . . .***na:=ata*** e=vae tete.
some=CLI 3SG.SBJ=REP enter
'. . .another [wave] hit.'
(1-T105-00:19:36.220)

(179) ***Na:=bau*** po manene=ina=i, a'aisi i=ae nao=i.
some=PL stay return=3PL.IPFV=IRR many 3PL.SBJ=NEG go=IRR
'Some (young women and men) will stay, many (young women and men) won't go.'
(1-T025-00:02:10.970)

(180) . . .*mama i=to usimu=ina=ina tena bau farm*
DEM1 3PL.SBJ=EMPH use=3PL.OBJ=3PL.IPFV OBL PL farm
*merei paga maria boro, na=marei tau **na:=bau** merei*
ATTRIB shoot thing pig SPEC[CLI]=bird and some=PL ATTRIB
***Second World War.** . .*
Second World War
'[The guns weren't strong] . . .those they used on the farms for shooting pigs, birds, and some (guns) from the Second World War. . .'
(1-T103-00:02:16.999)

(181) ***Na:=bau*** ora i=pei nao=i. . .
some=PL only 3PL.SBJ=PST.IPFV go=IRR
'Only some (people) would go. . .'
(1-T105-00:02:53.432)

Sometimes, there is another NP in apposition with this QP, which may follow or precede the QP as in (182)–(185) and (186)–(187) respectively (this reflects the variation in constituent order found elsewhere in Papapana). The class and/or number of the elided head of the complement NP is reflected by *ata, au*, or *bau*, and the referent of the elided head is anaphorically or cataphorically recoverable from the apposed NP. Note that in (187) the head of the apposed NP, *'usia* 'child', is a Class II noun so the Class I specific article marks plurality here (see §5.3.2 on inverse number marking).

(182) . . .*e=nai=a*   **na:=ata**   *na=maunu.*
  3SG.SBJ=marry=3SG.OBJ some=CLI SPEC[CLI]=woman
  '. . .he married another woman.'
  (1-T026-00:00:27.400)

(183) . . .*iara* **na:=au**   *nu='usia*   *e=vae*   *burisi=a.*
  then   some=CLII SPEC.CLII=child 3SG.SBJ=REP deliver=3SG.OBJ
  '. . .then she gave birth to another child.'
  (1-T029-00:23:26.570)

(184) **Na:=bau** *bau vesunu* *i=etawa=ina.*
  some=PL PL star 3PL.SBJ=big=3PL.IPFV
  'Some stars are big.'
  (2-E023)

(185) **Na:=bau ani**   *vanua,*   *nu=toa*   *e=oa=ina,*
  some=PL DIM.PL people SPEC.CLII=chicken 3SG.SBJ=cry=3PL.OBJ
  i=pei   *tua~tua*   *roro=ina*   *mai*   *Arigoa.*
  3PL.SBJ=PST.IPFV RD~paddle still=3PL.IPFV hither Arigoa
  'Some poor men were still paddling to Arigoa when the chicken cried out at them.'
  (1-T065-00:03:02.170)

(186) . . .*aia* **na=poana**   **na:=ata**   *e=nasi=a.* . .
  3SG   SPEC[CLI]=village some=CLI 3SG.SBJ=ask=3SG.OBJ
  '. . .he asked another village. . .'
  (1-T074-00:01:26.090)

(187) **Na='usia**   *na:=bau* *i=pei*   *magono=i*
  SPEC[CLI]=child some=PL 3PL.SBJ=PST.IPFV dislike=IRR
  avosia *mi=nao=i*   *te=na=skuru.*
  SUBR 1EXCL.SBJ=go=IRR OBL=SPEC[CLI]=school
  'Some children wouldn't want us to go to school.'
  (1-T011-00:01:40.060)

There is some variation in the corpus on the choice of article marking the head of the apposed NP when its referent is plural (see also (191) and (193) in §5.6.4). In (188) *vesunu* 'star' is a Class I noun and is marked by the singular Class I specific article *na=*, while in (189) *obutu* 'canoe' is a Class II noun and is marked by the singular Class II specific article *nu=*. This contrasts with (184) and (187) above where the heads of the apposed NPs are Class I *vesunu* 'star' and Class II *'usia* 'child' respectively yet they are marked with the plural article or inverse number marking. Within the time constraints of my fieldwork, it was not possible to determine the reason for the variable use of articles in NPs that are in apposition with *na:bau*. In fact, elicitation produced as much variation as had been attested in the text data.

(188) ***Na:=bau*** ***na=vesunu*** *i=etawa=ina*.
some=PL SPEC[CLI]=star 3PL.SBJ=big=3PL.IPFV
'Some stars are big.'
(2-E023)

(189) ***Na:=bau*** ***nu=obutu*** *i=po* *egoego=ina*.
some=PL SPEC.CLII=canoe 3PL.SBJ=stay well=3PL.IPFV
'Some canoes were fine.'
(2-E011)

In (174)–(175) in §5.6.2, *na:* has a complement NP marked by *bau*; this contrasts with example (184) where *na:* has a partial complement NP containing only *bau*, and then an apposed NP marked by *bau*. The fact that the complement NP of *na:* in (178)–(187) is not a whole NP raises questions for further research about Papapana NP structure and whether *ata*, *au* and *bau* should be considered phrasal heads (see also discussion in §5.5.3).

5.6.4 *a'aisi* 'many'

QPs headed by the quantifier *a'aisi* 'many' may or may not have a complement NP, which may precede or follow the quantifier. Dislocation of *a'aisi* from the NP, as in (195a), demonstrates quantifier float and is evidence that the quantifier is the head of a QP, rather than being an adnominal constituent in a NP.

The QP can either precede or follow its complement NP as in (190)–(191) and (192)–(194) respectively. This is another instance of the mixture of left-headedness and right-headedness found in Papapana. The head of the complement NP may be marked by a specific article (190)–(192) or the plural article (193)–(194). Note that in (191) and (193), both from text recording 1-T098, the speaker varies in their choice of article for the Class I noun *siodo* 'job', using the singular Class I specific article *na=* in (191) but the plural article *bau* in (193). This is similar to the variable use of articles in NPs that are in apposition with *na:bau* discussed in §5.6.3 and it is unclear whether this variation is free or not.

(190) . . .*a'aisi na=vanua*   *i=ara*   *atunu=ina*. . .
many   SPEC[CLI]=people 3PL.SBJ=PST attack-3PL.OBJ
'. . .they attacked many people. . .'
(1-T034-00:31:39.904)

(191) ***A'aisi na=siodo***   *i=ta~tavotu=ina.*
many SPEC[CLI]=work 3PL.SBJ=RD~arrive=3PL.IPFV
'Many jobs are appearing.'
(1-T098-00:04:25.611)

(192) . . .*avosia **na=vanua***   *a'aisi i=mate.*
SUBR   SPEC[CLI]=people many 3PL.SBJ=die
'. . .that many people had died.'
(1-T103-00:07:09.983)

(193) *Port Moresby va:gi **bau** siodo a'aisi o=peri=ina=i*
Port Moresby now PL   work many 2SG.SBJ=find=3PL.OBJ=IRR
Port Moresby.
Port Moresby
'You'll find many jobs in Port Moresby today.'
(1-T098-00:00:30.850)

(194) ***Bau** 'a'ade'e a'aisi e=ma'a=u.*
PL   narrative many 2SG.SBJ=find=3PL.OBJ=IRR
'He gave me a lot of stories.'
(1-T089-00:10:36.403)

Remarkably, *a'aisi* 'many' can even be dislocated from its complement NP as in (195). In an elicitation session, speakers confirmed this and reported that (195b) and (195c) were also acceptable, and they did not perceive a change in meaning. This dislocation is evidence that the quantifier is the head of a QP and not an adnominal constituent in a NP.

(195) a. ***Na=vanua***   *i=pei*   *mate~mate=ina=i*   ***a'aisi.***
SPEC[CLI]=people   3PL.SBJ=PST.IPFV   RD~die=3PL.IPFV=IRR   many
'Many people died.'
(1-T034- 00:07:36.480)

b. ***A'aisi na=vanua***   *i=pei*   *mate~mate=ina=i.*
many   SPEC[CLI]=people   3PL.SBJ=PST.IPFV   RD~die=3PL.IPFV=IRR
'Many people died.'
(2-E005)

c. ***Na=vanua***   ***a'aisi***   *i=pei*   *mate~mate=ina=i.*
SPEC[CLI]=people   many   3PL.SBJ=PST.IPFV   RD~die=3PL.IPFV=IRR
'Many people died.'
(2-E005).

A'aisi may be modified by the intensifiers *poto* and *mamangi* (see §4.7.3) as in (196) and (197) respectively.

(196) . . .*na=kauto*   ***a'aisi mamangi***   *i=mangano*
SPEC[CLI]=Terminalia.Catappa   many   INTS   3SG.SBJ=hang
i-ata.
LOC-above
'. . .very many Terminalia Catappa nuts were hanging above.'
(1-T033-00:01:12.240)

(197) . . .*na=vanua*   ***a'aisi poto***   *i=pei*   *ara*
SPEC[CLI]=people   many   INTS   3PL.SBJ=PST.IPFV   PST
po=ina=i.
stay=3PL.IPFV=IRR
'Very many people stayed. . . [here in our village in the past].'
(1-T029-00:00:19.890)

Some QPs headed by the quantifier *a'aisi* 'many' do not have an overt complement NP as in (198)–(199) but instead it is elided and the referent of the complement NP is anaphorically recoverable from the discourse context.

(198) *Na:=bau po manene=ina=i,* **a'aisi** *i=ae nao=i.*
some=PL stay return=3PL.IPFV=IRR many 3PL.SBJ=NEG go=IRR
'Some [young women and men] will stay, many [young women and men] won't go.'
(1-T025-00:02:10.970)

(199) ***A'aisi poto*** *u=to roroto vowa=ina=au. . .*
many INTS 1SG.SBJ=EMPH see be.like=3PL.OBJ=1SG.IPFV
'Very many [things] I look at. . .'
(1-T089-00:15:36.922)

Chapter 6
Verbs and the verb complex

This chapter describes verbs and the structure of the verb complex (§6.1), verbal derivation and compounding (§6.2), argument marking and alignment (§6.3), verb types (§6.4) and valency-changing operations (§6.5), and verb serialisation (§6.6). Verbs can be modified by directionals (§6.7) and adverbs (§6.8). Chapter 7 describes tense, aspect and mode marking, imperative marking and negation.

6.1 Verbs and verb complex structure

Verbs, including derived verbs and compound verbs (§6.2), belong to an open word class in Papapana and can be categorised according to their transitivity based on the presence/absence of object-indexing enclitics, the macrorole of the subject, and the valency-changing devices which can operate with the verb (see §6.4). Certain verbs can occur in serial verb constructions (SVC) (§6.6) while verbs may also be categorised into aspectual classes (§7.1.7). The defining characteristic of verbs in Papapana is that they are always marked by subject-indexing proclitics. Verbs do not have to be marked for tense, aspect or mode (TAM) but when they are, TAM distinctions are made through verbal reduplication and/or preverbal and postverbal markers. Verbs can be reduplicated in prohibitive constructions, reciprocal constructions or to mark imperfective aspect. Verbs can also be negated and/or modified by adverbs, directionals and an emphatic marker. A verb in Papapana functions primarily as a predicate but some verbs may also modify nouns in compounds (§4.4). The head of a verbal predicate may be a verb, or a verb derived from another lexical category (§6.2).

The *verb complex* (VC) is a traditional descriptive device in Oceanic research that captures the fixed structural relationship between the verbal head (or sequence of verbs in a serial construction) and its accompanying modifiers. I do not attempt to model the syntactic status of the VC here. The VC does not include arguments and the object-indexing enclitics are considered to be agreement rather than pronominal objects (see §6.3.2); therefore, without the inclusion of the object noun phrase (NP), the VC does not equate to a verb phrase (VP). Whether or not Papapana even has a VP is open to further research; certainly the fact that adjuncts can occur between the object NP and the VC (see §8) suggests that perhaps Papapana does not have a VP. Tables 6.1 and 6.2 show the VC structure in Papapana.

Table 6.1: Verb complex structure: preverbal.

	PREVERBAL									HEAD
SBJ=	EMPH	PST.IPFV	OPT or COND	NEG or APPR	PST	REP	Adverb	Seq.	CAUS- or DETR- or COM or R/R	VERB(S)

Table 6.2: Verb complex structure: postverbal.

HEAD	POSTVERBAL										
VERB(S)	Geog.	All.	COMPL	Adverb	Adverb	=TR or APPL	=OBJ	=PSI	Deic.	=IRR	=REP

The most minimal VC in Papapana consists of a head with subject-indexing proclitic attached to the leftmost margin of the VC as in (1). The head position includes the preverbal valency-changing morphemes: causative *va-* (§6.5.2), detransitivising *ta-* (§6.5.3), comitative *me* (§6.5.4) or reciprocal/reflexive *vei* (§6.5.6) as in (2). Inflectional verbal reduplication occurs in the VC in prohibitive constructions with *ae* or *te* (§7.3.2), reciprocal constructions with *vei* (§6.5.6.1) as in (2) or to mark continuous or habitual aspect in conjunction with postverbal subject-indexing (PSI) enclitics (§7.1.6).

(1) Nani te=na=garasi **mi=tamu.**
    there OBL=SPEC[CLI]=grass 1EXCL.SBJ=eat
    'We ate there on the grass.'
    (1-T071-00:05:52.450)

(2) Iara **i=pei** vae vei a~'adu=ina=i.
    then 3PL.SBJ=PST.IPFV REP R/R RD~destroy=3PL.IPFV=IRR
    'Then they kept hurting each other.'
    (1-T034-00:04:06.306)

There are ten preverbal positions. First are the subject-indexing proclitics (§6.3.2.1) then the emphatic marker *to* (§6.3.3) as in (3), then the past imperfective marker *pei* (§7.1.4.2) and the optative mode marker *eri* or conditional mode *awa* (whose relative order is unclear) (§7.1.5 and §7.1.4.4) as in (4). Next are the negative marker *ae* (§7.3.1) or apprehensive mode marker *te* (§7.1.4.3), then the past tense marker *ara* (§7.1.3) as in (5). Finally there are the repetitive aspect marker *vare ~ vae* (§7.1.7) as in (6), preverbal adverbs (§6.8.1) and the sequential directionals *mei* 'come and' or *no* 'go and' (whose order relative to *ara, vare ~ vae* and preverbal adverbs can vary) (§6.7.3).

There are ten postverbal positions. First are the geocentric directionals *tae* 'ascend/away from shore', *dini* 'descend/towards shore' as in (3) or *batabata* 'parallel' (§6.7.1) and the allative directional *vowa ~ vewa* 'towards' (§6.7.4). Next are the completive aspect marker *osi* (§7.1.8) as in (3), postverbal adverbs such as *egoego* in (5) (see §6.8.2), then transitive =*i* or applicative *i* (under certain conditions) (§6.5.1), object-indexing enclitics (§6.3.2.2) as in (6), postverbal subject-indexing (PSI) enclitics (§7.1.1) as in (4) and deictic directionals *mai* 'hither' and *nao* 'thither' (§6.7.2) as in (3). Finally at the rightmost margin of the VC are the irrealis mode enclitic =*i* (§7.1.4) and/or the discontinuous repetitive aspect enclitic =*re* (§7.1.8) as in (6). Usually only one adverb occurs postverbally, but two adverbs are attested; however, further data is required to establish whether there are any restrictions regarding the adverbs that can co-occur and their relative order (see §6.8.2.1).

(3) **U=to** tua dini osi mai...
1SG.SBJ=EMPH paddle down COMPL hither
'(When) I have paddled back...'
(2-E007-2B)

(4) **I=pei** eri agos=i=a=ina=i.
3PL.SBJ=PST.IPFV OPT hold=TR=3SG.OBJ=3PL.IPFV=IRR
'They wanted to hold her.'
(1-T029-00:23:46.299)

(5) *Tau Nathan e=ae ara tavotu egoego.*
and Nathan 3SG.SBJ=NEG PST arrive well
'And Nathan didn't turn out well.'
(1-T104-00:01:40.480)

(6) **U=vare   kaku   tae=a=i=re.**
    1SG.SBJ=REP bend up=3SG.OBJ=IRR=REP
    'I'll bend it up again.'
    (1-T062-00:03:39.980)

6.2 Verbal derivation and compounding

Papapana does not have extensive patterns of verbal derivation. This brief section describes the limited instances of zero derivation (§6.2.1), reduplication (§6.2.2) and verbal compounding (§6.2.3), as well as outlining valency-changing operations (§6.2.4).

6.2.1 Zero derivation

In most cases of verbal derivation from other lexical categories, verbs are derived through zero derivation, most notably from adjectives as in (7) and some nouns (8)–(11).

In (7a) the adjective *etawa* 'big' modifies the head noun *tama* 'father' while in (7b) *etawa* is an intransitive verb denoting 'be big' (see §4.6 and §6.4.1 for more examples).

(7) a. *E-sina-u*   *kaka'i ta*   *e-tama-u*
       PERS-mother-1SG.PSSR small   and PERS-father-1SG.PSSR
       etawa   *i=nao.*
       big   3PL.SBJ=go
       'My small mother and big father went.'
       (2-E004)
    b. *Aia   e=etawa=ena.*
       3SG 3SG.SBJ=big=3SG.IPFV
       'He is big.'
       (2-E011)

In (8a), (9a) and (10), where the verb has been derived from a noun, the resulting verb is intransitive and has a stative meaning: 'be afternoon', 'be night', 'be a man'. In (8b) and (9b), the resulting verb is monotransitive and denotes 'afternoon/night befall someone'. In (11) the resulting verb is monotransitive and denotes 'be friends with'. There are only three other instances attested in the corpus of verbs zero-derived from nouns: the directly possessed Personal noun *e-sina-na* 'its mother' is derived as the verb 'to be its mother'; *sikuru* 'school' is derived as the verb 'to go to school'; and the compound *tue-ni Papapana* 'Papapana language' is derived as the verb 'to speak Papapana'. These instances came from two elicitation sessions and fieldnotes and were not subsequently verified. Verbal derivation from nouns does not therefore appear to be a productive process, but further data is required to determine whether verbs can be zero-derived from other nouns and if so, which types of nouns and why.

(8) a. ***E=navi*** **tani.**
 3SG.SBJ=afternoon already
 'It's nearly evening (lit. it's afternoon already).'
 (1-T033-00:01:33.440)

 b. . . .*e=pei* *no* *siodo=ena=i*
 3SG.SBJ=PST.IPFV go.SEQ work=3SG.IPFV=IRR
 e=no ***navi=i=a.***
 3SG.SBJ=go.SEQ afternoon=TR=3SG.OBJ
 '. . .she was working until the afternoon fell on her.'
 (1-T052-00:02:16.580)

(9) a. *Enai=ma* ***e=to*** **boni mai,** *mi=aputu=ma.*
 after=ma 3SG.SBJ=EMPH night hither 1EXCL.SBJ=sleep=ma
 'Then it was night, we slept.'
 (1-T033-00:03:35.510)

 b. . . .*e=nao* ***e=to*** ***boni=i=a*** nani.
 3SG.SBJ=go 3SG.SBJ=EMPH night=TR=3SG.OBJ there
 '. . .he went until night fell on him there.'
 (1-T091-00:02:32.908)

(10) . . .***e=no*** *orawi-ota.*
 3SG.SBJ= go.SEQ man-AUG
 '[And they looked after him well] . . .he became a grown man.'
 (1-T034-00:11:03.010)

(11) a. *Na=au* *pupu* *va:gi* ***e=atamata*** *roro=a=na*
 SPEC=CLII hornbill now 3SG.SBJ=friend still=3SG.OBJ=3SG.IPFV
 cassowary.
 cassowary
 'The hornbill is still friends with the cassowary now.'
 (Fieldnotes 2013, pedagogical readers)

b. *Na=orawi   o=to   atamata=a=mu=i*
     SPEC[CLI]=man 2SG.SBJ=EMPH friend=3SG.OBJ=2SG.IPFV=IRR
     enai. . .
     DEM2
     'If you're friends with/dating the man. . . [he stays at his mother's].'
     (3-D001-00:03:55.447)

6.2.2 Reduplication

There are a limited number of examples in my data of verbs derived through reduplication from a noun, such as in (12). An intransitive verb is also derived by reduplication from the emphatic marker *tobi* (13).

(12) a. **Na=au**   *tu*
        SPEC=CLII utensil
        'a utensil'
        (Fieldnotes 2013)
     b. *Anau* **u=tu~tu**   *tamu~tamu.*
        1SG   1SG.SBJ=RD~utensil   RD~eat
        'I served food.'
        (Fieldnotes 2013)

(13) a. **Anau tobi**   *u=de=a=ma*   *na=po*   *mama.*
        1SG   EMPH 1SG.SBJ=take=3SG.OBJ=ma SPEC[CLI]=stay DEM1
        'I myself took this position (of chief).'
        (1-T079-00:00:42.730)
     b. *. . .na=po   e=ae   agai   tobi~tobi=ena.*
        SPEC[CLI]=stay 3SG.SBJ=NEG really RD~EMPH=3SG.IPFV
        '. . .life isn't really right.'
        (1-T093-00:03:07.067)

6.2.3 Verbal compounding

Compound verbs are not common in Papapana. Two attested compound verbs are *siopamata* 'trust' (from the noun *siopa* 'stomach' and adjective *mata* 'good') as in (14) and *atupapasi* 'hurry' (from the verb *atu* 'make' and the adverb *papasi* 'quickly') as in (15). These compounds are non-compositional, that is, the meaning of the compound is not the sum of the meanings of its parts, as (14) demonstrates. While verbs can be modified by adverbs such as *papasi*, *atu* is normally monotransitive, which it is not in (15), and the meaning of (15) is not 'make quickly' but instead denotes manner of movement. The semantic non-compositionality of these constructions and the fact they are phonologically one word is evidence that these are compounds.

(14) *Anau u=siopamata=i=o=u.*
 1SG   1SG.SBJ=trust=TR=2SG.OBJ=1SG.IPFV
 'I trust you.'
 (2-E014-2)

(15) *Ena=bau   adope   i=atupapasi   nao...*
 3SG.PSSR=PL grandchild 3PL.SBJ=hurry thither
 'His grandchildren hurried away...'
 (2-T022-00:02:21.590)

6.2.4 Valency

Verbal derivation which alters valency includes applicative *i*, causative *va-*, de-transitivising *ta-*, applicative comitative *me* (which attaches to suffixes reflecting the 3SG and 3PL object enclitics), reciprocal/reflexive *vei*, object incorporation and transitivity discord. All valency-changing operations will be discussed in detail in §6.5.

6.3 Argument marking

This section describes alignment and grammatical relations (§6.3.1), subject- and object-indexing clitics (§6.3.2) and the emphatic marker *to* (§6.3.3).

6.3.1 Alignment and grammatical relations

Papapana is nominative-accusative in its formal marking of core arguments and the person and number of all subjects are indexed by subject proclitics in the VC. There is thus no distinction between the subject of an intransitive (16), monotransitive (20) or ditransitive predicate (23), nor is the semantic role of the subject in an intransitive predicate differentiated, as shown in (16)–(18) for which the semantic roles are actor, undergoer and experiencer respectively (i.e. there is no difference between the subjects of unergative, unaccusative and psychological verbs).

(16) *Na=orawi   e=orete=ena.*
     SPEC[CLI]=man 3SG.SBJ=walk=3SG.IPFV
     'The man is walking.'
     (2-E009)

(17) *Na=orawi   e=to   pu.*
     SPEC[CLI]=man 3SG.SBJ=EMPH fall
     'The man fell.'
     (2-E009)

(18) *Na=orawi   e=nami=ena.*
     SPEC[CLI]=man 3SG.SBJ=sad=3SG.IPFV
     'The man is sad.'
     (2-E009)

If the predicate is monotransitive, object enclitics in the VC index the person and number of the only object, which may have the semantic role of patient (19), theme (20), addressee (21) or beneficiary (22).

(19) *Anau u=ani=a   na=tamute.*
     1SG   1SG.SBJ=eat=3SG.OBJ SPEC[CLI]=mango
     'I ate a mango.'
     (2-E009)

(20) *Na=orawi   e=ae=a   nu=gau~gaunu.*
     SPEC[CLI]=man 3SG.SBJ=buy=3SG.OBJ SPEC.CLII=RD~write
     'The man bought a book.'
     (2-E009)

(21) *Na=orawi   e=wa=i=a=na   Ellen.*
     SPEC[CLI]=man 3SG.SBJ=say=TR=3SG.OBJ=3SG.IPFV Ellen
     'The man is speaking to Ellen.'
     (2-E009)

(22) *Epa e=pei si~siodo=au=ena=i.*
Epa 3SG.SBJ=PST.IPFV RD~work=1SG.OBJ=3SG.IPFV=IRR
'Epa was working for me.'
(1-T043b-00:02:18.090)

If the predicate is ditransitive (23), the object enclitics index the person and number of the addressee, recipient or beneficiary while the object expressing the patient, or theme (such as the singular *iana* 'fish' in (23)) appears only as a NP without any object enclitic indexing it.

(23) *Ben e=ma'a=ina na=iana Jeff auana Ellen.*
Ben 3SG.SBJ=give=3PL.OBJ SPEC[CLI]=fish Jeff 3DU Ellen
'Ben gave the fish to Jeff and Ellen.'
(2-E018)

Papapana makes a distinction between *primary* and *secondary* objects, rather than a *direct/indirect* object distinction, because the only object of a monotransitive predicate (usually the patient (P)) is marked in the same way (by the object enclitics) as the addressee (A), recipient (R) or beneficiary (B) object of a ditransitive predicate, while the theme (T) of a ditransitive predicate occurs only as a NP. The difference between the two patterns can be illustrated by Figure 6.1 (adapted from Dryer 2007a: 256). This is also the case in the Northwest Solomonic language Hoava (Davis 2003: 111) and cross-linguistically this is not unusual: "if the verb agrees with only one of the two objects, it will normally agree with the primary object" (Kroeger 2005: 62).

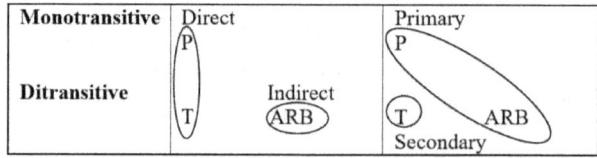

Figure 6.1: Objects: direct and indirect, primary and secondary.

In Papapana, there is no morphological case on NP arguments nor are there distinct subject and object independent pronouns to indicate grammatical relations. Constituent order is variable with both verb-medial and verb-final orders being prevalent (see §9.1); however, in pragmatically unmarked clauses, the subject is always clause-initial and thus constituent order does play a role in marking grammatical relations, but it is not the primary means of doing so.

6.3.2 Subject-indexing and object-indexing clitics

The Papapana VC utilises subject-indexing proclitics (see Table 6.3) and object-indexing enclitics (see Table 6.4) which belong to two of Papapana's six pronominal paradigms (see Appendix 1). The subject-indexing and object-indexing clitics mark the number and person of the subject (S) or object (O) referent in the VC and are agreement markers. Like all pronominal paradigms in Papapana, there is no gender[23] or case distinction, and referents are classified according to first, second or third person, with an inclusive and exclusive distinction in the first person plural. Like the possessor suffixes (§5.5.1) and possessor proclitics (§5.5.2), the subject-indexing and object-indexing clitics distinguish only singular and plural number, and not dual and trial number like the independent pronouns (§4.2.1). It is common in Oceanic languages for "non-singular numbers to be neutralised as plural in the subject and object paradigms" (Ross 2004c: 498). Papapana is typically Oceanic as Oceanic languages commonly have preverbal morphemes indicating the person and number of the subject and these are usually clitics (Lynch, Ross and Crowley 2002: 35), while postverbal morphemes, usually suffixes or enclitics, indicating the person and number of the object are quite often found in the Oceanic languages of Micronesia and Melanesia (Lynch, Ross, and Crowley 2002: 36, 46).

In Papapana, as in most canonic Oceanic languages (Ross 2004c: 499), the subject- and object-indexing clitics occur whether or not there is an overt subject or object NP (the motivation for the presence or absence of core argument NPs is discussed in §9.1). The only circumstance under which object enclitics are not present is when there is transitivity discord (see §6.5.5). A subject NP may be lexical as in (24) (*nia esinau etamau* 'my mother and father') or an independent pronoun as in (25) (*aia* '3SG'). Object NPs are usually lexical as in (25) (*enaaraoeta* 'his big brother') but occasionally they are co-expressed by a free conominal pronoun as in (24) (*anau* '1SG'). However, it should be noted that in such cases, the object pronoun is in Topic position, rendering the clause order Object-Subject-VC (OSV) (see §9.1.2), and this could be motivating the presence of the non-lexical object NP. Certainly in non-Topic position, be it SVO or SOV order (see §9.1.2), non-lexical object NPs are not attested in the corpus. Therefore, there is the possibility that the object enclitics are weak accusative pronouns, which are part of a VP, and that when a lexical object NP is present, it is in fact an adjunct. However, this requires further research to confirm and at this stage, I am working

---

[23] The term *gender* refers not to noun class, but to masculine and feminine participants, i.e. 'he' and 'she'.

on the basis that the object enclitics are not accusative pronouns, but agreement markers. In Siewierska's terms, the subject and object clitics in Papapana are "ambiguous agreement markers" since they "occur both in the presence of an overt controller in the same construction [. . .] and in the absence of such a controller" (Siewierska 2004: 126), the controller being "the element which determines the agreement" (Corbett 2006: 4), in this case the subject or object.

(24) "*Anau nia e-sina-u e-tama-u*
 1SG ASSOC.PL PERS-mother-1SG.PSSR PERS-father-1SG.PSSR
 i=ara asi=au. . ."
 3PL=PST leave=1SG.OBJ
 '"My mother and father left me. . ."'
 (1-T003-00:01:03.550)

(25) *Aia e=nutu varisi=a ena=arao-eta.*
 3SG 3SG.SBJ=refuse also=3SG.OBJ 3SG.PSSR[CLI]=brother-AUG
 'He refused his big brother.'
 (1-T035-00:06:11.957)

6.3.2.1 Subject-indexing proclitics

The subject-indexing proclitics in Papapana, shown in Table 6.3 are clear reflexes of PNWS subject clitics **u, gu, a* 1SG, **o, (mu)* 2SG, **i, e* 3SG, **mi* 1EXCL, **ta* 1INCL, **mu* 2PL, and **di, da* 3PL (Ross 1988: 365).

Table 6.3: Subject-indexing proclitics.

	1EXCL	1INCL	2	3
SG	u=		o=	e=
PL	mi=	si= ~ so=	mu=	i=
		sa=		

The subject-indexing proclitics are always the first element in the VC and cliticise to the next element in the VC, be that the verb itself (26), or one of the other preverbal morphemes like *ara* 'PST' (27). Their status as clitics is determined by the fact that they form phonological words with the host (see §3.5.3) and do not attach to a particular lexical category but to the left of preverbal morphemes or the verb itself.

(26) *Na=vanua* **i=nao=i** *i-ava.*
SPEC[CLI]=people 3PL.SBJ=go=IRR LOC-sea
'People would go to sea.'
(1-T077-00:01:57.360)

(27) *Na=orawi* **e=ara** **naomai**...
SPEC[CLI]=man 3SG.SBJ=PST come
'A man came...'
(1-T065-00:00:23.470)

In some Melanesian languages, subject-indexing morphemes are portmanteau forms that combine with the expression of the TAM categories of the verb (Lynch, Ross, and Crowley 2002: 45), but in Papapana this is not the case and there is one paradigm of subject-indexing proclitics for all voice and TAM distinctions. However, there is one exception: there are three 1INCL subject-indexing proclitics. As described in §3.1.3, the subject-indexing proclitics *si=* and *so=* are in free variation: there is no grammatical, semantic or pragmatic motivation for the variation but instead speakers reported that *so=* was used by younger speakers, as in (28).

(28) *Arira* **so=oi~oi=i=a=ira** *avosia* "mimis"...
1INCL INCL.SBJ=RD~call=TR=3SG.OBJ like mimis
'We call it like "mimis"...'[24]
(1-T029-00:15:40.480)

The form *sa=* on the other hand can be used instead of *si= ~ so=* but only in hortative clauses (29).

(29) "...*sa=nao=i* *i-daramu,* **sa=no**
1INCL.SBJ.HORT=go=IRR LOC-river 1INCL.SBJ.HORT=go.SEQ
tutuvu=i."
wash=IRR
"'...let's go to the river, let's go and wash.'"
(1-T033-00:03:03.510)

---

[24] *Mimis* are small shells, traditionally used as money or jewellery.

The interchangeable nature of these 1INCL subject-indexing proclitics is demonstrated in (30) where both *sa=* and *si=* are used and speakers confirmed that *si= ~ so=* could replace *sa=* in the first clause, while *sa=* or *so=*could replace *si=* in the second.

(30) "...*sa=asi=a=i* Pasa ta *si=nao=i*..."
INCL.SBJ.HORT=leave=3SG.OBJ=IRR Pasa and INCL.SBJ=go=IRR
"'...let's leave Pasa and go....'"
(1-T031-00:01:57.361)

6.3.2.2 Object-indexing enclitics

The object-indexing enclitics in Papapana, shown in Table 6.4, bear more resemblance to the independent pronouns (§4.2.1) than the subject-indexing proclitics do. Since cross-linguistically participant reference usually arises from a diachronic process which begins with independent pronouns, "participant reference markers are often similar in form to the free pronouns" (Payne 1997: 251), and this is especially the case for the independent pronouns and object markers in Oceanic languages (Lynch, Ross, and Crowley 2002: 36; Evans 2008: 289). The object-indexing enclitics in Papapana are clear reflexes of the POc object markers *=au* 1SG, *=ko* 2SG and *=a* 3SG (Evans 1995: 137) and the POc independent pronouns *ka[m]i* 1EXCL, *kita* 1INCL, *ka[m]u* 2PL, and *[k]ira* 3PL (Ross 1988: 367). The absence of initial /k/ in the Papapana forms is consistent with other areas of the lexicon where POc *k* is lost, or in some cases realised as /ʔ/ (see §3.1.2.4).

Table 6.4: Object-indexing enclitics.

	1EXCL	1INCL	2	3
SG	=au		=o	=a
PL	=ami	=ira	=amu	=ina

The status of object-indexing morphemes as clitics is determined by the fact that they form phonological words with the host and the fact they do not attach to a particular lexical category but to the rightmost postverbal morpheme or the verb itself. The object-indexing enclitics generally tend to attach directly to the verb (31) or the final verb in a verb series; however, geocentric directionals (32), the completive aspect marker (33) and adverbs (34) may intervene between the verb and the object-indexing enclitic, and if so, the object-indexing enclitic attaches to the rightmost of these postverbal morphemes.

(31) *Evea Marorakuraku e=to   burisi=a...*
     Evea Marorakuraku 3SG.SBJ=EMPH give.birth=3SG.OBJ
     'Evea gave birth to Marorakuraku...'
     (2-T001-1-00:02:10.405)

(32) *Nu=obutu   u=rasi   dini=a.*
     SPEC.CLII=canoe 1SG.SBJ=pull down=3SG.OBJ
     'I pulled down the canoe.'
     (1-T071-00:01:10.110)

(33) *Enai=ma i=to   va-tamu   osi=ira...*
     after=ma 3PL.SBJ=EMPH CAUS-eat COMPL=3PL.OBJ
     'After they finished feeding us'
     (1-T002-00:02:51.630)

(34) *Na=vanua   i=ari~ari   garigari=ina   bau ari.*
     SPEC[CLI]=people 3PL.SBJ=RD~dig always=3PL.OBJ PL   dig
     'The people always dug holes.'
     (2-E007-2A)

6.3.3 Emphatic *to*

The preverbal marker *to* is optional but prevalent in the data. When *to* is present, it immediately follows the subject-indexing proclitic and no other element is permitted to intervene between the two. It may co-occur with a lexical (35) or pronominal (36) subject NP. I have analysed *to* as an emphatic marker, after carefully considering several other hypotheses, which I outline below.

(35) *Na=daramu   e=to   mamaravi=ena.*
     SPEC[CLI]=water 3SG.SBJ=EMPH cold=3SG.IPFV
     'The water is cold.'
     (2-E024)

(36) *Anau* **u=to** *matono=i.*
 1SG 1SG.SBJ=EMPH awaken=IRR
 'I will wake up.'
 (2-E024)

It could be argued that *to* is a *predicate marker*, also referred to as *verb marker* or *verbalizer* in the Oceanic literature. In the Northwest Solomonic languages Teop and Taiof, the verb marker is *to*, derived from an earlier relativiser (Ross 1982: 50–51), so it is reasonable to question whether *to* in Papapana is also a verb marker. Ross (1988: 251) asserts that in Nehan-North Bougainville languages, subject pronominal proclitics have been reduced to a single verb marker, because the subject proclitics are rendered redundant by the addition of the "possessive pronominal suffixes" (referred to here as *postverbal subject-indexing* (PSI) and discussed in §7.1.1). This is clearly not the case in Papapana because, when present, *to* must co-occur with (non-reduced) subject-indexing proclitics (37) and furthermore, whether *to* is present or not, subject-indexing proclitics are not rendered redundant by PSI enclitics (38), which are only used to mark three TAM distinctions anyhow. More crucially, the optional nature of *to* means it cannot be a predicate marker.

(37) a. *Prime Minister* **e=to** *mate tani.*
    Prime Minister 3SG.SBJ=EMPH die already
    'The Prime Minister had already died.'
    (2-E008)
  b. **Prime Minister* **to** *mate tani.*
    Prime Minister to die already
    'The Prime Minister had already died.'
    (2-E008)

(38) "*Nua matuana* **i=to** *oa~oa=ina.*"
    two[CLI] spirit 3PL.SBJ=EMPH RD~cry=3PL.IPFV
    '"Two spirits are crying."'
    (1-T026-00:03:22.280)

In Halia, the verbalizer "has a cross reference to the person of the subject and also relates to the tense of the action [. . . and] is obligatory in all VPs except those involving imperative and obligative mode" (Allen 1978: 32). Thus, I considered whether *to* was a TAM marker but I found no evidence of this. However, like Halia's verbaliser, *to* is also not attested in imperative or hortative clauses. Otherwise, there are no restrictions with regard to TAM: *to* can occur with no

TAM markers (37), with PSI and reduplication expressing present imperfective (38), with the past tense marker *ara* (39) and the past imperfective marker *pei* (40), and with the aspect markers *vare ~ vae* (41) and *osi* (42). It may also occur in both intransitive declarative (41), monotransitive declarative (39), negative (43) and interrogative clauses (44).

(39) ***U=to   ara tu'u=i=a.***
     1SG.SBJ=EMPH PST meet=TR=3SG.OBJ
     'I met him.'
     (2-E014-1)

(40) ***E=to   pei   gaun=i=a=i   nu=pepa.***
     3SG.SBJ=EMPH PST.IPFV write=TR=3SG.OBJ=IRR SPEC.CLII=paper
     'He used to write a letter (every morning).'
     (2-E014-1)

(41) ***E=to   vae manene nao.***
     3SG.SBJ=EMPH REP return   thither
     'He went back again.'
     (1-T029-00:06:56.820)

(42) ***U=to   tutuvu osi. . .***
     1SG.SBJ=EMPH wash   COMPL
     '(After) I finish washing. . .'
     (1-T008-00:01:04.690)

(43) *Bikos   vituasi o   te:bau   i=to   ae   no~nongono=ina,*
     because young   or who.PL   3PL.SBJ=EMPH NEG RD~hear=3PL.IPFV
     aruai.
     no
     'Because young people or whoever don't listen, no.'
     (1-T089-00:05:43.302)

(44) "*Au=au   bareo   te:a   **e=to***
     1SG.PSSR=CLII breadfruit who.SG 3SG.SBJ=EMPH
     ani~ani=a=na?"
     RD~eat=3SG.OBJ=3SG.IPFV
     '"Who's eating my breadfruit?"'
     (1-T035-00:05:03.924)

I considered the hypothesis that *to* is a realis marker, as a more recent description of Taiof analyses *to* as a realis mode marker (Ross 2002b: 433). In Papapana however, this cannot be the case since *to* co-occurs with the irrealis mode enclitic =*i* as in (40) above, with the preverbal conditional marker *awa* and irrealis =*i* (45), and the preverbal optative mode marker *eri* in clauses expressing wishes (46) and in counterfactual conditional clauses with *eri* and *awa* (47).

(45) John **e=to**   awa   nao=i,   i=to
     John 3SG.SBJ=EMPH COND go=IRR 3PL.SBJ=EMPH
     atun=i=a=i.
     attack=TR=3SG.OBJ=IRR
     'If John goes, they will attack him.'
     (2-E022)

(46) **U=to**   eri   gaun=i=au   nu=pepa.
     1SG.SBJ=EMPH OPT write=TR=1SG.IPFV SPEC.CLII=paper
     'I want to write a letter.'
     (2-E014-1)

(47) **E=to**   eri awa aputu mata, va:gi e=eri   sare.
     3SG.SBJ=EMPH CF COND sleep good   now   3SG.SBJ=CF happy
     'If he had slept well, he would have been happy now.'
     (2-E014-2)

I observed in the text data that *to* often occurs in the first clause of a complex sentence but not in the second and therefore I hypothesised that *to* is a topic or focus marker. To test this, I designed and elicited ten complex sentences, of which (48)–(50) are representative examples: in (48) the subject of both clauses is the same, in (49) the object of both clauses is the same, and in (50) the object of the first clause is the subject of the second. For each of these sentences, speakers reported that *to* could be used in both clauses, but that it was not necessary to repeat it in the second clause. If *to* were a topic or focus marker one would expect that *to* could not be used in both clauses.

(48) John e=nao   Buka tau e=ae   mai   na=rice.
     John 3SG.SBJ=go Buka and 3SG.SBJ=buy hither SPEC[CLI]=rice
     'John went to Buka and bought some rice.'
     (2-E029-1)

(49) Tom na=iana   e=peri=a   tau
      Tom SPEC[CLI]=fish 3SG.SBJ=find=3SG.OBJ and
      e=muni=a.
      3SG.SBJ=hide=3SG.OBJ
      'Tom found a fish and hid it.'
      (2-E029-1)

(50) Wayne e=tepe   dini=a   nu=naono   tau e=pu
      Wayne 3SG.SBJ=cut   down=3SG.OBJ   SPEC.CLII=tree   and 3SG.SBJ=fall
      dini.
      down
      'Wayne cut a tree and it fell.'
      (2-E029-1)

It could be that the origins of *to* lie in the predicate markers of Nehan-North Bougainville languages, but synchronically the morphosyntactic behaviour of *to* differs from other predicate markers (except for the similarity to Halia in not occurring in imperative clauses). Predicate markers mark the verb or VC, but I am unconvinced about how meaningful this label is and I do not feel I have any evidence to suggest that *to* marks the verb or VC. The use of *to* is optional and is not motivated by the presence or absence of other morphemes in the VC, nor by tense, aspect or mode, nor by NP arguments or transitivity. No speaker has been able to adequately account for the difference in meaning between utterances with and without *to*, but Papapana speakers did insist that *to* "marks the man" and "stands for he/she/we . . . ". It could be then that *to* forms a subject pronoun with the subject proclitics, or perhaps emphasises the subject proclitic in the same way that the modifier *tobi* can emphasise an independent pronoun (see §4.2.1). Indeed, it could very well be that *to* derives from *tobi*. This analysis is also compatible with the fact that *to* is not attested in imperative clauses, because subject NPs (including pronominal ones) are not usually attested in imperative clauses either (see §9.2).

6.4 Verb types

Verbs in Papapana can be classified based on their transitivity into intransitive, monotransitive, ditransitive and ambitransitive verbs (which may be intransitive or monotransitive).

The framework adopted here follows Evans' (2003) classification of Proto-Oceanic verb roots based on "(i) the macrorole of the intransitive subject and the relationship between the intransitive and transitive forms of a verb; and (ii) the types of valency-changing devices with which a verb occurred" (Evans 2003: 305). Evans distinguishes between "U-Verbs" whose intransitive subject has the macrorole of Undergoer (U), and "A-Verbs", whose intransitive subject has the macrorole of Actor (A). The intransitive subject (S) of U-Verbs corresponds to the transitive object (O), whereas for A-verbs, the intransitive subject corresponds to the transitive actor (A). For intransitive verbs this classification broadly corresponds to the distinction between unaccusative and unergative verbs. Evans (2003: 23) characterises verbs as: *state* verbs denoting the state or condition of a referent, *process* verbs denoting that a referent has changed its state or condition, *action* verbs denoting activities which someone performs, and *process-action* verbs denoting a process involving a change in the condition of a patient and an action performed by an agent. Proto-Oceanic U-verbs are further subclassified into i) U-stative verbs, denoting states and ii) U-process verbs denoting processes and process-actions, including affect verbs, some motion verbs (which could take a non-volitional 'moving' participant) and verbs of opening, closing, beginning and smelling, while A-verbs denoted actions or process-actions and included corporeal verbs, verbs of mode/direction of motion, and verbs of cognition, emotion, tasting, throwing and hitting (Evans 2003: 88). U-stative, U-process and A-verb classes could then each be further divided based on whether they occurred with certain valency-changing devices: the causative prefix *pa[ka]-*, the transitive suffix *-i*, the detransitivising *ma-* or *ta-* prefix, and reduplication. Figure 6.2 shows these Proto-Oceanic verb class divisions.

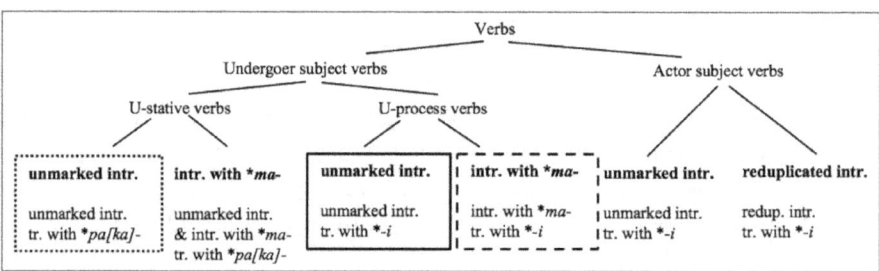

Figure 6.2: Proto-Oceanic verb classes (after Evans 2003: 87, 306).

In Papapana it is important to consider both word-level and clause-level transitivity when defining verb classes, because (i) in the case of ditransitive verbs, there is morphological marking of only the primary object in the VC (*Jeff auana Ellen* 'Jeff and Ellen' is marked by 3PL =*ina* in example (51)), but there may be both primary and secondary object NPs present in the clause (the secondary object in (51) being *naiana* 'the fish'), and (ii) in the case of transitivity discord, the clause contains an object NP but the VC does not mark the object morphologically (52) (see §6.5.5.2 for the difference between transitivity discord and object incorporation).[25]

(51) *Ben e=ma'a=ina na=iana Jeff auana Ellen.*
Ben 3SG.SBJ=give=3PL.OBJ SPEC[CLI]=fish Jeff 3DU Ellen
'Ben gave the fish to Jeff and Ellen.'
(2-E018)

(52) *I=to 'aria o'ovata na=uvi.*
3PL.SBJ=EMPH together roast SPEC[CLI]=yam
'They roasted yam together.'
(1-T029-00:11:03.590)

I classify Papapana verbs firstly as intransitive, monotransitive, ditransitive or ambitransitive. In their unmarked forms without any valency-changing morphology, intransitive verbs always occur without object-indexing enclitics in the VC, monotransitive and ditransitive verbs always occur with object-indexing enclitics in the VC, while ambitransitive verbs may occur either with or without object-indexing enclitics in the VC (see Table 6.5). I then consider the macrorole of the subject and the valency-changing devices that can function with these verb types: applicative *i*, the causative prefix *va-* and the detransitivising prefix *ta-* (see Table 6.5). Other valency-changing devices are discussed and exemplified in §6.5 but their use is not a defining characteristic of verb class so they are mentioned but not exemplified in the following subsections. Note that there are no avalent verbs in Papapana, that is, verbs without any argument.

Table 6.5: Valency and verb types in Papapana.

	Object-enclitic	Valency-changing	
Intransitive 1[26]	Without	Causative *va-*	§6.4.1
Intransitive 2	Without	Applicative *i* Causative *va-*	§6.4.1

---

25 See Hill (2011: 459) for a comparison of the syntactic approach to transitivity taken in much of the broader typological literature with the focus on word-level morphological transitivity widespread in Oceanist research.
26 This class reflects the POc unmarked intransitive U-stative verb class, indicated by a dotted-line in Figure 6.2.

Table 6.5 (continued)

	Object-enclitic	Valency-changing	
Monotransitive A-verbs	With	Applicative *i* Causative *va-*	§6.4.2.1
Monotransitive U-process verbs[27]	With	Detransitivising *ta-*	§6.4.2.2
Ditransitive	With	Ø	§6.4.3
Ambitransitive U-process[28]	With or Without	Ø	§6.4.4.1
Ambitransitive A-verbs 1	With or Without	Causative *va-*	§6.4.4.2
Ambitransitive A-verbs 2	With or Without	Applicative *i* Causative *va-*	§6.4.4.2

6.4.1 Intransitive verbs

All intransitive verbs in Papapana are morphologically unmarked for valency as in (53a) and (55a). The valency of an intransitive verb may be increased with the causative prefix *va-* (see §6.5.2) as in (53b) and (55b). There are two intransitive subclasses, differentiated by the fact that applicative *i* can increase valency only for the second subclass, as in (55c) below. The valency of an intransitive verb in the first subclass may also be increased by the applicative comitative *me* (see §6.5.4).

(53) a. *Francis e=umunu=ena.*
     Francis 3SG.SBJ=sit=3SG.IPFV
     'Francis is sitting.'
     (2-E009)
  b. *Jerry e=va-umun=i=a   Francis.*
     Jerry 3SG.SBJ=CAUS-sit=TR=3SG.OBJ Francis
     'Jerry seated Francis.'
     (2-E009)

---

[27] This class reflects the marked intransitive U-process verb class in POc, indicated by a dashed-line in Figure 6.2.
[28] This class reflects the POc unmarked intransitive U-process class, indicated by a solid-line box in Figure 6.2.

The morphosyntactic behaviour of Papapana intransitive verbs in the first subclass corresponds to the unmarked intransitive U-stative verb class in Proto-Oceanic (see Figure 6.2). However, in Papapana these verbs are not only semantically state verbs, but also process (including motion) and action (including motion) verbs, examples of which are shown in the non-exhaustive list in Table 6.6 (it is necessary for the discussion of serial verb constructions to distinguish motion verbs in Papapana; see §6.6).

Table 6.6: Intransitive 1 verbs.

State	*mate*	be dead
	po	stay/exist
Process	*mate*	die
	ngono	boil
	u'udu	catch fire
	aputu	sleep
Process (motion)	*pu*	fall
	dovo	sink
Action (motion)	*manene*	return
	tavotu	arrive
	naovo	fly
	tuvu	swim
	tonu	stand
Action	*oa*	cry
	pata	laugh
	tamu	eat
	vo'o	call out

It is worth noting that the intransitive verb *tamu* 'eat' has a monotransitive counterpart *ani* 'eat':

(54) a. *Aia   e=tamu.*
       3SG 3SG.SBJ=eat
       'She ate.'
       (2-E010)
   b. *Anau   u=ani=a   na=tamute.*
       1SG   1SG.SBJ=eat=3SG.OBJ SPEC[CLI]=mango
       'I ate a mango.'
       (2-E009)

The second subclass of intransitive verbs have been derived through zero derivation from adjectives (see §4.6). As with all intransitive verbs, these can be morphologically unmarked for valency (55a) and have valency increased with the causative prefix *va-* (55b). However, they can also have valency increased with applicative *i* (55c). The causative prefix introduces an agent argument, with the former intransitive subject corresponding to the new monotransitive object. The applicative marker introduces a singular object that is the comparand in a comparative construction. In §4.6 I explained that adjectives in Papapana are a distinct word class because despite having some things in common with nouns and verbs, they are different from these words in several ways. Here we can see that intransitive U-stative verbs derived from adjectives are different from other intransitive U-stative verbs because their valency can be increased by applicative *i*. They also differ from Proto-Oceanic where intransitive stative U-verbs expressing property concepts could only form a transitive with the causative prefix (Lynch, Ross, and Crowley 2002: 81).

(55) a. *Na=anianipeu* ***e=arava.***
SPEC[CLI]=dish 3SG.SBJ=dry
'The dishes have dried/are dry.'
(2-E009)
b. *Francis* ***e=va-arav=i=a*** *na=anianipeu.*
Francis 3SG.SBJ=CAUS-dry=TR=3SG.OBJ SPEC[CLI]=dish
'Francis made the dishes dry.'
(2-E009)
c. *Skiotu mama* ***e=arava*** *i=a=na mama.*
skirt DEM1 3SG.SBJ=dry APPL=3SG.OBJ=3SG.IPFV DEM1
'This skirt is drier than this.'
(2-E005)

6.4.2 Monotransitive verbs

Monotransitive (bivalent) verbs in Papapana occur in their root form and the VC is marked by an object-indexing enclitic. In Papapana, only the object-indexing enclitics in the VC are a defining feature of a monotransitive verb. Singular object enclitics may however be preceded by the transitive enclitic *=i* (56) but its presence is determined by the phonology of the verbal root (see §6.5.1.1). Since the transitive enclitic does not co-occur with plural object-indexing enclitics (57), then I do not consider it to be a defining characteristic of transitivity in Papapana, nor to be a synchronically productive valency-changing device (hence I call it *transitive* rather than *transitivising*, as it is sometimes referred to in the Oceanic literature). This contrasts with Proto-Oceanic, in which the transitive suffix was one of the defining characteristics of transitivity: a transitive verb is defined as "any verb which (a) carries a transitive suffix **-i* or **-aki(ni)*, and/or (b) carries a pronominal suffix or clitic determining person and number of the direct object" (Pawley and Reid 1979: 105).

(56) *Anau u=ri   'a'ade'e=i=a=u*
     1SG   1SG.SBJ=OPT   narrative=TR=3SG.OBJ=1SG.IPFV
     nu='a'ade'e. . .
     SPEC.CLII=narrative
     'I want to tell a story. . .'
     (1-T063-00:00:17.130)

(57) *Bau siodo   viviro'o   u=pei   no*
     PL   work   around   1SG.SBJ=PST.IPFV go.SEQ
     atu=ina=u.
     make=3PL.OBJ=1SG.IPFV
     'I was going and doing jobs all over the place.'
     (1-T087-00:02:43.390)

In Papapana, the majority of monotransitive verbs have no derived intransitive counterpart and these verbs are action verbs that prototypically have an actor as subject (§6.4.2.1). There is a small group of undergoer process verbs which do have a derived intransitive counterpart and for these verbs the monotransitive object corresponds to the derived intransitive subject (§6.4.2.2).

6.4.2.1 A-verbs

For monotransitive A-verbs (see examples in Table 6.7), valency may be increased by applicative *i*, deriving ditransitive verbs (compare (57) above and (58)). The new argument is the O1 and has the semantic role of addressee, recipient or beneficiary. Applicative *i* is only evident when the new argument is 2SG or 3SG (see §6.5.1). The valency of a monotransitive A-verb may also be decreased through object incorporation or transitivity discord if the object is generic (see §6.5.5), or with the reciprocal/reflexive marker *vei* (see §6.5.6), while some monotransitive verbs are attested with the valency-increasing causative prefix *va-*, which derives a ditransitive verb for which the introduced argument is an agent as in (59) (see §6.5.2). The prototypical A-verb has an actor as subject but even though not all of these verbs are prototypical, they nevertheless all behave morphosyntactically in the same way.

(58) Anau na=menaga u=atu i=o
 1SG SPEC[CLI]=creamed.banana 1SG.SBJ=make APPL=2SG.OBJ
 mai.
 hither
 'I made *menaga* for you.'[29]
 (2-E015)

(59) Jerry e=va-amunu=ina Francis tau Alan
 Jerry 3SG.SBJ=CAUS-look=3PL.OBJ Francis and Alan
 na=vu~vurau.
 SPEC[CLI]=RD~run
 'Jerry showed Francis and Alan the car.'
 (2-E015)

Table 6.7: Monotransitive A-verbs.

rasi	pull
tuna	push
de	take
atono	bring
noe	put
agoto	hold
amunu	look
tu'u	meet
ani	eat
atu	make
nata	ask
oi	call
atunu	attack
paga	shoot

6.4.2.2 U-process verbs

The class of monotransitive U-process verbs in Papapana reflects the marked intransitive U-process verb class in Proto-Oceanic (see Figure 6.2) because

---

[29] *Menaga* is a traditional dish served on special occasions. It is made from boiled bananas that are mashed, then rolled and baked in coconut cream.

these verbs can be detransitivised with the prefix *ta-* (see §6.5.3). The verb may occur in its unmarked monotransitive form (60a), occur in a monotransitive SVC (see §6.6.2.5) or be detransitivised with the verbal prefix *ta-* (60b). The object of the monotransitive verb corresponds to the undergoer subject of the derived intransitive verb. The only verbs attested are listed in Table 6.8.

(60) a. ***E=pus=i=a**   na=magura.*
   3SG.SBJ=break.off=TR=3SG.OBJ SPEC[CLI]=green.coconut
   'He broke off the green coconut.'
   (1-T012-00:01:59.930)

   b. *. . .pei naunu **e=ta-putu.***
   PART leaf   3SG.SBJ=DETR-break.off
   '. . .the leaf broke off.'
   (1-T035-00:04:30.596)

Table 6.8: Monotransitive U-process verbs.

puana	break (glass, pottery, fruit)
'a'u	break (wood)
bu	capsize
repi	split (wood)
putu	break off
apa	open/uncover

6.4.3 Ditransitive verbs

A ditransitive verb in Papapana is trivalent, that is, there are three arguments, the subject, the primary object (O1) and the secondary object (O2) as in (51) above and (61). When defining a ditransitive verb in Papapana it is necessary to consider both morphology and syntax: the VC marks only the O1 with object-indexing enclitics (which may be coreferential with an O1 NP outside the VC), while the O2 occurs as a NP only and is not morphologically marked within the VC. The presence of the transitive enclitic *=i* is dependent on the number of the object (compare (51) with (61)). As described in §6.3.1, the O1 is usually the addressee, recipient or beneficiary, and the O2 is the theme. The only underived ditransitive verb in Papapana is *ma'a* 'give'.

(61) **E=no** vae **ma'=i=a=re** na=maria
 3SG.SBJ=go.SEQ REP give=TR=3SG.OBJ=REP SPEC[CLI]=thing
 koko'i. . .
 taro
 'He went and gave her the what's-it-called, taro again. . .'
 (1-T029-00:08:30.295)

6.4.4 Ambitransitive verbs

An ambitransitive verb is one which may be intransitive or monotransitive without requiring valency-changing morphology; a limited number are U-process verbs (§6.4.4.1) while the rest are A-verbs (§6.4.4.2).

6.4.4.1 U-process verbs

These U-process verbs can occur underived as intransitive (62) or monotransitive (63). The only verbs attested are listed in Table 6.9. Like intransitive verbs, the intransitive form is unmarked, and like monotransitive verbs, the monotransitive form is the head of a VC marked by object-indexing enclitics (the presence of the transitive enclitic =i is again dependent on the phonology of the verb root and the number of the object). The intransitive subject (62) corresponds to the monotransitive object (63), thus these verbs are U-verbs, and their morphosyntactic behaviour outlined here corresponds to the unmarked intransitive U-process verb class in Proto-Oceanic (see Figure 6.2).

Table 6.9: Ambitransitive U-process verbs.

gini	be closed/close
vatago	be leant/lean
tapipi	be blocked/block

(62) Na=windoa **e=gini=ena.**
 SPEC[CLI]=window 3SG.SBJ=close=3SG.IPFV
 'The window is closed.'
 (2-E015)

(63) *Francis na=windoa* ***e=gini=a.***
Francis SPEC[CLI]=window 3SG.SBJ=close=3SG.OBJ
'Francis closed the window.'
(2-E015)

6.4.4.2 A-verbs

Ambitransitive A-verbs, such as those in Tables 6.10 and 6.11, can occur underived as intransitive or monotransitive. The intransitive forms are unmarked as in (64a) and (65a), and the monotransitive forms are the head of a VC marked by object-indexing enclitics as in (64b) and (65b), (the presence or absence of the transitive enclitic =*i* is again dependent on the phonological form of the verb, and object number).

(64) a. *Bikos vituasi o te:bau **i=to** ae*
because young or who.PL 3PL.SBJ=EMPH NEG
***no~nongono=ina**, aruai.*
RD~hear=3PL.IPFV no
'Because young people or whoever don't listen, no.'
(1-T089-00:05:43.302)
b. ***E=to** nongon=i=a na=au da...*
3SG.SBJ=EMPH hear=TR=3SG.OBJ SPEC=CLII noise
'He heard a noise...'
(2-E022)

(65) a. *Mamena boni~boni John **e=ga~gau~gaunu=ena.***
PL.COLL RD~day John 3SG.SBJ=RD~RD=write=3SG.IPFV
'John writes every day.'
(2-E029-2)
b. ***E=gau~gaun=i=a=ena** nu=pepa.*
3SG.SBJ=RD~write=TR=3SG.OBJ=3SG.IPFV SPEC.CLII=paper
'He is writing a letter.'
(2-E008)

While all ambitransitive A-verbs are attested with causative *va-*, those in Group 1 (Table 6.10) are not attested with applicative *i*, while those in Group 2 (Table 6.11) are attested with applicative *i* (see §6.5.1). For Group 2 verbs, applicative *i* has two functions: (i) it is used as a valency-increasing device to derive a ditransitive verb where the new argument that is singular in number has an addressee, recipient or beneficiary role and is the O1 as in (66), and (ii) to change the semantic role of the singular object in a monotransitive predicate from patient to addressee, recipient, or beneficiary as in (67) (or to comitative if valency has been increased by the applicative comitative *me*; see §6.5.4).

(66) *Te:a*   *e=gaunu*   *i=a*   *na=leta*   Eddy?
     who.SG   3SG.SBJ=write   APPL=3SG.OBJ   SPEC.CLII=letter   Eddy
     'Who wrote a letter to Eddy?'
     (3-E002)

(67) *Evan*   *e=gaunu*   *i=a*   Jane.
     Evan   3SG.SBJ=write   APPL=3SG.OBJ   Jane
     'Evan wrote to Jane.'
     (2-E018)

These ambitransitive verbs are also subject to the same valency-changing devices as monotransitive verbs: object incorporation or transitivity discord if the object is generic (see §6.5.5), and the reciprocal/reflexive marker *vei* (see §6.5.6), while some are attested with the valency-increasing causative prefix *va-*, which derives a ditransitive verb for which the introduced argument is an agent (see §6.5.2).

Table 6.10: Ambitransitive A-verbs: Group 1.

Process-Action	*iromo*	drink
	bio	sweep
	burisi	give birth
Action	*nai*	marry
	vavarai	wait
	roroto	see
	vori	talk
	varona	know
	nongono	hear
	matautu	fear
Action (motion)	*nao*	go
	umunu	sit
	vaene	jump
	vurau	run
	oto	board

Table 6.11: Ambitransitive A-verbs: Group 2.

Action	gaunu	write
	'a'ade'e	narrate
	moroko	lie
	siodo	work

As Tables 6.10 and 6.11 show, semantically, these verbs are process-action or action (including motion) verbs. In Group 1, the verbs of mode/direction of motion are most often intransitive and may have an adjunct expressing location, source or goal (as in (68a) and (69a)). When they are monotransitive verbs, the object is a location or goal, as shown in (68b) and (69b). Indeed in Proto-Oceanic transitive constructions with the transitive suffix *-i, the roles denoted by the object of a motion verb were location and goal (Evans 2003: 304).

(68) a. ***E=nao***   *te=na=kaukau.*
     3SG.SBJ=go   OBL=SPEC[CLI]=sweet.potato
     'He went to the garden.'
     (1-T029-00:20:07.670)

    b. ***E=nao=i=a***   ***nao***   *nu=tura.*
     3SG.SBJ=go=TR=3SG.OBJ   thither   SPEC.CLII=fire
     'He approached/went to the fire.'
     (1-T012-00:00:44.510)

(69) a. *Na=orawi*   ***e=vaene***   *tae* *te=na=au*   *naono.*
     SPEC[CLI]=man   3SG.SBJ=climb   up   OBL=SPEC=CLII   tree
     'The man climbed up the tree.'
     (2-E018)

    b. *Aina panapana* ***i=vaene***   *tae=a*   *na=namu.*
     3PL   all   3PL.SBJ=climb   up=3SG.OBJ   SPEC[CLI]=Malay.apple
     'They all climbed up the Malay apple tree.'
     (1-T022-00:01:07.630)

6.5 Valency-changing operations

Like other Oceanic languages (Lynch, Ross, and Crowley 2002; Evans 2003), Papapana has a number of valency-changing devices: an applicative marker (§6.5.1), a causative prefix (§6.5.2), a detransitivising prefix (§6.5.3), an applicative comitative marker (§6.5.4), object incorporation and transitivity discord (§6.5.5), and a reciprocal/reflexive marker (§6.5.6). As in canonical Oceanic languages, reduplication plays a role in valency-changing in Papapana, however, only when it occurs in combination with the reciprocal marker in reciprocal constructions. There is no passive in Papapana: if a passive construction in another language were translated into Papapana, it would be realised as a transitive clause in which the subject NP was omitted but indexed by third person subject proclitics in the VC as in (70), with a tendency for the object to be preverbal as in (71).

(70) *I=to atun=i=a na=toituna.*
3PL.SBJ=EMPH attack=TR=3SG.OBJ SPEC[CLI]=chief
'The king was attacked (lit. they attacked the king).'
(2-E008)

(71) *Na=mata i=buibui tani=a.*
SPEC[CLI]=door 3PL.SBJ=clean already=3SG.OBJ
'The door was already cleaned (lit. the door, they already cleaned it).'
(2-E007-2)

6.5.1 Transitive =*i* and applicative *i*

In transitive clauses in Papapana, singular object-indexing enclitics are sometimes immediately preceded by the transitive =*i* or applicative *i*. Before proceeding further with the synchronic description of Papapana, it is necessary to provide the diachronic and typological context of these morphemes.

POc is reconstructed as having a transitivising suffix **-i* which had either a causative or applicative function: for U-verbs the intransitive S corresponded to the transitive O and an actor subject was added, while for A-verbs, it added an O argument and the intransitive S corresponded to the transitive A (Evans 2003: 104–117; Ross 2004c: 506). In Proto-Oceanic, the applicative function of **-i* contrasted with that of **-akin[i]* in terms of the participant types expressed by the introduced O argument: **-i* tended to introduce an O argument that denoted patient, stimulus, goal and location roles, while **-akin[i]* introduced an O argument that denoted roles such as concomitant, instrument and beneficiary (Evans 2003: 93). In the Oceanic literature these objects are often referred to respectively as *close* and *remote* objects (Lynch, Ross, and Crowley 2002: 44).

Cross-linguistically, applicatives can apply to intransitive and transitive predicates. When an applicative applies to an intransitive predicate, it derives a monotransitive predicate, the intransitive S goes into A function, and a "peripheral argument (which could be explicitly stated in the underlying intransitive) is taken into the core, in O function" (Dixon and Aikhenvald 2000: 13). When an applicative applies to a monotransitive predicate, transitivity is maintained and the A argument remains the same, but a peripheral argument with a different semantic role fills the O function, while the former O argument is moved into the periphery of the clause and may even be omittable (Dixon and Aikhenvald 2000: 13–14).

6.5.1.1 Transitive =*i*
In Papapana transitive predicates, the use of the transitive enclitic =*i* is quite idiosyncractic and is motivated by the number of the object and the phonology of the verb root. In Papapana transitive predicates, =*i* occurs with object-indexing enclitics that mark patient objects, like POc transitivising *-*i*; however, Papapana =*i* does not derive a monotransitive predicate from an intransitive, because it can occur with monotransitive verbs that are never used intransitively. The fact that it only occurs when the object is singular shows that it is not a synchronically productive derivational morpheme and that it is not a necessary marker of transitivity. I therefore call it a *transitive* marker and not *transitivising*. Indeed, in many Melanesian languages the -*i* suffix is no longer productive and there is only vestigial transitive marking, or none at all (Lynch, Ross, and Crowley 2002: 45). Papanana =*i* could also be argued to be an idiosyncratic vestigial form with a low or no functional load.

Transitive =*i* can immediately precede the object-indexing enclitics, but only 2SG and 3SG (and sometimes 1SG) object-indexing enclitics. It is considered an enclitic as it forms a phonological word with its host and it attaches to the verb or one of the postverbal modifiers: geocentric directionals, completive aspect marker or postverbal adverb. The use of =*i* is conditioned by the phonology of the verb root. Furthermore, the phonology of the verb root may be altered when =*i* is present. Monotransitive or ambitransitive verbs can be categorised into three groups based on whether they occur without =*i* or with =*i*, with this latter group further subdivided into verbs which retain and those which lose their final vowel when it is attached. As Table 6.12 and the associated examples referenced there show, =*i* does not occur (i) when the final syllable of a verb root contains a vowel that is different from the penultimate vowel and (ii) when the verb root ends in /i/ (if =*i* were present one would expect a long vowel to occur, or for there to be some other change such as stress shift as there is in /i/-final verb roots in Hoava (Davis 2003: 127)). Transitive =*i* does occur (iii) when there are two adjacent vowels, which is also the case in Hoava (Davis 2003: 127), (iv) when the final vowel is /a/, and (v) when the vowels in the penultimate and final syllables are identical. In three syllable roots where the vowels in the penultimate and final syllables are identical (vi), the final vowel is replaced by =*i*.

Table 6.12: Transitive structures with singular objects.

Group	Root	Transitive Stem	Example
i)	(CV.)CVx.CVy	(CV.)CVx.CVy=OBJ	72, 73
ii)	(CV.)CV.Ci	(CV.)CV.Ci=OBJ	74, 75
iii)	CVx.Vy	CVx.Vy=TR=OBJ	76
iv)	CV.Ca	CV.Ca= TR=OBJ	77
v)	(CV.CV.)CVx.CVx	(CV.CV.)CVx.CVx=TR=OBJ	78, 79
vi)	CV.CVx.CVx	CV.CVx.C=TR=OBJ	80

(72) Anau na=menaga   *u=atu=a.*
 1SG   SPEC[CLI]=creamed.banana 1SG.SBJ=make=3SG.OBJ
 'I made *menaga*.'
 (2-E015)

(73) ***E=to***   ***averu=a***   *au=au*   *koko'i.*
 3SG.SBJ=EMPH   steal=3SG.OBJ   1SG.PSSR=CLII   taro
 'He stole my taro.'
 (2-E009)

(74) ***E=peri=a***   *na=kabekabe.*
 3SG.SBJ=find=3SG.OBJ   SPEC[CLI]=bag
 'He found a bag.'
 (2-E024)

(75) *Evea Marorakuraku **e=to***   ***burisi=a.** . .*
 Evea Marorakuraku 3SG.SBJ=EMPH give.birth=3SG.OBJ
 'Evea gave birth to Marorakuraku. . .'
 (2-T001-1-00:02:10.405)

(76) *Anau na=inu*   ***u=bio~bio=i=a=u.***
 1SG   SPEC[CLI]=house 1SG.SBJ=RD~sweep=TR=3SG.OBJ=1SG.IPFV
 'I am sweeping the house.'
 (2-E009)

(77) **E=tuna=i=a** na=bara.
3SG.SBJ=push=TR=3SG.OBJ SPEC[CLI]=ball
'She pushed the ball.'
(2-E010)

(78) Na=soida'o **e=tu'u=i=a.**
SPEC[CLI]=old.man 3SG.SBJ=meet=TR=3SG.OBJ
'He met an old man.'
(1-T091-00:02:13.795)

(79) Anau **u=ri** **'a'ade'e=i=a=u**
1SG 1SG.SBJ=OPT narrative=TR=3SG.OBJ=1SG.IPFV
nu='a'ade'e. . .
SPEC.CLII=narrative
'I want to tell a story. . .'
(1-T063-00:00:17.130)

(80) E-tama-na **e=nongon=i=a.**
PERS-father-3SG.PSSR 3SG.SBJ=hear=TR=3SG.OBJ
'His father heard him.'
(1-T031-00:08:52.960)

The interaction of =*i* and the verb root in Papapana reflects that of Proto-Oceanic and many modern Oceanic languages, where the presence of -*i* between the verb and object enclitic depends on the phonology of the verb root, as shown in Table 6.13 adapted from Evans (2008: 291). The loss of the final vowel in three syllable roots where the vowels in the penultimate and final syllables are identical, as in (80), can be explained diachronically: Northwest Solomonic languages often reflect a Proto-Northwest Solomonic echo vowel added after word-final Proto-Oceanic consonants (Ross 1988: 218) and therefore the three syllable Papapana verb roots actually reflect the Proto-Oceanic CVCVC roots and when =*i* is present, the echo vowel is deleted. Such behaviour is common in Northwest Solomonic languages such as Hoava (Davis 2003: 127), Kokota (Palmer 2002: 508), Marovo (Evans 2008: 291) and Roviana (Corston-Oliver 2002: 183).

Table 6.13: Proto-Oceanic transitive structures (adapted from Evans 2008: 291).

	CVCVC stems	CVCa stems	CVCV stems
INTR	CVCVC	CVCa	CVCV
TR	CVCVC-i=OBJ	CVCa-i=OBJ	CVCV=OBJ

In Papapana, in three syllable roots with identical penultimate and final vowels, a final syllable beginning with /t/ undergoes a sound change to [s] when =*i* replaces the final vowel: this reflects the sound change of POc and PNWS *t to s/_i (Ross 1988: 219):

(81) CV.CVx.tVx ⟶ CV.CVx.s=i=OBJ

    a. *Mamena boni~boni* **u=ni~nio~nioto=u.**
       PL.COLL RD~day   1SG.SBJ=RD~RD~dream=1SG.IPFV
       'Every day I dream.'
       (2-E028-1)

    b. *Anna* **e=nios=i=a**   *ena=sinoni.*
       Anna 3SG.SBJ=dream=TR=3SG.OBJ 1SG.PSSR[CLI]=husband
       'Anna dreamt of her husband.'
       (2-E024)

The replacement of a final vowel by =*i* in CVVCV roots such as *gaunu* 'write' also provides evidence to support my analysis that diphthongs are not phonemic in Papapana (see §3.1.1.3). In (82) the final /u/ is replaced by =*i* because it is identical to the penultimate vowel. If the diphthong /aʊ/ were phonemic, the final /u/ would not be an echo vowel.

(82) **E=gau~gaun=i=a=ena**   *nu=pepa.*
     3SG.SBJ=RD~write=TR=3SG.OBJ=3SG.IPFV SPEC.CLII=paper
     'He is writing a letter.'
     (2-E008)

When an adverb intervenes between the verb and the object enclitic, =*i* attaches to the adverb:

(83) *Enai* **e=tatu**   *muramura=i=a=na=ma.*
     DEM2 3SG.SBJ=mash firmly=TR=3SG.OBJ=3SG.IPFV=ma
     'He's mashing it firmly.'
     (1-T036-8-00:01:04.350)

(84) *"A:mani **mi=mate**   **poto=i=a=mani***
    1EXCL   1EXCL.SBJ=like INTS=TR=3SG.OBJ=1EXCL.IPFV
    enai pei   tanga   mama."
    DEM2 PART shell.money DEM1
    '"We really want that necklace (that you're wearing).'"
    (1-T029-00:16:03.170)

It is important to remember that the description presented thus far applies only to clauses in which the object is singular. The 2SG and 3SG object-indexing enclitics are monosyllabic and this could be why they occur with =*i*. Examples (85) to (88) show the absence of =*i* with other object enclitics. In Kubokota too, -*i* is only used with the 2SG and 3SG monosyllabic object enclitics (Chambers 2009: 113).

(85) ***I=to***   ***agoto=ami***   *te*   *oina=kara.*
    3PL.SBJ=EMPH hold=1EXCL.OBJ OBL 3PL.PSSR[CLI]=car
    'They held us in their car.'
    (1-T053-00:04:11.110)

(86) *Anna **e=nioto=ira.***
    Anna 3SG.SBJ=dream=1INCL.OBJ
    'Anna dreamt of us.'
    (2-E024)

(87) *"**Mi=no**   **atono=amu=i**   ini."*
    1EXCL.SBJ=go.SEQ bring=2PL.OBJ=IRR PROX
    '"We'll go and bring you here."'
    (1-T002-00:03:22.830)

(88) ***E=gaunu=ina***   *na=pepa.*
    3SG.SBJ=write=3PL.OBJ SPEC[CLI]=paper
    'He wrote letters.'
    (2-E008)

In Papapana, =*i* does sometimes co-occur with the 1SG object enclitic =*au*, but the variation has no apparent grammatical or semantic motivation as (89) and (90) demonstrate. The use of =*i* with =*au* could suggest that the use of =*i* was once less restricted or it might be analogous with the other singular object-indexing enclitics (as in (91) for example); speakers certainly deemed it more acceptable to not include =*i*.

(89) *"Aetau **o=moroko=au**?"*
why 2SG.SBJ=lie=1SG.OBJ
'"Why did you lie to me?"'
(1-T052-00:03:36.440)

(90) *"Aetau **o=mo~morok=i=au=omu**?"*
why 2SG.SBJ=RD~lie=TR=1SG.OBJ=2SG.IPFV
'"Why are you lying to me?"'
(1-T049-00:01:48.130)

(91) ***E=no*** ***morok=i=a=i*** *na=maunu.*
3SG.SBJ=go.SEQ lie=TR=3SG.OBJ=IRR SPEC[CLI]=woman
'He went and lied to the woman.'
(1-T088-00:32:07.907)

6.5.1.2 Applicative *i*

Applicative *i* in Papapana can function as a valency-increasing device. When applied to the subclass of intransitive verbs derived from adjectives, *i* introduces an object that is the comparand in a comparative construction (see §6.4.1). When applied to a monotransitive or ambitransitive verb, it derives a ditransitive verb where the new object is the O1 (i.e. it is indexed by the object enclitics) and expresses the semantic role of addressee, recipient or beneficiary, while the former O1 argument occurs only as a NP in the clause (see the O1 *Jane* in (97)). When applied to an ambitransitive verb of Group 2 Action verbs (see §6.4.4.2), it may also change the semantic role of the object in a monotransitive predicate from patient to addressee, recipient or beneficiary, as with *Jane* in (98). Example (98) contrasts with example (82) in §6.5.1.1 where *gaunu* is also monotransitive but the transitive enclitic is present and the object is a patient. Applicative *i* also functions with the applicative comitative *me* to derive a monotransitive verb with a comitative object from an intransitive verb, or to change the semantic role of the object of an ambitransitive A-verb to comitative (see §6.5.4).

Like transitive =*i*, applicative *i* immediately precedes the object-indexing enclitics, but only 2SG and 3SG object-indexing enclitics; however, unlike transitive =*i*, it is used with verb roots of all phonological shapes and it does not alter the verb root's phonology (see Table 6.14 and compare (82) and (98)). Applicative *i* is not considered a suffix or enclitic because it does not form a phonological word with the verb; for example, in (93) below, a long vowel is not formed, which one would expect if *i* formed a phonological word with the verb.

Table 6.14: Ditransitive structures with singular objects.

Root	Transitive Stem	Example
(CV.)CVx.CVy	(CV.)CVx.CVy APPL=OBJ	92
(CV.)CV.Ci	(CV.)CV.Ci APPL=OBJ	93
CVx.Vy	CVx.Vy APPL=OBJ	94
CV.Ca	CV.Ca APPL=OBJ	95
(CV.CV.)CVx.CVx	(CV.CV.)CVx.CVx APPL=OBJ	96
CV.CVx.CVx	CV.CVx.CVx APPL=OBJ	97, 98

(92) **E=averu** i=a na=gono aia.
 3SG.SBJ=steal APPL=3SG.OBJ SPEC[CLI]=banana 3SG
 'He stole a banana for him.'
 (2-E009)

(93) **E=peri** i=a ena=kabekabe.
 3SG.SBJ=find APPL=3SG.OBJ 3SG.PSSR[CLI]=bag
 'He found his bag for him.'
 (2-E024)

(94) Anau **u=bio** i=a e-sina-u
 1SG 1SG.SBJ=sweep APPL=3SG.OBJ PERS-mother-1SG.PSSR
 na=inu.
 SPEC[CLI]=house
 'I swept the house for my mother.'
 (3-E002)

(95) Anau **u=tuna** i=a John nu=obutu.
 1SG 1SG.SBJ=push APPL=3SG.OBJ John SPEC.CLII=canoe
 'I pushed the canoe for John.'
 (3-E001)

(96) Anau na='usia oina=bau 'a'ade'e
    1SG SPEC[CLI]=child 3PL.PSSR=PL narrative
    u='a'ade'e   **i=a**   e-sina-u.
    1SG.SBJ=narrative APPL=3SG.OBJ PERS-mother-1SG.PSSR
    'I told the children's stories for/to my mother.'
    (3-E002)

(97) Evan **e=gaunu**   **i=a**   na=pepa   Jane.
    Evan 3SG.SBJ=write APPL=3SG.OBJ SPEC[CLI]=paper Jane
    'Evan wrote Jane letters.'
    (2-E018)

(98) Evan **e=gaunu**   **i=a**   Jane.
    Evan 3SG.SBJ=write APPL=3SG.OBJ Jane
    'Evan wrote to Jane.'
    (2-E018)

As with transitive =*i*, the description presented thus far applies only to clauses in which the object is 2SG or 3SG singular, as a comparison of (99a) with (99b) and (99c) shows.

(99) a. Anau **u=atu**   **ma'ata** **i=a**   nu=koko'i.
       1SG 1SG.SBJ=make be.heated APPL=3SG.OBJ SPEC.CLII=taro
       'I cooked taro for him.'
       (2-E010)
    b. Anau **u=atu**   **ma'ata=amu**   nu=koko'i.
       1SG 1SG.SBJ=make be.heated=2PL.OBJ SPEC.CLII=taro
       'I cooked taro for you.'
       (2-E010)
    c. Anau **u=atu**   **ma'ata=ina**   nu=koko'i.
       1SG 1SG.SBJ=make be.heated=3PL.OBJ SPEC.CLII=taro
       'I cooked taro for them.'
       (2-E010)

Unlike transitive =*i*, applicative *i* can be derivational, albeit not especially productive since it is only applied with 2SG and 3SG objects. Since the object that is introduced by *i* has the semantic role of addressee, recipient, beneficiary, or comitative, this *i* is actually more similar to POc *-akin[i]* than it is to POc *-i*. It could be that in Papapana the functions of POc *-i* have been extended, but the morphophonological behaviour is clearly different so I hypothesise that applicative *i* actually reflects POc **-akin[i]*. Indeed, Evans proposes that an applicative form **=ni*, which occurs in a number of Northwest Solomonic languages, can be reconstructed for Proto-Meso-Melanesian, and "it seems likely that this **=ni* is a reduced reflex of POc **-akin[i]*" (Evans 2003: 233). In Papapana, I hypothesise that **=ni* has been further reduced to *i*.

6.5.2 Causative *va-*

A causative is a valency-increasing device which adds a controlling participant: the *causee* is the undergoer of the caused event and the *causer* is the agent of the predicate of cause. In Papapana, the causative prefix *va-* is a clear reflex of the POc causative prefix **pa-* (Lynch, Ross, and Crowley 2002: 83) and is clearly cognate with the causative prefix *va-* in other Northwest Solomonic languages such as Banoni (Lynch and Ross 2002: 447–448), Teop (Mosel and Thiesen 2007), Roviana (Corston-Oliver 2002: 482), Hoava (Davis 2003: 133) and Kubokota (Chambers 2009: 132). Causative *va-* is a productive morpheme that occurs frequently and attaches directly to the verb. It can function with intransitive, monotransitive and ambitransitive verbs.

With intransitive verbs, *va-* increases the valency and derives a monotransitive verb from an intransitive one. As shown in (100)–(101), the causer is the introduced agent participant, occurring as the A argument in the causative clause (*Francis* and 3PL in (100b) and (101b)), while the S argument of the intransitive form of the verb corresponds to the O argument of the causative form of the verb and is the causee (*nudaramu* 'the water' and 1PL in (100) and (101)), The causee object is indexed by the object enclitic, with the presence of the transitive enclitic *=i* again dependent on the phonology of the verb root and object number. Intransitive verbs can have their valency increased by *va-* regardless of the semantic role of the S argument of the underived verb; for example, the subject is an actor in (101a) and patient in (100a). Note that for the intransitive verb *tamu* 'to eat', the causative derives a monotransitive verb meaning 'to feed' which contrasts with the monotransitive verb *ani* 'to eat (something)'.

(100) a. *Nu=daramu*   ***e=ngono~ngono=ena.***
      SPEC.CLII=water   3SG.SBJ=RD~boil=3SG.IPFV
      'The water is boiling.'
      (2-E009)

b. *Francis e=va-ngon=i=a=na   nu=daramu.*
   Francis 3SG.SBJ=CAUS-boil=TR=3SG.OBJ=3SG.IPFV SPEC.CLII=water
   'Francis is boiling the water.'
   (2-E009)

(101) a. *Nani   te=na=garasi   **mi=tamu.***
         there OBL=SPEC[CLI]=grass   1EXCL.SBJ=eat
         'We ate there on the grass.'
         (1-T071-00:05:52.450)
      b. *Enai=ma   **i=to**   **va-tamu**   osi=ira...*
         after=ma   3PL.SBJ=EMPH   CAUS-eat   COMPL=3PL.OBJ
         'After they finished feeding us...'
         (1-T002-00:02:51.630)

With monotransitive and ambitransitive verbs, *va-* increases the clause-level valency to ditransitive as in (102)–(103). The causer is the introduced agent participant, occurring as the A argument in the causative clause (*Jerry* in both (102b) and (103b)), while the A argument of the transitive form of the verb corresponds to the O1 argument of the causative form of the verb and is the causee (*Francis tau Alan/Anna* 'Francis and Alan/Anna' in (102b) and (103b)). The former O argument of the transitive verb (*navuvurau* 'the car' and *nadaramu* 'the water' in (102) and (103)) is demoted to O2 and is therefore no longer indexed by the object enclitics. Again, the transitive enclitic =*i* only occurs with some verbs when the object is singular. Monotransitive and ambitransitive verbs can have their valency increased by *va-* regardless of the semantic role of the A argument of the underived verb; for example, the subject is an experiencer in (102) and actor in (103).

(102) a. *Ben nu=buku   e=amun=i=a.*
         Ben SPEC.CLII=book   3SG.SBJ=look=TR=3SG.OBJ
         'Ben saw a book.'
         (2-E007-2A)
      b. *Jerry **e=va-amunu=ina**   Francis tau Alan*
         Jerry 3SG.SBJ=CAUS-look=3PL.OBJ Francis and Alan
         na=vu~vurau.
         SPEC[CLI]=RD~run
         'Jerry showed Francis and Alan the car.'
         (2-E015)

(103) a. *Francis nu=daramu*   *e=irom=i=a.*
Francis SPEC.CLII=water 3SG.SBJ=drink=TR=3SG.OBJ
'Francis drank the water.'
(2-E015)
b. *Jerry e=va-iromo=ina*   *Francis tau Anna*
Jerry 3SG.SBJ=CAUS-drink=3PL.OBJ Francis and Anna
na=daramu.
SPEC[CLI]=water
'Jerry made Francis and Anna drink the water.'
(2-E015)

6.5.3 Detransitivising *ta-*

For the small class of monotransitive U-process verbs (see §6.4.2.2), the verb may occur in its unmarked monotransitive form (104a) or be detransitivised with the verbal prefix *ta-* (104b), in which case the monotransitive object (*nunanava* 'the pot') corresponds to the intransitive subject. In Papapana the detransitivising prefix *ta-* is a clear reflex of the POc detransitivising prefix **ta-* but its use appears to be restricted to only these U-process verbs and it does not occur very frequently in the data. Since these verbs are inherently inchoative, *ta-* derives a result state predicate, which is inherently intransitive, so an alternative analysis of *ta-* might be that it has a resultative function rather than detransitivising. In any case, *ta-* occurs rarely and does not apply to all verbs expressing a change of state; therefore, it is either extremely limited in its function or it is synchronically lexicalised.

(104) a. *Francis e=puan=i=a*   *nu=nanava.*
Francis 3SG.SBJ=break=TR=3SG.OBJ SPEC.CLII=pot
'Francis broke the pot.'
(2-E015-B)
b. *Nu=nanava*   *e=ta-puana.*
SPEC.CLII=pot 3SG.SBJ=DETR-break
'The pot broke.'
(2-E015-B)

6.5.4 Applicative comitative *me*

There are two ways of expressing a participant with a comitative role in Papapana: one involves a postposition phrase (see §8.3.4) and the other, discussed here, is an unusual construction consisting of an applicative comitative marker in the VC that appears to occupy the same preverbal position as the causative prefix *va-*, detransitivising prefix *ta-* and the reciprocal/reflexive marker *vei*.

The applicative comitative *me* marks a participant with a comitative role as a core object, and this object is usually indexed by the object enclitics. *Me* attaches to the suffixes *-a* when the new object is singular, and to *-na* when it is plural, resulting in the forms *me-a* (105)–(106) and *me-na* (107)–(109). The form *-a* is identical to the 3SG object enclitic while *-na* resembles the 3PL object enclitic =*ina* (it is feasible that *me-ina* has phonologically reduced to *me-na*); however, person is no longer distinguished, so *me-a* is used for all singular comitative objects (105)–(110) and *me-na* for all plural comitative objects (107)–(109). The choice between *me-a* and *me-na* is thus not motivated by the person and number of the subject, as there are a variety of subjects. If the object is singular, the applicative *i* may also be present (see §6.5.1.2) as in (106).

(105) *"Ani ini   o=me-a   po=au=omu=i."*
      2SG here 2SG.SBJ=COM-SG.OBJ stay=1SG.OBJ=2SG.IPFV=IRR
      '"You stay here with me."'
      (1-T023-00:04:32.013)

(106) *Na=vanua   i=me-a   tua   i=o   nao*
      SPEC[CLI]=people 3PL.SBJ=COM-SG.OBJ paddle APPL=2SG.OBJ thither
      Buka.
      Buka
      'The people paddled with you to Buka.'
      (2-E015B)

(107) *Ta   toituna iai   e=me-na   po   tani=ira.*
      and God   PROX 3SG.SBJ=COM-PL.OBJ stay already=INCL.OBJ
      'God already lives with us.'
      (1-T097-00:11:03.851)

(108) *"Anau u=eri   me-na   nao=amu=ou*
      1SG   1SG.SBJ=OPT COM-PL.OBJ go=2PL.OBJ=1SG.IPFV
      te=na='uru."
      OBL=SPEC[CLI]=island
      '"I want to go with you to the island."'
      (1-T029-00:04:56.730)

(109) *A:mani ini   mi=me-na   po=ina=mani   ini.*
1EXCL here 1EXCL.SBJ=COM-PL.OBJ stay=3PL.OBJ=1EXCL.IPFV here
'We'll stay here with them.'
(1-T002-00:03:15.610)

As shown below, in applicative comitative constructions, the object-indexing enclitics may be present or absent and there may or may not be a conominal object NP; however this variation is not yet understood. In the examples above, the object is indexed only by an object enclitic, so morphologically the verb's valency has been increased to monotransitive. In the following examples, the object is indexed by an object enclitic and an object NP, thus the verb is transitive at both the morphological and clause-level:

(110) *U=pei   me-a   siodo i=a=au*
1SG.SBJ=PST.IPFV COM-SG.OBJ work   APPL=3SG.OBJ=1SG.IPFV
au=avutei.
1SG.PSSR[CLI]=brother.in.law
'I was working with my brother-in-law.'
(1-T042-00:11:09.440)

(111) *I=no   me-na   po=ina=i   na=vanua.*
3PL.SBJ=go.SEQ COM-PL.OBJ stay=3PL.OBJ=IRR SPEC[CLI]=people
'They go and stay with the men.'
(1-T076-00:01:52.880)

In some of my data, such as (112) and (113), only the object NP is present and not an object-indexing enclitic, meaning that morphologically the verb's valency has not been increased to monotransitive. Given that the object is either 3SG or 3PL, it could be that the object enclitics are rendered redundant by the fact that *me* attaches to reflexes of the object enclitics *=a* and *=ina*. However, in (110) and (109) above, the object enclitics are actually used with 3SG and 3PL objects so it cannot be a matter of redundancy.

(112) *U=me-a*   tamu *e-sina-u.*
1SG.SBJ=COM-SG.OBJ eat   PERS-mother-1SG.PSSR
'I ate with my mother.'
(2-E009)

(113) . . .*e=pei*   *me-na*   *siodo=ena=i*   *na=siapani.*
3SG.SBJ=PST.IPFV COM-PL.OBJ work=3SG.IPFV=IRR SPEC[CLI]=Japan
'. . .he was working with the Japanese.'
(1-T034-00:13:27.980)

In a few instances, such as (114) and (115), there is no object enclitic and no object NP, which calls into question the status of these verbs as derived transitive verbs. Nevertheless, they are interpreted as having an object, and this suggests that the *-a* and *-na* attached to *me* are the object markers, and that *me* was diachronically a verb (see below).

(114) *I=me-a*   *tua*   *nao=i*   *i-ava.*
3PL.SBJ=COM-SG.OBJ paddle thither=IRR LOC-sea
'They would paddle out to sea with him.'
(1-T032-00:00:53.160)

(115) *Mi=pei*   *me-na*   *tua*   *tae* *nao=i. . .*
1EXCL.SBJ=PST.IPFV COM-PL.OBJ paddle up thither=IRR
'We used to paddle out with them. . .'
(1-T025-00:01:07.393)

Me occurs with intransitive verbs or ambitransitive verbs. With intransitive verbs, such as *tamu* in (112) above, *me* functions as a valency-increasing device, introducing an object with a comitative role, while with ambitransitive verbs, such as *nao* in (115) above, it changes the semantic role from patient or location to comitative. *Me* cannot occur with a solely monotransitive verb: in elicitation recordings ESD3-E001 and ESD3-E003 in April 2018, I tried to elicit utterances such as 'I ate mangoes with my mother' and 'I made food with my friend' (thus targeting the transitive verbs *ani* 'eat' and *atu* 'make') but speakers did not accept the use of *me*, let alone use it themselves. Instead the speakers used other strategies to express the comitative participant; either NP coordination with the coordinator *tau* 'and' (see §10.1.1.2) or a coordinate construction using a dual independent pronoun (see §10.1.1.3).

It is possible for *me* to be reduplicated instead of the verb in constructions that combine PSI enclitics and verbal reduplication patterns to express imperfective aspect (see §7.1.6), as the contrasting pair of examples in (116) and the examples in (117) and (118) show. There is also data, albeit limited, which shows that reciprocal/reflexive *vei* can be optionally reduplicated instead of the verb in prohibitive and reciprocal clauses (Smith 2016c: 546). The reduplication of *me* and *vei* instead of the verb could suggest that the reduplicant is a clitic and not an affix (Smith 2016c: 549–551).

(116) a. *Tom **e=me-a**   **tua~tua=na**   soida'o.*
Tom 3SG.SBJ=COM-SG.OBJ RD~paddle=3SG.IPFV old.man
'Tom is paddling with the old man.'
(2-E029-1)

b. *Tom **e=me~me-a**   **tua=na**   soida'o.*
Tom 3SG.SBJ=RD~COM-SG.OBJ paddle=3SG.IPFV old.man
'Tom is paddling with the old man.'
(2-E029-1)

(117) *... nu=obutu   **mi=me~me-a**   nao tae=mani.*
SPEC.CLII=canoe 1EXCL.SBJ=RD~COM-SG.OBJ go up=1EXCL.IPFV
'... we go out [to sea] with the canoe.'
(1-T099-00:01:23.520)

(118) *Buriatanana   bau sina-ina*
young.women PL mother-3PL.PSSR
*i=ae   **me~me-na**   orete=ina=ina.*
3PL.SBJ=NEG RD~COM-PL.OBJ walk=3PL.OBJ=3PL.IPFV
'Young women don't walk around with their mothers.'
(1-T040-00:00:52.130)

The optional reduplication of *me* instead of the verb and the fact that *me* hosts reflexes of object-indexing enclitics, could suggest that diachronically *me* was a verb, perhaps denoting 'be with'. Given its preverbal position, it may reflect a comitative "conjoined participant serialisation" like that found in Lewo (Vanuatu) (Early 1993: 68, 89). In such serialisations, "the subject and the object of the first verb become the combined subject of the second" (Early 1993: 89), as in (119).

(119) **Lewo**
Ne-mio-la   me-pano.
1SG.SBJ-with-3PL.OBJ 1EXCL.SBJ-REAL.go
'We went together (lit. I with them we went).'
(Early 1993: 89)

However, Papapana *me* appears to be cognate with comitative forms elsewhere in Northwest Solomonic languages that are not verbs: the comitative prepositions *me-* in Teop and Banoni and comitative case clitic *=me* in Taiof. In Banoni, *me-* attaches to a suffixed pronoun resembling the object set, and may precede a comitative NP in a preposition phrase (Lynch and Ross 2002: 452–453). In Taiof, *=me* is also followed by an object clitic, and is historically a preposition which has been captured by the verb and incorporated within the VC in a postverbal position, to increase the verb's valency (Ross 2002: 434). In Teop, *me* is a preposition that introduces a preposition phrase (PP) outside of the VC, but it may also be incorporated into the VC in a postverbal position in which it may host object enclitics, in order to increase valency and promote "the object of the preposition to the position of a primary object" (Mosel, in prep: 9, 14). The fact that in all three languages *me* hosts the object markers is likely a reflection of its history as a prepositional verb, as the special class of prepositional verbs common to Oceanic languages sometimes takes transitive morphology (Durie 1988: 2). Indeed, it is likely that *me* is a reflex of the POc comitative prepositional verb **ma-* (Pawley 1973: 142–147) and the PNWS comitative preposition **ma* (Ross 1988: 252): in Oceanic languages some prepositional verbs in SVCs have been reanalysed as adpositions when the serial construction has become unstable (Durie 1988: 3). In Teop and Taiof, these prepositions have then been incorporated into the VC. Papapana *me* could have the same history. It behaves similarly to *me* in Taiof and Teop: it also attaches to what appear to be reflexes of object-indexing enclitics (albeit only the 3SG and 3PL ones), it occurs within the VC and it increases valency, promoting a participant with a comitative role to the position of O1. However, Papapana *me* is not postverbal and instead seems to more closely reflect *mio* in Lewo. Either way, it seems likely that Papapana *me* was diachronically a serialised verb.

Me is no longer a verb in a SVC because (i) it does not occur as an independent verb, (ii) it may only be marked by reflexes of the 3SG and 3PL object-indexing enclitics, and (iii) *me-a* and *me-na* optionally co-occur with object-indexing enclitics. It could well be that the optional object-indexing enclitics in the VC in a *me* construction are a later development which occurred after *me* had been reanalysed, perhaps by analogy with other transitive clauses. Any semantic or pragmatic difference between constructions with or without object-indexing enclitics has yet to be identified, and awaits future research.

6.5.5 Object incorporation and transivity discord

In Papapana, the use of object incorporation (§6.5.5.1) and transitivity discord (§ 6.5.5.2) as valency-decreasing devices is a reflection on the specificity of the object and not on the verb class: that is, only generic objects can be incorporated into the VC or occur in transitivity discord constructions. It is common for a generic object to be incorporated into the VC in Oceanic languages (Lynch, Ross, and Crowley 2002: 46) and Northwest Solomonic languages such as Kokota

(Palmer 2002: 508), and this is also cross-linguistically common: following Hopper and Thompson (1980), Margetts (2008: 31) states that "highly individuated objects are likely to occur with transitive verbs, while less individuated objects are more likely to occur with intransitive verbs. What the crucial object properties are varies across languages, but the properties most often discussed as relevant are definiteness and specificity". Object incorporation in Papapana is a productive valency-decreasing process, though it is not overly prevalent in the text data, occurring mainly in elicitation. Transitivity discord in Papapana is a productive valency-decreasing process that seems to occur more often than object incorporation.

6.5.5.1 Object incorporation

Object incorporation is a particular type of *lexical compounding* "in which a V and N combine to form a new V. The N bears a specific semantic relationship to its host V – as patient, location, or instrument" (Mithun 1984: 848). In Papapana, the construction consists of a monotransitive or ambitransitive verb that syntactically incorporates its generic object (patient) argument, deriving an intransitive verb, which is thus not marked by object-indexing enclitics. Only a noun root is incorporated, not a NP, and it immediately follows the verb root. That the noun is part of the verb is evidenced by the fact that PSI enclitics and the irrealis enclitic =*i* attach to it as in (120)–(121) and (122) respectively. The semantic result of object incorporation in Papapana is that the attention is no longer on the effect of the process on the object but instead on the process itself, in most cases recognizing it as an institutionalized/culturally salient activity.

(120) A:*mani* **mi=ari~ari** *kaukau=emani.*
 1EXCL 1EXCL.SBJ=RD~dig sweet.potato=1EXCL.IPFV
 'We sweet potato-dig.'
 (2-E010)

(121) *Aina* **i=tuvi~tuvi** *obutu=ina.*
 3PL 3PL.SBJ=RD~build canoe=3PL.IPFV
 'They canoe-build.'
 (2-E014-2)

(122) **E=pei** *gaunu pepa=i.*
 3SG.SBJ=PST.IPFV write paper=IRR
 'He used to letter-write (after breakfast, last summer).'
 (2-E008)

6.5.5.2 Transitivity discord

Margetts (2008: 43) suggests that at the clause-level, some Oceanic languages should be described in terms of "at least four discrete morphosyntactic constructions" to adequately account for the range of semantic transitivity expressed in a language. In addition to intransitive and transitive clauses, she includes object incorporation and what she terms *transitivity discord*. Transitivity discord "occurs when an object is not cross-referenced on the verb" (Margetts 2008: 31) but the clause does include an object NP outside of the VC. There is therefore discord between verb-level transitivity (defined by the presence or absence of an object pronoun or other transitivity marker that is part of the verb or VC) and clause-level transitivity (defined by the overall number of arguments in the clause, whether inside or outside the VC) (Margetts 2008: 31).

In Papapana, transivitity discord constructions consist of a monotransitive verb and a generic object NP outside of the VC, but there are no object-indexing enclitics in the VC (123). That the object NP is not part of the VC is evidenced by the fact that when the clause order is SVO, the object follows the PSI enclitics (124) and the irrealis enclitic *=i* (125), while when the clause order is SOV, the object precedes subject-indexing proclitics (126). This distinguishes transitivity discord clauses from object incorporation, where the nominal object is incorporated inside the VC as part of the verb. The defining criterion for a transitive verb in Papapana is that the VC is marked by object-indexing enclitics, thus transitivity discord reduces valency morphologically, yet the clause itself is transitive. Note that in (123) and (126) the nouns are Class II and I nouns respectively, but display inverse number marking (§5.3.2) and are thus marked by the Class I and II specific articles respectively, rendering a plural, generic interpretation.

(123) ***I=to***   'aria   o'ovata   na=uvi.
      3PL.SBJ=EMPH   together   roast   SPEC[CLI]=yam
      'They roasted yams together.'
      (1-T029-00:11:03.590)

(124) *Aia*   *e=ae*   ***ani~ani=ena***   kaukau.
      3SG   3SG.SBJ=NEG   RD~eat=3SG.IPFV   sweet.potato
      'He doesn't eat sweet-potatoes.'
      (2-E011)

(125) *A:mani*   ***mi=atu=i***   ani   obutu   kaka'i.
      1EXCL   1EXCL.SBJ=make=IRR   DIM.PL   canoe   small
      'We'll make some small canoes.'
      (2-E009)

(126) *John na=au gono **e=averu=ena.***
John SPEC=CLII banana 3SG.SBJ=steal=3SG.IPFV
'John steals bananas.'
(2-E028-1)

6.5.6 Reciprocal/Reflexive *vei*

The valency-decreasing marker *vei* immediately precedes the verb and can function with monotransitive, ditransitive and ambitransitive verbs to express reciprocal and reflexive actions (see §6.5.6.1 and §6.5.6.2 respectively), with the verb being reduplicated in reciprocal clauses. Cross-linguistically, it is common for languages that have morphological reflexives to also have morphological reciprocals, and for such languages to "typically express reflexives and reciprocals with the same morphological operators" (Payne 1997: 201). Indeed, reciprocals and reflexives are conceptually similar as they both indicate that the agent and patient are coreferential (Payne 1997: 201). In Papapana, *vei* is a productive morpheme that occurs frequently, while the same form has a collective function in the NP (see §4.3, §4.4.4 and §4.6.1).

In Papapana, the reciprocal/reflexive marker *vei* is likely to be a reflex of the POc **paRi* and **pai-* and Proto-New Ireland **var-* and **vai-* prefixes, which commonly derived reciprocals and collective action verbs from transitives (Lynch, Ross, and Crowley 2002: 83; Ross 1988: 284). Pawley (1973: 150–151) reconstructed POc **paRi-* as a collective/associative, reciprocal, and iterative marker, referring to (i) "mutual interaction between the entities denoted by the subject of the verb", and to (ii) "unified or conjoined action by a plural subject, or repeated action by a singular subject, or unification of objects". Pawley (1973: 151–152) pointed out that the reciprocal meaning was restricted to a subclass of verbs and therefore labelling this prefix *reciprocal* was misleading. Dixon (1988: 178) similarly argues for Fijian that "to label [the prefix] *vei-* as reciprocal tends to obscure its other functions" and that reciprocal is a specification of the collective meaning. More recently, Lichtenberk (2000b: 58) suggested that POc **paRi-* expressed plurality of relationship (including reciprocal, collective, and chained actions), and argued that there is no evidence that the reciprocal function was historically primary (Lichtenberk 2000b: 32).

As the following subsections will demonstrate, in combination with *vei*, reciprocal and reflexive constructions in Papapana may also optionally use the verb *manene* 'return' as the second verb in a nuclear verb serialization. It is quite common for the sources of reciprocal and reflexive markers in Oceanic languages to be spatial notions such as 'downward', or 'return' (Moyse-Faurie

2008: 142–152) and indeed, Lichtenberk (1991: 503–504) identified reflexive markers as one of the grammaticalisation paths of the verb 'return' in the Oceanic languages Vangunu (Solomon Islands) and Paamese (Vanuatu).

6.5.6.1 Reciprocal

In a prototypical reciprocal clause, two participants equally act upon each other, i.e. both are equally agent and patient. Papapana reciprocal constructions are formed with monosyllabic or disyllabic verbal reduplication and the valency-decreasing marker *vei*, which immediately precedes the verb. The subject indicates the participants that are involved in the reciprocal action and is thus always non-singular. Whether the verb is monotransitive (127)–(131) or ditransitive (132), the VC is not marked by the object-indexing enclitics, and therefore in a reciprocal clause valency is reduced and the verb is morphologically intransitive, with the clause rendered intransitive or monotransitive respectively. When the clause has been rendered monotransitive (132), the only object NP is the theme (which in non-reciprocal constructions is the O2 and not indexed by object enclitics). Example (131) shows that non-human referents can be subjects of reciprocal constructions.

(127) *Va:sina, bau tubu-mani i=vei si~sia'a.*
before PL grandparent-1EXCL.PSSR 3PL.SBJ=R/R RD~look.after
'In the past, our ancestors looked after each other.'
(1-T078-00:00:25.890)

(128) *Natu~natu panapana i=vei ta~tavone=i.*
RD~clan all 3PL.SBJ=R/R RD~help=IRR
'All clans helped each other.'
(1-T093-00:02:57.580)

(129) *Aina i=vei ro~roroto.*
3PL 3PL.SBJ=R/R RD~see
'They saw each other.'
(2-E007-1)

(130) *Enai=ma mi=ara vei atu~atunu nani.*
after=ma 1EXCL.SBJ=PST R/R RD~attack there
'We fought each other there.'
(1-T088-00:12:47.027)

(131) *Nua=au   boro   **i=vei**   **tu'u~tu'u.**
      two=CLII pig   3PL.SBJ=R/R   RD~meet
      'Two pigs met each other.'
      (2-E014-2)

(132) *Bill   auana   John   **i=vei**   **ma'a~ma'a**   bau   basket   kaukau.*
      Bill   3DU   John   3PL.SBJ= R/R   RD~give   PL   basket   sweet.potato
      'Bill and John gave each other baskets of potatoes.'
      (2-E007-1)

As (127)–(132) show, verbal reduplication in reciprocal constructions may be monosyllabic or disyllabic but it is unclear what motivates the type of reduplication in reciprocals. Firstly, the type of reduplication in reciprocal constructions does not always correspond with the type of reduplication found in continuous aspect constructions (see §7.1.6). For example, *atunu* 'attack' (130) and *tu'u* 'meet' (131) undergo the same type of reduplication in both constructions, but *tavone* 'help' (128) and *roroto* 'see' (129) display no reduplication in continuous aspect constructions and monosyllabic reduplication in reciprocal constructions. Secondly, valency does not play a role as *sia'a* 'look after' (127) is monotransitive, but so too is *atunu* 'attack' (130) and these verbs display different reduplication patterns. Thirdly, the type of reduplication is not phonologically determined: *avoro* 'complain' and *atunu* 'attack' have the same syllable structure, as do *suga* 'trust' and *ma'a* 'give', but these verbs undergo different reduplication in reciprocal constructions.

Furthermore, some reciprocal constructions uttered in elicitation sessions show the use of PSI enclitics and express imperfective aspectual meanings (133)–(135). It should be noted that the 3PL object-indexing enclitic and the 3PL PSI enclitic are homophonous, but the object-indexing enclitics are definitely not used in reciprocal constructions as (133) shows, since the 1EXCL object enclitic is *=ami*. In the case of *tavone* 'help' (134), the reduplicant can be assumed to express reciprocity, as also shown in (128) above, because *tavone* belongs to Group 1 in imperfective aspect constructions and is not reduplicated to express continuous aspect (see §7.1.6). The verb *atunu* 'attack', however, belongs to Group 3 in imperfective aspect constructions and undergoes disyllabic reduplication to express continuous aspect (see §7.1.6). In (130) above and (136) below, which both express past tense, the reduplicant on the verb *atunu* expresses reciprocity; however, in (135), which expresses continuous aspect, it is unclear whether the reduplicant marks continuous aspect or reciprocity, and furthermore, why *atu~atu~atunu* is not possible, since Papapana does permit multiple reduplication in habitual aspect constructions (see §7.1.6). The fact that multiple reduplication can occur in imperfective constructions but not in constructions which express both imperfective and reciprocal meanings, calls into question the nature of Papapana multiple reduplication as a unitary or serial process (Smith 2016c: 551–557).

(133) ***Mi=pei***   *vei   a~'atutusi ora=emani=i.*
1EXCL.SBJ=PST.IPFV R/R RD~chase only=1EXCL.IPFV=IRR
'We were just chasing each other.'
(2-E014-2)

(134) *Na=vanua   i=vei   ta~tavone=ina*
SPEC[CLI]=people 3PL.SBJ=R/R RD~help=3PL.IPFV
te=na=kaukau.
OBL=SPEC[CLI]=sweet.potato
'The men help each other in the garden.'
(2-E014-2)

(135) ***I=vei   atu~atunu=ina.***
3PL.SBJ=R/R RD~attack=3PL.IPFV
'They are attacking each other.'
(2-E007-1)

(136) *Ben auana John i=vei   atu~atunu.*
Ben 3DU John   3PL.SBJ=R/R RD~attack
'Ben and John attacked each other.'
(2-E007-1)

As mentioned in §6.5.6, reciprocal constructions may optionally use the verb *manene* 'return' as the second verb (V2) in a nuclear verb serialization, as in (137), and in (138) where the PSI enclitics clearly show that *manene* is part of the VC in V2 position. It is not clear why the verb is not reduplicated in these reciprocal constructions.

(137) *Naonava   auana tobi   i=vei   roroto manene.*
Yesterday 3DU   EMPH 3PL.SBJ=R/R see   return
'Yesterday the two of them saw each other.'
(2-E014-1)

(138) *Auana   i=vei   roroto manene=ina.*
      3DU   3PL.SBJ=R/R   see   return=3PL.IPFV
      'The two of them see each other.'
      (2-E014-1)

6.5.6.2 Reflexive

In a prototypical reflexive construction, the subject and object are the same entity. In Papapana reflexive constructions *vei* immediately precedes the verb and the VC is not marked by the object-indexing enclitics (139), nor is the verb reduplicated as in reciprocal constructions. *Vei* therefore reduces valency by specifying that instead of two separate entities being involved, one entity fulfils two semantic roles and/or grammatical relations.

(139) *O=to   vei   tepe=i. . .*
      2SG.SBJ=EMPH   R/R   cut=IRR
      'If you cut yourself. . .'
      (1-T058-00:05:24.100)

As mentioned in §6.5.6, reflexive constructions may optionally use the verb *manene* 'return' in a nuclear verb serialization in V2 position, as in (140) where its use is optional and in (141) where the PSI enclitics clearly show that *manene* is part of the VC in V2 position.

(140) a. *Na=maunu   e=vei   tepe.*
         SPEC[CLI]=woman   3SG.SBJ=R/R   cut
         'The woman cut herself.'
         (2-E007-2A)
      b. *Na=maunu   e=vei   tepe manene.*
         SPEC[CLI]=woman   3SG.SBJ=R/R   cut   return
         'The woman cut herself.'
         (2-E007-2A)

(141) *John   e=vei   magono   manene=ena.*
      John   3SG.SBJ=R/R   dislike return=3SG.IPFV
      'John dislikes himself.'
      (2-E014-2)

The emphatic nominal modifier *tobi* (§4.7.5) may optionally modify the pronominal subject NP to emphasise reflexivity (142).

(142) **Ani tobi**　　o=vei　　　　　tepe.
　　　2SG EMPH 2SG.SBJ=R/R cut
　　　'You cut yourself.'
　　　(2-E007-2A)

6.6 Verb serialisation

In Papapana, verbs may occur in serial verb constructions (SVC). Verb serialisation is "the juxtaposition of two or more verbs, each of which would also be able to form a sentence of its own" (Bisang 1996: 533). The sequence of verbs (i) act together as a single predicate without any overt marker of dependency, (ii) share TAM and polarity values, (iii) share at least one and possibly more arguments, (iv) describe what is conceptualised as a single event, and (v) have the same intontational properties as a monoverbal clause (Aikhenvald 2006: 4–20; Durie 1997: 291).

In Papapana, two verbs can occur in a SVC. Papapana is therefore like other Northwest Solomonic languages such as Taiof (Ross 2002b), Banoni (Lynch and Ross 2002) and Sisiqa (Ross 2002a) which have two verbs in SVCs, whereas in Kokota (Palmer 2002) and Roviana (Corston-Oliver 2002) up to three or four verbs respectively may form a SVC. Example (143) shows that Papapana verbs act as a single predicate without a clause boundary or dependency marker because the verbs occur within one VC; the leftmost margin of the Papapana VC is marked by the subject-indexing proclitics, here 3SG, and the rightmost margin is marked by the irrealis mode enclitic =*i* (except when the repetitive aspect marker *vare ~ vae* occurs as a discontinuous morpheme; see §7.1.7). Example (143) also shows that SVCs in Papapana share TAM marking, but unfortunately there is no data showing that verbs in SVCs share negative marking.

(143) **E=pei**　　　　　　eri　　no　　vurau　tete=na=i
　　　3SG.SBJ=PST.IPFV OPT go.SEQ run　　enter=3SG.IPFV=IRR
　　　i-poana.
　　　LOC-village
　　　'He wanted to run inside the village.'
　　　(1-T035-00:10:55.920)

Subject-indexing proclitics precede the first component verb, while object-indexing enclitics follow the final component verb (see §6.6.2.1, §6.6.2.3 and §6.6.2.4 for examples), regardless of whether the final verb is a transitive verb or not, thus Papapana SVCs are *nuclear* or *contiguous*, that is "the verbs are bound together and have only a single set of arguments" (Lynch, Ross, and Crowley 2002: 47) and "no other elements intervene between the two verbs" (Reinig 2004: 93). In Western Oceanic languages, nuclear layer serializations are actually less common than *core* layer serializations (Bril 2004: 1), in which "the verbs remain separate words and usually share just one argument, any other argument [. . . belonging to] just one of the component verbs" (Lynch, Ross, and Crowley 2002: 47).

As Reinig (2004: 94) notes, not all of the criteria outlined above "have to be present at the same time, but on the other hand, a single feature would not be sufficient to classify a construction as a serial verb construction". Some authors have observed that eventhood and intonation are unreliable criteria for identifying SVCs and I do not use these criteria here. I agree with Reinig (2004: 94) that it is unclear how one can confidently determine what is conceptualised as a single event for a native speaker. Reinig (2004: 94) also finds the notion of single intonation pattern problematic as "it is unrealistic to assume that there is only one intonation pattern in a monoverbal clause". I also do not use intonation to identify SVCs in Papapana for the same reason and because prosodic analysis was beyond the scope of the current research.

The remainder of this section discusses the types of verbs found in Papapana SVCs and their component wordhood (§6.6.1), and the semantic types and composition of SVCs (§6.6.2).

6.6.1 Verb types and component wordhood

The types of verbs that occur in Papapana SVCs are intransitive verbs of movement in a geographic direction, intransitive locomotion verbs, monotransitive locomotion verbs, monotransitive action and process verbs and intransitive stative verbs (see Table 6.15). I have grouped verbs into these semantic categories in alignment with Proto-Oceanic SVC verb types (Ross 2004b: 300–301) to allow easier cross-linguistic comparison as these categories occur in other Northwest Solomonic languages such as Kubokota (Chambers 2009).

Intransitive verbs of movement in a geographic direction (GEOG) are those verbs which express movement relative to a specific location or physical ground. These verbs are intrinsically oriented because the "meaning of these verbs includes an orientation for the motion they describe" (Durie 1988: 9). In Proto-Oceanic, verbs denoting 'ascend' and 'descend' belonged to the GEOG category. In

Papapana *tae* 'ascend/away from shore', and *dini* 'descend/towards shore' semantically belong to this category but they are not independent verbs in synchronic Papapana, but postverbal geocentric directionals (see §6.7.1). Similarly, Proto-Oceanic had a group of deictic verbs which expressed movement in a deictic direction, referring to one of three persons. In Papapana reflexes of these verbs, *nao* 'go' and *naomai* 'come', have grammaticalised as postverbal deictic directionals and preverbal sequential directionals (see §6.7.2 and §6.7.3), while the postverbal allative directional likely reflects the POc deictic directional verb **ua* 'go: 2' (see §6.7.4).

Locomotion verbs (LOCO) are those verbs which express the manner of movement and entail no directionality. There are two groups of LOCO verbs in Papapana: intransitive and monotransitive. The monotransitive LOCO verbs can be subcategorised according to whether they occur as the first verb in the series (V1 position) or the second (V2 position). The V2 monotransitive LOCO verbs are extrinsically oriented because the verb takes "an object which specifies the spatial reference of the motion" (Durie 1988: 9).

The action, process and stative verbs that are attested in SVCs in my corpus are restricted to those shown in Table 6.15, except for when the V2 is *vowa ~ vewa* 'be like' and then a wide range of verbs can occur as V1.

Table 6.15: SVC verb types.

Verb type	Verbs	
GEOG	*nao*	go
	tete	enter
	manene	return
	votu	leave
	tavotu	arrive
LOCO-INTR	*orete*	walk
	vurau	run
	pu	fall
	tua	paddle/row
	para'a	jump
LOCO-TR-V1	*mamu*	throw
	de	take
	banu	carry
	oi	take
LOCO-TR-V2	*mumurina*	follow
	atutusi	chase
	tage	approach/near

Table 6.15 (continued)

Verb type	Verbs	
Action	*atunu*	attack
	atu	make
Process	*puana*	break (glass, pottery, fruit)
	'a'u	break (wood)
	putu	break off
	repi	split (wood)
Stative	*mate*	die/be dead
	ma'ata	be heated
	vovoi	be ready
	vowa ~ vewa	be like

Since verb serialisation involves juxtaposing two or more verbs, "each of which would also be able to form a sentence of its own" (Bisang 1996: 533), one cannot analyse a construction as verb serialisation unless one is certain that the morpheme/word in question can indeed function as an independent verb. While it is not possible here to prove this for every verb listed above, the following examples illustrate a verb from each of the categories in Table 6.15 being used as an autonomous nucleus:

(144) *Na=tonu-eta   e=to   ara tete.*
   SPEC[CLI]=wave-AUG 3SG.SBJ=EMPH PST enter
   'The tsunami came in.'
   (1-T105-00:10:46.026)

(145) ***E=to   para'a na=epio...***
   3SG.SBJ=EMPH jump   SPEC[CLI]=frog
   '(When) the frog jumped...'
   (1-T063-00:02:38.490)

(146) *Aia e=to   de=a   mai.*
   3SG 3SG.SBJ=EMPH take=3SG.OBJ hither
   'He took it back.'
   (1-T029-00:08:11.580)

(147) *Madonna Nathan **e=mumurina=i=a**. . .*
 Madonna Nathan 3SG.SBJ=follow=TR=3SG.OBJ
 'Madonna follows Nathan. . .'
 (1-T104-00:00:52.720)

(148) *Enai=ma e-sina-ina **e=atunu=ina.***
 after=ma PERS-mother-3PL.PSSR 3SG.SBJ=attack=3PL.OBJ
 'Then their mother attacked them.'
 (1-T007-00:01:10.140)

(149) *Francis **e=puan=i=a** nu=nanava.*
 Francis 3SG.SBJ=break=TR=3SG.OBJ SPEC.CLII=pot
 'Francis broke the pot.'
 (2-E015-B)

(150) *. . .na=sosopeni gono **e=to** ma'ata=i.*
 SPEC[CLI]=saucepan banana 3SG.SBJ=EMPH be.heated=IRR
 '[You wait until] . . .the saucepan of bananas is cooked.'
 (1-T036-3-00:00:38.070)

Vowa ~ vewa 'be like, in the way of' most often occurs in a SVC (§6.6.2.6) and rarely as an independent verb; however, the fact it can be used as an autonomous nucleus means that such constructions can be analysed as SVCs. As an independent verb, *vowa ~ vewa* 'be like, in the way of' may or may not have a complement, as shown by (151)–(152) respectively. Overt complements may also be PPs headed by *avosia* (see §8.3.3) but when an overt complement is lacking, the subject is being likened to something mentioned elsewhere in the discourse. The alternate forms *vowa* and *vewa* reflect the phonological variation described in §3.1.3. Additionally, *vowa ~ vewa* can function as an associative postnominal modifier (§4.7.6) and a postverbal allative directional (§6.7.4).

(151) *Ta iai **e=vewa.***
 and PROX 3SG.SBJ=be.like
 'And it is like this.'
 (1-T027-3-00:03:09.220)

(152) *Port Moresby va:sina e=pei ae vewa=na=i.*
 Port Moresby before 3SG.SBJ=PST.IPFV NEG be.like=3SG.IPFV=IRR
 'Port Moresby wasn't like (this) in the past.'
 (1-T098-00:01:13.583)

6.6.2 SVC semantic types and composition

The verb types described in §6.6.1 combine in various ways to form six types of SVC. Table 6.16 shows the verb types that are permitted in V1 and V2 positions in Papapana SVCs, and the permitted combinations. Papapana SVCs are *symmetrical* as they consist of "two or more verbs each chosen from a semantically and grammatically unrestricted class" (Aikhenvald 2006: 3).

Table 6.16: SVC semantic types and composition.

Type	V1	V2	Semantic type
1	LOCO-INTR	LOCO-TR-V2	Same-subject monotransitive directional
2	LOCO-INTR	GEOG	Intransitive directional
	LOCO-INTR	LOCO-INTR	
	GEOG	GEOG	
3	LOCO-TR-V1	GEOG	Switch-subject monotransitive directional
4	Action	Stative	Causative
5	Process	Process	Cause-effect
6	All verbs	*vowa ~ vewa* 'be like'	Similarity/manner

The first three types (see §6.6.2.1 to §6.6.2.3) are directional SVCs, in which "the first verb expresses movement, the second the direction of that movement or the position reached as result" (Lynch, Ross, and Crowley 2002: 47). The fourth type (see §6.6.2.4) is causative, in which "the first verb is transitive and the second expresses the result of the action of the first verb" (Lynch, Ross, and Crowley 2002: 47). The fifth type expresses cause and effect (see §6.6.2.5). Papapana is very much like other Northwest Solomonic languages, such as Banoni (Lynch and Ross 2002: 450) and Taiof (Ross 2002b: 435), which have only directional and causative SVCs. However, Papapana also has a SVC expressing similarity/manner where *vowa ~ vewa* 'be like' is the V2 but there are no restrictions on the type of verb which can occur as V1. *Vowa ~ vewa* 'be like' in a SVC may or may not have a complement: when one is lacking, the subject is being likened to something mentioned elsewhere in the discourse while when one is present, it may take the form of a PP headed by *avosia*, a finite complement clause introduced by *avosia* or the interrogative term *avoa* (see §6.6.2.6).

6.6.2.1 Same-subject monotransitive directional

In same-subject monotransitive directional SVCs (154)–(157), the subject is the moving participant while the object of the construction is the goal of the movement expressed by the V2. Although V1 is intransitive, the valency of the whole SVC is monotransitive due to the V2 being monotransitive.

(153) *Kapa e=para'a mumurina=au.*
Kapa 3SG.SBJ=jump follow=1SG.OBJ
'Kapa jumped after me.'
(1-T106-00:01:13.080)

(154) ***E=pei** tua mumurina=i=a=ena=i=ma.*
3SG.SBJ=PST.IPFV paddle follow=TR=3SG.OBJ=3SG.IPFV=IRR=ma
'He was paddling after him.'
(1-T031-00:09:23.770)

Further information about direction of movement in these SVCs can be expressed by postverbal deictic directionals *nao* 'thither' and *mai* 'hither':

(155) *Anau e-sina-u u=vu~vurau atutusi=a **nao**.*
1SG PERS-mother-1SG.PSSR 1SG=RD~run chase=3SG.OBJ thither
'I ran and chased my mother.'
(2-E007-2A)

(156) ***E=to** tua tage=a mai.*
3SG.SBJ=EMPH paddle approach=3SG.OBJ hither
'He paddled closer to it.'
(1-T026-00:03:53.243)

6.6.2.2 Intransitive directional

Intransitive directional SVCs contain a LOCO verb followed by a GEOG verb, though it is also possible for two intransitive LOCO verbs to co-occur (157), and for GEOG verbs to co-occur (158)–(159). These SVCs reflect the Proto-Oceanic intransitive geographical directional SVC (Ross 2004b: 302–308) and like that

SVC, this Papapana SVC may occur with a locative adjunct as in (158) and (159):

(157) *Aia e=pei   eri   para'a tuvu=ena=i.*
      3SG 3SG.SBJ=PST.IPFV OPT   jump   swim=3SG.IPFV=IRR
      'He wanted to dive (in).'
      (1-T042-00:06:07.730)

(158) ***E=nao***   ***manene*** te   ena=poana.
      3SG.SBJ=go   return   OBL   3SG.PSSR[CLI]=village
      'She went back to her village.'
      (1-T012-00:03:37.940)

(159) *Na=iana   e=to   no   nao   tete*
      SPEC[CLI]=fish 3SG.SBJ=EMPH   go.SEQ   go   enter
      te=na=vatu.
      OBL=SPEC[CLI]=stone
      'The fish went and went inside the rocks.'
      (1-T016-00:00:59.640)

In these SVCs, further information about direction of movement or position reached as a result can be expressed by preverbal sequential directionals (159), postverbal deictic directionals (160)–(163) and/or locative adjuncts (161)–(163). Although (161) appears to be three verbs in a SVC, I argue in §6.7.2 that *nao* in final position is not a serial verb but a deictic directional.

(160) *. . .tau u=to   vurau manene mai=i. . .*
      and   1SG.SBJ=EMPH   run   return hither=IRR
      '. . .and if I run back. . .'
      (1-T052-00:04:38.660)

(161) ***E=pu***   tete   ***nao=ma***   nani. . .
      3SG.SBJ=fall   enter thither=ma   there
      'He fell in there. . .'
      (1-T035-00:11:08.540)

(162) ***Mi=ara***   votu   ***manene mai***   i-poana.
      1EXCL.SBJ=PST   leave   return   hither   LOC-village
      'We went back to the village.'
      (1-T071-00:08:22.610)

(163) ***E=to***   ***tete***   ***manene nao***   *i-inu.*
3SG.SBJ=EMPH enter return thither LOC-house
'He went back inside the house.'
(1-T029-00:20:50.780)

6.6.2.3 Switch-subject monotransitive directional

In switch-subject monotransitive directional SVCs, the subject is the participant performing the action expressed by the monotransitive LOCO V1 while the object, such as *na'usia* 'the children' in (164), is affected by that action but also undergoes the movement expressed by the intransitive GEOG V2. Although V2 is intransitive, the valency of the whole SVC is monotransitive due to the V1 being monotransitive. This SVC reflects the Proto-Oceanic transitive geographical directional SVC (Ross 2004b: 303–308) and like that SVC, this Papapana SVC may occur with a locative adjunct:

(164) ***E=mamu~mamu***   ***tete=ina***   *na='usia*
3SG.SBJ=RD~throw enter=3PL.OBJ SPEC[CLI]=child
te=na=sirau   *te*   *aia.*
OBL=SPEC[CLI]=bag OBL 3SG
'He was throwing all the children inside his string bag.'
(1-T022-00:01:47.980)

Further information about direction of movement or position reached as a result can be expressed by postverbal deictic directionals as in (165) and/or locative adjuncts (166).

(165) *Ta*   ***e=banu***   ***votu=ina***   ***mai.***
and 3SG.SBJ=carry leave=3PL.OBJ hither
'And he carried them back home.'
(1-T052-00:00:45.920)

(166) ***E=pei***   ***de~de***   ***votu=ina=na***   ***mai=i***
3SG.SBJ=PST.IPFV RD~take leave=3PL.OBJ=3SG.IPFV hither=IRR
i-tanana. . .
LOC-road
'(When) he was carrying them home on the road. . .'
(1-T052-00:00:47.940)

6.6.2.4 Causative

In causative SVCs (167)–(169), the subject is the *causer* who does something to the object, the *causee*, which then results in the causee being in a particular state. The causer's actions are denoted by the monotransitive V1 while the causee's resulting state is denoted by the V2.

(167) *Jerry e=atunu   mate=a   Francis.*
Jerry 3SG.SBJ=attack die=3SG.OBJ Francis
'Jerry killed Francis.'
(2-E009)

(168) *Anau u=atu   ma'as=i=a   nu=koko'i.*
1SG   1SG.SBJ=make be.heated=TR=3SG.OBJ SPEC.CLII=taro
'I cooked taro.'
(2-E010)

(169) *Tamu~tamu na=vei   ma'ata*
RD~eat   SPEC[CLI]=COLL be.heated
i=to   ara atu   vovoi=ina.
3PL.SBJ=EMPH PST make be.ready=3PL.OBJ
'They prepared hot foods.'
(1-T076-00:01:49.670)

The SVC with *atunu* 'attack' and *mate* 'die' (167) is prevalent in Oceanic and Northwest Solomonic languages such as Banoni (Lynch and Ross 2002: 450) and Hoava (Davis 2003: 155, 158). The causative nature of the verbs *atunu* 'attack' and *atu* 'make' is highlighted by comparing (167)–(168) with the following elicited examples (170)–(171) in which the intransitive stative verb is transitivised by the causative prefix *va-*. Indeed, causative SVCs in Papapana are quite infrequent and do not appear to be particularly productive, and causation is instead productively expressed by the causative prefix *va-* (§6.5.2).

(170) *Jerry e=va-mat=i=a   Francis.*
Jerry 3SG.SBJ=CAUS-die=TR=3SG.OBJ Francis
'Jerry killed Francis.'
(2-E015)

(171) Aina **i=va-ma'ata** tani kaukau.
3PL 3PL.SBJ=CAUS-be.heated already sweet.potato
'They had already cooked the potatoes.'
(2-E014-2)

6.6.2.5 Cause-effect

The class of monotransitive U-process verbs in Papapana denote some kind of breaking (§6.4.2.2) and a few of them are attested in monotransitive cause-effect SVCs (172)–(173), though it is unclear if there are restrictions as to which verbs can occur in which position. The affected participant is the object of both verbs and this differentiates these SVCs from the causative SVCs above, in which the affected participant is the object of V1 and the subject of V2. Note that *soka* in (173) is a clear reflex of POc **soka* 'stab, spear' but is not attested as an independent verb in Papapana and therefore this type of SVC is largely lexicalised. Even for those verbs that do occur independently, cause-effect SVCs are very infrequent and unproductive.

(172) Anau **u=soka** **puan=i=a** na=ma'ata.
1SG 1SG.SBJ=stab break=TR=3SG.OBJ SPEC[CLI]=brown.coconut
'I split open a brown coconut.
(2-E009)

(173) **E=putu** **'a'u=a** na=maria na='overau.
3SG.SBJ=break.off break=3SG.OBJ SPEC[CLI]=thing SPEC[CLI]=bamboo
'He broke off the what's-it-called, the bamboo.'
(1-T064-00:02:56.640)

6.6.2.6 Similarity and manner

As discussed in §6.6.1, the verb *vowa ~ vewa* 'be like, in the way of' most often occurs in a SVC which expresses similarity or manner and which may or may not have a complement phrase or clause. When an overt complement is lacking, the subject is being likened to something mentioned elsewhere in the discourse, as in (174)–(176). Complements may be PPs headed by *avosia* 'like' (see §8.3.3), finite complements clauses introduced by the complementizer *avosia* (see §10.4.1), or the interrogative term *avoa* 'how' (see §9.3.2.3.4). *Vowa ~ vewa* 'be like, in the way of' always occurs as the V2, and there are no restrictions on the type of verb which can occur as V1. The valency of the whole SVC is determined by the V1.

(174) . . .*enai=ma* ***e=taosi***   ***vewa=i.***
      after=ma   3SG.SBJ=finish   be.like=IRR
      '. . .then it finishes like (that).'
      (1-T020-00:02:55.560)

(175) "*A:mani*   ***mi=tonu***   ***vewa=mani***   *va:gi.*"
      1EXCL   1EXCL.SBJ=stand   be.like=1EXCL.IPFV   now
      "'We're standing like (this) today.'"
      (1-T103-00:03:52.917)

(176) *Ini*   ***o=atu***   ***vewa=i=a=i.***
      here   2SG.SBJ=make   be.like=TR=3SG.OBJ=IRR
      'Here you make it like (this).'
      (1-T027-3-00:00:24.470)

6.7 Directionals

Directionals belong to a small closed class of words that can modify a verb, providing optional information about spatial location. There are four types of directional in Papapana and these have different syntactic positions in the VC, as shown in Tables 6.1 and 6.2 in §6.1: the three geocentric directionals immediately follow the verb before the completive aspect marker (§6.7.1), the two deictic directionals occur between PSI enclitics and the irrealis mode enclitic (§6.7.2), the two sequential directionals occur in the syntactic position that is immediately prior to the valency-changing morphemes *vei* and *va-* (§6.7.3) and the allative directional follows geocentric directionals but precedes object enclitics and, unlike adverbs, requires a goal (§6.7.4). Directionals are therefore distinct from adverbs (see §6.8), three of which occur preverbally immediately before valency-changing morphemes and many of which occur postverbally between the completive aspect marker and the object-indexing enclitics. For each of the four positions outlined for directionals, there is a choice of only one, two or three directionals which can fill that position, whereas the adverb positions can be filled by many adverbs with miscellaneous meanings. Furthermore, the directionals are all argued to be grammaticalised serial verbs.

6.7.1 Geocentric directionals *tae*, *dini* and *batabata*

One of the semantic systems Papapana uses in talking about space is an absolute system of fixed bearings in local space. As Figure 6.3 shows, there is a transverse axis parallel to the coastline in either direction and a vertical axis for which the shoreline is the centre, with movement away from the shoreline (either seawards or landwards/mountainwards) conceived as 'up' and movement towards the shoreline (either from the sea or from inland/the mountains) conceived as 'down'. In the Papapana VC, these geocentric coordinates may be expressed by the geocentric directionals *tae* 'ascend/away from shore' (177)–(178), *dini* 'descend/towards shore' (179)–(180) and *batabata* 'parallel' (181). The geocentric directionals *tae* and *dini* are also used on a vertical axis to refer to movement up away from the ground (182) and down towards the ground (183). These directionals do not modify nouns nor do they occur as clause-level adjuncts; however, the Relational Location nouns *ata* 'above' and *vuna* 'below' correspond to the geocentric directionals *tae* and *dini* and can function as case-marked locative NP adjuncts (see §8.1.2.3).

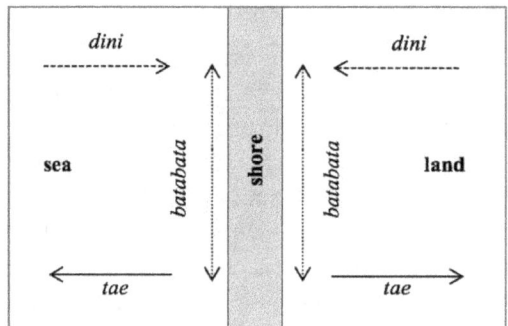

Figure 6.3: Geocentric coordinates.

(177) . . .*mi=vurau   tae nao   Panguna*. . .
      1EXCL.SBJ=run   up   thither Panguna
      '. . .we ran up to Panguna (mine). . .'
      (1-T034-00:32:48.796)

(178) ***E=pei***   *roroto tae=na   nao=i*
      3SG.SBJ=PST.IPFV   see   up=3SG.IPFV thither=IRR
      te=na='uru.
      OBL=SPEC[CLI]=island
      'He looked out to the island.'
      (1-T029-00:05:15.817)

(179) . . .*e=nao* **dini** *i-nongana.*
 3SG.SBJ=go down LOC-beach
 '. . .he went down to the beach.'
 (1-T029-00:13:09.703)

(180) *Ta* **mi=to** *tuvu* **dini** *nao.*
 and 1EXCL.SBJ=EMPH swim down thither
 'And we swam back (to the shore).'
 (1-T059-00:01:23.370)

(181) ***E=pei*** *tua batabata=ena* ***nao=i.***
 3SG.SBJ=PST.IPFV paddle parallel=3SG.IPFV thither=IRR
 'He was paddling along (the shore).'
 (2-T001-2-00:01:14.496)

(182) ***E=tonu*** *tae=ma.*
 3SG.SBJ=stand up=ma
 'He stood up.'
 (1-T052-00:05:14.460)

(183) ". . .*mu=ubete* **dini**. . ."
 2SG.SBJ=lay down
 "'. . .lie down. . .'"
 (1-T002-00:04:37.570)

These three geocentric dimensions reflect the dimensions reconstructed for POc: **sipo* '(go) downward' and **sake* '(go) upward' were opposed to each other on a vertical axis, with **pano* '(go) across' on a second axis transverse to the vertical axis (Ross 2004b: 302). On land, in coastal areas, 'up' was used for 'inland' and 'down' for 'seaward' with the undifferentiated transverse axis lying along the shore (François 2004: 8). However, in modern Oceanic languages, on a navigational scale at sea, the reflexes of **sipo* '(go) down' and **sake* '(go) up' were metaphorically extended to indicate 'go northwest' (i.e. 'downwind') and 'go southeast' (i.e. 'upwind') (François 2004: 18). As Chambers (2009: 360) explains, "the prevailing southeast wind was a highly salient feature of the environment for Proto-Oceanic navigators, and motivated a cardinal up-down axis running northwest-southeast".

In Papapana, however, *tae* does not correspond to southeast/upwind nor *dini* to northwest/downwind, since the coastline is oriented northwest-southeast; therefore, movement out to sea (*tae* 'up') from Teperoi is in a northeast, not southeast, direction, while movement in a northwest or southeast direction would be conceived as 'parallel'. As in Kubokota (Chambers 2009: 364) and Torau (Palmer, pers.comm.), small-scale orientation in Papapana therefore consists of two separate sets of axes, one land-based and one sea-based, whereas in most Oceanic languages, the inland-seaward axis extends out to sea. However, there is one utterance in my data which suggests that on a navigational scale, when describing long-distance travel at sea, 'down' and 'up' do correspond to northwest and southeast: in (184) *dini* 'down' is used to refer to paddling to Asitavi, which is northwest of Teperoi (see Figure 2.2 in §2.1).

(184) **Mi=tua** dini nao Asitavi.
1EXCL.SBJ=paddle down thither Asitavi
'We paddled to Asitavi.'
(1-T097-00:13:05.048)

As the examples above show, geocentric directionals occur immediately after the verb. These directionals precede all other postverbal elements including the completive aspect marker *osi* (185), adverbs such as *nanamoa* 'first' (186) and object-indexing enclitics (187):

(185) **U=to** tua dini osi mai...
1SG.SBJ=EMPH paddle down COMPL hither
'I finish paddling back down...'
(2-E007-2B)

(186) *Oina=au* kakau *i=mamu* dini nanamoa=i=a nao.
3PL.PSSR=CLII dog 3PL.SBJ=throw down first=TR=3SG.OBJ thither
'They threw their dog down first.'
(1-T007-00:01:55.930)

(187) **Mi=de** tae=a nao.
1EXCL.SBJ=take up=3SG.OBJ thither
'We took her up.'
(1-T030-00:03:06.276)

Since geocentric directionals immediately follow the verb and in Proto-Oceanic, verbs denoting 'ascend' and 'descend' belonged to the category of geographic direction verbs which occurred after locomotion verbs in SVCs (Ross 2004b: 300, 302–305), one might question whether *tae* and *dini* in Papapana are verbs in a series. Although diachronically it is likely that the geocentric directionals were serial verbs, I do not classify them as serial verbs because they are not independent verbs in synchronic Papapana. Instead, they have likely grammaticalised, especially as directionals in Oceanic languages are often descended from geographical direction verbs in geographical directional SVCs (Ross 2004b: 311). Indeed, the directional *batabata* is likely related to *babata* 'travel along coast' in Kubokota (Chambers 2009: 198–200) and *bata* 'simultaneous' in Teop (Mosel and Thiesen 2007).

Most often, these geocentric directionals are not reduplicated but there is some data that shows *tae* and *dini* occurring in a reduplicated form with both intransitive (188) and monotransitive verbs (189).

(188) a. . . .*e=vurau   tae~tae   nao.*
  3SG.SBJ=run RD~up thither
  '. . .he ran up.'
  (1-T067-00:02:46.330)
 b. *E=tua   dini~dini nao.*
  3SG.SBJ=paddle RD~down thither
  'He paddled down.'
  (1-T035-00:05:52.402)

(189) a. . . .*e=noe   tae~tae=a   te=na=tuvae.* . .
  3SG.SBJ=put RD~up=3SG.OBJ OBL=SPEC[CLI]=grate
  '. . .she put it up on the grate. . .'
  (1-T029-00:08:19.431)
 b. *E=atutusi   dini~dini=a   nao.*
  3SG.SBJ=chase RD~down=3SG.OBJ thither
  'He chased him down.'
  (1-T035-00:10:26.340)

It could be hypothesised that the geocentric directional is reduplicated instead of the verb in (188)–(189), much like the applicative comitative *me* and the reciprocal/reflexive *vei* can be reduplicated instead of the verb in imperfective constructions and prohibitive or reciprocal constructions respectively (see §6.5.4 and Smith 2016c). However, the utterances in (188)–(189) are not imperfective, prohibitive or reciprocal constructions as there are no PSI enclitics, or negative or reciprocal markers present. Some examples, such as (190), do contain a PSI enclitic and express imperfective aspect, however, the verbs belong to Group 1 (see §7.1.6.1) and are therefore not reduplicated to express continuous aspect anyway, so it cannot be the case that the geocentric directional is reduplicated instead of the verb.

(190) *Nu=dede'usia*   *e=pei*   *tonu*   *tae~tae=na=i.*
      SPEC.CLII=eagle 3SG.SBJ=PST.IPFV stand RD~up=3SG.IPFV=IRR
      'An eagle was standing above.'
      (1-T101-00:03:43.472)

There is no clear grammatical, semantic or pragmatic motivation for the variant forms of *tae* and *dini*, and unlike the reduplication of the applicative comitative *me* (§6.5.4), also derived from a serial verb, the reduplication of *tae* and *dini* is not productive. Further research is required to determine whether this variation is free or not.

6.7.2 Deictic directionals *mai* and *nao*

In the Papapana VC *mai* 'hither' and *nao* 'thither' optionally indicate the direction of the action in relation to a speech act participant. The deictic directionals follow PSI enclitics (191) but precede the irrealis mode enclitic (191)–(192) and discontinuous repetitive aspect =*re* (193).

(191) *Na=namu*   *e=pei*   *ta~tange=na*
      SPEC[CLI]=Malay.apple 3SG.SBJ=PST.IPFV RD~float=3SG.IPFV
      mai=i.
      hither=IRR
      'The Malay apple was floating down.'
      (1-T022-00:00:30.890)

(192) ***Mi=pei***   *orete   ora   nao=i*   *i-maria,*   *Vakonaia.*
      1EXCL.SBJ=PST.IPFV walk only thither=IRR LOC-thing Wakunai
      'We used to just walk to where's-it-called, Wakunai.'
      (1-T011-00:00:42.820)

(193) *Na:=ata   na=boni   **e=vae**   manene   **nao=re.***
    some=CLI SPEC[CLI]=day 3SG.SBJ=REP return   thither=REP
    'Another day he went back again.'
    (1-T029-00:06:53.220)

Proto-Oceanic had a group of deictic verbs which expressed movement in a deictic direction, making reference to one of three persons, and these deictic verbs could occur in a SVC following a locomotion or geographic direction verb (Ross 2004b: 300, 305–308). Diachronically it is likely that the Papapana deictic directionals were serial verbs, but I do not classify them as serial verbs because *mai* does not occur as an independent verb in synchronic Papapana, and when the form *nao* is a verb, it occurs in a different position in the VC and it may co-occur with the deictic directional *nao* (194). *Nao* thus has two lexical categories. Furthermore, synchronically in Papapana, deictic directionals may be separated from the verb by other elements, as for example in (194) and so they do not behave as similarly to serial verbs as geocentric directionals. Given that deictic directionals in Papapana clearly derive from the verbs *nao* 'go' and *naomai* 'come', it is likely that they are grammaticalised serial verbs. Indeed, it is common in Oceanic languages for directionals meaning 'hither' and 'thither' to be cognate with the verbs 'come' and 'go' and to descend from deictic direction verbs in deictic directional SVCs (Ross 2004b: 311).

(194) . . .*i=to   **nao** reareana   **nao=i.***
    3PL.SBJ=EMPH go   far   thither=IRR
    '. . .they go far away.'
    (1-T094-00:02:12.999)

6.7.3 Sequential directionals *mei* and *no*

In the Papapana VC *mei* 'come and' and *no* 'go and' are preverbal directionals that express the movement that is necessary to fulfil the action expressed by the main verb. They follow the subject proclitic (195), emphatic *to* (196), past imperfective *pei* (197), the optative mode marker *eri* (198) and the negative marker *ae* (199), but precede the valency-changing morphemes *vei* (200) and *va-* (201):

(195) ***E=mei***   *muni=a.*
    3SG.SBJ=come.SEQ hide=3SG.OBJ
    'He came and hid her.'
    (1-T003-00:01:50.870)

(196) *Aia* **e=to** *no* **de=a** *nu=kururu.*
3SG 3SG.SBJ=EMPH go.SEQ take=3SG.OBJ SPEC[CLI]=yellow.bamboo
'He went and got the yellow bamboo.'
(1-T031-00:06:51.160)

(197) *Arira ioi i-ata* **si=pei** *no*
1INCL DIST LOC-above 1INCL.SBJ=PST.IPFV go.SEQ
ta'opo=era=i.
hide=INCL.IPFV=IRR
'We were going and hiding up there.'
(1-T002-00:02:17.440)

(198) ***E=pei*** *eri no vurau tete=na=i*
3SG.SBJ=PST.IPFV OPT go.SEQ run enter=3SG.IPFV=IRR
i-poana.
LOC-village
'He wanted to go and run into the village.'
(1-T035-00:10:55.920)

(199) *"Obetana* **o=ae** *no mu~munu=i."*
under 2SG.SBJ=NEG go.SEQ RD~sit=IRR
'"Don't go and sit underneath."'
(1-T028-00:01:18.630)

(200) ***Mi=no*** *vei ta'opo=re.*
1EXCL.SBJ=go.SEQ R/R hide=REP
'We went and hid ourselves again.'
(1-T094-00:00:51.444)

(201) . . .*enai=ma* ***i=mei*** *va-apus=i=a.*
after=ma 3PL.SBJ=come.SEQ CAUS-sleep=TR=3SG.OBJ
'. . .then they came and made her sleep.'
(1-T003-00:02:16.010)

However, the sequential directionals are attested as both preceding (a) and following (b) the past tense marker *ara* (202) and the repetitive aspect marker *vare~ vae* (203):

(202) a. *Na=siodo   mama **u=no**   ara de=a.*
       SPEC[CLI]=work DEM1 1SG.SBJ=go.SEQ PST take=3SG.OBJ
       'I went and got this job.'
       (1-T097-00:13:36.867)
   b. *. . .**i=ara**   no   atu   tamu~tamu bau wallaby.*
       3PL.SBJ=PST go.SEQ make RD~eat   PL   wallaby
       '. . .the wallabies went and made a feast.'
       (1-T063-00:00:41.720)

(203) a. *"Iai   **mu=no**   vae vamaunisi=ma i-poana."*
       PROX 2PL.SBJ=go.SEQ REP rest=ma   LOC-village
       '"Go and rest again in the village."'
       (1-T042-00:04:50.200)
   b. *. . .iara **e=vare**   no   bua tae.*
       then   3SG.SBJ=REP go.SEQ full up
       '. . .then he was filled up again (with tears/water).'
       (1-T026-00:03:05.688)

The sequential directionals clearly derive from the verbs *naomai* 'come' and *nao* 'go'. Synchronically in Papapana, sequential directionals may be separated from the verb by other elements, such as in (203a), and so they do not behave like serial verbs, and they are certainly not independent verbs in Papapana. However it seems likely that they are grammaticalised serial verbs because in Proto-Oceanic, deictic verbs such as 'come' and 'go' could occur first in a sequential SVC and express 'come and' and 'go and' while the second verb expressed the main event of the predication (Ross 2004b: 309–311). In such SVCs, the verbs had the same subjects and a purposive relationship between the actions was usually implied (Ross 2004b: 309). Although the Proto-Oceanic sequential SVC has "resulted in far fewer grammaticalizations than the directional SVCs" across Oceanic languages (Ross 2004b: 314), this type of construction is present in other Northwest Solomonic languages such as Teop (Reinig 2004: 102–103) and Banoni (Lynch and Ross 2002: 448–449). However, in these languages the sequential directionals (termed *directional proclitics* and *sequential particles* respectively) occur immediately before the verb, reflecting the sequential SVC much more than in Papapana where *mei* and *no* do not have to occur immediately prior to the verb.

6.7.4 Allative directional *vowa ~ vewa*

The postverbal allative directional *vowa ~ vewa* 'towards' requires a goal, which may follow (204) or precede (205) the entire VC and may be a preposition phrase (204) or a Location noun such as *Arawa* (205). The alternate forms *vowa* and *vewa* reflect the phonological variation described in §3.1.3.

(204) . . .*ta e=tange   vowa   nao   te=na=poana.*
and   3SG.SBJ=float towards thither OBL=SPEC[CLI]=village
'. . .and it floated to the village.'
(1-T035-00:00:58.600)

(205) *Arawa i=no   vurau vowa.*
Arawa   3PL.SBJ=go.SEQ   run   towards
'They went and ran to Arawa.'
(1-T059-00:02:48.600)

The allative directional *vowa ~ vewa* 'towards' likely reflects the POc deictic directional verb *ua 'go: 2'. In many Oceanic languages, such as South New Ireland languages (Western Oceanic) and Longgu (Southeast Solomonic, Central-Eastern Oceanic) (Ross 2004b: 317–318), the POc verb *ua 'go: 2' has grammaticalised into an allative preposition or *relator*, forming a constituent with the following locative phrase. A *relator* is "a preposition-like morpheme which differs in its distribution from a preposition in that it precedes either a preposition phrase or a local noun" (Ross 2007a: 268). A reflex of *ua is also found in Teop with the preposition *vo* 'to, towards', which always governs a locative expression (Mosel, in prep). In Papapana however, *vowa ~ vewa* 'towards' is not a preposition nor relator as it does not form a constituent with the locative phrase, since the locative phrase can precede (205) or follow (204) the VC, and can be separated from *vowa ~ vewa* by other verbal elements, such as the deictic directional *nao* 'thither' (204). Allative *vowa ~ vewa* 'towards' is therefore clearly VC-internal. It follows geocentric directionals (206), but precedes object-indexing enclitics (207), PSI enclitics (208) and deictic directionals (209).

(206) *Na=vena   e=nao   dini   vewa   Vito.*
SPEC[CLI]=individual 3SG.SBJ=go down   towards Vito
'One went down to Vito.'
(1-T060-00:00:27.140)

(207) . . . *i=atono*   *vowa=au*   *nao*   *te*
3PL.SBJ=bring towards=1SG.OBJ thither OBL
e-tubu-u.
PERS-grandparent-1SG.PSSR
'. . .they took me over to my grandfather.'
(1-T051-00:02:09.041)

(208) *E=tua~tua*   *vowa=ena*   *nao*   *Makomako.*
3SG.SBJ=RD~paddle towards=3SG.IPFV thither OBL
'He is paddling to Makomako.'
(Fieldnotes 23/04/13)

(209) *Tai*   *Iraka*   *ini*   *i=vurau*   *vowa*   *mai.*
people Iraka here 3PL.SBJ=run towards hither
'The Iraka people ran here.'
(1-T034-00:36:41.440)

Since allative *vowa ~ vewa* 'towards' can be separated from the verb by geocentric directionals, it is not a verb in a SVC. The form *vowa ~ vewa* can however be an independent or serial verb denoting 'in the way of, be like' (see §6.6) which can occur with a PP headed by *avosia* 'like' (§8.3.3), with the interrogative term *avoa* 'how' (§9.3.2.3.4) or with a finite clause introduced by the complementizer *avosia* (§10.4.1). Additionally, it can function as an associative postnominal modifier (see §4.7.6). In Teop too, *vo* also denotes 'in the way of, like' and is described as polysemous (Mosel, in prep) whereas I argue (Smith-Dennis 2018a) that *vowa ~ vewa* is heterosemous and that it represents a case of polygrammaticalisation, whereby "a single morpheme is the source of multiple grammaticalisation chains" (Craig 1991: 455).

6.8 Adverbs in the VC

Adverbs belong to a small but seemingly open class of words that can optionally modify a verb or a clause, providing information about temporal location, aspect and mode, spatial location and manner. Two adverbs are derived from numerals, while others formally appear to be reduplicated but synchronically they are not. In Papapana there are three adverbs that occur in preverbal position (§6.8.1), while the rest occur in postverbal position in the VC (§6.8.2); see Table 6.1 and Table 6.2 in §6.1. There is no evidence that preverbal and postverbal adverbs can co-occur. One of the preverbal adverbs and some of the postverbal adverbs are also attested at the clause-level (§8.4), while others may function in the NP as modifiers (§4.7). Adverbs which operate exclusively at the clause-level are discussed in §8.4.

Adverbs in the VC are distinct from serialised verbs because they cannot occur as independent verbs. Adverbs in the VC are also distinct from directionals, which are also optional modifiers, because each type of directional has its own distinct position in the VC separate to that of the adverbs, and for each of the four positions outlined for directionals, there is a choice of only one, two or three directionals which can fill that position, whereas the preverbal and postverbal adverb positions can be filled by many adverbs with miscellaneous meanings. Furthermore adverbs do not form a class of words that are argued to be grammaticalised serial verbs (see §6.7).

6.8.1 Preverbal

Within the VC, there are three adverbs which occur exclusively in preverbal position, seemingly before sequential directional and valency-changing morphemes but after all other preverbal morphemes: *agai* 'really', *'aria* 'together' and *avirua* 'not yet'. Since these adverbs follow subject proclitics, they are part of the VC rather than clause-level adverbs.

The following examples demonstrate this syntactic position: in (210)–(212) the adverb follows emphatic *to* and/or the past imperfective marker *pei*, in (213)–(214) the adverb follows the negative marker *ae*, and in (215)–(218) *'aria* 'together' follows the optative mode marker *eri*, the past tense marker *ara* and the repetitive aspect marker *vare ~ vae*.

(210) . . .*avosia   na=naoi   e=to   pei   agai*
       SUBR   SPEC[CLI]=rain 3SG.SBJ=EMPH PST   really
       si'i=ena=i.
       rain=3SG.IPFV=IRR
       '. . .that the rain was really falling.'
       (1-T097-00:01:21.753)

(211) *I=pei   'aria   o'ovata=ina=i   na=uvi.*
       3PL.SBJ=PST.IPFV together   roast=3PL.IPFV=IRR SPEC[CLI]=yam
       'They were roasting yams together.'
       (2-E007-2A)

(212) ***U=pei*** *   avirua nai=ou.*
     1SG.SBJ=PST.IPFV not.yet marry=1SG.IPFV
     'I wasn't married yet.'
     (1-T042-00:00:33.390)

(213) *Anau u=ae   agai   varona=au*
     1SG   1SG.SBJ=NEG really know=1SG.IPFV
     tena atu=a   nu=maria,   nu=pute~pute.
     SUBR make=3SG.OBJ SPEC.CLII=thing SPEC.CLII=RD~wind
     'I don't really know how to make a what's-it-called, a fan.'
     (1-T027-3-00:02:07.200)

(214) ***I=to*** *   ae   'aria   o'ovata na=uvi.*
     3PL.SBJ=EMPH NEG together roast   SPEC[CLI]=yam
     'They didn't roast yams together.'
     (2-E007-2A)

(215) ***I=to*** *   eri   'aria   o'ovata=ina   na=uvi.*
     3PL.SBJ=EMPH OPT together roast=3PL.IPFV SPEC.CLII=yam
     'They wanted to roast yams together.'
     (2-E007-2A)

(216) ***I=ara*** *   'aria   o'ovata na=uvi.*
     3PL.SBJ=PST together roast   SPEC[CLI]=yam
     'They roasted yams together.'
     (2-E007-2A)

(217) ***I=to*** *   vare 'aria   o'ovata na=uvi.*
     3PL.SBJ=EMPH REP together roast   SPEC[CLI]=yam
     'They roasted yams again together.'
     (2-E007-2A)

While (218) shows that preverbal adverbs precede valency-changing morphemes like comitative *me*, the position relative to sequential directionals *no* 'go and' and *mei* 'come and' varies as (219) and (220) demonstrate. However, it should be noted that sequential directionals show variable position relative to other morphemes too, including past tense *ara* and repetitive aspect *vare ~ vae*.

(218) *Harry e=pei avirua me-a*
Harry 3SG.SBJ=PST.IPFV not.yet COM-SG.OBJ
vori~vori=au=ena=i.
RD~talk=1SG.OBJ=3SG.IPFV=IRR
'Harry hadn't spoken with me yet.'
(2-E026)

(219) *. . .i=pei avirua no de=a=ina=i.*
3PL.SBJ=PST.IPFV not.yet go.SEQ take=3SG.OBJ=3PL.IPFV=IRR
'. . .they hadn't yet gone and got it.'
(1-T092-00:00:30.040)

(220) *I=mei 'aria o'ovata na=uvi.*
3PL.SBJ=come.SEQ together roast SPEC[CLI]=yam
'They came and roasted yams together.'
(2-E007-2A)

The prevebal adverb *avirua* 'not yet' is used with anticipated events that have not yet taken place (221)–(222) or had not yet taken place at a point in time in the past as in (218)–(219). In the latter examples, the VC is marked by the past imperfective marker *pei* and the irrealis mode enclitic *=i* (note that *=i* does not occur when the 1SG PSI enclitic is present, as in (212) above; see also §7.1.4.2 and §7.1.5.1). In all examples, *avirua* co-occurs with PSI enclitics and I therefore originally analysed *avirua* as a TAM marker; however, the data is limited and the co-occurrence with PSI enclitics may not be compulsory. The co-occurrence could simply be because PSI enclitics can mark imperfective aspect and clauses with *avirua* refer to an ongoing situation (which is expected to change at some point). Furthermore, *avirua* may also occur outside of the VC as a clause-level adverb (see §8.4.2.2) which no TAM marker is able to do.

(221) *E-tubu-na e=avirua mate=ena.*
PERS-grandparent-3SG.PSSR 3SG.SBJ=not.yet die=3SG.IPFV
'His grandmother hasn't died yet.'
(2-E017)

(222) *Mi=avirua atu tamu~tamu=emani.*
1EXCL.SBJ=not.yet make RD~eat=1EXCL.SBJ
'We haven't made food yet.'
(2-E017)

Given its semantics, it is not surprising that *'aria* 'together' is only attested with plural subjects: either third person as in the examples above and (223), or first (224) or second person (225) plural. In the numeral system *'aria* denotes 'one' and this could be the origin of this adverb, since doing something 'together' is akin to do something 'as one'. Indeed, it is common for 'one' to grammaticalise as 'together' (Heine and Kuteva 2002: 225).

(223) ***I=to   'aria   o'ovata na=uvi.***
      3PL.SBJ=EMPH together roast   SPEC[CLI]=yam
      'They roasted yams together.'
      (1-T029-00:11:03.590)

(224) *"Maisia **sa='aria**   nao=i."*
      okay   INCL.SBJ.HORT=together go=IRR
      '"Let us go together."'
      (1-T029-00:19:01.380)

(225) *"...iara **mu='aria**   naovo manene nao=i*
      then   2PL.SBJ=together fly   return thither=IRR
      te=na='uru."
      OBL=SPEC[CLI]=island
      "...then you fly back to the island together."'
      (1-T101-00:11:32.269)

6.8.2 Postverbal

Within the VC there is a postverbal adverb position which follows the completive aspect marker position but precedes the transitive enclitic and/or object enclitic position. Given their position before the rightmost margin of the VC (usually marked by the irrealis enclitic), these adverbs are part of the VC rather than clause-level adverbs. As Table 6.17 shows, most adverbs that occur in this position do not appear elsewhere in Papapana, but there are some which function at the clausal level, and four which function in the NP as modifiers. The syntactic position of these adverbs is exemplified in §6.8.2.1, the alternate forms of some adverbs are discussed in §6.8.2.2, while interaction with TAM is discussed in §6.8.2.3.

Table 6.17: Postverbal adverbs: meanings and functions.

Meaning			Other functions
Temporal or Aspectual	tani	already	None
	roro	still	
	garigari	always	
	nanamoa	first	
	matamata	early	
Manner or Space	egoego	well	None
	muramura	firmly	
	gogoro	together	
	oata	across	
	banubanu	in a row	
	uru'uru	around and about	
Manner or Space	papasi	quickly	Clause-level adverbs (§8.4.1)
	viviro'o	around	
	reareana	far	
Limiter or Intensifier	ora	only	Nominal modifiers (§4.7)
	panapana	INTS	
	mamangi	INTS	
	poto	INTS	

6.8.2.1 Syntactic position

Within the VC, in postverbal position, the only elements that separate the adverb from the verb are the geocentric directionals such as *tae* 'ascend/away from shore' and *dini* 'descend/towards shore' as in (226)–(227), the allative directional *vowa ~ vewa* 'towards', and the completive aspect marker *osi* (228). All other postverbal elements follow the adverb: the adverb precedes the transitive enclitic, object enclitic and PSI enclitic in (229), the object enclitic and PSI enclitic in (230), and the deictic directional and irrealis enclitic in (231).

(226) *Na=nganangana e=nao   tae tani   mai.*
   SPEC[CLI]=moon 3SG.SBJ=go up already hither
   'The moon had already risen up.'
   (1-T065-00:02:59.990)

(227) *Oina=au   kakau i=mamu   dini nanamoa=i=a   nao.*
3PL.PSSR=CLII dog 3PL.SBJ=throw down first=TR=3SG.OBJ thither
'They threw their dog down first.'
(1-T007-00:01:55.930)

(228) *Anau u=atu   ma'ata osi   panapana=ina tamu~tamu.*
1SG 1SG.SBJ=make be.heated COMPL INTS=3PL.OBJ RD~eat
'I have already totally cooked the food.'
(2-E014)

(229) *Enai e=tatu   muramura=i=a=na=ma.*
DEM2 3SG.SBJ=mash firmly=TR=3SG.OBJ=3SG.IPFV=ma
'He's mashing it firmly.'
(1-T036-8-00:01:04.350)

(230) ***U=pei***   *tavone ora=ina=u   na=vanua...*
1SG.SBJ=PST.IPFV help only=3PL.OBJ=1SG.IPFV SPEC[CLI]=people
'I was just helping people...'
(1-T103-00:13:27.000)

(231) *...i=to   nao reareana nao=i.*
3PL.SBJ=EMPH go far thither=IRR
'...they go far away.'
(1-T094-00:02:12.999)

Usually only one adverb occurs in this postverbal position but it is also possible for two postverbal adverbs to co-occur, though this is not widely attested in my data. In (232) and (233) a manner adverb co-occurs with an aspectual and intensifying adverb respectively, while in (234) and (235) intensifying and aspectual adverbs co-occur. At least for the intensifier and aspectual adverb in (235), the order is interchangeable. Further data is required to establish whether there are any restrictions regarding the adverbs that can co-occur.

(232) *Anau u=usi   papasi tani=a   na=niunu.*
1SG 1SG.SBJ=scrape quickly already=3SG.OBJ SPEC[CLI]=coconut
'I already scraped the coconut quickly.'
(2-E007-2B)

(233) . . .*i=pei   vei   atamata egoego poto=ina=i.*
3PL.SBJ=PST.IPFV R/R friend well INTS=3PL.IPFV=IRR
'. . .they were really good friends.'
(Fieldnotes 2013, pedagogical readers)

(234) *Va:gi, cassowary e=vurau   mamangi roro=ena.*
now   cassowary 3SG.SBJ=run INTS   still=3SG.IPFV
'Today, the cassowary still really runs.'
(Fieldnotes 2013, pedagogical readers)

(235) a. *Anau u=atu   ma'ata   osi   panapana*
1SG   1SG.SBJ=make be.heated COMPL INTS
tani=ina   *tamu~tamu.*
already=3PL.OBJ   RD~eat
'I have already totally finished cooking the food.'
(2-E014)
b. *Anau u=atu   ma'ata   osi   tani*
1SG   1SG.SBJ=make be.heated COMPL already
panapana=ina *tamu~tamu.*
INTS=3PL.OBJ   RD~eat
'I have already totally finished cooking the food.'
(2-E014)

6.8.2.2 Reduplication and alternate forms

It is worth noting that the form of many adverbs might suggest the adverb has undergone reduplication, but synchronically this is not the case. There are some postverbal adverbs, *'uru'uru* 'around and about', *matamata* 'early' and *banubanu* 'consecutively', which may have undergone disyllabic reduplication, but synchronically there is no obvious link between the adverbs and the roots *'uru* 'island', *mata* 'eye' and *banu* 'carry'. Other postverbal adverbs (such as *papasi* 'quickly' and *muramura* 'firmly') appear to be reduplicated but are not synchronically reduplicated as no corresponding root exists. This is also the case for the postverbal adverbs *garigari* 'always' and *egoego* 'well', as *gari* and *ego* do not exist as roots. However, these two adverbs do occur in alternate forms, *gagari* and *e'ego*, which seem to display monosyllabic, rather than disyllabic, reduplication.

In the two instances in my data of *gagari* and in many instances of *e'ego* the verb is monotransitive and followed by the 3SG object enclitic (see examples (236b) and (237)), and this led me to question whether transitivity was the motivation for the alternate form. However, *garigari* and *egoego* also modify monotransitive verbs, such as in (238). Furthermore, intransitive verbs can be modified by both *gagari* and *e'ego* as in (239), and *garigari* and *egoego* as in (236a). Since reduplication can express augmentation of participants or events in Papapana, it could be suggested that *gagari* and *e'ego* are the forms used when the object is singular (236b) while *garigari* and *egoego* are used when the object is plural (238); however, in (240b) *egoego* is used when the object is singular.

(236) a. *Rob e=to   awa   ae   nao~nao **garigari**=ena=i*
       Rob 3SG.SBJ=EMPH COND NEG RD~go always=3SG.IPFV=IRR
       Wakunai,
       Wakunai
   b. *e=roroto   **gagari**=a=ena=i   ena=arao.*
      3SG.SBJ=see always=3SG.OBJ=3SG.IPFV=IRR 3SG.PSSR[CLI]=brother
      'If Rob did not always go to Wakunai, he would always see his brother.'
      (2-E027)

(237) *Tau i=pei   sia'a   **e'ego**=a=ina=i. . .*
      and 3PL.SBJ=PST.IPFV look.after well=3SG.OBJ=3PL.IPFV=IRR
      'And they looked after him well. . . [he became a grown man].'
      (1-T034-00:11:03.010)

(238) *. . .e=pei   ae   atu   **egoego**=ina=i.*
      3SG.SBJ=PST.IPFV NEG make well=3PL.OBJ=IRR
      '. . .he didn't used to do them well.'
      (1-T052-00:00:22.260)

(239) *". . .u=ae   tarami **e'ego**=au."*
      1SG.SBJ=NEG feel   well=1SG.IPFV
      "'. . .I'm not feeling well.'"
      (1-T029-00:22:27.600)

Furthermore, the examples in (240) were both produced in the same narrative by the same speaker and have almost identical verb complexes, yet there is alternation between *egoego* and *e'ego*. It is therefore likely that *gagari* and *e'ego* are features of casual speech or reflect a point in history when the reduplication of the roots *gari and *ego was productive.

(240) a. *"O=pei   ae   sia'a   e'ego=a=mu=i..."*
       2SG.SBJ=PST.IPFV NEG look.after well=3SG.OBJ=2SG.IPFV=IRR
       '"You didn't treat him well..."'
       (1-T031-00:10:43.450)

   b. *"Ia'a mama e=pei   ae   sia'a*
      Mum DEM1 3SG.SBJ=PST.IPFV NEG look.after
      ***egoego=au**=ena=i."*
      well=1SG.OBJ=3SG.IPFV=IRR
      '"Mum didn't treat me well."'
      (1-T031-00:10:14.590)

The intensifying adverb *mamangi* may also be diachronically reduplicated but **mangi* does not exist synchronically. However, there are a few instances where *mamangi* is reduplicated, seemingly to increase intensity:

(241) *E-tubu-na   e=sare   **ma~mamangi.***
      PERS-grandparent-3SG.PSSR 3SG.SBJ=happy RD~INTS
      'His grandmother was very, very happy.'
      (1-T029-00:08:57.760)

6.8.2.3 Interaction with TAM

There are three postverbal adverbs which express aspectual notions: *tani* 'already', *roro* 'still' and *garigari* 'always'. This section briefly discusses their interaction with the TAM system.

The adverb *tani* 'already' arises often in the corpus and expresses that something has already occurred in the past, either in relation to another time in the past (242) or in relation to the present (243). It thus has a completive meaning and can co-occur with the completive aspect marker *osi* (see §7.1.8) as in (235) above. *Tani* generally does not co-occur with other TAM markers but it is attested with the past tense marker *ara* when the event has occurred in relation to another time in the past (242).

(242) *Na:=bau ago~agoto paga **i=ara**   mei   tavotu **tani**...*
      some=PL RD~hold shoot 3PL.SBJ=PST come.SEQ arrive already
      'The armed men had already arrived...'
      (1-T002-00:00:26.690)

(243) ***E=to   roroto   tani=a   nu=buku   mama.***
3SG.SBJ=EMPH see   already=3SG.OBJ SPEC.CLII=book DEM1
'He has already read this book.'
(2-E014-1)

The adverb *roro* 'still' sometimes occurs in the corpus and expresses that something is still happening in relation to the present (244), past (245), or future time (246). It thus has a continuous meaning and may co-occur with PSI enclitics and verbal reduplication (for some verbs), which mark imperfective aspect (see §7.1.6):

(244) *"Aia **e=aputu   roro=ena.**"*
3SG 3SG.SBJ=sleep still=3SG.IPFV
"'He's still sleeping.'"
(1-T052-00:03:17.670)

(245) *Na='usia   **i=pei   gaganini roro=ina=i.***
SPEC[CLI]=child 3PL.SBJ=PST.IPFV play   still=3PL.IPFV=IRR
'The children were still playing.'
(1-T033-00:02:17.370)

(246) *"**Si=nao   roro=ra=i   **te=na=kaukau.*"
1INCL.SBJ=go still=1INCL.IPFV=IRR OBL=SPEC[CLI]=sweet.potato
"'We'll still be going to the garden.'"
(1-T033-00:01:35.760)

The adverb *garigari* 'always' sometimes appears in the corpus and expresses the frequency of an action. It thus has a habitual meaning and can co-occur with PSI enclitics and verbal reduplication (for some verbs), which mark imperfective aspect (see §7.1.6):

(247) *Na=vanua   **i=ari~ari   garigari=ina**   bau ari.*
SPEC[CLI]=people 3PL.SBJ=RD~dig always=3PL.OBJ PL   dig
'The people always dug holes.'
(2-E007-2A)

Chapter 7
Tense, aspect, mode and negation

This chapter describes tense, aspect and mode marking (§7.1), imperative and hortative marking (§7.2), and negation within the verb complex (§7.3).

7.1 Tense, aspect and mode

Papapana has a complex system of tense, aspect, mode (TAM) marking in which verbal reduplication and various combinations of preverbal and postverbal markers are used to make TAM distinctions. I initially analysed the TAM system from text recordings and elicitation sessions, but to more fully understand the system I carried out elicitation sessions using Part A of the TMA questionnaire (Dahl 1985: 198–206) and parts of the Progressive Aspect Questionnaire (Dahl 2000: 810–818).

7.1.1 Distinctions, markers and postverbal subject-indexing

Tense in Papapana always relates the event to the time of the speech event and therefore tense is *absolute,* and never relative. Papapana, has an unmarked present tense but marked past tense, and future time marked by the irrealis mode enclitic (see §7.1.3, §7.1.4.1 and §7.1.4.2). Papapana encodes five aspectual notions: proximative, habitual, continuous, repetitive and completive. These will be defined in the relevant sections (§7.1.5.2, §7.1.6, §7.1.7 and §7.1.8). The term *mode* is used here to refer to the speaker's attitudes toward a situation, including their belief in its reality or likelihood, with the highest-level distinction being between realis and irrealis (Payne 1997: 244).[30] Realis mode asserts that "a specific event or state of affairs has actually happened, or actually holds true" (Payne 1997: 244) while irrealis depicts situations that were not or are not yet a reality, but only possibilities (Whaley 1997: 225). Realis is morphologically

---

[30] As Velupillai (2012: 214) points out, the terms 'mood' and 'modality' are often used interchangeably. When distinguished, "mood tends to denote a higher level distinction for the whole clause of realis [. . .] versus irrealis [. . .] while modality denotes semantic labels of attitudes towards events" (Velupillai 2012: 214). The term 'mode' is sometimes used to cover both mood and modality, and it is 'mode' that I use here, since there is no clear divide between 'mood' and 'modality' in Papapana.

https://doi.org/10.1515/9781501509971-007

unmarked in Papapana (as in Proto-Oceanic (Lynch, Ross, and Crowley 2002: 84)). Papapana encodes four irrealis distinctions: apprehensive (§7.1.4.3), hypothetical conditional (§7.1.4.4), optative (§7.1.5.1) and counterfactual conditional (7.1.5.3).

Table 7.1 shows how the TAM markers combine to express the distinctions mentioned above, and their relative position in the verb complex (VC). These distinctions will be described and exemplified in the cross-referenced sections, and summarised now here. The preverbal marker *ara* marks past tense, and the postverbal enclitic =*i* marks irrealis mode (which may express future tense, or habitual aspect with a present time reference). The preverbal marker *pei* in combination with the irrealis mode enclitic =*i* marks past habitual, while preverbal *te* in combination with =*i* marks apprehensive mode (*te* is also used in prohibitives; see §7.3.2). The preverbal marker *awa* and irrealis =*i* mark hypothetical conditional mode in a dependent clause (with =*i* used in the main clause). The preverbal marker *eri* in combination with the postverbal subject-indexing (PSI) enclitics (see next paragraph) and irrealis =*i* mark optative mode, while *eri* and PSI enclitics mark proximative aspect. *Eri* combined with the conditional mode marker *awa* marks counterfactual conditionals in a dependent clause (with *eri* used in the main clause). The PSI enclitics also interact with different patterns of verbal reduplication to express continuous or habitual aspect, with a present time reference if there are no other TAM markers. The preverbal marker *vare ~ vae* marks repetitive aspect while the postverbal marker *osi* marks completive aspect.

Papapana, like most Northwest Solomonic languages, displays postverbal subject-indexing (PSI), which reflects former possessor indexing (see Palmer 2011: 723 for a detailed discussion of the diachronic functional shift fom nominal to verbal marking). This phenomenon was first noted by Capell (1971: 276) for the Buka languages, Lincoln (1976a: 427–428) for Mono, Torau and Uruava, and Ross (1982) for Nehan-North Bougainville languages, Piva-Banoni and Mono, Torau and Uruava. Papapana has PSI enclitics which index the person and number of all subjects (see Table 7.2), and express imperfective aspect (see §7.1.6), and also combine with optative mode marker *eri* to express optative mode or proximative aspect (see §7.1.5). In Papapana, PSI enclitics co-occur with the preverbal subject-indexing proclitics, which is typical of most Northwest Solomonic languages (Palmer 2011: 691). Their status as clitics is evidenced by the fact they form phonological words with their host (see §3.5.4) and may attach to either the verb or other lexical categories that follow the verb: geographical directionals, completive aspect *osi*, postverbal adverbs or object-indexing enclitics.

Table 7.1: TAM constructions.

	Preverbal						VERB	Postverbal			
	PST.IPFV	APPR	COND	OPT	PST	REP		COMPL	IPFV	IRR	
	pei	te	awa	eri	ara	vare ~ vae	Reduplication	osi	=PSI	=i	
Past					✓						§7.1.3
Future										✓	§7.1.4.1
Habitual (present)										✓	§7.1.4.1
Habitual, past	✓									✓	§7.1.4.2
Apprehensive		✓								✓	§7.1.4.3
Hypothetical conditional			✓							✓	§7.1.4.4
Optative				✓					✓	✓	§7.1.5.1
Proximative				✓					✓		§7.1.5.2
Counter-factual conditional			✓	✓							§7.1.5.3
Imperfective (present)							(✓)		✓		§7.1.6
Repetitive						✓					§7.1.7
Completive								✓			§7.1.8

Table 7.2: Postverbal subject-indexing (PSI) enclitics.

	1EXCL	1INCL	2	3
SG	=u		=mu	=na
	~ =eu		~ =emu	~ =ena
	~ =ou		~ =omu	
PL	=mani	=ra	=miu	=ina
	~ =emani	~ =era	~ =emiu	

The PSI enclitics displayed in bold typeface are identical to the Papapana direct possessor suffixes, except for 1INCL which has an initial /i/ in the direct possessor paradigm (see §5.5.1 and Appendix 1). In Northwest Solomonic languages, many of the PSI forms exhibit an initial vowel which reflects a possessor indexing host: PNWS *na- and *sa- expressed general possession and *ye expressed consumable possession. The hosts have varying functions in synchronic PSI in Northwest Solomonic languages (see Palmer 2011: 722–723). The variant forms in Papapana shown in Table 7.2 exhibit an initial vowel, either /o/ or /e/, which reflect the general and consumable possession hosts (Palmer 2011: 716); however, synchronically in Papapana there is no functional distinction between PSI enclitics without an initial vowel, PSI enclitics with /o/ and those with /e/. Speakers reported that the initial vowel may be dropped as a quicker way of saying the same thing as attested in the utterances in (1) which both occurred in the same elicitation session with an older and younger female speaker.

(1) a. *Francis e=tua~tua=**na**   nao   te=na='uru.*
       Francis 3SG.SBJ=RD~paddle=3SG.IPFV thither OBL=SPEC[CLI]=island
       'Francis is paddling to the island.'
       (2-E024)
    b. *Francis e=tua~tua=**ena**   nao   te=na='uru.*
       Francis 3SG.SBJ=RD~paddle=3SG.IPFV thither OBL=SPEC[CLI]=island
       'Francis is paddling to the island.'
       (2-E024)

It was also suggested by these two speakers that /o/ was used by younger speakers as in (2a) which was produced by the younger female speaker, in contrast with /e/ in (2b) which was produced by the older female speaker; this phonological variation is consistent with the second phonological change noted in §3.1.3.

(2) a. *Ani o=gaganini=**omu**.*
     2SG 2SG.SBJ=play=2SG.IPFV
     'You are playing.'
     (2-E024)
   b. *Ani o=gaganini=**emu**.*
     2SG 2SG.SBJ=play=2SG.IPFV
     'You are playing.'
     (2-E024)

It could also be suggested that the lack of or choice of initial vowel is related to the phonology of the verb root, but I have tested this and observed no regular patterns, and if verbal phonology did play a role then the variation in (1) and (2) would not occur.

To summarise this introductory section, it can be seen that only past tense *ara*, repetitive aspect *vare ~ vae* and completive aspect *osi* demonstrate *canonical exponence* whereby there is a one-to-one mapping between the morpheme and the feature value. The irrealis mode enclitic *=i* can express future time, or habitual aspect with a present time frame and it can also combine with other morphemes to express other distinctions. All other TAM distinctions are realised by combinations of morphemes and thus the exponence of a particular TAM value can be said to be *distributed*, that is, "morphosyntactic and morphosemantic properties are marked non-redundantly at multiple inflectional sites" (Carroll 2016: 286). While some Papapana TAM morphemes can function independently, others cannot. Consequently it is difficult to divide this chapter into tense, aspect and mode morphemes but I have tried as much as possible to do so: §7.1.2 discusses the times referenced when there are no TAM markers, §7.1.3 discusses the past tense marker *ara*, §7.1.4–§7.1.5 discuss mode and aspect, and §7.1.6–§7.1.8 discuss aspect. Tense is discussed throughout these sections, as are any other attested combinations of TAM distinctions, for example, repetitive aspect and future time.

7.1.2 Unmarked

A verb unmarked by TAM operators does not express any particular TAM value but its default reading is past time (3), unless there are non-past temporal adjuncts suggesting a different interpretation, such as present (4) or future time (5).

(3) *Nani te=na=garasi mi=tamu.*
there OBL=SPEC[CLI]=grass 1EXCL.SBJ=eat
'We ate there on the grass.'
(1-T071-00:05:52.450)

(4) *Jim e=oto te=na=au obutu va:gi.*
Jim 3SG.SBJ=board OBL=SPEC=CLII canoe now
'Jim is boarding the canoe at this moment.'
(2-E007-1)

(5) *U=naomai natui.*
1SG.SBJ=come tomorrow
'I'll come tomorrow.'
(2-E015)

Examples (6)–(9) show that an unmarked verb can be used to refer to events that have past time reference, regardless of whether the past event occurred at an unspecified time in the past (6), the day before the speech act (7), the same day as the speech act (8) or perhaps even very shortly before the speech act as in (9) where the past event has had consequences on the present situation.

(6) *Anau u=tu'u=i=a.*
1SG 1SG.SBJ=meet=TR=3SG.OBJ
'I met him (your father who died last year).'
(2-E008)

(7) *U=to tu'u=i=a ini naonava.*
1SG.SBJ=EMPH meet=TR=3SG.OBJ here yesterday
'I met him here yesterday.'
(2-E008)

(8) *U=to tu'u=i=a ini va:gi tuimatamata.*
1SG.SBJ=EMPH meet=TR=3SG.OBJ here now morning
'I met him here this morning.'
(2-E008)

(9) *U=to ate=a na=windoa.*
1SG.SBJ=EMPH open=3SG.OBJ SPEC[CLI]=window
'I opened the window (that is why it is cold in this room).'
(2-E008)

7.1.3 Past tense *ara*

The preverbal marker *ara* expresses past tense, as in (10)–(11), while the preverbal marker *pei* marks past tense and imperfective aspect (see §7.1.4.2). *Ara* expresses past tense only, rather than perfective aspect or, apparently, perfect aspect.

(10) *Na=orawi   e=**ara**   asi=au.*
     SPEC[CLI]=man 3SG.SBJ=PST leave=1SG.OBJ
     'The man left me.'
     (1-T039-00:01:28.296)

(11) *Mi=pei   po=mani=i   nani, aite e=**ara***
     1EXCL.SBJ=PST.IPFV stay=1EXCL.IPFV=IRR there Dad 3SG.SBJ=PST
     mate.
     die
     '(While) we were living there, Dad died.'
     (1-T030-00:02:34.020)

The possible co-occurrence of *ara* with the past tense imperfective aspect marker *pei* and irrealis mode enclitic =*i* in a clause expressing past tense and habitual aspect, as in (12), rules out a perfective hypothesis.

(12) *Jerry e=**pei**   ara ena=**i**.*
     Jerry 3SG.SBJ=PST.IPFV PST sing=IRR
     'Jerry used to sing.'
     (2-E007-1)

A VC marked by *ara* often expresses a past event occurring before another past event (13) or before the present (14)–(16), and therefore it could be that *ara* expresses perfect aspect. However, this is a tendency and further data is required to confirm whether *ara* has any aspectual meaning.

(13) *Na=orawi   e=**ara**   naomai ta   e=mei*
     SPEC[CLI]=man 3SG.SBJ=PST come   and 3SG.SBJ=come.SEQ
     wa=ami. . .
     say=1EXCL.OBJ
     'A man came and said to us. . .'
     (1-T065-00:00:23.470)

(14) E=to u'usi roro=na, e=to **ara** si'i.
 3SG.SBJ=EMPH wet still=3SG.IPFV 3SG.SBJ=EMPH PST rain
 'It is still wet, it rained.'
 (2-E008)

(15) Vavine-u e=to **ara** atu=a na=inu
 sibling-1SG.PSSR 3SG.SBJ=EMPH PST make=3SG.OBJ SPEC[CLI]=house
 mama.
 DEM1
 'My brother built this house (that we are standing in front of).'
 (2-E008)

(16) O=**ara** tu'u=i=a vavine-u?
 2SG.SBJ=PST met=TR=3SG.OBJ sibling-1SG.PSSR
 'Have you met my brother (yet)?'
 (2-E008)

7.1.4 Irrealis mode =i

When the postverbal enclitic =i occurs without any other TAM markers, it indicates irrealis mode. As such it is used to refer to future events, or habitual events with a present time reference (§7.1.4.1). On its own =i may also optionally be used in imperative, hortative and prohibitive clauses (see §7.2 and §7.3.2). It is an enclitic because it forms a phonological word with the verb or the rightmost postverbal morpheme (with the exception of the discontinuous repetitive aspect =re which follows the irrealis mode enclitic). Irrealis =i may be used in conjunction with the past tense imperfective aspect marker *pei* to express past tense and habitual aspect (§7.1.4.2), with the apprehensive mode marker *te* in apprehension-causing adverbial clauses (§7.1.4.3), with the conditional mode marker *awa* in hypothetical conditional adverbial clauses (§7.1.4.4) and with the optative mode marker *eri* and PSI enclitics to express optative mode (§7.1.5.1).

7.1.4.1 Future tense and present habitual: =i

The irrrealis enclitic =i is used to refer to future events, or habitual events with a present time reference. That irrealis =i is compatible with these different contexts of use is not surprising as cross-linguistically mode interacts significantly with tense and aspect. Future can be regarded as a prototypical irrealis category because it refers to events that have not yet happened and are therefore unreal (de Haan 2006: 41), while habitual aspect describes an event type that is instantiated from time to time by actual events, but is not a specific real event (Payne 1997: 245).

Examples (17)–(23) show that Papapana does not distinguish between different degrees of future time: a verb marked by =*i* may express future tense for events that are about to occur as in (17) and (18), will occur the day after the speech act (19), in the coming week after the speech act (20), or at an unspecified time in the future as in (21) and (22). Papapana also uses =*i* to mark future tense for events that the speaker is hypothesising will happen (23).

(17) *Va:gi u=gaun=i=a=**i**   nu=pepa.*
now   1SG.SBJ=write=TR=3SG.OBJ=IRR SPEC.CLII=paper
'Right now I'll write a letter.'
(2-E008)

(18) *Anne e=asi=a=**i**   na=poana.*
Anne 3SG.SBJ=leave=3SG.OBJ=IRR SPEC[CLI]=village
'Anne will leave the village (in a minute).'
(2-E016)

(19) *Natui   Anne e=asi=a=**i**   na=poana.*
tomorrow   Anne 3SG.SBJ=leave=3SG.OBJ=IRR SPEC[CLI]=village
'Tomorrow Anne will leave the village.'
(2-E016)

(20) *Anau u=matono   matamata=**i** tena siodo.*
1SG   1SG.SBJ=awaken   early=IRR   SUBR work
'(This week) I'll wake up early to work.'
(2-E008)

(21) *. . .na=au   tue   mama   tue-ni   Papapana*
SPEC=CLII language DEM1   language-CONST   Papapana
*e=taosi=**i**   mumurina.*
3SG.SBJ=finish=IRR future
'[His grandparents knew that] . . .this language, Papapana language, will die out in the future.'
(1-T083-00:01:59.430)

(22) Anau u=atu=a=**i**   nu=obutu   kaka'i.
     1SG   1SG.SBJ=make=3SG.OBJ=IRR SPEC.CLII=canoe small
     'I will make a small canoe.'
     (2-E007-1)

(23) Ben bea   e=oto=**i**   te=na=au   obutu.
     Ben maybe 3SG.SBJ=board=IRR   OBL=SPEC=CLII   canoe
     'Maybe Ben will board the canoe.'
     (2-E007-1)

The enclitic =*i* also expresses habitual aspect and if there is no further marker indicating tense, then the time reference is present (24). The clause may include temporal adjuncts (25)–(26).

(24) Mi=nao=**i**   i-ava.
     1EXCL.SBJ=go=IRR   LOC-sea
     'We (often) go to sea.'
     (1-T010-00:00:50.200)

(25) Mamena   boni~boni Maureen e=siodo=**i**,   e=gaganini=**i**,
     PL.COLL   RD~day   Maureen 3SG.SBJ=work=IRR   3SG.SBJ=play=IRR
     iara   e=no   aputu=**i**.
     then   3SG.SBJ=go.SEQ   sleep=IRR
     'Every day, Maureen works, plays then goes and sleeps.'
     (2-E016)

(26) Tena bau Sande   mi=ae   buibui=**i**,   mi=ae
     OBL   PL   Sunday 1EXCL.SBJ=NEG   clean=IRR   1EXCL.SBJ=NEG
     siodo=**i**,   mi=ae   atu   ma'ata=**i**.
     work=IRR   1EXCL.SBJ=NEG   make   be.heated=IRR
     'On Sundays we don't clean, we don't work and we don't cook.'
     (2-E024)

7.1.4.2 Past habitual: *pei* and =*i*

The preverbal marker *pei* marks past tense and imperfective aspect and always functions in combination with the irrealis mode enclitic =*i*. The only situation in which =*i* does not appear is if the 1SG PSI enclitic is also present (see §6.8.1 and §7.1.5.1); however, the motivation for this is unclear. Together, and without any other TAM markers present, *pei* and *=i* mark past tense and habitual aspect (27)–(29), and may co-occur with temporal adjuncts (29).

(27) *Mi=**pei**   matono=i   i-poana   Teperoi.*
1EXCL.SBJ=PST.IPFV awaken=IRR LOC-village   Teperoi
'We used to wake up in Teperoi village.'
(1-T011-00:00:42.820)

(28) *. . .u=**pei**   nao=i   te=na=kaukau. . .*
1SG.SBJ=PST.IPFV go=IRR OBL=SPEC[CLI]=sweet.potato
'[In the past, when I was small] . . . I used to go to the garden. . . [with my mother].'
(1-T004-00:00:33.780)

(29) *Tena bau Mande, a:mani mi=**pei**   nao=i*
OBL PL Monday 1EXCL 1EXCL.SBJ=PST.IPFV go=IRR
te=na=skuru.
OBL=SPEC[CLI]=school
'On Mondays, we used to go to school.'
(2-E024)

Pei and *=i* may also co-occur with the past tense morpheme *ara* (see §7.1.3), and with the preverbal marker *eri* and PSI enclitics to express past tense, optative mode (see §7.1.5.1). *Pei* and *=i* also co-occurs with PSI enclitics and, for some verbs, verbal reduplication to express past continuous (30) (see §7.1.6 for more examples). It is for this reason that I analyse *pei* as imperfective rather than habitual.

(30) *Na:=bau i=**pei**   ubete=ina=i   i-tanana. . .*
some=PL 3PL.SBJ=PST.IPFV lay=3PL.IPFV=IRR LOC-road
'Some were lying on the road. . . [while we were running back].'
(1-T002-00:04:51.530)

The occurrence of the irrealis mode enclitic *=i* in utterances expressing past continuous is admittedly problematic since the situation expressed by the VC is real and the irrealis mode enclitic *=i* is usually used to refer to 'unreal' events. For some of the utterances where *pei* and *=i* co-occur with PSI enclitics and verbal reduplication to express past continuous, the presence of *=i* could be explained by the fact that the utterances come from elicitation sessions or from traditional narratives, such as in (31), in which the speaker is arguably referring to imaginary situations. Other utterances, such as (32), could arguably be interpreted as past habitual, though the difference between utterances such as (32) and (27) would need explaining. In much of my data, however, the situation expressed by the VC is a real past event as in (30) and they are interpreted as expressing past continuous: the reason for the occurrence of =*i* in such utterances requires further research.

(31) *Rosu   e=**pei**   bae~baene=ena=i   na=orona.*
     Lucifer 3SG.SBJ=PST.IPFV RD~hunt=3SG.IPFV=IRR SPEC[CLI]=possum
     'Lucifer was hunting possums.'
     (1-T035-00:04:39.088)

(32) *. . .e=**pei**   me-na   siodo=ena=i   na=siapani.*
     3SG.SBJ=PST.IPFV COM-PL.OBJ work=3SG.IPFV=IRR SPEC[CLI]=Japan
     '. . .he was working with the Japanese.'
     (1-T034-00:13:27.980)

7.1.4.3 Apprehensive mode: *te* and =*i*

Apprehensives convey "the possibility of a state of affairs that is possible, but undesirable and best avoided" (Angelo and Schultze-Berndt 2016: 258). Lichtenberk (1995: 291–292) uses the term "apprehensional-epistemic modality" and points out that it is a "mixed modality" which is "both epistemic and attitudinal: it has to do with the speaker's degree of certainty about the factual status of the proposition and also with his or her attitude concerning the desirability of the situation encoded in the clause". Lichtenberk (1995) delimits three functions of apprehensive markers, one of which is the "precautioning" function. In this function, the apprehensive occurs in a complex sentence and encodes a possible, "apprehension-causing" situation; such a clause is associated with a "precaution" (Lichtenberk 1995) main clause expressing preventative action which can be taken to avoid the undesirable situation. In Papapana, the preverbal apprehensive mode marker *te* and the irrealis mode enclitic co-occur in the VC of the apprehension-causing adverbial clause, while the precaution main clause may be may be an imperative (33), hortative (34), or prohibitive (35). A declarative main precaution clause is attested only once in my data (36). *Te* does not co-occur with any other TAM markers apart from irrealis =*i*, nor does it co-occur with negative *ae*. For discussion of the subjects and order of clauses and the subordinate status of the apprehension-causing clause, see §10.3.2. *Te* is also used, along with verbal reduplication and sometimes irrealis =*i*, in prohibitives as in the precaution clause in (35) (see §7.3.2).

(33) Ta na=au dada o=noe a'aisi, e=**te** tuatuare=i.
 but SPEC=CLII coconut.milk 2SG.SBJ=put many 3SG.SBJ=APPR burn=IRR
 'But put lots of coconut milk (on your hands), (otherwise) it will burn.'/
 'But put lots of coconut milk (on your hands), (so that) it doesn't burn.'
 (1-T036-8-00:02:00.850)

(34) "Sa=nao tovoni nao=i, i=**te** moroko=ira=i."
 1INCL.SBJ.HORT=go check thither=IRR 3PL.SBJ=APPR lie=1INCL.OBJ=IRR
 "'Let's go check, (in case) they might be lying to us.'"
 (1-T034-00:30:12.380)

(35) O=te e~'esivo=i, i=**te** nongon=i=o=i.
 2SG.SBJ=APPR RD~sneeze=IRR 3PL.SBJ=APPR hear=TR=2SG.OBJ=IRR
 'Don't sneeze, (or) they might hear you.'
 (2-E017)

(36) . . .e=va-mamago=a pei tanga
 3SG.SBJ=CAUS-decorate=3SG.OBJ part shell.money
 tenava e=**te** uga poto=i. . .
 so.that 3SG.SBJ=APPR drown INTS=IRR
 '. . .she adorned him with the shell necklace, so that he didn't drown. . .'/
 '. . .she adorned him with the shell necklace, otherwise he might drown. . .'
 (1-T029-00:19:04.385)

7.1.4.4 Hypothetical conditional: *awa* and *=i*

Conditional constructions assert that the situation expressed in the conditional adverbial clause is prior to or the authority for the consequence expressed in the main clause. The conditional clause may refer to unreal situations for which the speaker imagines what might be, or imagines what might have been. The former type of conditional clause has been labelled "hypothetical" and the latter "counterfactual" in typological literature (Thompson, Longacre and Hwang 2007: 256). In Papapana, the preverbal conditional mode marker *awa* is used in both types of conditional clauses and is never the only TAM marker in a clause. In dependent hypothetical conditional clauses (37)–(39), *awa* must co-occur with the irrealis mode =*i*, while the main clause is marked by =*i* only and expresses the consequence (see §10.3.1 for more, and §7.1.5.3 for counterfactual conditional clauses).

(37) *Edward e=**awa**   roros=i=a=i   ena=arao,*
Edward 3SG.SBJ=COND see=TR=3SG.OBJ=IRR 3SG.PSSR[CLI]=brother
e=ba'o=a=i.
3SG.SBJ=beat=3SG.OBJ=IRR
'If Edward sees his brother, he'll beat him.'
(2-E022)

(38) *O=to   **awa**   nao=i,   i=no   atun=i=o=i.*
2SG.SBJ=EMPH COND go=IRR 3PL.SBJ=go.SEQ attack=TR=2SG.OBJ=IRR
'If you go, they will go and attack you.'
(2-E022)

(39) *U=to   **awa**   nao=i   te=na=skuru,   iara*
1SG.SBJ=EMPH COND go=IRR OBL=SPEC[CLI]=school then
u=peri   siodo=i.
1SG.SBJ=find work=IRR
'If I go to school, then I will find work.'
(2-E022)

Sometimes the situation is more certain or is predicted and can be interpreted as 'when' instead of 'if':

(40) *O=to   **awa**   manene mai=i,*
2SG.SBJ=EMPH COND return hither=IRR
anau u=gaunu   osi=ina=i   na=pepa.
1SG 1SG.SBJ=write COMPL=3PL.OBJ=IRR SPEC[CLI]=paper
'When you return, I will have finished writing the letters.'
(2-E008)

(41) *E=to   **awa**   nao=i Buka, e=no   ani=i*
3SG.SBJ=EMPH COND go=IRR Buka 3SG.SBJ=go.SEQ eat=IRR
na=toa.
SPEC[CLI]=chicken
'When she goes to Buka, she'll eat chicken.'
(2-E024)

Often in casual speech *awa* is reduced to *wa:*

(42) E=to   **wa**   de=a=**i**   na=vatu,
     3SG.SBJ=EMPH COND take=3SG.OBJ=IRR SPEC[CLI]=money
     e=ae   kaukau=i=a=**i**   ena=maunu.
     3SG.SBJ=buy sweet.potato=TR=3SG.OBJ=IRR 3SG.PSSR[CLI]=woman
     'If he gets the money, he will potato-buy for his wife.'
     (2-E008)

Some utterances do not exhibit *awa*, but only =*i* in both the main and dependent clause. Since the construction with *awa* only became transparent in elicitation sessions, it could be that in casual speech *awa* is often omitted. Indeed, the first clause has the same conditional function as one marked by *awa*, and impressionistically the intonation contour is the same as that of a hypothetical conditional sentence. Alternatively, it could be that sentences such as (43)–(44) are structurally two separate main clauses and the hearer is left to ascertain the relationship between the two clauses. Either way, the translations given by speakers suggest there is no difference between the two types of constructions in terms of function.

(43) Enai aina i=to   matono=**i**,   i=varona=**i**.
     after 3PL 3PL.SBJ=EMPH awaken=IRR 3PL.SBJ=know=IRR
     'If they wake up, they will know.'
     (1-T021-00:02:11.420)

(44) Na=vatu   o=to   noe=i=a=**i**
     SPEC[CLI]=stone 2SG.SBJ=EMPH put=TR=3SG.OBJ=IRR
     te=na=kabekabe,   e=tagoa=**i**.
     OBL=SPEC[CLI]=bag 3SG.SBJ=break=IRR
     'If you put a stone in the bag, it will break.'
     (2-E008)

Like counterfactual conditionals (§7.1.5.3), imperatives and prohibitives (see §7.2 and §7.3.2), when *po* 'stay, exist' is the verb in a hypothetical conditional construction, imperfective PSI enclitics are also employed (45). This could be because *po* is a state verb which reports ongoing situations and is thus compatible with imperfective aspect (see §7.1.6 for definitions of imperfective aspect and for Vendler's (1957) classification of verbal predicates). In imperative and prohibitive clauses, the subject is of course second person, but interestingly, the counterfactual and hypothetical conditional clauses with *po* also have a second person subject. Thus, it remains unclear whether the addition of PSI enclitics applies only to the verb *po* or to the verb *po* with a second person subject.

(45) O=to **po=mu=i,** na=ubetu
 2SG.SBJ=EMPH stay=2SG.IPFV=IRR SPEC[CLI]=hungry
 e=atun=i=o=**i.**
 3SG.SBJ=attack=TR=2SG.OBJ=IRR
 'If you stay, hunger will kill you.'
 (1-T098-00:02:48.801)

7.1.5 Optative mode *eri*

The preverbal optative mode marker *eri* operates with PSI enclitics and irrealis mode =*i* to express optative mode (§7.1.5.1), with PSI enclitics to express proximative aspect (§7.1.5.2), and with the conditional mode marker *awa* in counterfactual conditional constructions (§7.1.5.3).

7.1.5.1 Optative mode: *eri*, PSI and =*i*

The preverbal optative mode marker *eri* co-occurs with PSI enclitics and irrealis mode =*i* to express optative mode, which refers to wishes and desires (Payne 1997: 246), as in (46)–(47). Wishes "express attitudes towards propositions whose factual status is not known or propositions that relate to unrealised events" (Palmer 2001: 13) and thus the presence of irrealis mode =*i* is not surprising. If we see wishes and desires as ongoing states then the use of the imperfective aspect PSI enclitics would be compatible with optative mode; however, this is a hypothesis and further research is needed to determine why the PSI enclitics are used in this construction. As elsewhere (see §6.8.1 and §7.1.4.2), =*i* does not occur if the 1SG PSI enclitic is present (48)–(50).

(46) O mata o=to **eri** me-a ruvu=**omu=i**. . .
 or what 2SG.SBJ=EMPH OPT COM-SG.OBJ put=2SG.IPFV=IRR
 'Or whatever you want to put with it. . .'
 (1-T085-00:02:42.740)

(47) . . .te=na=kaukau　　　　　　i=to　　　　　　**eri**　nao=**ina**=**i**
　　　OBL=SPEC[CLI]=sweet.potato 3PL.SBJ=EMPH OPT go=3PL.IPFV=IRR
　　　mena　　　panu-na. . .
　　　DU.COLL　spouse-DER
　　　'. . .a couple wanted to go to the garden. . .'
　　　(1-T034-00:10:13.800)

(48) U=**eri**　　　　tamu=**ou.**
　　　1SG.SBJ=OPT　eat=1SG.IPFV
　　　'I want to eat.'
　　　(2-E007-1)

(49) U=**eri**　　　　gaun=i=a=**u**　　　　　　　nu=pepa.
　　　1SG.SBJ=OPT　write=TR=3SG.OBJ=1SG.IPFV　SPEC.CLII=paper
　　　'I want to write a letter.'
　　　(2-E008)

(50) "Anau u=**eri**　　　　me-na　　　　nao=amu=**ou**
　　　1SG　1SG.SBJ=OPT　COM-PL.OBJ　go=2PL.OBJ=1SG.IPFV
　　　te=na='uru."
　　　OBL=SPEC[CLI]=island
　　　'"I want to go with you to the island."'
　　　(1-T029-00:04:56.730)

In casual speech when *eri* is adjacent to emphatic *to*, it is often shortened to *ri* as in (51), or these two morphemes may also combine to form *teri* as in (52).

(51) "Mu=to=**ri**　　　　　　nao tae=**mu**=**i,**　　　moni
　　　2PL.SBJ=EMPH=OPT　go　up=2PL.IPFV=IRR　money
　　　mu=ma'a=ami. "
　　　2PL.SBJ=give=1EXCL.OBJ
　　　'"(If) you want to go up, give us money."'
　　　(1-T053-00:02:03.310)

(52) Ta　iara　na=vanua　　　　　i=t=**eri**　　　　　　nao=**ina**=**i**. . .
　　　and　then　SPEC[CLI]=people 3PL.SBJ=EMPH=OPT go=3PL.IPFV=IRR
　　　'And then the people want to go. . .'
　　　(1-T029-00:25:36.966)

The optative mode construction may be further marked by the past imperfective *pei* and the irrealis enclitic =*i* (see §7.1.4.2) to express optative mode in the past tense as in (53)–(54) (note that =*i* does not occur in (53) because the 1SG PSI enclitic is present), or in combination with the preverbal repetitive aspect marker *vare ~ vae* to express optative mode and repetitive aspect (55).

(53) *Naonava u=**pei** eri ena=**u**.*
yesterday 1SG.SBJ=PST.IPFV OPT sing=1SG.IPFV
'Yesterday I wanted to sing.'
(2-E014-2)

(54) *I=**pei** eri agos=i=a=**ina**=**i**.*
3PL.SBJ=PST.IPFV OPT hold=TR=3SG.OBJ=3PL.IPFV=IRR
'They wanted to hold her.'
(1-T029-00:23:46.299)

(55) *Maisia anau u=**ri** vare 'a'ade'e=i=a=**u***
okay 1SG 1SG.SBJ=OPT REP narrative=TR=3SG.OBJ=1SG.IPFV
nu='a'ade'e...
SPEC.CLII=narrative
'I want to tell a story again... [about two friends].'
(1-T064-00:00:19.860)

In contrast with this construction, the verbs *mate* 'like' (56)–(57) and *magono* 'dislike' (58) can also denote 'want' and 'not want' respectively. With *mate*, it is hard to know which meaning is intended, or if there is even such a distinction in Papapana, because to elicit these sentences I used the verb *laik(im)* in Tok Pisin, which also means both 'like' and 'want'.

(56) *Anau u=mate=i=a=u tamu~tamu.*
1SG 1SG.SBJ=like=TR=3SG.OBJ=1SG.IPFV RD~eat
'I want food.'
(2-E007-1)

(57) *Anau u=ae mate=i=a=u tena ena.*
1SG 1SG.SBJ=NEG like=TR=3SG.OBJ=1SG.IPFV SUBR sing
'I don't want to sing.'
(2-E007-1)

(58) *Anau u=magono=u   tena vare ena.*
　　　 1SG 1SG.SBJ=dislike=1SG.IPFV SUBR REP sing
　　　 'I don't want to sing again.'
　　　 (2-E007-1)

7.1.5.2 Proximative aspect: *eri* and PSI

There is some, albeit limited, evidence from elicitation sessions and from one dialogue recording which shows that *eri* functions with PSI enclitics to express proximative aspect, which is used to refer to events that are about to be realised, as in (59)–(62). Comrie (1976: 64) uses the term "prospective aspect" for this aspectual notion while in the Oceanic literature, Chambers (2009: 102) uses the term "immediate irrealis". Cross-linguistically, proximative aspect has been found to grammaticalise from verbs expressing 'want' or 'desire', as in some African languages (Heine 1992), Bulgarian (Kuteva and Heine 1995) and even Tok Pisin (from *laik* 'want/like/desire') (Romaine 1999), hence I have analysed *eri* as optative and believe that the proximative meaning has developed from the optative meaning. Whether this development has occurred independently in Tok Pisin and Papapana, or whether this is evidence of contact-induced change due to contact with Tok Pisin, remains open to further investigation, though it should be noted that I did not use *laik* when eliciting the utterances below. It is possible to distinguish between optative mode and proximative aspect because in the proximative aspect construction, irrealis =*i* is not present.

(59) *Na=kara   e=**eri**   nao=**na**=ma.*
　　　 SPEC[CLI]=car 3SG.SBJ=OPT go=3SG.IPFV=ma
　　　 'The car is about to go/is starting to go.'
　　　 (2-E016)

(60) *Ian e=**eri**   atu=a=**ena**   ena=siodo.*
　　　 Ian 3SG.SBJ=OPT make=3SG.OBJ=3SG.IPFV 3SG.PSSR[CLI]=work
　　　 'Ian is starting to do his work.'
　　　 (2-E024)

(61) *Ian e=**eri**   atuma'as=i=a=**ena**   nu=koko'i.*
　　　 Ian 3SG.SBJ=OPT cook=TR=3SG.OBJ=3SG.IPFV SPEC.CLII=taro
　　　 'Ian is starting to cook taro.'
　　　 (2-E024)

(62) *Era=au   atu~atu   e=**eri**   opi=**na**,*
     1INCL.PSSR=CLII RD~make 3SG.SBJ=OPT disappear=3SG.IPFV
     *e=**eri**   tosi=**ena**.*
     3SG.SBJ=OPT finish=3SG.IPFV
     'Our custom is starting to disappear, it's about to finish.'
     (3-D001-00:02:45.800)

In contrast with this construction, the verb *vuna* 'start' can express that the activity or event is imminent:

(63) *Ian e=vun=i=a   na=siodo.*
     Ian 3SG.SBJ=start=TR=3SG.OBJ SPEC[CLI]=work
     'Ian is starting the work.'
     (2-E024)

(64) *Ian e=vun=i=a   tena   atuma'as=i=a*
     Ian 3SG.SBJ=start=TR=3SG.OBJ SUBR cook=TR=3SG.OBJ
     nu=koko'i.
     SPEC.CLII=taro
     'Ian is starting to cook taro.'
     (2-E024)

7.1.5.3 Counterfactual conditional: *awa* and *eri*

The other TAM marker that *eri* co-occurs with is the preverbal conditional mode marker *awa* (which is never the only TAM marker in a clause). Together, these markers express counterfactual conditional situations, which describe situations which did not or could not happen. The dependent clause is marked by both *awa* and *eri*, expressing the conditional situation, while the main clause is marked by *eri* only and expresses the resulting situation if the conditional situation had been realised (see §10.3.1 for more information). Such constructions are attested only in elicitation data.

Counterfactuality refers to "grammatical constructions that express or make reference to situations that are "contrary to fact"" (Iatridou 2000: 231). Counterfactuality can occur in two environments: counterfactual wishes (where the subject expresses a desire for things to be different from what they are or were) and counterfactual conditions (Iatridou 2000: 231–232). Both wishes and counterfactual conditional constructions refer to situations which are unrealised.

In a wish, the speaker is expressing something they would like to happen and thus optative mode involves intention or willingness. In Papapana counterfactual conditional constructions, the speaker expresses what would inevitably have happened or what they would have wished to happen, if something else had happened (i.e. someone else's potential intention had been realised). Since there is this semantic link between optative and counterfactual, it is perhaps not surprising that Papapana speakers use the optative mode marker *eri* in counterfactual conditional constructions. Nevertheless, the construction is quite different as *eri* does not combine with PSI enclitics, but with conditional *awa*, and in the main clause *eri* is the only TAM marker; therefore, I gloss *eri* here as counterfactual (CF).

The relative ordering of *awa* and *eri* is quite variable as shown in (65), with speakers producing both orders and deeming both to be acceptable without any change in meaning. In casual speech *awa* is often shortened to *wa* as in (65a) while when *eri* is adjacent to emphatic *to*, it is often shortened to *ri* as in (65b) and (66).

(65) a. *Tamu~tamu i=to   **wa** eri ma'ata,   u=**eri***
        RD~eat   3PL.SBJ=EMPH COND CF   be.heated 1SG.SBJ=CF
        tamu.
        eat
        'If they had heated the food, I would have eaten.'
        (2-E014-2)
   b. *Tamu~tamu i=to   **ri** **awa** ma'ata,   u=**eri***
        RD~eat   3PL.SBJ=EMPH CF   COND be.heated 1SG.SBJ=CF
        tamu.
        eat
        'If they had heated the food, I would have eaten.'
        (2-E014-2)

(66) *Au=atamata   e=to   **awa** **eri** nao, anau tomana*
     1SG.PSSR[CLI]=friend 3SG.SBJ=EMPH COND   CF   go   1SG   too
     *u=**ri**   nao tani.*
     1SG.SBJ=CF go   already
     'If my friend had gone, I too would have already gone.'
     (2-E022)

Like hypothetical conditionals (§7.1.4.3), imperatives and prohibitives (see §7.2 and §7.3.2), when *po* 'stay, exist' is the verb in this construction, imperfective PSI enclitics are also employed (see §7.1.4.3 for further discussion):

(67) *O=to   ri   awa   po=mu   i-inu   te   anau*
     2SG.SBJ=EMPH CF   COND stay=2SG.IPFV LOC-house   OBL   1SG
     naonava,   o=ri   varon=i=a   Sue.
     yesterday 2SG.SBJ=CF   know=TR=3SG.OBJ   Sue
     'If you had been at home yesterday, then you would know Sue.'
     (2-E028-2)

(68) *O=to   ri   awa   po=mu   Buka, o=ri*
     2SG.SBJ=EMPH CF   COND stay=2SG.IPFV Buka   2SG.SBJ=CF
     roros=i=au.
     see=TR=1SG.OBJ
     'If you had been in Buka, you would have seen me.'
     (2-E027)

7.1.6 Imperfective aspect: PSI and reduplication

Papapana postverbal subject-indexing (PSI) enclitics interact with verbal reduplication in a complex way to express either continuous or habitual aspect, which are subtypes of imperfective aspect. Habitual aspect "describe[s] a situation which is characteristic of an extended period of time" (Comrie 1976: 27) and "makes extended states out of situations by repeating a situation over multiple occasions" (Timberlake 2007: 289). Continuous aspect is defined as "imperfectivity that is not occasioned by habituality" (Comrie 1976: 33) and can be further divided into progressive and non-progressive. Progressive aspect is traditionally defined as describing a situation in progress, and is the "combination of continuousness with non-stativity" (Comrie 1976: 12), that is, it describes "a process actually in progress at some contextual occasion" (Timberlake 2007: 294). The non-progressive can be seen, analogously, to describe a "state that holds at some contextual occasion" (Timberlake 2007: 294). In Papapana, there is no formal distinction between ongoing states and processes in progress, so I will use the term *continuous* to refer to both.

Continous aspect is expressed by PSI enclitics and either no verbal reduplication, monosyllabic reduplication or disyllabic reduplication, depending on the verb. Habitual aspect is expressed by the addition of a monosyllabic reduplicant to the continuous aspect constructions thus resulting in multiple reduplication (see Smith 2016c). When there are no additional TAM markers, the time reference is present (§7.1.6.1). However, the addition of irrealis =*i* can result in a construction which expresses continuous aspect with a future time reference (§7.1.6.2), while the addition of past tense imperfective aspect *pei* and irrealis =*i*, or *pei*, =*i* and past tense *ara*, can express continuous aspect with a past time reference (§7.1.6.3). These tense markers are not added to the habitual constructions and indeed past habitual is expressed in another construction consisting of just *pei* and =*i* (§7.1.4.2). Further research is needed to determine the difference between present habitual constructions expressed by PSI and reduplication, and present habitual expressed by irrealis =*i* (see §7.1.4.1).

7.1.6.1 Continuous and habitual aspect, present

In Papapana, monosyllabic or disyllabic verbal reduplication used in combination with PSI expresses imperfective aspect; however, Papapana displays the typologically unusual phenomenon of multiple reduplication to distinguish continuous and habitual aspect. Continuous aspect is expressed either by (i) PSI only, (ii) PSI and monosyllabic verbal reduplication or (iii) PSI and disyllabic verbal reduplication, depending on the group the verb belongs to; see Table 7.3 and examples (69a), (70a) and (71a) respectively. For all verb groups, the habitual constructions are identical to the continuous constructions but with the addition of a monosyllabic reduplicant; see Table 7.3 and examples (69b), (70b) and (71b) respectively. Quite often in natural speech and sometimes in elicited speech, the continuous construction may express habitual aspect if the context is clear, for example, if there is an adjunct such as *mamena boni-boni* 'every day'. It was only through detailed elicitation sessions that the habitual construction became completely transparent.

Table 7.3: Imperfective aspect: PSI and reduplication patterns.[31]

Group	1	2	3
Continuous	Verb=PSI	RD1~Verb=PSI	RD2~Verb=PSI
Habitual	RD1~Verb=PSI	RD1~RD1~Verb=PSI	RD1~RD2~Verb=PSI

---

31 *RD1* denotes monosyllabic copying, while *RD2* denotes disyllabic copying.

(69) a. *"A:mu BRA mu=me-na   **siodo=mu** awa aruai?"*
  2PL BRA 2PL.SBJ=COM-PL.OBJ work=2PL.IPFV correct NEG
  '"Are you working with the BRA or not?"'
  (1-T053-00:04:21.790)
 b. *Anau u=to   na~nao~nao=u*
  1SG 1SG.SBJ=EMPH RD~RD=go=1SG.IPFV
  *te=na=kaukau   u=**si**~siodo=**u**,*
  OBL=SPEC[CLI]=sweet.potato 1SG.SBJ=RD~work=1SG.IPFV
  u=no   kokopa=u.
  1SG.SBJ=go.SEQ cut.bush=1SG.IPFV
  'When I go to the garden, I work, I cut the bush.'
  (1-T008-00:00:29.130)

(70) a. *"Aetau o=**mo**~morok=i=au=**omu**?"*
  why 2SG.SBJ=RD~lie=TR=1SG.OBJ=2SG.IPFV
  '"Why are you lying to me?"'
  (1-T049-00:01:48.130)
 b. *E=**mo**~**mo**~moroko=au=**ena**.*
  3SG.SBJ=RD~RD~lie=1SG.OBJ=3SG.IPFV
  'He (always) lies to me.'
  (2-E029-2)

(71) a. *"Anau te ia'a u=**nao**~nao=**u**."*
  1SG OBL Mum 1SG.SBJ=RD~go=1SG.IPFV
  '"I'm going to Mum."'
  (1-T031-00:09:30.360)
 b. *Anau u=to   **na**~**nao**~nao=**u***
  1SG 1SG.SBJ=EMPH RD~RD=go=1SG.IPFV
  te=na=kaukau. . .
  OBL=SPEC[CLI]=sweet.potato
  'When I go to the garden. . .'
  (1-T008-00:00:29.130)

Papapana is not unusual in using PSI to express imperfective aspect, as across the Northwest Solomonic group, PSI often occurs in constructions expressing nonpast tense, negative propositions, permission or prohibition, or imperfective, continuous or progressive aspect (Palmer 2011: 703–713). It is also quite common in Northwest Solomonic languages for verbal reduplication to play a role in expressing imperfective aspect. For example, in Torau, there are two imperfective aspect markers which function morphologically as hosts for PSI suffixes (Palmer 2007a: 500). The aspectual reading of a clause with imperfective aspect marking depends on which imperfective marker is present, whether or not reduplication is present, the aspectual semantics of the verb itself and the presence of any other TAM markers (Palmer 2007a: 511–516). Like Papapana, habitual aspect in Torau is only expressed when there is verbal reduplication, and in Teop too, habitual aspect may be expressed by reduplication, which might co-occur with PSI (Palmer 2011: 707). Monosyllabic or disyllabic verbal reduplication can also express durative actions in Teop (Mosel and Thiesen, 2007) and progressive or habitual aspect in Hoava (Davis, 2003), though it is unclear what determines the type of reduplication in these languages. Monosyllabic verbal reduplication expresses a habitual or repetitive action or an ongoing state in Banoni (Lincoln, 1976a: 449; Lynch and Ross, 2002) while disyllabic verbal reduplication expresses iterative or continuous action in Kubokota (Chambers, 2009). Papapana is however unique as its patterns of multiple reduplication are not found anywhere else in Northwest Solomonic and are typologically rare (see Smith 2016c).

The verbs within each group are presented below. These groups are not phonologically determined, they do not reflect the transitivity categories described in §6.4 and they cannot be distinguished based on the aspectual semantics of the verb. To demonstrate the latter, verbs within each group are categorised according to Vendler's (1957) classification of verbal predicates: states, activities, accomplishments and achievements. Vendler's (1957) classification intuits that "there are two properties which are crucial in categorizing eventualities or event types" (Rothstein 2004: 11): (i) telicity and (ii) whether an event type can be analysed as progressing or developing, and is thus *dynamic*, or not. Accomplishments and achievements "report situations that change in a way that is discontinuous and irreversible" (Timberlake 2007: 285) and are *telic* as they have an inherent end point, whereas states and activities report continuous situations (Timberlake 2007: 284) and are thus *atelic*. Activities and accomplishments are dynamic as they involve change and stages, whereas states and achievements "do not go on or progress" because they are respectively "inherently non-dynamic" and "near instantaneous" (Rothstein 2004: 12).

As the non-exhaustive list in Table 7.4 shows, the verbs in Group 1 belong to a wide range of semantic classes, display a range of syllable structures and word shapes, and may be intransitive (such as *aputu* 'sleep'), monotransitive (such as *agoto* 'hold') or ambitransitive (such as *siodo* 'work'). Some of the verb roots appear to be reduplicated, such as *roroto* 'see' and *gaganini* 'play' but synchronically these are monomorphemic: **roto* and **ganini* do not exist as roots.

Table 7.4: Imperfective aspect: Examples of Group 1 verbs.

Atelic	State	dua	be bad	Non-dynamic
		mata	be good	
		ge:rere	be white	
		roroto	see	
		aputu	sleep	
		magono	dislike	
		varona	know	
		tonu	stand	
		umunu	sit	
		po	stay	
	Activity	gaganini	play	Dynamic
		siodo	work	
		agoto	hold	
Telic	Accomplishment	tatu	mash	
		ma	chew	
		sigi	wash	

The non-exhaustive list in Table 7.5 shows that the verbs in Group 2 belong only to three semantic classes, display a range of syllable structures and word shapes, and may be intransitive (such as *vurau* 'run'), monotransitive (*atu* 'make'), ditransitive (*ma'a* 'give') or ambitransitive (*iromo* 'drink').

Table 7.5: Imperfective aspect: Examples of Group 2 verbs.

Atelic	Activity	vurau	run	Dynamic
		nu	chase	
		iromo	drink	
		wa	say	
		vatana	tell	
		moroko	lie	
		siri	read	
Telic	Accomplishment	atu	make	
		erepe	peel	
	Achievement	ma'a	give	Non-dynamic

Finally, as the non-exhaustive list in Table 7.6 shows, Group 3 verbs belong to only three semantic classes, display a range of syllable structures and word shapes, and may be intransitive (such as *tamu* 'eat'), monotransitive (such as *tu'u* 'meet') or ambitransitive (such as *gaunu* 'write').

Table 7.6: Imperfective aspect: Examples of Group 3 verbs.

Atelic	Activity	oa	cry	Dynamic
		nioto	(day)dream	
		tamu	eat	
		gaunu	write	
		nao	go	
		votu	leave	
		naovo	fly	
		tua	paddle	
		vo'o	call out	
		ena	sing	
Telic	Accomplishment	atunu	attack	
		ngono	boil	
		peri	find	
		ari	dig	
		tuvi	build	
		bio	sweep	
		buibui	clean	
	Achievement	tu'u	meet	Non-dynamic
		sogo	push	
		muni	hide	

7.1.6.2 Continuous aspect, future

The irrealis mode enclitic =i may co-occur with the continuous construction to express future continuous. This is attested only in two elicited examples ((72) and another elicited example with the same verb and a plural object), but was subsequently confirmed as grammatical by other speakers. The verb in (72) belongs to Group 3, so continuous aspect is expressed by disyllabic verbal reduplication and PSI:

(72) E=**gau**~gaun=i=a=**na**=i   nu=pepa.
    3SG.SBJ=RD~write=TR=3SG.OBJ=3SG.IPFV=IRR   SPEC.CLII=paper
    '(When we arrive), he will be writing a letter.'
    (2-E008)

7.1.6.3 Continuous aspect, past

It is possible to add the preverbal past imperfective marker *pei* and the irrealis mode enclitic =i to the continuous construction to express past continuous. In (73) the verb belongs to Group 1, so continuous aspect is expressed by PSI enclitics only; in (74) the verb belongs to Group 2, so continuous aspect is expressed by monosyllabic verbal reduplication and PSI enclitics, and in (75) the verb belongs to Group 3, so continuous aspect is expressed by disyllabic verbal reduplication and PSI enclitics.

(73) *Sa=au   maunu   e=**pei**   **magono=ena=i***
     DIM=CLII woman   3SG.SBJ=PST.IPFV dislike=3SG.IPFV=IRR
     tena   asi=a   sa=au   'usia.
     SUBR leave=3SG.OBJ DIM=CLII   child
     'The poor girl didn't want to leave the poor boy.'
     (1-T029-00:12:29.810)

(74) *Enai   nana   na=vituasi   e=**pei**   **vu~vurau***
     after individual SPEC[CLI]=young 3SG.SBJ=PST.IPFV RD~run
     *tae=**na=i**. . .*
     up=3SG.IPFV=IRR
     'One of the young men was running away. . .'
     (1-T002-00:05:28.300)

(75) *. . .nu=otana   e=**pei**   **ngono~ngono=ena=i.***
     SPEC.CLII=pot 3SG.SBJ=PST.IPFV RD~boil=3SG.IPFV=IRR
     '[He saw] . . .the pot was boiling.'
     (1-T101-00:05:03.137)

It is also possible to add the preverbal past imperfective marker *pei* and the irrealis mode enclitic *=i*, as well as the preverbal past tense marker *ara* to the continuous construction to express past continuous. Further research is required to determine the difference in constructions with and without *ara*. In (76) the verb belongs to Group 1, so continuous aspect is expressed by PSI enclitics only while in (77) the verb belongs to Group 3, so continuous aspect is expressed by disyllabic verbal reduplication and PSI enclitics.

(76) *Na:=ata   na=poana   e=**pei**   ara*
     some=CLI SPEC[CLI]=village 3SG.SBJ=PST.IPFV PST
     po=ena=i.
     stay=3SG.IPFV=IRR
     'There was another village.'
     (1-T034-00:01:23.864)

(77) "...*e=**pei*** *ara gau~gaunu=i=a=**ena**=i* mai
3SG.SBJ=PST.IPFV PST RD~write=TR=3SG.OBJ=3SG.IPFV=IRR hither
nu=leta..."
SPEC.CLII=letter
"'[I didn't know that]...he was writing her letters...[and I didn't know].'"
(1-T043-00:02:04.430)

7.1.7 Repetitive aspect *vare ~ vae*

The preverbal aspect marker *vare ~ vae* expresses repetitive aspect, encoding that the specified event occurs again. *Vare ~ vae* follows past tense *ara* and generally precedes sequential directionals (see below). Example (78) shows *vare ~ vae* can co-occur with preverbal adverbs. While it might be argued that *vare ~ vae* is another adverb in preverbal position, there is no evidence that any other preverbal adverbs can co-occur and thus a hypothetical additional preverbal adverb position would only contain *vare ~ vae*. *Vare* (79a) may also be pronounced *vae* (79b), or occur as a discontinuous morpheme (79c), with *vare ~ vae* occurring preverbally and the enclitic *=re* as the final postverbal element in the VC. I analyse *=re* as an enclitic because it forms a phonological word with the host and it attaches to the rightmost postverbal morpheme or the verb itself, rather than to a particular lexical category. The form *=re* can also cliticise to the noun phrase (NP) head to denote '(an)other' (see §4.7.8).

(78) *I=to* *vare* *'aria* *o'ovata na=uvi.*
3PL.SBJ=EMPH REP together roast SPEC[CLI]=yam
'They yam-roasted again together.'
(2-E007-2A)

(79) a. *Natui* *u=**vare*** *nao=i* *Buka*
tomorrow 1SG.SBJ=REP go=IRR Buka
'Tomorrow I'll go to Buka again.'
(2-E024)
b. *Natui* *u=**vae*** *nao=i* *Buka*
tomorrow 1SG.SBJ=REP go=IRR Buka
'Tomorrow I'll go to Buka again.'
(2-E024)
c. *Natui* *u=**vare*** *nao=i=**re*** *Buka*
tomorrow 1SG.SBJ=REP go=IRR=REP Buka
'Tomorrow I'll go to Buka again.'
(2-E024)

The examples show that the repetitive marker may precede the reciprocal/reflexive marker *vei* (80), may follow the past tense marker *ara* to express past tense and repetitive aspect (81), and may co-occur with the irrealis mode enclitic =*i* to express either future tense and repetitive aspect (82), or both repetitive and habitual aspects (83).

(80) *Iara i=pei* **vae vei** *a~'adu=ina=i.*
 then 3PL.SBJ=PST.IPFV REP R/R RD~destroy=3PL.IPFV=IRR
 'Then they kept hurting themselves.'
 (1-T034-00:04:06.306)

(81) *Na:=ata na=boni e=**ara** **vae** gaunu mai.*
 some=CLI SPEC[CLI]=day 3SG.SBJ=PST REP write hither
 'One day he wrote again.'
 (1-T043-00:00:36.760)

(82) *U=**vare** kaku tae=a=**i**=**re**.*
 1SG.SBJ=REP bend up=3SG.OBJ=IRR=REP
 'I'll bend it up again.'
 (1-T062-00:03:39.980)

(83) . . .*mi=no* **vare** *tepe=i na=naunu.* . .
 1EXCL.SBJ=go.SEQ REP cut=IRR SPEC[CLI]=leaf
 '[After we've wrapped it] . . .we go and cut leaves again. . . [to cover the oven].'
 (1-T038-00:01:51.837)

As (84)–(85) show, sequential directionals show variable position relative to *vare ~ vae*, as they do with *ara* and preverbal adverbs.

(84) *Na:=ata na=boni=re,*
 some=CLI SPEC[CLI]=day=REP
 *mi=**vae** no gono mai=re na=kauto.*
 1EXCL.SBJ=REP go.SEQ collect hither=REP SPEC[CLI]=Indian.almond
 'Another day, we went and picked Indian almonds again.'
 (1-T010-00:00:37.460)

(85) E=**no**   vae   ma'=i=a=**re**   na=maria
    3SG.SBJ=go.SEQ REP   give=TR=3SG.OBJ=REP SPEC[CLI]=thing
    koko'i...
    taro
    'He went and gave her taro again...'
    (1-T029-00:08:30.295)

In Papapana, the repetitive aspect marker may be a reflex of the POc *paRi-* prefix which, as noted in §6.5.6, Pawley (1973: 150–151) reconstructed not only as a collective/associative and reciprocal marker but also as an iterative marker. Bril (2005: 27) reports that there is evidence that POc *paRi-* could combine with POc *-i* to express iterative actions, while various Oceanic languages combine the prefixes with root reduplication to express iterative actions; however, this is not the case in Papapana.

7.1.8 Completive aspect *osi*

The postverbal completive aspect marker *osi* expresses completion of an event and immediately follows the geocentric directionals in the VC, as in (86) and (87), and precedes any adverbs, including the completive adverb *tani* 'already', as in (88) and (89). Example (90) shows *osi* following the verb and preceding object-indexing enclitics.

(86) U=to   nao **tae osi**   o~'oema-na,
    1SG.SBJ=EMPH go   up   COMPL RD~taro.garden-DER
    iara u=ari~ari   kaukau.
    then 1SG.SBJ=RD~dig sweet.potato
    '(When) I have finished going up to the bush, then I dig potatoes.'
    (2-E007-2B)

(87) U=to   tua   **dini osi**   mai,
    1SG.SBJ=EMPH paddle down COMPL hither
    iara u=atu   ma'ata=i   tamu~tamu.
    then 1SG.SBJ=make be.heated=IRR RD~eat
    '(When) I have paddled back, then I cook food.'
    (2-E007-2B)

(88) *Anau   u=atu   ma'ata   **osi**   **tani**=ina   tamu~tamu.*
     1SG   1SG.SBJ=make   be.heated COMPL   already=3PL.OBJ   RD~eat
     'I have already finished cooking the food.'
     (2-E014)

(89) *A:mani   mi=to   usi   **osi**   **papasi**   tani=a=i*
     1EXCL   1EXCL.SBJ=EMPH   scrape   COMPL   quickly   already=3SG.OBJ=IRR
     na=niunu.
     SPEC[CLI]=coconut
     'We have already quickly scraped the coconut.'
     (2-E007-2B)

(90) *Mi=to   usi   **osi**=a=i*
     1EXCL.SBJ=EMPH   scrape   COMPL=3SG.OBJ=IRR
     na=ma'ata...
     SPEC[CLI]=brown.coconut
     'After we've scraped the brown coconut...'
     (1-T038-00:01:09.458)

I analyse *osi* as an aspect marker, having ruled out the hypotheses that it is an adverb or serial verb. *Osi* is not an adverb because there is already an adverb expressing completion, *tani* 'already' (see §6.8.2), which *osi* can co-occur with, as in (88) and (89). While it is possible that *osi* and *tani* could be synonymous adverbs, their co-occurrence as adverbs would result in semantic redundancy. *Osi* is not a serial verb because it can be separated from the verb by geocentric directionals, which I have established are not synchronically serial verbs (see §6.7.1), and *osi* cannot occur as a predicate on its own, an important criterion in identifying serial verbs (see §6.6.1). Nevertheless it is likely that diachronically *osi* has grammaticalised as an aspect marker from the verb *taosi* 'finish', which has a plural or singular object in (91) and (92). Indeed, in Oceanic languages, such as Toqabaqita (Malaita, Solomon Islands) (Lichtenberk 2006: 269), it is quite common to find postverbal aspect morphemes, especially for the completive, and these "seem mainly to be derived from verbs like 'finish' used in an ambient verb serialisation" (Lynch, Ross, and Crowley 2002: 85–86).

(91) *Anau   u=taosi=ina   au=bau   tamu~tamu.*
     1SG   1SG.SBJ=finish=3PL.OBJ   1SG.PSSR=PL   RD~eat
     'I finished my food.'
     (2-E014)

(92) *Anau u=taosi=a au=siodo.*
1SG 1SG.SBJ=finish=3SG.OBJ 1SG.PSSR[CLI]=work
'I finished my work.'
(2-E014)

7.2 Imperative and hortative

In Papapana, imperatives and hortatives are expressed by the same construction. Papapana does not have inflectional morphology dedicated exclusively to imperatives and hortatives, thus in Papapana *imperative* and *hortative* refer to a clause type. While this section describes marking of imperatives/hortatives within the VC, the presence and order, or absence, of NP arguments is discussed in §9.2.

In Papapana, imperative and hortative clauses may carry no TAM marking whatsoever as in (93) and (94) or the irrealis mode enclitic =*i* as in (95)–(97). The optionality of irrealis =*i* makes these clauses distinct from those described in §7.1.4.1 where =*i* also occurred on its own, but not optionally, to express future time or habitual events with a present time reference. In Northwest Solomonic languages such as Kokota, an imperative is also expressed as an irrealis clause (Palmer 2002: 520) and indeed, cross-linguistically imperative clauses are often irrealis. The lack of TAM markers is also typical of imperatives cross-linguistically because "it is simply pragmatically impossible to command someone to perform acts with certain TAM operations" (Payne 1997: 305).

(93) *O=nao te=na=skuru va:gi.*
2SG.SBJ=go OBL=SPEC[CLI]=school now
'Go to school now.'
(2-E026)

(94) *Mu=nao, mu=no ituvu=au mai nu=daramu."*
2PL.SBJ=go 2PL.SBJ=go.SEQ fetch=1SG.OBJ hither SPEC.CLII=water
"'Go, go and fetch me some water.'"
(1-T007-00:00:37.860)

(95) *"Nu=risi nu=kaka'i o=de=a=i. . ."*
SPEC.CLII=rope SPEC.CLII=small 2SG.SBJ=take=3SG.OBJ=IRR
"'Take a small rope. . .'"
(1-T035-00:03:44.985)

(96) *"Na:=bau taramina mu=asi=ina=**i**."*
　　　some=PL　thing　　　2PL.SBJ=leave=3PL.OBJ=IRR
　　　'"Leave some things."'
　　　(1-T002-00:00:54.230)

(97) *". . .sa=asi=a=**i**　　　　　　　　　　　Pasa　ta　si=nao=**i**. . ."*
　　　INCL.SBJ.HORT=leave=3SG.OBJ=IRR　Pasa　and　INCL.SBJ=go=IRR
　　　'". . .let's leave Pasa and go. . ."'
　　　(1-T031-00:01:57.361)

Some compound sentences in Papapana may even exhibit no TAM marking in the first clause and the irrealis mode enclitic in the second:

(98) *"Mu=nao　　i-daramu　ta　　mu=no　　　　　tutuvu=**i**."*
　　　2PL.SBJ=go　LOC-river　and　2PL.SBJ=go.SEQ　wash=IRR
　　　'"Go to the river and wash."'
　　　(1-T042-00:03:25.700)

Speakers reported that there was no semantic or pragmatic difference between the absence or presence of the irrealis mode enclitic *=i*, but that the lack of the irrealis mode enclitic *=i* was a shorter way of expressing the same thing. To check this, I elicited utterances, such as (99a), which corresponded to text recording data such as (99b), and I asked speakers to compare them; speakers reported that both were acceptable and meant the same thing (though of course the subject number is different here).

(99) a. *O=tuvu　　　tau　o=vurau=**i**.*
　　　　2SG.SBJ=swim　and　2SG.SBJ=run=IRR
　　　　'Swim and run away.'
　　　　(2-E026)
　　b. *"Mu=tuvu,　　mu=vurau."*
　　　　2PL.SBJ=swim　2PL.SBJ=run
　　　　'"Swim, run away."'
　　　　(1-T029-00:24:04.600)

Like hypothetical conditionals (§7.1.4.3), counterfactual conditionals (§7.1.5.3), and prohibitives (§7.3.2), when *po* 'stay, exist' is the verb in an imperative, imperfective PSI enclitics are also employed (100)–(102). This could be because *po* is a state verb which reports ongoing situations and is thus compatible with imperfective aspect (see §7.1.6 for definitions of imperfective aspect and for Vendler's (1957) classification of verbal predicates). In Teop too, imperfective aspect can be used in an imperative clause (Mosel and Thiesen 2007).

(100) *"Aite, o=po=**mu**."*
  Dad   2SG.SBJ=stay=2SG.IPFV
  '"Dad, stay."'
  (1-T031-00:09:30.360)

(101) *Ani   o=po=**mu**=i   ini.*
  2SG   2SG.SBJ=stay=2SG.IPFV=IRR   here
  'You must stay here.'
  (2-E014-2)

(102) *"A:mu   mu=po=**mu**=i."*
  2PL   2PL.SBJ=stay=2PL.IPFV=IRR
  '"You stay."'
  (1-T065-00:04:07.970)

There are also two examples from text data where the verb is reduplicated, but this could be because the postverbal adverbs appear to be reduplicated (and likely were reduplicated diachronically; see §6.8.2.2):

(103) *"Mu=**nao**~nao   **garigari**   te=na=skuru. . ."*
  2PL.SBJ=RD~go   always   OBL=SPEC[CLI]=school
  '"You must always go to school. . ."'
  (1-T011-00:02:08.530)

(104) *Iara   o=**rasi**~rasi   **egoego**=ina=i. . .*
  then   2SG.SBJ=RD~pull   well=3PL.OBJ=IRR
  'Then you pull them well. . .'
  (1-T027-2-00:04:57.630)

7.3 Negation

Mosel (1999: 5) outlines five basic functions of negatives in Oceanic languages: (i) the negative answer to questions, (ii) negative existential constructions, (iii) the negation of non-verbal assertive predicates, (iv) the negation of verbal assertive predicates and (v) the negation of imperatives. The first three functions are dealt with in §9.3, §9.5 and §9.6. This section discusses the fourth function which is expressed by the preverbal negative marker *ae* (§7.3.1), and the fifth function which is expressed by verbal reduplication and either the preverbal negative marker *ae* or the preverbal apprehensive marker *te* (§7.3.2). The apprehensive mode marker *te* may also be used in conjunction with the irrealis mode enclitic =*i* to denote 'lest' (§7.1.4.3).

7.3.1 Verbal assertive negation: *ae*

The preverbal negative marker *ae* negates verbal assertive predicates in Papapana. The use of a preverbal negative marker is a typical negation marking strategy in Oceanic languages and a number of these preverbal negators reflect forms beginning with *kai- (Lynch, Ross, and Crowley 2002: 51, 88). It could be that in Papapana *ae* derives from the negative verb *aruai*, as in a few Oceanic languages negators are "derived from a negative verb [that] has been grammaticalised to such a degree that it has become part of the VC" (Lynch, Ross, and Crowley 2002: 88).

In Papapana, the negative marker follows the subject proclitics and *to* (105), but precedes sequential directionals (106) and valency-changing morphemes (107):

(105) *Na=ava   e=to   ae   tete=na   nao...*
      SPEC[CLI]=sea 3SG.SBJ=EMPH NEG enter=3SG.IPFV thither
      'The sea wasn't coming inside...'
      (1-T105-00:09:06.675)

(106) *Mi=ae   no   vae   de~de   tamu~tamu=ma Vakonaia.*[32]
      1EXCL.SBJ=NEG go.SEQ REP RD~take RD~eat=ma   Wakunai
      'We didn't go and get food from Wakunai again.'
      (1-T096-00:02:04.171)

(107) *Mi=ae   vei   aporo=i   na=vunu   te   a:mani.*
      1EXCL.SBJ=NEG R/R groom=IRR SPEC[CLI]=hair OBL 1EXCL
      'We do not cut our hair.'
      (1-T019-2-00:00:37.245)

---

[32] It is unclear why the speaker reduplicates the verb in this utterance since there are no other markers of imperfective aspect, and this is not a prohibitive or reciprocal clause.

The negative marker is compatible with almost all TAM distinctions as examples (108)–(118) below show. It is not attested with the completive aspect marker *osi*; however, this is likely a matter of lack of data rather than of incompatibility. *Ae* is also not attested with apprehensive mode *te*, which is most likely because apprehension-causing clauses express possible, undesirable situations that the subject wants to not happen (see §7.1.4.3) and because *ae* and *te* are in complementary distribution in prohibitive clauses (see §7.3.2). Although negated clauses are often treated as irrealis in languages that make a realis-irrealis contrast (Palmer 2001: 173–176), this is not the case in Papapana; instead mode and negation are independent and the negative marker *ae* may occur in both realis clauses, such as (108), and irrealis clauses, such as (112). As the examples show, it is also not the case, as in many Oceanic languages, that the negative marker is "interposed between the last of the TAM markers and the verb" (Lynch, Ross, and Crowley 2002: 45).

Past

(108) *Tau Nathan e=ae ara tavotu egoego.*
and Nathan 3SG.SBJ=NEG PST arrive well
'And Nathan didn't turn out well.'
(1-T104-00:01:40.480)

Future

(109) *Natui si=ae siodo=i.*
tomorrow INCL.SBJ=NEG work=IRR
'Tomorrow we will not work.'
(2-E008)

Present habitual

(110) *. . .i=ae nongono=i.*
3PL.SBJ=NEG hear=IRR
'. . .they don't listen.'
(1-T025-00:01:47.050)

Past habitual

(111) *Na=vanua i=pei ae ari=ina=i*
SPEC[CLI]=people 3PL.SBJ=PST.IPFV NEG dig=3PL.OBJ=IRR
te=na=kavururu.
OBL=SPEC[CLI]=ground
'They didn't used to bury people in the ground.'
(1-T032-00:00:16.760)

Hypothetical conditional

(112) Anna e=to awa ae tamu=i, e=ubetu=i.
Anna 3SG.SBJ=EMPH COND NEG eat=IRR 3SG.SBJ=hungry=IRR
'If Anna doesn't eat, she will be hungry.'
(2-E022)

(113) Louise e=awa peri=a=i pei si'ini
Louise 3SG.SBJ=COND find=3SG.OBJ=IRR PART spear
e=**ae** atuni=a=i nu=toa.
3SG.SBJ=NEG attack=3SG.OBJ=IRR SPEC.CLII=chicken
'If Louise finds a spear, she will not attack the chicken.'
(2-E028-2)

Counterfactual conditional

(114) Maria e=to ri awa nongon=i=a
Maria 3SG.SBJ=EMPH CF COND hear=TR=3SG.OBJ
e-sina-na, e=eri ae mate.
PERS-mother-3SG.PSSR 3SG.SBJ=CF NEG die
'If Maria had listened to her mother, she would not have died.'
(2-E027)

(115) Sharon e=to ri awa ae nao Buka,
Sharon 3SG.SBJ=EMPH CF COND NEG go Buka
e=eri me-a nao=au te=na='uru.
3SG.SBJ=CF COM-SG.OBJ go=1SG.OBJ OBL=SPEC[CLI]=island
'If Sharon had not gone to Buka, she would have gone with me to the island.'
(2-E027)

Optative

(116) Na=siodo e=t=**eri** ae
SPEC[CLI]=work 3SG.SBJ=EMPH=OPT NEG
ma'=i=o=ena=i. . .
give=TR=2SG.OBJ=3SG.IPFV=IRR
'(If) he doesn't want to give you work. . .'
(1-T097-00:14:03.950)

Present Imperfective

(117) *"Aetau na=iana u=ae roroto=ina=u?"*
    why   SPEC[CLI]=fish   1SG.SBJ=NEG   see=3PL.OBJ=1SG.IPFV
    "'Why am I not seeing the fish?'"
    (1-T064-00:02:25.120)

Repetitive

(118) *"...ta u=ae ara vae nami=o."*
    and   1SG.SBJ=NEG   PST   REP   sad=2SG.OBJ
    "'...and I didn't miss you again.'"
    (1-T029-00:18:46.635)

7.3.2 Prohibitives: *ae/te* and verbal reduplication

Prohibitives (also called *negative imperatives*) in Papapana are formed with either monosyllabic (119)–(120) or disyllabic (121) verbal reduplication and either the preverbal negative marker *ae* (120–(121)) or the preverbal apprehensive marker *te* (119) (see §7.1.4.3 for discussion of apprehensives). The prohibitive meaning developed from the apprehensive meaning, and hence I gloss *te* as APPR (Smith-Dennis 2019; Smith-Dennis, in press). As with imperative and hortative clauses, the irrealis mode enclitic =*i* may be absent as in (119) and (121), or present (120), but other TAM marking does not occur. In a study of negation in Oceanic languages, Mosel (1999: 15) reports that with the exception of the Loyalty Islands languages, "all the languages in our sample formally distinguish the negation of assertive and imperative clauses", and therefore Papapana is typically Oceanic because although the negative marker *ae* is also used in the negation of assertives, reduplication and *te* are not.

(119) *O=**te** e~'esivo.*
    2SG.SBJ=APPR   RD~sneeze
    'Don't sneeze.'
    (2-E026)

(120) *"Mu=**ae** va~vatan=i=a=**i**."*
    2PL.SBJ=NEG   RD~tell=TR=3SG.OBJ=IRR
    "'Don't tell him.'"
    (1-T065-00:01:07.070)

(121) O=***ae***   ***oto~'oto***   te=na=au   obutu.
　　　 2SG.SBJ=NEG RD~board OBL=SPEC=CLII canoe
　　　 'Don't board the canoe.'
　　　 (2-E026)

During my 2011–2013 fieldwork, speakers reported no semantic or pragmatic difference between *ae* and *te;* these markers were judged to be interchangeable as shown in (122) and (123) from elicitation sessions.

(122) a. O=***ae***   ***to~***tonu,   o=te   pu=i.
　　　　 2SG.SBJ=NEG RD~stand 2SG.SBJ=APPR fall=IRR
　　　　 'Don't stand up, (otherwise/in case) you might fall.'
　　　　 (2-E028-2)
　　 b. O=***te***   ***to~***tonu,   o=te   pu=i.
　　　　 2SG.SBJ=APPR RD~stand 2SG.SBJ=APPR fall=IRR
　　　　 'Don't stand up, (otherwise/in case) you might fall.'
　　　　 (2-E028-2)

(123) a. O=***ae***   ***ago~***agos=i=a   pei   to'o~to'o.
　　　　 2SG.SBJ=NEG RD~hold=TR=3SG.OBJ PART   RD~cut
　　　　 'Don't hold the knife.'
　　　　 (2-E026)
　　 b. O=***te***   ***ago~***agos=i=a   pei   to'o~to'o.
　　　　 2SG.SBJ=APPR RD~hold=TR=3SG.OBJ PART   RD~cut
　　　　 'Don't hold the knife.'
　　　　 (2-E026)

However, during my 2018 visit, one speaker suggested that *ae* is used to prohibit someone from doing something they have not done yet (124a), while *te* is used to prohibit someone from doing something they have already started (124b).

(124) a. O=***ae***   ***vae~***vaene, o=te   pu=i.
　　　　 2SG.SBJ=NEG RD~climb   2SG.SBJ=APPR fall=IRR
　　　　 'Don't climb (that tree), (otherwise) you might fall.'
　　　　 (3-E001)
　　 b. O=***te***   ***vae~***vaene, o=te   pu=i.
　　　　 2SG.SBJ=APPR RD~climb   2SG.SBJ=APPR fall=IRR
　　　　 'Stop climbing (that tree), (otherwise) you might fall.'
　　　　 (3-E001)

This analysis is supported by the following example from a traditional narrative, where people are running with bows and clubs to attack a woman's 'bird husband' and she suddenly jumps down and tells them not to kill her husband:

(125) *"Mu=**te** **atu~**atun=i=a enai au=sinoni!"*
2PL.SBJ=APPR RD~attack=TR=3SG.OBJ DEM2 1SG.PSSR[CLI]= husband
"'Don't attack my husband!"
(1-T101-00:10:48.994)

Nevertheless, in example (126), from a personal narrative about the Bougainville Crisis, the speaker recounts how she and other women were travelling up into the bush and were stopped by soldiers who asked where they were going and then told them:

(126) *"Mu=**ae** **nao~**nao tae, mu=**ae** **nao~**nao=i."*
2PL.SBJ=NEG RD~go up 2PL.SBJ=NEG RD~go=IRR
"'Don't go up, don't go.'"
(1-T053-00:01:54.310)

When the women explained that they were looking for some women, the soldiers uttered (127). Since both *ae* and *te* are used in the same context (and the women had made no further progress with their journey), this supports the idea that *ae* and *te* could be interchangeable after all. On the other hand, it could be the case that at first, the soldiers did not know what the women were doing, but once they discovered their intentions, they perceived the women's journey as already being in progress and were instructing them to cease their activity. Therefore, the recently proposed analysis is again supported. For further discussion of the difference between *ae* and *te,* see Smith-Dennis (in press).

(127) *"Mu=**te** **nao~**nao=i."*
2PL.SBJ=APPR RD~go=IRR
"'Don't go.'"
(1-T053-00:02:01.450)

Verbal reduplication in negative clauses is not unknown in Northwest Solomonic languages as it also occurs in prohibitives in Banoni (Lynch and Ross 2002: 450), and in Torau verbal reduplication is obligatory when negation is expressed by the suffix *-ka* on the preverbal modal/subject indexing particle (Palmer 2009).

As the examples so far show, verbal reduplication in prohibitives may be monosyllabic or disyllabic. For some verbs, the type of reduplication found in prohibitives is the same as that in continuous aspect constructions (see §7.1.6); for example, *atunu* 'attack' displays disyllabic reduplication in both prohibitives (125) and continuous aspect constructions. However, for other verbs, the type of reduplication found in prohibitives is not the same as that in continuous aspect constructions; for example, *tonu* 'stand' is a Group 1 verb and is not reduplicated in continuous aspect constructions, yet in prohibitives, *tonu* undergoes monosyllabic reduplication (122). Transitivity also does not play a role as *tonu* and *vo'o* 'call out' are both intransitive, but *vo'o* displays disyllabic reduplication (128). Similarly, the type of reduplication is not phonologically determined: *esivo* 'sneeze' and *atunu* 'attack' have the same syllable structure, as do *tonu* 'stand' and *vo'o* 'call out', but these verbs undergo different reduplication in prohibitives. It is thus unclear what motivates the type of reduplication in prohibitives.

(128) *O=**te**   **vo'o~**vo'o,   i=te   matono=i.*
    2SG.SBJ=APPR RD~call.out 3PL.SBJ=APPR wake=IRR
    'Don't shout, (or) they might wake up.'
    (2-E028-2)

As in imperative clauses (§7.2), hypothetical conditionals (§7.1.4.3) and counterfactual conditionals (§7.1.5.3), the verb *po* 'stay/exist' in a prohibitive clause requires the imperfective PSI enclitics (see §7.2 for further discussion):

(129) *O=**te**   **po~**po=**mu**=i   te=na=mamaravi.*
    2SG.SBJ=APPR RD~stay=2SG.IPFV=IRR OBL=SPEC[CLI]=cold
    'Don't stay outside in the cold.'
    (2-E026)

Chapter 8
Obliques, adjuncts and clause-level adverbs

This chapter discusses the internal characteristics of obliques (adposition phrases) and other clause-level adjuncts, and the position of obliques and adjuncts in the clause. Clause-level adjuncts in Papapana can be noun phrases (NP) (§8.1), deictic locational words (§8.2), adposition phrases (§8.3), and clause-level adverbs (§8.4). Adposition phrases can also function as oblique arguments in Papapana. Oblique arguments are not prevalent in Papapana and since there is no formal distinction between oblique arguments and adjuncts, the two are discussed together here and reference is made to the status of an oblique as argument or adjunct at the appropriate points.

Clause order in Papapana is summarised in §1.4.6 and described in detail in §9.1–§9.3. Clauses are variably verb-medial or verb-final. (For the purposes of discussing clause order, 'V' refers not just to the verb but to the Verb Complex (VC) which begins with the subject proclitic (see chapter 6)). Overall, the position of adjuncts in the clause is variable: most often, they are clause-final, but they may also occur clause-initially, and sometimes they can occur between an argument NP and the VC. In Papapana, there is no correlation between the position of an oblique and its status as adjunct or argument, nor is there a correlation between the position of an adjunct and its status as an adposition phrase, NP or deictic locational, nor the semantic relation it expresses. Adjuncts can co-occur in sequences, while some NP adjuncts headed by Location nouns could be interpreted as being embedded in another NP adjunct headed by a Location noun. Sequences of adjuncts and embedded adjuncts are discussed in this chapter while coordinated preposition phrases are described in §10.1.1.2 since §10.1 describes coordinators and the coordination of clauses and phrases. Adverbs can also occur clause-initially, clause-finally or between an argument NP and the VC, though there are two adverbs which are restricted to a pre-VC position. Such variability in the position of adjuncts is not uncommon for a Northwest Solomonic language: in Banoni temporal phrases occur sentence-initially but other obliques usually occur after the object (Lynch and Ross 2002: 452); in Taiof temporal phrases occur clause-initially or finally (Ross 2002: 436); while in Teop, only temporal and locative adjuncts are found clause-initially with other adjuncts clause-final (Mosel and Thiesen 2007).

8.1 Adjunct noun phrases

Some Class I nouns referring to time can function as the head of a NP adjunct (§8.1.1), while Location nouns (§8.1.2) and the bound noun *peite-* 'own' (§8.1.3) can also function as the head of a NP adjunct.

8.1.1 Class I temporal nouns

Class I nouns (see §5.1.2) denoting units of time or periods of the day may function as the heads of NP adjuncts expressing temporal duration (§8.1.1.1) or temporal location (§8.1.1.2). Such Class I nouns may also head a NP complement in a preposition phrase (PP) with *te* (see §8.3). Generally adjuncts headed by Class I temporal nouns occur clause-finally but other positions are attested.

8.1.1.1 Temporal duration
Class I nouns denoting units of time can be modified by numerals and express durational time in NP adjuncts, in either clause-initial (1) or clause-final (2) position. Example (3) shows the NP adjunct preceding an oblique adjunct, while (4) shows the NP adjunct headed by a Class I noun following a NP adjunct headed by an Absolute Location noun.

(1) ***Pepeitaunima na='aria nganangana***
 five SPEC[CLI]=one month
 nani u=pei no po=u.
 there 1SG.SBJ=PST.IPFV go.SEQ stay=1SG.IPFV
 'I went and stayed there for six months.'
 (1-T088-00:09:29.235)

(2) *I-bana e=po=ena* ***tautoi na:ni.***
 LOC-inside 3SG.SBJ=stay=3SG.IPFV three.NHUM day
 'She stays inside for three days.'
 (1-T066-00:01:31.210)

(3) *Mi=to no po **na='aria wik***
 1EXCL.SBJ=EMPH go.SEQ stay SPEC[CLI]=one week
 te=na='uru.
 OBL=SPEC[CLI]=island
 'We went and stayed on the island for one week.'
 (1-T103-00:10:29.671)

(4) E=to   ara po=na=i   Australia **tautoi**   **yia.**
    3SG.SBJ=EMPH PST stay=3SG.IPFV=IRR Australia three.NHUM year
    'He lived in Australia for three years.'
    (2-E019)

8.1.1.2 Temporal location

Three nouns expressing periods of the day are Familiar Location nouns, which are marked by the locative case prefix *i-* (see §5.1.4): *navi* 'afternoon', *naviboni* 'evening' and *boni* 'night'. However, there are two more nouns which express periods of the day, *tuiboniboni* 'dawn' and *tuimatamata* 'morning', but these are Class I nouns, which are not marked by the locative case prefix *i-* (see §5.1.2), and can function as the head of a NP adjunct in clause-initial (5) or clause-final position (6)–(7). These forms may be diachronically polymorphemic, consisting of the root *tui* which denotes 'heart', *matamata* which denotes 'early' and *boni* which denotes 'night' or 'twenty-four hours'. Example (5) and (7) show that the adjunct NP can contain a nominal modifier, such as a demonstrative (see §4.5.1) or the intensifier *mamangi* (see §4.7.3).

(5) **Tuimatamata mama** e=nao   i-nongana.
    morning   DEM1 3SG.SBJ=go LOC-beach
    'On that morning, she went to the beach.'
    (2-E026)

(6) Na=mo'udo   i=pei   no   garu=i,
    SPEC[CLI]=dew   3PL.SBJ=PST.IPFV   go.SEQ   collect=IRR
    na=vanua,   **tuiboniboni.**
    SPEC[CLI]=people dawn
    'The people would go and collect the dew at dawn.'
    (1-T044-00:00:27.930)

(7) "Ta=boni   o=naovo=nao=i   **tuimatamata mamangi.**"
    NSPEC[CLI]=day   2SG.SBJ=fly=thither=IRR   morning   INTS
    '"One day, fly in the early morning."'
    (1-T101-00:04:33.397)

8.1 Adjunct noun phrases

Tuimatamata may co-occur in a sequence with an Absolute Location noun expressing time relative to the point of speaking:

(8) **Naonava tuimatamata** *u=ani*   *na=uvi.*
     yesterday morning   1SG.SBJ=eat SPEC[CLI]=yam
     'Yesterday morning I ate yam.'
     (2-E026)

(9) **Va:gi tuimatamata** *u=ani*   *koko'i.*
     now   morning   1SG.SBJ=eat taro
     'This morning I ate taro.'
     (2-E026)

(10) **Natui   tuimatamata** *u=ani*   *kaukau.*
     tomorrow morning   1SG.SBJ=eat sweet.potato
     'Tomorrow morning I'll eat sweet potato.'
     (2-E026)

The noun *boni* may be a Familiar Location noun denoting 'night' (see §5.1.4) or a Class I noun denoting 'twenty-four hour period' (see §5.1.2). As a Class I noun *boni* can head a NP adjunct, occurring in pre-VC (11), clause-initial (12) or clause-final (13) positions. Note that in (11), *boni* is modified by the augmentative suffix *-eta ~ -ota* (see §4.6.3) to denote 'midnight', in (12) *boni* heads a NP in apposition with a quantifier phrase (see §5.6.3) and in (13) *boni* is modified by the plural collective article.

(11) *Enai* **na=boni-eta**   *mi=matono=ma.*
     after SPEC[CLI]=night-AUG   1EXCL.SBJ=awaken=ma
     'Then at midnight we woke up.'
     (1-T103-00:19:15.880)

(12) **Na:=ata   na=boni**   *u=tua*   *dini* *nao*   *i-nongana.*
     some=CLI SPEC[CLI]=day 1SG.SBJ=paddle down   thither LOC-beach
     'Another day I paddled down to the beach.'
     (2-E026)

(13) *Ani* *o=mo~moroko=mu*   **mamena boni~boni.**
     2SG   2SG.SBJ=RD~lie=2SG.IPFV PL.COLL RD~day
     'You lie every day.'
     (2-E009)

8.1.2 Location nouns

Location nouns (§5.1.4) never occur in adposition phrases but function as the heads of adjunct NPs. Generally, these are positioned clause-finally but other positions are attested. The four subtypes of Location nouns are discussed separately in the following sections because the internal characteristics of the adjunct NP can differ and because the syntactic relationship with adjacent NPs and PPs can also differ. While it is attested that the Absolute Location noun *va:sina* 'before, past' can be modified, and all Relational Location nouns may be directly possessed (with a possible coreferential possessor NP), other Location nouns are not attested with modifiers in adjunct NPs. Adjuncts headed by the Absolute Location noun, *o'oemana* 'bush', and adjuncts headed by Absolute Location nouns referring to time can respectively occur in sequences with adjuncts headed by Relational Location nouns or Absolute Location nouns. Adjuncts headed by Familiar Location nouns (except those referring to time) and Relational Location nouns can occur in sequences with PP adjuncts headed by *te*, or NP adjuncts headed by Familiar Location nouns. Adjuncts headed by lexicalised Relational Location nouns do not occur in sequences with other adjuncts, but internally the NP contains the head noun and a complement NP or PP.

8.1.2.1 Absolute Location nouns

Absolute Location nouns (which are not marked by the locative case prefix *i-* and are never directly possessed; see §5.1.4) can function as the heads of adjunct NPs. Papapana is not unusual in this respect as in many Northwest Solomonic languages there are contexts in which an adjunct may be a bare NP without any adpositional element or case-marking and this often includes proper place names and local nouns. As Ross comments in relation to the Oceanic language Minigir, "the fact that the preposition is absent before placenames [...] seems unsurprising, as a placename by default denotes a location and needs no special marking to show that it is a locative expression" (Ross 2007b: 287).

Papapana proper place names can function as clause-final adjuncts expressing location (14), goal (15) and source (16).

(14) *Iara u=pei siodo=u* **Vakonaia**...
 then 1SG.SBJ=PST.IPFV work=1SG.IPFV Wakunai
 'Then (while) I was working in Wakunai...'
 (1-T105-00:19:36.220)

(15) *Iai=ma   si=nao   dini   nao   **Manetai**=ma.*
PROX=ma 1INCL.SBJ=go down thither Manetai=ma
'Then we went down to Manetai.'
(1-T002-00:02:58.630)

(16) *Ta   i=ara   naomai   **France**.*
and 3PL.SBJ=PST come   France
'And they came from France.'
(1-T097-00:03:30.147)

O'oemana is the only other Absolute Location noun which refers to spatial location and can also function as a clause-final adjunct expressing location (17), goal (18) and source (19). *O'oemana* may co-occur with other adjuncts as in (20) and (21). It is unclear whether (20) is a sequence of adjuncts or whether the second adjunct is embedded within and modifying the first adjunct NP. Example (21) however is a sequence of adjuncts; if it were 'inside of the bush' then the Relational Location noun *i-bana* would be directly possessed.

(17) *A:mani mi=ara   ta'opo **o~'oema-na**.*
1EXCL 1EXCL.SBJ=PST hide   RD~taro.garden-DER
'We hid in the bush.'
(2-E009)

(18) *. . . i=to   ara nao **o~'oema-na**,   bau Siapani, aina.*
3PL.SBJ=EMPH PST go RD~taro.garden-DER PL Japanese 3PL
'[Another day] . . .they went into the forest, the Japanese.'
(1-T034-00:12:10.880)

(19) *Na=vanua   i=tavotu   mai   ma:mido*
SPEC[CLI]=people 3PL.SBJ=arrive hither slowly
***o~'oema-na** . . .*
RD~taro.garden-DER
'People came back slowly from the bush . . .'
(1-T105-00:06:11.797)

(20) *E=nao   **o~'oema-na**   i-ata.*
3SG.SBJ=go RD~taro.garden-DER LOC-above
'He went to the bush to the top/to the bush at the top.'
(1-T063-00:03:08.460)

(21) Iara   i=to   tete   nao   **i-bana**   o~'oema-na.
     then   3PL.SBJ=EMPH   enter   go   LOC-inside   RD~taro.garden-DER
     'Then they went inside to the bush.'
     (1-T103-00:03:49.311)

The eight Absolute Location nouns which refer to time demonstrate more variety in their clause position: they can occur as the heads of NP adjuncts after the VC (22), after argument NPs but before the VC (23), or clause-initially (24). Note that to indicate intensity, the noun *va:sina* 'before' may be modified by the intensifier *poto* (see §4.7.3) as in (25) or be reduplicated (26). Example (27) shows that an Absolute Location noun with temporal deixis co-occurring in a sequence with an Absolute Location noun referring to a place.

(22) ...na=au   tue   mama   tue-ni   Papapana
     SPEC=CLII language DEM1   language-CONST   Papapana
     e=taosi=i   **mumurina.**
     3SG.SBJ=finish=IRR   future
     '[His grandparents knew that] . . . this language, Papapana language, will die out in the future.'
     (1-T083-00:01:59.430)

(23) "Taramina   mama   au=arao   **naonava**   e=to
     thing   DEM1   1SG.PSSR[CLI]=brother   yesterday   3SG.SBJ=EMPH
     goni=a."
     pick=3SG.OBJ
     '"My brother picked this thing yesterday."'
     (1-T035-00:03:13.267)

(24) **Nasipuna**   na=gitana   i=atu=a=i.
     sometimes   SPEC[CLI]=agreement   3PL.SBJ=make=3SG.OBJ=IRR
     'Sometimes they made an agreement.'
     (1-T077-00:01:53.940)

(25) **Va:sina poto,** sa=au   maunu   e=pei   ara
     before   INTS   DIM=CLII   woman   3SG.SBJ=PST.IPFV   PST
     po~po=na=i   te=na='uru.
     RD~stay=3SG.IPFV=IRR   OBL=SPEC[CLI]=island
     'Long ago, a young woman lived on an island.'
     (1-T003-00:00:31.890)

(26) **Va~va:sina,** *Teperoi mi=pei po~po=mani=i . . .*
RD~before Teperoi 1EXCL.SBJ=PST.IPFV RD~stay=1EXCL.IPFV=IRR
'Long ago, we lived in Teperoi . . .'
(1-T030-00:00:33.770)

(27) *Aipasi u=to tu'u=i=a* **naonava Vakonaia.**
yes 1SG.SBJ=EMPH meet=TR=3SG.OBJ yesterday Wakunai
'Yes I met him yesterday in Wakunai.'
(2-E008)

8.1.2.2 Familiar Location nouns

In adjunct NPs, the Familiar Location nouns that refer to geographic locations may express location (28), goal (29) or source (30). The examples here are all adjuncts. Most often adjuncts occur clause-finally (28)–(29), but (30) shows the adjunct occuring clause-initially before the VC.

(28) *Iara mi=no agosi=a* ***i-nongana,***
then 1EXCL.SBJ=go.SEQ hold=3SG.OBJ LOC-beach
mi=rasi=a.
1EXCL.SBJ=pull=3SG.OBJ
'Then we went and held him on the beach, we pulled him in.'
(1-T042-00:06:16.310)

(29) *Na=nganangana e=naovo tae nao* ***i-nganisi=ma.***
SPEC[CLI]=moon 3SG.SBJ=fly up thither LOC-sky=ma
'The moon . . . flew up to the sky.'
(1-T065-00:02:22.290)

(30) *Tau **i-ava** mi=de~de=a=mani mama.*
and OBL=sea 1EXCL.SBJ=RD~take=3SG.OBJ=1EXCL.IPFV DEM1
'And we got it from the sea.'
(1-T107-00:01:04.200)

Familiar Location noun adjuncts may co-occur with oblique adjuncts marked by *te* as in (31)–(33) or with other location noun adjuncts (34). In (31)–(34) the adjuncts occur clause-finally. Examples (31) and (32) are sequences of NP and PP adjuncts. Examples (33)–(34) may be sequences or it could be that the second adjunct is embedded within and modifying the first adjunct.

(31) I=to   pu   mai   i-nganisi te=na=au   epu.
     3PL.SBJ=EMPH fall hither LOC-sky   OBL=SPEC=CLII   cloud
     'They fell from the sky, from the clouds.'
     (2-E019)

(32) I=to   atu   ma'ata=ina   na=koko'i
     3PL.SBJ=EMPH make   be.heated=3PL.OBJ SPEC[CLI]=taro
     i-ngonana te=na=au   otana.
     LOC-beach   OBL=SPEC=CLII   pot
     'They cooked the taro on the beach, in the pot.'
     (2-E019)

(33) O=ruvu=ina   na=gono   **te=na=au   otana**
     2SG.SBJ=put=3PL.OBJ   SPEC[CLI]=banana   OBL=SPEC=CLII   pot
     i-ava.
     LOC-sea
     'Put the bananas in the pot, in the sea/Put the bananas in the pot in the sea.'
     (2-E019)

(34) Mi=to   ari=a   **i-nongana i-poana.**
     1EXCL.SBJ=EMPH   dig=3SG.OBJ   LOC-beach LOC-village
     'We buried her on the beach, in the village/We buried her on the beach in the village.'
     (2-E019)

Familiar Location nouns that refer to periods of the day express temporal location and may be clause-initial (35) or clause-final (36).

(35) **"I-navi**   u=to   ani=a=i."
     LOC-afternoon   1SG.SBJ=EMPH   eat=3SG.OBJ=IRR
     '"I'll eat it this afternoon."'
     (1-T031-00:01:37.150)

(36) I=to   naomai   **i-boni.**
     3PL.SBJ=EMPH   come   LOC-night
     'They came at night.'
     (1-T097-00:05:50.802)

8.1.2.3 Relational Location nouns

Relational Location nouns can express location as in (37), goal as in (38) or source as in (43). When occurring as the only adjunct, NPs headed by these Relational Location nouns are only attested in clause-final position as in (37)–(38).

(37) ... *avosia   na=maria   toituna   e=po=na   **i-ata.***
     SUBR   SPEC[CLI]=thing   God   3SG.SBJ=stay=3SG.IPFV   LOC-above
     '... that God lives above.'
     (1-T105-00:01:09.929)

(38) *I=to   naovo=ina=i   **i-ata** ...*
     3PL.SBJ=EMPH   fly=3PL.OBJ=IRR   LOC-above
     'They flew them above ...'
     (1-T034-00:29:00.380)

Relational Location noun adjuncts may precede Familiar Location noun adjuncts (39) or co-occur with other locative obliques marked by the preposition *te* as in (40)–(44), in which case they may precede or follow the PP (compare (40) and (41)). These examples are analysed as sequences of adjuncts because if the second adjunct were modifying the first adjunct, the Relational Location noun would be directly possessed with the second noun as its possessor as in (46) and (47) below. All the sequences of adjuncts in (39)–(44) express location, except (42) which is an adjunct expressing source. Such sequences tend to be clause-final, though the adjuncts occur between the VC and object NP in (40) and preceding the VC in (44).

(39) ... *tena   rasi=ina   na=iana   **i-ata**   **i-namana.***
     SUBR   pull=3PL.OBJ   SPEC[CLI]=fish   LOC-above   LOC-ocean
     '... to pull in fish out on the ocean.'
     (1-T099-00:03:37.380)

(40) ... *ta   e=rave=i=a   **i-ata**   te=na=au   naono*
     and   3SG.SBJ=hang=TR=3SG.OBJ   LOC-above   OBL=SPEC=CLII   tree
     pei   tanga.
     PART   shell.money
     '... and he hung the necklace above on a tree.'
     (1-T029-00:13:14.460)

(41) . . . *o=noe=ina=i=ma* **te=na=au** *'a'u i-bana.*
2SG.SBJ=put=3PL.OBJ=IRR=ma OBL=SPEC=CLII 'a'u LOC-inside
'. . . put them inside in the *'a'u*.'[33]
(1-T036-8-00:00:35.750)

(42) *I=pu mai i-ata te=na=au naono.*
3PL.SBJ=fall hither LOC-above OBL=SPEC=CLII tree
'They fell down from above from the tree.'
(1-T077-00:01:23.780)

(43) *Na=orawi e=tonu=ena i-bana*
SPEC[CLI]=man 3SG.SBJ=stand=3SG.IPFV LOC-inside
te=na=vu~vurau.
OBL=SPEC[CLI]=RD~run
'The man is standing inside in the truck.'
(2-E029-1)

(44) ***I-bana te=na=niunu*** *e=to*
LOC-inside OBL=SPEC[CLI]=coconut 3SG.SBJ=EMPH
po~po=na.
RD~stay=3SG.IPFV
'It lives on the inside in a coconut shell.'
(1-T058-00:06:18.730)

Relational Location nouns can be directly possessed as a comparison of (43) above and (46) below show. When Relational Location nouns are directly possessed, they may be marked only with the direct possessor suffixes as in (45) or with the direct possessor suffixes and a possessor NP as in (46)–(47).

(45) *Bau paga* **i-nguru-mani**
PL shoot LOC-mouth-1EXCL.PSSR
i=pei ma~manene ora=ina=i. . .
3PL.SBJ=PST.IPFV RD~return only=3PL.IPFV=IRR
'The guns were just pointing at our mouths. . .'
(1-T053-00:01:46.060)

---

[33] An *'a'u* is a cooking tool similar to a pestle and mortar, but it is wooden, thin and between one and two metres tall. It is used for mashing food such as bananas.

(46) *Na=orawi   e=tonu=ena   **i-bana-na***
    SPEC[CLI]=man 3SG.SBJ=stand=3SG.IPFV LOC-inside-3SG.PSSR
    na=vu~vurau.
    SPEC[CLI]=RD~run
    'The man is standing in the inside of the truck.'
    (2-E029-1)

(47) *O=no   sapo=a   **i-ata-na**   **na=inu.***
    2SG.SBJ=go.SEQ clean=3SG.OBJ   LOC-above-3SG.PSSR SPEC[CLI]=house
    'Go and clean the top of the house.'
    (2-E029-1)

Relational Location nouns may also be possessed using the prepositional possessive construction with *te* as in (48)–(49). Example (50) also shows that it is possible for the Relational Location noun to be directly possessed in addition to the possessor NP being inside a possessive PP headed by *te*.

(48) *Na=ma'ata   **i-vuna**   te   anau   e=po=na.*
    SPEC[CLI]=brown.coconut LOC-below   OBL   1SG   3SG.SBJ=stay=3SG.IPFV
    'The coconut is below me (lit. at the below of me).'
    (Fieldnotes 16/04/13)

(49) *Nu=pen   **i-butona**   tena nua   inu   e=po=na.*
    SPEC.CLII=pen LOC-middle OBL two[CLI] house 3SG.SBJ=stay=3SG.IPFV
    'The pen is in the middle of the two houses.'
    (Fieldnotes 16/04/13)

(50) *Na=orawi   nu=buku   e=noe=a*
    SPEC.CLI=man SPEC.CLI=book 3SG.SBJ= put=3SG.OBJ
    i-patu-na   te=na=au   'usia.
    LOC-head-3SG.PSSR OBL=SPEC=CLII child
    'The man put the book on the child's head.'
    (2-E015)

8.1.2.4 Lexicalised Relational Location nouns

There are three Relational Location nouns which may function as adjuncts but have a PP complement headed by *te*, or a NP complement headed by a Location noun: *obetena* 'under', *gegetena* 'next to' and *tage-* 'near'. These nouns are invariant in form regardless of the complement; for example, the complements below are 1SG (54), 3SG (55) and 3PL (58). The form *tage-* can however be directly possessed (see example (27) in §5.1.4) suggesting that the forms *obetena*, *gegetena* and *tagena* are lexicalised but may be diachronically divisible into a root and the 3SG possessor suffix *-na* (see §5.1.4).

These Relational Location nouns precede their PP complement in (51)–(55) and precede their locative NP complement in (56)–(57). In (51)–(53) the noun being marked by *te* is a Class I or II noun. The nominal that *te* governs may also be an independent pronoun (54) or Personal proper name (55). These adjuncts express location and typically occur clause-finally, although they may occur in several other positions, such as in (52) where the adjunct precedes the VC.

(51) *U=aputu* **obetena** *te=na=vuni* *kauto.*
1SG.SBJ=sleep under OBL=SPEC[CLI]=trunk terminalia.catappa
'I slept under the Terminalia catappa tree.'
(1-T033-00:00:51.630)

(52) *Anau* **gegetena** *te=na='uru* *u=pei*
1SG next.to OBL=SPEC[CLI=island 1SG.SBJ=PST.IPFV
tuvu=ou.
swim=1SG.IPFV
'I was swimming next to the island.'
(2-E026)

(53) *Mi=ari=a* *na=orawi* **tagena** *te=na=au*
1EXCL.SBJ=dig=3SG.OBJ SPEC[CLI]=man near OBL=SPEC=CLII
naono.
tree
'We buried the man near to the tree.'
(2-E019)

(54) *Aia* *e=tonu=ena* **tagena** *te* *anau.*
3SG 3SG.SBJ=stand=3SG.IPFV near OBL 1SG
'He is standing next to me.'
(2-E026)

(55) E=to   tua   **gegetena te**   **John.**
3SG.SBJ=EMPH paddle next.to   OBL John
'He paddled next to John.'
(2-E019)

(56) . . . *e=pei*   *bio~bio=na*   *nao=i*   **obetena**
3SG.SBJ=PST.IPFV RD~sweep=3SG.IPFV thither=IRR under
i-inu.
LOC-house
'. . . she was sweeping under the house.'
(1-T067-00:00:51.800)

(57) *Mi=ari=i=a*   *nani* *te=na=poana*
1EXCL.SBJ=dig=TR=3SG.OBJ there OBL=SPEC[CLI]=village
mama, ***gegetena i-tanana.***
DEM1   next.to   LOC-road
'We buried him there in that village, next to the road.'
(1-T030-00:03:47.956)

In (58)–(60) the Relational Location noun follows its PP or NP complement, thus it is right-headed rather than the left-headed constructions shown above. This is another instance of the mixture of left-headedness and right-headedness found in Papapana. The adjuncts in (58) and (59)–(60) express location and appear in clause-initial and clause-final position respectively.

(58) ***Tena bau etawa obetena*** *u=pei*   *me=na*
OBL   PL   big   under   1SG.SBJ=PST.IPFV COM=PL.OBJ
po=u=ma.
stay=1SG.IPFV=ma
'I stayed under the chiefs.'
(1-T103-00:09:52.475)

(59) . . .*na:=ata na=poana*   *mi=atu=a*   ***i-tanana***
some=CLI SPEC[CLI]=village 1EXCL.SBJ=make=3SG.OBJ LOC-road
gegetena.
next.to
'. . . we built another village next to the road.'
(1-T030-00:02:52.990)

(60) BRA   i=ara   ta'opo=ami   i-daramu gegetena...
    BRA   3PL.SBJ=PST   hide=1EXCL.OBJ   LOC-river   next.to
    Uruvaovi tagena.
    Uruvaovi near
    'The BRA were hiding from us near the river... near Uruvaovi.'
    (1-T053-00:00:58.440)

8.1.3 Bound noun *peite-* 'own'

The bound noun *peite-* 'own' always takes direct possessor suffixes (see §5.5.1) and denotes 'on one's own' or 'by one's self' in a NP adjunct. The possessed form of *peite-* can function as a clause-level adjunct most often before the VC (61)–(64) but also after the VC (65). Examples (61)–(65) show 1SG, 2SG, 3SG and 3PL possessor suffixes.

(61) "... ta **peite-u**   u=po~po=u   ini."
    and   own-1SG.PSSR   1SG.SBJ=RD~stay=1SG.IPFV   here
    "'... and I live here on my own.'"
    (1-T003-00:01:03.550)

(62) ... ani ara   **peite-mu**   o=nao=i.
    2SG   only   own-2SG.PSSR   2SG.SBJ=go=IRR
    '... you go only on your own.'
    (1-T001-00:02:38.892)

(63) **Peite-na**   e=pei   ena~ena=na   nao=i.
    own-3SG.PSSR   3SG.SBJ=PST.IPFV   RD~sing=3SG.IPFV   thither=IRR
    'She sang alone.'
    (1-T049-00:03:44.720)

(64) Va:gi buriatanana   **peite-ina**   i=re~rete=ina.
    now   young.women   own-3PL.PSSR   3PL.SBJ=RD~walk=3PL.IPFV
    'Today young women walk around by themselves.'
    (1-T040-00:01:19.690)

(65) *Na:=ata=ma   na=boni   e=pei   naomai=ma*
some=CLI=ma SPEC[CLI]=day 3SG.SBJ=PST.IPFV come=ma
peite-na.
own-3SG.PSSR
'One day he came back by himself.'
(1-T063- 00:03:04.390)

The status of *peite-* as a noun is confirmed by the fact it can be modified by the Class II diminutive article *sau* (see §5.3.4) as in (66), or by the limiter *ora ~ ara* 'only' (see §4.7.2) as in (67), or by both (68).

(66) *Anau u=pei   no   po~po=u   sa=au*
1SG   1SG=PST.IPFV go.SEQ RD~stay=1SG.IPFV DIM=CLII
peite-u.
own-1SG.PSSR
'I stayed on my own.'
(1-T098-00:03:37.517)

(67) *John   e=to   tuvu=ena   **peite-na   ora.***
John   3SG.SBJ=EMPH wash=3SG.IPFV own-3SG.PSSR only
'John is washing by himself.'
(2-E007-2A)

(68) *Taim mama u=pei   po=u   sa=au   peite-u*
time   DEM1 1SG=PST.IPFV stay=1SG.IPFV DIM=CLII own-1SG.PSSR
***ora*. . .**
only
'When I'm on my own . . .'
(1-T088-1635.000)

8.2 Deictic locationals

Deictic locationals form a small closed class of three words, which are never modified by any other constituent: *ini* 'here', *nani* 'there' and *inio* 'over there'. These deictic distinctions correspond with the demonstratives that are based on distance relative to the speaker, *iai* 'proximal', *ioi* 'medial', *io'o* 'distal' (see §4.5). Deictic locationals can function as adjuncts (69)–(71) and occur between an argument NP and the VC (69) or after the VC (70)–(71). They can also be the complement of the preposition *merei* (72b).

(69) *"Aruai, a:mani **ini** mi=po=mani."*
no   1EXCL here 1EXCL.SBJ=stay=1EXCL.IPFV
'"No, we're staying here."'
(1-T002-238.840)

(70) *Na=maunu   e=mate   **nani.***
SPEC[CLI]=woman   3SG.SBJ=die   there
'The woman died there.'
(1-T029-00:02:35.436)

(71) *". . . vavine-ira   mama e=to   nai=ena   **inio.**"*
sibling-1INCL.PSSR DEM1 3SG.SBJ=EMPH marry=3SG.IPFV over.there
'"[We're going to live with] . . . our cousin who is married there."'
(1-T042-00:00:48.110)

The excerpt in (72) is from a text in which the speaker recounts events that she experienced during the Bougainville Crisis. In this part of her story, she and some other women have been found out walking in the bush and are being questioned by the Papua New Guinea army about their contact with the Bougainville Revolutionary Army (BRA). In (72b) *nani* refers to the area in which they were walking and is the complement of the preposition *merei*, in a PP modifying the head noun *BRA*, while in (72c) *nani* refers to the police station where the army were holding them and is the goal adjunct of *noe* 'put'.

(72) a. *"Aipasi a:mani BRA mi=tu'u=ina   ta   enai*
       yes   1EXCL BRA 1EXCL.SBJ=meet=3PL.OBJ and DEM2
       oina=poana."
       3PL.PSSR[CLI]=village
       '"Yes we met the BRA but that's their home."'
       (1-T053-00:04:33.800)
   b. *"BRA **merei   nani** a:mani mi=tu'u=ina."*
       BRA ATTRIB there 1EXCL 1EXCL.SBJ=meet=3PL.OBJ
       '"The BRA from there, we met them."'
       (1-T053-00:04:37.340)
   c. *"I=noe=ami=ma   **nani**. . ."*
       3PL.SBJ=put=1EXCL.OBJ=ma   there
       'They put us there'
       (1-T053-00:04:40.130)

8.3 Adposition phrases

Papapana is like most Oceanic and Northwest Solomonic languages in having a small, closed class of adpositions which introduce participants with a wide range of semantic roles. The preposition *te* expresses temporal location, static spatial location, the goal to which movement or action is directed, the source from which movement or action originates, the semantic roles of instrument, addressee, recipient and beneficiary, and it can also mark possession. While a number of Northwest Solomonic languages have a preposition which is formally identical to *te*, Papapana's other prepositions attributive *merei* and *avosia* 'like' do not, to my knowledge, have cognates, while the preposition *eangoiena* 'until' and the nascent postposition *tomana* 'with' have likely arisen as adpositions due to processes of lexicalisation and grammaticalisation, induced by contact with Tok Pisin and the Papuan language Rotokas respectively.

Adpositions in Papapana are invariant in form (except for *te* which has the form *tena* when the NP is plural or marked by a diminutive article; see §8.3.1.4), they are all prepositions (except *tomana* 'with', a nascent postposition), and they all always have a complement NP with which they form a preposition or postposition phrase (PP). PPs with *te, avosia, eangoiena* and *tomana* function as clausal adjuncts: *te* expresses spatial location (location, goal, source) and temporal location, and sometimes the semantic roles of instrument, addressee, recipient and beneficiary (§8.3.1), *eangoiena* marks temporal duration (§8.3.2), *avosia* denotes similarity or manner (§8.3.3), while postposition *tomana* marks accompaniment (§8.3.4).

Possessive PPs headed by *te* and attributive PPs headed by *merei* function as postnominal modifiers (see §4.1, §4.8 and §5.5.5), while locative PPs with *te* and attributive PPs with *merei* function as predicates in a verbless clause (see §9.6.3 and §9.6.4). The description of the internal characteristics of PPs with *te* presented here in §8.3.1, also applies to adnominal and predicate PPs headed by *te*.

Tena, merei, avosia, and *eangoiena* are also subordinators introducing adverbial clauses (see §10.3), while *tena* and *avosia* are also subordinators introducing complement clauses (see §10.4). Although one could broaden the definition of a preposition and say that prepositions can have either NP or clausal complements, I am distinguishing between the two word classes because *tena, merei* and *avosia* have different meanings as subordinators and because not all prepositions can have clausal complements.

8.3.1 Preposition *te*

All nominals except Location nouns can occur in a PP with the preposition *te* which can express spatial location (location, goal, source) and temporal location, and sometimes the semantic roles of instrument, addressee, recipient and beneficiary. With regards to spatial location, the exact thematic role is determined by the verb and directionals and not by the preposition. Usually PPs are clause-final, following the VC and any core arguments. However, a few of the examples below show different clause orders. In (81) and (83), the oblique precedes the VC, while in (77) the oblique occurs between the subject NP and the VC.

The preposition *te* is a reflex of the POc preposition *i ta* which occurred with a common NP marked by an article (Ross 2007b: 284). The following sections describe the interaction of *te* with different kinds of nouns and prenominal modifiers. When the NP complement begins with a possessor proclitic (§8.3.1.1), or the NP head is a Personal noun that may be marked by the Personal specific article *e-* (§8.3.1.2), *te* does not form a long vowel with *e-* nor a phonological word with the possessor proclitic or Personal noun. This demonstrates that *te* is not a clitic. However, since *te* is monomoraic, it does not satisfy word minimality (see §3.3.2) and thus sometimes there is compensatory lengthening of the vowel /e/ in *te*. Furthermore, with NPs that begin with the specific articles *na=* or *nau*, *te* does cliticise to the article giving the forms *tena=* and *tenau* (§8.3.1.3). This may represent a change in progress, especially as there is evidence that *tena* has become a grammaticalised form (see §8.3.1.4, §10.3 and §10.4).

8.3.1.1 *te* with possessor proclitics

When the preposition *te* licences a NP with a possessor proclitic, *te* does not cliticise to the possessor proclitic, as shown in the oblique adjuncts (73) and (74), which express location and goal.

(73) *E=o'ovana* **te** *ami=pa'apena* ...
    3SG.SBJ=grow OBL 1EXCL.PSSR[CLI]=area
    'It grows in our area ...'
    (1-T058-00:01:35.970)

(74) *E=nao manene* **te** *ena=poana.*
    3SG.SBJ=go return OBL 3SG.PSSR[CLI]=village
    'She went back to her village.'
    (1-T012-00:03:37.940)

8.3.1.2 *te* with Personal nouns

When the preposition *te* licences a NP headed by a Personal kinship term noun, the Personal specific article *e-* remains prefixed to the head noun as in (75) and (78) and does not form a phonological word with *te*. Personal proper name nouns are not marked by an article whether they are in an oblique (76), or not (see §5.1.1), and they also do not form a phonological word with *te*. Examples (75)–(77) are all oblique adjuncts expressing goal, while (78) could be interpreted as a goal or addressee of the intransitive verb *vo'o* 'call out'.

(75) E=de   tae=a   nao   **te**   **e-tubu-na.**
     3SG.SBJ=take up=3SG.OBJ thither OBL PERS-grandparent-3SG.PSSR
     'He took it up to his grandmother.'
     (1-T035-00:01:20.880)

(76) E=to   naovo **te**   **Maravuruai.**
     3SG.SBJ=EMPH fly   OBL Maravuruai
     'It flew to Maravuruai.'
     (1-T074-00:01:21.350)

(77) "Anau **te**   ia'a   u=nao~nao=u."
     1SG   OBL Mum   1SG.SBJ=RD~go=1SG.IPFV
     "'I'm going to Mum.'"
     (1-T031-00:09:30.360)

(78) E=to   vo'o   nao   **te**   **e-sina-na.**
     3SG.SBJ=EMPH call.out thither OBL PERS-mother-3SG.PSSR
     'He shouted to his mother.'
     (1-T016-00:01:14.000)

In (79a) the oblique adjunct has the semantic role of beneficiary, though as (79b) shows, applicative *i* has been added to the monotransitive A-verb *atono* 'bring' (see §6.4.2.1) to increase valency and promote the beneficiary to primary object. Similarly in (80a) the oblique adjunct has the semantic role of beneficiary but, in (80b), applicative *i* derives a ditransitive verb where the new argument is a primary object with a beneficiary role.

(79) a. *Tauvita   koko'i Anna   e=atono=ina   **te**   **John?**
        how.many taro   Anna   3SG.SBJ=bring=3PL.OBJ OBL John
        'How many taros did Anna bring for John?'
        (2-E029-1)

b. *Tauvita koko'i Anna e=atono i=a Bob?*
how.many taro Anna 3SG.SBJ=bring APPL=3SG.OBJ Bob
'How many taros did Anna bring for Bob?'
(2-E029-1)

(80) a. *Te:a ena=au gono Peter e=to averu=a*
who 3SG.PSSR=CLII banana Peter 3SG.SBJ=EMPH steal=3SG.OBJ
te Emma?
OBL Emma
'Whose banana did Peter steal for Emma?'
(2-E029-1)

b. *Nu=marei e=averu i=a na=iana*
SPEC.CLII=bird 3SG.SBJ=steal APPL=3SG.OBJ SPEC[CLI]=fish
nu=kakau.
SPEC.CLII=dog
'The bird stole the fish for the dog.'
(2-E026)

8.3.1.3 *te* with Class I/II nouns

When the preposition *te* licences a NP headed by a Class I or II noun, the Class I specific article *na=* and the Class II specific article *nau* usually form a phonological word with the preposition *te*, resulting in the forms *tena=* and *tenau* as in (81)–(85). As (81) shows, the form is *tenau* even with Class II nouns such as *daramu* 'water' which, when not in oblique constructions, are marked by the Class II specific article allomorph *nu=*. The cliticisation of *te* to the article could be motivated by the fact that *te* is monomoraic and does not satisfy word minimality (see §3.3.2).

Example (81) is an oblique adjunct expressing location, (82) is an oblique adjunct expressing source, (83) is an oblique adjunct expressing temporal location, (84) is an oblique argument with a recipient role (which is usually a core argument for the ditransitive verb *ma'a* 'give') and (85) is an oblique adjunct with the semantic role of instrument.

(81) ***Te=na=perete te=na=au*** *daramu e=to*
OBL=SPEC[CLI]=plate OBL=SPEC=CLII water 3SG.SBJ=EMPH
ruvu=i=a.
put=TR=3SG.OBJ
'He put it on the plate in the water.'
(1-T073-00:00:57.900)

(82) ... *mi=no   de   mai   **te=na=kaukau.***
     1EXCL.SBJ=go.SEQ take   hither OBL=SPEC[CLI]=sweet.potato
     '[Okay if we want to grate tapioca] . . . we go and get it from the garden.'
     (1-T038-00:00:21.280)

(83) "***Te=na=na:ni***   *mama iai   u=to   nao=i . . .*"
     OBL=SPEC[CLI]=day   DEM1 PROX 1SG.SBJ=EMPH go=IRR
     "'When I go on this day . . .'"
     (1-T026-00:02:17.850)

(84) *Emma e=ma'=i=a   na=tamute*
     Emma 3SG.SBJ=give=TR=3SG.OBJ SPEC[CLI]=mango
     te=na=orawi   *mama e=to   roros=i=a*
     OBL=SPEC[CLI]=man REL   3SG.SBJ=EMPH see=TR=3SG.OBJ
     naonava.
     yesterday
     'Emma gave the mango to the man whom she saw yesterday.'
     (2-E021-1)

(85) *Ben e=tepe=a   nu=naono   **te=na=tora:ra.***
     Ben 3SG.SBJ=cut=3SG.OBJ SPEC.CLII=tree   OBL=SPEC[CLI]=axe
     'Ben cut the tree with an axe.'
     (2-E026)

Quite often, NPs with the semantic role of instrument do not appear in a PP with *te* as for example in (86)–(89) (note that (86) contrasts with (85) above).

(86) *Ben e=tepe=a   nu=naono   **na=tora:ra.***
     Ben 3SG.SBJ=cut=3SG.OBJ SPEC.CLII=tree   SPEC[CLI]=axe
     'Ben cut the tree with an axe.'
     (2-E026)

(87) *Na=orawi   e=o'omu=a   nu=ovata   **pei***
     SPEC[CLI]=man   3SG.SBJ=cut=3SG.OBJ   SPEC.CLII=bread PART
     to'o~to'o.
     RD~cut
     'The man cut the bread with a knife.'
     (2-E009)

(88) *E=to   vagasi=a   nu=obutu   **nu=risi***
     3SG.SBJ=EMPH tie=3SG.OBJ SPEC.CLII=canoe SPEC.CLII=rope
     nu=ae   itaita.
     SPEC.CLII=NEG strong
     'He tied up the canoe with a weak rope.'
     (1-T035-00:04:18.208)

(89) ***O'opuaiboro iai***   na='usia   iai
     plant.sp   PROX SPEC[CLI]=child PROX
     mi=si~sigi=ina=amani.
     1EXCL.SBJ=RD~wash=3PL.OBJ=1EXCL.IPFV
     'We wash children with this *o'opuaiboro*.'
     (1-T058-00:01:22.970)

I considered whether (86)–(89) were ditransitive, with the instrument being one of the objects. Teop has this type of ditransitive clause, in which the O1 is patient and the O2 is instrument (Mosel 2007: 14). However, the Papapana verbs in these examples are monotransitive (see §6.4.2) and there is no applicative *i* to increase valency and promote the instrument to O1. Even if the instrument were being promoted to O2, one would still expect to see applicative *i* since the verbs would be derived ditransitives. It could be the case that the instrument is actually the object or the subject as is feasible in, (90) and (91a) and (92a) respectively. However, this is not feasible for (86)–(87) above where there are three overt NPs, nor for (89) above where the subject proclitic is 1EXCL but the overt NP referents are 3SG and 3PL. The instrument is thus an adjunct and it could simply be the case that instruments can sometimes be NP adjuncts rather than PP adjuncts. Alternatively, *te* is being dropped by some speakers: indeed in an elicitation session when I asked speakers to add in a certain NP as the actor or patient to (88)–(89) and (91)–(92) (thus increasing the number of NPs to three), they then used *te* to introduce the instrument as (91b) and (92b) show.

(90) ***Na=tuma***   o=tavi=a=i.
     SPEC[CLI]=coconut.shaving 2SG.SBJ=rub=3SG.OBJ=IRR
     'You rub it with the coconut shavings./You rub the coconut shavings.'
     (1-T036-7-00:00:24.630)

(91) a. ***Nu=sipa***   *e=ta~taguv=i=a=i*
SPEC.CLII=grill   3SG.SBJ=RD~cover=TR=3SG.OBJ=IRR
nu=patu-na.[34]
SPEC.CLII=head-3SG.PSSR
'He covered his head with a grill./A grill covered his head.'
(1-T052-00:03:04.710)
b. *John e=ta~taguv=i=a*   *nu=patu-na*
John 3SG.SBJ=RD~cover=TR=3SG.OBJ   SPEC.CLII=head-3SG.PSSR
te=na=au   ***si:pa.***
OBL=SPEC=CLII   grill
'John covered his head with a grill.'
(2-E018)

(92) a. *E=nopa*   *dini=a*   *mai*   ***nu=maria,***
3SG.SBJ=shoot   down=3SG.OBJ   hither   SPEC.CLII=thing
nu=api.
SPEC.CLII=bamboo
'He shot him down with the what's-it-called, the bamboo./The bamboo shot him down.'
(1-T049-00:01:18.700)
b. *John e=nopa*   *dini=a*   *mai*   Peter ***te=na=au***
John 3SG.SBJ=shoot   down=3SG.OBJ   hither   Peter   OBL=SPEC=CLII
api.
bamboo
'John shot down Peter with the bamboo.'
(2-E018)

8.3.1.4 *te* with other articles and numerals

In oblique constructions, the plural article *bau*, the Class I and II diminutive articles *si=* and *sau ~ su=* and the cardinal numeral modifiers follow *tena* regardless of the noun class of the noun. This contrasts with core argument NPs, where the plural article *bau* does not distinguish noun class and never co-occurs with the specific articles *e-*, *na=* or *nau ~ nu=* (see §5.3.2), where the Class I and II diminutive articles *si=* and *sau ~ su=* also do not co-occur with the specific articles (see §5.3.4), and where the cardinal numeral modifiers (except 'one') do not co-occur

---

[34] The *=i* after the verb is clearly the transitive marker and not the applicative marker because it alters the verb root's phonology from *taguvu* to *taguv* (see §6.5.1.1). Furthermore, it is unclear why the speaker reduplicates the verb in example (91) and uses the irrealis marker in (91a).

with the specific articles either but may be marked by the Class II noun marker *au* (see §5.4.2). The fact that in obliques, all of these prenominal modifiers co-occur with *tena* regardless of the noun class of the noun, suggests that the combination of the preposition *te* and the Class I specific article *na* has become a grammaticalized form (see also §10.3 and §10.4 where *tena* is a subordinator):

Examples (93)–(95) show *tena bau* in oblique adjuncts expressing spatial location and temporal location with Class I nouns; (96) shows *tena bau* in an oblique argument expressing goal with a Class II noun (*oto* 'board' is usually a transitive verb); (97) shows *tena* with the numeral modifier *nua* 'two' and the Class II marker *au* in an oblique adjunct expressing source; (98) shows *tena* with Tok Pisin loanwords in an oblique adjunct expressing temporal location, and (99) shows *tena* with the Class II diminutive article *sau* in an oblique adjunct expressing goal.

(93) Avosia   a:mani   mi=pei   ta'opo=ina=i   **tena   bau**
     SUBR   1EXCL   1EXCL.SBJ=PST.IPFV   hide=3PL.OBJ=IRR   OBL   PL
     tanana.
     road
     'So we used to hide from them on the roads.'
     (1-T034- 00:28:14.155)

(94) **Tena   bau   Sande,**   mi=to   matono=i . . .
     OBL   PL   Sunday   1EXCL.SBJ=EMPH   awaken=IRR
     'On Sundays, we wake up . . .'
     (2-E024)

(95) **Tena   bau   tuimatamata**   mi=to   matono=i,
     OBL   PL   morning   1EXCL.SBJ=EMPH   awaken=IRR
     mi=tutuvu=i . . .
     1EXCL.SBJ=wash=IRR
     'Every morning we wake up, we wash . . .'
     (1-T011-00:00:51.670)

(96) . . .mi=oto   **tena   bau   obutu** . . .
     1EXCL.SBJ=board   OBL   PL   canoe
     '. . .we got into the canoes . . .'
     (1-T043a-00:01:15.740)

(97) *Ta   nani   **tena nua=au**   'usia mama*...
     and there OBL two=CLII child DEM1
     'And there from these two children...'
     (1-T083-00:03:43.200)

(98) *"O=naomai   **tena naen kirok**."*
     2SG.SBJ=come OBL nine o'clock
     '"Come at nine o'clock."'
     (1-T088-00:44:58.400)

(99) *Mi=ru~ruvu=i=a   nao=i   **tena sa=au   pe'uri**.*
     1EXCL.SBJ=RD~put=TR=3SG.OBJ thither=IRR OBL DIM=CLII basket
     'We put it into small baskets.'
     (1-T085-00:04:03.810)

8.3.2 Preposition *eangoiena* 'until'

Durational time may be expressed in an oblique adjunct with the preposition *eangoiena* 'until' and an Absolute Location noun that expresses a time relative to the time of speaking, in either clause-initial (100)–(101) or clause-final position (101). In (101) *eangoiena* also expresses durational time but the speaker switches to English for the NP, which contains a numeral and a noun expressing a unit of time. *Eangoiena* 'until' may also be a subordinator, introducing an adverbial clause that expresses the end point of a duration of time (see §10.3.4.2).

(100) *Enai **eangoiena** va:gi na:=bau   vanua-i   sikuna i=ara*
      after until   now   some=PL   people-CONST   ship   3PL.SBJ=PST
      naomai.
      come
      'So until today some foreigners (lit. ship people) come.'
      (1-T034-00:39:15.380)

(101) ***Eangoiena**=ma six year-s   iai   u=po   ora=u*
      until=ma   six year-PL   PROX 1SG.SBJ=stay only=1SG.IPFV
      i-poana=ma.
      LOC-village=ma
      'I've just been in the village for six years.'
      (1-T087-00:03:20.820)

(102) *Aia e=aputu=i* **eangoiena natui.**
 3SG 3SG.SBJ=sleep=IRR until tomorrow
 'He will sleep until tomorrow.'
 (2-E019)

Eangoiena is likely to be a lexicalised form of the modal verb *eangoi* and the 3SG postverbal subject-indexing (PSI) enclitic *=ena*. This modal verb may occur inside the VC with PSI enclitics in which case it expresses ability and requires a clausal complement (see §10.4.1 and §10.4.2). *Eangoiena* is also a lexicalised clause-level adverb expressing ability (see §8.4.2.1). The fact that *eangoiena* is also a preposition denoting 'until' is likely to be due to contact with Tok Pisin where *inap* is also a verb expressing ability as well as a preposition denoting 'until' (Smith-Dennis 2017).

8.3.3 Preposition *avosia* 'like'

The preposition *avosia* 'like' and its NP complement function as clause-final oblique adjuncts expressing similarity or manner as in (103). *Avosia* may also be a subordinator, introducing finite adverbial clauses expressing similarity or manner (§10.3.9) or finite complement clauses (§10.4).

(103) "*O=nao maisia,* **avosia aniau iai.**"
 2SG.SBJ=go okay like 1SG PROX
 '"Go okay, like me."'
 (1-T072-00:01:09.760)

Most often, PPs headed by *avosia* are the complement of the verb *vowa ~ vewa* 'be like, in the way of', which can be an independent verb (104) but usually occurs in a serial verb construction (105)–(107) (see §6.6.1 and §6.6.2.6). *Vowa ~ vewa* 'be like, in the way of' is always the second verb in the series, and there are no restrictions on the type of verb which can be the first verb in the series. Other complements of *vowa ~ vewa* 'be like, in the way of' include finite complements clauses introduced by *avosia* (§10.4.1) or the interrogative term *avoa* (§9.3.2.3.4).

(104) ...*e=ae*   *vewa=na*   *avosia iai*   *na=po*
3SG.SBJ=NEG be.like=3SG.IPFV like   PROX SPEC[CLI]=stay
mama va:gi.
DEM1   now
'[The lifestyle I saw] . . . wasn't like this lifestyle now.'
(1-T025-00:00:35.560)

(105) "... *i=to*   *pei*   *togana vowa=ina=i*   *avosia*
3PL.SBJ=EMPH PST.IPFV smell   be.like=3PL.IPFV=IRR like
na=maria   ***na=menaga.***"
SPEC[CLI]=thing SPEC[CLI]=creamed.banana
"'[Mother, I was carrying the banana leaves] . . . they smelt like what's-it-called, *menaga*.'"
(1-T052-00:01:22.000)

(106) *Na=orawi*   *e=etawa*   *vowa=ena*   *avosia*
SPEC[CLI]=man 3SG.SBJ=big be.like=3SG.IPFV like
na=maunu.
SPEC[CLI]=woman
'The man is big like the woman./The man is as big as the woman.'
(2-E005)

(107) *E=no*   *tavotu vewa=i*   *avosia na='o'o.*
3SG.SBJ=go.SEQ arrive be.like=IRR like   SPEC[CLI]=k.o.basket
'It turns out like an *'o'o* basket.'[35]
(1-T102-00:04:10.210)

8.3.4 Nascent postposition *tomana* 'with'

Obliques expressing accompaniment are formed with the comitative marker *tomana* as in (108)–(111). *Tomana* follows the head noun as in (108)–(109), or follows a directly possessed head noun as in (110). In (111) the head noun is a compound. *Tomana* as a comitative marker is not attested with independent pronouns. Oblique adjuncts with *tomana* are clause-final in the attested data.

---

[35] This is a traditional basket made from a type of vine.

(108) *Mi=gaganini   viviro'o=mani   **na='usia   tomana.***
      1EXCL.SBJ=play around=1EXCL.IPFV SPEC[CLI]=child COM
      'We used to play around with the children.'
      (1-T010-44.830)

(109) *...sibuava nani   si=asi=ina   **seida'o   tomana.***
      old.women there 1INCL.SBJ=leave=3PL.OBJ old.man   COM
      '[Then in the afternoon] . . . we left the old women there with an old man.'
      (1-T002-130.690)

(110) *Auana ora   i=pei   ara   po~po=ina=i*
      3DU   only   3PL.SBJ=PST.IPFV   PST   RD~live=3PL.IPFV=IRR
      tubu-ina   tomana.
      grandparent-3PL.PSSR   COM
      'Only the two of them lived with their grandmother.'
      (1-T035-00:02:18.656)

(111) *Na:=ata   na=boni   u=pei   gaganini=ou   i-nongana*
      some=PL   SPEC[CLI]=day   1SG.SBJ=PST.IPFV play=1SG.IPFV   LOC-beach
      au=nua   arao   nanasi tomana.
      1SG.PSSR=two[CLI]   brother   cousin COM
      'One day I was playing on the beach with my two cousins.'
      (1-T042-00:00:23.710)

There are a few examples which show *tomana* following the head noun but preceding a possessive PP (112)–(113) or a relative clause (114). Note that in (112) the NP is the complement of a quantifier.

(112) *Ta   na=orawi   tena   vono e=naomai   **na:=bau   kakau***
      and   SPEC[CLI]=man   SUBR   hunt 3SG.SBJ=come   some=PL   dog
      tomana te   aia.
      COM   OBL   3SG
      'And a man came to hunt pigs with some dogs of his.'
      (1-T049-00:03:49.260)

(113) ***Ami=stasiu   tomana te   a:mani.***
      1EXCL.PSSR[CLI]=statue   COM   OBL   1EXCL
      'With our statue.'
      (1-T065-00:03:29.190)

(114) *E=pei   po=ena=i,   **ena=maunu   tomana***
3SG.SBJ=PST.IPFV stay=3SG.IPFV=IRR 3SG.PSSR[CLI]=woman COM
mama i=to   ma'=i=a.
REL   3PL.SBJ=EMPH give=TR=3SG.OBJ
'He lived with his wife that they gave him.'
(1-T029-00:01:51.702)

Syntactically *tomana* is therefore inside the NP in a particular position after possessor suffixes but before possessive PPs and relative clauses, and as such it is not the head of a postposition phrase. Although speakers confirmed that (112)–(114) were grammatical, it should be noted that these are the only examples I have found of this sort in the corpus. When I tried to elicit further examples of nouns with a comitative semantic role that had possessive PPs or relative clauses modifying them, speakers used the applicative comitative construction in which the comitative NP is the object of the verb (see §6.5.4). Although *tomana* has not yet developed its own category projection, it has nevertheless taken on the characteristics of a postposition because it follows the noun to mark a comitative relation; this may be the result of contact with neighbouring Papuan languages as Oceanic languages generally have prepositions and not postpositions (see Smith 2016a). In particular, it seems *tomana* may have grammaticalised as a comitative marker from the Papapana additive marker denoting 'too' (see §4.7.7), again perhaps under the influence of neighbouring Papuan language Rotokas, in which *tapo(ro)* also denotes 'also' and 'with' (see Smith 2015a: 340–341).[36] This history might explain why *tomana* as a comitative marker precedes PPs and relative clauses, as (115) and (116) show that *tomana* as an additive marker also precedes PPs and relative clauses. In either language, it is not surprising that an additive marker and a comitative marker (addition of participants) are polysemous since such semantic notions cluster around an "additive" perspective.

(115) *U=to   po=u   avosia **na=etawa   tomana***
1SG.SBJ=EMPH stay=1SG.IPFV like   SPEC[CLI]=big too
***merei   i-poana*. . .**
ATTRIB LOC-village
'I'm like chief of the village too . . .'
(1-T093-00:04:09.878)

---

[36] Despite the publication year, the analysis of *tomana* in Smith (2015a) postdates that of Smith (2016a).

(116) *Na=skuru*   **tomana iai**   **so=umunu=era**...
SPEC[CLI]=school too   PROX   1INCL.SBJ=sit=1INCL.IPFV
'The school where we're sitting too... [during the war we looked after it].'
(1-T029-00:34:44.343)

8.4 Clause-level adverbs

As discussed in §6.8, adverbs belong to a small but seemingly open class of words which can optionally modify a verb or a clause, providing information about temporal location, aspect and mode, spatial location and manner. In Papapana, adverbs operating at the clausal level include spatial, manner and modal adverbs which can occur clause-initially, clause-finally or between an argument NP and the VC (§8.4.1). Three of the manner and spatial adverbs are also attested inside the VC in postverbal position (see §6.8.2). There is no correlation between the position of the adverb and its semantics. There are two further clause-level modal adverbs that are restricted to preceding the VC (§8.4.2). One of these, *avirua* 'not yet' also occurs inside the VC in preverbal position (§6.8.1), while the other, *eangoiena* expresses ability and has likely lexicalised from the modal verb *eangoi* and the 3SG PSI enclitic =*ena* (§8.4.2.1).

8.4.1 Spatial, manner and modal adverbs

There are five clause-level adverbs that can precede or follow the VC: the spatial adverbs *viviro'o* 'around' and *reareana* 'far', the manner adverbs *ma:mido* 'slowly' and *papasi* 'quickly' and the epistemic adverb *bea* 'maybe'. The adverbs *papasi* 'quickly', *viviro'o* 'around' and *reareana* 'far' are also attested within the VC (see §6.8.2).

These adverbs can immediately precede the VC as in (117)–(120). In (117) there is no preverbal argument NP but in (118)–(119) the adverb occurs between a preverbal subject NP and the VC, and in (120) between a preverbal object NP and the VC.

(117) **Ma:mido** *e=pei*   *gau~gaunu=a=na=i*
slowly 3SG.SBJ=PST.IPFV RD~write=3SG.OBJ=3SG.IPFV=IRR
nu=pepa.
SPEC.CLII=letter
'He was writing the letter slowly.'
(2-E008)

(118) *Ami=bau   'usia iai **reareana** i=pei*
      1EXCL.PSSR=PL child PROX far   3PL.SBJ=PST.IPFV
      po=ina=i.
      stay=3PL.IPFV=IRR
      'Our children lived far away.'
      (1-T090-00:01:22.484)

(119) *Robert **bea**   e=vau~vau=i=a=na*
      Robert maybe 3SG.SBJ=RD~look.after=TR=3SG.OBJ=3SG.IPFV
      nu=boro.
      SPEC.CLII=pig
      'Maybe Robert is looking after the pig.'
      (2-E016)

(120) *Bau siodo **viviro'o** u=pei   no*
      PL work around   1SG.SBJ=PST.IPFV go.SEQ
      atu=ina=u.
      make=3PL.OBJ=1SG.IPFV
      'I was going and doing jobs all over the place.'
      (1-T087-00:02:43.390)

These adverbs can also immediately follow the VC as in (121)–(124).

(121) *...iara tena bau vuni   naono na=iana   i=pagana   **viviro'o**.*
      then OBL PL trunk tree SPEC[CLI]=fish 3PL.SBJ=stick around
      '...then the fish got stuck all over the place in the tree trunks.'
      (1-T105-00:05:40.391)

(122) *Na=vanua   i=tavotu   mai   **ma:mido***
      SPEC[CLI]=people 3PL.SBJ=arrive hither slowly
      o~'oema-na...
      RD~taro.garden-DER
      'People came back slowly from the bush...'
      (1-T105-00:06:11.797)

(123) *Casilda e=vamamatau=ena   **bea**.*
      Casilda 3SG.SBJ=teach=3SG.IPFV maybe
      'Maybe Casilda is teaching.'
      (2-E016)

(124) ". . . avosia   e=taosi   **papasi,** nu=risi   merei   obutu."
     SUBR   3SG.SBJ=finish quickly, SPEC.CLII=rope ATTRIB canoe
     "'. . . so that it breaks quickly, the canoe rope.'"
     (1-T035-00:04:07.880)

The adjaceny of the adverbs to the VC might suggest that there are additional adverb positions inside the VC not already accounted for, that is, that the VC does not begin with the subject proclitic and end with the irrealis mode =*i* or discontinuous repetitive aspect =*re*. However, examples (125)–(127) show that the adverb can be separated from the VC by other adjuncts when the adverb is postverbal (125) and preverbal (126) and by the subject NP when the adverb is in preverbal position (127). Therefore these adverbs are not part of the VC.

(125) *E=no*   *peri=a=i*   *tena bau naono* **viviro'o.**
     3SG.SBJ=go.SEQ find=3SG.OBJ=IRR OBL PL tree   around
     'She went and looked for it in all the trees around.'
     (1-T029-00:03:52.620)

(126) *Na=vanua*   **ma:mido**   *nani*
     SPEC[CLI]=people slowly   there
     i=pei   *te~tete*   *vewa=ina*   *mai=i*   *tena bau*
     3PL.SBJ=PST.IPFV RD~enter be.like=3PL.IPFV hither=IRR OBL PL
     poana
     village
     'Slowly people were joining like that there from the villages.'
     (1-T034-00:25:34.605)

(127) *Enai* **bea**   *John* *e=oto=i*   *te=na=au*   *obutu.*
     after maybe John   3SG.SBJ=board=IRR OBL=SPEC=CLII canoe
     'Then maybe John will board the canoe.'
     (2-E007)

8.4.2 Modal adverbs *eangoiena* and *avirua*

There are two clause-level modal adverbs: *eangoiena* expresses ability and *avirua* denotes 'not yet'. These adverbs only precede the VC. These adverbs are discussed separately in the following two sections as *eangoiena* is thought to derive from a verb and can also be a preposition or subordinator, while *avirua* is also found as a VC-internal adverb.

8.4.2.1 Ability: *eangoiena*

As a clause-level adverb expressing ability (CAP[ability]), *eangoiena* only precedes the VC as in (128)–(131). Before *eangoiena*, there may be an argument NP as in (129)–(131), where the NP is headed by an independent pronoun, Personal proper noun or Personal kinship noun respectively. The form *eangoiena* has likely lexicalised from the modal verb *eangoi* and the 3SG PSI enclitic =*ena*: as a verb, *eangoi* expresses ability and is always marked by one of the PSI enclitics and requires a clausal complement (see §10.4.1 and §10.4.2). The modal adverb *eangoiena* or the modal verb *eangoi* are the only ways of expressing ability in Papapana. In its lexicalised form, *eangoiena* may also be a preposition or subordinator denoting 'until' (see §8.3.2 and §10.3.4.2).

(128) **Eangoiena** o=adu~adu=i=a=i na=orawi . . .
      CAP   2SG.SBJ=RD~destroy=TR=3SG.OBJ=IRR SPEC[CLI]=man
      'You can harm a man . . .'
      (1-T034-00:19:35.952)

(129) *"Ani* **eangoiena** *o=oi dini=ina nao=i."*
      2SG CAP   2SG.SBJ=take down=3PL.OBJ thither=IRR
      '"You can take them down."'
      (1-T071-00:07:47.800)

(130) *Jerry* **eangoiena** *e=atun=i=a=i nu=boro.*
      Jerry CAP   3SG.SBJ=attack=TR=3SG.OBJ=IRR SPEC.CLII=pig
      'Jerry can attack the pig.'
      (2-E007-1)

(131) *Bau sina-mani* **eangoiena** *i='ire'ire=i nani.*
      PL mother-1EXCL.PSSR CAP   3PL.SBJ=be.angry=IRR there
      'Our mothers could get cross there.'
      (1-T094-00:01:21.314)

8.4.2.2 *avirua* 'not yet'

The adverb *avirua* 'not yet' precedes the VC and refers to anticipated events that have or had not yet taken place, with *avirua* either preceding the VC (132), preceding the VC and a postverbal subject NP (133), or *avirua* following the subject NP but preceding the VC and object NP (134). It is notable that none of these utterances contain tense, aspect or mode marking. This contrasts with the use of *avirua* as a preverbal adverb inside the VC (and thus following the subject-indexing proclitics), where it is attested with the imperfective aspect PSI enclitics, or the PSI enclitics, past imperfective *pei* and irrealis *=i* (see §6.8.2).

(132) **Avirua** mi=atu tamu~tamu.
 not.yet 1EXCL.SBJ=make RD~eat
 'We haven't made the feast yet.'
 (1-T030-00:03:41.935)

(133) *Aruai,* **avirua** *e=mate e-tubu-na.*
 no not.yet 3SG.SBJ=die PERS-grandparent-3SG.PSSR
 'No, his grandmother hadn't died yet.'
 (1-T029-00:14:11.120)

(134) *Anau* **avirua** *u=ani=ina ta:=bau gono.*
 1SG not.yet 1SG.SBJ=eat=3PL.OBJ some=PL banana
 'I haven't eaten any bananas yet.'
 (2-E017)

It could be argued that there is an adverb position before the subject proclitics in the VC and that *avirua* is inside the VC; however, (135) shows that *avirua* may be separated from the VC by a PP adjunct.

(135) *Sue* **avirua** *te=na='uru e=tua.*
 Sue not.yet OBL=SPEC[CLI]=island 3SG.SBJ=paddle
 'Sue hadn't paddled to the island yet.'
 (2-E026)

Chapter 9
Clause types and structures

This chapter is structured according to clause types. Within the discussion of each clause type I will discuss clause structure. The clause types discussed are declarative verbal clauses with core arguments (§9.1), imperative and hortative verbal clauses (§9.2), interrogative verbal clauses (§9.3), verbal existential clauses (§9.4), verbal negative clauses (§9.5) and finally verbless clauses (§9.6). When discussing clause order, it should be noted that 'V' refers not just to the verb but to the Verb Complex (VC) as outlined in chapter 6.

9.1 Declarative clauses and core arguments

Core arguments are represented by noun phrases (NP) (though complement clauses can function as objects; see §10.4). The expression of arguments in Papapana follows a nominative-accusative alignment, therefore the *subject* of a clause, designated here as 'S', is either the sole argument in an intransitive clause, or the argument which behaves syntactically like the actor argument of a *primary transitive verb* (Andrews 2007: 138). In Papapana, the subject of a clause is the argument indexed in the VC by subject proclitics (see §6.3.2). The *primary object* is the object indexed by the object enclitics (see §6.3.2). In a monotransitive clause, this is the only object and will thus be marked as 'O'. O may have the semantic role of patient, theme, addressee, recipient or beneficiary depending on the semantics of the verb. In ditransitive clauses the primary object has the semantic role of addressee, recipient or beneficiary, while the *secondary object* has the semantic role of theme (see §6.3.1). The primary object will be marked 'O1' and the secondary object as 'O2'.

Subject- and object-indexing clitics are required in all transitive clauses except for transitivity discord clauses in which object enclitics are not present (see §6.5.5.2). Overt subject and object NPs are not obligatory. As explained in §6.3.2, the subject- and object-indexing clitics are "ambiguous agreement markers" (Siewierska 2004: 126) since they occur in the presence and absence of overt NPs expressing the subject and object. Indeed in Proto-Oceanic, "the presence or absence of a subject proclitic was in no way dependent on the presence or absence of a subject NP, and the same was true of an object enclitic with regard to the object noun phrase" and, as in many modern Oceanic languages, "the typical clause [. . .] had no core noun phrase, or at most one, as the task of referent tracking was performed by the clitics, which also remained when the relevant noun phrase was present" (Lynch, Ross and Crowley 2002: 83). Papapana is thus typically Oceanic in its use of subject- and object-indexing clitics and the presence or absence of argument NPs.

Argument NPs can be omitted if they are retrievable, either extra-linguistically or within the linguistic context. When all argument NPs are present, there is considerable variation in clause order, with both left- and right-headed clauses. In intransitive clauses (see §9.1.1), verb-final clause order is the basic clause order and the pragmatically marked clause order when the subject is Topic, while verb-initial clause order is highly restricted. *Topic* is the "framework within which the main predication holds" (Chafe 1976: 50) and for this framework to serve as the context for the proposition expressed by the predication, it must "be meaningful for the hearer, and therefore invoke information already known to the hearer [. . .] in order to background it, signalling its role as the context for the associated proposition" (Palmer 2009: 218). In pragmatically unmarked monotransitive clauses (see §9.1.2), both SVO and SOV order are prevalent while the pragmatically marked monotransitive clause order involves a clause-initial Topic position. In ditransitive clauses (see §9.1.3) both verb medial (S V O2 O1) and verb final (S O2 O1 V) orders are attested. Verb-final clause order is not typical of Oceanic languages and is argued to be the result of contact-induced grammatical change under the influence of the Papuan languages of Bougainville which exhibit SOV basic clause order (Smith 2016a).

9.1.1 Intransitive

In intransitive clauses, verb-final clause order (SV) is the basic clause order while verb-initial clause order is highly restricted. The pragmatically marked intransitive clause order in Papapana involves a clause-initial Topic position. Topic subjects are not marked morphologically, and they are preverbal like non-Topic subjects, therefore it is not immediately apparent whether the sole argument of an intransitive verb is in the Subject or Topic position. It was only by analysing the features of the discourse context that I could ascertain that an argument like *Nabebe* in (1b) was the Topic, in this case because it is the object in (1a) and thus already known to the hearer.

(1) a. *Iara   Ebauka   e=vo'u=i=a*   *Nabebe.*
       then   Ebauka   3SG.SBJ=call=TR=3SG.OBJ   Nabebe
       'Then Ebauka called Nabebe.'
       (2-T001-2-00:01:42.141)

b. *Nabebe **e=to** tua dini nao.*
Nabebe 3SG.SBJ=EMPH paddle down thither
'Nabebe paddled in.'
(2-T001-2-00:01:44.817)

When the subject of an intransitive clause has the same referent as the subject of the preceding intransitive clause, the subject NP of the second clause is often omitted, as in (2).

(2) a. *Aina na=vanua nani i=pei*
3PL SPEC[CLI]=people there 3PL.SBJ=PST.IPFV
tagumu=ina=i.
assemble=3PL.IPFV=IRR
'The people were assembled there.'
(1-T035-00:10:48.280)
b. ***I=pei vavarai=ina=i.***
3PL.SBJ=PST.IPFV wait=3PL.IPFV=IRR
'They were waiting.'
(1-T035-00:10:49.950)

If omitting the subject NP might result in a semantically ambiguous utterance, the subject NP may be repeated, as in (3) where omission of the subject NP in the second clause might have rendered the interpretation that it was the newborn child who died.

(3) *Na=maunu=ma **e=to** burisi, na=maunu*
SPEC[CLI]=woman=ma 3SG.SBJ=EMPH give.birth SPEC[CLI]=woman
e=mate.
3SG.SBJ=die
'The woman gave birth, the woman died.'
(1-T029-00:02:31.108)

Nevertheless, there are instances in which there is no potential for ambiguity and the subject NP is still repeated as in (4) where the women are the only 3PL referents.

(4) a. *Enai=ma burimaunu i=va-puna~puna=ina=i.*
after=ma women 3PL.SBJ=CAUS-RD~celebrate=3PL.IPFV=IRR
'Then the women celebrate.'
(1-T066-00:01:52.580)

b. *Enai=ma **i=to**   maria osi=i,*
   after=ma 3PL.SBJ=EMPH thing COMPL=IRR
   i=va-puna~puna   *osi=i*
   3PL.SBJ=CAUS-RD~celebrate COMPL=IRR
   *burimaunu **i=nao=ma**   i-inu   te   aina.*
   women   3PL.SBJ=go=ma LOC-house OBL 3PL
   'Then (when) they finish what's-it-called, celebrating, the women go to their houses.'
   (1-T066-00:01:56.910)

In intransitive clauses, verb-initial clause order (VS) occurs very rarely (only nine tokens in a selected twenty-five texts, totalling 2 hours 39 minutes), it does not occur across a range of text genres nor is it produced by a range of speakers. Verb-initial clause order is highly restricted as it only occurs in asyndetic coordinate constructions in which the first clause is verb-final (SV) and the second clause verb-initial (VS). These constructions are considered coordinate as impressionistically they have the intonation contour of a single sentence. In such sentences, there is either repetition of the subject and predicate but with reversed clause order as in (5), or the subjects of the two clauses make reference to the same participant as in (6) where the subject of the second clause, *sau maunu* 'the poor woman' is co-referential with the subject of the first clause in which the same woman is the possessor.

(5) *Rosu   **e=to**   naomai, e=to   naomai Rosu.*
    Lucifer 3SG.SBJ=EMPH come 3SG.SBJ=EMPH come   Lucifer
    'Lucifer came, come did Lucifer.'
    (1-T035-00:08:05.626)

(6) *Iara ena=nganangana=ma   merei   burisi   **e=to***
    then 3SG.PSSR[CL1]=month=ma ATTRIB give.birth 3SG.SBJ=EMPH
    naomai, e=burisi   *sa=au   maunu.*
    come   3SG.SBJ=give.birth DIM=CLII woman
    'Then her due date came, the poor woman gave birth.'
    (1-T029-00:02:24.061)

9.1.2 Monotransitive

In pragmatically unmarked monotransitive clauses, both SVO and SOV orders are prevalent and when presented with such clauses in a text, speakers judged both orders to be acceptable and interchangeable with no difference in meaning. Both the verb-medial SVO clause order and verb-final SOV clause order are found across a variety of text genres and are produced by a range of speakers. In one elicitation session, the speaker even produced a clause with SOV order despite me eliciting in Tok Pisin, with its SVO order. There are no formal morphological markers for a particular clause order, and there is no grammatical motivation for the variant clause order, such as the animacy of the argument referents, as the following discussion demonstrates. Instead, SOV order is likely to be the result of contact-induced grammatical change under the influence of the Papuan languages of Bougainville (Smith 2016a).

Examples (7)–(10) show that utterances with equivalent information structure exhibit clause order variation. The clauses in (7) and (8) begin the respective narratives; therefore, all the arguments in each clause are being introduced for the first time and are unpredictable elements in the utterance, and thus are not Topics (according to the definitions given in §9.1). Nevertheless, despite the information structure in (7) being the same as that in (8), (7) displays SVO order and (8) displays SOV order. Examples (7) and (8) also show that animacy does not motivate clause order as both the subject referents are animate while both the object referents are inanimate.

(7) Va:sina na=vanua ***i=pei*** ae
before SPEC[CLI]=people 3PL.SBJ=PST.IPFV NEG
varona=ina=i
know=3PL.IPFV=IRR
nu=maria nu=bareo.
SPEC.CLII=thing SPEC.CLII=breadfruit
'Before, people didn't know (about), the what's-it-called, the breadfruit tree.'
(1-T035-00:00:17.250)

(8) Maisia sa=au 'usia=ma na=vutunu ***e=to***
okay DIM=CLII child=ma SPEC[CLI]=bow 3SG.SBJ=EMPH
de=a e=nao.
take=3SG.OBJ 3SG.SBJ=go
'Okay, a young boy got a bow (and) went.'
(1-T012-00:00:20.480)

The clauses in (9) and (10) also demonstrate equivalent information structure: all the arguments in each clause have already been introduced and even referred to in the preceding utterances, yet (9) displays SVO order, and (10) demonstrates SOV order. Examples (9) and (10) demonstrate that clause order is not motivated by the presence of independent pronouns nor by specificity as both subject referents are expressed by pronouns and both object referents are possessed nouns.

(9) Aia e=nutu   varisi=a   ena=arao-eta.
     3SG 3SG.SBJ=refuse also=3SG.OBJ   3SG.PSSR[CLI]=brother-AUG
     'He refused his big brother.'
     (1-T035-00:06:11.957)

(10) "Ani au=maunu   bea   o=pei   ae
     2SG   1SG.PSSR=woman   maybe 2SG.SBJ=PST.IPFV   NEG
     mate=a=amu=i."
     like=3SG.OBJ=2SG.IPFV=IRR
     "'Maybe you don't like my wife.'"
     (1-T067-00:02:55.770)

The pragmatically marked monotransitive clause order in Papapana involves a clause-initial Topic position. As described in §9.1.1, Topic subjects are not marked morphologically, and like non-Topic subjects, they precede both the verb and object (whatever the relative ordering of V and O is), therefore it is not immediately apparent whether the subject of a transitive verb is in the Subject or Topic position: I could only ascertain that by analysing the features of the discourse context. Both verb-medial and verb-final clause orders are widespread in pragmatically marked monotransitive clauses in which the subject is Topic. As with pragmatically unmarked monotransitive clauses, both the verb-medial and verb-final clause order are found across a variety of text genres and are produced by a range of speakers, and the clause order variation is not motivated by the grammatical features of the NP arguments nor is it marked morphologically. Instead, the clause-order variation is likely motivated by language contact (Smith 2016a). In both (11) and (12), the subject refers to a participant that is already known and was last referred to several utterances beforehand, and is therefore Topic (according to the definitions given in §9.1). The object referents on the other hand are introduced for the first time in these clauses. Clause order is not motivated by the presence of proper nouns since both subject referents in (11) and (12) are expressed by proper nouns.

(11) *Rosu* **e=pei** *bae~baene=ena=i* *na=orona.*
Lucifer 3SG.SBJ=PST.IPFV RD~hunt=3SG.IPFV=IRR SPEC[CLI]=possum
'Lucifer was hunting possums.'
(1-T035-00:04:39.088)

(12) *Isio na=sirao* **e=de=a.**
Satan SPEC[CLI]=string.bag 3SG.SBJ=take=3SG.OBJ
'Satan got a string bag.'
(1-T022-00:01:36.350)

If the object is Topic, the clause order is OSV, as in (13) where the object referent was referred to by the subject in the previous utterance, and in (14) where the object referent was referred to by the object in the previous utterance.

(13) *Arira tana* **e=ae** *amunu=ira=i.*
1INCL individual 3SG.SBJ=NEG look=1INCL.OBJ=IRR
'Nobody saw us.'
(1-T002-00:01:08.160)

(14) *Kaukau te aia burimaunu* **i=nao=i** *tau*
sweet.potato OBL 3SG women 3PL.SBJ=go=IRR and
i=no *ari=a=i.*
3PL.SBJ=go.SEQ dig=3SG.OBJ=IRR
'Women go and dig her (sweet potato) garden.'
(1-T066-00:00:43.100)

9.1.3 Ditransitive

Ditransitive verbs are generally derived with the applicative *i* in Papapana (see §6.5.1.2) but there is one underived ditransitive verb *ma'a* 'give'. In the text data, I have not found any ditransitive clauses in which all three arguments are expressed as NPs at the same time. In the elicitation data however, ditransitive clause order was generally S V O2 O1 as in (15).

(15) *Ben* **e=ma'a=ina** *na=iana Jeff auana Ellen*
Ben 3SG.SBJ=give=3PL.OBJ SPEC[CLI]=fish Jeff 3DU Ellen
'Ben gave a fish to Jeff and Ellen.'
(2-E018)

To confirm this clause order, I presented speakers with clauses such as (16)–(19) in which all three NP arguments are 3SG and have the same type of head noun (e.g. Personal proper noun, Class I/II noun, pronoun). Admittedly, this resulted in some semantically odd utterances, so I asked speakers to be imaginative! For these clauses, speakers identified the first NP as the actor (S), the second as the theme (O2) and the third as the addressee, recipient or beneficiary (O1).

(16) Sue *e=averu* *i=a* Daniel Ian.
Sue 3SG.SBJ=steal APPL=3SG.OBJ Daniel Ian
'Sue stole Daniel for Ian.'
(2-E026)

(17) *Nu=marei* *e=averu* *i=a* *na=iana*
SPEC.CLII=bird 3SG.SBJ=steal APPL=3SG.OBJ SPEC[CLI]=fish
nu=kakau.
SPEC.CLII=dog
'The bird stole the fish for the dog.'
(2-E026)

(18) *Matilda* *e=ma'=i=a* Nicholas Rose.
Matilda 3SG.SBJ=give=TR=3SG.OBJ Nicholas Rose
'Matilda gave Nicholas to Rose.'
(2-E015)

(19) *Nu=marei* *e=ma'=i=a* *nu=pusi*
SPEC.CLII=bird 3SG.SBJ=give=TR=3SG.OBJ SPEC.CLII=cat
nu=kakau.
SPEC.CLII=dog
'The bird gave the cat to the dog.'
(2-E026)

I also tested whether a ditransitive clause could be verb-final, as in (20), and speakers indicated that verb-final order was indeed grammatical. In the same way as above, I created four different clauses (of which (20) was one) in which the NP arguments were all 3SG and proper nouns, and occurred in a different order. When asked to identify the semantic roles of the NP arguments, the same order of objects pertained, as in (20): O2 before O1.

(20) *Matilda Nicholas Rose **e=ma'=i=a**.*
Matilda Nicholas Rose 3SG.SBJ=give=TR=3SG.OBJ
'Matilda gave Nicholas to Rose.'
(2-E015)

Not only is there variation in the position of the verb in ditransitive clauses, but it is also possible to vary the order of the objects, as demonstrated by the pair of contrasting utterances in (21). Such variation could be possible because the semantics of the two objects exclude the possibility of amibiguity.

(21) a. *Danny **e=atu** ma'ata i=a Lucy koko'i.*
Danny 3SG.SBJ=make be.heated APPL=3SG.OBJ Lucy taro
'Danny cooked taro for Lucy.'
(2-E018)
b. *Danny **e=atu** ma'ata i=a koko'i Lucy.*
Danny 3SG.SBJ=make be.heated APPL=3SG.OBJ taro Lucy
'Danny cooked taro for Lucy.'
(2-E018)

9.2 Imperative and hortative clauses

As described in §7.2, imperative clauses either carry no tense, aspect or mode (TAM) marking whatsoever, or they are marked by the irrealis mode enclitic =*i* in the VC. The optionality of irrealis =*i* makes these clauses distinct from those described in §7.1.4.1 where =*i* expressed future time or habitual events with a present time reference. This short section discusses the presence and order, or absence of NP arguments in imperative and hortative clauses.

As with all VCs in Papapana, VCs in imperative and hortative clauses are marked by subject-indexing proclitics in the VC, either 2SG *o=* or 2PL *mu=* for imperative clauses as in (22)–(24), or 1INCL *si=* ~ *so=* or 1INCL hortative *sa=* (see §6.3.2.1) for hortative clauses (25). Subject NPs were not produced in imperative or hortative clauses in the text or elicitation data, which suggests these clauses are different from declaratives and interrogatives where subject NPs referring to first, second and third person, are attested in text and elicitation data, though they are not obligatory. However, subject NPs in imperative clauses are not judged as unacceptable by speakers: when presented with the clauses (22), (23) and (24) speakers reported it was possible to use pronouns *ani* 2SG or *a:mu* 2PL as subject NPs in preverbal position (22), though the position of the object NP may vary and result in clause orders SVO (23b), SOV (24b), or OSV (24c).

(22) a. *"Maisia, **o=tamu**."*
    Okay   2SG.SBJ=eat
    '"Okay, eat."'
    (1-T012-00:01:16.550)
  b. *Maisia, ani **o=tamu**.*
    Okay   2SG   2SG.SBJ=eat
    'Okay, eat.'
    (2-E017)

(23) a. *"**Mu=de=ina**   taramina te   a:mu..."*
    2PL.SBJ=take=3PL.OBJ thing   OBL   2PL
    '"Get your things..."'
    (1-T002-00:00:51.115)
  b. *A:mu **mu=de=ina**   taramina te   a:mu.*
    2PL   2PL.SBJ=take=3PL.OBJ thing   OBL   2PL
    'Get your things.'
    (2-E017)

(24) a. *"Na:=bau taramina **mu=asi=ina=i**."*
    some=PL thing   2PL.SBJ=leave=3PL.OBJ=IRR
    '"Leave some things."'
    (1-T002-00:00:54.230)
  b. *A:mu na:=bau   taramina **mu=asi=ina=i**.*
    2PL   some=PL   thing   2PL.SBJ=leave=3PL.OBJ=IRR
    'Leave the other things.'
    (2-E017)
  c. *na:=bau taramina a:mu **mu=asi=ina=i**.*
    some=PL thing   2PL   2PL.SBJ=leave=3PL.OBJ=IRR
    'Leave the other things.'
    (2-E017)

(25) *"...**sa=asi=a=i**   Pasa ta   **si=nao=i**..."*
    INCL.SBJ.HORT=leave=3SG.OBJ=IRR Pasa and INCL.SBJ=go=IRR
    '"...let's leave Pasa and go..."'
    (1-T031-00:01:57.361)

9.3 Interrogative clauses

Papapana differentiates two interrogative subtypes: polar questions (a.k.a. yes/ no questions) and content questions (a.k.a. wh-questions, information questions or constituent interrogatives). The affirmative and negative responses to polar questions in Papapana are *aipasi* 'yes' and *aruai* 'no'.

9.3.1 Polar questions

In Papapana, polar questions may be expressed by specific intonation patterns or the addition of tags. In Oceanic in general, and Northwest Solomonic languages in particular, polar questions tend to exhibit only an intonation change (Lynch, Ross, and Crowley 2002: 52).

In Papapana, polar questions exhibit rising then falling intonation at the end of the clause as found in (26), or only rising intonation as found in (27) and (28). It should be noted that this is an impressionistic analysis only; it was beyond the scope of the current research to carry out an instrumental analysis of prosody. In the attested data, polar questions do not exhibit a subject NP, but can exhibit object NPs and these always precede the VC.

(26) *"Mi=no atono=amu=i=ma?"*
1EXCL.SBJ=go.SEQ bring=2PL.OBJ=IRR=ma
'"Shall we go and take you?"'
(1-T042-00:07:04.970)

(27) *"So=nao=i i-poana?"*
1INCL.SBJ=go=IRR LOC-village
'"Shall we go home?"'
(1-T029-00:18:58.210)

(28) *"Na=magura o=no pus=i=a=i?"*
SPEC[CLI]=green.coconut 2SG.SBJ=go.SEQ break.off=TR=3SG.OBJ=IRR
'"Are you going to pick the green coconut?"'
(1-T012-00:01:51.190)

Polar questions in Papapana may employ an interrogative tag such as *awa* 'correct' or *o aruai* 'or not'. These tags request confirmation or disconfirmation of the declarative clause that precedes them, and can thus be argued to bias the addressee in their answer. In the attested data, both subject and object NPs precede the VC. The intonation patterns are variable, with (29) exhibiting a falling intonation and (30) exhibiting a rising intonation on the tag.

(29) "*A:mu iai mu=atun=i=a, awa?*"
2PL PROX 2PL.SBJ=attack=TR=3SG.OBJ correct
"'You've killed him, right?'"
(1-T029-00:25:06.160)

(30) "*Na=pute e=togaru=o o aruai?*"
SPEC[CLI]=wind 3SG.SBJ=blow.down=2SG.OBJ or no
"'Did the wind blow you down or not?'"
(1-T022-00:01:19.095)

The presence of the preverbal negative marker *ae* in a polar interrogative clause could also be perceived as contributing a certain bias, for example, that the speaker expects that the addressee has not seen their brother (31) and does not miss their mother (32). It is unknown whether tags could occur in such clauses.

(31) "*Au=arao mu=ae amun=i=a?*"
1SG.PSSR[CLI]=brother 2PL.SBJ=NEG look=TR=3SG.OBJ
"'Have you not seen my brother?'"
(1-T074-00:01:26.090)

(32) "*E-sina-mu o=ae nami=a=i?*"
PERS-mother-2SG.PSSR 2SG.SBJ=NEG sad=3SG.OBJ=IRR
"'Don't you miss your mother?'"
(1-T074-00:02:11.880)

9.3.2 Content questions and interrogative terms

As in many Oceanic languages, content questions in Papapana are formed by employing one of seven interrogative terms, which mark the clause as a question and indicate what information is being requested. As Table 9.1 shows, two of these interrogative terms can function as core arguments, four of these interrogative terms have an adnominal function, modifying and requesting information about an explicity expressed nominal, and three interrogative terms modify a verb or clause, seeking information about temporal location, reason, spatial location and manner. Interrogative terms can also function as non-verbal predicates (§9.6.2). *Avoa ~ avea* denotes 'where' but in conjunction with a serial verb

Table 9.1: Functions of interrogative terms in verbal clauses.

Function	Interrogative	
Argument	te:na ~ te:a	who
	mata	what
Adnominal	te:na ~ te:a	whose
	mata	what kind
	avete	which
	tauvita	how many
Adjunct	nongovita	when
	avetau ~ aetau	why
	avoa ~ avea	where/how

construction (SVC) containing the verb *vowa ~ vewa* 'be like', *avoa* denotes 'how'. When *avete* 'which' and *mata* 'what kind' modify a Class II noun, they are marked by the Class II noun marker *au*; otherwise, these interrogative terms are invariant and cannot be modified by any other constituent.

In interrogative clauses which inquire about core arguments (§9.3.2.1) the interrogative term is preverbal, though not necessarily clause-initial because other arguments can precede the questioned constituent. In interrogative clauses where the interrogative term has an adnominal function (§9.3.2.2), the questioned constituent is clause-initial, regardless of its grammatical relation or status as an adjunct. In interrogative clauses which elicit information about temporal location, reason, spatial location and manner (§9.3.2.3) the interrogative term varies in position: *nongovita* 'when' and *avetau ~ aetau* 'why' occur clause-initially, while *avoa ~ avea* occurs between the subject and VC. In addition to their use in interrogative clauses, *te:na ~ te:a* 'who (singular)' and *mata* 'what/what kind', along with *te:bau* 'who (plural)' can function as arguments or adnominally in declarative clauses, where they denote 'whoever' and 'whatever/whatever kind of' (see §9.3.2.4). Meanwhile, *avoa* has the same form as the subordinator *avoa* 'where' which introduces adverbial clauses (see §10.3.5), but further research is required to determine which word is derived from which.

9.3.2.1 Core arguments

Two interrogative terms in Papapana, *te:na* 'who' and *mata* 'what', elicit the identity of a human or non-human core argument respectively. The form *te:a* is a phonologically reduced form of *te:na* and speakers were unable to account for, or are unaware of, a semantic or pragmatic difference between the two forms, nor is there any grammatical motivation for the variation. These interrogative terms cannot be modified by any other constituent.

There is limited data on intransitive interrogative clauses which inquire about the sole core argument, but one attested utterance in my data suggests that they have SV structure, that is, the interrogative term (i.e. the subject) is preverbal:

(33) **Te:na**   e=to   po=na   i-bana   i-inu?
     who.SG 3SG.SBJ=EMPH stay=3SG.IPFV LOC-inside LOC-house
     'Who is inside in the house?'
     (2-E020)

Monotransitive interrogative clauses which inquire about core arguments are always verb-final, with the interrogative term occurring clause-medially and the other, known argument occuring clause-initially. If the interrogative clause inquires about the subject, the constituent order is therefore OSV (34) whereas if the interrogative clause inquires about the object, the constituent order is SOV (35). This is unusual as an interrogative is a focused constituent and therefore cross-linguistically we would expect it to precede other arguments; however, the interrogative clause order does align with the pragmatically marked declarative clause order in Papapana in which there is a Topic initial position (see §9.1).

(34) "Au=bosara   **te:na**   e=atu   sisipo=a?"
     1SG.PSSR[CLI]=design who.SG 3SG.SBJ=make copy=3SG.OBJ
     'Who copied my design?'
     (1-T058-00:05:44.760)

(35) "Ani **mata** o=pe~peri=a=mu?"
     2SG what   2SG.SBJ=RD~find=3SG.OBJ=2SG.IPFV
     '"What are you looking for?"'
     (1-T012-00:02:32.754)

An alternative clause order appears to be possible in which the interrogative term occurs clause-initially and the object NP follows the VC, giving SVO order. However, this is attested only in the two elicited examples (36)–(37). This variation in clause order likely reflects the clause order variation demonstrated in declarative clauses (see §9.1) which is argued to be the result of language contact (Smith 2016a).

(36) **Te:a**   e=to   atu=a   na=inu   mama?
     who.SG 3SG.SBJ=EMPH make=3SG.OBJ SPEC[CLI]=house DEM1

'Who made this house?'
(2-E026)

(37) **Te:a**   e=to   paga=i=a   na=orawi   mama?
who.SG 3SG.SBJ=EMPH shoot=TR=3SG.OBJ SPEC[CLI]=man DEM1
'Who shot this man?'
(2-E026)

Unlike monotransitive interrogative clauses, which are verb-final (with the exception of (36) and (37)), ditransitive interrogative clauses are verb-medial. Ditransitive interrogative clauses which inquire about the subject can be subject-initial with S V O2 O1 constituent order as in (38). Alternatively the primary object precedes the interrogative term giving O1 S V O2 constituent order as in (39).

(38) **Te:na**   e=to   ma'=i=a   na=gono   John?
who.SG 3SG.SBJ=EMPH give=TR=3SG.OBJ SPEC[CLI]=banana John
'Who gave the banana to John?'
(3-E002)

(39) John **te:na**   e=to   ma'=i=a   na=gono?
John who.SG 3SG.SBJ=EMPH give=TR=3SG.OBJ SPEC[CLI]=banana
'Who gave the banana to John?'
(3-E002)

Ditransitive interrogative clauses which inquire about one of the objects are subject-initial, with the interrogative term occurring between the subject and the VC, and the other object following the VC. If the clause inquires about the O1, the constituent order is S O1 V O2 (40), whereas if the clause inquires about the O2, the constituent order is S O2 V O1 (41).

(40) Anna **te:a**   e=ma'=i=a   na=gono?
Anna who.SG 3SG.SBJ=give=TR=3SG.OBJ SPEC[CLI]=banana
'Who did Anna give the banana to?'
(2-E026)

(41) Anna **mata** e=ma'=i=a   Jason?
Anna what 3SG.SBJ=give=TR=3SG.OBJ Jason
'What did Anna give to Jason?'
(2-E026)

9.3.2.2 Adnominal

There are four interrogative terms in Papapana which elicit information about a noun's referent and are in prenominal position: *te:na ~ te:a* 'whose', *avete* 'which', *mata* 'what kind' and *tauvita* 'how many'.

The interrogative term *te:na ~ te:a* can function as a possessor NP denoting 'whose' and modify a possessed noun, which is either marked by the possessor suffixes or possessor proclitics (see §5.5.1 and §5.5.2). *Te:na ~ te:a* 'whose' seeks information about the identity of the possessor. Although possessor NPs may precede or follow the head noun in declarative clauses, *te:na ~ te:a* 'whose' only occurs in prenominal position, like other interrogative terms. Also like other NPs containing interrogative terms, the questioned constituent occurs clause-initially, whether it is the S argument of a NP predicate (42), the S argument of an intransitive clause (43), monotransitive clause (44) or ditransitive clause (45), the O argument of a monotransitive clause (46), or the O1 (47) or O2 argument of a ditransitive clause (48).

(42) **Te:na   e-tama-na   i-nongana?**
who.SG PERS-father-3SG.PSSR LOC-beach
'Whose father is on the beach?'
(2-E019)

(43) **Te:a   ena=inu   i-nongana   e=tonu=ena?**
who.SG 3SG.PSSR=house LOC-beach   3SG.SBJ=stand=3SG.IPFV
'Whose house is on the beach?'
(2-E019)

(44) **Te:na   e-sina-na   e=atun=i=a**
who.SG PERS-mother-3SG.PSSR 3SG.SBJ=attack=TR=3SG.OBJ
nu='usia?
SPEC.CLII=child
'Whose mother hit the child?'
(3-E002)

(45) **Te:na   e-sina-na   e=ma'=i=a**
who.SG PERS-mother-3SG.PSSR 3SG.SBJ=give=TR=3SG.OBJ
na=tamute   John?[37]
SPEC[CLI]=mango John
'Whose mother gave the mango to John?'
(3-E002)

---

[37] This clause shows S V O2 O1 order, but S V O1 O2 was also produced.

(46) ***Te:a   ena=au   obutu*** Ben *e=to*
     who.SG 3SG.PSSR=CLII canoe Ben 3SG.SBJ=EMPH
     oto=i=a?
     board=TR=3SG.OBJ
     'Whose canoe did Ben board?'
     (2-E019)

(47) ***Te:na   e-sina-na   na=tamute***
     who.SG PERS-mother-3SG.PSSR SPEC[CLI]=mango
     e=ma'=i=a   Emma?[38]
     3SG.SBJ=give=TR=3SG.OBJ Emma
     'Whose mother did Emma give mangoes to?'
     (3-E002)

(48) ***Te:a   ena=au   gono***   Emma *e=to*
     who.SG 3SG.PSSR=CLII banana Emma 3SG.SBJ=EMPH
     ma'=i=a   Sam?
     give=TR=3SG.OBJ Sam
     'Whose banana did Emma give to Sam?'
     (2-E028-2)

The interrogative terms *avete* 'which' and *mata* 'what kind' do not co-occur with articles, but the unmarked forms modify singular Class I nouns as in (49) and (51), while for Class II nouns these interrogative terms are marked by Class II noun marker *au* as in (50) and (52).

(49) ***Avete   gono***   Emma *e=ani=a?*
     which[CLI] banana Emma 3SG.SBJ=eat=3SG.OBJ
     'Which banana did Emma eat?'
     (2-E026)

(50) ***Avete=au   koko'i*** *si=ani=a?*
     which=CLII taro   1INCL.SBJ=eat=3SG.OBJ
     'Which taro did we eat?'
     (2-E026)

---

38 This clause shows O1 O2 V S order, but S O1 O2 V or S O1 V O2 order was also produced.

(51) **Mata** iana Joseph e=mate=i=a=ena?
what[CLI] fish Joseph 3SG.SBJ=like=TR=3SG.OBJ=3SG.IPFV
'Which kind of fish does Joseph like?'
(2-E026)

(52) **Mata=au kaukau** Joseph e=mate=i=a=ena?
what=CLII sweet.potato Joseph 3SG.SBJ=like=TR=3SG.OBJ=3SG.IPFV
'Which kind of sweet potato does Joseph like?'
(2-E026)

Interrogative clauses which inquire about quantity use the modifier *tauvita* 'how many'. Given the sound correspondences described by Ross (1988: 219–222), it is likely that *tauvita* is diachronically divisible as *tau-vita*, the second element reflecting POc *pica(n)* 'how many' which could co-occur with the counting prefix *ka-* (Lynch, Ross, and Crowley 2002: 89), and that *tauvita* is cognate with *to-(v)isa* 'how many' in Banoni (Lynch and Ross 2002: 454), *kavisa* 'how many/much' in Roviana (Corston-Oliver 2002: 494) and 'how many/much' *ka=viza* 'how many' in Kubokota (Chambers 2009: 85). The noun which *tauvita* modifies may or may not have an article (53)–(54).

(53) **Tauvita na=niunu** Ben auana Anna i=to
how.many SPEC[CLI]=coconut Ben 3DU Anna 3PL.SBJ=EMPH
ani=ina?
eat=3PL.OBJ
'How many coconuts did Ben and Anna eat?'
(2-E026)

(54) **Tauvita kaukau** Anna auana Bob i=atono=ina
how.many sweet.potato Anna 3DU Bob 3PL.SBJ=bring=3PL.OBJ
mai?
hither
'How many sweet potatoes did Anna and Bob bring?'
(2-E026)

Furthermore, *tauvita* was sometimes pronounced *tauvitai* as in (55). The presence of *i* may be a variation in pronunciation, but it may also be the construct suffix found in compounds (see §4.4.1). In this case, *tauvita* would be the head noun and the following noun would be the modifier. The lack of article in (55) is consistent with this analysis as in compounds only the head noun is marked by an article and the modifying noun is not. In addition, the frequent occurrence of *tauvita* without *i* is consistent with the compounds as the construct suffix is regularly deleted in these constructions. Compounds in Papapana reflect Proto-Oceanic inalienable and alienable non-specific possessor constructions and it would not be unusual for a numeral to occur in a possessor construction in an Oceanic language; indeed, as mentioned in §5.4.1, Ross (1988: 313) proposes a Proto-New Ireland NP structure in which the numeral was the head of the phrase and the enumerated noun was the grammatical possessor.

(55) **Tauvita-i   magura   u=to   de=ina   mai?**
how.many-CONST green.coconut 1SG.SBJ=EMPH take=3PL.OBJ hither
'How many green coconuts did I bring?'
(2-E019)

The NP containing the interrogative term may be the subject of an intransitive (56), monotransitive (57) or ditransitive clause (58), the object of a monotransitive clause (59), the O2 of a ditransitive clause (60) or an adjunct (61). In all cases, the questioned constituent is clause-initial giving the orders **SV**, **SVO**, **S V O1 O2**, **OSV**, and **O2 S V O1**. When the questioned constituent is an adjunct, it is clause-initial, followed by the subject NP and the VC (61a). Other adjuncts may also be present and could intervene between the questioned adjunct and the subject (61b), or follow the VC (61c).

(56) **Mata   maunu   e=nao~nao   te=na=lotu?**
what[CLI] woman 3SG.SBJ=RD~go OBL=SPEC[CLI]=worship
'Which kind of woman goes to church?'
(2-E026)

(57) **Tauvita   na='usia   i=to   ani=a**
how.many SPEC[CLI]=child 3PL.SBJ=EMPH eat=3SG.OBJ
na=tamute?
SPEC[CLI]=mango
'How many children ate mangoes?'
(3-E002)

(58) **Tauvita   na='usia   i=ma'=i=a**
how.many SPEC[CLI]=child 3PL.SBJ=give=TR=3SG.OBJ
na=orawi   na=tamute?
SPEC[CLI]=man SPEC[CLI]=mango
'How many children gave mangoes to the man?'
(3-E002)

(59) **Avete inu** Alex e=ara atu=a?
which[CLI] house Alex 3SG.SBJ=PST make=3SG.OBJ
'Which house did Alex build?'
(2-E026)

(60) **Mata=au gono** Emma e=to ma'=i=a Sam?
what=CLII banana Emma 3SG.SBJ=EMPH give=TR=3SG.OBJ Sam
'What kind of banana did Emma give to Sam?'
(2-E028-2)

(61) a. **Avete skuru** Alex e=nao?
which[CLI] school Alex 3SG.SBJ=go
'Which school does Alex go to?'
(2-E026)
b. **Tauvita yia** i-poana ani o=pei
how.many year LOC-village 2SG 2SG.SBJ=PST.IPFV
po=mu=i?
stay=2SG.IPFV=IRR
'How many years have you lived in the village?'
(2-E028-2)
c. **Tauvita yia** John e=pei po=na=i
how.many year John 3SG.SBJ=PST.IPFV stay=3SG.IPFV=IRR
i-poana?
LOC-village
'How many years has John lived in the village?'
(2-E028-2)

SOV can also be the order for a monotransitive clause in which the NP containing the interrogative term is the object, i.e. the questioned constituent occurs clause-medially instead of clause-initially (62)–(63). Similarly (64) shows S **O1** V O2 order for a ditransitive clause in which the NP containing the interrogative term is primary object. This variation in clause order also likely reflects the clause order variation demonstrated in declarative clauses.

(62) *Anau* **avete** *po'uri u=de=a=i?*
 1SG which[CLI] basket 1SG.SBJ=take=3SG.OBJ=IRR
 'Which basket shall I take?'[39]
 (2-E019)

(63) *Arira* **mata=au koko'i** *si=ani=a=i?*
 1INCL what=CLII taro 1INCL.SBJ=eat=3SG.OBJ=IRR
 'What kind of taro shall we eat?'
 (2-E019)

(64) *Emma* **tauvita na='usia** *e=ma'a=ina*
 Emma how.many SPEC[CLI]=child 3SG.SBJ=give=3PL.OBJ
 na=tamute?
 SPEC[CLI]=mango
 'How many children did Emma give mangoes to?'
 (3-E002)

9.3.2.3 Clausal adjunct

There are four interrogative terms in Papapana which elicit information about temporal location, reason, spatial location and manner: *nongovita* 'when' and *avetau* 'why' occur clause-initially, while *avoa* occurs between the subject and VC, whether it denotes 'where' or whether it denotes 'how' in conjunction with a SVC containing the verb *vowa ~ vewa* 'be like'.

9.3.2.3.1 Temporal

The interrogative term *nongovita* 'when' inquires about the temporal location of an event or state and always occurs clause-initially in intransitive (65), monotransitive (66) and ditransitive clauses (67). In the examples below, the subject NP is always preverbal and objects are postverbal. *Nongovita* appears to be cognate with *no-(v)isa* 'when' in Banoni (Lynch and Ross 2002: 454).

(65) **Nongovita** *Ben e=oto=i te ena=au obutu?*
 when Ben 3SG.SBJ=board=IRR OBL 3SG.PSSR=CLII canoe
 'When does Ben board onto his canoe?'
 (2-E019)

---

[39] A *po'uri* [pɔʔuri] is a type of basket woven from palm tree leaves and is also pronounced [peʔuri].

(66) **Nongovita** nu=kakau   e=ara   atun=i=a
     when   SPEC.CLII=dog   3SG.SBJ=PST   attack=TR=3SG.OBJ
     nu=pusi?
     SPEC.CLII=ca
     'When did the dog attack the cat?'
     (2-E026)

(67) **Nongovita** Jane e=ma'=i=a   na=gono   John?
     when   Jane 3SG.SBJ=give=TR=3SG.OBJ   SPEC[CLI]=banana   John
     'When did Jane give the banana to John?'
     (2-E028-2)

9.3.2.3.2 Reason

The interrogative term *avetau* 'why' inquires about the reasons for an event or state. It is sometimes shortened to *aetau* in casual speech. It generally occurs clause-initially in intransitive and monotransitive clauses, as in (68) and (69) where the clause orders are SV and SVO. Alternatively, the order can be VS in an intransitive clause, but this is attested only in text data example (70). A ditransitive interrogative clause with *avetau* 'why' is attested only once, in elicited example (71), where *aetau* is in clause-initial position and the clause order is S O2 V O1.

(68) **Avetau** Rose auana Max i=orete   viviro'o=ina?
     why   Rose 3DU   Max 3PL.SBJ=walk   around=3PL.IPFV
     'Why are Rose and Max walking around?'
     (2-E019)

(69) **Avetau** Albert e=averu=ina   au=bau   tamu~tamu?
     why   Albert 3SG.SBJ=steal=3PL.OBJ   1SG.PSSR=PL   RD~eat
     'Why did Albert steal my food?'
     (2-E019)

(70) **Aetau** i=re~rete   vowa=ina   nua   anua   mama?
     why   3PL.SBJ=RD~walk   be.like=3PL.IPFV   two[CLI]   person   DEM1
     'Why are those two people walking around like that?'
     (1-T094)

(71) **Aetau** Ben na=iana e=ma'=i=a Jerry?
why Ben SPEC[CLI]=fish 3SG.SBJ=give=TR=3SG.OBJ Jerry
'Why did Ben give a fish to Jerry?'
(3-E001)

In elicitation sessions speakers indicated that the interrogative term *avetau* 'why' can also occur between the subject and VC in intransitive and monotransitive clauses, as in (72b), (73b) and (74), where the clause orders are SV and SVO.

(72) a. **Avetau** aia e=nao?
why 3SG 3SG.SBJ=go
'Why does he go?'
(2-E026)
b. *Aia* **avetau** e=nao?
3SG why 3SG.SBJ=go
'Why does he go?'
(2-E026)

(73) a. **Avetau** aina i=ae ara nao?
why 3PL 3PL.SBJ=NEG PST go
'Why did they not go?'
(2-E026)
b. *Aina* **avetau** i=ae ara nao?
3PL why 3PL.SBJ=NEG PST go
'Why did they not go?'
(2-E026)

(74) *John* **avetau** e=atunu=ina Bob auana Adam?
John why 3SG.SBJ=attack=3PL.OBJ Bob 3DU Adam
'Why did John attack Bob and Adam?'
(2-E026)

9.3.2.3.3 Location

The interrogative *avoa* 'where' inquires about the location of an event or state and may be variably pronounced as *avea*. The alternate forms are a reflection of the phonological variation described in §3.1.3. Unlike other interrogative terms, *avoa* ~ *avea* occurs between the subject NP and VC in both intransitive (75) and monotransitive clauses (76)–(77), and before any object NPs. The position of the object NP in a monotransitive clause may be postverbal (76) or preverbal (77).

A ditransitive interrogative clause with *avoa* 'where' is attested only once, in elicited example (78), where *avoa* occurs between the subject NP and VC.

(75) Ani **avoa** o=nao~nao=mu?
2SG where 2SG.SBJ=RD~go=2SG.IPFV
'"Where are you going?"'
(1-T033-00:00:26.530)

(76) Ani **avoa** o=to ae=a koko'i?
2SG where 2SG.SBJ=EMPH buy=3SG.OBJ taro
'Where do you buy taro?'
(2-E026)

(77) John **avoa** na=pe'uri te anau e=to
John where SPEC[CLI]=basket OBL 1SG 3SG.SBJ=EMPH
ruvu=i=a?
put=TR=3SG.OBJ
'Where did John put my basket?'
(2-E019)

(78) Betty **avoa** e=atu ma'ata i=a
Betty where 3SG.SBJ=make be.heated APPL=3SG.OBJ
Terese-Anne kaukau?
Terese-Anne sweet potato
'Where did Betty cook food for Terese-Anne?'
(3-E001)

9.3.2.3.4 Manner

When the interrogative *avoa* is used in conjunction with a SVC containing the verb *vowa ~ vewa* 'be like' (see §6.6 for SVCs with this verb and §8.3.3 and §10.4.1 for its phrasal and clausal complements respectively), it denotes 'how' and the clause inquires about the manner in which an event occurred. *Avoa* occurs between the subject and VC in intransitive (79) and monotransitive clauses (80), and precedes objects. The position in ditransitive clauses requires further data to determine.

(79) John **avoa** e=siodo vewa?
John how 3SG.SBJ=work be.like
'How did John work?'
(2-E028-2)

(80) *Joe **avoa** e=atu   vewa=i=a   na=inu?*
    Joe   how 3SG.SBJ=make be.like=TR=3SG.OBJ SPEC[CLI]=house
    'How did Joe make the house?'
    (2-E026)

Example (81) shows *avoa* in clause-initial position in an intransitive clause with VS order, but as with *avetau* 'why', this VS order is attested only once, in elicited data (81).

(81) ***Avoa** e=to   mate vewa   Robert?*
    how   3SG.SBJ=EMPH die   be.like Robert
    'How did Robert die?'
    (2-E019)

9.3.2.4 Interrogative terms in declarative clauses

In declarative clauses, the interrogative terms *te:na ~ te:a* 'who (singular)' and *mata* 'what/what kind' (see Table 9.1), along with *te:bau* 'who (plural)', can function as arguments or adnominal constituents and denote 'whoever' and 'whatever/whatever kind of'.

In (82)–(84) *te:na ~ te:a* and *te:bau* denote 'whoever' and refer to a participant whose identity is uncertain. In (82) and (83) *te:bau* and *te:a* are the subject of the verb (which is reflected in the 3PL and 3SG subject proclitics respectively), whereas in (84) *te:bau* is the object of the verb, though it is unclear why there is no object enclitic in the VC.

(82) *Bikos   vituasi o   **te:bau** i=to   ae   nongono=ina,*
    because young   or who.PL   3PL.SBJ=EMPH NEG hear=3PL.IPFV
    aruai.
    no
    'Because young people or whoever don't listen, no.'
    (1-T089-00:05:43.302)

(83) *"Maisia **te:a**   e=to   mate=i=a=na=i,*
    okay   who.SG 3SG.SBJ=EMPH like=TR=3SG.OBJ=3SG.IPFV=IRR
    mu=naomai."
    2PL.SBJ=come
    '"Okay whoever wants it, come."'
    (1-T029-00:16:07.136)

(84) . . .o u=ae   varona=u   **te:bau.** . .
     or   1SG.SBJ=NEG know=3SG.IPFV who.PL
     '[And the B.R.A]. . . or I don't know who. . . [they hid on the road].'
     (1-T103-00:12:36.225)

In (85)–(86) *mata* denotes 'whatever' and is the object of the verb.

(85) **Mata** o=to   noe=i=a=i   te=na=kabekabe,
     what   2SG.SBJ=EMPH put=TR=3SG.OBJ=IRR OBL=SPEC[CLI]=bag
     e=ae   tagoa=i.
     3SG.SBJ=NEG break=IRR
     'Whatever you put into this bag, it (the bag) won't break.'
     (2-E008-1)

(86) "**Mata** e=to   vatan=i=o=i,
     what   3SG.SBJ=EMPH tell=TR=2SG.OBJ=IRR
     o=atutusi=a=i."
     2SG.SBJ=chase=3SG.OBJ=IRR
     '"Whatever he tells you, follow it."'
     (1-T035-00:06:33.970)

Mata can also modify a noun and denote 'whatever kind of'. The unmarked *mata* modifies singular Class I nouns (87) while for Class II nouns, *mata* is marked by Class II noun marker *au* (88).

(87) **Mata**   taramina o=to   wa=i=a=i,
     what[CLI] thing   2SG.SBJ=EMPH say=TR=3SG.OBJ=IRR
     e=ae   vatana manene=i.
     3SG.SBJ=NEG tell   return=IRR
     'Whatever kind of thing you tell him, he won't answer.'
     (2-E008-1)

(88) **Mata=au** vori~vori i=to   me-a   naomai. . .
     what=CLII RD~talk   3PL.SBJ=EMPH COM-3SG.OBJ come
     'Whatever kind of message they came with. . . [the chief used to blow the coneshell].'
     (1-T107-00:00:51.225)

9.4 Existential clauses

In Papapana, existential clauses may be verbless (see §9.6.7) or verbal. Verbal existential clauses in Papapana employ three existential verbs: *po* 'stay/exist', *tonu* 'stand' and *a'aisi* 'be many'. Existential clauses employing the verb *tonu* 'stand' always contain an adjunct expressing the existence of an entity in a location, while those employing *po* 'stay/exist' may or may not contain such an adjunct.

9.4.1 Existential verb *po* 'stay/exist'

In Papapana, the intransitive verb *po* 'stay/exist' may denote 'stay' or 'live', but it can also be used in existential constructions. The subject NP is always preverbal, and refers to the participant(s) whose existence is predicated by the clause, be it in the present (89)–(90) or past (91)–(92):

(89) *Toituna* **e=po=na.**
     God   3SG.SBJ=stay=3SG.IPFV
     'There is a God.'
     (2-E017)

(90) *Tamu~tamu* **i=po=ina.**
     RD~eat   3PL.SBJ=stay=3PL.IPFV
     'There is food.'
     (2-E017)

(91) *Na:=ata   na=poana   **e=pei**   ara*
     some=CLI SPEC[CLI]=village 3SG.SBJ=PST.IPFV PST
     po=ena=i.
     stay=3SG.IPFV=IRR
     'There was another village.'
     (1-T034-00:01:23.864)

(92) *Mena   sina-na   **i=pei**   **po~po=ina=i.**...*
     DU.COLL mother-DER 3PL.SBJ=PST.IPFV RD~stay=3PL.IPFV=IRR
     'There was a mother and son. . . [and his father died].'
     (1-T067-00:00:28.150)

The verb *po* 'stay/exist' may also be used as a predicate in a clause in which an adjunct expresses the existence of an entity in a location. As with simple existential clauses, the subject NP is always preverbal in verbal locational clauses, and refers to the participant(s) whose location is expressed by the clause, while the adjunct may occur clause-finally (93), clause-initially (94)–(95) or clause-medially (96).

(93) a. *John   e=pei   po=ena=i*
John   3SG.SBJ=PST.IPFV   stay=3SG.IPFV=IRR
te=na=ereere.
OBL=SPEC[CLI]=mountain
'John was in the mountains.'
(2-E017)

b. *Aina   i=pei   po=ina=i   o~'oema-na.*
3PL   3PL.SBJ=PST.IPFV   stay=3PL.IPFV=IRR   RD~taro.garden-DER
'They were in the bush.'
(2-E017)

(94) ***Australia*** *bau   kangaroo   i=po=ina.*
Australia   PL   kangaroo   3PL.SBJ=stay=3PL.IPFV
'In Australia there are kangaroos.'
(2-E017)

(95) ***I-ata***   *bau   vanao   na=vei   etawa   poto*
LOC-above   PL   tree sp.   SPEC[CLI]=COLL   big   INTS
i=pei   po=ina=i.
3PL.SBJ=PST.IPFV   stay=3PL.IPFV=IRR
'There were really big *vanao* trees above.'
(1-T034-00:07:48.090)

(96) *Nua=au   kakau   te=na=inu   mama   i=po=ina.*
two=CLII   dog   OBL=SPEC[CLI]=house   DEM1   3PL.SBJ=stay=3PL.IPFV
'There are two dogs in the house.'
(2-E017)

9.4.2 Existential verb *tonu* 'stand'

The intransitive verb *tonu* 'stand' is mainly used to denote human posture but it can also be used as an existential verb in a clause in which an adjunct expresses the existence of an entity in a location. The subject NP is preverbal but the adjunct can be situated before the subject NP (97)–(98) or between the subject NP and the VC (99)–(100). In (98) the speaker first produced the utterance with the verb *po* before repeating the utterance with *tonu* instead. Similarly, in (100) the speaker produced this utterance first before repeating it with *po*. Therefore it seems *po* and *tonu* are interchangeable and that *tonu* really is being used as an existential verb in these clauses rather than as a posture verb. Furthermore, I did not use the Tok Pisin verb *sanap* 'stand' to elicit (97)–(100), I used *i gat* 'there is' for (98) and (100) and *stap* 'stay' for (99).

(97) **I-bana te=na=board,** na=vanua mama
LOC-inside OBL=SPEC[CLI]=board SPEC[CLI]=people DEM1
i=tonu=ina.
3PL.SBJ=stand=3PL.IPFV
'These people are on the (school) board.'
(1-T081-00:00:11.840)

(98) *Va:sina* **pei mama** *na=stasiu* **e=pei**
before part DEM1 SPEC[CLI]=statue 3SG.SBJ=PST.IPFV
tonu=ena=i.
stand=3SG.IPFV=IRR
'In the past there was a statue in this place.'
(2-E017)

(99) *Te:a ena=inu* **i-nongana e=tonu=ena?**
who.SG 3SG.PSSR=house LOC-beach 3SG.SBJ=stand=3SG.IPFV
'Whose house is on the beach?'
(2-E019)

(100) *Naonava tautoi boro* **i-poana i=pei**
yesterday three.NHUM pig LOC-village 3PL.SBJ=PST.IPFV
tonu=ina=i.
stand=3PL.IPFV=IRR
'Yesterday there were three pigs in the village.'
(2-E026)

9.4.3 Existential verb *a'aisi* 'be many'

The quantifier *a'aisi*, as in (101) (see §5.6.4 for more), is also a zero-derived verb meaning 'be many' (102)–(104). The meaning of examples (102)–(104) could be quantification, or they could mean that an entity exists in abundance: further research is required to determine the underlying interpretation.

(101) . . .*na=vanua*   *a'aisi poto i=pei*   *ara*
SPEC[CLI]=people many INTS 3PL.SBJ=PST.IPFV PST
po=ina=i.
stay=3PL.IPFV=IRR
'[Okay before here in our village] . . .there were very many people.'
(1-T029-00:00:19.890)

(102) "*Na=iana*   *i=a'aisi?*"
SPEC[CLI]=fish 3PL.SBJ=be.many
'"Are there many fish?"'
(1-T064-00:02:33.040)

(103) *I-nongana*   *i=a'aisi=ina*   *nu=kokirako*
LOC-beach 3PL.SBJ=be.many=3PL.IPFV SPEC.CLII=tamanu
'There are lots of tamanu on the beach.'
(1-T058-00:02:15.340)

(104) . . .*ta na=vanua*   *e=pei*   *a'aisi*
and SPEC[CLI]=people 3SG.SBJ=PST.IPFV be.many
poto=ina=i.
INTS=3PL.IPFV=IRR
'. . .and there were lots of people.'
(1-T034-00:20:22.129)

9.5 Negative clauses

Section 7.3 described the negation of verbal assertive predicates with the preverbal negative marker *ae* and the negation of imperatives with verbal reduplication and either the preverbal negative marker *ae* or the preverbal apprehensive marker *te*. Section 9.3.1 discussed the negative answer to questions *aruai* 'no' and the interrogative tag *o aruai* 'or not'. Clause order in negative assertive and negative imperative clauses does not differ from affirmative assertive or affirmative imperative clauses. Clause order in negative subordinate clauses also does not differ from clause order in affirmative subordinate clauses, and negative subordinate clauses also employ *ae* (see chapter 10 for subordinate clauses).

This section describes the use of *aruai* as a zero-derived negative existential verb, and as a clausal negative marker with verbal assertive predicates, which may or may not be marked by the preverbal negative marker *ae*. The negation of non-verbal assertive predicates also employs *aruai* and is discussed in §9.6. Note that *aruai* also denotes 'zero' in the counting system (§5.4.1).

It is not unusual for a negative word in an Oceanic language to serve more than one function. Mosel (1999) outlines three types of negatives used as negative answers in Oceanic languages and one of these is "a negative verb which has the same form as those used in negative existential constructions" (Mosel 1999: 11). Mosel (1999) also states that "in most of the languages in our sample, the same negative can be used with verbal and non-verbal predicates" (Mosel 1999: 11): in Papapana this is true of *aruai* but not of *ae*. Papapana confirms three of the working hypotheses suggested by Mosel (1999: 17): (i) Oceanic negatives tend to distinguish three functions: the negation of existential constructions, predicates and imperatives, (ii) if a language has negative verbs and particles, it will use the verb for existential constructions and the particle for predicates, and (iii) the negative prosentence (i.e. negative answers to questions) tends to have the same form as the existential negative.

9.5.1 Negative existential verb *aruai* 'be not'

In Papapana, the negative existential verb *aruai* expresses the non-existence of an entity (105). In (106)–(107), the subject NP occurs preverbally, and refers to the entity that is lacking:

(105) ***E=to   aruai.***
    3SG.SBJ=EMPH be.not
    'There was nothing.'
    (1-T049-00:05:05.970)

(106) *Na=vatu   e=to   aruai=ena=i,   enai*
    SPEC[CLI]=money 3SG.SBJ=EMPH be.not=3SG.IPFV=IRR after
    i=ubetu=i.
    3PL.SBJ=hungry=IRR
    'If there is no money, then they'll be hungry.'
    (1-T098-00:03:17.518)

(107) *Taramina a'aisi na=vei mata **i=pei***
thing many SPEC[CLI]=COLL good 3PL.SBJ=PST.IPFV
be.not=3PL.IPFV=IRR
aruai=ina=i. . .
'There were not many good things. . .'
(1-T034-00:16:53.740)

Negative existential clauses may also be formed by negating an existential clause containing the existential verbs *po* 'stay/exist' or *a'aisi* 'be many' (see §9.4) with the preverbal negative marker *ae*:

(108) *Ta bau bareo i=pei **ae po~po=ina=i***
and PL breadfruit 3PL.SBJ=PST.IPFV NEG RD~stay=3PL.IPFV=IRR
i-poana.
LOC-village
'And there were no breadfruits in the village.'
(1-T035-00:00:22.220)

(109) *Taim mama buriatanana i=pei **ae** agai*
time DEM young.women 3PL.SBJ=PST.IPFV NEG really
a'aisi=ina=i. . .
be.many=3PL.IPFV=IRR
'At that time, there weren't very many young women. . .'
(1-T034-00:14:08.010)

9.5.2 Verbal assertive negation: *aruai* 'no'

A verbal assertive predicate which has been negated with the preverbal negative marker *ae*, may also employ *aruai* in clause-final position to emphasise the negation (110)–(112). *Aruai* is thus very similar to *ahiki* in Teop which, without tense-aspect marking, can function as a negative answer to questions, as a question tag *ge ahiki* 'or not', and can follow negative statements for emphasis, but may also be used in negative existential constructions when combined with tense-aspect markers (Mosel and Spriggs 1999b: 48–49).

(110) . . .*tau va:gi iai **e=ae** agai mata=na **aruai**.*
and now PROX 3SG.SBJ=NEG really good=3SG.IPFV NEG
'. . .and today it's not very good.'
(1-T001-00:00:31.071)

(111) *Mi=**ae***   *ani~ani na=miti*   ***aruai.***[40]
     1EXCL.SBJ=NEG RD~eat SPEC[CLI]=meat NEG
     'We don't eat meat.'
     (1-T015-00:02:14.030)

(112) *"Ani o=**ae***   *muni=au **aruai.**"*
     2SG 2SG.SBJ=NEG hide=1SG NEG
     '"You didn't hide me."'
     (1-T052-00:04:25.310)

9.6 Verbless clauses

In verbless clauses in Papapana the predicate may be a NP and express identity, possession or location, or be negated (§9.6.1). The predicate of a verbless clause may also be an interrogative term (§9.6.2) a locative preposition phrase (PP) (§9.6.3), an attributive PP (§9.6.4), a numeral phrase (§9.6.5), or an adjective phrase (§9.6.6). A verbless existential clause can consist of just the predicate NP with no subject NP, but the predicate noun must be modified by a numeral or negative marker (§9.6.7). There is also a compound-like construction which predicates possession (§9.6.8).

9.6.1 Nominal predicates

Verbless clauses in which the predicate is a NP may express identity (§9.6.1.1) and possession (§9.6.1.2). When the head noun is a Location noun referring to spatial location, the nominal predicate expresses the location in which the subject referent is situated (§9.6.1.3). A nominal predicate may be negated with *aruai* (§9.6.1.4). In all verbless clauses containing nominal predicates, the subject NP and the predicate NP are juxtaposed and there is no overt marking to indicate the function of the NP, though the subject NP tends to precede the predicate NP.

---

40 This utterance expresses habitual aspect but it is unclear why the verbal reduplication is not accompanied by PSI enclitics.

9.6.1.1 Identity

Nominal predicates expressing identity consist of two juxtaposed NPs. It is possible to interpret slight differences in the meaning of the nominal predicate; some express proper inclusion and others equation.

In nominal predicate clauses which express proper inclusion, it is asserted that an entity is among the class of items specified in the predicate. In nominal predicate clauses expressing proper inclusion in Papapana (113)–(115), the subject NP occurs first, while the predicate NP follows the subject, as is also the case in Northwest Solomonic languages such as Banoni (Lynch and Ross 2002: 451) and Sisiqa (Ross 2002: 463). Note that the nominal predicate in (115) is a compound noun construction which denotes a trait of habitually carrying out the action denoted by the reduplicated verb (see §4.4.4).

(113) *"Aruai, a:mani **na=vanua** merei i-poana."*
   no   1EXCL SPEC[CLI]=people ATTRIB LOC-village
   '"No, we are villagers."'
   (1-T059-00:02:08.660)

(114) *Ta sa=au 'usia mama **sa=au maru.***
   and DIM=CLII child DEM1 DIM=CLII orphan
   'And this poor child was an orphan.'
   (1-T035-00:01:23.910)

(115) *Anau **nu=mata ro~romo=u.***
   1SG SPEC.CLII=trait RD~drink=1SG.IPFV
   'I'm an alcoholic (lit. I drink (a lot) / I'm a drinker).'
   (1-T088-00:27:26.500)

Nominal predicate clauses which express equation assert that an entity (the subject) is identical to the entity specified in the predicate. In equational clauses in Papapana (116)–(117), the subject NP precedes the predicate NP.

(116) *Anau **na=treasurer.***
   1SG SPEC[CLI]=treasurer
   'I'm the treasurer.'
   (1-T081-00:00:20.610)

(117) *Na=orawi   mama* **Peter.**
    SPEC[CLI]=man DEM1 Peter
    'That man is Peter.'
    (2-E017)

The predicate NP expressing equation may be a possessed NP marked by possessor suffixes (118) or proclitics (119), or by the possessor suffixes and a coreferential possessor NP (120)–(121). Note that (120) and (121) show that possessor NPs can be preposed or postposed (see §5.5). When the subject NP is headed by a noun referring to the possessum as in (122), the predicate NP does not need to contain the possessum, thus it is elided, leaving the possessor proclitic which attaches to the Class I marker *ata* (122), Class II marker *au* or plural article *bau*, which agree with the elided noun in class and/or number, and thus also agree with the subject NP (see §5.5.3 for further discussion).

(118) *Iai   **nu=ie-u.***
    PROX SPEC.CLII=leg-1SG.PSSR
    'This is my leg.'
    (2-E028-2)

(119) *"Iai   **amu=maunu.**"*
    PROX 2SG.PSSR[CLI]=woman
    '"This is your wife."'
    (1-T029-00:01:38.624)

(120) *Mama **nu=boro**   **nu=ie=na.***
    DEM1 SPEC.CLII=pig SPEC.CLII=leg-3SG.PSSR
    'This is the pig's leg.'
    (2-E028-2)

(121) *Mama **nu=nima-na**   **John.***
    DEM1 SPEC.CLII=hand-3SG.PSSR John
    'This is John's hand.'
    (2-E028-2)

(122) *Avete   inu   **amu=ata?***
    Which house 2SG.PSSR=CLI
    'Which house is yours?'
    (2-E019)

9.6.1.2 Possession

In examples (118)–(122) above, which express possession, the predicate NP consisted of a possessed noun and this nominal predicate was equated with the subject NP referent. This differs from the nominal clauses which express possession in this section; in these, the structure of the clause is also composed of two juxtaposed NPs, but the subject NP refers to the possessor and is followed by the nominal predicate which refers to the possessum, with no possessive morphology required. Since the structure of identity and possession verbless clauses is the same, it is possible that ambiguity (between an identity or possession interpretation) could result but it was beyond the scope of this research to test for such ambiguity.

The nominal predicate expressing the possessum may consist simply of a noun marked by an article as in (123), or by a noun modified by an interrogative (124) or a numeral (125). In (126) the noun is modified by a numeral phrase consisting of the numeral and the limiter *ora*. These examples are not numeral phrase predicates (see §9.6.5) because the noun is not marked by an article, which it would if the numeral were a separate phrase.

(123) *"Ani **na=kari?**"*
 2SG SPEC[CLI]=kina.shell
 '"Do you have a kina shell?"'
 (1-T022-00:02:52.730)

(124) *Aina **taovita** **na='usia?***
 3PL how.many SPEC[CLI]=child
 'How many children do they have?'
 (2-E017)

(125) *Ta Port Moresby **tautoi** ta'apena.*
 and Port Moresby three.NHUM area
 'And Port Moresby has three areas.'
 (1-T098-00:05:02.721)

(126) *Aia **tauvasi ora kukuraka.***
 3SG four only finger
 'He has only four fingers.'
 (2-E017)

9.6.1.3 Location

Nominal predicates which consist of a Familiar Location noun (thus marked by the locative case prefix *i-*) express the existence in a location of the subject NP referent. The subject NP precedes the predicate NP. Since there is no TAM marking in verbless locational clauses, time reference is either ambiguous (127)–(128) or can be indicated by temporal adjuncts as in (129)–(130).

(127) *Na=bara*   ***i-ava.***
      SPEC[CLI]=ball   LOC-sea
      'The ball is/was in the sea.'
      (2-E026)

(128) *Ena=inu*   ***i-nongana.***
      3SG.PSSR[CLI]=house   LOC-beach
      'His house is/was on the beach.'
      (1-T105-00:18:07.300)

(129) *Va:gi tautoi epu* ***i-nganisi.***
      now   three.NHUM   cloud   LOC-sky
      'Now three clouds are in the sky.'
      (2-E017)

(130) *Naonava tautoi boro* ***i-poana.***
      yesterday   three.NHUM   pig   LOC-village
      'Yesterday three pigs were in the village.'
      (2-E028-2)

Nominal predicates which consist of an Absolute Location noun expressing time can express the existence in temporal location of the subject NP referent. Unlike (127)–(130), the subject NP follows the predicate NP:

(131) ***Va:sina*** *sa=au 'usia.*
      before   DIM=CLII   child
      'Long ago there was a poor child.'
      (1-T050-00:00:17.340)

(132) ***Naonava*** *na=naoi-eta.*
      yesterday   SPEC[CLI]=rain-AUG
      'Yesterday there was a lot of rain.'
      (2-E017)

9.6.1.4 Negative nominal predicates

As mentioned in §9.5, *aruai* can function as a clausal negative marker with verbal predicates, but it may also function inside a nominal predicate, where it usually follows the head noun. When the negative nominal predicate negates identity (133)–(135) the subject NP precedes the predicate NP.

(133) *Nu='a'ade'e   nu=moroko   aruai.*
      SPEC.CLII=narrative SPEC.CLII=lie   NEG
      'The story is no lie.'
      (1-T044-00:06:33.600)

(134) *"A:mani   na='usia   aruai."*
      1EXCL   SPEC[CLI]=child   NEG
      '"We aren't children."'
      (1-T053-00:02:12.920)

(135) *Toituna **Charlie aruai.***
      chief   Charlie   NEG
      'The paramount chief is not Charlie.'
      (2-E026)

Aruai may also negate possessed NPs functioning as non-verbal predicates (136)–(139). In these examples the subject NP is situated before the predicate NP that it is being equated with.

(136) *Enai   vavine-u   aruai.*
      DEM2 sibling-1SG.PSSR NEG
      'That is not my brother.'
      (2-E026)

(137) *"Anau amu=au   'usia   aruai."*
      1SG   2SG.PSSR=CLII   child   NEG
      '"I'm not your child."'
      (1-T088-00:29:53.873)

(138) *"Ini   iai   Pasa ena=kavururu   aruai."*
      here PROX   Pasa 3SG.PSSR[CLI]=ground   NEG
      '"This here is not Pasa's land."'
      (1-T035-00:01:06.280)

(139) *Na=iana   mama **au=ata**   **aruai**.*
      SPEC[CLI]=fish DEM1 1SG.PSSR=CLI NEG
      'This fish is not mine.'
      (2-E026)

The negative *aruai* is also used in non-verbal clauses in which the subject refers to the possessor and the predicate to the possessum. Except for *aruai*, the possessum NP may contain no nominal modifiers (140)–(141), or an article (142), or a numeral modifer (143)–(144).

(140) *Ta   a:mani **moni**   **aruai**.*
      and 1EXCL   money NEG
      'And we had no money.'
      (1-T053-00:02:05.860)

(141) *Arira **kavururu aruai**.*
      3PL   land   NEG
      'They have no land.'
      (2-E017)

(142) *Anau **na=vu~vurau**   **aruai**.*
      1SG   SPEC[CLI]=RD~run NEG
      'I have no car.'
      (2-E026)

(143) *Peter **nua=au   kakau aruai**.*
      Peter two=CLII dog   NEG
      'Peter doesn't have two dogs.'
      (2-E026)

(144) *Pauline tau Kingsford **atono**   'usia **aruai**.*
      Pauline and Kingsford three.HUM child NEG
      'Pauline and Kingsford don't have three children.'
      (2-E026)

Aruai may also precede the head noun in the nominal predicate, as in (145)–(146), although this is infrequent; other nominal modifiers such as possessors also occur prenominally and postnominally and this variation is thought to be the result of contact with neighbouring Papuan languages (Smith 2016a).

(145) *Anau **aruai na=vatu.***
    1SG   NEG SPEC[CLI]=money
    'I have no money.'
    (2-E017)

(146) *Aina **aruai tamu~tamu.***
    3PL   NEG RD~eat
    'They have no food.'
    (2-E017)

9.6.2 Interrogative predicates

An interrogative can function as a predicate expressing equation as in (147) or location (148)–(149). The subject NP may follow or precede the predicate as in (150) and (147)–(149) respectively.

(147) *Na=orawi   mama **te:na?***
    SPEC[CLI]=man DEM1 who.SG
    'Who is this man?'
    (2-E019)

(148) *"Aia **avea?"***
    3SG   where
    '"Where is he?"'
    (1-T029-00:25:20.510)

(149) *"Amu=poana   **avea?"***
    2SG.PSSR[CLI]=village where
    '"Where is your village?"'
    (1-T029-00:06:12.170)

(150) *"Awa   ta   **avea**   na=maunu   mama?"*
    correct and   where SPEC[CLI]=woman DEM1
    '"Right and where is this woman?"'
    (1-T029-00:18:51.720)

9.6.3 Locative PP predicates

Locational clauses refer to the location in which the subject referent is situated. In Papapana locational clauses may have the existential verb *po* 'stay/exist' or *tonu* 'stand' as their predicate and a locative adjunct (see §9.4.1 and §9.4.2), but they may also have a locative PP as the predicate (151)–(153). There is no apparent functional difference between the two, though verbal locational clauses can be specified for TAM, as this can only be marked by verbal morphology in Papapana. In the attested verbless locational clauses, the subject NP (be it a pronoun or lexical NP) precedes the locative PP predicate, whose head is the preposition *te* (see §8.3.1):

(151) *Enai a:mani **te=na=ereere**.*
 after 1EXCL OBL=SPEC[CLI]=mountain
 'Then we were in the mountains.'
 (1-T034-00:28:02.921)

(152) *Pepeitaunima vuri **te=na=epita**.*
 five egg OBL=SPEC[CLI]=nest
 'Five eggs are in the nest.'
 (2-E026)

(153) *Matthew **te=na='uru**.*
 Matthew OBL=SPEC[CLI]=island
 'Matthew is on the island.'
 (2-E028-2)

9.6.4 Attributive PP predicates

PPs headed by the preposition *merei* (see §4.8 and §8.3) may function as the predicate in a verbless clause, assigning an attribute to the subject NP. As in other verbless clauses, the two phrases are juxtaposed, with the subject NP occurring first. In these examples the complement of the preposition is a deictic locational word (154) or an Absolute Location noun (155).

(154) *Nu='a'ade'e mama **merei** nani.*
 SPEC.CLII=narrative DEM1 ATTRIB there
 'This story is from there.'
 (2-E005)

(155) *Tau nu='a'ade'e mama **merei** va~va:sina.*
and SPEC.CLII=narrative DEM1 ATTRIB RD~before
'And this story is from long ago.'
(1-T026-00:00:15.180)

9.6.5 Numeral predicates

A numeral phrase may function as the predicate in a verbless clause expressing that the subject referent occurs in a certain number (156). If the subject is a NP that is modified by a possessor as in (157) and (158) the idiomatic English translation is a possessive clause. The predicate numeral phrase may contain just the head numeral (156)–(158), or the numeral modified by the limiting modifier *ora ~ ara* and marked by an article which agrees with the the head of the subject NP (159)–(161) (see also §5.4.2). If the numeral denotes 'one' (159)–(162), 'two' or 'three' (158), it makes a noun class or human/nonhuman distinction that agrees with that of the subject NP (see §5.4.2).

These constructions are not nouns being modified by numerals because the subject NP can be a pronoun, which is never modified by numerals (156), or as (157)–(158) show, the head of the subject NP is marked by an article, thus distinguishing it as its own phrase (except *toituna*[41] (159) which is never marked by an article). There may be a locative or temporal adjunct in the clause as in (156) and (161). The order of the subject NP and the numeral phrase predicate is variable as (162) demonstrates.

(156) *A:mani **numanoa** te=na=inu mama.*
1EXCL ten OBL=SPEC[CLI]=house DEM1
'There are ten of us in this house (lit. We are ten in the house).'
(2-E017)

(157) *Au=bau boro **pepeitaunima.***
1SG.PSSR=PL pig five
'I have five pigs (lit. My pigs are five).'
(2-E017)

---

41 *Toituna* is likely a compound composed of the noun *toi* 'person' and the modifier *tuna*, though the meaning of *tuna* is unknown. *Toi* itself is hypothesised to be a lexicalisation of the head noun *to* 'person' and the construct suffix *-i* (see §4.4.3).

(158) *Bau tubu-mani* **atono.**
PL grandparent-1EXCL.PSSR three.HUM
'We have three grandparents (lit. Our grandparents are three).'
(1-T060-00:00:22.490)

(159) . . .*avosia toituna mama enai* **na='aria** **ora.**
SUBR God DEM1 DEM2 SPEC[CLI]=one only
'[I want to tell you] . . .that there is only one god (lit. This God is only one).'
(1-T097-00:08:48.840)

(160) **Na='aria** **ora** *na=ato.*
SPEC[CLI]=one only SPEC[CLI]=sun
'There is only one sun (lit. The sun is only one).'
(2-E017)

(161) *Va:gi* **nu='aria** **ora** *nu=kakau.*
now SPEC.CLII=one only SPEC.CLII=dog
'Today there is only one dog (lit. Today the dog is only one).'
(2-E028-2)

(162) a. *Na=matuana* **na='aria.**
SPEC[CLI]=devil SPEC[CLI]=one
'There is one devil (lit. The devil is one).'
(2-E017)
b. **Na='aria** *na=matuana.*
SPEC[CLI]=one SPEC[CLI]=devil
'There is one devil (lit. The devil is one).'
(2-E017)

9.6.6 Adjectival predicates

Adjective phrases (AP) (see §4.6.1) may function as the predicate in a verbless clause, assigning an attribute to the subject NP. As in other verbless clauses, the two phrases are juxtaposed, with the subject NP occurring first. The AP consists of an adjective preceded by an article that agrees in noun class with the subject NP (163)–(167). Note that (165) shows two coordinated verbless clauses while the subject NP consists of a compound noun in (166) and a pronoun in (167).

(163) *Na=iana* **na=mamaravi.**
SPEC[CLI]=fish SPEC[CLI]=cold
'The fish is cold.'
(2-E004)

(164) *Nu='usia* **nu=kokobunu.**
SPEC.CLII=child SPEC.CLII=short
'The child is short.'
(2-E004)

(165) *Nu=kakau mama* **nu=etawa** *ta mama* **nu=kaka'i.**
SPEC.CLII=dog DEM1 SPEC.CLII=big and DEM1 SPEC.CLII=small
'This dog is big and this (dog) is small.'
(2-E004)

(166) *Na=guvi-ni niunu* **na=bua.**
SPEC[CLI]=bottle-CONST coconut SPEC[CLI]=full
'The coconut bottle was full.'
(1-T044-00:01:22.630)

(167) "*Ani* **na=au** *dua.*"
2SG SPEC=CLII bad
'"You're bad."'
(1-T052-00:05:14.460)

If the subject NP head is modified by a numeral, the predicate AP is marked with the same numeral:

(168) . . .*bikos nua=au ie-na ta nua=au nima-na*
because two=CLII leg-3SG.PSSR and two=CLII arm-3SG.PSSR
nua=au sirorai.
two=CLII long
'. . .because his two legs and his two arms were long.'
(1-T063-00:02:53.250)

(169) *Nua iana mama* **nua** *mata.*
two[CLI] fish DEM1 two[CLI] good
'These two fish are good.'
(2-E021)

When the subject NP is plural, the predicate AP does not take the same article as the subject NP head but is instead marked with *na=vei:*

(170) *Bau katopo-na* **na=vei** *sirorai...*
PL nail-3SG.PSSR SPEC[CLI]=COLL long
'His nails were long... [on his arm and his leg].'
(1-T035-00:00:34.430)

(171) *Bau inu mama* **na=vei** *vaunu.*
PL house DEM1 SPEC[CLI]=COLL new
'All these houses were new.'
(2-E004)

The predicate AP may also be postmodified by the intensifier *poto*:

(172) *Aia nu=visio-na* **nu=etawa poto.**
3SG SPEC.CLII=body-3SG.PSSR SPEC.CLII=big INTS
'His body was really big'
(1-T034-00:11:10.850)

(173) *Na=dede mama* **na=nabu poto.**
SPEC[CLI]=bag DEM1 SPEC[CLI]=heavy INTS
'This bag is very heavy.'
(2-E004)

Unlike NP predicates, AP predicates (and indeed AP modifiers, see §4.6.1) are not negated by *aruai* but are premodified by the negative marker *ae*, the negative marker found in the VC. The negative marker occurs between the article and the adjective root:

(174) *Na=inu* **na=ae** *mata.*
SPEC[CLI]=house SPEC[CLI]=NEG good
'The house wasn't good.'
(1-T071-00:07:06.780)

(175) *Nu=urisi* **nu=ae** *itaita*
SPEC.CLII=rope SPEC.CLII=NEG strong
'The rope wasn't strong.'
(1-T035-00:04:18.208)

(176) . . .bau   paga   mama   **na=vei**   ae   *itaita.*
        PL   shoot   DEM1   SPEC[CLI]=COLL   NEG   strong
    '. . .all these guns were not strong.'
    (1-T103-00:02:13.229)

9.6.7 Existential clauses

Verbless existential clauses in Papapana may consist only of the NP whose referent is said to exist; however, there is usually some kind of modification: a numeral modifier or the negative marker *aruai*.

Verbless existential clauses may consist of a nominal predicate whose head noun has been modified by a numeral; such clauses express the existence of a number of things. Example (177) is not a numeral phrase predicate (see §9.6.5) because the noun does not occur with an article, which it would if the numeral were a separate phrase.

(177) **Nua=au   pepeitaunima   manoa   vesunu.**
        two=CLII   five   ten   star
    'There are a hundred stars.'
    (2-E017)

Verbless existential clauses may also consist of a nominal predicate whose head noun has been modified by the negative marker *aruai*; these clauses express the non-existence of an entity. *Aruai* occurs postnominally (178)–(180).

(178) **Na=vu~vurau   aruai.**
        SPEC[CLI]=RD~run   NEG
    'There was no car.'
    (1-T042-00:06:42.900)

(179) **Ta=matuana   aruai.**
        NSPEC[CLI]=devil   NEG
    'There is no devil.'
    (2-E017)

(180) *A:mani* *mi=nao*   *te=na=stoa,*   **na=rice**   ***aruai.***
        1EXCL   1EXCL.SBJ=go   OBL=SPEC[CLI]=store   SPEC[CLI]=rice   NEG
    'We went to the store but there was no rice.'
    (2-E017)

9.6.8 Possessive clauses with *pea*

Pea 'possession' occurs in a compound-like construction in which *pea* is followed by a possessum noun marked by a possessor suffix. The construction functions as a predicate expressing possession and the coreferent lexical possessor NP is the subject, and is always clause-initial. Examples (181)–(186) show that the lexical possessor NP can be 1SG, 2SG, 3SG or 3PL, but 1st and 2nd person plural subjects are not attested. Examples (181)–(184) also show that the lexical possessor NP can be animate or inanimate (185), while the possessum noun can also be animate (184) or inanimate. The possessum noun may be either alienable (181)–(182) or inalienable as in (183) and (185). NPs headed by alienable nouns are not ordinarily marked by possessor suffixes but by possessor proclitics, which may or may not directly attach to the possessum noun (see §5.5) and therefore I tentatively analyse this construction as a compound with *pea* as an inalienable head noun. The prototypical inalienable noun in Papapana expresses a part-whole relation, and indeed in some cases such as (183) and (185), this construction is used to refer to something which is part of a larger entity. These possessive clauses differ from nominal predicates expressing possession (§9.6.1.2) because there, the clause is composed of a NP referring to the possessor and a NP referring to the possessum, but the clause lacks possessive morphology.

(181) *Anau* **pea** *vu~vurau-u.*[42]
 1SG possession RD~run-1SG.PSSR
 'I have a car.'
 (2-E026)

(182) *Ani* **pea** *inu-mu.*
 2SG possession house-2SG.PSSR
 'You have a house.'
 (2-E026)

(183) *Aia nu='usia mama* **pea** *apu-na*
 3SG SPEC.CLII=child DEM1 possession sore-3SG.PSSR
 i=to nasi=a. . .
 3PL.SBJ=EMPH ask=3SG.OBJ
 'They asked him, the child with sores. . .'
 (1-T022-00:02:52.730)

---

[42] The noun *vuvurau* 'car' has been derived from the verb *vurau* 'run' through reduplication; see §4.3.2.1.

(184) *Na=orawi* **pea** *boro-na.*
 SPEC[CLI]=man possession pig-3SG.PSSR
 'The man has a pig.'
 (2-E026)

(185) *Nu=naono mama* **pea** *vua-na.*
 SPEC.CLII=tree DEM1 possession fruit-3SG.PSSR
 'This tree has fruit.'
 (1-T058-00:07:04.470)

(186) *Sue tau Bob* **pea** *koko'i-ina.*
 Sue and Bob possession taro-3PL.PSSR
 'Sue and Bob have taros.'
 (2-E026)

It is also possible for the possessum noun to be modified by a numeral:

(187) *Peter* **pea** *nua=au kakau-na.*
 Peter possession two=CLII dog-3SG.PSSR
 'Peter has two dogs.'
 (2-E026)

(188) *Pauline tau Kingsford* **pea** *atono 'usia-ina.*
 Pauline and Kingsford possession three.HUM child-3PL.PSSR
 'Pauline and Kingsford have three children.'
 (2-E026)

Examples (189)–(191) show that the whole construction can be negated with *ae*, which precedes *pea*. *Ae* is the negative marker found in the VC (see §7.3.1) and adjective phrases can also be negated with *ae* (see §4.6.1). The negation of these possessive clauses differs from nominal predicates expressing possession, which are negated with *aruai* (§9.6.1.4), the clausal negative marker (see §9.5).

(189) *Anau ae pea pepeitaunima boro-u.*
 1SG NEG possession five pig-1SG.PSSR
 'I don't have five pigs.'
 (2-E017)

(190) *Iai   o'onata, iai **ae   pea   vua-na.***
PROX plant.sp PROX NEG possession fruit-3SG.PSSR
'This is *o'onata*, this doesn't have its fruit.'
(1-T058-00:01:55.150)

(191) ***Pauline tau Kingsford ae   pea   'usia-ina.***
Pauline and Kingsford NEG possession child-3PL.PSSR
'Pauline and Kingsford don't have children.'
(2-E026)

The use of *ae*, the negative marker found in the VC, might suggest that *pea* is a verb and not a noun. Indeed, speakers in elicitation session ES2-E017 translated *pea* as "i gat" (Tok Pisin for 'to have, to own, to possess' or 'there is'). Furthermore, in Hoava, there is a very similar construction consisting of the existential verb *ari*, which is "used to state the existence of something that is regarded as part of a larger entity or as belonging to someone" (Davis 2003: 183). Hoava *ari* has an obligatorily incorporated possessive NP, consisting of a possessum noun and possessor pronominal, and the subject of such clauses is the coreferent possessor NP (Davis 2003: 183–185), as shown in (192). *Ari* can also be negated by the negative particle *kipu*, as in (193).

(192) **Hoava**
    Ari sigoto-na   sa   bore.
    exist anchor-3SG ART:SG canoe
    'The canoe has an anchor.'
    (Davis 2003: 183)

(193) **Hoava**
    Kipu ari tama-mi *gamu   karu.*
    NEG exist father-2PL PRO:2PL two
    'You two do not have a father.'
    (Davis 2003: 183)

There are some crucial differences between the Hoava and Papapana constructions though, that provide evidence against analysing Papapana *pea* as a verb. Firstly, in Hoava, the possessive NP does not have to be marked by the inalienable suffixes because the independent "exclusive" (i.e. not inalienable and not edible) possessive forms can also be used (Davis 2003: 183). Secondly, the future tense marker can precede Hoava *ari*, *ari* can be reduplicated and intensifiers usually used with verbs can be placed after the possessum (Davis 2003: 183–184). In contrast, in Papapana, the alienable possessive forms are not used and aside from negative *ae*, no verbal morphology is used with *pea*. Moreover, *pea* may be preceded by an article (194)–(197), even those which have been negated (196)–(197). Speakers in elicitation session ES2-E017 said that in "original Papapana language" articles were not used but that some people do add *nu=*, *na=* and *bau*. Perhaps diachronically *pea* was a verb, but synchronically it has more in common with nouns.

(194) "...bau vituasi mama **bau pea** **paga-ina**."
PL young DEM1 PL possession shoot-3PL.PSSR
'"[Let's call them]...all these young with guns."'
(1-T103-00:02:05.900)

(195) *Bau api mama* **bau pea** * tatopu-ina.*
PL young DEM1 PL possession hole-3PL.PSSR
'These bamboos have holes.'
(2-E017)

(196) *Aia* **nu=ae** * ***pea** * 'usia-na.*
3SG SPEC.CLII=NEG possession child-3SG.PSSR
'He doesn't have children/a child.'
(2-E017)

(197) *Sa=au maunu mama* **nu=ae** * ***pea** * ***ngisi-na**.
DIM=CLII woman DEM1 SPEC.CLII=NEG possession teeth-3SG.PSSR
'This little girl doesn't have teeth (yet).'
(2-E017)

Chapter 10
Complex sentences

This chapter describes coordination and subordination. Coordinating constructions are symmetrical and involve linking independent clauses (§10.1). Section 10.1 will also discuss the coordination of phrases. Subordination is asymmetrical because one clause is embedded inside another. Papapana has three types of subordination: relative clauses (§10.2), adverbial clauses (§10.3), and complement clauses (§10.4). A relative clause is embedded within a noun phrase (NP) and depends on the matrix noun for the interpretation of one of its arguments, while a complement clause is embedded within a matrix clause of which it is an argument. Adverbial clauses are either i) non-finite and introduced by a subordinator, ii) finite but the particular combination of mode markers, or the combination of the predicate and the type of noun heading the subject NP, does not occur in independent clauses, or iii) finite and introduced by a subordinator, and are semantically dependent on the main clause, corresponding to the circumstances under which the event expressed by the main clause takes place.

10.1 Coordination and coordinators

Papapana coordinating constructions may be syndetic and employ a coordinator, or they may be asyndetic in which case the units are simply juxtaposed without an overt coordinator (§10.1.4). Papapana has three coordinators: *tau ~ ta* 'and' marks conjunction and may also be interpreted as expressing adversative coordination (§10.1.1), *o* 'or' marks disjunction (§10.1.2), and *iara* 'then' and *enai* 'after' mark sequential coordination (§10.1.3). The use of such a small set of coordinators is typically Oceanic (Lynch, Ross and Crowley 2002: 53). The coordinator *o* 'or' is likely a loan from Tok Pisin which might explain why, despite being monomoraic, it constitutes a word (see §3.3.2). *Enai* 'after' is formally identical to the person-based demonstratives *enai* 'near addressee' (see §4.5) but further research is required to determine whether there is a diachronic relationship between these two words. Coordinators are invariant in form and coordination is monosyndetic as there is always just one coordinator, which immediately precedes the last coordinate.

10.1.1 Conjunction and adversative coordination

The coordinator *tau ~ ta* 'and' marks conjunction, which is an interpropositional relation that obtains between coordinate clauses. The specific semantics and context of the clause may conspire to express adversative coordination which presents a contrast between two clauses and denotes 'but'. *Tau* and *ta* are allomorphs in free variation: there is no grammatical motivation for the variation and speakers report no difference in meaning, but instead reported that *ta* was a shorter means of uttering *tau*. The coordinator *tau ~ ta* is used to conjoin clauses (§10.1.1.1), and it may also link NPs and preposition phrases (PP) (§10.1.1.2). In addition, dual independent pronouns may also coordinate NPs (§10.1.1.3).

Some Oceanic languages use coordinators in *numeral coordination*, which is a type of additive coordination in which units are coordinated with tens in numerals (Moyse-Faurie and Lynch 2004: 488). In Papapana, this is largely not the case but as described in §5.4.1, counting between 'one hundred' and 'one thousand' involves counting in fifties, and it is the decades in between fifties that are formed additively with the coordinator *tau ~ ta*.

10.1.1.1 Clause coordination

Papapana allows clauses to be coordinated with *tau ~ ta* regardless of whether the subjects of the clauses are different or the same. Examples (1)–(2) show sentences in which the clauses each have their own subject and predicate. The coordinator *tau ~ ta* marks conjunction in (1); this sentence was elicited with Tok Pisin *na* 'and'. In (2) a translation expressing adversative coordination was given but these sentences could equally express conjunction. Note that the sentence in (2) also begins with *ta*, linking it to the previous sentence; sentences being joined in this way is common in speech and in fact it seems to be a stylistic feature of this particular narrative as many of the sentences begin with *ta*.

(1) Ben   e=ani   na=iana   **tau** anau u=ani
    Ben   3SG.SBJ=eat   SPEC[CLI]=fish and   1SG 1SG.SBJ=eat
    na=rice.
    SPEC[CLI]=rice
    'Ben ate fish and I ate rice.'
    (2-E021-1)

(2) Ta   e-tama-na   e=ara   mate **tau** enai
    and PERS-father-3SG.PSSR 3SG.SBJ=PST die   and DEM2
    e-sina-na   ara   e=pei   ara
    PERS-mother-3SG.PSSR only 3SG.SBJ=PST.IPFV PST
    po=na=i.
    stay=3SG.IPFV=IRR
    'And his father was dead and/but only his mother was alive.'
    (1-T029-00:01:46.046)

Examples (3)–(7) show sentences in which the clauses have the same subject but different predicates. For (3)–(5) a translation expressing conjunction was given for text data, or the example was elicited with Tok Pisin *na* 'and', while for (6)–(7) a translation expressing adversative coordination was given for text data, or the example was elicited with Tok Pisin *tasol* 'but'. Further research is required to establish whether there are criteria for assuming a conjunction or adversative reading. Note that (5) does not have subject NPs as the clauses are imperative and imperative clauses frequently lack subject NPs (see §9.2, where there are also more examples of syndetic coordinate imperative clauses). In the other sentences, the second clause does not require a subject NP as the subject of both clauses is identical. It could thus be argued that there is *coordination reduction* in Papapana but as shown in §10.1.4, this is not the case. Even though the second clause does not require a subject NP, when presented with (3) and (6) speakers indicated that it was possible for the second clause to repeat the lexical subject NP of the first clause or to have a coreferential independent pronoun subject NP, and that this would not alter the interpretation of the sentence.

(3) Va:sina na=vanua   i=pei
    before   SPEC[CLI]=people 3PL.SBJ=PST.IPFV
    tu~tuv=i=a=ina=i   iai
    RD~swim=TR=3SG.OBJ=3PL.IPFV=IRR PROX
    tau i=pei   sa~saremu=i=a=ina=i.
    and   3PL.SBJ=PST.IPFV RD~sell=TR=3SG.OBJ=3PL.IPFV=IRR
    'In the past people used to dive for this and they used to sell it.'
    (1-T107-00:04:42.200)

(4) *Ben e=pei umunu=ena=i **tau***
Ben 3SG.SBJ=PST.IPFV sit=3SG.IPFV=IRR and
e=pei ani~ani gono=ena=i.
3SG.SBJ=PST.IPFV RD~eat banana=3SG.IPFV=IRR
'Ben was sitting and he was eating bananas.'
(2-E021-1)

(5) *O=nao **tau** o=de mai ta:=bau iana.*
2SG.SBJ=go and 2SG.SBJ=take hither some=PL fish
'Go and catch some fish.'
(2-E026)

(6) *Na=tsunami e=ara tete i-poana **ta** e=ae*
SPEC[CLI]=tsunami 3SG.SBJ=PST enter LOC-village and 3SG.SBJ=NEG
ara maria egoego.
PST thing well
'The tsunami hit the village but it didn't do much (damage).'
(1-T105-00:08:39.189)

(7) *Bau vanua-eta i=roros=i=a **ta** i=ae*
PL people-AUG 3PL.SBJ=see=TR=3SG.OBJ and 3PL.SBJ=NEG
ma'=i=a na=maunu.
give=TR=3SG.OBJ SPEC[CLI]=woman
'The chiefs saw him but they didn't give him a wife.'
(2-E021-1)

10.1.1.2 Phrase coordination

NPs and PPs may be coordinated by *tau ~ ta* in Papapana. Unlike some Oceanic languages, there is no distinction between *tight* and *loose* nominal coordination (that is, between items which are more or less closely associated in the real world), nor are there different coordinating morphemes depending on the animacy or class of the coordinated nouns (Moyse-Faurie and Lynch 2004: 450, 453).

When subject NPs are linked in Papapana, the coordination may be *segregatory* or *combinatory*. Examples (8)–(11) show segregatory coordination in which the two subject NPs could each be expanded into their own clause (note the differing subject proclitics in each), whereas (12)–(14) demonstrate combinatory coordination in which the two subject NPs combine to function as one unit of meaning, with reference to the rest of the clause; these subject NPs cannot be expanded into separate clauses. Note that (14) shows that coordination of clauses, as well as phrases, may arise within one sentence.

(8) **"E-tama-u tau e-sina-u i=ri**
PERS-father-1SG.PSSR and PERS-mother-1SG.PSSR 3PL.SBJ=OPT
amun=i=o=ina."
look=TR=2SG.OBJ=3PL.IPFV
'"My mother and father want to meet you."'
(1-T029-00:10:46.140)

(9) . . .*i=mei tue=ami*
3PL.SBJ=come.SEQ scold=1EXCL.OBJ
bau sina-mani ta bau tama-mani.
PL mother-1EXCL.PSSR and PL father-1EXCL.PSSR
'. . .our mothers and fathers scolded us.'
(1-T011-00:01:47.979)

(10) **Anau ta aia** *mi=ara nao.*
1SG and 3SG 1EXCL.SBJ=PST go
'He and I went.'
(2-E021-1)

(11) **Anau ta ani** *si=ara nao.*
1SG and 2SG 1INCL.SBJ=PST go
'You and I went.'
(2-E021-1)

(12) *Nasipuna,* **na=orawi ta na=maunu**
sometimes SPEC[CLI]=man and SPEC[CLI]=woman
i=to re~rete=ina=i auana.
3PL.SBJ=EMPH RD~walk=3PL.IPFV=IRR 3DU
'Sometimes, a man and woman go about together.'
(1-T094-00:01:41.203)

(13) **E-sina-u tau e-tama-u** *i=vei nai*
PERS-mother-1SG.PSSR and PERS-father-1SG.PSSR 3PL.SBJ=R/R marry
numanoa yia i=nao tani.
ten year 3PL.SBJ=go already
'My mother and father married each other ten years ago.'
(2-E021-1)

(14) Va~va:sina, Teperoi   mi=pei   po~po=mani=i
     RD~before   Teperoi 1EXCL.SBJ=PST.IPFV   RD~stay=1EXCL.IPFV=IRR
     tau **aite tau na:=bau na=vanua**   i=ara   vei
     and Dad and some=PL SPEC[CLI]=people   3PL.SBJ=PST   R/R
     va-ireire=ma.
     CAUS-be.angry=ma
     'Long ago, we were living in Teperoi and Dad and some people argued with each other.'
     (1-T030-00:00:33.770)

When object NPs are linked, the object enclitic is generally singular as in (15), but it is possible for the object enclitic to be plural (16). Speakers reported that the plural object enclitics in (17b) and (18b) were more acceptable than the singular object enclitics in (17a) and (18a), yet plural enclitics only occurred in elicitation sessions, and often only when prompted.

(15) U=to   vatan=i=a=i   **e-sina-u**   tau
     1SG.SBJ=EMPH   tell=TR=3SG.OBJ=IRR   PERS-mother-1SG.PSSR   and
     e-tama-u.
     PERS-father-1SG.PSSR
     'I will tell my mother and my father.'
     (2-E021-1)

(16) Richard   e=tu'u=**ina**   Kate   ta   ena=au   'usia.
     Richard 3SG.SBJ=meet=3PL.OBJ   Kate   and   3SG.PSSR=CLII   child
     'Richard met Kate and her child.'
     (2-E027)

(17) a. Anau   u=roros=i=**a**   Kate tau Sarah.
        1SG   1SG.SBJ=see=TR=3SG.OBJ   Kate and Sarah
        'I saw Kate and Sarah.'
        (2-E021-1)
     b. Anau   u=roroto=**ina**   Kate tau Sarah.
        1SG   1SG.SBJ=see=TR=3PL.OBJ   Kate and Sarah
        'I saw Kate and Sarah.'
        (2-E021-1)

(18) a. *Peter e=ara irom=i=a* **nu=daramu** *ta*
Peter 3SG.SBJ=PST drink=TR=3SG.OBJ SPEC.CLII=water and
na=Cocacola.
SPEC[CLI]=Cocacola
'Peter drank water and Coca-Cola.'
(2-E027)
b. *Peter e=ara iromo=**ina** nu=daramu ta*
Peter 3SG.SBJ=PST drink=3PL.OBJ SPEC.CLII=water and
na=Cocacola.
SPEC[CLI]=Cocacola
'Peter drank water and Coca-Cola.'
(2-E027)

The object enclitic agrees with the first of the coordinated object NPs, as in (19) where the object NPs exhibit different person categories. In (20a) the object enclitic agrees with the person category of the first of the coordinated object pronoun *ani* '2SG' but the object enclitic is plural. When both of the coordinated object NPs are pronouns, then the first pronoun may be omitted and instead be reflected in the object enclitic as in (20b). Example (20b) supports the suggestion in §6.3.2 that object enclitics might be weak accusative pronouns, or it could be that there is no phrasal coordination in this clause but that the subject and verb complex (VC) of the second clause are not overtly expressed (i.e. 'I want to talk to you and (I want to talk to) him').

(19) *Eugene e=roros=i=a* **Helen** *ta* **ani.**
Eugene 3SG.SBJ=see=TR=3SG.OBJ Helen and 2SG
'Eugene saw Helen and you.'
(2-E027)

(20) a. *Anau u=eri vori~vori=**amu**=ou* **ani** *ta* **aia.**
1SG 1SG.SBJ=OPT RD~talk=2PL.OBJ=1SG.IPFV 2SG and 3SG
'I want to talk to you and him.'
(2-E027)
b. *Anau u=eri vori~vori=i=**o**=u ta* **aia.**
1SG 1SG.SBJ=OPT RD~talk=TR=2SG.OBJ=1SG.IPFV and 3SG
'I want to talk to you and him.'
(2-E027)

In (21)–(22) the object NPs are also linked but there is no object enclitic as these clauses demonstrate transitivity discord (§6.5.5.2).

(21) *Arira si=ani=i* **bau kaukau** *ta na=iana.*
 1INCL 1INCL.SBJ=eat=IRR PL sweet.potato and SPEC[CLI]=fish
 'We'll eat sweet potatoes and fish.'
 (2-E021-1)

(22) *A:mani mi=ani* **na=koko'i,** **na=uvi** *tau*
 1EXCL 1EXCL.SBJ=eat SPEC[CLI]=taro SPEC[CLI]=yam and
 na=gono.
 SPEC[CLI]=banana
 'We eat taro, yam and banana.'
 (2-E021-1)

The coordinator *tau ~ ta* can conjoin PPs which are headed by the preposition *te* (23)–(24). It is not possible for a preposition to dominate a pair of conjoined NPs.

(23) *...si=boto* **te** *ia'a tau te aite.*
 1INCL.SBJ=be.born OBL Mum and OBL Dad
 '...we were born to Mum and to Dad.'
 (1-T089-00:09:53.802)

(24) *E=nao* **te=na=skuru** *tau te=na=stoa.*
 3SG.SBJ=go OBL=SPEC[CLI]=school and OBL=SPEC[CLI]=store
 'He goes to school and to the store.'
 (2-E021-1)

The coordinator *tau ~ ta* can also conjoin oblique NP adjuncts (25), or a NP adjunct and a PP adjunct headed by the preposition *te* (26)–(27).

(25) *Mamena boni~boni e=nao* ***i-nongana tau i-daramu.***
 PL.COLL RD~day 3SG.SBJ=go LOC-beach and LOC-river
 'Every day he goes to the beach and to the river.'
 (2-E021-1)

(26) *Mamena boni~boni e=nao* **te=na=skuru** *ta*
PL.COLL RD~day 3SG.SBJ=go OBL=SPEC[CLI]=school and
i-daramu.
LOC-river
'Every day he goes to school and to the river.'
(2-E021-1)

(27) *Mamena boni~boni e=nao* **i-ava** *ta* **te=na='uru.**
PL.COLL RD~day 3SG.SBJ=go LOC-sea and OBL=SPEC[CLI]=island
'Every day he goes to sea and to the island.'
(2-E021-1)

10.1.1.3 Phrase coordination with dual independent pronouns

Papapana has two sets of dual independent pronouns. The first set in Table 4.3 in §4.2 begin with *aua* while the remainder of the form is similar to the possessor suffixes. These dual independent pronouns can coordinate NPs, as in the following examples in which the dual independent pronoun occurs between the coordinated NPs, which are the subject of the verb (28) or the object (29).

(28) *Tauvita koko'i* **Anna auana Bob** *i=atono i=a*
how.many taro Anna 3DU Bob 3PL.SBJ=bring APPL=3SG.OBJ
Emma?
Emma
'How many taros did Anna and Bob bring for Emma?'
(2-E029-1)

(29) *. . .nia* **aite auana ia'a** *mi=to ari=ina.*
ASSOC.PL Dad 3DU Mum 1EXCL.SBJ dig=3PL.OBJ
'. . .we had buried Dad and Mum.'
(1-T030-00:03:12.127)

In (30)–(32) the dual independent pronoun has an *inclusory* function as it "identifies a set of participants that includes the one [. . .] referred to by the lexical noun phrase" (Lichtenberk 2000a: 1). The inclusory pronoun precedes the included NP and there is no overt marker of the relation between them; therefore, inclusory constructions in Papapana are *implicit* (Lichtenberk 2000a: 4). The construction is coordinate and the inclusory pronoun and the included NP together form a phrase, which is reflected in the plural subject proclitic in the VC.

(30) Na:=ata   na=boni   **auami**   **Josep** mi=nao   tena
some=CLI SPEC[CLI]=day 1EXCL.DU Josep 1EXCL.SBJ=go SUBR
ai~aini.
RD~hook
'One day Joseph and I went to fish.'
(1-T017-00:00:18.970)

(31) **Auami   e-maria   Willis** enai   na=poana
1EXCL.DU PERS-thing Willis DEM2 SPEC[CLI]=village
mi=asi=a.
1EXCL.SBJ=leave=3SG.OBJ
'What's-their-name, Willis and I left that village.'
(1-T034-00:37:13.280)

(32) "E-tama-na   e-sina-na   e=mate   ta
PERS-mother-3SG.PSSR PERS-mother-3SG.PSSR 3SG.SBJ=die and
auana e-tubu-na   i=po~po=ina.
3DU   PERS-grandparent-3SG.PSSR 3PL.SBJ=RD~stay=3PL.IPFV
'His father, his mother died and he and his grandmother lived.'
(1-T029-00:10:11.620)

10.1.2 Disjunction

The coordinator *o* 'or' coordinates alternative clauses, that is, clauses which represent events or states that are alternative possibilities, and thus exhibit disjunction. *O* may join clauses which have the same subject but different predicates (§10.1.2.1), or join subject NPs, object NPs, or adjunct PPs (§10.1.2.2). In the attested data, *o* does not join clauses which each have their own subject and predicate, nor do coordinated object NPs exhibit different person categories. Generally the conjoined elements occur alongside each other with *o* intervening.

10.1.2.1 Clause coordination

In (33)–(34) the coordinator *o* 'or' joins clauses which have the same subject but different predicates. These examples represent quite complex sentences: in (33) the conjoined clauses are preceded by a conditional adverbial clause, while in (34) the conjoined clauses are joined to another clause with the sequential coordinator *iara* 'then'. The subject NP in the second clause of (33) is optional.

(33) *John e=to   ani=a=i   pei   naono mama,* **[***John***]**
John 3SG.SBJ=EMPH eat=3SG.OBJ=IRR PART tree   DEM1 John
e=mate=i   o e=matemate=i.
3SG.SBJ=die=IRR or 3SG.SBJ=sick=IRR
'If John eats that piece of tree, he'll die or he'll get sick.'
(2-E021-1)

(34) **Tena bau Sande   Theresa e=nao~nao=na**
OBL PL Sunday Theresa 3SG.SBJ=RD~go=3SG.IPFV
te=na=vei   toko   o e=po=na   i-poana,
OBL=SPEC[CLI]=COLL worship or 3SG.SBJ=stay=3SG.IPFV LOC-village
iara tena bau Mande   e=si~siodo=ena.
then OBL PL Monday 3SG.SBJ=RD~work=3SG.IPFV
'On Sundays Theresa goes to church or she stays at home, then on Mondays she works.'
(2-E027)

10.1.2.2 Phrase coordination

The coordinator *o* 'or' may also join subject NPs (35), object NPs (36) and adjuncts (37). Example (36) shows that more than one NP can be coordinated and in this particular example there is actually more than one coordinator.

(35) *. . .na=orawi   o na=maunu   e=to   mate=i.*
SPEC[CLI]=man or SPEC[CLI]=woman 3SG.SBJ=EMPH die=IRR
'[I want to talk about the time that] . . .a man or a woman dies.'
(1-T069-00:00:15.850)

(36) *I=to   taga=i=a=i*
3PL.SBJ=EMPH burn=TR=3SG.OBJ=IRR

   na=kara   o na=inu   o na=paga   enai.
   SPEC[CLI]=car or SPEC[CLI]=house or SPEC[CLI]=shoot DEM2
   'They burnt cars or houses or guns.'
   (1-T034-00:27:06.026)

(37) Na='usia   i=pei   gaganini=i **i-nongana**
     SPEC[CLI]=child 3PL.SBJ=PST.IPFV play=IRR   LOC-beach
     o **te=na='uru.**
     or OBL=SPEC[CLI]=island
     'In the past, children used to play on the beach or on the island.'
     (2-E027)

10.1.3 Sequential coordination

The temporal coordinators *iara* 'then' and *enai* 'after' coordinate clauses that express events that occur sequentially. *Iara* 'then' generally occurs between the conjoined elements and may join clauses that each have their own subject and predicate (38)–(39) or clauses which have the same subject but different predicates (40)–(42). The first clause expresses the event which happened first. Often the first clause contains the completive aspect marker *osi* as in (38) and (40), but other attested data show no tense, aspect, mode (TAM) marking (41), or the use of the irrealis mode enclitic =*i* as in (39) and (42).

(38) U=to   tovu osi   **iara** mi=po~poni=a=i.
     1SG.SBJ=EMPH husk COMPL then 1EXCL.SBJ=RD~shell=3SG.OBJ=IRR
     'I finish husking then we shell it.'
     (1-T009-00:00:45.080)

(39) U=to   manene mai=i   **iara** so=nao=i.
     1SG.SBJ=EMPH return hither=IRR then 1INCL.SBJ=go=IRR
     'I'll come back then we'll go.'
     (2-E022)

(40) Ben e=to   ani osi   na=gono,   **iara**
     Ben 3SG.SBJ=EMPH eat COMPL SPEC[CLI]=banana then
     e=nao   i-nongana.
     3SG.SBJ=go LOC-beach
     'Ben finished eating the banana then he went to the beach.'
     (2-E021-1)

(41) E=to   roroto=au   **iara** e=atun=i=au.
     3SG.SBJ=EMPH see=1SG.OBJ then 3SG.SBJ=attack=TR=1SG.OBJ
     'He saw me then he killed me.'
     (2-E021-1)

(42) *Mamena boni~boni Maureen e=siodo=i,   e=gaganini=i,*
     PL.COLL RD~day Maureen 3SG.SBJ=work=IRR 3SG.SBJ=play=IRR
     ***iara** e=no   aputu=i.*
     then 3SG.SBJ=go.SEQ sleep=IRR
     'Every day, Maureen works, plays then goes and sleeps.'
     (2-E016)

Enai 'after' precedes the two clauses, the first of which expresses the event which happened first. *Enai* can coordinate clauses that each have their own subject and predicate (43), or clauses which have the same subject but different predicates (44). Occasionally, *enai* occurs between the conjoined elements and its meaning can be interpreted as 'then' as in (45) (see also §10.3.1). In all these examples, *=ma* attaches to *enai*, but this is not always the case (as noted in §5.3.1, *=ma* attaches to all word classes and may be a discourse marker).

(43) ***Enai**=ma sispaia   e=to   ara tosi, i-poana*
     after=ma ceasefire 3SG.SBJ=EMPH PST finish LOC-village
     mi=manene   mai.
     1EXCL.SBJ=return hither
     'After the ceasefire finished, we went back to our village.'
     (1-T018-00:01:22.060)

(44) ***Enai**=ma u=to   tepe=a=i   na=teari,*
     after=ma 1SG.SBJ=EMPH cut=3SG.OBJ=IRR SPEC[CLI]=betelnut
     u=depana=i=a=i.
     1SG.SBJ=shell=TR=3SG.OBJ=IRR
     'After I cut the betelnut, I shell it.'
     (1-T006-00:00:43.280)

(45) *U=pei   po=u=ma   **enai**=ma u=nai.*
     1SG.SBJ=PST.IPFV stay=1SG.IPFV=ma after=ma 1SG.SBJ=marry
     'I lived then I got married.'
     (1-T005-00:01:00.880)

10.1.4 Asyndesis

Papapana also expresses coordination by asyndesis. These constructions are considered coordinate as impressionistically they have the intonation contour of a single sentence. Asyndetic coordinate constructions may express conjunction, adversative coordination or sequential coordination but do not mark disjunction, nor link phrases. Asyndesis may also coordinate clauses referring to events that occur simultaneously. Speakers did not report, or were unaware of, a difference in meaning between syndetic and asyndetic coordinate constructions in Papapana: when I presented speakers with asyndetic coordinate constructions such as (46) and (47) below, they indicated that the addition of a coordinator did not affect meaning, and both constructions were grammatical. The relationship between the two clauses is derived from the context and the TAM marking. In (46)–(47) the clauses each have their own subject and predicate, though there are no overt subject NPs in (47). Adversative coordination and sequential coordination are expressed in (46) and (47) respectively. Possible differences in function or distribution between sentences with and without a coordinator are left for future research.

(46) *Burimaunu i=nao te=na=tago Vakonaia,*
women 3PL.SBJ=go OBL=SPEC[CLI]=exchange Wakunai
na=vanua i=nao te=na=siodo.
SPEC[CLI]=people 3PL.SBJ=go OBL=SPEC[CLI]=work
'The women went to the market in Wakunai (but) the men went to the plantations.'
(2-E027)

(47) *U=to votu mai naonava, e=gaunu=ina*
1SG.SBJ=EMPH leave hither yesterday 3SG.SBJ=write=3PL.OBJ
nua=au pepa.
two=CLII paper
'When I left yesterday, (then) he wrote two letters.'
(2-E008)

In (48)–(53) the clauses have the same subject but different predicates; (48)–(49) express conjunction, (50)–(51) express adversative coordination, and (52)–(53) express sequential coordination. Note that in (48), the coordinator *tau* occurs at the beginning of the sentence, linking it to the previous sentence; it is common in speech for sentences to be joined in this way. In (49) and (51), asyndesis connects imperative clauses and therefore there are no subject NPs (see §9.2 where there are also more examples of asyndetic coordinate imperative clauses). In (52) and (53) the completive aspect marker *osi* is present and therefore although the clauses are ordered iconically in (52), in (53) the second clause expresses the event that occurred first and this is signalled by the completive aspect.

(48) *Tau na:=bau bau vanua-ota i-poana i=to*
and some=PL PL people-AUG LOC-village 3PL.SBJ=EMPH
amun=i=a, i=ma'=i=a na=maunu.
look=TR=3SG.OBJ 3PL.SBJ=give-TR=3SG.OBJ SPEC[CLI]=woman
'And some elders in the village saw him (and) gave him a wife.'
(1-T029-00:01:15.510)

(49) *"Mu=matono, mu=de=ina taramina te a:mu..."*
2PL.SBJ=awaken 2PL.SBJ=take=3PL.OBJ thing OBL 2PL
'"Wake up (and) get your things..."'
(1-T002-00:00:49.505)

(50) *Na='usia i=nao te=na=skuru,*
SPEC[CLI]=child 3PL.SBJ=go OBL=SPEC[CLI]=school
i=ae de=a ta=matau.
3PL.SBJ=NEG take=3SG.OBJ NSPEC[CLI]=knowledge
'The children went to school (but) they didn't learn anything.'
(2-E027)

(51) *O=ae ani~ani kaukau, koko'i o=ani.*
2SG.SBJ=NEG RD~eat sweet.potato taro 2SG.SBJ=eat
'Don't eat the sweet potato, (but do) eat the taro.'
(2-E028-2)

(52) *Mi=to usi osi=a=i*
1EXCL.SBJ=EMPH scrape COMPL=3SG.OBJ=IRR
na=ma'ata, mi=pitu=a=i
SPEC[CLI]=brown.coconut 1EXCL.SBJ=squeeze=3SG.OBJ=IRR
na=ma'ata.
SPEC[CLI]=brown.coconut
'After we finish scraping the brown coconut, we squeeze the coconut.'
(1-T038-00:01:09.458)

(53) *Ben e=nao i-nongana, e=to ani osi*
Ben 3SG.SBJ=go LOC-beach 3SG.SBJ=EMPH eat COMPL
na=gono.
SPEC[CLI]=banana
'Ben went to the beach after he finished eating the banana.'
(2-E021-1)

In examples (48)–(53) above (and (3)–(7) in §10.1.1.1), there is no overt subject NP in the second clause and this missing subject NP is controlled by (i.e. is coreferential with) the subject of the first clause. Therefore it could be argued that there is *coordination reduction,* also known as "ellipsis" or "deletion" (Haspelmath 2004: 31). However, most canonic Oceanic languages do not have coordination reduction constructions; therefore, "if the third person subjects of successive clauses are omitted (as they often are), leaving only the prefix or proclitic to the verb to indicate the person and number of the subject, then the identity of the missing subject must be inferred from context" (Ross 2004: 517). Indeed it is not always the case in Papapana that the missing subject NP of the second clause is coreferential with the subject of the first clause: in (54) the 3PL object of the first clause (which was earlier expressed by *navanua* 'the men') is the subject of the second clause, while in (55) the 3SG object of the first clause, *Ben,* is the subject of the second clause. If there were coordination reduction in Papapana, then the 3PL *bau sinaina* 'their mothers' or 3SG *Maureen* would be the subject of both clauses, but they are not and instead the subject of the second clause is inferred from the context and understood to actually be coreferential with the object of the first clause. Since there is no coordination reduction, the subject proclitic does not have a reference tracking function, which is also the case in canonic Oceanic languages (Ross 2004: 518).

(54) *Bau sina-ina   i=vori~vori=ina=ina=i,*
PL   mother-3PL.PSSR 3PL.SBJ=RD~talk=3PL.OBJ=3PL.IPFV=IRR
i=ae   nongono=i.
3PL.SBJ=NEG hear=IRR
'Their mothers talk to them but they don't listen.'
(1-T025-00:01:47.050)

(55) *Maureen e=oi=a   Ben, e=to   ani*
Maureen 3SG.SBJ=call=3SG.OBJ Ben 3SG.SBJ=EMPH eat
osi=a=i   na=gono.
COMPL=3SG.OBJ=IRR SPEC[CLI]=banana
'Maureen called Ben (after) he finished eating his banana.'
(2-E021-1)

Asyndesis may coordinate clauses which express events that happen simultaneously, such as in (56) where both clauses have past imperfective marking (see §7.1.4.2). Asyndesis may also coordinate clauses which occur simultaneously but one of the events is signalled by continuous aspect marking to be the context or background for the other foregrounded event, which is not marked for continuous aspect, as in (57)–(59). The backgrounded event may precede or follow the foregrounded event. Cross-linguistically, the use of a continuative, durative or imperfective aspect marker is one of the two most common methods of expressing a backgrounded event (Thompson, Longacre and Hwang 2007: 254).

(56) *Na:=bau   i=pei   ubete=ina=i   i-tanana,*
     some=PL   3PL.SBJ=PST.IPFV   lay=3PL.IPFV=IRR   LOC-road
     mi=pei   vurau=emani   mai=i.
     1EXCL.SBJ=PST.IPFV   run=1EXCL.IPFV   hither=IRR
     'Some were lying on the road while we were running back.'
     (1-T002-00:04:51.530)

(57) *E=pei   no   po=na=i   nani,*
     3SG.SBJ=PST.IPFV   go.SEQ   stay=3SG.IPFV=IRR   there
     na=maunu   e=mei   tu'u=i=a.
     SPEC[CLI]=woman   3SG.SBJ=come.SEQ   meet=TR=3SG.OBJ
     'While he was there, the girl came and met him.'
     (1-T029-00:14:30.850)

(58) *Mi=pei   po=mani=i   nani, aite e=ara*
     1EXCL.SBJ=PST.IPFV   stay=1EXCL.IPFV=IRR   there Dad   3SG.SBJ=PST
     mate.
     die
     '(While) we were living there, Dad died.'
     (1-T030-00:02:34.020)

(59) *E=udua   tae=ami   mi=pei*
     3SG.SBJ=light   up=1EXCL.OBJ   1EXCL.SBJ=PST.IPFV
     tua~tua=mani=i.
     RD~paddle=1EXCL.IPFV=IRR
     'It lit us up while we were paddling.'
     (1-T071-00:01:49.850)

10.2 Relative clauses

This section describes the position of a relative clause within the matrix NP in relation to the noun it modifies, and the way in which the two are linked (§10.2.1), and relativised functions permitted in Papapana and the strategies used to indicate them (§10.2.2). There are no restrictions in Papapana on the external grammatical relations in the matrix clause of a NP containing a relative clause. There is no structural difference between restrictive and non-restrictive relative clauses in Papapana, so the discussion below applies to both.

10.2.1 Position and relativiser

As mentioned in §4.1, and shown in (60), relative clauses in Papapana are externally headed and postnominal, that is, the matrix noun occurs outside of the relative clause and the relative clause follows the matrix noun. Relative clauses typically follow the matrix noun in Oceanic languages (Lynch, Ross, and Crowley 2002: 43), and cross-linguistically, even in languages where modifiers are prenominal (as they can be in Papapana), there is a tendency for relative clauses to be postnominal due to the universal pragmatic principle that shifts heavy elements to later in a clause (Payne 1997: 326).

(60) *Anau u=roros=i=a   nu=kakau   **mama na=orawi***
     1SG 1SG.SBJ=see=TR=3SG.OBJ SPEC.CLII=dog REL   SPEC[CLI]=man
     e=to   ba'o=a.
     3SG.SBJ=EMPH   beat=3SG.OBJ
     'I saw the dog that the man hit.'
     (2-E021-1)

In Papapana, *mama* signals the beginning of the relative clause and connects the relative clause to the matrix noun. *Mama* does not introduce other subordinate clauses. *Mama* is invariant and does not indicate the relativised function (which is instead indicated by the gapping strategy, see §10.2.2), therefore *mama* is a relativiser and not a relative pronoun; for example, in (60) the matrix noun has a non-human 3SG referent while in (61) it has a human 3PL referent. *Mama* has the same form as the person-based demonstrative *mama* 'near speaker' (§4.5). This is typical of Oceanic languages in which relative clause markers "are often similar or identical in shape to demonstratives" (Lynch, Ross, and Crowley 2002: 53).

(61) *Kevin e=siodo=ina   sibuava   **mama Ben***
     Kevin 3SG.SBJ=work=3PL.OBJ old.women REL   Ben
     e=to   tavone=ina   naonava.
     3SG.SBJ=EMPH   help=3PL.OBJ yesterday
     'Kevin works for the old women whom Ben helped yesterday.'
     (2-E027)

Sometimes *mama* is omitted and the relative clause is connected to the matrix noun asyndetically, that is, it is embedded in the matrix clause with no overt marking. As a comparison of (62a) and (62b) shows, there is no grammatical, semantic or pragmatic motivation for which strategy is employed, though speakers indicated that it was more acceptable to link the relative clause and the matrix noun syndetically. It seems likely that the omission of *mama* is a feature of casual speech and therefore I do not distinguish between syndetic and asydentic constructions, but will highlight examples of asydensis.

(62) a. *Anau u=roros=i=a   na=orawi   e=to*
    1SG 2SG.SBJ=see=TR=3SG.OBJ SPEC[CLI]=man 3SG.SBJ=EMPH
    ba'o=a   nu=kakau.
    beat=3SG.OBJ SPEC.CLII=dog
    'I saw a/the man who hit a dog.'
    (2-E027)
  b. *Anau u=roros=i=a   na=orawi   mama*
    1SG 2SG.SBJ=see=TR=3SG.OBJ SPEC[CLI]=man REL
    e=to   ba'o=a   nu=kakau.
    3SG.SBJ=EMPH beat=3SG.OBJ SPEC.CLII=dog
    'I saw a/the man who hit a dog.'
    (2-E027)

10.2.2 Relativised function

In Papapana, all grammatical relations within the relative clause can be relativised except the object of a comparative, though a relativised NP as genitive is rare. Papapana is thus like many Oceanic languages which allow relativisation of NPs well down the universal Accessibility Hierarchy (Lynch, Ross, and Crowley 2002: 43). It should be noted here that I have described Papapana as making a distinction between *primary* and *secondary* objects rather than *direct* and *indirect* objects (see §6.3.1), which are the terms used on the Accessibility Hierarchy (Keenan and Comrie 1977). Thus, to avoid any confusion here, I will simply describe objects in terms of their semantic roles and whether they are objects of a monotransitive or ditransitive predicate.

Since *mama* is not a relative pronoun, it does not indicate the relativised function. Instead the relativised function may be indicated by the gap strategy. In (63) the relative clause is missing a locative adjunct, while in (64) the relative clause is missing a subject NP. The matrix noun is interpreted as filling the gap and the grammatical relation of the missing argument is the relativised function. In (63) there is no overt expression, such as a preposition, of the locative adjunct in the relative clause. In (64) however, the subject proclitic in the relative clause is an overt expression of the missing argument and agrees in person and number with the matrix noun, indicating that the matrix noun is coreferential with the relativised noun. It is common in Oceanic languages for a pronominal form to remain in the relative clause as an expression of the relativised noun (Lynch, Ross, and Crowley 2002: 80). This could be interpreted as the pronoun retention strategy; however, I treat subject and object clitics as agreement and not independent pronouns (see §6.3.2) and therefore they are different to the resumptive pronouns found in other languages that use the pronoun retention strategy. The following sections will demonstrate these strategies in more detail.

(63) *E=adu~adu=i=a*   *na=inu*   **mama**
3SG.SBJ=RD~destroy=TR=3SG.OBJ SPEC[CLI]=house REL
na=kaukau   *i=to*   *ruvu=ina.*
SPEC[CLI]=sweet.potato 3PL.SBJ=EMPH put=3PL.OBJ
'He destroyed the house in which they put sweet potatoes.'
(2-E021-2)

(64) *Anau u=roros=i=a*   *na=maunu*   **mama**
1SG 1SG.SBJ=see=TR=3SG.OBJ SPEC[CLI]=woman REL
e=pei   *de~de=ina=ena=i*   *na=pe'uri.*
3SG.SBJ=PST.IPFV RD~take=3PL.OBJ=3SG.IPFV=IRR SPEC.CLII=basket
'I saw a/the woman who was carrying baskets.'
(2-E027)

In Papapana, relative clauses are always finite: aside from the gapped argument or adjunct, they have the same structure as an independent clause. Like independent clauses, clause order may be variable; this will be described in each of the following sections.

10.2.2.1 Relativised NP as subject
This section demonstrates that the relativised NP can be subject of an intransitive or monotransitive clause. The relativised NP is not attested as subject of a ditransitive clause in my data, but this is most likely a gap in the data rather than it being ungrammatical.

In the following examples the function of the relativised NP is subject of an intransitive clause. The relativiser is followed by the VC which, like all other

VCs, is obligatorily marked by a subject proclitic, here coreferential with the matrix noun. Note that there is no relativiser in (66). In (65) the external grammatical relation is subject of a monotransitive clause which is embedded within an asydentic finite complement. In (66) and (67) the external grammatical relation is object of a monotransitive clause with the semantic roles of patient and beneficiary respectively, while in (68) the matrix NP is a postposed possessor.

(65) "*Au=nua   arao   i=wa   vavine-ina*
     1SG.PSSR=two[CLI] brother 3PL.SBJ=say sibling-3PL.PSSR
     mama e=to   nai=ena   e=mei
     REL   3SG.SBJ=EMPH marry=3SG.IPFV 3SG.SBJ=come.SEQ
     va-oto=ina=i. . ."
     CAUS-board=3PL.OBJ=IRR
     '"My two cousins said their cousin who is married will come take them. . ."'
     (1-T042-00:01:51.940)

(66) *Iara na:=bau   na=siapani   **i=to   pei***
     then some=PL   SPEC[CLI]=Japanese 3PL.SBJ=EMPH PST.IPFV
     averu=i, i=pei   *vae   atunu=ina=i=ma.*
     steal=IRR 3PL.SBJ=PST.IPFV REP attack=3PL.OBJ=IRR=ma
     'Then they killed some Japanese who used to steal.'
     (1-T034-00:12:02.800)

(67) *Na='usia   i=no   siodo i=a   soida'o*
     SPEC[CLI]=child 3PL.SBJ=go.SEQ work APPL=3SG.OBJ old.man
     mama e=pei   matemate=ena=i.
     REL   3SG.SBJ=PST.IPFV sick=3SG.IPFV=IRR
     'The children worked for an old man who was sick.'
     (2-E027)

(68) *E-tubu-na   maunu e=de=a,*
     PERS-grandparent-3SG.PSSR woman 3SG.SBJ=take=3SG.OBJ
     *e-sina-na   na=orawi   **mama e=to***
     PERS-mother-3SG.PSSR SPEC[CLI]=man REL   3SG.SBJ=EMPH
     ara mate.
     PST die
     'His grandmother took him, the mother of the man who died.'
     (1-T029-00:02:42.780)

In the following examples the function of the relativised NP is subject of a monotransitive clause. The relativiser is followed by the VC which is marked by a subject proclitic that is coreferential with the matrix noun, and an object enclitic. The position of the object NP is generally postverbal but as a comparison of (70a) and (70b) shows, the object NP may occur preverbally as well. Example (69) shows that a relative clause follows other postnominal modifiers such as *panapana* 'all'. In both examples, the external grammatical relation is object (patient) of a monotransitive clause.

(69) "*Mu=oi=ina   na=vanua   panapana **mama***
    2PL.SBJ=call=3PL.OBJ SPEC[CLI]=man all   REL
    i=to   ***atun=i=a***   ***na=orawi***   ***mama*. . ."
    3PL.SBJ=EMPH   attack=TR=3SG.OBJ SPEC[CLI]=man DEM1
    "'Call everyone who killed this man. . .'"
    (1-T029-00:25:26.170)

(70) a. *Jim e=ara   roroto=ina   nua=au   kakau **mama***
       Jim   3SG.SBJ=PST see=3PL.OBJ   two=CLII dog   REL
       i=pei   ***ani~ani=a=ina=i***   ***nu=ki:roko.***
       3PL.SBJ=PST.IPFV RD~eat=3SG.OBJ=3PL.IPFV=IRR SPEC.CLII=rat
       'Jim saw two dogs which were eating a rat.'
       (2-E027)
    b. *Jim e=ara   roroto=ina   nua=au   kakau **mama***
       Jim   3SG.SBJ=PST see=3PL.OBJ   two=CLII dog   REL
       nu=ki:roko   ***i=pei***   ***ani~ani=a=ina=i.***
       SPEC.CLII=rat 3PL.SBJ=PST.IPFV RD~eat=3SG.OBJ=3PL.IPFV=IRR
       'Jim saw two dogs which were eating a rat.'
       (2-E027)

10.2.2.2 Relativised NP as object

This section demonstrates that the relativised NP can be object of a monotransitive or ditransitive clause and have various semantic roles.

In the following examples the function of the relativised NP is patient or theme object of a monotransitive clause. The relativiser is followed by a subject NP and the VC, which is marked by a subject proclitic, and an object enclitic that is coreferential with the matrix noun. Note that (71) and (73) do not have subject NPs. The external grammatical relation is subject of a monotransitive clause in (71), object (comitative) of a monotransitive clause in (72) and adjunct in (73).

(71) *Na=orawi* **mama** *i=to* *va-dovi=a*
SPEC[CLI]=man REL 3PL.SBJ=EMPH CAUS-sink=3SG.OBJ
e=wa...
3SG.SBJ=say
'The man whom they sank said. . .'
(1-T072-00:01:09.760)

(72) *Tom e=me-a* *tua* *na=maunu* **mama**
Tom 3SG.SBJ=COM-SG.OBJ paddle SPEC[CLI]=woman REL
na=orawi *e=to* *atun=i=a.*
SPEC[CLI]=man 3SG.SBJ=EMPH attack=TR=3SG.OBJ
'Tom paddled with the woman whom the man attacked.'
(2-E027)

(73) *Jeff e=ruvu=i=a* *na=vatu*
Jeff 3SG.SBJ=put=TR=3SG.OBJ SPEC[CLI]=stone
te=na=table **mama** *e=to* *atu=a.*
OBL=SPEC[CLI]=table REL 3SG.SBJ=EMPH make=3SG.OBJ
'Jeff put the stone on the table that he built.'
(2-E021-1)

In the following examples the function of the relativised NP is comitative object of a monotransitive clause. The relativiser may or may not be followed by a subject NP, while the VC is marked by a subject proclitic and the applicative comitative *me*. Ordinarily, *me* is always marked with -*a* when the object is singular and -*na* when it is plural, and the clause may have an object enclitic in the VC or an object NP, or both, which identifies the comitative object (see §6.5.4). In a relative clause however, there is no object enclitic and no object NP, so the relativised noun is indicated by a gap. The -*a* or -*na* attached to *me* do nevertheless agree with the coreferential matrix noun in number. In (74) the external grammatical relations is object (beneficiary) of a ditransitive clause, while in (75) the matrix NP is a preposed possessor.

(74) *Anau u=tavui* *i=a* *koko'i na=orawi* **mama**
1SG 1SG.SBJ=plant APPL=3SG.OBJ taro SPEC[CLI]=man REL
Alex *e=to* *me-a* *siodo=na.*
Alex 3SG.SBJ=EMPH COM-SG.OBJ work=3SG.IPFV
'I planted taros for the man whom Alex worked with.'
(2-E021-2)

464 —— Chapter 10 Complex sentences

(75) *Na=orawi* **mama** *u=to* *me-a* *naomai*
SPEC[CLI]=man REL 1SG.SBJ=EMPH COM-SG.OBJ come
vatono-na Billy.
name-3SG.PSSR Billy
'The man who I came with's name is Billy.'
(2-E021-1)

In the following example the function of the relativised NP is beneficiary object of a monotransitive clause. The relativiser is followed by the subject NP and the VC, which is marked by a subject proclitic, and an object enclitic that is coreferential with the matrix noun. The external grammatical relation here is subject of an intransitive clause.

(76) *Na=orawi* **mama** Alex *e=pei* *ara*
SPEC[CLI]=man REL Alex 3SG.SBJ=PST.IPFV PST
siodo i=a=ena=i *Teperoi e=po=na.*
work APPL=3SG.OBJ=3SG.IPFV=IRR Teperoi 3SG.SBJ=stay=3SG.IPFV
'The man whom Alex was working for lives in Teperoi.'
(2-E021-2)

In the following example the function of the relativised NP is beneficiary object of a ditransitive clause. The relativiser is followed by the subject NP and the VC, which is marked by a subject proclitic, and an object enclitic that is coreferential with the matrix noun. The patient object is a NP in postverbal position. The matrix NP here is an adjunct.

(77) *Anau u=umunu* *tae te=na=orawi* **mama Nick**
1SG 1SG.SBJ=sit up OBL=SPEC[CLI]=man REL Nick
e=to *atu* *i=a* *na=inu.*
3SG.SBJ=EMPH make APPL=3SG.OBJ SPEC[CLI]=house
'I sat on the man whom Nick built a house for.'
(2-E027)

In the following examples the function of the relativised NP is recipient object of a ditransitive clause. The relativiser is followed by the subject NP and the VC, which is marked by a subject proclitic, and an object enclitic that is coreferential with the matrix noun. The theme object generally occurs as a NP in postverbal position, though (78) shows a preverbal position. The external grammatical relation is object (patient) of a monotransitive clause in (78) and object (recipient) of a ditransitive clause in (79).

(78) *Chris e=roroto=ina   na=vanua   **mama Alex***
     Chris 3SG.SBJ=see=3PL.OBJ SPEC[CLI]=people REL   Alex
     na=gono   e=to   ara ma'a=ina.
     SPEC[CLI]=banana 3SG.SBJ=EMPH PST give=3PL.OBJ
     'Chris saw the people whom Alex gave the banana to.'
     (2-E027)

(79) *Anau u=ma'=i=a   na=tamute*
     1SG   1SG.SBJ=give=TR=3SG.OBJ SPEC[CLI]=mango
     *na=orawi   **mama Alex e=ma'=i=a**   koko'i.*
     SPEC[CLI]=man REL   Alex 3SG.SBJ=give=TR=3SG.OBJ taro
     'I gave a mango to the man whom Alex gave the taro to.'
     (2-E021-2)

10.2.2.3 Relativised NP as adjunct

In the following examples the relativised NP is an adjunct (80)–(82). In (80)–(81) the matrix NP is also adjunct, while in (82) the the external grammatical relation is subject of a nominal predicate. In the relative clause, the relativiser is followed by the object NP and the VC (and a reiterated object NP) in (80), the subject NP and VC in (81), and the VC and object NP in (82). There is no adposition to mark the adjunct and so the relativised noun is indicated by a gap. This is unusual for Oceanic languages as with "relativised NPs lower on the [accessibility] hierarchy, there is generally some kind of obligatory free form trace" (Lynch, Ross, and Crowley 2002: 43).

(80) *Te=na   inu   **mama na=maria**   i=to*
     OBL=SPEC[CLI] house REL   SPEC[CLI]=thing 3PL.SBJ=EMPH
     ru~ruvu=ina=ina,   bau taramina na=vei   takarau,
     RD~put=3PL.OBJ=3PL.IPFV PL   thing   SPEC[CLI]=COLL rusty
     mu=no   ruvu=ina=i   taramina te   a:mu nani.
     2PL.SBJ=go.SEQ put=3PL.OBJ=IRR thing   OBL   2PL   there
     'In the house in which they used to put the things, the rusty things, go put your things there.'
     (1-T071-00:03:54.110)

(81) *Mi=to   no   va-tonu   i-nongana   nani*
    1EXCL.SBJ=EMPH go.SEQ CAUS-stand   LOC-beach   there
    *te=na=pei   **mama na=barusu**   **e=to***
    OBL=SPEC[CLI]=place   REL   SPEC[CLI]=plane 3SG.SBJ=EMPH
    pu~pu=ena.
    RD~fall=3SG.IPFV
    'We went and parked on the beach there at the place on which planes land.'
    (1-T042-00:07:54.370)

(82) *Sa=au   naono **mama** e=to   **ba'o=a=i***
    DIM=CLII   tree   REL   3SG.SBJ=EMPH   beat=3SG.OBJ=IRR
    ***nu=kakau**   nu=etawa   poto.*
    SPEC.CLII=dog   SPEC.CLII=big INTS
    'The wood with which he hit the dog is very big.'
    (2-E027)

10.2.2.4 Relativised NP as genitive

In the following examples the function of the relativised NP is possessor of one of the arguments in the relative clause. The relativiser is followed by the possessum which is marked by a possessor suffix coreferential with the matrix noun. In (83) the possessum is the comitative object of the relative clause, while in (84) it is the recipient object. The relative clause thus contains a subject NP, the VC and in (84) a theme object NP. In both these examples, the external grammatical relation of the NP modified by the relative clause is patient object of the verb *nai* 'marry'.

(83) *Anau   u=nai=a=au   nu='usia   **mama***
    1SG   1SG.SBJ=marry=3SG.OBJ=1SG.IPFV   SPEC.CLII=child   REL
    e-tama-na**   **e-tama-u**   **e=me-a
    PERS-father-3SG.PSSR PERS-father-1SG.PSSR 3SG.SBJ=COM-SG.OBJ
    siodo=ona.
    work=3SG.IPFV
    'I married the child whose father my father works with.'
    (2-E028-2)

(84) *Emma e=nai=a   nu='usia   **mama***
    Emma 3SG.SBJ=marry=3SG.OBJ SPEC.CLII=child REL
    e-tama-na   Alex e=ma'=i=a
    PERS-father-3SG.PSSR Alex 3SG.SBJ=give=TR=3SG.OBJ
    na=kaukau.
    SPEC[CLI]=sweet.potato
    'Emma married the child whose father Alex gave sweet potatoes to.'
    (2-E028-2)

It proved very difficult to elicit examples such as (83) and (84), and more often speakers produced sentences such as (85) which is asyndetically coordinated.

(85) *Anau u=roros=i=a   na=maunu   mama,*
    1SG   1SG.SBJ=see=TR=3SG.OBJ SPEC[CLI]=woman REL
    na=orawi   e=to   ba'o=a   ena=au   kakau
    SPEC[CLI]=man 3SG.SBJ=EMPH beat=3SG.OBJ 3SG.PSSR=CLII dog
    'I saw this woman, the man hit her dog.'
    (2-E021-2)

10.3 Adverbial clauses and subordinators

Adverbial clauses in Papapana include conditional clauses, apprehension-causing adverbial clauses, and adverbial clauses expressing purpose, temporal location, spatial location, reason, result, concession and similarity or manner.

One type of temporal adverbial clause expressing elapsed time consists of an enumerated Class I temporal noun as the subject of the predicate *inao tani* 'they went already' and this adverbial clause is asyndetically linked to the main clause. All other adverbial clauses are linked to the main clause that they modify asyndetically or by a subordinator. In addition to the relativiser *mama* which is dedicated to introducing relative clauses (see §10.2.1), Papapana has ten subordinators: *tena* 'in order to', *tenava* 'so that', *merei* 'in order to', *eangoiena* 'until', *avoa* 'where', *avisi* 'because', *arogani* 'therefore', *marana* 'even though', *po'ovira* 'even though' and *avosia* 'like, so that, because' (see Table 10.1). Subordinators are invariant in form, do not occur in independent clauses, and there is always just one subordinator, which occurs immediately before the subordinate clause. *Tena* and *avosia* also introduce complement clauses but are not referred to as *complementizers* because they are not dedicated solely to introducing complement clauses (see §10.4). *Tena, merei, avosia,* and *eangoiena* are also prepositions which have NP complements (see §8.3

where I also discuss why I distinguish the two word classes). Meanwhile, *avoa* has the same form as the interrogative term *avoa* (see §9.3.2) but further research is required to determine which word is derived from which.

Table 10.1 shows the functions of adverbial clauses in Papapana, the mode of linking the adverbial clause to the main clause, and the section in which the function is discussed. There is a tendency for an adverbial clause to follow the main clause and adverbial clauses may contain other subordinate clauses: these issues will be discussed in the following sections.

Table 10.1: Adverbial clauses.

Function	Mode of linking clauses		
Condition	Asyndesis		§10.3.1
	sometimes *enai*	after	
	iara	then	
Apprehensive	Asyndesis		§10.3.2
	sometimes *tenava*	so that	
	avosia	so that	
Purpose	*tena*	in order to	§10.3.3.1
	tenava	so that	§10.3.3.2
	avosia	so that	§10.3.3.3
	merei	in order to	
Temporal location (elapsed time)	Asyndesis		§10.3.4.1
Temporal location (duration)	*eangoiena*	until	§10.3.4.2
Spatial location	*avoa*	where	§10.3.5
Reason	*avisi*	because	§10.3.6
	avosia	because	
Result	*arogani*	therefore	§10.3.7
Concession	*marana*	even though	§10.3.8.1
	po'ovira	even though	§10.3.8.2
Similarity and manner	*avosia*	like	§10.3.9

10.3.1 Condition

This section will recap the TAM marking described in §7.1 for complex sentences containing an adverbial clause expressing hypothetical condition (§7.1.4.4) and counterfactual condition (§7.1.5.3), and then discuss how the two clauses may be linked.

Hypothetical conditional adverbial clauses refer to unreal situations for which the speaker imagines what might be. The situation expressed in the conditional clause is prior to or the authority for the consequence expressed in the main clause. The adverbial clause is marked by the preverbal conditional mode marker *awa* and the irrealis enclitic *=i*, while the main clause is marked only by *=i*:

(86) Jim e=to **awa** nao=**i** Buka,
Jim 3SG.SBJ=EMPH COND go=IRR Buka
e=no peri=a=**i** na=siodo.
3SG.SBJ=go.SEQ find=3SG.OBJ=IRR SPEC[CLI]=work
'If Jim goes to Buka, he'll go and find work.'
(2-E027)

Counterfactual conditional adverbial clauses refer to unreal situations for which the speaker imagines what might have been. Again the situation expressed in the conditional clause is prior to or the authority for the consequence expressed in the main clause. The adverbial clauses is marked by the conditional mode marker *awa* and the optative mode marker *eri* (sometimes shortened to *ri*), while the main clause is marked only by *eri*:

(87) Albert e=to **ri awa** roros=i=a nu=muvi,
Albert 3SG.SBJ=EMPH CF COND see=TR=3SG.OBJ SPEC.CLII=movie
e=**eri** sare
3SG.SBJ=CF happy
'If Albert had watched the movie, he would have been happy.'
(2-E027)

As (86)–(87) show, the main clause and adverbial clause do not have a subordinator to link them. The position of the adverbial clause in relation to the main clause is fixed: conditional adverbial clauses occur before the main clause. These adverbial clauses are considered subordinate, as opposed to main clauses in a sequence, because the combinations of *awa* and *=i*, and *awa* and *eri*, do not occur in independent clauses.

Although the two clauses usually do not have a subordinator to link them as in (86)–(87), sometimes *enai* 'after' or *iara* 'then' link the clauses in a hypothetical conditional sentence:

(88) Sara e=to   **awa** ba'o=a=**i**   nu=toa,
    Sara 3SG.SBJ=EMPH COND   beat=3SG.OBJ=IRR   SPEC.CLII=chicken
    enai e=mate=**i**.
    after 3SG.SBJ=die=IRR
    'If Sarah hit the chicken, then it would die.'
    (2-E028-2)

(89) Au=atamata   e=to   **wa**   nao=**i**, **iara** anau
    1SG.PSSR[CLI]=friend   3SG.SBJ=EMPH   COND   go=IRR   then   1SG
    u=nao=**i**.
    1SG.SBJ=go=IRR
    'If my friend goes, then I will go.'
    (2-E022)

10.3.2 Apprehensive

This section will recap the TAM marking described in §7.1 for complex sentences containing an apprehension-causing adverbial clause (§7.1.4.3), and then discuss how the two clauses may be linked.

An apprehension-causing adverbial clause encodes the high probability and undesirability of a situation and is associated with a precaution clause expressing preventative action which can be taken to avoid the undesirable situation. Lichtenberk (1995: 298) identifies two subtypes of apprehension-causing clauses: the avertive function and the 'in case' function. In the former, there is a direct causal link between the two clauses; the precaution can avert the apprehension-causing event (X so that not Y), or if no precaution is taken, the apprehension-causing situation will occur (if not X, then Y). In the latter, there is no causal link; the precaution can only avert the consequences of the apprehension-causing event should it occur, rather than the event itself (X in case Y). In Papapana there is no formal distinction between the two and therefore I do not use the term *negative purpose*, used in my doctoral thesis (Smith 2015a), because this term only covers the avertive function.

In Papapana the preverbal apprehensive mode marker *te* occurs in conjunction with the irrealis mode enclitic *=i* in the apprehension-causing adverbial clause, while the main precaution clause may be a hortative (90), an imperative (often marked by the irrealis mode enclitic *=i*) (91) or a prohibitive marked with verbal reduplication and either the preverbal negative marker *ae* (92) or the preverbal negative mode marker *te* (93). There is only one example in the corpus of a declarative precaution main clause (94).

(90) *"Sa=nao tovoni nao=i, i=te moroko=ira=i."*
1INCL.SBJ.HORT=go check thither=IRR 3PL.SBJ=APPR lie=1INCL.OBJ=IRR
"'Let's go check, (in case) they might be lying to us.'"
(1-T034-00:30:12.380)

(91) *O=nabe=i, o=te mate=i.*
2SG.SBJ=swim=IRR 2SG.SBJ=APPR die=IRR
'Swim, (otherwise) you might die.'/ 'Swim, (so that) you don't die.'
(2-E028-2)

(92) *O=ae ago~agos=i=a pei to'o~to'o,*
2SG.SBJ=NEG RD~hold=TR=3SG.OBJ PART RD~cut
e=te tepe=i=o=i.
3SG.SBJ=APPR cut=TR=2SG.OBJ=IRR
'Don't hold the knife, (or) it might cut you.'/'Don't hold the knife, (so that) it doesn't cut you.'
(2-E028-2)

(93) *O=te ta~tavotu, o=te maragini=i.*
2SG.SBJ=PROH RD~arrive 2SG.SBJ=APPR cold=IRR
'Don't come, (or) you might get cold.'/'Don't come, (so that) you don't get cold.'
(2-E028-2)

(94) *. . .e=va-mamago=a pei tanga*
3SG.SBJ=CAUS-decorate=3SG.OBJ part shell.money
tenava e=te uga poto=i. . .
so.that 3SG.SBJ=APPR drown INTS=IRR
'. . .she adorned him with the shell necklace, so that he didn't drown. . .'/
'. . .she adorned him with the shell necklace, otherwise he might drown. . .'
(1-T029-00:19:04.385)

The precaution clause in Papapana usually has a second person subject as in (91)–(93) but can have a first or third person subject as in the hortative and declarative clauses in (90) and (94). The apprehension-causing clause can have a second person subject as in (91) and (93), or third person subject as in the other examples, and there is no preference for non-co-referential subjects (unlike in Schmidtke-Bode's (2009) typological study).

The position of the two clauses is fixed: the precaution main clause precedes the apprehension-causing adverbial clause. This is a common cross-linguistic tendency (Dixon 2009: 48) and is iconic since the precaution clause has directive illocutionary force, aiming to prevent the probable and undesirable event in the apprehension-causing clause from subsequently occurring. As (91)–(93) show, the main clause and adverbial clause are usually linked asyndetically. However, it is possible for a subordinator to occur, as in (94) above and (95) below. The subordinators *tenava* 'so that' and *avosia* are used elsewhere in finite purposive adverbial clauses when the subject is not coreferential with that of the main clause (see §10.3.3.2). These apprehension-causing adverbial clauses are analysed as syntactically dependent because a subordinator can be employed and because there is no strong evidence that the combination of the apprehensive mode marker *te* and the irrealis enclitic *=i* can arise as an independent apprehensive clause (Smith-Dennis 2019; Smith-Dennis, in press).

(95) *O=tavia   o'ogo=a=i,   **avosia** saviako te   ani o*
     2SG.SBJ=rub well=3SG.OBJ=IRR SUBR   tapioca OBL 2SG or
     na=gono,   mata=au   o=to   atuma'as=i=a=i,
     SPEC[CLI]=banana what=CLII 2SG.SBJ=EMPH cook=TR=3SG.OBJ=IRR
     *e=**te**   ravarava=i o=to   eri*
     3SG.SBJ=APPR black=IRR   2SG.SBJ=EMPH OPT
     tatu=ina=mu=i.
     mash=3PL.OBJ=2SG.IPFV=IRR
     'You rub it well, so that your tapioca or the banana, whatever you cooked, won't be black when you want to mash them.'
     (1-T036-3-00:00:26.430)

10.3.3 Purpose

Purposive adverbial clauses express the purpose of the event or state expressed by the main clause. When the subjects of both clauses are coreferential, the subordinator *tena* 'in order to' introduces the adverbial clause (§10.3.3.1), but when they are not, the subordinator *tenava* 'so that' (§10.3.3.2) or *merei* 'in order to' (§10.3.3.3) introduce the adverbial clause, depending on whether the clause is finite or non-finite.

10.3.3.1 *tena* 'in order to'
In a purposive adverbial clause which begins with the subordinator *tena* 'in order to', the subject is coreferential with that of the main clause. *Tena* is also a

preposition (see §8.3.1). The adverbial clause introduced by *tena* is desententialised: there is no tense, aspect or mode, and there are no subject proclitics or subject NPs. It is common for a subject to be deleted in a desententialised subordinate clause when it is coreferential with an argument in the main clause (Ross 2004c: 518). The adverbial clause is clearly subordinate because it cannot function as an independent clause.

A purposive adverbial clause beginning with *tena* follows the main clause (97)–(101), though there are two examples, such as (96), where it occurs between the subject NP and VC of the main predicate. The adverbial clause may contain an object NP (97)–(98), an object enclitic (99), or both (100)–(101).

(96) *Na=orawi* **tena ai~aini** *e=to ara nao.*
SPEC[CLI]=man SUBR RD~hook 3SG.SBJ=EMPH PST go
'A man went to fish.'
(1-T003-00:00:47.710)

(97) *I=to nao* **tena ituvu daramu.**
3PL.SBJ=EMPH go SUBR fetch water
'They went to fetch water.'
(1-T007-00:00:43.600)

(98) *E=to nao te=na=tago* **tena**
3SG.SBJ=EMPH go OBL=SPEC[CLI]=exchange SUBR
ae kaukau.
buy sweet.potato
'He went to the market to buy sweet potatoes.'
(2-E008)

(99) *Anau u=to naomai* **tena amun=i=o**
1SG 1SG.SBJ=EMPH come SUBR look=TR=2SG.OBJ
'I came to see you.'
(2-E022)

(100) *Reareana i=pei nao=i* **tena**
far 3PL.SBJ=PST.IPFV go=IRR SUBR
vono=ina *na=vanua.*
hunt=3PL.OBJ SPEC[CLI]=people
'They used to go far away to hunt humans.'
(1-T021-00:01:47.620)

(101) *I=to   nao **tena** **amun=i=a**   **na=orawi.**
3PL.SBJ=EMPH go   SUBR   look=TR=3SG.OBJ SPEC[CLI]=man
'They went to see/look at the man.'
(2-E022)

The adverbial clause may also contain the reciprocal/reflexive marker *vei* as in (102) where there is also a pronominal object NP and in (103) where an oblique adjunct marked by the preposition *te* is also part of the adverbial clause.

(102) *I=to   nao **tena** **vei** **amunu aina tobi.**
3PL.SBJ=EMPH go   SUBR   R/R   look   3PL   EMPH
'They went to see/look at each other.'
(2-E014)

(103) *I=to   nao tae mai   i-nongana   **tena** **vei**
3PL.SBJ=EMPH go   up   hither LOC-beach SUBR   R/R
manenu te=na=ato.
warm   OBL=SPEC[CLI]=sun
'They came up on the beach to warm themselves in the sun.'
(1-T029-00:26:32.990)

Cristofaro's (2003) hierarchy of adverbial desentententialisation (Figure 10.1) claims that in a given language no adverbial clause type on the hierarchy will be more desententialised than any type to its left. It is expected then that purposive adverbial clauses will be one of the most desententialised types and this is indeed the case in Papapana.

purpose < before < after, when < reason, reality condition

Figure 10.1: Adverbial Desententialisation Hierarchy.

Complement clauses may also be desententialised and in Papapana purposive adverbial clauses are formally similar to non-finite complement clauses, which are also are introduced by the subordinator *tena* (§10.4.2).

Desententialisation in adverbial clauses is rare in canonic Oceanic languages, even in purpose clauses (Ross 2004c: 519) and therefore Papapana is unusual in having desententialised adverbial clauses. Nevertheless, Teop has two kinds of purposive clauses, one of which is marked by *tea*, lacks TAM marking and has an implied but not overt subject that is coreferential with an argument in the main clause (Mosel and Thiesen 2007). *Tea* in Teop and *tena* in Papapana are likely cognate forms. Like Papapana, a purposive clause marked by *tea* in Teop is formally similar to a complement clause. This is also the case in Banoni where a locative preposition is used both as a purposive conjunction and as a complementiser (Lynch and Ross 2002: 455).

10.3.3.2 *tenava* 'so that'
In a purposive adverbial clause which begins with the subordinator *tenava* 'so that', the subject is not coreferential with that of the main clause. The adverbial clause is verbal and may occur after (104) or before (105) the main clause.

(104) *I=no   uvu=i*
3PL.SBJ=go.SEQ clear=IRR
tenava e-sina-na   e=siod=i=a=i
so.that PERS-mother-3SG.PSSR 3SG.SBJ=work=TR=3SG.OBJ=IRR
na=uvu   mama.
SPEC[CLI]=clear DEM1
'They cleared grass so that his mother could work the clearing.'
(1-T027-2-00:01:48.000)

(105) ***Tenava** na='usia   i=aputu=i,*
so.that   SPEC[CLI]=child 3PL.SBJ=sleep=IRR
iai   pei   ena mama i=atu=a=i.
PROX PART sing DEM1 3PL.SBJ=make=3SG.OBJ=IRR
'So that the children will sleep, they sing this little song.'
(1-T048-00:00:36.670)

Avosia may also be used instead of *tenava* at the beginning of a purposive adverbial clause (106)–(108). Indeed in (106) below speakers reported that *tenava* and *avosia* were interchangeable. It seems *avosia* is becoming a general subordinator, perhaps under the influence of Tok Pisin, in which *olsem* is also a general subordinator with several denotations including 'as if, like, therefore, so'

(Smith-Dennis 2017). The purposive adverbial clause again follows the main clause and only verbal adverbial clauses are attested in the data:

(106) "O=mei tua=i
2SG.SBJ=come.SEQ paddle=IRR
avosia e=taosi papasi nu=risi merei obutu."
SUBR 3SG.SBJ=finish quickly SPEC.CLII=rope ATTRIB canoe
"'Come paddle so that the canoe rope breaks quickly.'"
(1-T035-00:04:07.880)

(107) *Anau u=vatan=i=o* **avosia o=varona=i.**
1SG 1SG.SBJ=tell=TR=2SG.OBJ SUBR 2SG.SBJ=know=IRR
'I told you so that you would know.'
(2-E028-2)

(108) *Anau u=de=ina na=iana*
1SG 1SG.SBJ=take=3PL.OBJ SPEC[CLI]=fish
avosia so=ani=ina=i.
SUBR 1INCL.SBJ=eat=3PL.OBJ=IRR
'I caught some fish so that we could eat.'
(2-E028-2)

10.3.3.3 *merei* 'in order to'

In a purposive adverbial clause which begins with the subordinator *merei* 'in order to', the adverbial clause is desententialised: there is no tense, aspect or mode, and there are no subject proclitics or subject NPs. *Merei* may also function as an attributive preposition expressing origin or purpose (see §4.8). The purposive adverbial clause follows the main clause and is clearly subordinate because it cannot function as an independent clause. In the attested examples, the adverbial clause may consist only of a verb (109), of a verb and an object NP (110), or of a verb marked with the causative prefix *va-* with an object enclitic and object NP (111). The object of the main clause is coreferential with the subject of the adverbial clause in (109) and (111) and coreferential with the locative adjunct of the adverbial clause in (110).

(109) *Na=vanua i=pei*
SPEC[CLI]=people 3PL.SBJ=PST.IPFV
peri~peri=ina=i=ma **merei tavone.**
RD~find=3PL.OBJ=IRR=ma PURP help
'They would look for people to help them.'
(1-T034-00:24:08.015)

(110) *Pei   arivava   o=va-ubete   egoego=i **merei***
      PART banana.leaf 2SG.SBJ=CAUS-lay well=IRR PURP
      noe tamu~tamu.
      put RD~eat
      'Lay a banana leaf well in order to put food on.'
      (1-T061-00:14:07.800)

(111) *Sibuava   i=to   me-a   po=ina=i*
      old.women 3PL.SBJ=EMPH COM-SG.OBJ stay=3PL.IPFV=IRR
      merei va-aputu=ina   na='usia.
      PURP CAUS-sleep=3PL.OBJ SPEC[CLI]=child
      'Old women use it [a story] in order to put children to sleep.'
      (1-T048-00:00:32.810)

Example (112) is a particularly complex sentence consisting of a main clause and a purposive adverbial clause introduced by *tena*. This adverbial clause consists of a verb, object enclitic and two object NPs, and is further modified by a purposive adverbial clause introduced by *merei*. In this second adverbial clause, there is a serial verb construction (SVC) which has been transitivised with the causative prefix *va-*.

(112) *Tavea   mama mi=roa~roa=ina=mani*
      plant.sp DEM1 1EXCL.SBJ=RD~plant=3PL.OBJ=1EXCL.IPFV
      tena   birasi=ina   nu=ari~ari   bau tanana
      SUBR decorate=3PL.OBJ SPEC.CLII=RD~dig PL road
      merei va-amunu mata=ina.
      PURP CAUS-look good=3PL.OBJ
      'We plant this *tavea* to decorate cemeteries and roads in order to make them look good.'
      (1-T058-00:00:54.420)

10.3.4 Temporal location

In Papapana, time may be expressed by adjunct NPs (§8.1) or adjunct PPs (§8.3), as adverbs in the VC (§6.8) or at the clause-level (§8.4), or as an adverbial clause. Adverbial clauses expressing time signal the time elapsed between a past event and the present (§10.3.4.1) or the duration of time between two events in the past or present (there are no examples of that in the future) (§10.3.4.2).

10.3.4.1 Elapsed time: *inao tani* 'ago'

To express the time elapsed between the present and an event in the past, the elicitation data shows that Papapana can use an adverbial clause in which the subject NP is an enumerated Class I temporal noun and the predicate literally denotes 'they already went' (113)–(115). Although the predicate may occur with other subject NPs in independent clauses, the combination of this predicate and an enumerated temporal noun is not attested as an independent clause. Instead the adverbial clause is conventionalised, semantically dependent on the main clause and occurs in a fixed position after the main clause, which expresses the past event.

(113) I=vei   nai   **numanoa yia   i=nao   tani.**
      3PL.SBJ=R/R marry ten   year 3PL.SBJ=go   already
      'They married each other ten years ago.'
      (2-E021)

(114) Na=vei   atu~atunu e=ara   tosi   tani,
      SPEC[CLI]=COLL   RD~attack 3SG.SBJ=PST finish already
      numanoa tauvasi yia   i=nao   tani.
      ten   four   year 3PL.SBJ=go already
      'The war finished fourteen years ago.'
      (2-E026)

(115) Jim e=ara   vun=i=a   ena=siodo
      Jim 3SG.SBJ=PST start=TR=3SG.OBJ   3SG.PSSR[CLI]=work
      nua   yia   i=nao   tani.
      two[CLI]   year 3PL.SBJ=go already
      'Jim started his work two years ago.'
      (2-E026)

10.3.4.2 Duration: *eangoiena* 'until'

As described in §8.3.2, durational time may be expressed in an oblique adjunct containing the preposition *eangoiena* 'until' and a NP complement whose head noun is an Absolute Location noun that expresses a time relative to the time of speaking. *Eangoiena* 'until' may also function as a subordinator, introducing an adverbial clause that expresses the end point of a duration of time. Adverbial clauses introduced by *eangoiena* follow the main clause (116)–(118).

Example (119) is one exception to this but speakers reported that the order of the clauses could be changed without altering the semantics (though future research might show a difference, perhaps pragmatically).

(116) *O=dari=a=i* **eangoiena na=au dada**
2SG.SBJ=rub=3SG.OBJ=IRR until SPEC=CLII coconut.milk
e=to **taosi.**
3SG.SBJ=EMPH finish
'You rub it until the coconut milk is done.'
(1-T036-9-00:01:24.920)

(117) *U=pei siodo=i te=na=stoa*
1SG.SBJ=PST.IPFV work=IRR OBL=SPEC[CLI]=store
eangoiena au=bau 'usia i=podo.
until 1SG.PSSR=PL child 3PL.SBJ=born
'I used to work in the store until my children were born.'
(2-E019)

(118) *U=pei me-a po=u,*
1SG.SBJ=PST.IPFV COM-SG.OBJ stay=1SG.IPFV
eangoiena au=au 'usia e=no etawa.
until 1SG.PSSR=CLII child 3SG.SBJ=go.SEQ big
'I stayed with her until my child grew up.'
(1-T039-00:01:41.343)

(119) **Eangoiena tenpela nani mi=va-tavotu=ina,**
until ten there 1EXCL.SBJ=CAUS-arrive=3PL.OBJ
Mabiri mi=pei po~po=mani=i,
Mabiri 1EXCL.SBJ=PST.IPFV RD~stay=1EXCL.IPFV=IRR
'Until we had given birth to ten children there, we stayed in Mabiri.'
(1-T030-00:01:42.880)

As discussed in §8.3.2, *eangoiena* is likely to be a lexicalised form of the modal verb *eangoi* 'be able' and the 3SG postverbal subject-indexing (PSI) enclitic *=ena*; the verb *eangoi* requires a clausal complement (see §10.4.1 and §10.4.2). *Eangoiena* is also a lexicalised clause-level adverb expressing ability (see §8.4.2.1). The fact that *eangoiena* is also a preposition/subordinator denoting 'until' is likely to be due to contact with Tok Pisin where *inap* is also a verb expressing ability as well as a preposition denoting 'until' (Smith-Dennis 2017).

10.3.5 Spatial location: *avoa* 'where'

In Papapana, location may be expressed by an oblique (see §8.1–8.3), as adverbs in the VC (§6.8) or at the clause-level (§8.4), or as an adverbial clause. Adverbial clauses expressing location are not frequent in the data, however the few examples that exist show that they are verbal and are introduced by the subordinator *avoa* 'where' which is polysemous with the interrogative term *avoa* 'where'. *Avoa* occurs at the beginning of the adverbial clause and the adverbial clauses may follow or precede the main clause, as in (120)–(121) respectively. Note that in (121) the adverbial clause and the main clause it modifies are part of a conjunctive coordinate construction, and joined to the sentence-initial clause asydentically.

(120) *Mi=ma'=i=a nao=i*
1EXCL.SBJ=give=TR=3SG.OBJ thither=IRR
avoa mi=to eri ma'=i=a=mani.
where 1EXCL.SBJ=EMPH OPT give=TR=3SG.OBJ=1EXCL.IPFV
'We'll sell it wherever we want to sell it.'
(1-T106-00:01:58.740)

(121) *Mi=pei gaganini egoego=i,*
1EXCL.SBJ=PST.IPFV play well=IRR
avoa mi=to=ri nao=mani, *mi=nao=i.*
where 1EXCL.SBJ=EMPH=OPT go=1EXCL.IPFV 1EXCL.SBJ=go=IRR
'We used to play nicely (and) wherever we wanted to go, we would go.'
(1-T094-00:01:12.629)

10.3.6 Reason: *avisi* 'because'

An adverbial clause which begins with the subordinator *avisi* 'because' denotes an event or state which is considered to be the reason why the event or state expressed in the main clause occurs. A reason adverbial clause always follows the main clause. Examples (122)–(124) show verbal adverbial clauses while in (125) the adverbial clause is a verbless clause with a nominal predicate. In (124) the main clause and adverbial clause together form the complement of the verb *wa* 'say' introduced by *avosia*.

(122) *E=to   atun=i=au   **avisi   u=to***
    3SG.SBJ=EMPH attack=TR=1SG.OBJ because 1SG.SBJ=EMPH
    ara   morok=i=a.
    PST lie=TR=3SG.OBJ
    'He attacked me because I lied to him.'
    (2-E022)

(123) *Na=tonu   mama   e=to   ara tete mai*
    SPEC[CLI]=wave DEM1 3SG.SBJ=EMPH PST enter hither
    avisi   na:=bau   i=pei   vae   tue   visivisi=i.
    because some=PL 3PL.SBJ=PST.IPFV REP scold rubbish=IRR
    'This wave came inside because some (people) would always complain.'
    (1-T105-00:11:07.837)

(124) *I=wa=ina   avosia na=nganangana iai=ma*
    3PL.SBJ=say=3PL.OBJ SUBR   SPEC[CLI]=moon PROX=ma
    e=ara   naovo tae
    3SG.SBJ=PST fly   up
    avisi   e-noa-na   e=to   ara
    because PERS-son.in.law-3SG.PSSR 3SG.SBJ=EMPH PST
    no   araravi=a.
    go.SEQ surprise=3SG.OBJ
    'They tell them that the moon flew up because her son-in-law surprised it.'
    (1-T070-00:02:34.470)

(125) *Iai   e=ae   agai   mata=na   aruai*
    PROX 3SG.SBJ=NEG really good=3SG.IPFV NEG
    avisi   nu=maria,   nu=petai   na=au   dua.
    because SPEC.CLII=thing SPEC.CLII=palm.leaf SPEC=CLII bad
    'This isn't very good because the thing, the palm leaf is bad.'
    (1-T027-3-00:04:48.850)

Avosia can also be used instead of *avisi* at the beginnning of a reason adverbial clause, as in (126). As mentioned in §10.3.2.2, it seems *avosia* is becoming a general subordinator, perhaps under the influence of Tok Pisin, in which *olsem* is also a general subordinator with several denotations including 'as if, like, therefore, so' (Smith-Dennis 2017). The reason adverbial clause again follows the main clause and the adverbial clause is verbal. I did consider that this example could be a complement clause, since *avosia* can introduce complement clauses, but in elicitation session ESD3-E001 I asked a speaker to translate the sentence and she translated it as 'I got angry because I didn't know' and stated that *avosia* means 'because'.

(126) "*U=to* 'ire *avosia u=pei ae*
1SG.SBJ=EMPH be.angry SUBR 1SG.SBJ=PST.IPFV NEG
varona=u."
know=1SG.IPFV
'"I got cross because I didn't know."'
(1-T043-00:01:57.790)

Sometimes, both in text data and elicited data, a reason adverbial clause was not linked to the preceding main clause by a subordinator, as in (127)–(129). Of course these could be separate clauses, but for the elicited data I had used the Tok Pisin subordinator *bikos* 'because' to join the clauses.

(127) *E=to oa~oa=na=i,* ***e=to***
3SG.SBJ=EMPH RD~cry=3SG.IPFV=IRR 3SG.SBJ=EMPH
ubetu=ena.
hungry=3SG.IPFV
'He is crying, (because) he is hungry.'
(2-E022)

(128) *Iai u=tape=i=a=i,* ***e=to agai***
PROX 1SG.SBJ=tear=TR=3SG.OBJ=IRR 3SG.SBJ=EMPH really
sirorai=ena.
long=3SG.IPFV
'I'll tear it, (because) it's too long.'
(1-T062-00:07:41.130)

(129) *Anau u=vei va-nami=ou,*
1SG 1SG.SBJ=R/R CAUS-sad=1SG.IPFV
au=bau atamata i=to vurau asi=au.
1SG.PSSR=PL friend 3PL.SBJ=EMPH run leave=1SG.OBJ
'I feel sad, (because) all my friends ran away from me.'
(2-E022)

Four different speakers also used Tok Pisin *bikos* 'because' to introduce reason adverbial clauses, which were either verbal (131) or verbless (132).

(130) *I=pei si~sire=a=ina*
3PL.SBJ=PST.IPFV RD~stare=3SG.OBJ=3PL.IPFV
bikos nu=visio-na e=ravaravai=ena.
because SPEC.CLII=body-3SG.PSSR 3SG.SBJ=black=3SG.IPFV
'They stared at him because his skin was black.'
(1-T029-00:19:19.350)

(131) *E=no nao panapana na=wallaby*
3SG.SBJ=go.SEQ go all SPEC[CLI]=wallaby
bikos nua=au ie-na ta nua=au
because two=CLII leg-3SG.PSSR and two=CLII
nima-na nua=au sirorai.
arm-3SG.PSSR two=CLII long
'The wallaby went (and jumped) all the way because his two legs and his two arms were long.'
(1-T063-00:02:53.250)

10.3.7 Result: *arogani* 'therefore'

An adverbial clause which begins with the subordinator *arogani* 'therefore' denotes an event or state which is considered to be the result of the event or state expressed in the main clause. A resultative adverbial clause always follows the main clause, though (135) is one exception. Examples (132)–(135) show verbal adverbial clauses except (133) which shows a verbless adverbial clause with a nominal predicate.

(132) *Jim e=pei tongana=ena=i,*
Jim 3SG.SBJ=PST.IPFV smell=3SG.IPFV=IRR
arogani i-ava e=no tutuvu.
therefore LOC-sea 3SG.SBJ=go.SEQ wash
'Jim was sweaty, therefore he went to wash in the sea.'
(2-E027)

(133) *Bau Catholic a'aisi i=ara naomai,*
PL   Catholic many 3PL.SBJ=PST come
arogani iai arira panapana bau Catholic.
therefore PROX 1INCL all   PL Catholic
'Lots of Catholics came, therefore we are all Catholic.'
(1-T097-00:08:22.048)

(134) *"E=pei   ae   ara si~sia=au=na=i,*
3SG.SBJ=PST.IPFV NEG PST RD~look.after=1SG.OBJ=3SG.IPFV=IRR
arogani iai u=atu."
therefore PROX 1SG.SBJ=make
'"He wouldn't look after me, therefore I did this."'
(1-T088-00:38:07.541)

(135) ***Arogani u=ae   ani~ani=ou   na=iana,***
therefore 1SG.SBJ=NEG RD~eat=1SG.IPFV SPEC[CLI]=fish
e=to   ara va-matemate=au.
3SG.SBJ=EMPH PST CAUS-sick=1SG.OBJ
'That's why I don't eat fish, it makes me sick.'
(2-E027)

10.3.8 Concession

An adverbial clause which begins with the subordinator *marana* or *po'ovira* 'even though' expresses concession: the event or state expressed by the main clause occurred despite the event or state expressed by the adverbial clause. The difference between *po'ovira* and *marana* seems to be that *po'ovira* expresses an event that almost eventuated but did not eventuate, thus allowing the situation expressed by the main clause to occur.

10.3.8.1 *marana* 'even though'

An adverbial clause introduced by *marana* 'even though' is attested as both following and preceding the main clause. Adverbial clauses that follow the main clause may be verbal as in (136) and (137), or verbless as in (138) where it is a verbless existential clause (see §9.6.7), and in (139) where it is a negative verbless existential clause (see §9.6.1.4).

(136) *O=nao   roro   te=na=lotu   **marana**   **o=to***
    2SG.SBJ=go still OBL=SPEC[CLI]=worship even.though 2SG.SBJ=EMPH
    magono.
    dislike
    'You must still go to church even though you don't want to.'
    (2-E022)

(137) *. . .i=vamamatau=ina=i   oina=bau   'usia,*
    3PL.SBJ=teach=3PL.OBJ=IRR   3PL.PSSR=PL   child
    marana   *avosia aina i=to   nai=ina   nao*
    even.though   SUBR   3PL   3PL.SBJ=EMPH marry=3PL.OBJ thither
    na:=bau   i-ota.
    some=PL LOC-outside
    '. . .they should teach their children (Papapana), even though they married others from outside.'
    (1-T083-00:04:43.740)

(138) *Alex e=nao   roro=ena=i   te=na=kaukau,*
    Alex 3SG.SBJ=go still=3SG.IPFV=IRR OBL=SPEC[CLI]=sweet.potato
    marana   ***na=naui.***
    even.though   SPEC[CLI]=rain
    'Alex will still go to the garden, even though there is rain.'
    (2-E022)

(139) *Anau u=ae=ina   taramina a'aisi, **marana***
    1SG   1SG.SBJ=buy=3PL.OBJ thing   many   even.though
    moni-eta   aruai.
    money-AUG NEG
    'I buy lots of things, even though I don't have much money.'
    (2-E022)

Adverbial clauses that precede the main clause may also be verbal (140)–(141). In (142) two adverbial clauses are coordinated through same-subject clausal disjunction.

(140) ***Marana*** u=to po reareana=u i-poana te
even.though 1SG.SBJ=EMPH stay far=1SG.IPFV LOC-village OBL
anau, u=sare roro=u.
1SG 1SG.SBJ=happy still=1SG.IPFV
'Even though I live far away from my home, I'm still happy.'
(2-E022)

(141) ***Marana*** i=to vitu=a=i
even.though 3PL.SBJ=EMPH speak=3SG.OBJ=IRR
ta=pei tue
NSPEC[CLI]=part language
te=na=tue-ni sikuna,
OBL=SPEC[CLI]=language-CONST ship
mi=vamamatau manene=ina=ami.
1EXCL.SBJ=teach return=3PL.OBJ=1EXCL.IPFV
'Even though they say some words in Tok Pisin (lit. ship language), we teach them back (in Papapana).'
(1-T083-00:03:57.410)

(142) ***Marana*** tamu~tamu e=to dua=na=i
even.though RD~eat 3SG.SBJ=EMPH bad=3SG.IPFV=IRR
o e=to mata=na=i,
or 3SG.SBJ=EMPH good=3SG.IPFV=IRR
u=ani=a=i.
1SG.SBJ=eat=3SG.OBJ=IRR
'Whether the food is bad or good, I eat it.'
(2-E022)

10.3.8.2 *po'ovira* 'even though'

An adverbial clause introduced by *po'ovira* 'even though' generally follows the main clause (143)–(144), though in (145), the adverbial clause precedes the main clause. Only verbal adverbial clauses are attested in the data.

(143) *Anau* nu=naono mama u=no tepe=a,
1SG SPEC.CLII=tree DEM1 1SG.SBJ=go.SEQ cut=3SG.OBJ
po'ovira i=to tue osi=au.
even.though 3PL.SBJ=EMPH scold COMPL=1SG.OBJ
'I went and cut this tree even though they tried to stop me.'
(2-E027)

(144) *Aina i=vei tu'u va:gi,* **po'ovira** **u=ara**
3PL 3PL=R/R meet now even.though 1SG.SBJ=PST
tue osi=ina.
scold COMPL=3PL.OBJ
'They came today, even though I tried to stop them.'
(2-E027)

(145) *Pei wire mama iai*
PART wire DEM1 PROX
po'ovira *na=iana-eta na=ngisi-na*
even.though SPEC[CLI]=fish-AUG SPEC[CLI]=teeth-3SG.PSSR
***e=ani~ani** poto, e=ae eangoi=ena putu*
3SG.SBJ=RD~eat INTS 3SG.SBJ=NEG be.able=3SG.IPFV break.off
osi=a=i na=string.[43]
COMPL=3PL.OBJ=IRR SPEC[CLI]=string
'This bit of wire here, even though big fish's teeth really bite (this wire), it cannot break the string.'
(1-T099-00:02:38.740)

10.3.9 Similarity and manner: *avosia* 'like'

As described in §8.3.3, the preposition *avosia* 'like' and its NP complement occur as oblique adjuncts expressing similarity or manner. An adverbial clause which begins with the subordinator *avosia* 'like' also expresses similarity or manner, comparing an event or state with the event or state expressed in the main clause (146)–(147). Such clauses follow the main clause.

(146) *E=to nongon=i=a na=au da,*
3SG.SBJ=EMPH hear=TR=3SG.OBJ SPEC=CLII noise
***avosia** na=pira e=dao.*
SUBR SPEC[CLI]=thunder 3SG.SBJ=fire.up
'He heard a noise, like thunder rumbled.'
(2-E022)

---

43 It is unclear why the speaker reduplicates the verb in this utterance.

(147) *I=ani=a=i*   *nani   enai*
       3PL.SBJ=eat=3SG.OBJ=IRR there DEM2
       avosia   nua=au   orona=ma   i=pu   mai.
       SUBR   two=CLII   possum=ma   3PL.SBJ=fall   hither
       'They ate it (fallen coconut) there, like two possums had fallen down.'
       (1-T077-00:01:19.170)

10.4 Complement clauses

In Papapana, complement clauses only function as object of the matrix clause, and not as subject. There are two types of complement clauses in Papapana: finite (§10.4.1) and non-finite (§10.4.2). Finite and non-finite complements in reported speech sentences are described in §10.4.3. Finite complements, may be formally unmarked, as is typical of Oceanic languages (Lynch, Ross, and Crowley 2002: 53), or linked to the matrix clause by a subordinator. There are no dedicated complementizers in Papapana as the subordinators occuring with complement clauses, *avosia* and *tena*, also introduce adverbial clauses.

A complement introduced by a subordinator in Papapana may or may not be indexed by object enclitics in the VC of the matrix clause. Non-finite complement clauses are introduced by a subordinator. Complement clauses follow the matrix clause and can themselves contain subordination and coordination.

In the following discussion, I categorise the verbs that require object complements in Papapana according to Noonan's (2007: 120–145) classification of complement-taking predicates: *utterance* predicates involve a transfer of information; *modal* predicates involve expressing obligation, necessity and ability; *desiderative* predicates express a desire that the complement proposition be realised; *propositional attitude* predicates express an attitude regarding the truth of the complement proposition; *knowledge* predicates describe the state, or the manner of acquisition, of knowledge; and *immediate perception* predicates name the sensory mode by which the subject directly perceives the event coded in the complement. There is not however a one-to-one correspondence between the verb category and the structural type of the complement in Papapana, and even a single verb may take different types of complement.

10.4.1 Finite complements

Finite complements follow the matrix clause in Papapana. They may be linked asyndetically with the matrix clause or linked to the matrix clause by the subordinator *avosia*, in which case they may or may not be indexed by object enclitics in the VC of the matrix clause. Some verbs are also attested with interrogative terms introducing the complement clause. For some of the verbs which select a complement introduced by *avosia*, *avosia* is occasionally omitted; these will be discussed below, but it should be noted that in many languages, a subordinator can be omitted in certain constructions when, like *avosia*, the subordinator primarily signals syntactic dependence and does not carry meaning (Whaley 1997: 249).

In Papapana, finite complement clauses can be the objects of the following categories of verbs: modal, desiderative, propositional attitude, knowledge and the immediate perception verb *amunu* 'look' which occurs in an SVC with *vowa ~ vewa* 'be like, in the way of' (see §6.6 for SVCs with this verb and §8.3.3 and §9.3.2.3.4 for its phrasal complements). In reported speech sentences, finite complement clauses may be the object of utterance verbs (see §10.4.3). Table 10.2 shows which categories of verbs are attested with which structural type of clausal complement and the section in which they are discussed.

Table 10.2: Verb categories and finite clausal complement types.

Complement Clause Structure	Verb Category	Verbs		
Asyndesis	Modal	*eangoi*	be able	§10.4.1.1
Subordinator *avosia*	Desiderative	*magono*	dislike	§10.4.1.2
	Propositional attitude	*mataiwa*	think	
	Knowledge	*varona*	know	
	Perception	*nongono*	hear	
		amunu	look	
Subordinator *avosia* and Object-indexing enclitic	Desiderative	*mate*	like/want	§10.4.1.3
	Propositional attitude	*stuna*	believe	
Interrogative complementizers	Propositional attitude	*stuna*	believe	§10.4.1.4
	Knowledge	*varona*	know	

10.4.1.1 Asyndesis

The modal verb *eangoi* expresses ability and always requires a clausal complement. *Eangoi* is always marked by PSI enclitics (see §7.1.1), and may take a nonfinite clausal complement introduced by *tena* (§10.4.2) or a finite clausal complement which is linked asydentically to the matrix clause containing *eangoi*

(148)–(152). The complement clause may be intransitive with an adjunct (148) or monotransitive with an object NP in either preverbal (149) or postverbal (150) positions. In (148)–(149) *eangoi* is negated.

(148) *Anau u=ae eangoi=ou **u=nao=i***
 1SG 1SG.SBJ=NEG be.able=1SG.IPFV 1SG.SBJ=go=IRR
 tagena abata.
 near bachelor.house
 'I cannot go near a bachelor (traditional male initiation) house.'
 (2-E017)

(149) *Anau u=ae eangoi=ou*
 1SG 1SG.SBJ=NEG be.able=1SG.IPFV
 na='uru u=amun=i=a=i.
 SPEC[CLI]=island 1SG.SBJ=look =TR=3SG.OBJ=IRR
 'I cannot see the island.'
 (2-E019)

(150) *Cicilia e=eangoi=ena*
 Cicilia 3SG.SBJ=be.able=3SG.IPFV
 e=mei sapo=a=i na=inu?
 3SG.SBJ=come.SEQ clean=3SG.OBJ=IRR SPEC[CLI]=house
 'Can Cicilia come and clean the house?'
 (2-E026)

In (151) the complement clause itself contains a purposive adverbial clause introduced by the subordinator *tena* (see §10.3.3.1) while in (152) an apprehension-causing adverbial clause is dependent on the matrix clause and its clausal complement. In (152) *eangoi* is negated.

(151) *Cicilia e=eangoi=ena*
 Cicilia 3SG.SBJ=be.able=3SG.IPFV
 e=naomai tena sapo=a na=inu?
 3SG.SBJ=come SUBR clean=3SG.OBJ SPEC[CLI]=house
 'Can Cicilia come to clean the house?'
 (2-E026)

(152) O=ae   eangoi=emu   **o=tamu=i,**
2SG.SBJ=NEG be.able=2SG.IPFV 2SG.SBJ=eat=IRR
o=te   ou=i.
2SG.SBJ=APPR   cough=IRR
'You can't eat, lest you cough.'
(2-E026)

As the sentences in (153) show, there is no grammatical motivation for the fact that *eangoi* can take either a finite clausal complement, or a non-finite clausal complement, and both sentences were translated in the same way.

(153) a. *Ani   o=eangoi=omu*   **o=nao   Wakunai?**
2SG   2SG.SBJ=be.able=2SG.IPFV 2SG.SBJ=go Wakunai
'Can you go to Wakunai?'
(2-E028-2)
b. *Ani   o=eangoi=omu*   **tena   nao Wakunai?**
2SG   2SG.SBJ=be.able=2SG.IPFV SUBR   go   Wakunai
'Can you go to Wakunai?'
(2-E028-2)

10.4.1.2 Subordinator *avosia*

Some verbs require a finite clausal complement that is introduced by the subordinator *avosia*. The complement clause follows the matrix clause. The verbs that select this type of complement include the desiderative verb *magono* 'dislike', the propositional attitude verb *mataiwa* 'think', and the knowledge verbs *varona* 'know' and *nongono* 'hear'. The immediate perception verb *amunu* 'look' is the first verb in an SVC with *vowa ~ vewa* 'be like, in the way of' which can also select this type of complement. Other complements of this verb include PP complements headed by *avosia* (§8.3.3), finite complements clauses introduced by *avoa* (§10.4.1.4) or the interrogative term *avoa* (§9.3.2.3.4). Utterance verbs also select this type of complement but are discussed in §10.4.3. The verbs *magono* 'dislike', and *varona* 'know' may also select a non-finite complement when the subject of the matrix and complement clause are coreferential (see §10.4.2) but select a finite complement when the subjects of the matrix and complement clauses are not coreferential.

The complement clause may be intransitive (154)–(156), intransitive with an adjunct (157), monotransitive with an object enclitic only (158)–(160), monotransitive with an object enclitic and object NP (161)–(162) or the complement clause may be verbless and have a nominal predicate (163).

(154) *I=to   nongono **avosia ta=tsunami***
   3PL.SBJ=EMPH hear   SUBR NSPEC[CLI]=tsunami
   e=tavotu=i.
   3SG.SBJ=arrive=IRR
   'They heard that a tsunami will arrive.'
   (2-E022)

(155) *Anau u=mataiwa=u   **avosia e=ae***
   1SG 1SG.SBJ=think=1SG.IPFV SUBR 3SG.SBJ=NEG
   agai mata=na.
   really good=3SG.IPFV
   'I think that it's not very good.'
   (2-E022)

(156) *E=varona   **avosia au=arao**   **e=mate**   **tani.***
   3SG.SBJ=know SUBR 1SG.PSSR[CLI]=brother 3SG.SBJ=die already
   'He knew that my brother was already dead.'
   (1-T035-00:09:35.960)

(157) *Na='usia   na:=bau   i=pei   magono=i*
   SPEC[CLI]=child some=PL 3PL.SBJ=PST.IPFV dislike=IRR
   avosia mi=nao=i   te=na=skuru.
   SUBR   1EXCL.SBJ=go=IRR OBL=SPEC[CLI]=school
   'Some children wouldn't want us to go to school.'
   (1-T011-00:01:40.060)

(158) *A:mani mi=magono=emani   **avosia***
   1EXCL 1EXCL.SBJ=dislike=1EXCL.IPFV SUBR
   o=vatan=i=a=i.
   2SG.SBJ=tell=TR=3SG.OBJ=IRR
   'We don't want you to tell him.'
   (2-E022)

(159) *Anau u=mataiwa* **avosia** *si=atu=a=i.*
 1SG 1SG.SBJ=think SUBR 1INCL.SBJ=make=3SG.OBJ=IRR
 'I think that we'll make it.'
 (2-E022)

(160) *Tai ago~agoto paga i=ae varona*
 people RD~hold shoot 3PL.SBJ=NEG know
 avosia *i=oi~oi ora=ira.*
 SUBR 3PL.SBJ=RD~take only=1INCL.OBJ
 'The soldiers didn't know that they (the Bougainville Revolutionary Army) were just taking us.'
 (1-T002-00:01:11.460)

(161) *I=varona tani* **avosia** *i=de=a na=orawi.*
 3PL.SBJ=know already SUBR 3PL.SBJ=take=3SG.OBJ SPEC[CLI]=man
 'They (the villagers) already know that they (the cannibals) took the man.'
 (1-T021-00:02:20.190)

(162) *"U=pei ae varona=u*
 1SG.SBJ=PST.IPFV NEG know=1SG.IPFV
 avosia *e=pei ara gau~gaunu i=a=na*
 SUBR 3SG.SBJ=PST.IPFV PST RD~write APPL=3SG.OBJ=3SG.IPFV
 mai=i *nu=leta. . ."*
 hither=IRR SPEC.CLII=letter
 '"I didn't know that he was writing her letters. . . [and I didn't know]."'
 (1-T043-00:02:04.430)

(163) *I=mataiwa=ina*
 3PL.SBJ=think=3PL.IPFV
 avosia tue-ni *sikuna oina=au tue te aina.*
 SUBR language-CONST ship 3PL.PSSR=CLII language OBL 3PL
 'They think that Tok Pisin (lit. ship language) is their language.'
 (1-T083-00:00:45.550)

In (164)–(165), the verb *mataiwa* 'think' selects a finite complement clause, but the subordinator *avosia* is omitted. As mentioned in §10.4.1, subordinators that lack meaning can be omitted in many languages. Further data is required to establish whether other verbs may permit the omission of *avosia*, but there is no apparent grammatical, semantic or pragmatic difference between sentences in which *mataiwa* 'think' does and does not select *avosia*. As (165) shows, a complement clause may contain a relative clause.

(164) *Aia e=pei   mataiwa=na=i*
       3SG 3SG.SBJ=PST.IPFV think=3SG.IPFV=IRR
       na=orawi   enai   nu=abeabe-na   enai.
       SPEC[CLI]=man DEM2 SPEC.CLII=image-3SG.PSSR DEM2
       'He thought that his reflection was a man.'
       (1-T052-00:04:00.260)

(165) *I=pei   mataiwa=ina=i*
       3PL.SBJ=PST.IPFV think=3PL.IPFV=IRR
       bau tubu-ina   i=to   mate tani
       PL   grandparent-3PL.PSSR 3PL.SBJ=EMPH die   already
       va~va:sina iai   i=manene   mai.
       RD~before   PROX 3PL.SBJ=return hither
       'They thought that all their ancestors who had died in the past had come back.'
       (1-T097-00:06:52.147)

An SVC containing the immediate perception verb *amunu* 'see' and *vowa ~ vewa* 'be like, in the way of' can select a finite clausal complement that is introduced by the subordinator *avosia*. The complement clause follows the matrix clause. In (166) the complement clause makes a comparison, in much the same way that PPs headed by *avosia* do (see §8.3.3). However in (167)–(168) the predicate is arguably not one of perception but a knowledge predicate which describes the manner of knowledge acquisition. Indeed, perception predicates such as 'see' can be used in a knowledge/acquisition of knowledge sense (Noonan 2007: 129).

(166) *Aia e=amunu   vewa=na   avosia e=eri*
       3SG 3SG.SBJ=look be.like=3SG.IPFV SUBR   3SG.SBJ=OPT
       aputu=ena.
       sleep=3SG.IPFV
       'He's looking like he wants to sleep.'
       (2-E022)

(167) *Burimaunu i=**amunu** voa=ina **avosia***
women 3PL.SBJ=look be.like=3PL.IPFV SUBR
si=vanga~vanga=era.
1INCL.SBJ=RD~crazy=1INCL.IPFV
'The women see that we're drunk.'
(2-E027)

(168) *Na=vanua i=**amunu** vowa=ina*
SPEC[CLI]=people 3PL.SBJ= look be.like=3PL.IPFV
***avosia** mi=ara asi=a na=poana.*
SUBR 1EXCL.SBJ=PST leave=3SG.OBJ SPEC[CLI]=village
'The men see that we left the village.'
(2-E027)

10.4.1.3 Subordinator *avosia* and object-indexing

The desiderative verb *mate* 'like/want' and the propositional attitude verb *stuna* 'believe' require a finite clausal complement that is introduced by the subordinator *avosia* and indexed by an object enclitic in the matrix VC (169)–(171). It is clear that the object enclitic indexes the complement clause because the object enclitic is always 3SG, regardless of the person and number of the subject of the complement clause. The complement clause follows the matrix clause. Elicitation data shows that the complement clauses can be intransitive (169), intransitive with an adjunct (170), or monotransitive with an object enclitic only (171). The verb *mate* 'like/want' may also select a non-finite complement when the subject of the matrix and complement clause are coreferential (see §10.4.2) but select the finite complements described here when the subjects of the matrix and complement clauses are not coreferential.

(169) *Aia e=ae stun=i=**a**=ena*
3SG 3SG.SBJ=NEG believe=TR=3SG.OBJ=3SG.IPFV
***avosia** na=maunu e=atu ma'ata=i.*
SUBR SPEC[CLI]=woman make be.heated=IRR
'He doesn't believe that the woman will cook.'
(2-E024)

(170) A:mani   mi=ae   mate=i=**a**=emani
      1EXCL   1EXCL.SBJ=NEG   like=TR=3SG.OBJ=1EXCL.IPFV
      avosia o=manene   Australia.
      SUBR   2SG.SBJ=return   Australia
      'We don't want you to return to Australia.'
      (2-E027)

(171) E=to   mate=i=**a**=ena
      3SG.SBJ=EMPH   like=TR=3SG.OBJ=3SG.IPFV
      avosia si=no   amun=i=a=i.
      SUBR   1INCL.SBJ=go.SEQ   look=TR=3SG.OBJ=IRR
      'He wants us to go and see him.'
      (2-E022)

10.4.1.4 Interrogative complementizers

A finite complement clause can also be linked to the matrix clause by an interrogative: *nongovita* 'when' (172), *avoa ~ avea* 'where' (173), *avoa* 'how' (174) and *mata* 'what' (175). The only verbs attested in such a matrix clause are the knowledge verb *varona* 'know' (172)–(174) and the propositional attitude verb *stuna* 'believe' (175). As when these verbs select complements introduced by *avosia*, *varona* does not index the complement in the matrix VC whereas *stuna* indexes the complement as an object in the matrix VC. In (172)–(173) the complement clause is intransitive with the interrogative terms *nongovita* 'when' and *avoa* 'where' referring to a temporal adjunct (172) and spatial adjunct (173), while in (174) the complement clause predicate is an SVC with the perception verb *amunu* and *vowa ~ vewa* 'be like, in the way of' which is taking *avoa* as its own complement and giving the 'how' rather than 'where' meaning (see §9.3.2.3.4). In (175) the complement clause is monotransitive with the interrogative term *mata* 'what' referring to an object.

(172) Ta   e=varona=na   **nongovita o=mate=i.**
      and   3SG.SBJ= know=3SG.IPFV   when   2SG.SBJ=die=IRR
      'And he knows when you'll die.'
      (1-T097-00:14:11.015)

(173) E=pei   ae   varona=ena=i   avoa   e=nao
      3SG.SBJ=PST.IPFV   NEG   know=3SG.IPFV=IRR   where   3SG.SBJ=go
      nu='usia.
      SPEC.CLII=child
      'He didn't know where the child went.'
      (1-T035-00:06:02.208)

(174) . . .*u=ae   varona=au   na=tonu=ma*
      1SG.SBJ=NEG know=1SG.IPFV SPEC[CLI]=wave=ma
      *na=etawa   poto **avoa**   e=amunu   **vowa=ena.***
      SPEC[CLI]=big INTS where 3SG.SBJ=look be.like=3SG.IPFV
      '[And I was small so] . . .I didn't know how a tsunami looks.'
      (1-T105-00:15:30.000)

(175) *Anau u=ae   stun=i=a=u*
      1SG   1SG.SBJ=NEG believe=TR=3SG.OBJ=1SG.IPFV
      mata e=to   wa=i=a.
      what 3SG.SBJ=EMPH say=TR=3SG.OBJ
      'I don't believe what he said.'
      (2-E024)

10.4.2 Non-finite complements

In Papapana, non-finite complements follow the matrix clause and are introduced by the subordinator *tena*. With two verbs, discussed below, the complement is indexed by object enclitics in the matrix clause VC. There is no subject NP or subject proclitic in the VC and instead the notional subject is equi-deleted: equi-deletion "deletes subjects of complements when they are coreferential with [. . .] some argument in the matrix [clause]" (Noonan 2007: 76). In Papapana non-finite complement clauses, the subject of the complement is always coreferential with the subject of the matrix clause. Table 10.3 shows which categories of verbs select non-finite complement clauses. Those that are in bold typeface may also take finite complements; the motivation for which complement is selected has been discussed in §10.4.1 and will be repeated below for the verbs concerned.

Table 10.3: Verb categories with non-finite complements.

Verb Category	Verbs	
Phasal	*vuna*	start
	iovoto	stop
Modal	***eangoi***	be able
Desiderative	***magono***	dislike
	mate	like/want
Knowledge	***varona***	know
	namiaruve	forget

In indirect speech sentences, non-finite complement clauses may be the object of utterance verbs (see §10.4.3).

The phasal verbs *vuna* 'start' and *iovoto* 'stop' and the knowledge verb *namiaruve* 'forget' are only attested with non-finite complements and these constructions are only attested in the elicitation data. In (176) the matrix clause and its non-finite complement form a conditional adverbial clause. The non-finite clause itself is monotransitive by virtue of the applicative comitative *me* and the object is expressed overtly as a NP.

(176) *O=to   ae   iovoto=i **tena me-a***
  2SG.SBJ=EMPH NEG stop=IRR SUBR COM-SG.OBJ
  gaganini na=bara,   *u=de=a=i.*
  play   SPEC[CLI]=ball 1SG.SBJ=take=3SG.OBJ=IRR
  'If you don't stop playing with the ball, I'll take it.'
  (2-E008)

In (177) and (178) the non-finite complement clause is indexed by an object enclitic in the matrix VC. This is contrary to all other attested non-finite complement clauses, which are not indexed by object enclitics. In both non-finite complement clauses, the verb is monotransitive and there is an object NP as well as an object-indexing enclitic in the VC:

(177) *Ian e=vun=i=a   tena   atuma'as=i=a*
  Ian 3SG.SBJ=start=TR=3SG.OBJ SUBR cook=TR=3SG.OBJ
  nu=koko'i.
  SPEC.CLII=taro
  'Ian started to cook the taro.'
  (2-E024)

(178) *Naonava   u=namiaruve=a   tena   atu=a*
  yesterday 1SG.SBJ=forget=3SG.OBJ SUBR make=3SG.OBJ
  na=siodo   te   anau.
  SPEC[CLI]=work OBL 1SG
  'Yesterday I forgot to do my work.'
  (2-E024)

The desiderative verbs *magono* 'dislike' and *mate* 'like/want', and the knowledge verb *varona* 'know' are attested with finite complement clauses when the subjects of the matrix and complement clauses are not coreferential (§10.4.1) and non-finite complement clauses when the subject of the matrix and complement clause are coreferential (179)–(183). The complement clause may be intransitive (179)–(180), intransitive with an adjunct (181), monotransitive with an object enclitic and object NP (182), or monotransitive with the applicative comitative *me* (183). The matrix clause and complement clause may be the complement of an utterance verb (180) or occur in a direct quotation as in (181).

(179) O=varona=i **tena gaunu.**
2SG.SBJ=know=IRR SUBR write
'You must know how to write.'
(2-E009)

(180) *Tau u=eri 'a'ade'e=au avosia va~va:sina*
and 1SG.SBJ=OPT narrative=1SG.IPFV SUBR RD~before
e=pei ae varona=na=i **tena para'a,**
3SG.SBJ=PST.IPFV NEG know=3SG.IPFV=IRR SUBR jump
na=wallaby.
SPEC[CLI]=wallaby
'And I want to tell a story that in the past it didn't know how to jump, the wallaby.'
(1-T063-00:00:33.670)

(181) *U=wa=i=a e-sina-u*
1SG.SBJ=say=TR=3SG.OBJ PERS-mother-1SG.PSSR
"*anau u=magono=u* **tena nao**
1SG 1SG.SBJ=dislike=1SG.IPFV SUBR go
te=na=kaukau".
OBL=SPEC[CLI]=sweet.potato
'I said to my mother, "I don't want to go to the garden".'
(1-T033-00:01:50.350)

(182) *Anau u=ae agai varona=au*
1SG 1SG.SBJ=NEG really know=1SG.IPFV
tena atu=a nu=maria, nu=pute~pute.
SUBR make=3SG.OBJ SPEC.CLII=thing SPEC.CLII=RD~wind
'I don't really know how to make a what's-it-called, a fan.'
(1-T027-3-00:02:07.200)

(183) *"Mi=to   magono=emani   **tena   me-a   agoto***
1EXCL.SBJ=EMPH dislike=1EXCL.IPFV SUBR COM-SG.OBJ hold
nima-na   i=a   na=maria,   na=iana   enai."
hand-3SG.PSSR APPL =3SG.OBJ SPEC[CLI]=thing SPEC[CLI]=fish DEM2
'"We don't want to shake hands with the what's-it-called, that mermaid."'
(1-T029-00:23:05.410)

The modal verb *eangoi* expresses ability and requires a clausal complement. *Eangoi* is always marked by PSI enclitics and may take a finite clausal complement which is linked asydentically to the matrix clause containing *eangoi* (§10.4.1.1) or a non-finite clausal complement introduced by *tena* (184)–(191). As (153) in §10.4.1.1 shows, there is no grammatical motivation for the fact that *eangoi* can take either a finite clausal complement, or a non-finite clausal complement. In the attested elicitation examples below, the non-finite complement clause is intransitive but can contain a deictic directional and temporal adjunct (184), a geocentric directional and a spatial adjunct (185), a spatial and temporal adjunct (186), and a deictic directional, geocentric directional and spatial adjunct (187).

(184) *Alex e=eangoi=ena   **tena   mei   tamu va:gi?***
Alex 3SG.SBJ=be.able=3SG.IPFV SUBR come.SEQ eat   now
'Can Alex come and eat here today?'
(2-E028-2)

(185) *John e=eangoi=ena   **tena   nao tae***
John 3SG.SBJ=be.able=3SG.IPFV SUBR go   up
te=na=ereere.
OBL=SPEC[CLI]=mountain
'John can go up to the mountain.'
(2-E007-1)

(186) *Alex auana Jane i=vae   eangoi=ina   **tena***
Alex 3DU   Jane 3PL.SBJ=REP be.able=3PL.IPFV SUBR
nao Wakunai va:gi?
go Wakunai now
'Are Alex and Jane able again to go to Wakunai today?'
(2-E026)

(187) *Alex e=eangoi=ena   tena no*
　　　Alex 3SG.SBJ=be.able=3SG.IPFV SUBR go.SEQ
　　　tua   tae te=na='uru?
　　　paddle up   OBL=SPEC[CLI]=island
　　　'Can Alex go and paddle out to the island?'
　　　(2-E028-2)

A non-finite complement clause may also be monotransitive as in (188) where there is transitivity discord (§6.5.5.2) and so the object NP is not indexed on the verb, or as in (189)–(190) where the object NP is indexed by an object enclitic in the VC. Example (190) also shows a geocentric directional in the complement clause. The complement clause in example (191) is monotransitive by virtue of the causative prefix but there is transitivity discord and the object is not indexed on the verb.

(188) *Naonava   u=pei   ae   eangoi=eu   tena peri*
　　　yesterday 1SG.SBJ=PST.IPFV NEG be.able=1SG.IPFV SUBR find
　　　tamu~tamu.
　　　RD~eat
　　　'Yesterday I wasn't able to find food.'
　　　(2-E014-2)

(189) *John e=ae   eangoi=ena   tena*
　　　John 3SG.SBJ=NEG be.able=3SG.IPFV SUBR
　　　amun=i=a   na='uru.
　　　look=TR=3SG.OBJ SPEC[CLI]=island
　　　'John isn't able to see the island.'
　　　(2-E028-2)

(190) *Jerry e=eangoi=ena   tena vaene*
　　　Jerry 3SG.SBJ=be.able=3SG.IPFV SUBR climb
　　　tae=a   na=ereere.
　　　up=3SG.OBJ SPEC[CLI]=mountain
　　　'Jerry is able to climb up the mountain.'
　　　(2-E007-1)

(191) *Na=vanua   i=eangoi=ina*
      SPEC[CLI]=people 3PL.SBJ=be.able=3PL.IPFV
      tena   va-tonu   na=inu   tena bau naono.
      SUBR CAUS-stand SPEC[CLI]=house OBL PL   tree
      'People are able to build houses from trees.'
      (2-E028-2)

10.4.3 Reported speech

Direct speech attempts to represent the exact words spoken by a person, embedded in a matrix clause. Indirect speech is intended to represent the content of what was said, but not the speaker's exact words, and is deictically adapted to the matrix clause speech situation in person, tense and location. Direct and indirect speech in Papapana are introduced by a reporting clause which is the matrix clause and employs an intransitive or monotransitive utterance verb, depending on whether the addressee object is specified. The reported clause is selected by the matrix clause as a clausal complement. The complement clause always follows the matrix clause. Indirect speech may be introduced by the subordinator *avosia* while direct speech follows the reporting clause, with no subordinator. Generally the complement clause is finite (§10.4.3.1) but non-finite complement clauses occasionally occur when indirect speech is imperative (§10.4.3.2).

10.4.3.1 Finite complements
In reported speech sentences with finite complements the reported clause follows the reporting clause when the speech is direct (§10.4.3.1.1), but follows and is introduced by *avosia* when it is indirect (§10.4.3.1.2).

10.4.3.1.1 Direct
The utterance verb *wa* 'say' (see §10.4) may be found in matrix reporting clauses without an addressee object (192)–(195). Although there is no subordinator introducing the direct speech, sometimes *ini* 'here' occurs immediately before the direct speech as in (194)–(195), though its exact function is unclear.

(192) *Anau   u=wa   "Colin   e=atu=a=i   nu=tura".*
      1SG   1SG.SBJ=say Colin   3SG.SBJ=make=3SG.OBJ=IRR SPEC.CLII=fire
      'I said "Colin will make the fire".'
      (2-E027)

10.4 Complement clauses — 503

(193) *Billy e=wa* **"*Maureen e=nao tani mai*".**
Billy 3SG.SBJ=say Maureen 3SG.SBJ=go already hither
'Billy said "Maureen has already come".'
(2-E022)

(194) *E=to wa ini* **"*arira si=nao=i*".**
3SG.SBJ=EMPH say here 1INCL 1INCL.SBJ=go=IRR
'He said like "let's go".'
(2-E022)

(195) *Vavine-u e=wa ini,*
sibling-1SG.PSSR 3SG.SBJ=say here
"*na=daramu e=pei mamaravi=ena=i naonava*".
SPEC[CLI]=river 3SG.SBJ=PST.IPFV cold=3SG.IPFV=IRR yesterday
'My brother says like "the river was cold yesterday".'
(2-E008)

The utterance verb *wa* 'say' may also be found in matrix reporting clauses with an addressee object (196), as can the verbs *vatana* 'tell' (197) and *nata* 'ask' (198).

(196) *Vavine-u e=wa=au* **"*na=daramu***
sibling-1SG.PSSR 3SG.SBJ=say=1SG.OBJ SPEC[CLI]=river
***e=mamaravi=ena*".**
3SG.SBJ=cold=3SG.IPFV
'My brother said to me "the water is cold".'
(2-E008)

(197) *Aia e=vatana=**ina*** **"*aia 'usia mama***
3SG 3SG.SBJ=tell=3PL.OBJ 3SG child DEM1
e=pei me-na siodo=na=i
3SG.SBJ=PST.IPFV COM-PL.OBJ work=3SG.IPFV=IRR
***na=siapani. . .*".**
SPEC[CLI]=Japanese
'He told them "that boy was working with the Japanese. . .".'
(1-T034-00-00:13:49.920)

(198) Billy enata=au   "Maureen e=nao   tani   mai
      Billy 3SG.SBJ=ask=1SG.OBJ Maureen 3SG.SBJ=go already hither
      o   aruai?"
      or   no
      'Billy asked me "has Maureen come already or not?".'
      (2-E022)

10.4.3.1.2 Indirect

The utterance verb *wa* 'say' and *'a'ade'e* 'narrate' (see §10.4) may be found in matrix reporting clauses without an addressee object (199)–(200). Utterance verbs such as *moroko* 'lie' and *vastuna* 'promise' also do not require an addressee object (201)–(202). The indirect speech complement clause is introduced by *avosia*, and the subject of the two clauses may (201)–(202) or may not (199)–(200) be coreferential. Note that in (200), the utterance verb occurs in an SVC with *vowa ~ vewa* 'be like, in the way of'.

(199) *Sue e=wa   avosia Brian e=nao=i   Buka.*
      Sue 3SG.SBJ=say SUBR   Brian 3SG.SBJ=go=IRR Buka
      'Sue said that Brian will go to Buka.'
      (2-E022)

(200) *E-tama-u   e=ara   'a'ade'e   vowa*
      PERS-father-1SG.PSSR   3SG.SBJ=PST   narrative   be.like
      avosia   na=tonu   mama e=to   ara   tete   mai
      like   SPEC[CLI]=wave DEM1 3SG.SBJ=EMPH PST enter hither
      avisi   na:=bau   i=pei   vae   tue   visivisi=i.
      because some=PL 3PL.SBJ=PST.IPFV REP scold rubbish=IRR
      'My father recounted how this wave came inside because some (people) would criticise (religion).'
      (1-T105-00:11:07.837)

(201) *E=moroko   avosia e=naomai=i.*
      3SG.SBJ=lie   SUBR   3SG.SBJ=come=IRR
      'He lied that he would come.'
      (2-E022)

(202) *Anau u=vastuna* **avosia u=naomai=i.**
 1SG 1SG.SBJ=promise SUBR 1SG.SBJ=come=IRR
 'I promise that I'll come.'
 (2-E022)

The complement clause itself may contain coordinated clauses:

(203) *Na:=bau na=vanua nani i=pei wa=i*
 some=PL SPEC[CLI]=people there 3PL.SBJ=PST.IPFV say=IRR
 avosia na='usia nani
 SUBR SPEC[CLI]=child there
 i=pei vae mate~mate vewa=ina=i
 3PL.SBJ=PST.IPFV REP RD~die be.like=3PL.IPFV=IRR
 na=maria ta haus sik e=to mata aruai.
 SPEC[CLI]=thing and house sick 3SG.SBJ=EMPH good NEG
 'Some people there used to say said that the children there kept dying like (that), and the hospital wasn't good.'
 (1-T034-00:39:01.400)

The utterance verbs *wa* 'say', *'a'ade'e* 'narrate' and *vatana* 'tell' may occur in a reported clause with an addressee object and introduce a declarative statement (204)–(206), while *nata* 'ask' may have an address object and introduce an interrogative (207). The complement clause is introduced by *avosia*, and the subject of the complement clause in these examples is not coreferential with an argument in the matrix clause.

(204) *E=wa=au* **avosia na:=ata na=room**
 3SG.SBJ=say=1SG.OBJ SUBR some=CLI SPEC[CLI]=room
 e=po=na.
 3SG.SBJ=stay=3SG.IPFV
 'He said to me that there is another room.'
 (1-T088-00:24:42.360)

(205) *U='a'ade'e=i=a=i Ellen*
 1SG.SBJ=narrative=TR=3SG.OBJ=IRR Ellen
 avosia a:mani mi=ara asi=a Teperoi.
 SUBR 1EXCL 1EXCL.SBJ=PST leave=3SG.OBJ Teperoi
 'I'll recount to Ellen that we left Teperoi.'
 (1-T030-00:00:26.276)

(206) *U=vatan=i=a*   ***avosia si=orete.***
1SG.SBJ=tell=TR=3SG.OBJ   SUBR   1INCL.SBJ=walk
'I told him that we walked about.'
(2-E022)

(207) *Billy e=nata=au*   ***avosia Maureen e=naomai***
Billy 3SG.SBJ=ask=1SG.OBJ   SUBR   Maureen 3SG.SBJ=come
o aruai.
or no
'Billy asked me if Maureen had come or not.'
(2-E022)

The utterance verb *vatana* 'tell' may also occur in a reported clause with an addressee object and introduce an imperative (208)–(210). The complement is introduced by *avosia* and the object of the matrix clause is coreferential with the subject of the complement clause, that is, there is raising. *Vatana* may also select a non-finite complement to introduce an imperative when the subject of the complement is coreferential with the object of the matrix clause (§10.4.3.2), but it is unclear if there is a difference between the two. In (210) the reporting clause is an imperative and the complement clause contains asydentic coordination.

(208) *Sue e=vatan=i=a*   Brian ***avosia e=nao=i***   ***Buka.***
Sue 3SG.SBJ=tell=TR=3SG.OBJ   Brian   SUBR   3SG.SBJ=go=IRR   Buka
'Sue told Brian to go to Buka.'
(2-E022)

(209) *Anau vatan=i=a*   Colin
1SG   1SG.SBJ=tell=TR=3SG.OBJ   Colin
avosia e=atu=a=i   ***nu=tura.***
SUBR   3SG.SBJ=make=3SG.OBJ=IRR   SPEC.CLII=fire
'I told Colin to make a fire.'
(2-E027)

(210) *". . .o=no   vatana=**ina**=i*
  2SG.SBJ=go.SEQ tell=3PL.OBJ=IRR
  avosia   i=mumurina=ira   mai   i=mei
  SUBR   3PL.SBJ=follow=1INCL.OBJ hither 3PL.SBJ=come.SEQ
  peri=ira=i."
  find=1INCL.OBJ=IRR
  "'. . .go and tell them to follow us (and) find us.'"
  (1-T002-00:01:16.030)

10.4.3.2 Non-finite complements

When indirect speech is imperative, a non-finite complement clause introduced by *tena* may be selected by the utterance verb in the matrix clause (211)–(212). The utterance verbs attested with non-finite complements are *wa* 'say', *vatana* 'tell' and *nata* 'ask'. The verbs *wa* 'say', and *nata* 'ask' may also select finite complements but select non-finite complements as in (211) when the addressee object of the matrix clause is coreferential with the subject of the complement clause; that is, when the subject of the complement clause (which has a different subject to that of the matrix clause) is raised to be the object of the matrix clause. As mentioned at the end of §10.4.3.1.2, *vatana* may also select a finite complement to introduce an imperative when the subject of the complement is coreferential with the addresee object of the matrix clause but it is unclear if there is a difference between the two. Certainly a comparison of (208) above and (212) below suggest that there is none.

(211) *Billy e=wa=**au**   **tena   nao.***
   Billy 3SG.SBJ=say=1SG.OBJ SUBR   go
   'Billy told me to go.'
   (2-E022)

(212) *Sue e=vatan=i=**a**   Brian **tena nao** Buka.*
   Sue 3SG.SBJ=tell=TR=3SG.OBJ Brian SUBR   go   Buka
   'Sue told Brian to go to Buka.'
   (2-E027)

References

Aikhenvald, Alexandra Y. 2000. *Classifiers: A typology of noun categorization devices*. Oxford: Oxford University Press.
Aikhenvald, Alexandra Y. 2006. Serial verb constructions in typological perspective. In Alexandra Y. Aikhenvald & Robert M. W. Dixon (eds.), *Serial verb constructions*, 1–68. Oxford: Oxford University Press.
Allen, Gerald N. 1978. *Halia verb morphology: from morpheme to discourse*. Arlington: The University of Texas MA thesis.
Allen, Jerry, & Conrad Hurd. 1963. *Languages of the Bougainville district*. Ukarumpa: Papua New Guinea Summer Institute of Linguistics.
Andrews, Avery D. 2007. The major functions of the noun phrase. In Timothy Shopen (ed.), *Language typology and syntactic description, Volume 1: Clause structure, 2nd edn.*, 132–223. Cambridge: Cambridge University Press.
Angelo, Denise & Eva Schultze-Berndt. 2016. Beware *bambai* – lest it be apprehensive. In Felicity Meakins & Carmel O'Shannessy (eds.), *Loss & renewal: Australian languages since colonisation*, 255–96. Berlin: Mouton de Gruyter.
Austin, Peter K. 2006. Data and language documentation. In Jost Gippert, Nikolaus P. Himmelmann & Ulrike Mosel (eds.), *Essentials of language documentation*, 87–112. Berlin: Mouton de Gruyter.
Austin, Peter K. & Lenore A. Grenoble. 2007. Current trends in language documentation. In Peter K. Austin (ed.), *Language documentation and description, Volume 4*, 12–25. London: Hans Rausing Endangered Languages Project, Department of Linguistics, SOAS.
Baerman, Matthew. 2007. Morphological reversals. *Journal of Linguistics* 43. 33–61.
Baker, Phillip. 1993. Australian influence on Melanesian Pidgin English. *Te Reo* 36. 3–67.
Baker, Phillip. 1995. Some developmental influences from the historical studies of pidgin and creoles. In Jacques Arends (ed.), *The early stages of creolization*, 1–24. Amsterdam & Philadelphia: John Benjamins Publishing Company.
Baker, Phillip. 1996. Australian and Melanesian Pidgin English and the fellows in between. In Phillip Baker & Anand Syea (eds.), *Changing meanings, changing functions: Papers relating to grammaticalisation in contact languages*, 243–258. London: University of Westminster Press.
Bisang, Walter. 1996. Areal typology and grammaticalization: Processes of grammaticalization based on nouns & verbs in East and Mainland South East Asian Languages. *Studies in Language* 20 (3). 519–597.
Blust, Robert. 2001. Reduplicated colour terms in Oceanic languages. In Andrew Pawley (ed.), *The boy from Bundaberg: Studies in Melanesian linguistics in honour of Tom Dutton*, 23–49. Canberra: Pacific Linguistics.
Bowern, Claire. 2008. *Linguistic fieldwork: A practical guide*. Basingstoke: Palgrave Macmillan.
Bril, Isabelle. 2004. Complex nuclei in Oceanic languages: Contribution to an areal typology. In Isabelle Bril & Françoise Ozanne-Rivierre (eds.), *Complex predicates in Oceanic languages: Studies in the dynamics of binding and boundness*, 1–48. Berlin: Mouton de Gruyter.
Bril, Isabelle. 2005. Semantic and functional diversification of reciprocal and middles prefixes in New Caledonian and other Austronesian languages. *Linguistic Typology* 9. 25–76.

Capell, Arthur. 1971. Austronesian languages of Cape of Australian New Guinea. In Thomas A. Sebeok (ed.), *Current trends in linguistics, Volume 8, Linguistics in Oceania*, 240–340. The Hague: Mouton.
Carroll, Matthew. 2016. *The Ngkolmpu language with special reference to distributed exponence*. Canberra: Australian National University PhD thesis.
Chafe, Wallace L. 1970. *Meaning and structure of language*. Chicago: The University of Chicago Press.
Chafe, Wallace L. 1976. Givenness, contrastiveness, definiteness, subjects, topics, and point of view. In C. N. Li (ed.), *Subject and topic*, 22–55. New York: Academic Press.
Chambers, Mary. 2009. *Which way is up? Motion verbs and paths of motion on Kubokota, an Austronesian language of the Solomon Islands*. London: School of Oriental & African Studies, University of London PhD thesis.
Cleary-Kemp, Jessica. 2007. Universal uses of demonstratives: Evidence from four Malayo-Polynesian Languages. *Oceanic Linguistics* 46 (2). 325–347.
Comrie, Bernard. 1976. *Aspect*. Cambridge Cambridge University Press.
Comrie, Bernard. 1985. *Tense*. Cambridge: Cambridge University Press.
Corbett, Greville. 1991. *Gender*. Cambridge: Cambridge University Press.
Corbett, Greville. 2000. *Number*. Cambridge: Cambridge University Press.
Corbett, Greville. 2006. *Agreement*. Cambridge: Cambridge University Press.
Corston, Simon. 1996. *Ergativity in Roviana, Solomon Islands*. Canberra: Australian National University.
Corston-Oliver, Simon. 2002. Roviana. In John Lynch, Malcolm Ross & Terry Crowley (eds.), *The Oceanic Languages*, 467–497. Richmond: Curzon Press.
Cristofaro, Sonia. 2003. *Subordination: A typological study*. Oxford: Oxford University Press.
Craig, Colette. 1991. Ways to go in Rama: A case study in polygrammaticalization. In Elizabeth C. Traugott & Bernd Heine (eds.), *Approaches to Grammaticalization, Volume 2*, 455–492. John Benjamins Publishing Company.
Crowley, Terry. 2002. Southeast Ambrym. In John Lynch, Malcolm Ross & Terry Crowley (eds.), *The Oceanic Languages*, 660–670. Richmond: Curzon Press.
Dahl, Östen. 1985. *Tense and aspect systems*. Oxford: Basil Blackwell Limited.
Dahl, Östen. 2006. Diminutives and augmentatives. In Keith Brown (ed.), *Encyclopedia of language and linguistics*, 594–595. Amsterdam & Boston: Elsevier Limited.
Dahl, Östen (ed.). 2000. *Tense and aspect in the languages of Europe*. Berlin & New York: Mouton de Gruyter.
Davis, Karen. 2003. *A grammar of the Hoava language, Western Solomons*. Canberra: Pacific Linguistics.
de Haan, Ferdinand. 2006. Typological approaches to modality. In William Frawley (ed.), *The expression of modality*, 27–69. Berlin & New York: Mouton de Gruyter.
Devos, Maud & Daniël Van Olmen. 2013. Describing and explaining the variation of Bantu imperatives and prohibitives. *Studies in Language* 37 (1). 1–57.
Dixon, Robert M. W. 1968. Noun classes. *Lingua* 21. 104–125.
Dixon, Robert M. W. 2004. Adjective classes in typological perspective. In Robert M. W. Dixon & Alexandra Y. Aikhenvald (eds.), *Adjective classes*, 1–49. Oxford: Oxford University Press.
Dixon, Robert M. W. 2009. The semantics of clause linking in a typological perspective. In Robert M. W. Dixon & Alexandra Y. Aikhenvald (eds.), *The semantics of clause linking: A cross-linguistic typology*, 1st edn., 1–55. Oxford: Oxford University Press.

Dixon, Robert M. W. 2010. *Basic linguistic theory, Volume 1, Methodology*. Oxford: Oxford University Press.
Dixon, Robert M. W. & Alexandra Y. Aikhenvald. 2000. Introduction. In Robert M. W. Dixon & Alexandra Y. Aikhenvald (eds.), *Changing valency: Case studies in transitivity*, 1–29. Cambridge: Cambridge University Press.
Dobrin, Lise M. 2005. When our values conflict with theirs: Linguists and community empowerment in Melanesia. In Peter K. Austin (ed.), *Language documentation and description, Volume 3*, 42–52. London: Hans Rausing Endangered Languages Project, Department of Linguistics, SOAS.
Dryer, Matthew S. 2006. Descriptive theories, explanatory theories and Basic Linguistic Theory. In Felix K. Ameka, Alan Dench & Nicholas Evans (eds.), *Catching language: The standing challenge of grammar writing*, 207–234. Berlin: Mouton de Gruyter.
Dryer, Matthew S. 2007a. Clause types. In Timothy Shopen (ed.), *Language typology and syntactic description, Volume 1: Clause Structure*, 2nd edn., 224–275. Cambridge: Cambridge University Press.
Dryer, Matthew S. 2007b. Noun phrase structure. In Timothy Shopen (ed.), *Language typology and syntactic description, Volume 2: Complex Constructions*, 2nd edn., 151–205. Cambridge: Cambridge University Press.
Durie, M. 1988. Verb serialization and "verbal-prepositions" in Oceanic languages. *Oceanic Linguistics* 27 (1). 1–23.
Durie, Mark. 1997. Grammatical structures in verb serialization. In J. B. Alex Alsina & Peter Sells (ed.), *Complex predicates*, 289–354. Stanford, CA: Center for the Study of Language and Information.
Dwyer, Arienne M. 2006. Ethics and practicalities of cooperative fieldwork and analysis. In Jost Gippert, Nikolaus P. Himmelmann & Ulrike Mosel (eds.), *Essentials of language documentation*, 31–66. Berlin: Mouton de Gruyter.
Early, Robert. 1993. Nuclear layer serialization in Lewo. *Oceanic Linguistics* 32 (1). 65–93.
Evans, Bethwyn. 1995. *Reconstructing object markers in Oceanic languages*. Canberra: Australian National University BA Honours thesis.
Evans, Bethwyn. 2003. *A study of valency-changing devices in Proto-Oceanic*. Canberra: Pacific Linguistics and Centre for Researh on Language Change, Research School of Pacific & Asian Studies, Australian National University.
Evans, Bethwyn. 2008. Third person plural as a morphological zero: Object marking in Marovo. In Claire Bowern, Bethwyn Evans & Luisa Miceli (eds.), *Morphology and language history*, 281–298. Amsterdam & Philadelphia: John Benjamins Publishing Company.
Evans, Bethwyn. 2009. Beyond pronouns: Further evidence for South Bougainville. In Bethwyn Evans (ed.), *Discovering history through language: Papers in honour of Malcolm Ross*, 73–101. Canberra: Pacific Linguistics.
Evans, Bethwyn & Bill Palmer. 2011. Contact-induced change in South Bougainville. *Oceanic Linguistics* 50 (2). 489–529.
Everett, Daniel L. 2001. Monolingual field research. In Paul Newman & Martha Ratliff (eds.), *Linguistic fieldwork*, 166–188. Cambridge: Cambridge University Press.
Fagan, Joel L. 1986. *A grammatical analysis of Mono-Alu (Bougainville Straits, Solomon Islands)*. Canberra: Pacific Linguistics.
Florey, Margaret. 2005. Language shift and endangerment. In K. Alexander Adelaar & Nikolaus P. Himmelmann (eds.), *The Austronesian languages of Asia and Madagascar*, 43–64. London: Routledge.

François, Alexandre. 2004. Reconstructing the geocentric system of Proto-Oceanic. *Oceanic Linguistics* 43 (1). 1–31.
François, Alexandre. 2005. Unraveling the history of the vowels of seventeen Northern Vanuatu languages. *Oceanic Linguistics* 44 (2). 443–504.
Frostad, Benedicte H. 2012. *A grammar of Ughele: An Oceanic language of Solomon Islands*. Utrecht: Landelijke Onderzoekschool Taalwetenschap.
Givón, Talmy. 2001. *Syntax: An introduction, Volume I*. Amsterdam & Philadelphia: John Benjamins Publishing Company.
Glennon, John J. 2014. *Syntactic ergativity in Nehan*. Dallas: The Graduate Institute of Applied Linguistics M.A. thesis.
Gordon, Matthew K. 2017. *Phonological typology*. Oxford: Oxford University Press.
Goulden, Rick J. 1990. *The Melanesian content in Tok Pisin*. Canberra: Australian National University.
Grenoble, Lenore A. & Lindsay J. Whaley. 1998. Toward a typology of language endangerment. In Lenore A. Grenoble & Lindsay J. Whaley (eds.), *Endangered languages: current issues and future prospects*, 22–54. Cambridge: Cambridge University Press.
Griffin, James. 2005. Origins of Bougainville's boundaries. In Anthony J. Reagan & Helga-Maria Griffin (eds.), *Bougainville before the conflict*, 72–76. Canberra: Pandanus Books.
Grinevald, Colette. 2003. Speakers and documentation of endangered languages. In Peter K. Austin (ed.), *Language documentation and description, Volume 1*, 52–72. London: Hans Rausing Endangered Languages Project, Department of Linguistics, SOAS.
Haspelmath, Martin. 2004. Coordination constructions: an overview. In Martin Haspelmath (ed.), *Coordinating constructions*, 3–39. Amsterdam & Philadelphia: John Benjamins Publishing Company.
Heine, Bernd. 1992. Grammaticalisation chains. *Studies in Language* 16 (2). 335–368.
Heine, Bernd & Tania Kuteva. 2002. *World lexicon of grammaticalization*. Cambridge: Cambridge University Press.
Hill, Deborah. 2011. Transitivity in Longgu: The interdependence of verb classes and valency-changing derivations. *Oceanic Linguistics* 50 (2). 458–482.
Hill, Deborah & Cliff Goddard. 1997. Spatial terms, polysemy and possession in Longgu (Solomon Islands). *Language Sciences* 19 (3). 263–275.
Himmelmann, Nikolaus P. 1996. Demonstratives in narrative discourse: A taxonomy of universal uses. In B. Fox (ed.), *Studies in anaphora*, 205–254. Amsterdam & Philadelphia: John Benjamins Publishing Company.
Himmelmann, Nikolaus P. 2006. Language documentation: What is it and what is it good for? In Jost Gippert, Nikolaus P. Himmelmann & Ulrike Mosel (eds.), *Essentials of language documentation*, 1–30. Berlin: Mouton de Gruyter.
Himmelmann, Nikolaus P. 2010. Language endangerment scenarios: A case study from Northern Central Sulawesi. In Margaret Florey (ed.), *Endangered languages of Austronesia*, 45–72. Oxford: Oxford University Press.
Hooper, Robin. 1985. Proto-Oceanic *qi. In Andrew K. Pawley & Lois Carrington (eds.), *Austronesian linguistics at the 15th Pacific Science Congress*, 141–167. Canberra: Australian National University.
Hopper, Paul & Sandra Thompson. 1980. Transitivity in grammar and discourse. *Language* 56. 251–99.

Iatridou, Sabine. 2000. The grammatical ingredients of counterfactuality. *Linguistic Inquiry* 31 (2). 231–270.
Jenkins, Rebecca S. 2005. *Language contact and composite structures in New Ireland*. Dallas, Texas: Summer Institute of Linguistics International.
Kahn, Daniel. 1976. *Syllable-based generalizations in English phonology*. Cambridge, MA: Massachusetts Institute of Technology PhD thesis.
Keenan, Edward L., & Bernard Comrie. 1977. Noun phrase accessibility and universal grammar. *Linguistic Inquiry* 8. 63–99.
Keesing, Roger M. 1988. *Melanesian Pidgin and the Oceanic substrate*. Stanford, CA: Stanford University Press.
Krauss, Michael. 1992. The world's languages in crisis. *Language* 68 (1). 4–10.
Kroeger, Paul. 2005. *Analyzing grammar: An introduction*. Cambridge: Cambridge University Press.
Kulick, D. 1992. *Language shift and cultural reproduction: Socialization, self, and syncretism in a Papua New Guinean village*. Cambridge: Cambridge University Press.
Kuteva, Tania & Bernd Heine. 1995. The proximative. Paper presented at the Fourth International Cognitive Linguistics Association Meeting, University of Albuquerque, 1 July.
Lacrampe, Sébastien. 2014. *Lelepa: Topics in the grammar of a Vanuatu language*. Canberra: Australian National University PhD thesis.
Lanyon-Orgill, P. A., & Chung King. 1942. A Polynesian dettlement in New Britain. *The Journal of the Polynesian Society* 51 (2). 87–114.
Laracy, Hugh. 1969. The Torau speakers of Bougainville – an historical note. *Oceania* 39 (3). 234–235.
Laracy, Hugh. 1976. *Marists and Melanesians: A history of Catholic missions in the Solomon Islands*. Honolulu: The University Press of Hawai'i.
Laracy, Hugh. 2005a. 1914: Changing the guard at Kieta. In Anthony J. Reagan & Helga-Maria Griffin (eds.), *Bougainville before the conflict*, 136–140. Canberra: Pandanus Books.
Laracy, Hugh. 2005b. 'Imperium in Imperio'? The Catholic Church in Bougainville. In Anthony J. Reagan & Helga-Maria Griffin (eds.), *Bougainville before the conflict*, 125–135. Canberra: Pandanus Books.
Lewis, M. Paul, Gary Simons & Charles Fennig. 2014. *Ethnologue: Languages of the world, 17th edn*. Dallas, Texas: Summer Institute of Linguistics International.
Lichtenberk, Frantisek. 1985. Possessive constructions in Oceanic languages and Proto-Oceanic. In Andrew K. Pawley & Lois Carrington (eds.), *Austronesian linguistics at the 15th Pacific Science Congress* 93–140. Canberra: Australian National University.
Lichtenberk, Frantisek. 1991. Semantic change and heterosemy in grammaticalization. *Language* 67 (3). 475–509.
Lichtenberk, Frantisek. 1995. Apprehensional epistemics. In Joan Bybee & Suzanne Fleischman (eds.), *Modality in grammar and discourse*, (Typological Studies in Language 32), 293–327. Amsterdam & Philadelphia: John Benjamins Publishing Company.
Lichtenberk, Frantisek. 2000a. Inclusory pronominals. *Oceanic Linguistics* 39 (1). 1–32.
Lichtenberk, Frantisek. 2000b. Reciprocals without reflexives. In Zygmunt Frajzyngier & Traci S. Curl (eds.), *Reciprocals: forms and functions*, (Typological Studies in Language 41), 31–62. Amsterdam & Philadelphia: John Benjamins Publishing Company.
Lichtenberk, Frantisek. 2006. Serial verb constructions in Toqabaqita. In Alexandra Y. Aikhenvald & Robert M. W. Dixon (eds.), *Serial verb constructions*, 254–272. Oxford: Oxford University Press.

Lincoln, Peter C. 1976a. Austronesian languages: Bougainville province. In Stephen A. Wurm (ed.), *New Guinea area languages and language study, Volume 2, Austronesian Languages*, 419–440. Canberra: Australian National University.

Lincoln, Peter C. 1976b. *Describing Banoni, an Austronesian language of southeast Bougainville*. Honolulu: University of Hawai'i PhD thesis.

Litteral, Robert. 2001. Language development in Papua New Guinea. *Radical Pedagogy* 3 (1). http://www.radicalpedagogy.org/radicalpedagogy/Language_Development_In_Papua_New_Guinea.html (3 July 2018).

Lüpke, Friederike. 2009. Data collection methods for field-based language documentation. In Peter K. Austin (ed.), *Language documentation and description, Volume 6*, 53–100. London: Hans Rausing Endangered Languages Project, Department of Linguistics, SOAS.

Lynch, John 2001. Article accretion and article creation in southern Oceanic. *Oceanic Linguistics* 40 (2). 224–46.

Lynch, John & Malcolm Ross. 2002. Banoni. In John Lynch, Malcolm Ross & Terry Crowley (eds.), *The Oceanic Languages*, 440–455. Richmond: Curzon Press.

Lynch, John, Malcolm Ross & Terry Crowley. 2002. *The Oceanic Languages*. Richmond: Curzon Press.

Margetts, Anna. 2008. Transitivity discord in some Oceanic languages. *Oceanic Linguistics* 47 (1). 30–44.

McHardy, Emmet. 1935. *Blazing the trail in the Solomons*. Sydney: Visitor Printing Company.

Mithun, Marianne. 1984. The evolution of noun incorporation. *Language* 60. 847–94.

Moravcsik, Edith. 1978. Reduplicative constructions. In Charles A. Ferguson & Edith A. Moravcsik (eds.), *Universals of human language, Volume 3: Word structure*, 297–334. Stanford, CA: Stanford University Press.

Mosel, Ulrike. 1984. *Tolai syntax and its historical development*. Canberra: Pacific Linguistics B92.

Mosel, Ulrike. 1999. Towards a typology of negation in Oceanic languages. In Even Hovdhaugen & Ulrike Mosel (eds.), *Negation in Oceanic languages: Typological studies*, 1–19. München: Lincom Europa.

Mosel, Ulrike. 2007. Ditransitivity and valency change in Teop – a corpus based study. *Tidsskrift for Sprog forskning* 5. 1–40.

Mosel, Ulrike. 2010. Ditransitive constructions and their alternatives in Teop. In Andrej Malchukov, Martin Haspelmath & Bernard Comrie (eds.), *Studies in ditransitive constructions: A comparative handbook*, 486–509. Berlin & New York: De Gruyter Mouton.

Mosel, Ulrike. in prep. *Analogical levelling across constructions – incorporated prepositions in Teop*. https://www.academia.edu/7931337/Analogical_levelling_across_constructions_1_Analogical_levelling_across_constructions_incorporated_prepositions_in_Teop_Ulrike_Mosel

Mosel, Ulrike & Ruth Spriggs 1999a. Gender in Teop. In Barbara Unterbeck & Matti Rissanen (eds.), *Gender in grammar and cognition*, (Trends in Linguistics. Studies and Monographs [TiLSM] 124), 321–349. Berlin: Mouton de Gruyter.

Mosel, Ulrike & Spriggs, R. 1999b. Negation in Teop. In Even Hovdhaugen & Ulrike Mosel (eds.), *Negation in Oceanic languages: Typological studies*, 45–56. München: Lincom Europa.

Mosel, Ulrike & Yvonne Thiesen. 2007. The Teop sketch grammar. http://www.linguistik.uni-kiel.de/Teop_Sketch_Grammar_May07.pdf (17 May 2011).

Moyse-Faurie, Claire. 2008. Constructions expressing middle, reflexive & reciprocal situations in some Oceanic languages. In Ekkehard König & Volker Gast (eds.), *Reciprocals and reflexives: Theoretical and typological explorations*, 105–168. Berlin & New York: Mouton de Gruyter.

Moyse-Faurie, Claire & John Lynch. 2004. Coordination in Oceanic languages and Proto-Oceanic. In Martin Haspelmath (ed.), *Coordinating constructions*, 445–497. Amsterdam & Philadelphia: John Benjamins Publishing Company.

Mühlhäusler, Peter. 1976. Samoan Plantation Pidgin and the origins of New Guinea Pidgin: An introduction. *Journal of Pacific History* 11 (2). 122–125.

Mühlhäusler, Peter. 1979. *Growth and structure of the lexicon of New Guinea Pidgin*. Canberra: Australian National University.

Mühlhäusler, Peter. 1982. Tok Pisin in Papua New Guinea. In Richard Bailey & Manfred Görlach (eds.), *English as a world language*, 439–466. Ann Arbor: University of Michigan Press.

Mühlhäusler, Peter. 1987. On the origins of the predicate marker in Tok Pisin. In John W.M. Verhaar (ed.), *Melanesian Pidgin and Tok Pisin: Proceedings of the first international conference on pidgins and creoles in Melanesia, Volume 20*, 235–250. Amsterdam & Philadelphia: John Benjamins Publishing Company.

Mühlhäusler, Peter, Malcolm Philpott & Rachel Trew. 1996. Modern media in the Pacific area and their role in intercultural communication. In Stephen A. Wurm, Peter Mühlhäusler & Darrell T. Tryon (eds.), *Atlas of languages of intercultural communication in the Pacific, Asia, and the Americas, Volume II.2*, 1389–1454. Berlin: Mouton de Gruyter.

NDOE. 2003. *Elementary Language Syllabus*. Waigani: National Department of Education.

NDOE. 2015. *Elementary Language Syllabus*. Waigani: National Department of Education.

Nettle, Daniel & Suzanne Romaine. 2000. *Vanishing voices: the extinction of the world's languages*. Oxford: Oxford University Press.

Noonan, Michael. 2007. Complementation. In Timothy Shopen (ed.), *Language typology and syntactic description, Volume 2: Complex constructions*, 2nd edn., 52–150. Cambridge: Cambridge University Press.

Ogan, Eugene. 2005. An introduction to Bougainville cultures. In Anthony J. Reagan & Helga-Maria Griffin (eds.), *Bougainville before the conflict*, 47–56. Canberra: Pandanus Books.

Oliver, Douglas. 1973. *Bougainville: A personal history*. Carlton: Melbourne University Press.

Oliver, Douglas. 1991. *Black islanders: A personal perspective of Bougainville 1937–1991*. Melbourne: Hyland House.

Palmer, Bill. 2002. Kokota. In John Lynch, Malcolm Ross & Terry Crowley (eds.), *The Oceanic Languages*, 498–524. Richmond: Curzon Press.

Palmer, Bill. 2007a. Imperfective aspect and the interplay of aspect, tense and modality in Torau. *Oceanic Linguistics* 46 (2). 499–519.

Palmer, Bill. 2007b. Papapana dictionary, Version 2.1. http://www.smg.surrey.ac.uk/languages/northwest-solomonic/papapana/dictionary/ (3 July 2018).

Palmer, Bill. 2007c. Papapana elicitation materials. http://www.smg.surrey.ac.uk/languages/northwest-solomonic/papapana/elicitation-materials/ (3 July 2018).

Palmer, Bill. 2007d. Uruava (Poraka) dictionary, Version 3.0. http://www.smg.surrey.ac.uk/languages/northwest-solomonic/uruava/uruava-dictionary/ (3 July 2018).

Palmer, Bill. 2009. *Kokota Grammar*. Honolulu: University of Hawai'i Press.

Palmer, Bill. 2011. Subject-indexing and possessive morphology in Northwest Solomonic. *Linguistics* 49 (4). 685–747.
Palmer, Bill. 2012. *Nominal number in Meso-Melanesian*. Paper presented at the 17th International Lexical Functional Grammar Conference, Udayana University, 28 June–1 July.
Palmer, Bill. 2014. *Mono-Uruavan cognates*. Unpublished manuscripts, The University of Newcastle, Australia.
Palmer, Frank R. 2001. *Mood and modality, 2nd edn*. Cambridge: Cambridge University Press.
Pawley, Andrew. 1973. Some problems in Proto-Oceanic grammar. *Oceanic Linguistics* 12 (1). 103–188.
Pawley, Andrew. 2006. Explaining the aberrant Austronesian languages of Southeast Melanesia: 150 years of debate. *Journal of the Polynesian Society* 115. 215–258.
Pawley, Andrew K. & Lawrence A. Reid. 1979. The evolution of transitive constructions in Austronesian. In Paz B. Naylor (ed.), *Austronesian studies: Papers from the second Eastern conference on Austronesian languages*, (Michigan Papers on South and Southeast Asia 15), 103–130. Ann Arbor: Center for South and Southeast Asian Studies, The University of Michigan.
Payne, Thomas E. 1997. *Describing morphosyntax: a guide for field linguists*. Cambridge: Cambridge University Press.
Regan, Anthony J. 2005. Identities among Bougainvilleans. In Anthony J. Reagan & Helga-Maria Griffin (eds.), *Bougainville before the conflict* 418–446. Canberra: Pandanus Books.
Regan, Anthony J. & Helga-Maria Griffin (eds.). 2005. *Bougainville before the conflict*. Canberra: Pandanus Books.
Reinig, Jessika. 2004. Serial and complex verb constructions in Teop. In Isabelle Bril & Françoise Ozanne-Rivierre (eds.), *Complex predicates in Oceanic languages: Studies in the dynamics of binding and boundness*, 89–106. Berlin: Mouton de Gruyter.
Robinson, Stuart. 2011. *Split intransitivity in Rotokas, a Papuan language of Bougainville*. Nijmegen: Max Planck Institute for Psycholinguistics.
Romaine, Suzanne. 1999. The grammaticalization of the proximative in Tok Pisin. *Language* 75 (2). 322–346.
Ross, Malcolm. 1982. The development of the verb phrase in the Oceanic languages of the Bougainville region. In Amran Halim, Lois Carrington & Stephen A. Wurm (eds.), *Papers from the Third International Conference on Austronesian Linguistics, Volume 1: Currents in Oceanic*, (Pacific Linguistics C74), 1–57. Canberra: Department of Linguistics, Research School of Pacific Studies, Australian National University.
Ross, Malcolm. 1988. *Proto-Oceanic and the Austronesian languages of Western Melanesia*. Canberra: Australian National University.
Ross, Malcolm. 1996. Mission and church languages in Papua New Guinea. In Stephen A. Wurm, Peter Mühlhäusler & Darrell T. Tryon (eds.), *Atlas of languages of intercultural communication in the Pacific, Asia, and the Americas, Volume II.1*, 595–618. Berlin: Mouton de Gruyter.
Ross, Malcolm. 1998a. Possessive-like attribute constructions in the Oceanic languages of Northwest Melanesia. *Oceanic Linguistics* 37 (2). 234–276.
Ross, Malcolm. 1998b. Proto-Oceanic adjectival categories and their morphosyntax. *Oceanic Linguistics* 37 (1). 85–119.

Ross, Malcolm. 2002a. Sisiqa. In John Lynch, Malcolm Ross & Terry Crowley (eds.), *The Oceanic Languages*, 456–466. Richmond: Curzon Press.
Ross, Malcolm. 2002b. Taiof. In John Lynch, Malcolm Ross & Terry Crowley (eds.), *The Oceanic Languages*, 426–439. Richmond: Curzon Press.
Ross, Malcolm. 2004a. Demonstratives, local nouns and directionals in Oceanic languages: a diachronic perspective. In Gunter Senft (ed.), *Deixis and demonstratives in Oceanic languages*, 175–204. Canberra: The Australian National University.
Ross, Malcolm. 2004b. The grammaticization of directional verbs in Oceanic languages. In Isabelle Bril & Françoise Ozanne-Rivierre (eds.), *Complex predicates in Oceanic languages: Studies in the dynamics of binding and boundness*, 297–329. Berlin: Mouton de Gruyter.
Ross, Malcolm. 2004c. The morphosyntactic typology of Oceanic Languages. *Language & Linguistics* 5 (2). 491–541.
Ross, Malcolm. 2007a. Talking about space: terms of location and direction. In Malcolm Ross, Andrew Pawley & Meredith Osmond (eds.), *The lexicon of Proto Oceanic: The culture and environment of ancestral Oceanic society, Volume 2: The physical environment*, 229–294. Canberra: Pacific Linguistics.
Ross, Malcolm. 2007b. Two kinds of locative construction in Oceanic languages: A robust distinction. In Jeff Siegel, John Lynch & Diana Eades (eds.), *Language description, history and development: Linguistic indulgence in memory of Terry Crowley* (Creole Language Library Volume 30), 281–295. Amsterdam & Philadelphia: John Benjamins Publishing Company.
Ross, Malcolm, & Åshild Næss. 2007. An Oceanic origin for Äiwoo, the language of the Reef Islands? *Oceanic Linguistic* 46 (2). 457–498.
Rothstein, Susan. 2004. *Structuring events: A study in the semantics of lexical aspect*. Oxford: Blackwell Publishing Limited.
Sack, Peter. 2005. German colonial rule in the Northern Solomons. In Anthony J. Reagan & Helga-Maria Griffin (eds.), *Bougainville before the conflict*, 77–107. Canberra: Pandanus Books.
Siewierska, Anna. 2004. *Person*. Cambridge: Cambridge University Press.
Sillitoe, Paul. 1998. *An introduction to the anthropology of Melanesia*. Cambridge: Cambridge University Press.
Smith, Ellen. 2015a. *A grammar of Papapana, with an investigation into language contact and endangerment*. Newcastle: The University of Newcastle, Australia PhD thesis.
Smith, Ellen. 2015b. Documenting Papapana, a highly endangered Northwest Solomonic language of the Autonomous Region of Bougainville, Papua New Guinea. SOAS. URL: http://elar.soas.ac.uk/deposit/0313
Smith, Ellen. 2016a. Contact-induced change in a highly endangered language of Northern Bougainville. *Australian Journal of Linguistics* 36 (3). 369–405.
Smith, Ellen. 2016b. Measuring and understanding ethnolinguistic vitality in Papapana. In L. Filipović & M. Pütz (eds.), *Endangered languages and languages in danger: Issues of documentation, policy and language rights*, (IMPACT: Studies in Language & Society 42), 249–279. Amsterdam & Philadelphia: John Benjamins Publishing Company.
Smith, Ellen. 2016c. Papapana re~redu~reduplicates: multiple reduplication in an endangered Northwest Solomonic language. *Oceanic Linguistics* 55 (2). 522–560.

Smith-Dennis, Ellen. 2017. *Contact with a contact language: language endangerment and linguistic change*. Paper presented at the 7th Conference on Language Endangerment, University of Cambridge, 4 July.

Smith-Dennis, Ellen. 2018. *'This way, like': the polygrammaticalisation of an Oceanic deictic directional serial verb*. Paper presented at the 10th Austronesian and Papuan Languages and Linguistics Conference, University of Surrey, 4–5 May.

Smith-Dennis, Ellen. 2019. *Don't feel obligated, lest it be undesirable: The relationship between prohibitives and apprehensives in Papapana and beyond*. Paper presented at the 13th Association of Linguistic Typology Conference, University of Pavia, 4–6 September.

Smith-Dennis, Ellen. in press. Don't feel obligated, lest it be undesirable: The relationship between prohibitives and apprehensives in Papapana and beyond. *Linguistic Typology*.

Spriggs, Matthew. 2005. Bougainville's early history: An archaeological perspective. In Anthony J. Reagan & Helga-Maria Griffin (eds.), *Bougainville before the conflict*, 1–19. Canberra: Pandanus Books.

Taita, Luke. 2013. Language policy in all schools, Secretary's circular No. 4/2013. https://www.gurl?sa%3Dt%26rct%3Dj/url?sa%3Dt%26rct%3Dj%26q%3D%26esrc%3Ds%26source%3Dweb%26cd%3D1%26cad%3Drja%26uact%3D8%26ved%3D2ahUKEwj0n7fO-9LlAhXgSxUIHTUuCf8QFjAAegQIABAC%26url%3Dhttps%3A%2F%2Fjoyellen.files.wordpress.com%2F2013%2F03%2F04-2013-language-policy-in-all-school.pdf&usg=AOvVaw3UnRDKMlAsG6cMMdyras5L (3 July 2018).

Terrell, John E. & Geoffrey J. Irwin. 1972. History and tradition in the Northern Solomons: An analytical study of the Torau migration to southern Bougainville in the 1860s. *The Journal of the Polynesian Society* 81 (3). 317–349.

Thompson, Sandra A., Robert E. Longacre & Shin Ja J. Hwang. 2007. Adverbial clauses. In Timothy Shopen (ed.), *Language typology and syntactic description, Volume 2: Complex constructions*, 2nd edn., 237–300. Cambridge: Cambridge University Press.

Timberlake, Alan. 2007. Aspect, tense, mood. In Timothy Shopen (ed.), *Language typology and syntactic description, Volume 3: Grammatical categories and the lexicon*, 2nd edn., 280–333. Cambridge: Cambridge University Press.

Todd, Evelyn M. 1978. A sketch of Nissan (Nehan) grammar. In Stephen A. Wurm & Lois Carrington (eds.), *Second International Conference on Austronesian Linguistics: Proceedings. Fascicle 2: Eastern Austronesian*, (Pacific Linguistics C61), 1181–1239. Canberra: Research School of Pacific Linguistics, Australian National University.

Togolo, Melchior. 2005. Torau response to change. In Anthony J. Reagan & Helga-Maria Griffin (eds.), *Bougainville before the conflict*, 274–290. Canberra: Pandanus Books.

Tryon, Darrell. 2005. The languages of Bougainville. In Anthony J. Reagan & Helga-Maria Griffin (eds.), *Bougainville before the conflict*, 31–46. Canberra: Pandanus Books.

van Lier, Eva. 2016. Lexical flexibility in Oceanic languages. *Linguistic Typology* 20 (2). 197–232.

Velupillai, Viveka. 2012. *An introduction to linguistic typology*. Amsterdam/Philadelphia: John Benjamins Publishing.

Vendler, Zeno. 1957. Verbs and times. *Philosophical Review* 66. 143–60.

Vernon, Don. 2005. The Panguna mine. In Anthony J. Reagan & Helga-Maria Griffin (eds.), *Bougainville before the conflict*, 258–273. Canberra: Pandanus Books.

Whaley, Lindsay J. 1997. *Introduction to typology*. London: SAGE Publications.

Wilkins, David. 1999. The 1999 demonstrative questionnaire: 'this' & 'that' in comparative perspective. In David Wilkins (ed.), *Manual for the 1999 field season, 1–24*. Nijmegen: Max Planck Institute for Psycholinguistics.

Woodbury, Anthony C. 2003. Defining documentary linguistics. In Peter K. Austin (ed.), *Language documentation and description, Volume 1*, 35–51. London: Hans Rausing Endangered Languages Project, Department of Linguistics, SOAS.

Wurm, Stephen A. 2003. The language situation and language endangerment in the Greater Pacific area. In Mark Janse & Sijmen Tol (eds.), *Language death and language maintenance: Theoretical, practical and descriptive approaches*, 15–47. Amsterdam & Philadelphia: John Benjamins Publishing Company.

Wurm, Stephen A. 2012. Australasia and the Pacific. In C. Moseley (ed.), *Encyclopedia of the world's endangered languages*, 425–466. Oxon: Routledge.

Wurm, Stephen A. & Shirô Hattori (eds.). 1981–83. *Language atlas of the Pacific area* (Pacific Linguistics C66–67). Canberra: The Australian Academy of the Humanities in collaboration with the Japan academy.

Appendix 1
Pronominal paradigms

Independent pronouns

	1EXCL	1INCL	2	3
SG	anau ~ aniau		ani ~ anio	aia
DU	auami	auara	auamu	auana
	ami=nua anua	era=nua anua	amiu=nua anua	nua anua
TR	ami=atono	era=atono	amiu=atono	oina=atono
PL	a:mani	arira	a:mu	aina

Direct possessor suffixes

	1EXCL	1INCL	2	3
SG	-u		-mu	-na
PL	-mani	-ira	-miu	-ina

Indirect possessor proclitics

	1EXCL	1INCL	2	3
SG	au=		amu=	ena=
PL	ami=	era=	amiu=	oina=

Subject-indexing proclitics

	1EXCL	1INCL	2	3
SG	u=		o=	e=
PL	mi=	si= ~ so=	mu=	i=
		sa=		

Object-indexing enclitics

	1EXCL	1INCL	2	3
SG	=au		=o	=a
PL	=ami	=ira	=amu	=ina

Postverbal subject-indexing (PSI) enclitics

	1EXCL	1INCL	2	3
SG	=u		=mu	=na
	~ =eu		~ =emu	~ =ena
	~ =ou		~ =omu	
PL	=mani	=ra	=miu	=ina
	~ =emani	~ =era	~ =emiu	

Appendix 2
25 demonstrative scenes (Wilkins 1999)

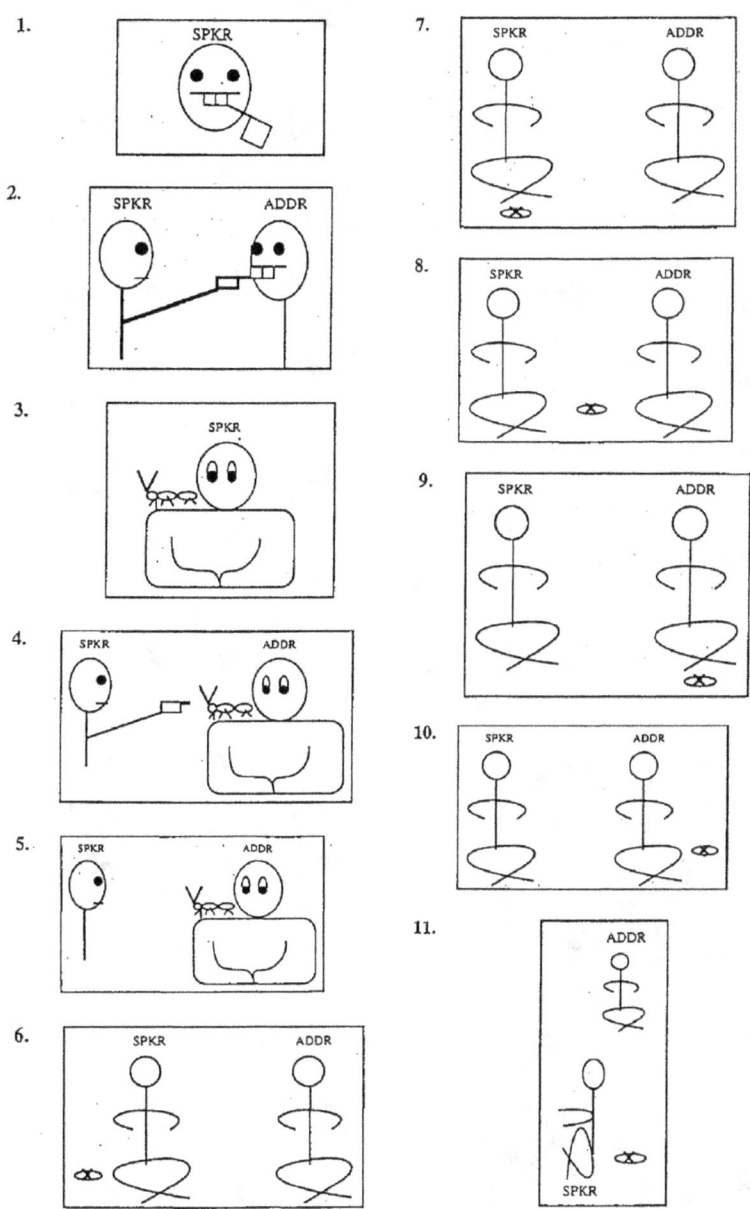

https://doi.org/10.1515/9781501509971-013

524 — Appendix 2 25 demonstrative scenes (Wilkins 1999)

12.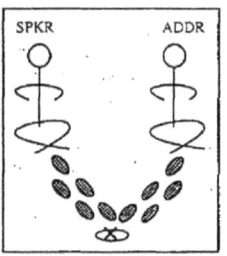

13.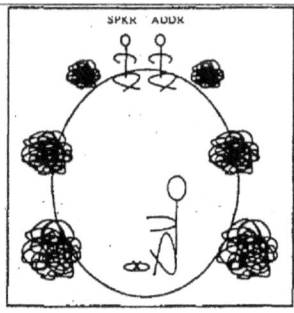

14.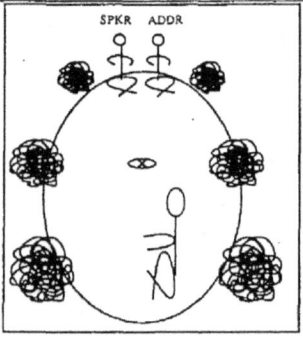

15.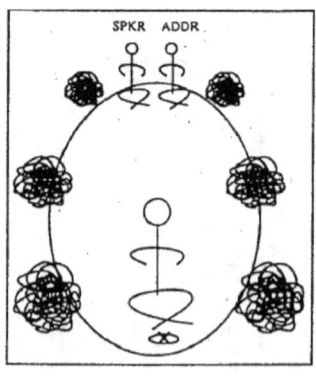

16.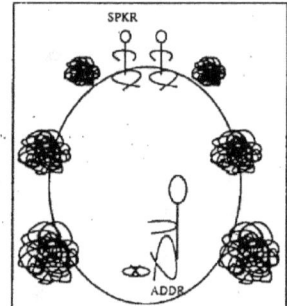

17.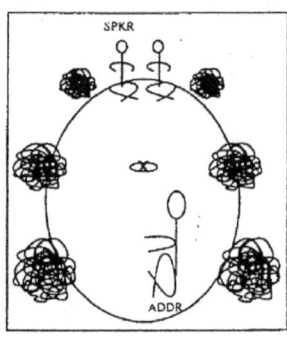

18.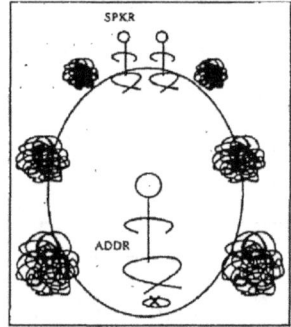

Appendix 2 25 demonstrative scenes (Wilkins 1999) — **525**

19.

20.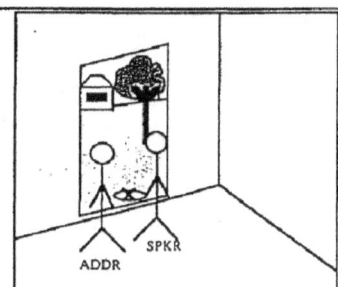

21.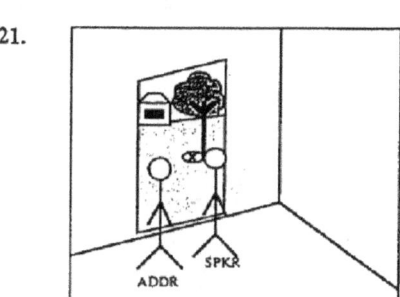

22.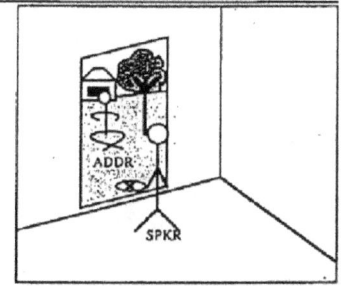

23.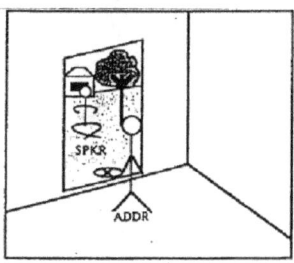

24.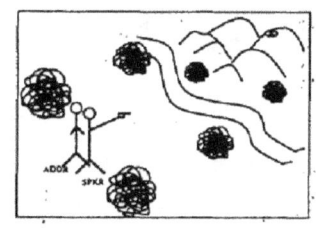

25.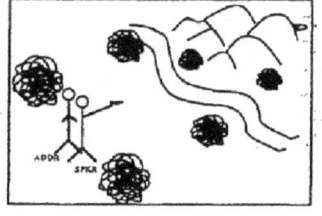

Index

Ability 382, 389, 488–491, 497, 500–502
Additive marker 150, 385
Adjectives 100, 102, 103, 121, 135–144, 146, 157, 190, 231, 233, 250, 264, 433–436
Adverbial clauses 321, 325, 326, 441, 450, 467–488, 490, 498
Adverbs 124, 144, 230, 233, 234, 293, 303–313, 342, 344, 345, 348, 356, 386–390
Affixes.
See also augmentative; case, locative; causative prefix; derivational suffix; valency-changing operations, detransitivising prefix
–construct suffix 101, 116–119, 121–123, 201, 408, 409, 432
–Personal specific article 169, 178–181, 374, 375
–possessor suffixes 99, 101, 117, 125, 126, 167, 168, 204–206, 368, 437, 466
–stress 97
Agreement
–adjective 190
–numeral 202, 203
–possession 205, 213, 425
–verb 171, 228, 229, 236–238, 391, 460
Alignment 234
Allomorphs 82, 137, 151, 178, 181, 188, 197, 376, 442
Allophones 70, 77–79, 84
Ambitransitive verbs 245, 247, 248, 254–257, 259, 264, 268, 272, 275, 277, 338, 339
Animacy in numerals 196, 197, 199, 203, 213
Articles. See collective articles; diminutive articles; non-specific articles; partitive article; plural article; specific articles
Aspect
–completive 230, 312, 314–316, 318, 344–346, 350, 452, 454
–continuous 279, 298, 313–316, 324, 325, 335–342, 355, 456, 457
–habitual 123, 279, 313–316, 318, 321–325, 335–342, 350
–perfect, lack of 320

–proximative 314–316, 332
–repetitive 151, 230, 301, 305, 314–316, 318, 331, 342–344, 352
Associative marker 149
Associative plural 100, 102, 154, 155, 173–175
Asyndesis 394, 453, 454, 456, 459, 467–469, 472, 488, 489
Augmentative 101, 117, 119, 142, 143, 170, 175, 359
Avalent verbs, lack of 247

Banoni language 3, 43, 52, 58, 72, 113, 125, 130, 199, 207, 216, 267, 273, 282, 287, 291, 301, 315, 338, 354, 356, 408, 411, 424, 475
Bougainville Crisis 52, 53, 55, 129, 354, 372
Bound nouns 156, 206, 370

Case
–lack of 104, 236, 237
–locative 128, 155, 165–167, 169, 427
Causative
–causative prefix 199, 229, 247, 248, 250, 251, 255, 256, 267–269, 291, 477
–causative serial verb construction 287, 291, 292
Clans 45, 46
Classifiers, lack of 211, 317
Clitics.
See also agreement, verb; aspect, repetitive; diminutive articles; mode, irrealis; non-specific articles; specific articles; transitive marker
–enclitic =ma 111, 126, 127, 148, 153, 157, 166, 169, 182, 196, 209, 232, 233, 241, 262, 268, 278, 286, 288, 289, 293, 295, 300, 301, 309, 332, 349, 359, 361, 363, 366, 369, 371, 372, 381, 393–395, 401, 446, 453, 461, 476, 481, 488, 497
–possessor proclitics 99, 101, 105, 155, 158, 161, 180, 208–215, 219, 374
–postnominal enclitic =re 151

–postverbal subject-indexing enclitics 97, 124, 125, 229, 230, 242, 279, 306, 315–318, 323, 328, 329–333, 335–338, 340, 341, 347, 355, 382, 389, 390, 479, 500
–stress 95–97
Cognates 25, 46, 81, 125, 157, 168, 180, 185, 208, 267, 273, 297, 299, 373, 408, 411, 475
Collective articles 100, 114, 115, 126, 175, 176, 191, 209, 359
Collective marker 101–102, 106–108, 111, 123, 124, 136, 139, 144, 176, 177, 277, 435
Collective nouns 115, 120, 159
Comitative. *See* postposition, nascent; valency-changing operations
Comparative construction 145, 250, 264, 459
Complement clauses 441, 474, 480, 482, 488–507
Compounding
–compound nouns 101, 115–124, 184, 432
–compound numerals 194–197
–compound, possession 437–440
–compound verbs 233, 234
Consonant clusters 85
Consonants 76–81, 83–85
Constituent order 30, 236, 356–365, 368, 369, 371, 374, 381–383, 386, 391–406, 409–415, 417–421, 423, 424, 426–428, 430–433, 437, 458, 468, 469, 473, 475, 476, 478, 480, 481, 483–488
Coordination 173, 272, 394, 441–457, 467, 480, 485, 505, 506
Coordinators 173, 193, 441–449, 450–454
Copula, lack of 30
Core arguments, marking of 234–241, 283, 391, 392, 459, 460 *See also* agreement, verb

Definiteness 180, 181, 185, 275
Deixis. *See also* directionals, deictic; demonstratives
–deictic locationals 371
–temporal deixis 166, 359, 362, 381, 478
Demonstratives 100, 102, 103, 127–135, 189, 371, 458

Derivation.
See also valency-changing operations
–causative prefix and numerals 199
–derivational reduplication 87, 88, 90, 91, 106, 109–115, 126, 127, 136, 137, 166, 192, 233
–derivational suffix 87, 88, 101, 106, 112–115, 126, 127, 192
–zero-derivation 25, 107–109, 152, 153, 231–233, 250, 303, 403, 420, 421
Diminutive articles 99, 101, 139, 140, 154, 155, 157, 158, 161, 176, 177, 186–189, 209, 373, 379, 380
Diphthongs 72–75, 79, 80, 82, 83, 85, 86, 89, 91, 93, 96–98, 179, 186, 262
Directionals
–allative 230, 284, 293, 302, 303
–deictic 230, 284, 288–290, 293, 298, 299
–geocentric 230, 284, 293–298
–sequential 230, 284, 289, 293, 299–302, 305, 343
Ditransitive verbs 234–236, 245–248, 251, 253, 255, 256, 264, 265, 268, 277, 278, 339, 375, 376, 378, 391, 392, 397–399, 405, 406, 409–412, 414, 459, 460, 462–464
Dual number
–dual collective article 114, 126, 176, 191
–dual pronouns 104–106, 173, 272, 449

Echo vowels 74, 76, 261, 262
Ellipsis
–coordination reduction 443, 456
–elided nouns 143, 144, 202, 203, 213–215, 222–224, 226
Emphasis
–emphatic marker 230, 233, 241–245, 330, 334
–emphatic, nominal modifier 148, 149, 282
–negation 422
–possession 218
English 41, 51, 53, 56, 57, 61, 62, 64, 65, 82, 85, 381
Epenthesis
–glides 75, 79, 80
–glottal stop 80, 84, 90, 94

Ethnolinguistic vitality 65–67
Existential clauses 417–422, 436, 439
Exponence, distributed 318

Frames of reference 294–296

Gender. *See* noun class
Gender, biological 104, 154, 237
Generic reference 118, 143, 180, 274–276
Grammaticalisation 144, 149, 150, 274, 278, 284, 293, 297, 299, 301–303, 307, 332, 345, 349, 380, 385

Halia language 43, 56–58, 135, 242, 245
Headedness, variation 2, 27, 131, 138, 195, 200, 204, 224, 225, 369, 385, 392, 394–396, 398, 399, 404, 410, 429
Hoava language 3, 70, 89, 110, 236, 259, 261, 267, 291, 338, 439
Hortatives 239, 242, 321, 325, 346–348, 399, 400, 470

Imperatives 242, 245, 321, 325, 346–348, 399, 400, 443, 454, 470, 502, 506
Inclusory pronoun 449
Intensifiers 139, 146, 148, 308, 309, 312, 362, 435
Interrogatives 100, 102, 401–416, 430, 468, 480, 489, 496, 497
Interrogative tags 401, 402
Intonation
–complex sentences 328, 394, 453
–interrogatives 401, 402
–serial verb constructions 283
Intransitive verbs 124, 135, 136, 231, 233, 234, 245–250, 254, 255, 257, 258, 264, 267, 272, 275, 278, 283, 284, 287, 288, 290, 338, 339, 391–394, 404, 406, 409, 411–415, 417, 419, 460, 502
Inverse number marking 182–185, 189, 223, 224, 276

Kinship terms 114, 115, 125–127, 154, 156, 157, 159, 160, 162–164, 173, 180, 206–208, 212

Kokota language 3, 70, 130, 199, 261, 274, 282, 346
Kubokota language 3, 113, 130, 157, 174, 175, 180, 263, 267, 283, 296, 297, 338, 408

Language change, contact-induced 150, 332, 382, 385, 412, 442, 475, 479 *See also* headedness, variation
Language death process 171
Language variation, phonological 81, 82, 105, 317, 328, 330, 334 *See also* allophones; allomorphs
Lexicalisation 121, 127, 141, 165–168, 175, 269, 292, 382, 389, 479
Loanwords 85, 114, 154, 159, 192, 441, 483

Mode
–apprehensive 230, 315, 316, 321, 325, 326, 350, 352, 467, 470–472
–counterfactual conditional 315, 316, 333–335, 351, 468–470
–hypothetical conditional 230, 315, 316, 321, 326–329, 351, 468–470
–irrealis 230, 314, 315, 318, 321–332, 340, 341, 346–348, 350–355
–optative 230, 315, 316, 321, 324, 329–332, 334, 351
Mono *See* Mono-Alu language
Mono-Alu language 3, 37, 125, 204, 315
Monotransitive verbs 168, 231, 234, 236, 245, 247, 248, 250–257, 259, 264, 268, 269, 271, 272, 275–278, 283, 284, 287, 288, 290–292, 338, 339, 375, 378, 391, 392, 395–397, 404, 406, 409–414, 459, 460, 462, 464, 502
Multilingualism 38–40, 42, 48, 55, 57, 58, 60, 67

Negation 230, 348–355, 401, 402, 420–423, 428–430, 435, 436, 490
–adjectives 136, 140
–compound, possession 438–440
Negative imperatives *See* prohibitives
Negative purpose *See* apprehensive

530 — Index

Nehan language 3, 42, 43, 56, 58, 135, 182
Nehan-North Bougainville languages 37, 135, 242, 245, 315
Non-specific articles 99, 101, 154, 155, 176, 177, 185, 186, 208
Northwest Solomonic languages 37, 38, 43, 72, 77, 87, 109, 110, 113, 130, 157, 169, 170, 176, 180, 182, 183, 194, 195, 199, 204, 216, 236, 242, 261, 266, 267, 273, 274, 282, 283, 287, 291, 301, 315, 317, 337, 346, 354, 360, 373, 401, 424
Noun class 121, 233
–Class I 99–101, 105, 107, 110, 111, 120, 123, 140, 154, 155, 157–161, 169–171, 177–189, 191, 194, 195, 199, 200, 208–210, 214, 216, 357–359, 376–379, 407, 416, 425, 478
–Class II 99–101, 107, 110, 111, 127, 140, 154, 155, 157, 161–164, 169–171, 177–190, 194, 195, 199, 209, 210, 214, 216, 376–379, 407, 416, 425
–Class I marker 99, 213–215, 221–224
–Class II marker 99, 101, 102, 155, 161, 176–178, 183, 185, 189–191, 200, 208–210, 213, 221–224
–Location nouns 99, 100, 112, 148, 154, 155, 164–170, 205–207, 216, 294, 302, 359, 360–370, 381, 427, 478
–Personal 99, 101, 140, 154–157, 173–175, 177–181, 183, 185–187, 189, 195, 199, 206, 216, 231, 232, 374, 375
Noun phrase structure 100–103, 176–178, 200–202, 213–215
Nouns 99–103, 106–127, 231
Numerals 99, 101–103, 112, 146, 158, 161, 192–203, 209, 307, 379, 380, 409, 432, 433, 434, 436
–numeral coordination 442

Oblique arguments 356, 376, 380
Oceanic languages, typological features of 24, 68, 72, 77, 85, 92, 104, 105, 109, 118, 128, 130, 135, 136, 157, 165, 166, 170, 204, 206, 207, 211, 237, 240, 257, 258, 261, 274, 276–278, 283, 295–297, 299, 301, 302, 344, 345, 348–350, 352, 385, 391, 392, 402, 421, 442, 444, 456, 458–460, 465, 474, 488

Papapana, typologically unusual features of 2, 72, 81, 87, 182, 194, 204, 336, 338, 404
Papuan languages 2, 27, 30, 36, 42–44, 46, 48, 55–57, 61, 65, 150, 194, 204, 385, 392, 395, 429
Partitive
–partitive article 100, 176, 190
–partitive noun 119, 120
Petats language 43, 125
Plurality.
See also associative plural; collective articles; collective marker; diminutive articles; dual number; inverse number marking; numerals; trial number
–lexical plurals 172
–plural article 100, 136, 157, 175–177, 182–185, 209, 213, 214, 220–222, 224, 225, 373, 379, 425
–reduplication 111, 166, 123, 175, 176, 221
Polysemy 107, 144, 169, 303, 385, 421, 480
Possession, alienability 99, 206, 207, 212
Possessive constructions 103, 105, 125–127, 155, 156, 161, 167, 168, 203–219, 365–368, 370, 374, 406, 407, 425, 426, 428, 429, 432, 433 *See also* compound, possession
Postposition, nascent 356, 373, 383–386
Predicate marker, lack of 242
Prepositions 100, 103, 151–153, 155, 158, 161, 167, 178, 216–220, 302, 356, 365, 371, 373–383, 431, 432, 448
Prohibitives 272, 297, 321, 325, 352–355, 470
Pronominal paradigms 104, 205, 208, 238, 240, 317, 521–522
Pronouns.
See also dual pronouns; inclusory pronoun
–demonstrative pronouns 99, 133–135
–independent pronouns 99, 104–106, 206, 211, 216, 236, 240, 460

Proto-New Ireland 194, 201, 277, 409
Proto-Northwest Solomonic 3, 74, 76, 194, 211, 238, 261, 262, 274, 317
Proto-Oceanic 46, 74, 76, 77, 81, 112, 117, 118, 125, 135, 149, 154, 157, 165, 175, 178, 185, 189, 194, 201, 203, 204, 207, 240, 245, 246, 249–252, 254, 257–259, 261, 262, 266, 267, 269, 274, 277, 283, 284, 288, 290, 292, 295, 297, 299, 301, 302, 315, 344, 374, 391, 409
Purpose
–adnominal preposition phrase 151, 152
–adverbial clauses 467, 468, 472–477

Quantifiers 144, 146, 152, 218–227, 420
Questions *See* interrogatives

Reduplication.
See also aspect, continuous; aspect, habitual; derivational reduplication; plurality; prohibitives; valency-changing operations, reciprocal
–adverbs 310–312
–applicative comitative 272, 273
–formal properties 87–92
–geocentric directionals 284, 293–298
–multiple reduplication 91, 92, 279, 280, 335, 336–338
–stress 94, 95
Relative clauses 100, 103, 441, 457–467, 494
Roviana language 3, 78, 113, 195, 216, 261, 267, 282, 408

Serial verb constructions 228, 273, 274, 277, 280–293, 297, 299, 301, 303, 345, 403, 477
Sisiqa language 3, 194, 195, 207, 216, 282, 424
Solos language 43, 125
Speakers
–fluent speakers 1, 9, 15, 38–41, 55, 57–62
–passive bilinguals 15, 38–41, 55, 58–60
–semi-speakers 15, 38–41, 55–60
Specific articles 95, 96, 99, 101, 137, 154–156, 158, 161, 169, 176–186, 189, 194, 198, 200, 202, 205, 208, 215, 224, 225, 374–376, 379, 380
Stress 70, 71, 86, 92–98, 179
–extrametricality 97, 98
–lexical stress, lack of 92
–secondary stress 92
Subordinators 373, 403, 441, 467, 472, 475, 476, 478–481, 483, 484, 486–491, 493–497, 502
Superlative 145

Taoif language 3, 77, 137, 157, 180, 185, 194, 204, 207, 208, 242, 244, 273, 274, 282, 287, 356
Tense
–future 313–316, 318, 321–323, 336, 340, 343, 350
–past 230, 301, 305, 312–316, 318, 320, 323–325, 331, 336, 340–343, 350, 456
–present 313–315, 321–323, 336–340, 350, 352
Teop language 3, 43, 46, 56–58, 119–121, 130, 137, 169, 180, 182, 183, 185, 186, 189, 216, 242, 267, 273, 274, 297, 301–303, 338, 348, 356, 378, 422, 474, 475
Tok Pisin 41, 48, 51–53, 56–58, 61, 62, 64–67, 82, 85, 114, 154, 159, 192, 332, 380, 382, 441, 475, 479, 481, 483
Topic 237, 392, 396, 397, 404
Torau language 37, 42, 45, 52, 56–58, 81, 89, 183, 204, 296, 315, 337, 338, 354
Transitive marker 230, 250, 251, 253–255, 258–264, 379
Trial number 104

Unproductive processes 25, 113, 175, 232, 250, 259, 266, 291, 298
Uruava language 33, 37, 42, 43, 45, 46, 125, 172, 204, 315

Valency-changing operations.
See also causative prefix; transitive marker
–applicative 136, 230, 247, 248, 250, 251, 255, 256, 258, 259, 264–267, 375, 378, 379

–applicative comitative 229, 256, 264, 269–274
–detransitivising prefix 229, 247, 248, 253, 269
–object incorporation 111, 113, 122, 274–276
–passive, lack of 258
–reciprocal 107, 113, 229, 272, 277–281
–reflexive 107, 277, 278, 281, 282
–transitivity discord 246, 274–277, 448
Verb complex structure 228–231, 315, 316
Verbless clauses 213, 373, 423–440
Verbs 121, 123, 228–234, 417–422

Vowels
–monophthongs 68–70, 82, 83, 85, 93
–vowel length 70–72, 82, 83, 85, 86, 93, 96–98, 179, 374
–vowel sequences 72–76, 79, 80, 85, 90

Word classes 24, 25, 99, 100, 127, 128, 135, 176, 192, 195, 218, 228, 250, 293, 303, 304, 371, 373, 386, 402–403, 441, 467, 468

www.ingramcontent.com/pod-product-compliance
Lightning Source LLC
Chambersburg PA
CBHW051552230426
43668CB00013B/1821